THIRD EDITION

Human Resource Management

Linking Strategy to Practice

Instructor's Edition

GREG L. STEWART

KENNETH G. BROWN

*To Lisa, Brandon, Ryan, Jason, and Analisa—***GLS**

*For my Mom—***KGB**

VICE PRESIDENT & EXECUTIVE PUBLISHER   George Hoffman
EXECUTIVE EDITOR   Lisé Johnson
PROJECT EDITOR   Brian Baker
EDITORIAL ASSISTANT   Jacqueline Hughes
ASSOCIATE DIRECTOR OF MARKETING   Amy Scholz
MARKETING MANAGER   Kelly Simmons
DESIGN DIRECTOR   Harry Nolan
PRODUCT DESIGNER   Allison Morris
ASSOCIATE PRODUCTION MANAGER   Joyce Poh
PRODUCTION EDITOR   Eugenia Lee
COVER DESIGNER   Wendy Lai

This book was set in 10/12pt TimesLTStd by Laserwords Private Limited, Chennai, India and printed and bound by Courier Kendallville.
The cover was printed by Courier Kendallville.

This book is printed on acid free paper.

Founded in 1807, John Wiley & Sons, Inc. has been a valued source of knowledge and understanding for more than 200 years, helping people around the world meet their needs and fulfill their aspirations. Our company is built on a foundation of principles that include responsibility to the communities we serve and where we live and work. In 2008, we launched a Corporate Citizenship Initiative, a global effort to address the environmental, social, economic, and ethical challenges we face in our business. Among the issues we are addressing are carbon impact, paper specifications and procurement, ethical conduct within our business and among our vendors, and community and charitable support. For more information, please visit our website: www.wiley.com/go/citizenship.

ISBN-13 978-1-1189-1123-5

Printed in the United States of America

10 9 8 7 6 5 4 3 2 1

About the Authors

GREG L. STEWART, PH.D.

Greg L. Stewart is the Henry B. Tippie Research Professor of Management and Organizations in the Henry B. Tippie College of Business at the University of Iowa. He received his Ph.D. in human resource management from Arizona State University and has been a faculty member at Vanderbilt University and Brigham Young University. His research has been published in top academic journals, including *Journal of Applied Psychology, Personnel Psychology, Academy of Management Journal, Organizational Dynamics,* and *Organization Science.* He served as an Associate Editor for *Journal of Management.* He has taught human resource management courses to undergraduate, MBA, and Executive MBA students, including international programs in Hong Kong, Italy, and India. He has received numerous teaching awards including GREAT Instructor of the Year for Executive MBA, the Dean's Award for Teaching Excellence, and MBA Professor of the Year at the Consortium Institute of Management and Business Analysis (CIMBA). He has worked with a variety of large and small organizations including Eli Lilly, LG Electronics, Newton Manufacturing, and the National Federation of Independent Business. He is currently involved in a number of projects working to improve the delivery of healthcare within the Veterans Health Administration.

KENNETH G. BROWN, SPHR, PH.D.

Kenneth G. Brown is a Professor and Tippie Research Fellow in the Henry B. Tippie College of Business at the University of Iowa. He also serves by courtesy appointment as a Professor of Educational Policy and Leadership Studies. He received his Ph.D. in industrial and organizational psychology from Michigan State University and his B.S. from the University of Maryland, and he is certified as a senior professional in human resource management (SPHR). He has taught courses in training and career development, organizational behavior, and general management to undergraduate, MBA, and Ph.D. students. He is the recipient of numerous teaching awards, including the Student's Choice for Faculty Excellence Award, the Dean's Teaching Award, the Collegiate Teaching Award, the James N. Murray Faculty Award for outstanding teaching and assistance to students, and the President and Provost Award for Teaching Excellence. His work using experiential learning was recognized as a finalist for the inaugural Academy of Management Human Resources Division Innovative Teaching Award in 2006 and for the 2007 Iowa Campus Compact Faculty Award. He has published articles in human resource management and organizational behavior for both academic and applied audiences. His academic work appears in such top journals as *Journal of Applied Psychology, Personnel Psychology,* and *Organizational Behavior and Human Decision Processes.* His applied work has been published by the American Society of Training and Development in *T&D* magazine and by the UK-based Chartered Institute of Personnel and Development. His consulting clients have included the Ford Motor Company, Rosetta Stone, the Society of Human Resource

Management, Toyota Motor Credit Corporation, the University of Iowa, and numerous local non-profit organizations. From 2012 to 2014, Brown serves as the editor-in-chief of the *Academy of Management Learning and Education*, a premiere journal of research on helping students acquire management knowledge and skill. From 2014–2016, Brown also serves as a Director of the HR Certification Institute, the worldwide leader in certifying HR competency.

The last decade has been an interesting period of change and survival for businesses. The worst economic recession in over 50 years forced many companies to rethink the way they did business. More recently, recovery from the recession has presented organizations with a number of different opportunities and threats. Only the best companies survive and thrive in such trying times. But what makes some companies more successful than others? What gives organizations an advantage over their competitors? One answer emphasizes the benefit of having the right people as members of the organization. It is often said that "the people make the place," which tells us that employees are the most important asset of any organization. Practices that help obtain and motivate employees are the core focus of human resource management, which is the field of study presented in this textbook.

As you read this book, we hope you will agree that human resource management is an exciting field of study. In order to make ideas and concepts come to life, we include a number of examples from real companies that illustrate how effective human resource management is helping companies achieve success. Each chapter explains how an organization can increase its effectiveness by improving its processes for hiring and motivating top-performing employees. We also specifically link human resource practices to competitive strategies. This linkage is critical, as it shows how a company can use human resource management to gain a competitive advantage over other companies.

WHY LINK HUMAN RESOURCE PRACTICE TO STRATEGY?

The field of human resource management has evolved a great deal during the past 20 years. Today, many practitioners and researchers argue that human resource management should extend beyond its traditional focus on legal compliance and adopt a more strategic perspective for managing employees. Perhaps more importantly, successful organizations are taking a more strategic approach to managing people. Many human resource textbooks have added material to reflect some of this change, but most books still lack a consistent strategic framework—even though this framework is rapidly becoming the norm within the field.

We have written *Human Resource Management: Linking Strategy to Practice, Third Edition,* in order to more fully develop and integrate the strategic perspective. Throughout the book, we emphasize the theme that organizations excel when they have consistent human resource practices that align with their strategic direction. We begin by establishing a strategic framework that illustrates how different approaches to human resource management fit with basic competitive strategies. We then integrate this strategic perspective into our discussion of traditional human resource practices, such as work design, staffing, performance management, training, compensation, and labor relations. At the same time, we clearly illustrate how these specific human resource practices help increase organizational effectiveness.

WHAT IS NEW IN THIS EDITION?

The practice of human resource management continues to evolve and improve. New research is being published at a rapid pace, and organizations are constantly innovating. This third edition of *Human Resource Management: Linking Strategy to Practice* reflects these changes. We have combed through research studies conducted since the first and second editions to identify and include new and updated ideas. This edition contains a number of "How Do We Know?" features that describe recently published research that informs our understanding of human resource management. We have also updated our case examples to reflect innovative ideas being carried out in contemporary organizations. These additions to the third edition ensure that students are exposed to the latest ideas and innovative thinking.

One particular area of change in the revision concerns updated material related to finding balance between work and family demands. Both academic studies and organizational practices provide new insights for organizations seeking to help organizations reduce conflict between these important, yet sometimes competing, aspects of life. In particular, Chapter 4 provides an array of concepts and illustrations explaining how companies benefit from making work more family friendly. New laws and government practices, such as the Affordable Care Act (Obamacare), also present new challenges and opportunities for businesses. Many of the critical issues that organizations will face as they implement these new policies are discussed in the section of Chapter 12 that describes how health insurance is becoming a legally required rather than discretionary benefit.

We continue to emphasize the impact of globalization. The importance of thinking globally is emphasized in each chapter with specific examples of ways that human resource practices are similar and different across national boundaries.

The revision also continues to emphasize the strategic approach. New research supporting the benefits of aligning human resource practice with organizational strategy is included. Company illustrations are also used to describe how many of the companies that have performed well during the economic downturn did so largely because of their human resource strengths. In this way, the third edition continues our unique approach to integrating strategy and practice.

HOW CAN STUDENTS BENEFIT FROM A STRATEGIC PERSPECTIVE?

A book designed around a strategic framework, such as the guiding model presented in Chapters 1 and 2, helps students not only to develop a set of human resource tools but also to know when each tool is most appropriate. The overall objective of *Human Resource Management: Linking Strategy to Practice* is thus to provide students with both an understanding of traditional human resource concepts and a framework for making decisions about when specific practices can be most beneficial. This link between strategy and practice is necessary for students to be able to correctly apply human resource tools to improve organizations.

The strategic perspective is critical for students because most people enrolled in an introductory course will not spend their careers working as human resource professionals. A majority will, however, work someday as managers with the charge to lead and direct others. Understanding the strategic benefits of good human resource management can help future managers better secure and motivate talented employees. The strategic perspective also provides a valuable framework for the future study of those students who do choose to become human resource professionals. Information from additional courses that provide more in-depth coverage of topics such as staffing, training, and compensation will easily fit within the strategic orientation of this book and provide guidance for knowing when to use specific tools.

HOW IS THIS BOOK ORGANIZED?

Human Resource Management: Linking Strategy to Practice is organized to provide coverage of both strategic topics and specific practices, as illustrated in the accompanying schematic. We open the book in Chapter 1 by examining the value of aligning human resource practices with organizational strategies. Chapter 2 describes the strategic perspective in more detail. It discusses various ways organizations try to be more effective than their competitors, and it illustrates how human resource management can help organizations carry out their strategies. Chapter 3 discusses legal and safety issues. Laws and regulations drive many human resource practices, and knowledge of these legal realities is necessary for understanding several issues related to securing and motivating employees. Chapters 2 and 3 thus provide information that establishes a strategic perspective and provides a context for much of the material in later chapters.

Chapters 4 through 7 focus on the process of securing employees. Chapter 4 describes work design, which creates job descriptions that clarify who does what. The work design process also identifies the characteristics of people most likely to carry out tasks successfully. The result is a type of shopping list that defines the types of people most likely to succeed in specific jobs and

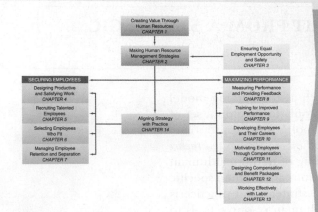

Figure 1.6 Framework and Chapter Outline Illustrating How Human Resource Management Practice Links to Strategy.

the specific activities the organization uses to secure and motivate employees. Activities aimed at securing employees include work design, recruiting, selection, and retention; these are discussed in Chapters 4 through 7. Activities that relate to motivating workers, which include performance management, career development, training, compensation, and labor relations, are discussed in Chapters 8 through 13. All these activities must be coordinated with each other as well as with the overall human resource strategy. The importance of coordination is discussed in Chapter 14.

Human resource management is an exciting field that provides critical benefits to organizations. Studying human resource management can help you develop knowledge and skills that will make you more effective throughout your career. Even if you don't become a human resource specialist, knowing why human resource specialists do what they do will enable you to work more cooperatively with them. Furthermore, knowing about methods for hir-

organizations. Chapters 5 and 6 build on this information by discussing how to locate and identify people who have these characteristics. Chapter 5 gives details about recruiting and illustrates methods for attracting people to apply for jobs with the organization. Faced with a pool of applicants, the organization must decide which of them to hire. Chapter 6 develops several selection methods useful in carrying out this task. Chapter 7 then explains ways of keeping good employees, as well as removing low performers. Taken together, Chapters 4 through 7 provide information that helps guide efforts to get the right people doing the right tasks. These chapters combine a strategic perspective of securing employees with a review of specific activities associated with recruiting, hiring, and retaining workers.

Once the right people have been placed in the right jobs, the next step is to maximize their performance. Chapters 8 through 13 focus on this process. Chapter 8 describes performance management, which provides methods for measuring what individuals contribute to the organization. Performance assessments are used to create feedback that teaches employees how to improve. Chapter 9 discusses the training process. Chapter 10 emphasizes career development and offers guidance for planning how employees can continue to contribute to the organization over the long term. Through training, people learn new things and become more valuable employees. Chapters 11 and 12 focus on compensation and illustrate how pay and benefits can increase motivation. Chapter 13 emphasizes the need for good labor relations and discusses methods for working with labor unions and treating employees fairly. In sum, this set of chapters provides information about developing skills and increasing motivation to ensure that employees are reaching peak performance. The overall emphasis is on ensuring that employees have the skills and motivation necessary to carry out the organization's strategy for competing with other firms.

The final chapter, Chapter 14, describes strategic alignment. The human resource practices of successful organizations align with organizational strategies for doing things better than competitors. Good human resource practices also work together. Staffing practices, for example, combine with compensation practices to help the organization hire and motivate people with certain characteristics. Performance management measures areas where people need to improve, and training teaches them how to improve. The final chapter thus presents the big picture by illustrating how different pieces of human resource management fit together to create successful organizations.

We have developed a number of pedagogical features for *Human Resource Management: Linking Strategy to Practice, Third Edition,* to support the strategic framework and enhance student interest and learning.

A MANAGER'S PERSPECTIVE AND A MANAGER'S PERSPECTIVE REVISITED

Each chapter opens with a real-life scenario describing a decision faced by an individual employee, manager, or human resource professional. These scenarios, labeled "A Manager's Perspective," highlight the importance of strategic decision making and help students see exactly how the chapter material is relevant to their future careers. Each scenario ends with five thought questions designed to get students thinking about core concepts from the upcoming chapter. A section labeled "A Manager's Perspective Revisited" at the end of each chapter provides answers to the thought questions and once again emphasizes how the material covered in the chapter can help students build successful careers.

A MANAGER'S PERSPECTIVE

ANGELA CLOSES HER CELL PHONE AND TAKES A DEEP BREATH. WAS IT REALLY A GOOD IDEA TO ACCEPT THE JOB AS RESTAURANT MANAGER? IT SOUNDED LIKE SUCH A GOOD IDEA WHEN MARK, THE REGIONAL MANAGER, OFFERED HER THE POSITION TWO MONTHS AGO. SHE WON'T GRADUATE WITH HER DEGREE IN ELEMENTARY EDUCATION FOR TWO MORE YEARS. BEING THE MANAGER PROVIDES HER WITH FLEXIBILITY TO TAKE CLASSES WHEN SHE WANTS, BUT TRYING TO SCHEDULE OTHER EMPLOYEES IS MUCH MORE STRESSFUL THAN SHE EXPECTED.

Just now Barbara—a new cook hired last month—called to tell Angela that she is quitting and will not work the hours scheduled during the upcoming week. This is the third time in two months that someone has quit with little or no advance notice. It will be difficult to schedule other employees to co... for Barbara during the upcom... ... someone to hire as ... ows that cooks ... o stay with the

same restaurant for long. Yet surely it should be possible to create a fun working atmosphere that would make employees less likely to leave. Might it help to pay higher wages? Would older workers and people with family responsibilities be more likely to stay than the college students she currently hires?

Angela's thoughts quickly shift to the other disagreeable task she faces today. The very thought of meeting with Simon is enough to make Angela want to quit, herself. Yesterday Simon was late for work the second time this week. Once he arrived, he spent much of his shift wasting time. Working with first graders will surely be easier than supervising Simon. Should she just fire him?

Thinking about firing someone scares Angela. Would Simon become emotional? When should she meet with him if she decides to deliver the bad news? What should she say? As questions about

A MANAGER'S PERSPECTIVE REVISITED

IN THE MANAGER'S PERSPECTIVE THAT OPENED THE CHAPTER, ANGELA FELT CONCERN ABOUT AN EMPLOYEE WHO HAD JUST QUIT. SHE WAS ALSO THINKING ABOUT CONFRONTING AN EMPLOYEE WHOSE PERFORMANCE WAS UNACCEPTABLE. FOLLOWING ARE THE ANSWERS TO THE "WHAT DO YOU THINK?" QUIZ THAT FOLLOWED THE MANAGER'S PERSPECTIVE. WERE YOU ABLE TO CORRECTLY IDENTIFY THE TRUE STATEMENTS? CAN YOU DO BETTER NOW?

1. Workers are less likely to quit when they feel the organization cares about their personal needs. TRUE. *Individuals who feel they receive support from the organization are more likely to remain with the organization, even if they have experiences that cause them to think about leaving.*

2. Decisions to quit often begin with a specific event that causes employees to evaluate their work situation. TRUE. *In most cases, a specific event can be identified as the point where the employee begins to think about leaving the organization.*

3. It doesn't really matter how you fire people, as long as you make it clear that their employment is being terminated. FALSE. *It is important for the person doing the firing to make it clear that the person is being dismissed, but a number of other issues should be addressed to minimize*

4. In order to defend against potential lawsuits, an organization should carefully document methods of disciplining problem employees. TRUE. *Principles of due process and progressive discipline suggest that employees should receive clear written warnings as part of the disciplinary process.*

5. Employees who see coworkers losing their jobs become more committed to staying with the organization. FALSE. *In many cases, layoff survivors begin to look for jobs at other organizations.*

Angela's frustration with employees who quit and employees who perform poorly is not uncommon. High employee turnover is costly. Angela is therefore wise to consider ways to increase the chances of good employees staying with the restaurant. She is also being an effective leader when she takes actions to help low performers such as Simon improve. The principles of due process and the steps of progressive discipline can guide Angela's efforts. These and other concepts in this chapter provide information about effective methods of retaining employees, as well as effective ways to discipline and dismiss employees

BUILDING STRENGTH THROUGH HR

The opening section of each chapter includes a discussion that illustrates how a specific company has used the concepts discussed in the chapter to increase effectiveness. Trader Joe's, Southwest Airlines, Marriott, and General Electric are just a few of the firms included in these in-depth examinations of strategic HR. Each of the company descriptions ends with a "Building Strength Through HR" feature that clearly summarizes how the firm has used specific human resource practices to become more effective and competitive.

Additional "Building Strength Through HR" features appear throughout each chapter. These brief cases illustrate how specific companies have benefited from implementing particular human resource practices—for example, how Leicester Royal Infirmary, a large teaching hospital in England, improved efficiency and patient satisfaction through work redesign and how LG Electronics created a global instructional program to connect company vision and values with leadership development practices. These discussions clearly illustrate how effective human resource practices have translated into success for a number of organizations. The inclusion of foreign-based firms points up the fact that the usefulness of strategic HR crosses international boundaries.

 Building Strength Through HR

LG ELECTRONICS

LG Electronics is a South Korea–based firm that designs and manufactures a wide variety of consumer electronics including smartphones, refrigerators, air conditioners, and televisions. To help fuel its growth, LG makes substantial investments in leadership development. In recent years they have sought to build a single standard Global Leadership Framework that connects to the company's vision and values and guides leadership development practices. Working with a consulting firm, LG created a list of behaviors needed by leaders at each level in the company. Then they launched a leadership academy that began with a multi-source assessment of participants' leadership behaviors. With data in hand, participants worked through custom-designed learning modules to enhance those skills. To further develop their skills, participants are given work assignments that help

©Andrew Kent/Corbis

improve particular skills. Finally, the consulting firm offered coaching to help participants practice behaviors on the job.

Source: Information from Erin Wilson Burns, Laurence Smith, and Dave Ulrich, "Competency Models with Impact: Research findings from the Top Companies for Leaders," *People & Strategy*, 35 (2012): 16-23.

HOW DO WE KNOW?

Research is an important part of the field of human resources. Each chapter therefore includes a number of features describing specific research studies. These features—labeled "How Do We Know?"—use nontechnical language to summarize research studies that have been published in scholarly journals. Each concludes with a "Bottom Line" summary that shows how the findings of the study contribute to our understanding of effective human resource management. These research summaries help students understand how knowledge is generated and help them see the science behind many of the principles discussed throughout the textbook.

 How Do We Know?

DOES HOW MUCH YOU MAKE DEPEND ON HOW MUCH YOU WEIGH?

Do people who are overweight make less money than their thinner peers? Is the effect of weight the same for men and women? Timothy Judge and Daniel Cable sought to answer these questions by examining data from two long-term studies. The first study obtained information from 11,340 German workers. The second study captured measures from 12,686 American workers. In both studies workers reported their weight and salaries over a number of years.

The results suggest that wages and salary decline as weight increases for women. The effect is such that additional weight is most harmful for women who were relatively thin. Specifically, a woman 25 pounds below average is expected to make $15,572 more than a woman of average weight, whereas the woman of average weight is predicted to make $13,847 more than a woman 25 pounds

above average. There is thus a wage premium for very thin women. The effect was opposite for men. Men who weighed more had higher salaries.

The Bottom Line. Weight has a negative relationship with earnings for women but a positive relationship for men. The negative effect of additional weight is most pronounced for women who are already below average, meaning that women appear to be rewarded most when they are very thin. Professors Judge and Cable conclude that this effect is consistent with media portrayals of the ideal woman as being unrealistically thin.

Source: Timothy A. Judge and Daniel M. Cable, "When It Comes to Pay, Do the Thin Win? The Effect of Weight on Pay for Men and Women," *Journal of Applied Psychology* 96 (2011): 95-112.

TECHNOLOGY IN HR

Technological change has had a pervasive influence on every aspect of management, and human resource management is no exception. "Technology in HR" features describe how technological advances are affecting the field of human resource management. The information included in this feature illustrates how the Internet and other forms of electronic communication are affecting human resource practices in areas such as employee selection, training, and compensation. These discussions show students how advancements in technology are being incorporated to increase the effectiveness of human resource management.

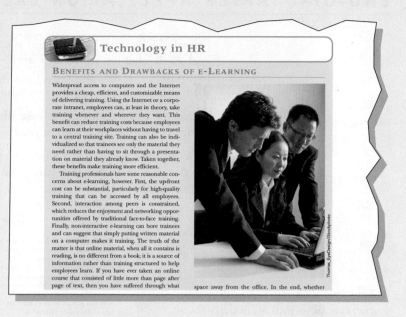

Technology in HR

BENEFITS AND DRAWBACKS OF e-LEARNING

Widespread access to computers and the Internet provides a cheap, efficient, and customizable means of delivering training. Using the Internet or a corporate intranet, employees can, at least in theory, take training whenever and wherever they want. This benefit can reduce training costs because employees can learn at their workplaces without having to travel to a central training site. Training can also be individualized so that trainees see only the material they need rather than having to sit through a presentation on material they already know. Taken together, these benefits make training more efficient.

Training professionals have some reasonable concerns about e-learning, however. First, the up-front cost can be substantial, particularly for high-quality training that can be accessed by all employees. Second, interaction among peers is constrained, which reduces the enjoyment and networking opportunities offered by traditional face-to-face training. Finally, non-interactive e-learning can bore trainees and can suggest that simply putting written material on a computer makes it training. The truth of the matter is that online material, when all it contains is reading, is no different from a book; it is a source of information rather than training structured to help employees learn. If you have ever taken an online course that consisted of little more than page after page of text, then you have suffered through what space away from the office. In the end, whether

RECALL FEATURES

A number of features included in each chapter help students focus on and learn key concepts.

- *Learning Objectives.* A list of learning objectives opens each chapter and prepares readers for the key concepts to be discussed.

- *Key Terms and Definitions.* Key terms shown in boldface in the chapter text and linked to margin definitions highlight critical concepts and provide an opportunity for review.

- *End-of-Section Review Questions.* Each major section concludes with review questions that focus students' attention on major topics.

- *End-of-Chapter Summaries.* Each chapter ends with a summary of key concepts linked to the chapter's learning objectives and major sections.

- *Discussion Questions.* End-of-chapter discussion questions revisit major topics, providing readers with an opportunity not only for review but also for critical thinking and interpretation.

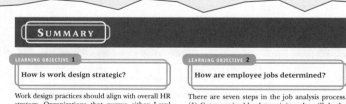

SUMMARY

LEARNING OBJECTIVE 1

How is work design strategic?

Work design practices should align with overall HR strategy. Organizations that pursue either Loyal Soldier or Bargain Laborer HR strategies benefit from efficiency. Efficiency comes from designing work so that employees have relatively little autonomy, meaning that they have little freedom to alter the way tasks are carried out. Efficiency is also increased with sequential processing, which occurs when people use assembly lines to complete work tasks. Competitive strategy that focuses on cost reduction thus aligns with work design practices that limit autonomy and create sequential processing.

Organizations that pursue either Committed Expert or Free Agent HR strategies benefit from innovation and creativity. Innovation comes from designing work so that employees have substantial autonomy, meaning that they have freedom to make decisions and ongoing adjustments to the work process. Reciprocal processing, which occurs when employees work closely together and share

LEARNING OBJECTIVE 2

How are employee jobs determined?

There are seven steps in the job analysis process. (1) Get organized by determining who will do the analysis and by gaining the support of top management. (2) Choose jobs that are critical for success and have a sufficient number of employees. (3) Review what has already been written about the job. (4) Select job agents, such as incumbents, supervisors, or experts. (5) Collect job information through interviews, questionnaires, and observations. (6) Create a job description that specifies the actions that workers do when performing the job. (7) Create job specifications that list the knowledge, skills, abilities, and other characteristics that workers need in order to successfully perform the job.

In order to guide other human resource practices, job analysis information needs to be translated into a "shopping list" of the characteristics needed by people who perform the job. Some worker-oriented job analysis procedures, such as the Position Analysis Questionnaire, provide a list

END-OF-CHAPTER APPLICATION EXERCISES

Knowledge is most useful when it can be applied to solve real problems. We end each chapter with cases and experiential exercises that help students begin the process of applying the concepts to solve actual problems associated with effective human resource management.

- *Example Cases.* An example case illustrates how a specific company implements the human resource practice discussed in the chapter.

- *Discussion Cases.* A discussion case provides background information about a fictional company that can serve as the launching point for a class discussion.

- *Experiential Exercises.* An experiential exercise describes an activity that a student can complete, often online, to actively learn more about the topic discussed in the chapter.

1. Why are effective human resource practices often a better competitive resource than equipment and buildings?
2. What are some external opportunities and threats that you think organizations will face in the next 10 years? What types of organizations will benefit most?
3. Why can groups be more effective than individuals for making decisions?
4. What are the primary differences between a cost leadership and a differentiation strategy?
5. What are the key elements of the commitment strategy from the universalistic approach? Why does this approach generally contribute to success for organizations?
6. What human resource practices might be associated with a cost reduction emphasis?

What practices might be associated with a differentiation emphasis?
7. What are the strengths and weaknesses of internal and external labor orientations?
8. Choose a company where you or someone you know works. Which of the four human resource strategies do you think is most common in the company?
9. What are the key elements of the four human resource strategies: Loyal Soldier, Bargain Laborer, Committed Expert, and Free Agent?
10. The chapter text pointed out that a majority of organizations have a human resource strategy that fits their competitive strategy. What should an organization do if the strategies don't match?

EXAMPLE CASE *United Parcel Service*

Of course, every company wants to attract the best people it can. Equally important at UPS is attracting people who fit the company culture, which encourages high energy, hard work, fairness, inclusiveness, teamwork, and sharing the wealth.

4. What has happened to the stock price of the company over the past 10 years?

4. Compare and contrast the strategies and practices of the companies that are direct competitors.

INTERACTIVE EXPERIENTIAL EXERCISE

HR Strategy in Action: Selling the HR Function at Mega Manufacturing
http://www.wiley.com/college/sc/stewart

Access the companion website to test your knowledge by completing a Mega Manufacturing interactive role-playing exercise.
In this exercise, you meet with senior management at Mega and try to convince other members of the management team that HR needs to have a "seat at the table" and function as a business partner within the company. The CFO, however, expresses the opinion that HR is just a "touchy feely" department that adds no legitimate business value. Your objective is to gain credibility and show that a strategic approach to HR can improve Mega Manufacturing. Based on previous discussions, you have learned that Mega believes that its products are better than those of its competitors. You also know that the company prefers to hire experienced people who won't require much training. How will you defend the HR function to the CFO and others in the meeting who may share the same opinion of HR? •

- *Interactive Experiential Exercises.* An interactive experiential exercise provides a link to the companion website where students can go to participate in a role-play that tests their knowledge of the basic concepts discussed in the chapter.

ENDNOTES

1. Jeffrey Pfeffer, "Competitive Advantage Through People," *California Management Review* 34, no. 2 (1992): 9–28; Jon Birger, "The 30 Best Stocks from 1972 to 2002," *Money* 31, no. 11 (2002): 88.
2. Birger, "The 30 Best Stocks," 88.
3. Daniel Fisher, "Is There Such a Thing as Nonstop Growth?" *Forbes* 170, no. 1 (2002): 82.
4. Wendy Zeller and Michael Arndt, "Holding Steady as Rivals Sputter, Can Southwest Stay on Top?" *BusinessWeek*, Issue 3818 (February 2003): 66.
5. Pfeffer, "Competitive Advantage Through People," 9–28.

Supplements

Several supplements have been designed to make both teaching and learning easier and more interesting for users of *Human Resource Management: Linking Strategy to Practice, Third Edition.* We are especially grateful to the following people for helping us to provide such a comprehensive teaching and learning package: Dyanne J. Ferk, University of Illinois–Springfield; Marcia Marriott, Monroe Community College and Rochester Institute of Technology.

Companion Website

The companion website for *Human Resource Management: Linking Strategy to Practice, Third Edition,* contains a myriad of tools and links to aid both teaching and learning, including nearly all of the resources described in this section. To access the site, go to **www.wiley.com/college/stewart**.

Instructor's Resource Manual

The *Instructor's Resource Manual* includes an introduction with sample syllabi, chapter outlines, chapter objectives, teaching notes on how to integrate and assign special features, and suggested answers for all quiz and test questions found in the text. The *Instructor's Resource Manual* also includes additional discussion questions and assignments that relate specifically to the cases, as well as case notes, self-assessments, and team exercises.

Test Bank

The robust test bank consists of over 100 true/false, multiple-choice, and short-answer questions per chapter. Furthermore, it is specifically designed so that questions vary in degree of difficulty, from straightforward recall to challenging, to offer instructors the most flexibility when designing their exams. Adding still more flexibility is the *computerized test bank*, which requires a PC running Windows. The computerized test bank, which contains all the questions from the manual version, includes a test-generating program that allows instructors to customize their exams.

PowerPoint Presentations

This resource provides another visual enhancement and learning aid for students, as well as additional talking points for instructors. This set of interactive PowerPoint slides includes lecture notes to accompany each slide.

Personal Response System

Personal Response System questions (PRS or "clicker" content) were designed for each chapter in order to spark additional discussion and debate in the classroom. For more information on PRS, please contact your local Wiley sales representative.

Web Quizzes

Online quizzes, available on the student portion of the *Human Resource Management: Linking Strategy to Practice, Third Edition,* companion website, include questions varying in level of difficulty, designed to help students evaluate their individual progress through a chapter. Each chapter's quiz includes 10 questions, including true/false and multiple-choice questions. These review questions, developed in conjunction with the test bank, were created to provide the most effective and efficient testing system. Within this system, students have the opportunity to "practice" the type of knowledge they'll be expected to demonstrate on the exam.

Pre- and Post-Lecture Quizzes

The pre- and post-lecture quizzes, found on the student companion website, consist of 10 to 15 questions (multiple-choice and true/false) per chapter, varying in level of detail and difficulty, but all focusing on that chapter's key terms and concepts. This resource allows instructors to quickly and easily evaluate their students' progress by monitoring their comprehension of the material from before the lecture to after it.

Videos

A set of short video clips from CBS News provides an excellent starting point for lectures or for general classroom discussion. Teaching notes, including clip introductions and assessment questions, are included for class discussion or assignment.

Acknowledgments

This book could not have happened without contributions from an outstanding team. We thank Lisé Johnson for her outstanding efforts to make this third edition a reality. Brian Baker guided us, kept us on task, and answered numerous questions throughout the process. Eugenia Lee provided superb production and editorial help. We also thank Judy Joseph, Jayme Heffler, Leslie Kraham, Joan Kalkut, and Beverly Peavler for their assistance with many features of earlier editions of this book.

Our efforts have also been aided by a number of outstanding colleagues who have read different manuscript versions and provided valuable input. Their feedback has improved our coverage of topics and helped us identify areas of weakness. These colleagues include

Muriel Anderson, *SUNY—Buffalo;* Vondra Armstrong, *Pulaski Technical College;* Tim Barnett, *Mississippi State University;* Myrtle Bell, *University of Texas— Arlington;* Jerry Bennett, *Western Kentucky University;* Stephen Betts, *William Paterson University;* Thomas Bock, *DeVry Institute of Technology—Long Island;* Walter Bogumil, *University of Central Florida;* Angela Boston, *University of Texas— Arlington;* H. Michael Boyd, *Bentley College;* Gene Brady, *Southern Connecticut State University;* Lynda Brown, *University of Montana;* April Cobb, *Oakland University;* Patrick Coughlin, *Kean University;* Ralph Covino, *Bridgewater State College;* Craig Cowles, *Bridgewater State College;* Carol Cumber, *South Dakota State University;* Tammy Davis, *University of Houston—Downtown;* Diana Deadrick, *Old Dominion University;* Paula Donson, *University of Alaska—Anchorage;* Karen Eastwood, *Florida Gulf Coast University;* Dyanne Ferk, *University of Illinois—Springfield;* Bill Ferris, *Western New England College;* Mary Gowan, *George Washington University;* Brooke Hargreaves-Heald, *University of Massachusetts—Lowell;* John Hendon, *University of Arkansas—Little Rock;* Kim Hester, *Arkansas State University;* John Hulsebus, *Chapman University College;* Samira Hussein, *Johnson County Community College;* Jennie Johnson, *University of Texas;* Roy Johnson, *Iowa State University;* Kathleen Jones, *University of North Dakota;* Deborah Kelly, *Siena College;* Mukta Kulkarni, *University of Texas—San Antonio;* Wendall Lawther, *University of Central Florida;* Dane Loflin, *York Technical College;* Lucy McClurg, *Georgia State University;* Margie McInerney, *Marshall University;* Jon Monat, *California State University—Long Beach;* Byron Morgan, *Texas State University—San Marcos;* Darlene Motley, *Robert Morris University;* Dorothy Mulcahy, *Bridgewater State College;* James Myers, *Tarleton State University;* Rebecca Neilson, *University of Texas—Arlington;* Kay Nicols, *Texas State University;* Laura Parks, *James Madison University;* Sue Pogue, *Tennessee Tech University—Cookeville;* John Poirier, *Bryant College;* Alexander P. Portnyagin, *Johnson & Wales University Graduate School;* Richard Posthuma, *University of Texas— El Paso;* Gary Potts, *University of Nevada—Las Vegas;* Ross Prizzia, *University of Hawaii—West Oahu;* Herve Queneau, *Brooklyn College;* Gail Sammons, *University of Nevada—Las Vegas;* John Shaw, *Mississippi State University;* Carol Spector, *University of North Florida;* Howard Stanger, *Canisius College;* Gary Stroud, *Franklin University;* Abe D. Tawil, *SUNY—Baruch College;* Linda Urbanski, *University of Toledo;* Phillip Varca, *University of Wyoming;* Steve Warner, *University of Houston;* Paige Wolf, *George Mason University;* Laura Wolfe, *Louisiana State University;* Michael Wolfe, *University of Houston—Clear Lake;* and Ryan Zimmerman, *Texas A & M University.*

Brief Contents

Contents

Chapter 2
Making Human Resource Management Strategic

Chapter 3
Ensuring Equal Employment Opportunity and Safety

PART 2 Securing Effective Employees

Chapter 4
Designing Productive and Satisfying Work

Chapter 5
Recruiting Talented Employees

Chapter 6
Selecting Employees Who Fit

Chapter 7
Managing Employee Retention and Separation

PART 3 Improving Employee Performance

Chapter 8
Measuring Performance and Providing Feedback

Chapter 9
Training for Improved Performance

Chapter 10
Developing Employees and Their Careers

PART 4 Motivating and Managing Employees

Chapter 11
Motivating Employees Through Compensation

Chapter 12
Designing Compensation and Benefit Packages

Chapter 13
Working Effectively with Labor

Chapter 14
Aligning Strategy with Practice

APPENDICES   (available online at www.wiley.com/college/stewart)

Part 1
Seeing People as a Strategic Resource

Chapter 1 • Creating Value Through Human Resources

Chapter 2 • Making Human Resource Management Strategic

Chapter 3 • Ensuring Equal Employment Opportunity and Safety

Chapter 1
Creating Value Through Human Resources

A MANAGER'S PERSPECTIVE

MIGUEL DISCONNECTS HIS PHONE AND BREATHES A SIGH OF RELIEF. THE JOB OFFER IS EVERYTHING HE HOPED IT WOULD BE. HE IS PRETTY CERTAIN HE WILL ACCEPT THE AUDITOR POSITION IN A COUPLE OF DAYS, BUT HE WANTS TO DO A LITTLE MORE RESEARCH FIRST. TWO YEARS AGO MIGUEL TOOK HIS FIRST ACCOUNTING CLASS AND INSTANTLY KNEW WHAT HE WANTED TO DO FOR A CAREER. HE LOVES THE STRUCTURE AND LOGIC OF ACCOUNTING. PUTTING ALL THE NUMBERS IN THE RIGHT PLACE AND MAKING SURE THEY ADD UP GIVES HIM A SENSE OF ACCOMPLISHMENT. NOW HE JUST NEEDS TO BE SURE THAT HE IS JOINING THE RIGHT FIRM.

As Miguel reflects back on his day of interviews with the firm, he recalls a number of insightful conversations. One thing that impresses him is the firm's strong reputation for excellence. In the last few years, he has seen many of his friends lose their jobs. Seeing their pain has steered Miguel toward business organizations that he feels are unlikely to have financial difficulties. He knows that profitability is one key to success. But why is the firm that is offering him a position so profitable? Of course, much of it has to do with the firm's excellent operating procedures. From everything he has learned, the firm is simply superior at meeting customer needs. According to some of the managers who interviewed him, being profitable helps the firm invest more money to improve working conditions. The firm also has a strong reputation for helping people in the community, which is very important to Miguel.

Something that really attracts Miguel to the company is how they treated him during the job interviews. Sarah, a human resource staff member, told Miguel that he has already progressed farther than 90 percent of job applicants. Sarah also described how the company focuses on finding and keeping only the best employees. This makes Miguel feel good and leads him to believe he will have competent coworkers. The firm seems to have good human resource practices. It offers numerous training opportunities and pays above-market wages. Insurance benefits are much better than most

AFP/Getty Images

THE BIG PICTURE *Human Resource Management Practices Help Successful Organizations Meet the Needs of Employees, Customers, Owners, and Society.*

competitors'. According to Sarah, the firm also emphasizes internal promotions, making it likely that Miguel will have an opportunity to become a manager.

The firm also seems to have a strategic plan for dealing with important changes that are likely to occur both in the marketplace and among future employees. Cutting-edge technology allows the firm to keep up with constantly changing accounting rules and procedures. Now that he has received an offer, Miguel plans to discuss things with his parents and a friend who works for the firm. Unless something changes his mind, he plans to take the offer and is convinced that he has the potential for a great career with the firm.

WHAT DO YOU THINK?

Suppose you are listening to a conversation between Miguel and his parents. His parents make the following statements as they and Miguel discuss his decision about the job offer. Which of the statements do you think are true?

T OR F Companies with good human resource practices have more satisfied workers.

T OR F Companies with happy employees are more profitable.

T OR F Companies lose money when they try to be good social and environmental citizens.

T OR F Having a successful career in the future workplace will require young employees to work effectively with older people.

T OR F Human resource specialists can provide critical information and support that helps make life better for employees.

After reading this chapter you should be able to:

LEARNING OBJECTIVE 1 Explain how human resource management, from the organizational life-cycle and stakeholder perspectives, can facilitate organizational success.

LEARNING OBJECTIVE 2 List the core functions of human resource management.

LEARNING OBJECTIVE 3 Explain what human resource professionals do to help create successful organizations.

LEARNING OBJECTIVE 4 Identify important labor trends that are affecting organizations and their human resource practices.

LEARNING OBJECTIVE 5 Explain how effective human resource management requires a combination of strategic and functional perspectives.

How Can Human Resource Management Make an Organization Effective?

Human resource management
The field of study and practice that focuses on people in organizations.

Human resource management focuses on people in organizations. Of course, people are a major component of any organization, so it follows that organizations with more productive employees tend to be more successful. Employee productivity increases when organizations hire and motivate employees effectively. In addition, good human resource practices create more satisfied employees, who in turn work harder to satisfy customers.[1]

One prosperous organization that traces much of its success to effective management of people is Trader Joe's. The chain now includes over 365 stores in more than 30 different states, but it began in the 1960s as three convenience stores seeking to survive the introduction of 7-Eleven. Seeing the difficulty of competing head-to-head with 7-Eleven, the founder—Joe Coulombe—decided to change Trader Joe's to a specialty store selling unique products. Trader Joe's has since become well known for providing foods and beverages that cannot be found in other stores. Products, which usually carry the store's own label, include gourmet and specialty foods such as soy ice-cream cookies, black rice, and stuffed salmon.[2]

Keeping prices low is one key to success for Trader Joe's. However, customers describe their shopping experience as something more than a simple hunt for bargains. Trader Joe's works hard to attract educated customers who develop a loyal relationship with the company. Many of these customers say they have fun shopping at Trader Joe's. They look forward to searching store aisles and finding interesting products. They also enjoy their interactions with helpful store employees dressed in casual Hawaiian shirts. The real key to success for Trader Joe's, then, seems to be finding and keeping great employees.[3]

What does Trader Joe's do to develop and maintain a productive workforce? Flexible job design certainly plays a role. Employees have a great deal of autonomy in determining how the store can best serve customers. Every employee is encouraged to sample products and make recommendations. Employees are free to tell customers when they don't like something. Workers at Trader Joe's are not limited to performing certain tasks but help out wherever they are needed. Managers, for example, often sweep floors and stock shelves.[4]

Of course, not everyone would fit equally well into the job environment at Trader Joe's. Employee selection focuses on hiring people with personalities that fit the productive and creative culture. Trader Joe's looks for employees who are upbeat, outgoing, and motivated by challenge. Employees also need a good sense of humor and a strong customer orientation.

Convincing people to take jobs with Trader Joe's does not seem to be difficult. The store has a reputation as a desirable place to work, and a large number of people apply whenever job openings are advertised.[5] One reason people like to work at Trader Joe's is the company's compensation practices. Employees are paid substantially more than they could make doing similar jobs in other companies. Full-time crew members begin at salaries around $50,000. They receive health insurance and participate in an excellent retirement savings program, including a plan that contributes over 15 percent of gross income to a tax-deferred retirement account. Excellent pay not only helps get people interested in working at Trader Joe's but also helps ensure that employees will stay with the company. Managers are almost always promoted from within the company, and few employees leave to work elsewhere.[6]

Both employees and customers see Trader Joe's as a successful company. It is a profitable company, with annual sales exceeding $8 billion. More important, Trader Joe's generates twice as many dollars in sales per square foot of store space as competitors such as Whole Foods. This profitability has helped the company expand the number of stores without taking on debt. Profits grew tenfold over a 10-year period.[7]

The success of Trader Joe's clearly illustrates how a company can thrive in difficult and changing times. Rather than giving up to a formidable competitor, Joe Coulombe identified an unmet need and created an organization to fill that need. Human resource practices at Trader Joe's help attract and motivate employees who provide great customer service. Doing things differently from the competition, and doing them better, has created a culture where people like to go to work. Happy employees make shoppers happy.

Building Strength Through HR

TRADER JOE'S

Trader Joe's is a privately owned chain of about 365 specialty grocery and wine stores. Human resource management at Trader Joe's builds competitive strength by

AFP/Getty Images

- Designing work to give people autonomy to complete tasks in creative ways.
- Identifying and hiring people who have fun, outgoing personalities.
- Providing high pay and excellent benefits to attract the best workers.
- Matching human resource practices with a competitive strategy of providing unique products.

How Is Organizational Success Determined?

As you begin studying human resource management, it is important to think about what you want to gain from your efforts. How can understanding human resource management better prepare you for success in your upcoming career? The most basic answer is that human resource skills will help you hire, manage, and motivate employees more effectively. Clearly, human resource skills are useful not only to human resource professionals but also to everyone who has responsibility for leading and managing others. Furthermore, even if you don't plan to work either as a human resource specialist or as a manager, learning the concepts of human resource management will help you to understand why the places where you work do much of what they do.

The goal of human resource management is, of course, to make organizations more effective. Thus, a starting point for learning about the field of human resource management is to explore the concept of organizational success. We know that some organizations are more successful than others. Can differences in human resource management explain why?

Most observers agree that Trader Joe's is a successful organization. This is supported by top rankings from publications such as *Consumer Reports*. But what exactly does it mean to say an organization is successful? Does it mean the organization makes a lot of money? Does it mean the organization makes the world a better place? Perhaps success is meeting the demands of different stakeholders, such as Trader Joe's recent agreement with a farmworker organization concerning employee fair treatment as part of tomato-growing practices.[8] Maybe success simply means the organization has been around for a long time. Because organizational success has many faces, each of these perspectives is partly true. Different viewpoints capture different meanings of success. Here, we briefly examine the meaning of organizational success from two perspectives—the life-cycle model and the stakeholder perspective—and consider how human resource management plays a role in making organizations effective from each viewpoint.

SUCCESS IN LIFE-CYCLE STAGES

Think about success for you as an individual. Being successful now doesn't guarantee you will be successful in 10 years. Having just enough money to buy pizza and books may equal success when you are 20, for example, but probably isn't enough when you are 40. Similarly, the life-cycle approach to organizational success suggests that measures of effectiveness change as an organization grows. Twenty-five years ago, Trader Joe's was successful simply because it didn't close when 7-Eleven entered the market. Success today depends on expansion into a national chain.

Organizational life cycle
Stages through which an organization moves after its founding.

At the heart of this model of success is the **organizational life cycle**, a series of stages through which an organization moves during its lifetime. Stages of growth begin when the organization is founded and end when it ceases to exist. Since goals and objectives change as the organization moves from stage to stage, the nature and meaning of success also change. Here, we examine four common stages in the organizational life cycle: the entrepreneurial stage, the communal stage, the formalization stage, and the elaboration stage.[9] As

Table 1.1	Human Resources Across the Organizational Life Cycle	
Stage	**Goal**	**Human Resource Contribution**
Entrepreneurial	Survival and growth	Need to hire and maintain employees; emphasis on creating plans for measuring performance and deciding pay
Communal	Develop identity and overcome conflict	Need to develop clear communication channels; emphasis on building strong loyalty among employees
Formalization	Efficient production	Need to create formalized practices for hiring, training, and compensating; emphasis on continual improvement of employee skills and motivation
Elaboration	Adaptation and renewal	Need to alter practices to meet changing demands; emphasis on new ways of organizing work tasks

you will see, human resource management plays an important role in every stage. Table 1.1 summarizes key differences across the stages.

Entrepreneurial Stage

An organization enters the **entrepreneurial stage** when it is first created. This stage is a lot like infancy for human beings. The main goal is survival and growth. Organizations in the entrepreneurial stage need to develop an identity and obtain resources. Success during this stage is often measured simply in terms of staying alive. Organizations that survive are successful. The early history of the Internet company Yahoo! is a good example. Yahoo! wasn't profitable in the beginning, but it showed innovation and growth when many competitors were going out of business.

Effective human resource management is very important for the survival and growth of newly formed organizations. Organizations must find and hire a sufficient number of high-quality employees. They must also develop basic plans for measuring performance and paying people.

A typical organization employs one human resource specialist for every 100 employees.[10] This means that organizations in the entrepreneurial stage of development are typically too small to have a full-time, dedicated human resource staff. As a result, it is likely that owners and managers of firms with relatively few employees perform many human resource duties themselves or hire outside consultants to do this work.

Given the importance of human resources for entrepreneurial organizations, it is not surprising that firms with better-developed plans and methods of obtaining and paying employees are more likely to survive. For instance, one study found that new organizations lacking clear human resource and pay plans have just a 34 percent chance of surviving the first five years. Firms with good human resource plans, in contrast, have a 92 percent chance of survival.[11] Organizations with better plans for hiring and motivating workers are thus more likely to survive—and survival is a key indicator of success during the entrepreneurial stage.

Communal Stage

Organizations that survive the entrepreneurial stage enter the **communal stage**, which is marked by expansion, innovation, and cooperation. This stage is much like the teenage years for human beings. The main objective is to gain a unique identity and overcome internal conflict. Learning who you are and improving your skills are the essence of life during these years. Similarly, organizations in the communal stage focus on developing and improving processes

Entrepreneurial stage
First stage in the organizational life cycle; focuses on survival.

Communal stage
Second stage in the organizational life cycle; focuses on expansion and innovation.

for effectively producing goods and services. Members of the organization begin to feel a sense of commitment. Survival is still important, but organizational success is measured increasingly by the extent to which employees feel a sense of cohesion or belonging. It is important for employees to build strong feelings of attachment to coworkers and to the mission of the organization. Such attachment is an important part of success at Trader Joe's, where employees feel connected. The company's managers listen to employees, which encourages employees to communicate effectively with customers.[12]

Organizations with effective human resource management practices in the communal stage continue to hire good employees and provide training. They also communicate well with employees. Employees, aware of these activities, develop a feeling that the organization is committed to taking care of them. Such feelings increase job satisfaction and feelings of empowerment, so that organizations with better human resource practices have happier employees who are more committed to making the organization successful and helping others.[13] Employees are also less likely to leave organizations with good human resource practices. The accompanying "How Do We Know?" feature describes a study that demonstrates how effective human resource practices in call centers increase the likelihood of retaining workers, which in turn increases profitability.

 # How Do We Know?

DOES EFFECTIVE HUMAN RESOURCE MANAGEMENT INCREASE ORGANIZATIONAL SUCCESS?

Have you phoned a company's call center in the past to ask a question or complain about a product or service? Perhaps a call center representative has phoned you to try to sell you something. Many companies have call centers, and some centers employ thousands of people. As you can probably imagine, working in a call center is not always fun, and employees frequently quit shortly after being hired.

An important question therefore is whether good human resource practices can improve work in call centers. Rosemary Batt conducted a study to learn about the effect of human resource practices on organizational performance in call centers. She asked call center managers about the skill level of employees, the amount of freedom employees had to choose how to do their work, and human resource incentives. She also measured employee quit rates and sales growth.

The study found higher sales growth in call centers with better human resource practices. Higher-performing centers had ongoing training, more employees working full-time rather than part-time, and more elaborate performance management

systems. Better centers allowed employees to exercise greater control in determining things like work pace, scheduling, and technology design. Much of the effect of the human resource practices on performance came through employee retention. Fewer employees left call centers that had better practices, which in turn helped these centers to experience increased sales growth.

The Bottom Line. Organizations are more successful when they have good human resource practices. Success comes from having a stable workforce, which develops when fewer people leave the organization. People are less likely to leave when they have freedom to make choices about how to do their work. They also stay longer when they have full-time jobs that pay them well. Professor Batt thus concluded that good human resource practices lead to lower quit rates, which in turn increase growth in customer sales.

Source: Rosemary Batt, "Managing Customer Services: Human Resource Practices, Quit Rates, and Sales Growth," *Academy of Management Journal* 45, no. 3 (2002): 587–597.

Formalization Stage

The **formalization stage** occurs as organizations become stable and develop clear practices and procedures for doing work. In humans, the formalization stage often begins just after graduation from college, when people tend to settle into stable jobs. Organizations in the formalization stage focus on improving efficiency and finding better ways to accomplish tasks. They develop clear goals for guiding their efforts. Making goods and services as efficiently as possible becomes a key goal. Making a good profit is also important.

Effective management of people is beneficial for increasing efficiency and goal accomplishment in this stage. Organizations with formalized human resource practices that develop employee skills and motivate workers generate more sales per employee.[14] IBM represents a company in this stage. IBM has been in existence 100 years and currently employs over 430,000 people. Keeping in touch with so many employees is difficult. However, IBM has a database that contains a profile for every employee. The profile lists each employee's skills. Maintaining such a database takes a great deal of effort, but cost savings from improved matching of employees and jobs has saved IBM $1.4 billion. Effective formalization of human resource practices has thus improved the efficiency and profitability of IBM.[15]

Formalization stage
Third stage in the organizational life cycle; focuses on establishing clear practices and procedures for carrying out work.

Elaboration Stage

The **elaboration stage** occurs when organizations need to adapt and renew. This stage is similar to middle age for human beings. Success often depends on redefining objectives and identifying new opportunities. People in this stage sometimes go through midlife crises, perhaps changing occupations and developing new hobbies. Organizations in the elaboration stage, like middle-aged people, have existed for some time, but shifting trends and preferences require them to change. For example, years ago Hallmark became successful as a producer of greeting cards, but changes in technology have forced the company to innovate and adapt to produce electronic greetings and family-based media.

Good human resource management is critical for successful adaptation. In fact, one survey found change management to be the most important skill that human resource professionals can contribute to an organization.[16] An example of an organization in this stage is Crouse Hospital in Syracuse, New York. At one point the company had a net loss of $15 million. About half of the hospital's employees were quitting each year. Hospital leaders took note and began to involve employees in an effort to change the culture of the organization. Numerous employee groups met and made suggestions. Employee efforts to turn around hospital performance took time but were successful. Financial problems were reversed to a net profit, and the employee quit rate dropped to 18 percent. Overall job satisfaction has increased to 96 percent.[17] Improved human resource management thus helped move Crouse Hospital from the elaboration stage back to the formalization stage.

Elaboration stage
Final stage in the organizational life cycle; focuses on reinvention and adaptation to change.

SUCCESS FROM STAKEHOLDER PERSPECTIVES

A second approach for assessing organizational effectiveness is the stakeholder perspective. According to this view, organizations are successful to the extent that they meet the needs of their stakeholders. **Stakeholders** are defined as individuals or groups of people who can affect or who are affected

Stakeholders
Individuals or groups who are affected by or who affect an organization.

by an organization.[18] This definition is quite broad, since almost every living person could in some way potentially affect or be affected by an organization. Fortunately, research suggests that employees, customers, and owners (shareholders) are the primary stakeholders. Their participation is crucial for the survival of the organization.[19] Society as a collective group is also seen by many as an important stakeholder.

Employees

Employees make up an important group of stakeholders. Because employees complete tasks to make goods and services, they obviously influence the organization's ability to achieve its objectives. Their lives are also obviously influenced by the organization. Meeting the needs of employees is a critical component of organizational success.

Many human resource practices protect the interests of employees. For instance, the human resource department often plays a major role in ensuring that the organization complies with employment and safety laws. A number of these laws are designed to make sure the organization treats employees fairly. Helping design work tasks to make them more enjoyable is another way human resource management makes life better for employees. Human resource professionals help individuals plan and advance their careers, which keeps employees happy and reduces the chance that they will leave for jobs in other organizations. Thus, good human resource practices reduce **employee turnover**, which happens when employees quit and take jobs elsewhere.[20] Low turnover is a strong sign that employees' needs are being met. Simply put, people are less likely to look for new work opportunities when they are satisfied with their current jobs.[21] As you can imagine, most companies prefer employee turnover to be low.

Employee turnover
The process in which employees leave the organization and are replaced by other employees.

Customers

Customers are another important group of stakeholders. An organization obviously will have trouble achieving its goals if customers don't buy its goods or services, so the influence of customers on the organization is immense. The goods and services available to customers can also affect their lives both positively and negatively.

Research evidence strongly supports the notion that good human resource management improves customer satisfaction, largely through customers' interactions with employees. Employees tend to treat customers the same way they believe managers treat them. If employees feel the organization values them and treats them with respect, they reproduce these good attitudes and behaviors in their interactions with customers. If they believe management doesn't care about them, they are less likely to be positive and helpful to customers.[22] For example, one study of hairstylists found that those who were most satisfied with their jobs were helpful to clients and coworkers and in turn had more satisfied customers.[23] Human resource practices that demonstrate care and concern for employees thus translate into increased customer satisfaction. Hiring and keeping skilled employees can also improve customer satisfaction. Just think of an experience you have had shopping for something like a new computer. Getting information from a knowledgeable employee is much more satisfying than trying to get information from someone who knows less than you do.

How Do We Know?

WHY ARE SOME ORGANIZATIONS MORE EFFECTIVE THAN OTHERS?

Human resource specialists often claim that differences in employee skill and ability represent a primary source of competitive advantage for firms. In short, having skilled and knowledgeable employees is seen as a valuable resource that firms can draw on to outperform competitors. Of course, there are many other things, such as firm strategy and economic conditions, that affect organizational performance. An important research question is thus whether organizations with better employees—those that have greater human capital—are indeed more effective than their competitors. Russell Crook, Samuel Todd, James Combs, David Woehr, and David Ketchen sought a clear answer to this question by summarizing the results of 66 different existing studies.

Human capital was scored as higher when employees have more work experience, higher levels of education, more desirable traits such as greater intelligence, and more knowledge of work processes. Organizational performance was captured through financial measures such as profitability and return on assets. As predicted, organizations with greater human capital were found to have higher profitability. The relationship was strongest when specific measures of human capital were used, suggesting that effective organizations develop and utilize employee skills and knowledge that are unique to them and not easily transferred to other organizations.

The Bottom Line. Having high-quality employees is a key to organizational success. Hiring and retaining the best employees pays off. The researchers thus conclude that organizations should emphasize acquiring and retaining the best and brightest workers.

Source: T. Russell Crook, Samuel Y. Todd, James G. Combs, David J. Woehr, and David J. Ketchen, Jr., "Does Human Capital Matter? A Meta-Analysis of the Relationship Between Human Capital and Firm Performance," *Journal of Applied Psychology* 96 (2011): 443–456.

Owners

A third group of important stakeholders is made up of owners, including stockholders. Owners influence organizations by determining who leads and makes decisions. In most cases their chief concern is the organization's profits, and the extent to which the organization returns profits and provides them with money influences them in many ways.

A great deal of research has linked human resource practices to organizational profits. As discussed in the "How Do We Know?" feature, this research illustrates how good human resource management makes a difference. Organizations are more profitable when they ensure high levels of employee skill by properly designing jobs, carefully selecting employees, and providing useful training. Effective practices also motivate employees by carefully measuring performance, making fair promotion decisions, and linking pay to performance.[24] In short, employees who have better skills, are well paid, and feel their jobs are secure have higher individual performance, which translates into desirable organizational improvements like growth in sales.[25]

Society

Society represents the broader community in which the organization operates. Although further removed from the organization than the stakeholder

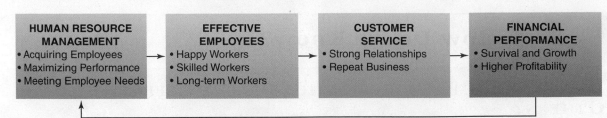

Figure 1.1 The Chain of Success.

groups discussed so far, society still serves as an important stakeholder. On the one hand, organizations affect society through their environmental practices, as well as their support of community charities and other such activities. On the other hand, various political and social forces can strongly influence organizations. For example, think about how changes in attitudes toward conservation and large automobiles affect the U.S. automobile industry.

Interestingly, organizations that are better community citizens are generally more profitable than organizations that ignore environmental and social concerns. Although there are exceptions, expending effort to do things such as protect the environment and improve local communities usually leads to improved financial performance for organizations.[26] In addition, effective human resource management within the organization results in other benefits to society. It provides employees with open channels of communication, which can reduce instances of unethical corporate behavior. Skilled and motivated employees also produce goods and services that help make the world a better place. Taking care of people at work can thus translate into important benefits for society as a whole.

THE CHAIN OF SUCCESS

Successful firms must meet the needs of each group of stakeholders, and these needs vary from group to group.[27] Fortunately, meeting the needs of one group can often help meet the needs of others. First, effective human resource management acquires high-quality employees, motivates them to maximize performance, and helps meet their psychological and social needs. This leads to long-term relationships with skilled and happy employees. Effective employees provide good customer service, which results in repeat business. Better customer service leads to improved financial performance that ensures profitability and success. Increased profitability allows organizations to spend money on improving human resource practices, which loops back and continues the chain of success. Properly managing people is therefore a critical part of the chain of success, which is shown in Figure 1.1 and summarizes the relationship among employee, owner, and customer interests. Obtaining and keeping excellent employees gives an organization an advantage in meeting customer needs, which translates into profitability and thereby provides organizations with resources to further improve human resource practices. This cycle of success was supported by a study that concluded that companies rated by *Fortune* as "The 100 Best Companies to Work for in America" are more profitable than their competitors.[28]

CONCEPT CHECK

1. *What are the four stages of the organizational life cycle, and what is the main goal of each stage?*
2. *How does human resource management contribute to success at each stage?*
3. *What four primary groups make up an organization's key stakeholders?*

LEARNING OBJECTIVE 2

What Does Human Resource Management Provide to an Organization?

Anyone who has applied for a job with a moderately large organization has probably interacted with a human resource department. But human resource functions go far beyond processing employment applications. From an overall strategic perspective, effective human resource management builds human capital that in turn increases organizational performance. In this section, we thus look at a number of activities that human resource professionals carry out in their role of managing the organization's employees.

CORE HUMAN RESOURCE FUNCTIONS

Core human resource functions can be summarized as people management activities. As shown in Table 1.2, these activities represent the primary purpose for having a human resource department. The Society for Human Resource Management (SHRM) and its affiliated Certification Institute have identified

Table 1.2	*Core Human Resource Functions*
Function	**Description**
Business Management and Strategy	Working with other parts of the organization to establish goals and provide high-quality goods and services
Workforce Planning and Employment	Identifying jobs that capture employee tasks; recruiting and selecting desirable employees
Human Resource Development	Measuring employee performance; teaching employees new knowledge, skills, and abilities
Compensation and Benefits	Paying employees fairly; administering benefits such as insurance
Employee and Labor Relations	Establishing and managing relationships between the company and employees; working with labor unions
Risk Management	Establishing procedures to provide a safe and secure working environment

Source: Information from Society for Human Resource Management (SHRM) and affiliated Certification Institute. See the PHR and SPHR Body of Knowledge at http://www.hrci.org/uploadedfiles/Content/Resource_Library/Certification_Handbooks_and_Other_Publications/PHR-SPHR%20BOK.pdf/

six broad functional areas of human resource management. These functions are business management and strategy, workforce planning and employment, human resource development, compensation and benefits, employee and labor relations, and risk management.[29]

Business management and strategy
The human resource function concerned with strategic planning, change processes, and evaluating organizational effectiveness.

Business management and strategy focuses on planning how the organization will produce and market goods and services. Strategic tactics guide efforts to do things better than competitors. For instance, an electronics manufacturer might decide to open a new plant that can produce parts less expensively. A hotel might initiate a marketing campaign to attract higher-paying customers. A healthcare provider may decide to structure work around teams of doctors, nurses, and clerical workers. Input from several different sources, including human resource specialists, guides these strategic plans. For the company opening a new plant, human resource data can help determine whether employees have the skills needed to carry out the new processes. For the hotel, human resource data can identify training needs that could result from focusing on a different type of customer. For the healthcare provider, data could help determine new skills that team members might need to learn. Effective strategic practice also requires ongoing measurement to assess the value that human resource management provides to the organization. Making and carrying out strategy is thus an important function that the human resource department shares with other departments throughout the organization. Human resource management also plays an important role in carrying out strategies of global companies. Employee expectations for compensation and benefits vary greatly from country to country. Human resource departments provide valuable assistance that guides organizations as they adapt their policies and practices to fit with local cultures and laws.[30]

Workforce planning and employment
The human resource function concerned with designing jobs and successfully placing people in those jobs.

Another important human resource function is getting people into jobs. **Workforce planning and employment** consists of designing jobs and then placing people in them. This function generates information about tasks that need to be done and about the knowledge and skills people must have in order to do those tasks. People with the necessary talents are then recruited and hired from outside the organization or are promoted from within. Once on board, new employees are oriented to company policies and procedures. In some organizations, the human resource department carries out the entire process of planning and hiring. These human resource specialists do everything from placing employment advertisements to conducting interviews to making final selection decisions. In other organizations, the human resource department acts more like a consulting agency. Line managers do the actual recruiting and hiring, while human resource specialists provide assistance. Regardless of who does what, the human resource department is almost always a major player in recruiting and hiring activities.

Human resource development
The human resource function concerned with helping employees learn knowledge and skills.

The **human resource development** function ensures that employees learn the knowledge, skills, and abilities required for current and future performance. Surveys and assessments provide information about areas where training might be needed. Individual employees receive performance appraisals and develop individualized plans for improvement. The human resource department also uses assessment information to design formal training and development programs. For example, a survey about computer skills may highlight the need for classes to teach people how to use specific software. In many cases, human resource specialists carry out training in such areas as communication skills and organizational policies. The human resource department also coordinates programs designed to accomplish goals such as increasing employee diversity and helping employees balance work and family concerns.

Human resource departments typically carry out the function of **compensation and benefits** by managing salary and insurance plans. Compensation practices include finding and analyzing information to determine how much to pay each employee. Identifying and pursuing methods of using pay to increase employee motivation is an important contribution of human resource management. Most human resource departments also take primary responsibility for payroll activities such as preparing and distributing paychecks. Administering benefits, especially health insurance, can be quite complicated and usually requires a number of technical contributions from human resource professionals. Compliance with numerous laws and regulations concerning compensation also calls for specialized knowledge, which usually comes from the human resource department. As described in the Technology in HR feature, Web-based information can help human resource departments communicate critical compensation and benefit policies.

Compensation and benefits
The human resource function concerned with managing employee pay and benefits.

Technology in HR

USING WEB-BASED INFORMATION TO MANAGE PEOPLE

An important question is whether technology can help human resource departments better serve the needs of managers and employees. The answer is a clear yes. Evidence shows that the various functions of human resource management benefit substantially from adopting appropriate technologies.

Some forms of technology are common. For instance, approximately 89 percent of organizations now use some type of self-service interface to help managers and employees solve human resource problems. An organization may use a Web-based Internet site to provide information about employee benefits, compensation agreements, organizational policies, and the like. Encouraging members of the organization to go to these sites for information reduces the need for face-to-face conversations and thereby reduces administrative costs.

Other forms of technology are not yet as widespread. Recent trends, however, suggest that cutting-edge firms are using technology to better link human resource practices to organizational strategy. In particular, technologies are being developed to improve methods of measuring productivity. In addition, information about individual employees is being incorporated into extensive databases that help organizations take advantage of the wide array of skills that employees have to offer. Being able to locate information about the skills of individual employees makes workforce planning easier

Jon Feingersh/Getty Images, Inc.

and more effective. Many technologically advanced organizations are also creating Web-based learning tools to help with human resource development.

Of course, organizations may face obstacles as they implement new technologies. One problem with Web-based information systems, for example, is that poorly designed user interfaces can make them so difficult to use that people avoid them. Another problem is that tools developed for U.S. employees are often difficult to adapt to employees in other countries. Nevertheless, companies that effectively use technology to manage people tend to be more effective than companies that lag behind.

Source: Information from "HR Technology Trends to Watch in 2007," *HR Focus* 84, no. 1 (2007): 1–15.

Employee and labor relations
The human resource function concerned with building and maintaining good relationships with employees and labor unions.

Good relationships between managers and employees improve organizational effectiveness. Building and maintaining effective working conditions and relationships are tasks associated with the **employee and labor relations** function. In organizations whose employees are represented by labor unions, much of this function is directed toward working with the unions. The human resource department plays a major role in negotiating terms of union contracts, which define not only pay levels but also work rules and procedures. Human resource specialists also coordinate procedures for filing and resolving employee grievances. When labor unions are not present, the human resource department works directly with managers and employees to ensure fair treatment of workers. The department may oversee disciplinary actions and provide communication channels so that employees can safely register complaints about such things as sexual harassment. Carrying out the employee and labor relations function thus provides critical support for both the organization and individual employees.

Risk management
The human resource function concerned with providing a safe and secure working environment, as well as protecting the organization from liability.

The function of **risk management** promotes the physical and mental well-being of people in the workplace. Because important laws govern workplace health and safety, carrying out this function requires specialized knowledge of government regulations. Human resource departments often take the lead in developing plans for reducing accidents. They make policies to protect employee rights of privacy. They also establish procedures to make sure that employees wear proper safety equipment. In many instances, the human resource department plans and coordinates the organization's response to natural disasters, such as hurricanes and earthquakes. Reducing workplace violence is also part of the risk-management function.

SPREADING KNOWLEDGE ABOUT HUMAN RESOURCE PRACTICES

Many of the core human resource functions just discussed require cooperation between the human resource department and other parts of the organization. Human resource inputs about workforce planning, for example, must be coordinated with operational plans for increasing or decreasing production. Efforts to develop new employee skills also must be coordinated with strategic and marketing plans. Such cooperative efforts are important, and the value of people management increases when leaders throughout the organization know what human resource specialists bring to the table. An important aspect of spreading knowledge is thus to help managers and others throughout the organization know the special capabilities that human resource specialists provide.

Another potentially important contribution of human resources is to teach organizational leaders effective practices for attracting and keeping talented workers. In this sense, human resource specialists function like internal consultants and teachers. They help managers learn and improve methods for hiring employees, assessing training needs, and making pay decisions. This function goes beyond simply informing managers about what human resource specialists can do. The emphasis is on helping the managers themselves develop better human resource skills. Human resource departments thus have an important responsibility for training managers throughout the organization.

An important part of spreading knowledge involves overcoming common misconceptions about human resources. Many organizational leaders believe that good human resource management is "common sense." They think, in other words, that hiring and motivating workers requires no special knowledge. But people who hold this view are mistaken. Managers generally are unfamiliar with many practices that provide clear direction for improving job performance. For instance, many managers resist using employment tests to select employees, even though evidence strongly shows that such tests can help them to make better hiring decisions.

Of course, human resource specialists must have knowledge before they can share it. Unfortunately, even professionals working within human resource departments often have misconceptions about good practices. This is shown by a survey that asked human resource leaders a number of questions about specific employment, staffing, and compensation practices. On average, these professionals knew the correct answer only about 60 percent of the time. Those with higher scores had been promoted more often, had received certification as human resource professionals, and read academic studies more frequently.[31] Simply reading trade journals and popular magazines may not be enough to learn cutting-edge practices. Many of the most important research findings do not make their way into publications written for practicing managers.[32] Overall, researchers in the field of human resource management need to do a better job of communicating their findings, and practitioners need to better test and implement best practices.

Another aspect of spreading human resource knowledge is building relationships of trust. Human resource departments need to provide managers with solutions to problems. Managers are more likely to believe and act on information from the human resource department when they see that it helps them. Human resource professionals earn managers' trust by listening to and understanding their problems and then providing solutions that work.[33] This requires people working in the human resource department to be capable of doing a wide array of things that help managers do their jobs better.

CONCEPT CHECK

1. *What are the six core human resource functions?*
2. *Why is it important for human resource professionals to educate others in their organizations about human resource functions?*

LEARNING OBJECTIVE 3

What Do Human Resource Specialists Do?

We have looked at some ways human resource management helps organizations and have explored some of the functions that human resource departments carry out. We can gain additional insight into the field by looking at the people who work in human resources. An example of someone who works in human resource management is Jen Martens, who works at University of Nevada–Las Vegas (UNLV). UNLV is a state-supported, nonprofit organization with nearly 28,000 students and 3,000 employees.[34] Just like any other large organization, UNLV must recruit and hire many employees every year.

Jen Martens assists in this process through her work as manager of employment. Her work includes managing employee recruitment programs, teaching managers how to hire effective employees, and assuring compliance with government regulations. Jen also leads other human resource specialists who do things like write job postings and develop interview questions.

Human resource professionals like Jen Martens, who is a certified Professional in Human Resources (PHR), work by themselves and with managers to "plan, direct, and coordinate human resource activities of an organization to maximize the strategic use of human resources and maintain functions such as employee compensation, recruitment, personnel policies, and regulatory compliance."[35] A more specific list of tasks is provided in Table 1.3.

The list in Table 1.3 is helpful, but it does not cover important ways human resource departments provide strategic contributions. Frameworks for capturing this more strategic contribution emphasize roles and competencies. Let's look more closely at these two areas.

HUMAN RESOURCE ROLES

Human resource roles involve people and processes. Part of the human resource professional's role is spending time interacting with employees individually. For instance, employees usually contact an organization's human resource department with questions about retirement benefits, health concerns, and harassment policies. Another part of the human resource role focuses on developing organizational processes aimed at hiring and motivating talented workers. Human resource specialists contribute in these roles through activities such as placing recruiting advertisements, helping develop compensation plans, and creating performance measures.

We can also look at human resource roles by contrasting long-term and short-term contributions. Short-term activities generally involve day-to-day

Table 1.3	*Typical Human Resource Specialist Tasks*

Administer compensation, benefits, and performance management systems and safety and recreation programs.

Identify staff vacancies and recruit, interview, and select applicants.

Allocate human resources, ensuring appropriate matches between personnel.

Provide current and prospective employees with information about policies, job duties, working conditions, wages, opportunities for promotion, and employee benefits.

Perform difficult staffing duties, including dealing with understaffing, refereeing disputes, firing employees, and administering disciplinary procedures.

Advise managers on organizational policy matters such as equal employment opportunity and sexual harassment and recommend needed changes.

Analyze and modify compensation and benefits policies to establish competitive programs and ensure compliance with legal requirements.

Plan and conduct new employee orientation to foster positive attitude toward organizational objectives.

Serve as a link between management and employees by handling questions, interpreting and administering contracts, and helping resolve work-related problems.

Source: The National O*Net Consortium at http://online.onetcenter.org/.

projects and focus on conducting surveys, maintaining databases, and counseling employees. Long-term activities are more strategic in nature and include developing organizational strategies, managing change processes, and planning ways to create new skills.

Combining the people and process dimension with the long-term and short-term dimension results in the grid shown in Figure 1.2. The figure identifies four critical roles for human resource professionals: functional expert, employee advocate, strategic partner, and human capital developer.[36] Understanding these four roles provides insight into the actual activities of human resource specialists.

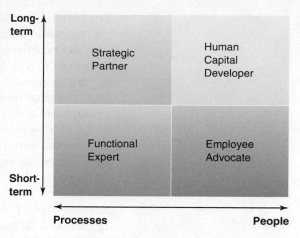

Figure 1.2 Human Resource Roles. *Source:* Figure based on information from Dave Ulrich, Human Resource Champions: (Boston: Harvard Business Press, 1997); and Dave Ulrich and Wayne Brockbank, The HR Value Proposition (Boston: Harvard Business Press, 2005).

Functional Expert

The role of functional expert is the most basic human resource role. Most of the activities listed in Table 1.3 fit this role, and many of the chapters in this book examine aspects of this role in more detail. The **functional expert role** focuses on providing technical expertise related to hiring and motivating employees. In this role, an effective human resource specialist helps build systems and practices to ensure that an organization is using state-of-the-art methods to manage people. This might include creating a testing program to screen potential employees or developing a compensation plan that pays employees more when they produce exceptional results. Human resource specialists also serve as consultants who teach managers ways to improve their interactions with employees. For example, the human resource department might offer managers training in such things as giving appropriate feedback and asking better interview questions.

One such functional expert is Dana Winkowitsch, who works for Johnson County in Iowa. Dana works as a human resources coordinator and spends a lot of her time answering questions and responding to requests from department heads and elected officials. She conducts orientation sessions to provide safety training, explain benefit programs, and help new employees complete paperwork. She leads the county safety committee and coordinates efforts to investigate accidents and maintain logs of work-related illnesses. Her duties include verifying payroll forms for accuracy and using the information database to create new employee positions. Because Johnson County only has a handful of human resource employees, Dana works mostly as a human resource generalist.

An organization can gain an advantage over its competitors when its human resource staff members are true functional experts. Experts help make sure that the best employees are hired and then trained to maintain high levels of skill and ability. Experts also increase employees' motivation by helping to ensure that each employee's contribution to the organization is accurately measured and rewarded. Performance in the functional expert role therefore represents a primary way human resource specialists such as Dana Winkowitsch can contribute something to the organization that other managers and employees cannot contribute.

Employee Advocate

Human resource professionals in the **employee advocate role** listen to employees and provide them with the resources they need to be effective. They look

Functional expert role
A human resource role concerned with providing technical expertise related to functions such as hiring, training, and compensating employees.

Employee advocate role
A human resource role concerned with looking out for the interests of employees and ensuring that they are treated fairly.

out for the interests of employees and often serve as advocates to make sure management treats employees fairly. Sometimes, too, they help employees who are experiencing personal problems. For instance, human resource professionals may help employees obtain medical care, attend funeral services for family members of employees, and help employees' spouses find work.[37] Showing genuine interest in employees communicates how much an organization cares about its employees. As a result, loyalty and motivation increase, and employees feel a stronger obligation to work hard.

Another important part of being an employee advocate is making sure the interests of employees are recognized when decisions are made. In the event of layoffs, human resource leaders can help ensure that these actions are carried out in ways that minimize the hurt for individuals. In their advocacy role, human resource leaders are often seen as the organization's conscience. By ensuring that employees are properly informed about organizational policies and procedures, they can play an important role in preventing members of the organization from engaging in unethical conduct. They do this by pointing out implications of decisions and asking leaders throughout the organization to think about the effect of decisions on individual employees. They also help develop and enforce policies that protect employees from being taken advantage of by more powerful supervisors. True leadership also requires human resource professionals to display high ethics in their own actions.

Strategic Partner

Strategic partner role
A human resource role concerned with providing inputs that help an organization put its competitive strategy into action.

In the increasingly important **strategic partner role**, human resource specialists work with other organizational leaders to put company strategy into action. True partners go beyond providing support to other leaders and expertise in human resource practices. An example of a strategic partner is Tracy Hulsebus, who works as the human resource manager for contingent staffing at the international media company Pearson. Tracy is the business partner for operations as well as other groups. She is responsible for developing strategy and goals to meet business partner objectives, identifying internal and external risks, and providing appropriate solutions. She manages a team of nine professionals who handle hiring, on-boarding, and employee relations for the contingent workforce at Pearson. To be strategic partners, human resource professionals like Tracy need to know about other business activities, such as finance, accounting, and marketing. They must also know a great deal about the organization's products and services. Finally, they must know how these activities, products, and services fit with the company's strategic objectives. With this knowledge, human resource partners can provide important input to help guide organizational decisions and actions. An example of a company where this human resource role is carried out effectively is Edwards Lifesciences, which is described in the accompanying "Building Strength Through HR" feature. Top-level managers at Edwards Lifesciences work closely with human resource professionals to make sure that employees are organized in a way that helps the company achieve its strategic objectives.

One particularly important aspect of the strategic partner role involves managing change. With organizations changing continually, the people within them must continually adapt to shifting conditions. The ability to apply concepts related to psychological reactions, power and influence, motivation, and group dynamics can help human resource professionals take a leadership role in facilitating change.

Building Strength Through HR

EDWARDS LIFESCIENCES

Edwards Lifesciences is a maker of cardiovascular medical devices. The company that now employs nearly 8,000 people was spun off from the larger Baxter International in 2000. Since 2000 the stock price has risen from $14 to $92 per share. During the down economy, Edwards Lifesciences experienced stock returns approximately five times the average return, and the company is ranked #8 by Forbes for innovation. Leaders in the organization credit much of this success to effective human resource management.

Success through human resource management begins with the CEO, Michael Mussallem. He spends about 20 percent of his time working on hiring and developing employees. He is described as a person who cares about relationships and treats others with respect. Even though he is a busy CEO, he will often pick up the telephone and talk to people who are being recruited for key positions. He also meets each year with leaders to conduct talent reviews that assess how well the company is doing in terms of utilizing key personnel to meet strategic objectives. Employee recruitment and job planning are included on every agenda for top-management meetings.

As part of the focus on maximizing human resource effectiveness, Edwards Lifesciences has identified approximately 75 key positions within the company. The key positions are not all at the top of the organization but represent numerous areas where work is critical to meeting strategic objectives. Training is used to ensure that one or two current employees are ready to take over a key

Ana Venegas/ZUMA Press/NewsCom

job if someone gets promoted or quits. This helps ensure that about 70 percent of job openings are filled within the company.

Edwards Lifesciences competes with other companies by providing customers with top-quality products. Creativity and excellence are required from employees. The company thus relies on the acquisition, development, and retention of top-notch employees to fill key positions. These efforts have paid off as the company has seen great success even in times of economic difficulty.

Source: Information from Gian Ruiz, "Edwards Lifesciences: The Cardiovascular Device Maker Pinpoints and Tracks Mission-Critical Jobs to Stay ahead of Business Needs and Build a Deep Bench of Important Talent," *Workforce Management*, March 26, 2007, p. 24; Tony Bingham and Pat Galagan, "Finding the Right Talent for Critical Jobs," *T + D* 61 No. 2 (2007): 30–36; http://www.forbes.com/companies/edwards-lifesciences/.

Human Capital Developer

Organizations are only successful when they learn faster than their competitors. The **human capital developer role** focuses on helping employees improve their skills. Sometimes facilitating learning requires human resource specialists to work as trainers who teach formal classes. Other times, the developer role requires sitting down with individuals and helping them make individualized plans for the future. In both cases, the objective is to make sure that employees continue to learn and improve.

Like the strategic partner role, the human capital developer role is becoming increasingly important in today's organizations. Rapid changes in

Human capital developer role
A human resource role concerned with facilitating learning and skill development.

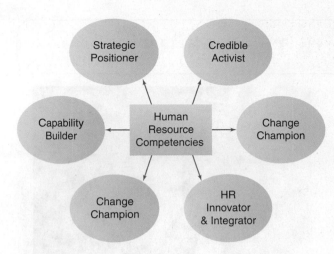

FIGURE 1.3 Human Resource Competencies.
Source: Content adapted from Dave Ulrich, Jon Younger, Wayne Brockbank, and Mike Ulrich, HR From the Outside In: Six Competencies For the Future of Human Resources (New York: McGraw-Hill, 2012).

Competencies
Characteristics and capabilities that human resource professionals need to succeed in their work assignments.

Strategic positioner
Knowledge and skills associated with accurately placing an organization in its business context through understanding finance, strategy, stakeholders, and competitive context.

Credible activist
Knowledge and skills for influencing others through acting with integrity, sharing information, and building trust.

Capability builder
Knowledge and skills related to understanding what the organization is capable of doing successfully.

technology necessitate frequent changes in work processes, which require new inputs from employees. Employees who do not learn new skills become less capable of helping the organization meet the needs of customers. The human capital developer role thus adds value to the organization by helping employees build and maintain cutting-edge skills.

HUMAN RESOURCE COMPETENCIES

Another way of understanding what human resource professionals do is to examine the competencies they need. **Competencies** represent characteristics and capabilities that human resource professionals need to succeed in their work assignments. To fill their various roles, human resource specialists need competencies in many areas. One recent model suggests that human resource professionals need six basic competencies. These competencies are shown in Figure 1.3 and include strategic positioner, credible activist, capability builder, change champion, HR innovator and integrator, and technology proponent.[38]

Strategic Positioner
In today's global business environment human resource specialists must increasingly demonstrate the **strategic positioner** competency, which means they must know the language of business and be able to converse with other organizational leaders. Specific areas of expertise include finance and strategy. Knowledge about stakeholders such as customers and investors is also required. Truly effective human resource specialists go even further to anticipate and plan for future trends in technology, politics, and workforce demographics. This requires a clear vision of the future, as well as an understanding of what the organization must do in order to perform at a high level. This competency is particularly important for the strategic partner role, which requires human resource specialists to be key contributors in determining what makes the organization superior to competitors.

Credible Activist
Credible activists must be proactive and constantly seek opportunities to influence others. They meet their obligations and follow through on commitments. The interpersonal relationships these leaders develop make others more willing to follow them. One key for effective influence is taking an interest in others and the greater good rather than pursuing selfish interests. Effective written and oral communication are also part of this competency.

Capability Builder
The **capability builder** competency focuses on knowing an organization's strengths and weaknesses. Human resource professionals must understand what an organization can do better than its competitors, and then steer activity to maximize unique capabilities. They help focus energy on the things that really matter. Part of this comes from being familiar with the core values of

the organization. Mastery of this competency helps connect employees to the mission and goals of the organization. As described in the Building Strength Through HR feature, these efforts to develop capable employees help companies succeed.

Change Champion

Effective organizations are constantly adapting and adjusting. The **change champion** competency encompasses skills and abilities needed to facilitate

Change champion
Knowledge and skills necessary to initiate and carry out change.

Building Strength Through HR

McDonald's

McDonald's has 34,000 restaurants located in 119 different countries. Chances are pretty good that you know someone who either works or has worked at McDonald's, as one in eight people have worked for the restaurant at some point in time. Today over 1.7 million people work for McDonald's. These employees have helped make McDonald's one of the most successful companies of all time. Annual revenue is over $27 billion each year, and net income exceeds $5 billion. McDonald's has increased shareholder dividends for 25 consecutive years.

A key to success at McDonald's is employee recruiting. Finding enough employees to fill jobs is a constant task. McDonald's focuses specifically on hiring students. Relationships with school principals, coaches, and counselors help steer students toward jobs at McDonald's. Flexible work schedules help balance work with social interests. McDonald's also focuses on hiring people with physical and mental disabilities. These and other recruiting practices allow McDonald's to maintain a steady flow of job applicants who are willing to work in entry-level positions, which helps minimize overall labor costs.

Once employees are hired, McDonald's helps them feel a connection to the company and coworkers. One method of building connections is StationM, which is a private networking site similar to Facebook and MySpace. Hourly employees can use the site to post comments, share photos, and participate in contests. This technology creates bonds and helps young employees feel a connection that builds loyalty.

Justin Sullivan/Getty Images

McDonald's also emphasizes skill development. The company actually runs a Hamburger University, where many managers receive extensive training. Although many companies cut training during tough economic times, McDonald's does not. Effective training helps explain why most managers began their careers as cashiers and cooks. Once they become managers, fewer quit than at competitors.

Overall, McDonald's successfully manages a very large number of employees. Its business results clearly show that more effective human resource management equates with improved performance. Restaurants with the highest levels of employee satisfaction and commitment have the highest customer satisfaction. They are also the most profitable.

Sources: Diana Thomas, "McDonald's Continues to Invest in Talent," *T + D* 63, No. 11 (2009): 15; Amy Garber, "McD Takes HR Strides to Cement Worker Loyalty," *Nation's Restaurant News*, March 7, 2005; Anonymous, "Human Resources: A Challenge Best Addressed One Unit at a Time," *Nation's Restaurant News* (2005): 100–101; stationM.com.

learning and growth. A first step in proactive change leadership is helping develop a sense of dissatisfaction with the status quo. Employees and leaders need to feel urgency to improve. This requires human resource professionals to guide the use of resources such as time, money, and information. Effort must also be put forth to ensure that new patterns of behavior continue once change has occurred. Change management thus requires true leadership.

HR Innovator and Integrator

HR innovator and integrator competencies are closely aligned with the functional expert role. Human resource professionals display this competency when they use research-based principles to help them establish effective processes for hiring and motivating employees. Human resource specialists must know how to properly divide work duties, create reporting relationships, and design motivating jobs. They also need to know about staffing procedures that help attract, select, and promote the right people. Of course, they must carry out these activities in ways that help the organization take advantage of its unique capabilities and effectively pursue its strategy. Each of the human resource practices benefits from being in alignment with other practices to develop a synergistic method of managing and leading employees.

Technology Proponent

Modern organizations require the management of massive amounts of information, which is aided by the **technology proponent** competency. Effective human resource specialists not only use technology themselves but also facilitate use by others. Understanding computing resources and software packages ensures that human resource specialists organize and retrieve information about employees. They also use technology to connect people to one another, which often comes through effective use of social media.

HR innovator and integrator Knowledge and skills that ensure HR practices such as work design, staffing, and compensation are aligned in ways that facilitate organizational success.

Technology proponent Knowledge and skills used to help organizations effectively adopt technology to manage information and connect individuals.

CONCEPT CHECK

1. *What are the four critical human resource roles, and what are some key features of each?*
2. *What is a competency, and what six competencies do human resource professionals need to develop?*

LEARNING OBJECTIVE 4

How Will Current Trends Affect Human Resource Management?

We've already seen that the ability to manage change is a key aspect of human resource management. The labor market is one important area in which changes can influence the organization's human resource practices. Of course, nobody can predict the future with perfect accuracy, but a review of trends in the labor market suggests some areas of expected change. In response, organizations and their human resource practices may need to change as well. One good source of information about labor market trends is the Bureau of Labor Statistics (BLS), an agency within the U.S. Department of Labor. BLS surveys and analyses predict particularly important trends related to changes in population, the labor force, employment opportunities, and education and training.[39] One such trend is an increasing move toward globalization and multinational corporations.

POPULATION TRENDS

How much will the U.S. population grow in the coming years? Will the proportion of young people in the population get bigger or smaller? What about the balance of minority groups? Each of these questions focuses on U.S. **population trends**, which are general movements over time in the number and characteristics of people living in the United States. Organizations are interested in population trends for two main reasons: to help them determine how the demand for their goods and services might change and to provide insight into the number and type of workers that are likely to be available in the future.

Population trends
Demographic trends related to the characteristics of people in a certain population.

The U.S. population grew 11.9 percent over the past ten years, and current projections indicate that the country's total population will grow by about 10.6 percent during the next decade. The rate of growth is thus expected to be somewhat lower than in the past. We might conclude, then, that the demand for goods and services will increase, more jobs will be created, and a growing number of workers will enter the workforce during this period. Like the rate of population growth, however, the rates of growth in these areas will be somewhat lower than in the past.

The balance between young and old people in the U.S. population is also changing. By 2018 the number of people between the ages of 16 and 24 will stay about the same, the number between 25 and 34 years old will grow. Those between 45 and 54 will shrink, and the number older than 55 will increase by almost 30 percent. Demand for goods and services desired by older people should thus increase considerably. The workforce will also become older, with more people near the ends of their careers. As a result, attracting and motivating older workers will become a more important task for human resource departments.

LABOR FORCE TRENDS

Of course, not everybody in the population works. **Labor force trends** focus not on the population as a whole but on the number and characteristics of people who will be working or looking for work. Racial proportions will also continue to change. The percentage of non-Hispanic white employees is expected to decrease from approximately 70 to 65 percent of the workforce, whereas the percentage of Hispanic workers will increase from about 15 to 19 percent of the workforce. Another important trend concerns women in the workforce. The number of female employees is expected to continue growing slightly faster (7 percent growth) than the number of male employees (6 percent growth).

Labor force trends
Trends concerning the number and types of people who are working or looking for work.

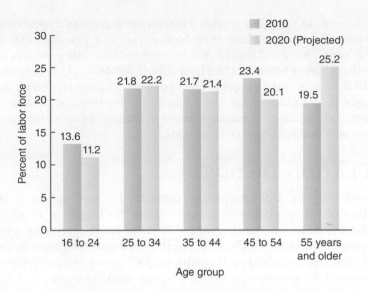

Figure 1.4 Labor Force by Age. *Source:* http://bls.gov/ooh/About/Projections-Overview.htm#educationandtraining.

Attracting and keeping minority and female employees will become increasingly important. We might thus expect to see more programs that offer convenience to working mothers, such as flexible working hours and on-site daycare. Organizations will also need to find better ways to meet the needs of minority workers. One such approach is to create ongoing groups of people with underrepresented backgrounds and needs who can meet together and discuss issues. These groups can also provide important feedback and suggestions to help leaders understand the unique perspectives of minority workers. As shown in Figure 1.4, the population trend for age will also result in a greater proportion of older workers by 2020. Integrating diverse workers will thus be increasingly critical.

EMPLOYMENT TRENDS

Employment opportunity trends

Trends concerning the types of jobs that will be available in the future.

Nobody wants to work in a company or an industry without a future. Therefore, an important question that arises is, Where will the jobs be in the years to come? **Employment opportunity trends** identify the type of work opportunities that will likely be available in the future. One ongoing trend that is expected to continue is the shift from goods-producing to service-providing employment. Most new jobs will be in areas that produce services. Figure 1.5 provides an overview of industies where jobs are expected to be created over the next decade. The fastest-growing industries will be health services, professional services, and education. The need for healthcare services will continue to increase as the population ages, and the demand for childcare will grow as more women enter the workforce.[40]

Organizations in growing industries often find it difficult to attract and retain enough high-quality workers. Good human resource management is particularly beneficial in these organizations because it helps them win the war for talent. Effective recruiting, hiring, and compensation are therefore expected to be particularly critical for high-growth occupations such as nurses, computer programmers, and teachers. The outlook is bright for occupations such as health aide and medical secretary, but it is rather bleak for production workers who make and assemble goods such as clothing.

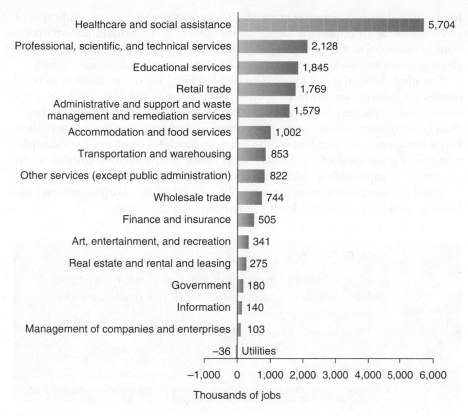

Figure 1.5 Trends In Service Industry Jobs between 2010 and 2020.
Source: http://bls.gov/ooh/About/Projections-Overview.htm#educationandtraining.

TRENDS IN EDUCATION AND TRAINING

Education and training trends tell us something about what competencies people will need to perform jobs in the future and how organizations can better focus their recruitment efforts. Growth is expected for a number of jobs that require advanced education. Indeed, the growth of jobs requiring doctoral or professional degrees is expected to be above 20 percent, whereas the growth of jobs requiring a high school diploma or less are expected to be below 15 percent. Yet, even with higher growth in jobs that require more education, approximately 60 percent of new jobs will still require only a high school diploma or less.

Training sometimes comes on the job rather than from formal education, and some jobs in high-growth areas will require this sort of training. Healthcare aides, who perform tasks in areas such as physical therapy, home care, and social services, represent such jobs. Organizations that need employees with these skills must develop on-the-job training programs that will ensure that new employees learn the necessary knowledge and skills.

GLOBALIZATION TRENDS

Globalization trends influence human resource management at many companies. Globalization refers to a process in which companies move beyond their national borders to do business in other countries. For global companies, the entire world represents not only their marketplace but also their place of production.

Education and training trends
Trends concerning the knowledge and skills workers will need in the future.

Globalization trends
Trends concerning the process by which companies move from doing business within one country to doing business in many countries.

International trade is growing at nearly 10 percent per year, a sure indicator of globalization as an important force.[41] Numerous large corporations have operations in countries scattered across the globe; even many small companies are purchasing goods and seeking sales from people living in more than one country.

The globalization trend appears to be beneficial for organizations, as companies on average are more profitable when greater portions of their sales, assets, and employees are foreign.[42] Nevertheless, having operations in more than one country does increase the complexity of human resource activities. Fairly compensating employees who work in foreign countries, for example, requires a great deal of expertise. Legal issues across various countries can also make it impossible to adopt standardized practices. Developing an international perspective for managing people is thus crucial as organizations continue to develop in multiple locations throughout the world.

CONCEPT CHECK

1. *How are current population trends and labor force trends likely to affect organizations and their human resource practices in the future?*
2. *What do employment opportunity trends tell us?*
3. *How does globalization complicate human resource management?*

LEARNING OBJECTIVE 5

How Do Strategic and Functional Perspectives Combine to Direct Human Resource Practices?

This chapter provides a broad introduction to human resource management, a field that focuses on people in organizations. Through good human resource practices, organizations can become more successful in a number of ways. The human resource management field has changed somewhat in recent years. Historically, it has emphasized functional skills, which represent day-to-day activities such as developing specific hiring methods, conducting pay surveys, and providing training. Today, however, it also requires strategic skills, which represent broader aspects of business and include activities such as planning and change management. Successful organizations require leaders and human resource professionals to pay attention to both strategic objectives and taking care of people.[43]

Accordingly, this textbook integrates the functional and strategic perspectives. The overall outline of the book is shown in Figure 1.6. Specifically, chapters are built around a strategic framework that illustrates how human resource decisions and practices fit with organizational strategy. Most chapters also discuss a key functional area.

As shown in the figure, an organization's competitive business strategy, along with legal and safety issues, influences the organization's choice of a human resource strategy. In turn, the human resource strategy chosen shapes

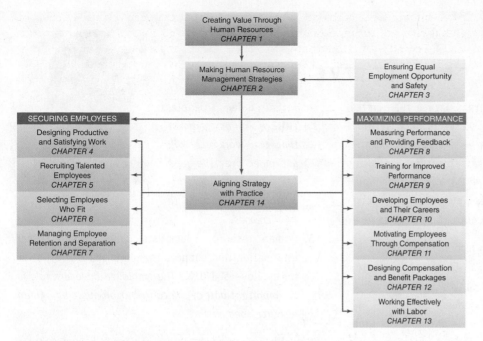

Figure 1.6 Framework and Chapter Outline Illustrating How Human Resource Management Practice Links to Strategy.

the specific activities the organization uses to secure and motivate employees. Activities aimed at securing employees include work design, recruiting, selection, and retention; these are discussed in Chapters 4 through 7. Activities that relate to motivating workers, which include performance management, career development, training, compensation, and labor relations, are discussed in Chapters 8 through 13. All these activities must be coordinated with each other as well as with the overall human resource strategy. The importance of coordination is discussed in Chapter 14.

Human resource management is an exciting field that provides critical benefits to organizations. Studying human resource management can help you develop knowledge and skills that will make you more effective throughout your career. Even if you don't become a human resource specialist, knowing why human resource specialists do what they do will enable you to work more cooperatively with them. Furthermore, knowing about methods for hiring and motivating others can provide you with important leadership skills. As you grow into leadership positions, you will be better equipped to meet the needs of others. Gaining knowledge about human resources will also make you a better strategic planner, enabling you to see how the needs of people and programs can be integrated to promote high performance. Taking a course in human resource management and reading this text can thus be important in determining your future success.

CONCEPT CHECK

1. *How do the functional perspective and the strategic perspective combine to create success?*

A MANAGER'S PERSPECTIVE REVISITED

Photolnc/iStockphoto

IN THE MANAGER'S PERSPECTIVE THAT OPENED THE CHAPTER, MIGUEL WAS EXCITED ABOUT THE PROSPECTS OF ACCEPTING A JOB OFFER. HE FELT LIKE THE FIRM WAS SUCCESSFUL AND THAT IT WOULD PROVIDE HIM WITH A BRIGHT FUTURE. FOLLOWING ARE THE ANSWERS TO THE "WHAT DO YOU THINK?" QUIZ THAT FOLLOWED THE CASE. WERE YOU ABLE TO CORRECTLY IDENTIFY THE TRUE STATEMENTS? COULD YOU DO BETTER NOW?

1. Companies with good human resource practices have more satisfied workers. **TRUE.** *Companies who treat employees well have more satisfied workers, who in turn provide better customer service.*

2. Companies with happy employees are more profitable. **TRUE.** *High employee satisfaction has been consistently linked to good organizational performance.*

3. Companies lose money when they try to be good social and environmental citizens. **FALSE.** *More socially responsible companies actually have higher profits on average.*

4. Having a successful career in the future workplace will require young employees to work effectively with older people. **TRUE.** *Trends suggest that the workforce will get older over the next few years as the percentage of people aged 55 to 64 increases.*

5. Human resource specialists can provide critical information and support that help make life better for employees. **TRUE.** *The employee advocate role is an important part of the contribution made by human resource specialists.*

Miguel is wise to think about a company's human resource practices before deciding whether to accept a job offer. Effective human resource management is a key determinant of employee satisfaction and is an important part of organizational success. Joining a company with effective human resource practices will mean that Miguel is more likely to enjoy his work—and that his new employer is likely to be around for all the years that Miguel wants to work there.

SUMMARY

LEARNING OBJECTIVE 1

How is organizational success determined?

The contribution of human resources to success can vary across an organization's life cycle. In the entrepreneurial stage, survival equals success. Human resource management helps the organization find employees. Success during the communal stage is marked by expansion and innovation. Building a sense of belonging and satisfying the needs of employees are critical. During the formalization stage, success comes from developing clear and efficient procedures. Human resource management builds structured programs that provide consistent procedures. An organization must change and adapt in the elaboration stage. This change is facilitated by hiring and rewarding people who have new ideas and different ways of doing things.

The stakeholder perspective focuses on people who affect and are affected by an organization. Human resource practices protect the interests of employees, and organizations with good practices experience lower employee turnover. Skilled and motivated employees effectively meet the needs of customers. Organizations with more effective human resource management practices have higher profits. Better human resource management can also benefit society as a whole by protecting the environment and helping disadvantaged people.

What does human resource management provide to an organization?

Human resource departments provide organizations with a number of key functions. In the function of business management and strategy, the human resource department works with other parts of the organization to plan effective methods of delivering goods and services. The function of workforce planning and employment determines who will do what tasks and recruits and selects people into jobs. The function of human resource development focuses on measuring the contributions of employees and teaching them new knowledge and skills. In the function of compensation and benefits, the human resource department plays an important role in making sure that employees are paid fairly and receive the proper insurance benefits. A fifth function is employee and labor relations, which captures efforts to work with labor unions and to ensure fair treatment of workers. The final human resource function is risk management.

What do human resource specialists do?

Human resource specialists add value to an organization through a number of different roles. In the functional expert role, they build systems and practices that help the organization better manage people. Human resource specialists contribute knowledge and skills that many other organizational members do not have. The employee advocate role provides an opportunity for meeting the needs of individual employees. Specialists filling this role listen to employee concerns and try to help them solve problems. The human resource perspective is integrated into other parts of the organization through the strategic partner role. The role of human capital developer facilitates learning and makes sure that employees in the organization continue to develop new knowledge and skills.

Performing the human resource roles requires competency in six different areas. One area is strategic positioning. Effective human resource specialists understand business issues such as finance, strategy, stakeholders, and competitive context. The second competency relates to becoming a credible activist who can successfully influence others. The third competency focuses on being a capability builder, which occurs when human resource specialists help the organization understand and leverage its unique strengths. The fourth competency emphasizes becoming a change champion. The fifth competency is most closely related to traditional HR skills and emphasizes the proper alignment of staffing and motivation processes. Being a technology proponent encompasses the final competency, which emphasizes the importance of embracing the use of new tools for managing information and connecting people.

How will current trends affect organizations and human resource management?

The U.S. population will increase, though at a lower rate than in the past, and will get older. As the population ages, the demand for products and services purchased by older people, such as healthcare, will grow. Older workers will also make up a greater percentage of the workforce. The proportion of Hispanic workers and women in the workforce will increase as well. Human resource departments will thus benefit from finding ways to meet the needs of older people, women, and members of minority groups. Job growth is expected in the fields of healthcare and social assistance services. Globalization will require human resource departments to create processes that effectively manage people working in various foreign countries.

How do strategic and functional perspectives combine to direct human resource practices?

In order to be truly effective, human resource management must combine strategic planning with day-to-day functional activities. Specific areas where this combination can take place include improving methods for securing employees and then maximizing their performance.

KEY TERMS

Business management and strategy   14
Capability builder competencies   22
Change champion competencies   23
Communal stage   7
Compensation and benefits   15
Competencies   22
Credible activist competencies   22
Education and training trends   27
Elaboration stage   9
Employee advocate role   19
Employee and labor relations   16
Employee turnover   10
Employment opportunity trends   26
Entrepreneurial stage   7
Formalization stage   9

Functional expert role   19
Globalization trends   27
HR innovator and integrator competencies   24
Human capital developer role   21
Human resource development   14
Human resource management   4
Labor force trends   25
Organizational life cycle   6
Population trends   25
Risk management   16
Stakeholders   9
Strategic partner role   20
Strategic positioner competencies   22
Technology proponent competencies   24
Workforce planning and employment   14

DISCUSSION QUESTIONS

1. Why might a newly formed organization be considered successful even if it is losing money?

2. Think of stores where you shop. Do employees of some stores seem happier than employees of other stores? What human resource practices might explain differences in employee happiness?

3. How can socially responsible organizations have high profits even though they spend money on things like environmental protection?

4. Why do managers and human resource specialists often do poorly on tests about the best ways of hiring and paying employees?

5. What are some specific things that can be done to teach company leaders how human resource management can contribute to organizational success?

6. Which human resource role do you think is most important? employee advocate? functional expert? strategic partner? human capital developer? Explain your answer.

7. Why do you think change is so difficult for organizations? What can human resource specialists do to make change easier?

8. What are some challenges you might face if you join an organization with a lot of older workers?

9. What are some things an organization could do to better meet the needs of women and members of minority groups?

10. How do you think the field of human resource management will change in the next 10 years?

 *Zappos*

Keeping employees happy at Zappos.com takes a little weirdness and a willingness to make work fun. You may not expect a woman whose footwear of choice is tennis shoes to work at one of the world's largest online shoe companies, but for senior HR manager Hollie Delaney, PHR, Zappos.com Inc. is a comfy fit.

Staff members in six HR functions report to Delaney at this intense, high-energy company where a worker might spring onto a table during a meeting and perform an impromptu break dance, and the computer log-on requires identifying the photo of a randomly selected employee. Conference rooms at corporate headquarters in Henderson, Nevada, are named after casinos in a nod to the famed Strip 6.7 miles away. In fact, the company plans to relocate to downtown Las Vegas sometime in 2012 or 2013. Job applicants at the 24/7 operation are interviewed in a room resembling a talk show set, and employees have been asked to submit creative ideas in various scenarios such as coming up with their own designs for Steve Madden creations. During annual Bald & Blue Day, CEO Tony Hsieh and other employees volunteer to shave their heads or dye their hair blue.

HR Magazine talked to Delaney about her career and how Zappos delivers happiness to its customers—and its 3,000 employees.

Question: Before Zappos, you worked in HR at a casino. What was that like?

It was big and impersonal, with thousands of employees and so many rules between unions and nonunions. There was a rule for everything—even that I had to wear pantyhose if I worked in HR. It made it difficult to be yourself. At the time, I thought HR was not for me.

Question: Describe your Zappos job interview.

During the phone interview, I described myself as "fun but a little weird." The interviewer said "Wow, that's one of our core values." I met everyone in HR and interviewed with 10 managers, including Tony. He was sitting in a cubicle alongside other employees; I didn't know he was the CEO at first. I started crying while telling him about my "miracle baby" and thought I'd blown the job interview.

Question: During on-boarding, Zappos offers new hires $3,000 to leave if they don't think they and the company are a good fit. Were you tempted?

It was $1,000 when I started, but no. Everybody here was so happy. They were so invested in this company. You could see it, and you could feel it. I was floored. I was skeptical, but I knew there had to be something special here for people to behave that way.

Question: How can you tell if a candidate is a good fit?

When people tour our company, they're kind of shellshocked. Some cannot get over the fact that people aren't in offices and it's so loud. Or, they want to work 9 to 5 and call it a day. Our environment is not the ideal place to meet those types of expectations. A state of consistent change, the open environment, and team aspect do not work for everyone. We move around a lot; you get to build relationships with people you haven't met before. You can be in senior management in four to seven years. In our call center, employees bid for different shifts every six months. You can wear pajamas or bunny ears to a meeting and be taken seriously—actually, they're more responsive to you.

The recruiting team interviews candidates for culture fit and a willingness to change and to learn. They notice how applicants interact at lunch. Do they talk with others or just the person they think makes the hiring decision? Our shuttle drivers tell us what candidates say during the ride back to their hotels.

Question: When did you know you had embraced the culture?

It took me about a year to change from focusing on the 10 percent of employees who cause problems to the 90 percent who do not. I remember Tony wanted to let all employees give out one $50 monthly bonus to any employee they chose. My traditional HR response was "You're insane." I thought people would give it to their friends, but some didn't even give it out at all: They were waiting for people to "wow" them the same way they were expected to wow customers. I didn't have any skepticism left by the time we started the Wishez Program in 2010. Employees' wishes have ranged from asking for homemade frosted sugar cookies to wanting to jump off the Stratosphere Hotel. One worker's wish for a car was granted when an employee bought a new car and gave him his old vehicle.

Question: I understand you wrestled with staying in HR at Zappos. What happened?

I'd been here nearly two years. People did not like HR when I started. It had the stigma of being the Debbie Downer Department, the rules enforcer. No one wants to be a part of that. HR was in a transitional period. We didn't have a Zappos identity. I felt like an outsider looking in. Headhunters started calling me. I wasn't sure what I wanted to do, where I stood with the company. I realized when I was talking to the life coach on staff that I had a huge opportunity to do something awesome at this awesome company. We started asking different managers what they needed from HR. An HR generalist started sitting in each department for eight months. Now, they include us in termination discussions. We are invited to teams' happy hours. We work with them to be part of the good things they do and not just the "You're getting written up" conversations. Zappos' ZCON team, which moved to HR from merchandising in January and handles areas such as reception, shuttle services, travel, and concierge services, is bringing a new face to HR. I'm having fun now. I could never go back to a traditional HR job. Here, our job is to educate employees. I'm more of a teacher, not a policeman. Our job is to protect the culture. If HR says "no," it doesn't mean no. You have to know all the rules of HR but be able to throw them out. If it's a rule, is it a good rule?

QUESTIONS

1. Does Zappos sound like a place you would want to work? Why?

2. Do you think it makes sense to offer new employees a $3,000 incentive to quit?

3. How do you think the role of HR might change as Zappos matures as a company?

4. How does the role of HR at Zappos differ from typical companies such as the casinos referenced in the article?

Source: Originally published as "Delivering HR at Zappos" by Kathy Guchiek c 2011, Society for Human Resource Management, Alexandria, VA. Used with permission. All rights reserved.

Curt's Cowboy Corner

Curt's Cowboy Corner is a chain of 15 stores that sells cowboy boots and western clothing. Curt opened the first store 10 years ago in a small Rocky Mountain town and quickly gained a following of loyal customers. Based on input from customers and friends, Curt decided to expand his business and began opening new stores in nearby towns. He plans to open 10 more stores in the next few years.

Each of Curt's stores has a manager, three full-time sales representatives, and five or six part-time employees. In the early days, Curt worked closely with each store manager to plan day-to-day operations, helping to make all hiring decisions. He and a secretary also spent many days each month working on payroll. Lately, however, Curt has found that he does not have enough time to interview job candidates and handle several other of his customary tasks. He thinks this might be one reason some of the newer employees aren't working out so well. In addition, last month, he was two days late completing the payroll, thereby creating numerous problems for employees. Curt knows that he needs to do a better job of delegating tasks. Another of his concerns focuses on the potential liabilities of having a growing workforce. One employee recently told him that she felt uncomfortable about some sexual comments her boss had made to her. Curt spent several hours talking to both the employee and her boss, and although he feels pretty good about how he handled the situation, he acknowledges that he does not have the requisite knowledge or skill to resolve such matters.

Curt's brother, who owns a number of automobile dealerships in a distant city, has encouraged Curt to hire a human resource professional. But Curt has been reluctant to hire staff members who do not spend time selling in stores. His philosophy has always been that staff members who don't make sales are an expense without much return. At the same time Curt knows that he must do something or else things will get worse. If he is able to grow the business as he plans, he will soon have nearly 100 full-time employees.

QUESTIONS

1. What are some specific tasks that a human resource specialist could do for Curt?
2. Are there any financial benefits that might come from hiring a human resource specialist?
3. How might labor trends affect Curt's ability to continue expanding his stores?
4. What benefits and problems might result if Curt hires a human resource specialist to provide support to all stores? Would it be better to simply delegate all human resource activities to each store manager?

EXPERIENTIAL EXERCISE — *Visit the SHRM Website*

The Society for Human Resource Management (SHRM) is a professional association devoted to human resource management. Visit the SHRM website at shrm.org and learn about the human resources field.

Look for information related to the following questions:

1. How many members are there in SHRM?
2. What types of careers are available in the field of human resource management?
3. What is the SHRM Code of Ethics, and how does it guide the efforts of human resource specialists?
4. What kind of resources does SHRM offer to help people learn new skills?
5. What are chapter/member groups? Who can join?
6. What are some current news issues that relate to human resource management?

INTERACTIVE EXPERIENTIAL EXERCISE — *Building an HR Department at Mega Manufacturing*

http://www.wiley.com/college/sc/stewart

Access the companion website to test your knowledge by completing a Mega Manufacturing role-playing exercise.

In this exercise, you're an HR consultant and will be assisting a small but established company (Mega Manufacturing) who will be going through significant expansion due to a new government contract. With the growth, the owner knows that it will be a good idea to add a dedicated HR person to his management team and wants you to help. As he's talking about the beliefs and vision of the company, you consider the organizational life cycle model, core HR functions, and critical HR roles. He then asks for your suggestions, and you realize that this assignment may be a great opportunity to align this new HR department with the strategy of the company. •

ENDNOTES

1. Michael Riketta, "The Causal Relation Between Job Attitudes and Performance: A Meta-Analysis of Panel Studies," *Journal of Applied Psychology* 93 (2008): 472–481; Ingrid Smithey Fulmer, Barry Gerhart, and Kimberly S. Scott, "Are the 100 Best Better? An Empirical Investigation of the Relationship Between Being a 'Great Place to Work' and Firm Performance," *Personnel Psychology* 56 (2003): 965–993; Benjamin Schneider and David E. Bowen, "Employee and Customer Perceptions of Service in Banks: Replication and Extension," *Journal of Applied Psychology* 70 (1985): 423–433.
2. John A. Byrne, "Lessons from Our Customer Champions," *Fast Company* 87 (October 2004):16; "Trader Joe's Targets 'Educated' Buyer," *Seattle Post-Intelligencer*, August 30, 2003; Stan Abraham, "Dan Bane, CEO of Trader Joe's," *Strategy & Leadership* 30, no. 6 (2002): 30–32.
3. Irwin Speitzer, "The Grocery Chain That Shouldn't Be," *Fast Company* 79 (February 2004): 31. Abraham, "Dan Bane," 30–32.
4. Jena McGregor, "Leading Listener: Trader Joe's," *Fast Company* 87 (October 2004): 82–83; Len Lewis, excerpts from *Trader Joe's Adventure*, (Chicago: Dearborn Trade Publishing, 2005). Reported in "Fostering a Loyal Work force at Trader Joe's," *Workforce Management Online*, June 2005, www.workforce.com/archive/feature/24/06/51/index.php.
5. http://company.monster.com/trader; Lewis, *Trader Joe's Adventure.*
6. Lewis, *Trader Joe's Adventure;* Beth Kowitt, "Inside the Secret World of Trader Joe's," Fortune International 162, no. 4 (2010): 32–39.
7. Larry Armstrong, "Trader Joe's: The Trendy American Cousin," *BusinessWeek,* 3880 (April 26, 2004): 62; Kowitt, "Inside the Secret World of Trader Joe's," 32–39.
8. http://www.traderjoes.com/about/customer-updates-responses.asp?i=60
9. Robert E. Quinn and Kim Cameron, "Organizational Life Cycles and Shifting Criteria of Effectiveness: Some Preliminary Evidence," *Management Science* 29 (1983): 33–51; I. M. Jawahar and Gary L. McLaughlin, "Toward a Descriptive Stakeholder Theory: An Organizational Life Cycle Approach," *Academy of Management Review* 26 (2001): 397–414.

10. BNA, Inc. HR Department Benchmarks and Analysis™: (Washington, DC: Bureau of National Affairs, 2004).

11. Theresa M. Welbourne and Alice O. Andrews, "Predicting the Performance of Initial Public Offerings: Should Human Resource Management Be in the Equation?" *Academy of Management Journal* 39 (1996): 891–919.

12. Speitzer, "The Grocery Chain That Shouldn't Be," 31.

13. Jake G. Messersmith, Pankaj C. Patel, David P. Lepak, and Julian S. Gould-Williams, "Unlocking the Black Box: Exploring the Link Between High-Performance Work Systems and Performance," Journal of Applied Psychology 96 (2011): 1105–1118.

14. Mark A. Huselid, "The Impact of Human Resource Management Practices on Turnover, Productivity, and Corporate Financial Performance," *Academy of Management Journal* 38 (1995): 635–672.

15. Jeremy Smerd, "IBM: Optimas Award Winner for Financial Impact," *Workforce Management*, October 20, 2008, 22.

16. Dave Ulrich, Wayne Brockbank, Arthur K. Yeung, and Dale G. Lake, "Human Resource Competencies: An Empirical Assessment," *Human Resource Management* 34 (1995): 473–495.

17. Patrick J. Keger, "Crouse Hospital: Optimas Award for General Excellence," *Workforce Management*, October 20, 2008, 16–17; http://www.crouse.org/careers/.

18. R. Edward Freeman, *Strategic Management: A Stakeholder Perspective* (Marshfield, MA: Pittman Publishing, 1984).

19. Max B. E. Clarkson, "A Stakeholder Framework for Analyzing and Evaluating Corporate Social Performance," *Academy of Management Review* 20 (1995): 92–117.

20. Huselid, "The Impact of Human Resource Management Practices," 635–672; Rosemary Batt, "Managing Customer Services: Human Resource Practices, Quit Rates, and Sales Growth," *Academy of Management Journal* 45, no. 3 (2002): 587–597.

21. Peter W. Hom and Angelo J. Kinicki, "Toward a Greater Understanding of How Dissatisfaction Drives Employee Turnover," *Academy of Management Journal* 44 (2001): 975–987; Rodger W. Griffeth, Peter W. Hom, and Stefan Gaertner, "A Meta-Analysis of Antecedents and Correlates of Employee Turnover: Update, Moderator Tests, and Research Implications for the Next Millennium," *Journal of Management* 26 (2000): 463–488. Schneider and Bowen, "Employee and Customer Perceptions," 423–433.

22. Huselid, "The Impact of Human Resource Management Practices," 635–672.

23. Stephanie C. Payne and Sheila Simsarian Webber, "Effects of Service Provider Attitudes and Employment Status on Citizenship Behaviors and Customers' Attitudes and Loyalty Behavior," *Journal of Applied Psychology* 91 (2006): 365–378.

24. Batt, "Managing Customer Services," 587–597.

25. Mahesh Subramony, Nicole Krause, Jacqueline Norton, and Gary N. Burns, "The Relationship between Human Resource Investments and Organizational Performance: A Firm-Level Examination of Equilibrium Theory," *Journal of Applied Psychology* 93 (2008): 778–788.

26. Mark Orlitzky, Frank L. Schmidt, and Sara L Rynes, "Corporate Social and Financial Performance: A Meta-Analysis," *Organization Studies* 24 (2003): 403–441; W. Gary Simpson and Theodore Kohers, "The Link Between Corporate Social and Financial Performance: Evidence from the Banking Industry," *Journal of Business Ethics* 35 (2002): 97–109; Bernadette M. Ruf, Krishnamurty Muralidhar, Robert M. Brown, Jay J. Janney, and Karen Paul, "An Empirical Investigation Between Change in Corporate Social Performance and Financial Performance: A Stakeholder Theory Perspective," *Journal of Business Ethics* 32 (2001): 143–156.

27. Pedro Lorca and Julita Garcia-Biez, "The Relation between Firm Survival and the Achievement of Balance among Its Stakeholders: An Analysis," *International Journal of Management* 21 (2004): 93–99.

28. Ingrid Smithey Fulmer, Barry Gerhart, and Kimberly S. Scott, "Are the 100 Best Better? An Empirical Investigation of the Relationship Between Being a 'Great Place to Work' and Firm Performance," *Personnel Psychology* 56 (2003): 965–993.

29. http://www.hrci.org/uploadedfiles/Content/Resource_Library/Certification_Handbooks_and_Other_Publications/PHR-SPHR%20BOK.pdf

30. Judy Greenwald, "Multicountry Benefits Require Delicate Touch," *Business Insurance* 40, no. 50. (2006): 12–13.

31. Sara L. Rynes, Amy E. Colbert, and Kenneth G. Brown, "HR Professionals' Beliefs about Human Resource Practices: Correspondence between Research and Practice," *Human Resource Management* 41 (2002): 149–174.

32. Sara L. Rynes, Tamara L. Giluk, and Kenneth G. Brown, "The Very Separate Worlds of Academic and Practitioner Periodicals in Human Resource Management: Implications for Evidence-Based Management," *Academy of Management Journal* 50 (2007): 987–1008.

33. Dave Ulrich and Wayne Brockbank, *The HR Value Proposition* (Boston: Harvard Business Press, 2005).

34. http://www.unlv.edu/main/highlights.html.

35. Occupational Information Network, O*net Online see http://online.onetcenter.org/link/summary/11–3040.00

36. Ulrich and Brockbank, *The HR Value Proposition.*

37. Susan Quinn, "Putting the Human Back into Human Resources," *Public Management* 80, no. 9 (1998): 23–28.

38. Dave Ulrich, Jon Younger, Wayne Brockbank, and Mike Ulrich, HR from the Outside In: Six Competencies for the Future of Human Resources (New York: McGraw Hill, 2012).

39. Statistics taken from U.S. Department of Labor Bureau of Labor Statistics website, http://bls.gov/ooh/About/Projections-Overview.htm.

40. Ibid.

41. A. T. Kearney, Inc. "The Globalization Index," *Foreign Policy* 157 (2006): 75–81.

42. Sally Sledge, "Globalization and Performance in the New Millennium: A Look at Firms from Developed and Developing Nations," *Journal of American Academy of Business* 10, no. 2 (2007): 51–57.

43. Mathis Schulte, Cheri Ostroff, Svetlana Shmulyian, and Angelo Kinicki, "Organizational Climate Configurations: Relationships to Collective Attitudes, Customer Satisfaction, and Financial Performance," *Journal of Applied Psychology* 94 (2009): 618–634.

Chapter 2
Making Human Resource Management Strategic

A MANAGER'S PERSPECTIVE

alynst/iStockphoto

ELIZABETH CLOSES HER OFFICE DOOR AND BEGINS THINKING ABOUT THE SMALL CHAIN OF CONVENIENCE STORES SHE PURCHASED LAST MONTH. THE PREVIOUS OWNER WORKED HARD AND SUCCESSFULLY GREW FROM A SINGLE STORE TO THE CURRENT FOUR OUTLETS. ELIZABETH WAS EXCITED WHEN SHE LEARNED THAT HE HAD ACCEPTED HER BID TO PURCHASE THE STORES. HOWEVER, NOW THAT THE DEAL HAS CLOSED, SHE KNOWS SHE NEEDS TO MAKE SOME CHANGES. THE STORES ARE ALL LOCATED IN DESIRABLE LOCATIONS AND ARE CURRENTLY PROFITABLE, BUT SHE HAS ALREADY FOUND IT DIFFICULT TO WORK WITH SOME OF HER MANAGERS. THE LACK OF QUALITY EMPLOYEES HAS REQUIRED HER TO SPEND SEVERAL HOURS DOING MANAGERIAL DUTIES IN TWO OF THE STORES. ELIZABETH HAS ALSO HEARD RUMORS THAT A LARGE NATIONAL CHAIN IS THINKING OF EXPANDING INTO HER TERRITORY. EVEN IF THE COMPETITOR DOES NOT EXPAND, SHE IS CONVINCED THAT THE STORES WILL FAIL UNLESS SHE MAKES SOME CRITICAL DECISIONS AND DEVELOPS A BETTER STRATEGIC PLAN.

Elizabeth knows that effective human resource management must be a big part of her strategic plan. She honestly believes that making employees happy is the key to making customers happy. Obviously, raising wages would make employees happy; yet, Elizabeth also understands that her choices are constrained by a need to produce profit. Paying too much in wages could result in losses that threaten her ability to keep the stores open. An even bigger issue is thus her need to develop a plan for ensuring loyal customers and earnings sufficient to cover her business expenditures.

Elizabeth remembers a few years back when she attended an educational retreat and took a strategic management course that focused on different ways businesses compete with each other to deliver services and goods. She doesn't think her stores currently have a clear strategy. Do people shop at her stores because she sells products that are superior to those sold by other stores? Perhaps customers are loyal only because prices are cheaper. As she reflects on these questions, Elizabeth realizes that she doesn't really have a plan for how she will compete with other stores, particularly a large national chain.

Ned Dishman/NBAE/Getty Images

THE BIG PICTURE *Human Resource Management Is Most Successful When Aligned with an Organization's Competitive Business Strategy*

She wonders if her human resource decisions might need to be different depending on her strategy.

The previous store owner emphasized developing loyalty and trying to make sure that employees stayed at the stores for long periods of time. She thinks this approach offers a lot of benefits. But she sometimes wonders if it would help to bring in more new people. What about diversity? Can her stores benefit from new skills and ways of thinking? Given the current economy and relatively high rate of unemployment, Elizabeth is quite certain that she would be able to identify and hire some very good new employees. Would now be a good time to bring in some outside talent?

As she thinks about her decisions, Elizabeth reminds herself that this is a big opportunity. She is excited by the prospect of making a difference and helping her new stores rise to even greater heights.

WHAT DO YOU THINK?

Suppose Elizabeth hears the following comments during a meeting with some friends who are entrepreneurs. Which of the statements do you think are true?

T OR F Having good employees is more important than having good production equipment.

T OR F Much of the workforce lacks needed skills, so high-quality employees are difficult to find and retain.

T OR F The most effective way for an organization to compete with other organizations is to produce similar goods and services at lower prices.

T OR F Organizations are most effective when they develop a highly committed workforce.

T OR F An organization seeking to produce the highest-quality products should have different human resource practices from an organization seeking to produce inexpensive products.

LEARNING OBJECTIVES

LEARNING OBJECTIVES

After reading this chapter you should be able to:

LEARNING OBJECTIVE 1 Describe the strategy formulation process.

LEARNING OBJECTIVE 2 Describe two generic competitive business strategies that organizations use.

LEARNING OBJECTIVE 3 Explain the universalistic and contingency approaches to human resource strategy, including key characteristics of the commitment strategy.

LEARNING OBJECTIVE 4 Describe four human resource strategies that organizations commonly use.

LEARNING OBJECTIVE 5 Explain how human resource strategies and competitive business strategies are aligned.

How Can a Strategic Approach to Human Resources Improve an Organization?

Suppose someone gave you $10,000 to invest in a single company, with the condition that you must leave the money invested in the same company for the next 30 years. At the end of 30 years, you get to keep all the profits from the investment. What company would you choose? Would it be a technology-focused company like Microsoft? How about a global leader like Coca-Cola? Maybe a large company with numerous products, such as General Electric? What would be the most important factors to consider when making this choice?

As discussed in Chapter 1, profitability is an important part of organizational effectiveness and a factor you would certainly want to consider in choosing an investment. In fact, business researchers and stock analysts spend a lot of time trying to learn why some companies are consistently more profitable than others. One possible explanation is that highly profitable companies are simply in desirable industries. Perhaps it is just easier to earn profits doing some types of work. Another potential explanation is that profitable companies have better technological capabilities—better equipment and processes. Still another possibility is that highly profitable companies are just bigger. Their large size might provide them with more power and resources, making it easier to produce goods and services. Yet none of these theories really explains why some companies are more profitable than others. In any industry, and at any size, some companies do well, and others do not.

Research suggests that a major key for long-term profitability is a clear strategy for being better than competitors, along with a highly effective workforce that carries out that strategy.[1] A good example is Southwest Airlines. The combination of a clear strategy and high-quality workforce allowed Southwest Airlines to earn the highest stock return of any company over a 30-year period.[2]

Southwest started out as a small company with three airplanes. Government regulations prohibited it from flying to states not bordering Texas. In the ensuing years Southwest Airlines has been consistently profitable, even at a time when other airlines have consistently lost money and many have faced bankruptcy. Just think about it. If you had been able to invest your $10,000 in

Southwest Airlines over a recent 30-year period, that investment would have grown to over $10.2 million.

As mentioned, one element of Southwest's success is its clear strategic direction. What are the elements of the company's strategy? First, it has a clear strategy of offering low fares. Unlike other major airlines, Southwest does not use a complicated price structure whereby some passengers pay much more than others. Instead, it aims to have the lowest available fare. The fact that other airlines are forced to substantially cut their fares once Southwest enters a market indicates how successful Southwest's low-fare strategy is.[3] Unfortunately for competitors, their costs to fly passengers are as much as 70 percent higher than Southwest's costs.[4] Why? Southwest is simply more efficient. This makes it possible for Southwest to earn profits while selling tickets at prices that would represent losses for other airlines.

What makes Southwest so much more efficient than other airlines? The company gets more productivity out of its employees. Southwest needs only about one-third as many employees as its competitors to fly the same number of customers.[5] How can it do this? The secret seems to be best captured by the company's founder, Herb Kelleher, who has said that Southwest's order of top priorities is employees, customers, and then shareholders.[6] In short, Southwest Airlines uses human resource practices to find and keep a large number of loyal employees who concentrate on reducing costs.

One way that Southwest reduces cost is by encouraging each employee to pitch in and help finish tasks, even if those tasks are not part of that person's normal job. For instance, flight attendants help clean airplane cabins, and pilots help move luggage. This practice greatly reduces the time that a plane is on the ground between flights.[7] Southwest has also developed a culture that makes it fun to work there. The company receives as many as 100 job applications for each open position.[8] Southwest is thus in the position of being able to hire only the very best employees. In particular, it focuses on hiring people who have the right attitude and who are willing to work hard to meet customer needs.[9] The company also pays well and was one of the first airline companies to share profits with employees.

The pattern of long-term success doesn't, however, prevent Southwest Airlines from continually facing strategic challenges. Herb Kelleher was followed as CEO by James Parker, who led the company through three somewhat troubling years. First, terrorist attacks and rising fuel costs made it increasingly difficult for airlines to earn profits. Then employees demanded higher wages, with negotiations frequently creating conflict between managers and employees.[10] Nevertheless, Southwest continued to outperform its competitors and return profits.[11] Gary Kelly, who took over in 2004 after Parker's retirement, makes it clear that he will not deviate from Southwest's core strategy: to be the airline with the lowest fares and the lowest cost structure. He also continues to emphasize the development of highly committed employees who spend their entire careers working to improve Southwest Airlines.[12] This consistent approach of adopting a low-cost strategy and emphasizing commitment to employees has been helpful during recent times of economic difficulty. Southwest did post financial losses during the recession that began in 2008,[13] but its lean structure and efficient practices helped it recover more quickly than competitors.[14] Success relative to competitors even allowed Southwest to expand by purchasing AirTran Airways in 2011, which among other benefits has allowed expansion of cross-border routes to Mexico and Caribbean destinations while retaining its cost focus.[15]

Building Strength Through HR

SOUTHWEST AIRLINES

Southwest Airlines is a low-cost airline that employs over 46,000 people to move over 100 million passengers each year. Human resource management at Southwest builds competitive advantage by

Ned Dishman/NBAE/ Getty Images

- Having a clear strategic direction for competing with other airlines.
- Creating a company culture where everyone is committed to success and doing whatever it takes to serve customers.
- Being highly selective and hiring only the very best employees.
- Paying above-average wages to obtain and keep the best employees.

The Southwest Airlines example illustrates how a strategic approach to human resource management increases organizational effectiveness. For Southwest, employees are a critical resource in meeting the needs of customers. The overall strategic direction of the organization guides decisions about how people are recruited, selected, trained, and compensated. These human resource practices help create a workforce that provides the talent necessary to serve customers well. Organizations such as Southwest that have clear strategies for effectively meeting the needs of customers, and clear human resource practices that match those strategies, simply get better results than other organizations.

LEARNING OBJECTIVE **1**

How Is Strategy Formulated?

Strategy
Coordinated choices and actions that provide direction for people and organizations.

Competitive business strategy
Strategy that focuses on different ways to provide goods and services that meet customer needs.

Human resource strategy
Strategy that focuses on different ways of managing employees of an organization.

We use the term *strategy* to discuss many things in our lives. We talk about strategies for taking exams, strategies for getting jobs, and strategies for saving money. But just what are we talking about when we use this term? We can think of a **strategy** as a set of coordinated choices and actions. Strategy concerns where you want to go and how you want to get there. Strategy is more than just decisions, however; it also concerns putting choices into practice.

With regard to human resource management in organizations, there are actually two types of strategy. One is **competitive business strategy**, which focuses on choices and actions about how to serve the needs of customers. The other is **human resource strategy**, which focuses on choices and actions concerning the management of people within the organization. These two types of strategy must work together to ensure high organizational effectiveness— as they do at Southwest Airlines.

One way of understanding similarities and differences in these two forms of strategy is to examine the common elements of strategy formulation. The first step in strategy formulation is gathering information (see Figure 2.1).

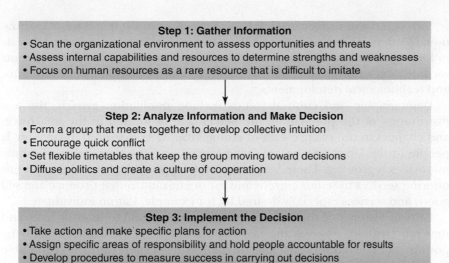

Figure 2.1 Strategy Formulation Process.

Information gathering commonly involves assessments both of the external environment and of internal capabilities. Once relevant information has been gathered, it is analyzed, and decisions are made. The set of decisions made constitutes a strategic plan, which must then be implemented. In the following sections, we look at the first two steps.

GATHERING INFORMATION

Effective strategic leaders seek a great deal of information. They constantly scan their external environment in an effort to understand their internal resources and capabilities. Such assessments may not allow them to predict the future perfectly but can help them better understand what has already happened, an understanding that will enable them to make better decisions.[16]

Assessing the External Environment

An **external environment** consists of all the physical and social factors outside of an organization's boundaries.[17] Some of these elements provide an organization with potentially favorable conditions and are labeled **opportunities**; other elements provide potentially unfavorable conditions and are labeled **threats**. Although opportunities are generally easier to control than threats, a clear understanding of both is critical for effective strategy formulation.[18]

One way of thinking about the importance of assessing threats and opportunities is to consider them in relation to your future goal of finding a job. A successful job search depends on a clear strategy, which requires an understanding of environmental conditions. Features of the environment might include the number of businesses hiring people in your field, the number of other new graduates looking for similar jobs, and the geographic location of potential employers. If the economy is bad and few businesses are hiring new employees, or if a large number of new graduates are highly qualified for the position you desire, you will face a threat. In contrast, a new technology that makes your skills valuable to a large number of organizations represents an opportunity. Having information about the job market in general helps you develop a good plan, or strategy, for finding a job.

External environment
Forces outside the organization's boundaries that influence the organization and its outcomes.

Opportunities
Positive elements of an organization's external environment.

Threats
Negative elements of an organization's external environment.

Just as you will use environmental information in finding a job, organizational leaders use information about environmental opportunities and threats to form their strategies.[19] Important elements of organizational environments include demographic and cultural trends, economic and political conditions, and technological developments.[20]

Demographic and cultural trends include population growth, the age distribution of the population, the percentage of women in the workforce, and changes in the relative sizes of ethnic groups. As discussed in Chapter 1, people in the United States are living longer, and the percentage of ethnic minorities is growing. These features provide opportunities for organizations offering services to senior citizens and for organizations that produce and sell goods and services especially desired by, for example, Latino individuals.

Critical features of the economic environment include interest rates and new job creation, whereas the political environment includes laws and the positions of elected officials. Recent changes associated with the Affordable Care Act have created numerous opportunities and threats for organizations, particularly those working in the healthcare industry. Other important threats and opportunities concern legal changes related to international trade. Stories about trade opportunities and threats in countries such as China appear almost every day.

An especially important aspect of current organizational environments is technological change. Trends such as improving manufacturing technologies and increased availability of information create opportunities for some organizations and threats for others. An example of technological innovation is Twitter, which is discussed in the accompanying Technology in HR feature.

Effective strategy formulation thus begins with information about threats and opportunities outside the organization. In formulating competitive business strategy, a company's understanding of these trends can help determine what goods and services to provide. Knowledge can also guide choices about whether to focus on lowering costs or on providing goods with superior features. Understanding broad changes outside the organization is also critical for human resource strategy. Organizations need information about demographic and cultural changes, for example, to forecast how many workers with particular skills will be available in the future. An interesting example of how environmental changes influence organizations is currently seen in Taiwan. The rapid rise and economic development of China has opened doors and markets for many companies located in Taiwan. Moreover, the job market in Taiwan has been depressed due to the economic downturn, but workers have found many opportunities in China. At least 1.5 million people from Taiwan are now working in China.[21] The changing nature of the global market thus provides both opportunity and threat for companies located in Taiwan and China. Problems occurring in one area often create opportunities for companies and workers in other areas.

Assessing Internal Capabilities

Strategy formulation also requires assessment of an organization's internal resources and capabilities. Areas of high capability are labeled **strengths**, and areas of low capability are called **weaknesses**.

The example of a job search can be helpful for thinking about strengths and weaknesses. Threats and opportunities focus on the environment—in the case of your job search, environment signifies things other than you. Strengths and weaknesses focus internally—in the job search example, on your own

Strengths
Positive elements that define areas in which an organization has high internal capability.

Weaknesses
Negative factors that define areas in which an organization has low internal capability.

Technology in HR

TWITTER AS AN OPPORTUNITY FOR BUSINESS

The micro-blogging service Twitter offers an exciting opportunity for businesses. Companies can use Twitter to send short messages not only to customers but also to current and prospective employees.

Companies such as Southwest Airlines, KFC, and General Mills have found success in communicating with customers. Southwest uses Twitter to connect with first-time customers by sending them an inexpensive yet personalized message of thanks and invitation for future service. Twitter was an important part of KFC's strategy for launching its grilled chicken product. Potential customers received information and links to vouchers for a free meal. In a similar way, General Mills found success by encouraging tweets about its new line of gluten-free baking products. The benefits of new products were extolled by customers rather than by a marketing department.

Human resource practices can also benefit from micro-blogging. For example, in the United Kingdom the Royal Air Force has employees continually sending short messages about what it is like to work in different roles. These posts on Twitter, along with responses to questions, serve as an important recruiting tool. Twitter can also be used as a training tool. Employees in training classes become more engaged by sending messages to instructors and other participants. Experienced employees can send tweets that help teach others the steps of completing important work tasks.

Of course, companies can also make mistakes as they get involved in social networking. In contrast to traditional communication such as advertising and job posting, micro-blogging creates two-way communication. Customers and potential employees talk back and share their thoughts with many

others. Blatant attempts to sell products or make a company look good are often met with criticism. Here are some steps to keep in mind to avoid some common pitfalls:

1. **Listen before you speak.** Successful companies begin their interactions by first finding out what is being said about them.
2. **Follow key people.** Identify people who frequently send tweets that relate to your company and its services or products.
3. **Respond with help.** Respond to tweets by offering help and addressing customer service issues.

Sources: Tim Bradshaw, "It Pays to Think Before You Tweet; Twitter May Be the Latest Hot Marketing Tool, but Companies Need to Ensure the Tone of Their Message Suits the Medium before Launching a Campaign," Financial Times, July 21, 2009, p. 14; Anonymous, "Make Twitter an Effective Business Tool in 4 Steps," PR News 65, no. 29 (2009); Emily Bryson York, "Social Media Allows Giants to Exploit Niche Markets," Advertising Age 80, no. 25 (2009): 3-4; Pat Gallagan, "Twitter as a Learning Tool. Really," Training and Development 63, no. 3 (2009): 28–30; Anonymous, "RAF Uses Twitter and Flickr to Show Potential Recruits Life in Force," New Media Age, July 23, 2009, p. 3.

characteristics. Your strengths might include past experience working in the industry or your graduation from a school with a strong reputation for producing high-quality graduates. These are all capabilities that help set you apart from other job seekers. At the same time, you probably have some weaknesses. Perhaps you have decided you must live in a certain city, or maybe your grades are lower than you wish. These weaknesses might work against your ability to obtain a desirable job. The strengths and weaknesses of companies are similar in that they focus on characteristics that are part of the organization itself.

Obviously it is more desirable to have strengths than weaknesses, but an understanding of both is essential for true success. Just as an honest assessment can help you get a job, organizations do better when they continually assess both strengths and weaknesses. Most strengths and weaknesses can be thought of in terms of the resources that an organization has. Some are tangible, such as money and equipment; others are intangible, such as reputation.

From a resource-based view of organizations, resources—including human resources—are true strengths when they are both valuable and rare. Accordingly, the ability to attract and keep high-quality employees represents a strength for the organization only when high-quality employees are hard to find. After all, if such employees are easy to find, every company will have them.

Consistent with the resource-based perspective, good management of skilled people is critical because high-quality employees are relatively rare. A recent report by the Task Force on Workforce Development concluded that much of the workforce lacks required skills. There is a shortage not only of technological and computer skills but also of more general skills such as critical thinking and communication.[22] This shortage is not confined to the United States; similar issues have been identified in other countries, such as the United Kingdom, France, and Germany.[23] Thus, effective ways to attract and keep employees do, in fact, represent sources of internal strength that can give an organization a competitive advantage.

Yet to be true strengths, human resource practices must also provide something that is difficult to imitate and for which there is no substitute. As you will see later in this chapter, creating an integrated set of human resource practices is extremely difficult. Competitors are often able to imitate parts of a human resource strategy, but they can rarely imitate the entire package.[24] This is particularly true when an organization is able to retain high-quality employees throughout long careers. In terms of substitutability, there is always the possibility that machines can replace employees, as has already occurred in some manufacturing organizations. However, people are still needed to design and operate the machines. Given the current emphasis on knowledge and service work, it appears that most organizations will continue to need employees, and thus human resource strategies, well into the future.

In summary, human resource practices can represent a critical internal strength for organizations. Conversely, lack of effective human resource management can represent a major weakness. Gathering information about human resource capabilities is therefore a vital part of an effective assessment of organizational strengths and weaknesses.

ANALYZING INFORMATION AND MAKING DECISIONS

Once information has been gathered, the next step in the strategy-formulation process is to analyze the information and make decisions. Spending time and effort to gather information is of little value unless it is used to arrive at high-quality decisions that are then carried out.

Research suggests four steps that can be used to make decisions effectively.[25] These steps are illustrated in Figure 2.2. The first step, to build collective intuition, develops when a group of people meet together often to discuss the information that has been gathered. Through these meetings, each member

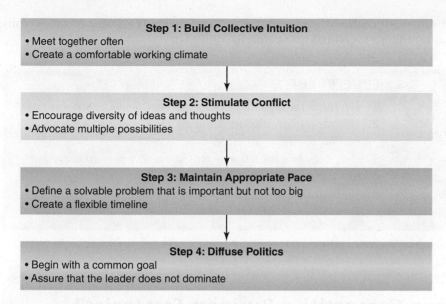

Figure 2.2 Effective Decision Making. *Source: Information from Kathleen M. Eisenhardt, "Strategy as Strategic Decision Making," Sloan Management Review 40 (1999): 65–72.*

can share what he or she knows with other group members. The outcome is a sense of intuition, or "gut feel," about the proper strategic direction.

The second step is to stimulate conflict. It may seem strange, but experiencing conflict about how to do things is very important for making good decisions.[26] In the absence of conflict, important threats and weaknesses are often ignored. Making sure that the team of decision makers includes people with different backgrounds can be helpful. Experienced managers and younger employees, for example, bring different insights to the decision-making process, as do marketing personnel and operations personnel. Another way to encourage conflict is to assign team members to advocate different possibilities, even if they don't really believe those possibilities are best.

The third step in good decision making is to maintain an appropriate pace. Decision makers too often see their task as so large that they become paralyzed. The key to effective decisions is to focus on issues that are large enough to be meaningful but small enough to be resolved. In this way, the team can view each decision as part of a larger set of decisions. The best plan is to set a flexible timeline that provides guidance for moving the decision forward but does not force the group to make the decision prematurely.

The final step is to diffuse politics. Bad decisions result when members of the decision-making team focus on making themselves look good at the expense of others. To avoid this problem, the team should begin with a common goal that develops a sense of cooperation rather than competition. Each team member should have a clear area of responsibility, in which he or she can provide expert input.

Strategy formulation is best done by a group of decision makers working together to carefully analyze the information obtained from assessing the organization's external environment and internal capabilities. The group then makes decisions about the best way to provide goods and services. This process of gathering and analyzing information is fundamental in determining how to compete with other organizations. Good decision making also provides plans for building a high-quality workforce.

CONCEPT CHECK

1. *What are the three steps in the strategy-formulation process?*
2. *What are some components of an organization's external environment?*
3. *Why does human resource management represent an important potential strength for organizations?*
4. *What four steps are necessary for effective decision making?*

LEARNING OBJECTIVE 2

What Are Common Competitive Business Strategies?

Corporate-level strategy
A competitive strategy that concerns the different businesses and diversity of products and services that an organization produces.

Business-level strategy
A competitive strategy that concerns how an organization, or part of an organization, will compete with other organizations that produce similar goods or services.

Cost leadership strategy
A business-level strategy that seeks to produce goods and services inexpensively.

Differentiation strategy
A business-level strategy that seeks to produce goods and services that are in some manner superior to what is produced by competitors.

Earlier we made the point that competitive business strategy and human resource strategy must work together to ensure high organizational effectiveness. In this section, we look more closely at competitive business strategies, which encompass various types of strategies. For instance, large corporations have strategies that guide their choices concerning the types of businesses they will pursue. Some corporations are made up of business units that are very similar; Whirlpool Corporation, for example, focuses only on making and selling appliances. Other corporations are made up of business units that are very different from one another. At General Electric, business units do very different things: some make small appliances, others provide financial services, and still others manufacture plastics. Decisions related to business types make up **corporate-level strategy**.

Good corporate-level strategy is important, but a different kind of strategy is most critical for day-to-day human resource activities. This other type of strategy is **business-level strategy**, which concerns how the organization will compete with other companies that provide similar goods and services. A corporation with several different business units needs a business-level strategy for each unit. Because each unit provides a specific type of good or service to meet a particular set of customer needs, strategies for the various units might be similar, or they might be very different. In any case, it is within business units that strategic human resource practices add the most value. Throughout this textbook we therefore focus on business-level competitive strategy.

Organizations can pursue a wide variety of strategies, but two generic business-level strategies capture the main ways business units compete: cost leadership and differentiation. Organizations with a **cost leadership strategy** seek to become low-cost producers of goods and services; their goal is to develop efficient production methods that enable them to sell at a lower price than competitors. Organizations with a **differentiation strategy** seek to produce goods and services that are somehow superior to the goods and services provided by competitors; their goal is to create unique value for which customers are willing to pay a higher price.[27]

COST LEADERSHIP STRATEGY

An organization chooses the cost leadership strategy when its decisions and actions focus on providing value by reducing cost. The goal of a business pursuing cost leadership is to become highly efficient, which will allow the organization to create value by producing goods and services at lower cost. Many organizations using a cost leadership strategy sell at prices lower than their competitors. However, not every company that sells at low prices is using a cost leadership strategy. Cost is, of course, not the same thing as price. Cost captures the expenses associated with creating the product, whereas price is what the organization receives for the product. The difference between cost and price creates profit. The key to the cost leadership strategy is in controlling expenses, not in simply setting low prices.

Southwest Airlines provides a good example of a firm with an effective cost leadership strategy. Southwest tries to have the lowest prices, but that is not the real basis of its strategy. Its strategy, rather, is to reduce the expenses associated with providing air travel. Other airlines often sell tickets at prices similar to Southwest's, but their costs are higher, which results in lower profits. These firms are sometimes forced to match Southwest's ticket prices, even when the matching price is below what it costs them to fly passengers. The practice of setting prices below costs is one reason for the high bankruptcy rate in the airline industry.

Organizations with a successful cost leadership strategy usually produce basic and standardized products and services and often have a relatively large share of the market. They pay lower prices for raw materials because they buy them in large quantities, and they use technology to develop efficient manufacturing methods. Walmart is another organization that has succeeded with a cost leadership strategy. Walmart has extremely efficient operations. It buys in high volume, which enables it to obtain favorable prices from suppliers. It also has a very efficient transportation system, which allows it to move goods at relatively low cost. Overall, this efficiency enables Walmart to sell products at low prices but still earn a profit.

A focus on cost reduction cannot come at the expense of producing goods and services with at least acceptable levels of quality and desirable features. Even if an organization's products are lower-priced than competing products, customers will not purchase them if their quality is unacceptable. Of course, it isn't always easy to tell what customers will consider when making the tradeoff between price and desirable features. For instance, observers long thought that Southwest's policy of no assigned seats would cause problems, but customers don't seem to care enough about seat choice to pay a higher price. In fact, the CEO once posted a blog about doing away with the open seating policy, but quickly received over 700 email messages that were mostly against such a move.[28] In contrast, even though it costs more, Southwest is updating its planes to include Internet connectivity and personal entertainment stations. Such updates are needed because competitors began including similar amenities and passengers communicated a desire for the benefits, even at a slightly higher cost. The key to success is not necessarily providing all the unique features that other airlines offer but rather reducing costs while providing enough of those features to satisfy passengers.

One problem with a cost leadership strategy is that usually just one organization can be the lowest-cost provider in any industry, and this is often an organization that has a large share of the market and is defending its territory.[29]

Therefore, only a relatively small number of business organizations can be successful with a cost leadership strategy. Another problem occurs when the market changes in such a way that the goods or services provided are no longer valued. Changes in technology can have this effect. Such changes can result in an organization that is a highly efficient provider of goods or services that no one needs or wants.

In the end, the cost leadership strategy can result in long-term success for organizations such as Walmart and Southwest Airlines. But what is it that allows firms such as these to succeed with a cost leadership strategy? Both firms are obsessed with cost reduction. They have cultures that create a sense of frugality, discipline, and attention to detail, as well as tight control structures that carefully track cost changes, and they continually focus on learning how to do what they do more efficiently. Much of their cost leadership ability stems from their strategic human resource management practices: Their employees work more efficiently than employees at other organizations.

DIFFERENTIATION STRATEGY

An organization following the differentiation strategy focuses on offering value by providing something better than competitors—something for which customers are willing to pay a higher price. The organization may differentiate its goods or services in any one of several ways. For example, the product itself may be unique, as when a pharmaceutical firm has a drug that no other firm has. A marketing approach is another way of differentiating goods and services. Most advertising is created to generate perceptions that goods or services are somehow different from those offered by competitors. Yet another area for differentiation is excellent customer service. Customers are often willing to pay more for a product if they know that the organization will help them if a problem arises. The effect of differentiation for fast-food restaurants is described in the accompanying "How Do We Know?" feature.

Target is a retail store that employs a business-level strategy of differentiation, seeking to set prices close to those of retailers such as Walmart. But the source of competitive advantage is not the cost structure itself. Rather, Target seeks to provide something slightly different from Walmart at a similar but perhaps slightly higher price. Target has store designer brands that are geared toward slightly more upscale customers. It also focuses on having clean, well-organized stores, as well as enough employees to ensure rapid checkout. In the end, Target tries to beat Walmart not by having lower cost but rather by providing a different value. Target's unique value is attractive to a certain set of customers as long as costs are only slightly higher. This differentiation strategy works best when economic conditions are generally favorable. For example, early in the recession of 2008, consumers appeared to be less willing to shop at Target instead of Walmart, but relative profits at Target have substantially improved as the economy has recovered.[30]

Another example of a firm with a differentiation strategy is BMW, which produces automobiles that are more expensive than those of many of its competitors. Consumers are willing to pay a higher price for a BMW because they perceive it has greater value, particularly in the areas of reliability, comfort, and image. People expect a BMW to be a more enjoyable car to drive than a less-expensive alternative.

Whereas few organizations in a given industry can successfully use the cost leadership strategy, a large number of organizations can simultaneously pursue

How Do We Know?

WHAT DIFFERENTIATES FAST-FOOD RESTAURANTS?

Have you ever wondered why some people like to eat at McDonald's, but others prefer Burger King? What sets one fast-food chain apart from another? To find out, Bonnie Knutson asked 200 college students about their perceptions of Arby's, Burger King, KFC, McDonald's, Subway, Taco Bell, and Wendy's. She asked the students to rate these restaurants on features such as atmosphere, menu choices, consistency, and price.

The study found that students have common beliefs about differences between fast-food restaurants. McDonald's received the highest overall ratings. Students saw McDonald's as particularly strong in terms of combination meals, kid's meals, consistency, and value. They gave Taco Bell the highest rating for low-priced food. Subway received the highest rating for good nutrition, and Wendy's for menu variety.

The Bottom Line. The results of this study illustrate the concepts of cost leadership and differentiation. Taco Bell is seen as a low-cost provider, which can be an effective strategy as long as the cost structure really allows it to produce and serve food at low cost. Subway has been successful at differentiating itself based on nutrition, and Wendy's has differentiated based on menu variety. These restaurants also have different human resource strategies that help support their competitive strategies. Professor Knutson concludes that fast-food restaurants should place high importance on creating a clear brand image that is consistent with their strategy for competing with other restaurants.

Source: Bonnie J. Knutson, "College Students and Fast Food: How Students Perceive Restaurant Brands," *Cornell Hotel and Restaurant Administration Quarterly* 41, no. 3 (2000): 68–74.

differentiation strategies. Each simply seeks to differentiate in a unique way. The key is to create value that is perceived as high enough to warrant a higher price. Of course, organizations with a differentiation strategy cannot simply ignore cost. Usually, their cost structures—and associated prices—must be close to those of competitors. If costs and prices are too far out of line, the added value of the unique features may not be sufficient to encourage purchases.

The requirements for succeeding with a differentiation strategy are quite different from those associated with the cost leadership strategy. Organizations using a differentiation strategy must continually struggle to show that their products are truly unique, which often requires them to adapt rapidly to changing customer preferences. Differentiators must also be highly innovative, and they must take risks and continually prospect for new ways of doing things. But differentiation and cost leadership are similar in one respect: Organizations that succeed with differentiation do so because of their human resource practices. Organizations using the differentiation strategy are creative and innovative because they have employees who do things better than the employees of their competitors, which helps them to be perceived as providing something with higher value.

COMBINATION STRATEGY

An interesting question is whether an organization can simultaneously pursue both cost leadership and differentiation. Theoretically, this is difficult. Organizations trying to purse both strategies often end up doing neither very well; they are stuck in the middle with no real competitive advantage.

Their desire to add unique features creates a cost structure that does not allow them to produce goods and services at the lowest cost. Yet their focus on cost does not allow them to develop features that are truly exceptional.

Most organizations must therefore choose one or the other approach and make strategic decisions accordingly. An organization with a primary cost leadership strategy should seek to differentiate only as long as doing so does not harm its ability to be the lowest-cost producer. Similarly, an organization with a primary differentiation strategy should seek to reduce costs wherever possible. But cost reduction only makes sense if it does not destroy the features that make the organization's product unique and valuable.

Cases where an organization is successful at simultaneously pursuing cost leadership and differentiation strategies are rare and tend to occur in markets where competition is not strong. If the market does not include a truly low-cost provider, and if most competitors are stuck between cost and differentiation, then an organization may be able to have it both ways for a time. An organization may also pioneer a unique innovation that provides it with a secret or protected way of doing things that is both unique and low in cost. Unfortunately, such scenarios do not typically last very long.[31]

CONCEPT CHECK

1. *What are the basic characteristics of the cost leadership strategy?*
2. *What are the main features of the differentiation strategy?*

LEARNING OBJECTIVE 3

What Are Basic Approaches to Human Resource Strategy?

Our discussion of competitive strategy shows that successful organizations create value by doing things for customers that other organizations do not do as well. The continued success of these organizations depends on their possessing capabilities that competitors cannot easily copy. One source of potential capability is physical resources, such as technology and equipment, which are often easy for competitors to duplicate. As we have seen, another source of potential capability—one that is less easy to copy—is human resources.[32] Effective human resource practices create a rare and difficult-to-imitate capability by increasing employee skills, motivation, and opportunity, which in turn translate to positive operational and financial outcomes.[33]

Effective human resource management capabilities are particularly difficult to copy because effectiveness comes not from a single practice but from a number of related practices. These practices are developed over extended periods of time. Social relationships that arise from human resource practices are also extremely difficult to copy. Taken together, these factors make human resource capabilities a source of potentially sustainable competitive advantage.[34]

The same characteristics that make human resource practices difficult to duplicate can sometimes make their results difficult to understand and predict. Nevertheless, research has identified consistent patterns of good human resource management. Researchers have taken two basic approaches in investigating human resource patterns:

- The **universalistic approach** seeks to identify a set of human resource practices that is beneficial for all organizations. The goal of universalistic research is therefore to find the one best way of managing human resources.
- The **contingency approach** seeks to match human resource practices with competitive business strategies. In this view, the human resource practices that work best for organizations pursuing a certain competitive strategy will not necessarily work best for organizations pursuing a different strategy.[36]

Research supports both approaches. Fortunately, the two approaches are not contradictory. Whereas some human resource practices are beneficial for all organizations, the benefits of other practices seem to depend on the organization's competitive business strategy. Furthermore, the two approaches have different areas of interest. The universalistic approach tends to focus on broad principles, whereas the contingency approach focuses more on specific practices.[37] The two approaches are thus complementary and often work together to form an overall human resource strategy.

THE UNIVERSALISTIC APPROACH

The universalistic approach, as we have seen, seeks to identify the best practices for all organizations to follow. One important finding of universalistic research is that human resource practices are most effective when they are bundled together into internally consistent clusters.[38] A single effective human resource practice, such as the use of a good employee-selection test, provides only limited benefits unless it is combined with other effective practices. For instance, using a computer knowledge test to select employees offers more benefits when such testing is combined with a compensation system that rewards people who actually use the computer skills to do their jobs. In a similar way, a training program that encourages innovation is most effective when it is combined with appraisal and compensation systems that measure and reward the behaviors taught during training. Sets of human resource practices that are internally consistent and that reinforce each other are known as **human resource bundles**.

Many practices related to hiring and motivating employees cluster naturally into two bundles. One bundle is based on a **control strategy**; the primary focus of human resource practices in this bundle is standardization and efficiency. The second bundle is based on a **commitment strategy**; the primary focus of practices in this bundle is to empower workers and build a strong sense of loyalty and commitment.[39]

Both the control and commitment strategies have been found in a number of different settings.[40] For example, in the steel production industry, researchers found that the practices of a distinct group of plants represented a commitment strategy. These plants reported widespread use of incentive pay, careful screening of recruits, high teamwork, and extensive sharing of information. Another group of plants used practices representing a control strategy. These practices included close supervision, strict work rules, narrow job responsibilities, and little formal training.[41] Similar observations were

Universalistic approach
A human resource perspective that seeks to identify methods of managing people that are effective for all organizations.

Contingency approach
A human resource perspective that seeks to align different ways of managing people with different competitive strategies for producing goods and services.

Human resource bundles
Groups of human resource practices that work together to create a consistent work environment.

Control strategy
A human resource bundle that emphasizes managerial control and tries to streamline production processes.

Commitment strategy
A human resource bundle that builds strong attachment to the organization and emphasizes worker empowerment.

made in a study of automobile assembly plants. One set of plants reported using commitment strategy practices such as extensive recruiting, employee involvement groups, and widespread training. These practices fostered a strong sense of cooperation between employees and managers. Other assembly plants reported using control strategy practices such as narrowly defined jobs and close supervision. The control practices created large status differences between employees and managers.[42]

Studies comparing the control and commitment strategies almost always conclude that the commitment strategy is better. Organizations with commitment strategies have higher productivity, and they generally produce higher-quality goods and services.[43] The superiority of a commitment strategy is consistent across various types of organizations and industries, but it is particularly strong in manufacturing organizations.[44] Moreover, its benefits have been documented in countries other than the United States, such as New Zealand and South Korea.[45] A strong research conclusion from the universalistic approach is therefore that organizations should adopt a commitment strategy.

The commitment strategy is often summarized as a human resource bundle that encourages high involvement. (The major human resource practices in the commitment strategy bundle are summarized in Table 2.1.) What do these practices have in common? Why are they consistently related to higher productivity and quality?

One answer to the question of what the practices have in common is that they communicate a message that management cares about employees. Organizations with managers who value people tend to use good human resource practices

Table 2.1	*Examples of Commitment Strategy Practices*
Practice Area	**Typical Examples**
Job Tasks	Broad job responsibilities
	Meaningful tasks
	Rotation across a variety of tasks
Empowerment	Inclusive decision making
	High levels of responsibility
	Building employee confidence
Teams	Organizing around work teams
	Self-management within teams
Communication	Two-way communication
	Quality-of-life surveys
	Encouraging suggestions
Training	Extensive new employee training
	Formal training for everyone
	Multiple job skill development
Compensation	Pay for performance
	High levels of pay
	Ownership forms of pay such as stock
Staffing	Highly selective recruiting
	Identification of skilled workers
	Long-term relationships with employees

to effectively deliver goods and services.[46] These organizations provide employees with opportunities for personal growth. Selective hiring, extensive training, and pay linked to performance provide employees opportunities to excel, which lead to deeper commitment to the organization.[47] The organizational climate conveys a sense of concern for employees, which increases job satisfaction and employee commitment.[48] Extensive training also improves employee skills. Employees develop a strong attachment to the organization and are less likely to quit.[49] Employees who think that human resource actions simply minimize cost at the expense of employees are less committed and satisfied than employees who see personnel actions as increasing quality and ensuring their well-being.[50] In essence, the commitment strategy bundle of human resources is beneficial because these practices treat employees as a critical resource.

Such strong support for the commitment strategy may seem to suggest that all organizations should simply adopt this strategy and the related human resource practices. Unfortunately, it's not quite this simple. The commitment strategy is a broad concept that includes few specific details. The strategy recommends that organizations hire high-quality employees and give them freedom and responsibility. As explained in the "How Do We Know?" feature, the commitment bundle creates a climate of trust and cooperation, which in turn leads to knowledge exchange and ultimately increased performance. However, the commitment strategy is not clear and consistent about specific ways to do these things.[51]

 # How Do We Know?

DO GOOD HUMAN RESOURCE PRACTICES IMPROVE PERFORMANCE?

Is it wise for an organization to spend money to find, hire, and train good employees? What are the effects of better hiring, training, and compensation? Are the benefits that these practices bring worth the costs? Christopher Collins and Ken Smith set out to answer these questions by obtaining data from 136 technology firms. They measured high-involvement work practices, which are consistent with the commitment strategy. Specific items asked about human resource practices of selection, training, compensation, and performance appraisals. The researchers linked these practices to revenue from new products and sales growth. They also assessed climates for trust and cooperation, as well the exchange of knowledge.

The study found that organizations using the commitment strategy had increased revenue and growth. The data also provided insight into the process by which human resource practices improve financial returns. Better methods for hiring, training, and paying employees create a climate of trust and cooperation. This good organizational climate leads to more learning and exchange of information among employees. The improved learning and sharing of ideas in turn corresponds with increased financial performance.

The Bottom Line. Effective human resource practices build a sense of trust and cooperation among workers, which leads them to share information and learn from each other. These positive interactions among employees, which are set in motion by good human resource management, help innovative firms grow and make money. Professors Collins and Smith conclude that leaders of technology firms should carefully choose their human resource practices used to manage knowledge workers.

Source: Christopher J. Collins and Ken G. Smith, "Knowledge Exchange and Combination: The Role of Human Resource Practices in the Performance of High-Technology Firms," Academy of Management Journal 49 (2006): 544–560.

THE CONTINGENCY APPROACH

The contingency approach to human resource strategy seeks to align people-management practices with competitive business strategies. Because this book takes a strategic view of human resource management, we emphasize the contingency approach. In this section, we look at two key differences in organizations: whether they have a cost leadership or a differentiation strategy and whether they have an internal or an external labor orientation. In the remainder of the chapter, we examine how these differences combine to define an organization's human resource strategy.

Cost Leadership Versus Differentiation

We've already discussed the differences between the competitive business strategies of cost leadership and differentiation. We've also suggested that these two strategies differ in terms of human resource practices. Table 2.2 summarizes important differences in how organizations with these strategies approach human resource management.

Organizations with a cost leadership strategy focus their efforts on increasing efficiency and hire generalists who work in a variety of different positions.[52] They tightly control work processes and carefully define what employees should do. Appropriate behavior is specifically prescribed for employees, and human resource practices focus on minimizing labor costs.[53]

A cost leadership strategy with a focus on tightly controlled processes makes sense when the organization knows exactly what it wants people to do. This situation usually arises when the preferences of consumers are well known and seldom change. The result is mass production of standardized goods or services at the lowest possible cost. As described earlier, Walmart is a good example of a company pursuing this strategy. The company carefully standardizes practices and focuses on reducing deviations within its processes. Employees focus their efforts on shipping and selling goods as efficiently as possible.

In contrast, organizations using a differentiation strategy focus their human resource efforts on innovation and quality enhancement. Employees in these organizations are often specialists who perform very specific tasks. Rather than seeking to control processes, these organizations concentrate on outcomes. Workers have more choice about how things should be done,[54] and accordingly, they are held accountable for outputs such as quality of the goods and services they produce.

Table 2.2	*Strategic Human Resource Differences*
Cost Strategy	**Differentiation Strategy**
Emphasis on group contribution	Emphasis on individual contribution
Focus on improving processes	Focus on outcomes and results
Development of general employee skills	Development of specific employee skills
Cooperation among employees	Moderate competition among employees
Efficiency culture	Innovation culture
Clearly prescribed tasks	Flexible task assignments
Rules and procedures that standardize work	Few rules and procedures; exceptions to rules allowed

A differentiation strategy with a focus on outcomes is particularly beneficial when organizations produce customized goods or services. In these organizations, the best process for completing work is often unknown, and employees are expected to continually look for different ways of doing things.[55] Service organizations such as investment firms and healthcare providers frequently have an outcome focus because their customers have very different needs and expectations. Unique customer expectations require employees to change their actions to best serve each client.[56] For instance, the investment banking firm Morgan Stanley works to build long-term relationships and meet the specific needs of clients, adapting its services for each client. This customization approach has helped Morgan Stanley obtain important clients such as Google.[57]

Internal Versus External Orientation

In addition to differing in competitive strategy, organizations differ in the extent to which they develop employees' skills within the organization. An organization with an **internal labor orientation** seeks to make its own talent and to keep employees for long periods of time. In contrast, an organization with an **external labor orientation** seeks to buy talent. These organizations hire people who already have the needed skills and in many cases keep them for only a short period of time.[58] Internal and external orientations have been identified across a number of organizations and industries, including sales, manufacturing, technology, food, and legal firms.[59] Basic differences between the two orientations are summarized in Table 2.3.

Organizations with an internal labor orientation generally hire young employees; a primary goal of hiring is to identify people who will have long careers within the organization. Because employee turnover is undesirable, human resource practices focus on developing loyalty and commitment. The idea is to develop a close relationship with employees and to provide them with a sense of stability and security. In exchange, employees agree to sacrifice some of their own personal interests. For example, they agree to develop skills that may not be valuable to other organizations, which decreases their chances of receiving other job offers.[60]

An internal orientation has several potential strengths. Organizations are able to predict what skills and capabilities will be available to them in the future, and employees build strong relationships with one another, so coordination

Internal labor orientation
A human resource perspective that emphasizes hiring workers early in their careers and retaining those workers for long periods of time.

External labor orientation
A human resource perspective that limits attachment to a specific organization and emphasizes hiring workers who already possess the skills they need to complete specific tasks.

Table 2.3	*Differences in Labor Orientation*
Internal	**External**
Hiring of people early in their careers	Hiring of people who have already developed skills
Extensive orientation for new employees	Limited orientation of company policies
Focus on internal promotions	Focus on bringing in new talent
Ongoing training opportunities	Limited training opportunities
Development of skills valuable only to the specific organization	Development of skills valuable to many organizations
Bias against laying off employees	Acceptance of employee layoffs
Employees contribute because of loyalty	Employees contribute because of money
People identify closely with the organization	People identify closely with a profession

and cooperation are high. Organizations with an internal labor orientation also save money because they reduce expenses for recruiting, interviewing, and hiring employees. One company that has benefited from emphasizing an internal labor orientation is the British grocery producer Fenmarc, which is profiled in the accompanying "Building Strength Through HR" feature.

An internal labor orientation has potential weaknesses as well. Organizations develop long-term commitments that make it difficult for them to adapt. Changes in strategic direction are complicated because workers have been encouraged to develop specific skills necessary for carrying out the old strategy. Long-term commitments may also make it difficult for organizations to replace workers whose skills are not up to date. In addition, such organizations tend to develop bureaucratic structures that make them inflexible.[61]

Organizations with an external labor orientation look very different. These organizations seek out people who have already developed skills, and the primary goal of hiring is to identify people who are able to contribute without additional training. Employee turnover can be desirable in some cases

Building Strength Through HR

FENMARC PRODUCE LTD

Fenmarc Produce is a vegetable processor and packer located in the United Kingdom. For a number of years, the company was not consistently profitable. A few years ago, the privately held company was purchased by a leadership team that placed special emphasis on linking competitive strategy to human resource management. Company leaders, recognizing that vegetables are commodities, decided to focus on making the company a low-cost producer. Fenmarc also sought to become a preferred supplier for the Walmart affiliate Asda, which is a supermarket giant in the United Kingdom.

In order to improve its production processes and ensure the delivery of safe produce, Fenmarc implemented a widespread training program. The program uses case studies, group activities, and coaching to improve the individual skills of employees. Employees who complete the training report more confidence in their abilities.

Fenmarc sees each of its over 400 employees as a valuable contributor. An important part of the organizational philosophy is that every individual has important opinions that should be valued. Six key principles capture this emphasis on people:

- Say it as it is.
- Challenge it, improve it, learn from it.

Noel Hendrickson/Getty Images

- Integrity before profit.
- Make it fun, make it happen.
- One team, one purpose.
- Respect for the individual.

Treating people well has helped Fenmarc retain its employees and has also improved efficiency. In a two-year period, the company received 2,200 suggestions for continuous improvement, and accidents fell by 20 percent. Investing more in people has paid off by improving company profitability.

Source: Information from David Pollitt, "Investment in Training and Development Bears Fruit for Fenmarc," *Human Resource Management International Digest* 15, no. 1 (2007): 27–29; www.fenmarc.com/

because it provides a way to make sure that the organization is able to continually hire people with the most up-to-date skills. Long-term commitments are avoided. The relationship between the organization and its employees is weak and based on contractual agreements. Employees work because they are paid, not necessarily because they are loyal. They usually do not develop a strong feeling of attachment to the organization.

A primary strength of the external orientation is flexibility; it allows the organization to respond quickly to changing conditions. Workers trained by universities or other employers can be added quickly in areas that demand new skills. Labor costs are not fixed, and the total number of employees can be increased or decreased. A primary weakness of this orientation is lack of consistency. Employees do not really provide a unique competitive advantage. Employees are essentially shared with other organizations, which makes it more difficult to create a rare resource that cannot be imitated.[62]

What is the basis for choosing an internal or an external labor orientation? Several considerations are important:

- Will the organization continue to need certain skills and inputs over a long period of time? If so, the organization is more likely to find an internal orientation useful.
- Does the organization produce goods and services that require unique labor inputs? If so, the organization may not be able to buy the labor inputs it needs. Employees must be trained to perform tasks that exist only in that organization, so an internal orientation is more appropriate than an external one.
- Does the organization know exactly what it needs employees to do? Sometimes an organization is unclear about what it wants from employees in certain areas. Organizational leaders may know that they need to improve a certain area, but they may be unfamiliar with the employee skills needed to carry out the improvement. Of course, an internal labor strategy allows the organization to enter into a long-term agreement that enables a new employee to become a committed member of the team and change the way some work tasks are completed. In contrast, an external labor strategy allows an organization to quickly acquire specialized skills that are taught in other places, such as universities. Organizational leaders know the skills and abilities needed, and they also know that current employees are unable to fill the needs. In many cases it is easier to hire specialized workers such as computer programmers with the latest skills than it is to train them.[63]

CONCEPT CHECK

1. *How does the contingency approach to human resource management differ from the universalistic approach?*
2. *What human resource practices are associated with cost reduction strategies? differentiation strategies?*
3. *What are the differences between an internal labor orientation and an external labor orientation?*

What Are Common Human Resource Strategies?

As we have just seen, the contingency approach identifies two strategic choices underlying an organization's human resource strategy: whether to focus on cost leadership or differentiation and whether to make or buy talent. We can combine the two choices into a grid describing four different forms of human resource strategy, as shown in Figure 2.3. Based on the grid, we could call these four HR strategies the internal/cost, external/cost, internal/differentiation, and external/differentiation approaches. For ease of reference in this book, though, we will call the strategies the Loyal Soldier HR strategy, the Bargain Laborer HR strategy, the Committed Expert HR strategy, and the Free Agent HR strategy.

A word about these terms is in order before we begin our discussion. The strategies we will discuss reflect common differences related to managing people at work, but even human resource professionals do not have terms that describe these strategic differences clearly. Because the technical terms are somewhat awkward and hard to conceptualize, we have developed the descriptive terms just mentioned. We believe these descriptive terms make this textbook more interesting and easier to read, but you should be aware that the terms may not be the exact terms you will hear used in other courses or in the business world. So it is important to remember that you may sometimes need to explain the meaning of the terms when you talk to others who have not read this book. However, using the terms Loyal Soldier, Bargain Laborer, Committed Expert, and Free Agent should help you get a clearer picture of what we mean when we describe the four different strategies.

INTERNAL/COST HR STRATEGY: THE LOYAL SOLDIER

Loyal Soldier HR strategy
A human resource strategy that combines emphasis on long-term employees with a focus on reducing costs (an internal/cost approach).

Combining an internal orientation with a cost leadership strategy results in what we will call a **Loyal Soldier HR strategy**. We chose this label because this strategy emphasizes hiring and retaining loyal employees who do whatever the company asks of them. Organizations with this strategy design work so that employees have broad roles and perform a variety of different tasks. People are recruited and hired because they fit the organization culture and because of their potential to become loyal employees. Efforts are made to satisfy the needs of employees and build a strong bond that reduces the likelihood of employee turnover. Organizations with this human resource strategy hire people early in their careers and provide them with extensive training in a number of different skills. Careers often include a number of very different positions, with promotions often made into positions that are not closely related to previous experiences. Performance appraisals are designed to facilitate cooperation rather than competition. Compensation includes long-term incentives and benefits and is often linked to the overall performance of the organization. Unions, which can help build feelings of unity, are frequently observed in these organizations.

United Parcel Service (UPS) is a good example of a company with a Loyal Soldier HR strategy. UPS's competitive strategy is to provide low-cost shipping. UPS has a strong internal promotion policy. A typical employee enters UPS as a part-time worker moving and sorting boxes. As employees work their way through the ranks, they may perform several different jobs, such as driver and

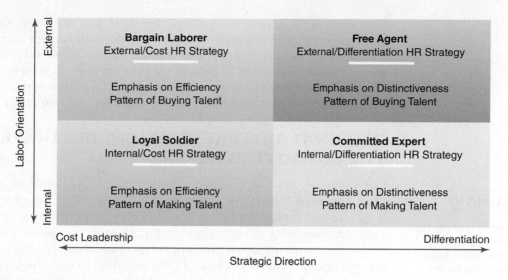

Figure 2.3 Strategic Framework for Human Resources.

facility manager. The company provides training in a number of areas, with an emphasis on teaching the company's philosophy and policies. Teamwork, cooperation, and a strong work ethic are encouraged. Long-term incentives are tied specifically to UPS, and over half of the drivers and full-time employees own stock in the company. Extensive benefit packages include excellent medical and dental plans. The company takes an interest in employees and offers wellness programs that encourage physical activity. These programs help reduce injuries and absenteeism.[64] The end result is a strong bond between UPS and its employees. Most employees report a great sense of pride in working for UPS. The bottom-line result is that even during difficult economic times, UPS has seen profits that are higher than competitors.[65]

EXTERNAL/COST HR STRATEGY: THE BARGAIN LABORER

Combining an external orientation with a cost leadership strategy results in a **Bargain Laborer HR strategy**. The emphasis of this strategy is on obtaining employees who do not demand high wages. Organizations with this strategy design work so that managers can tightly control employee efforts. Each employee is given clearly defined tasks that can be learned easily. People are recruited and hired to perform simple tasks that do not require clearly developed skills. Little attention is paid to meeting the long-term needs of employees. Organizations with this human resource strategy do not provide careers with clear paths for promotion and advancement. Performance appraisal focuses on day-to-day feedback and rarely incorporates formal measures. Training is mostly limited to on-the-job techniques that teach specific methods for completing particular tasks. Compensation is frequently based on hours worked, and benefits and long-term incentives are minimal. Short-term employment tends to make unions somewhat rare in organizations that pursue cost efficiency through an external labor orientation.

The Bargain Laborer HR strategy is very common for many positions in the hotel industry. For instance, a regional hotel located in Phoenix, Arizona is constantly searching for employees to work in jobs such as housekeeping and

Bargain Laborer HR strategy
A human resource strategy that combines emphasis on short-term employees with a focus on reducing costs (an external/cost approach).

food services. Most people who apply for these jobs are hired. Once hired, employees are given minimal on-the-job training that focuses on how to perform specific tasks. They are expected to carefully follow their supervisor's instructions. Pay is based on the number of hours worked. Most employees do not receive benefits. The hotel's focus is on reducing labor costs, and employees who receive better job offers from other companies frequently leave.

INTERNAL/DIFFERENTIATION HR STRATEGY: THE COMMITTED EXPERT

Committed Expert HR strategy
A human resource strategy that combines emphasis on long-term employees with a focus on producing unique goods and services (an internal/differentiation approach).

Combining an internal orientation with a differentiation strategy results in the **Committed Expert HR strategy**. The primary objective of this strategy is to hire and retain employees who specialize in performing certain tasks. Organizations using this strategy design work so that employees have a great deal of freedom to innovate and improve methods of completing tasks. People are recruited and hired because of their potential fit with the organizational culture, as well as their aptitude for becoming experts in particular areas. These organizations hire people early in their careers and train them to be experts in specific fields, such as accounting or sales. Performance appraisals are designed to balance cooperation and competition among employees. Careers generally include numerous promotions into similar jobs with increasing responsibility. Employees receive long-term training that helps them develop strong expertise. Compensation is relatively high and usually includes a good benefits package that ties employees to the organization.

Merck, the pharmaceutical company, employs a Committed Expert HR strategy, focusing a great deal of attention on developing employees during long careers. When employees enter Merck, they choose a career in research, sales and marketing, manufacturing and engineering, finance, or information services. They receive extensive training to provide them with the latest information and skills in their chosen area of expertise. Many Merck employees have a mentor who guides their careers and shares important information about the organizational culture. Compensation includes base pay and bonuses for exceptional performance. Many employees also receive long-term incentives, such as stock options. Merck's human resource practices help support a culture that stimulates creativity and innovation.[66]

EXTERNAL/DIFFERENTIATION HR STRATEGY: THE FREE AGENT

Free Agent HR strategy
A human resource strategy that combines emphasis on short-term employees with a focus on producing unique goods and services (an external/differentiation approach).

Combining an external orientation with a differentiation strategy forms what we refer to as a **Free Agent HR strategy**. The main emphasis associated with this strategy is hiring people who have critical skills but who are not necessarily expected to remain with the organization for a long period of time. Organizations using this strategy design work so that employees have extensive responsibility within specific areas and substantial freedom to decide how to go about their work. Long-term commitments are avoided, and no efforts are made to encourage strong attachments between employees and the organization. People are recruited because they already have the skills and experience they need to perform specific jobs. They are not led to expect long-term careers in the organization. Higher-level positions are frequently given to people from outside the organization. Performance appraisal focuses on outcomes and results. Training is rare. Short-term compensation is usually high, which is necessary if the organization is to obtain people with top skills. Pay is linked specifically to individual performance results. Benefits and long-term compensation packages, which tie employees to the organization, are avoided. We rarely see unions in these organizations.

Free Agent HR strategies are quite common for information technology firms. Information technology changes rapidly, and top skills are often in short supply. Many companies in information technology offer relatively high salaries to get skilled people to leave jobs with competitors. People with in-demand skills earn high salaries by frequently jumping from one firm to the next. At the extreme, many companies hire technology specialists on short-term contracts.[67] As a result of these practices, people working in the field of information technology are often more loyal to the profession than to a particular company.

CONCEPT CHECK

1. *What two human resource strategies are associated with the cost leadership strategy? How do these two HR strategies differ?*
2. *What two human resource strategies are associated with the differentiation strategy? How do these two HR strategies differ?*

LEARNING OBJECTIVE 5

How Do Human Resource Strategies Align with Competitive Business Strategies?

The four strategies just outlined provide a general framework for describing human resource practices. Of course, most organizations don't fit perfectly into one of the four boxes shown in Figure 2.3. For a majority of organizations, human resource practices fall mostly into one of the categories, with some practices that don't exactly fit. Some organizations have a more equal mix of two different strategies. In general, however, organizations fall on one continuum from internal to external and another continuum from cost leadership to differentiation, which means that they fit somewhere within the framework. The four basic categories are therefore useful for illustrating important issues and discussing differences across organizations. We will examine many specific human resource strategies within the framework of the four strategies in Chapters 4 through 13. In Chapter 14, we will return to the question of how well the practices of actual organizations fit into the four basic strategies.

Recall that the four basic human resource strategies arise from the contingency approach. The core idea of the contingency perspective is the notion that human resource strategies are most effective when they match competitive business strategies. Accordingly, organizations with a cost leadership competitive strategy are expected to do best when they have either a Bargain Laborer or Loyal Soldier HR strategy. Organizations with a competitive business strategy of differentiation are expected to do best when they have either a Committed Expert or Free Agent HR strategy. How well does research support these expectations? We answer this question next.

RESEARCH SUPPORTING THE CONTINGENCY PERSPECTIVE

The strategic approach to human resource management is relatively new. Researchers have only been studying the contingency perspective for a few years, which means that there are still a number of things we don't clearly understand. However, preliminary research generally supports the notion that organizations are most successful when they take a strategic approach to managing people. Research related to the contingency perspective provides three specific insights.

1. Many organizations do have human resource strategies that fit their competitive strategies.
2. Organizations are more successful when they broadly adapt their human resource practices to fit their competitive strategies.
3. Organizations with a cost leadership or differentiation strategy do perform better when they have a matching human resource strategy.

Let's look more specifically at the research related to each insight.

A starting point for contingency research has been simply to determine the percentage of organizations that report matching strategies. For instance, research in steel manufacturing mills examined whether plants pursuing a cost leadership or differentiation strategy had matching human resource strategies. About 90 percent of the plants with a cost leadership strategy had human resource practices consistent with the Bargain Laborer or Loyal Soldier HR strategies. About 60 percent of the plants with a competitive business strategy of differentiation had practices consistent with the Committed Expert HR strategy.[68] Other studies have found support for the notion that organizations naturally tend to adopt the human resource practices that match their competitive strategies.[69] Other factors, such as organizational structure and values that correspond with strategy, have also been linked to different approaches to human resource management that range from minimizing cost to maximizing employee commitment.[70]

The next question is whether organizations with matching strategies really have better performance. Although research related to this question does not always use the four human resource strategies outlined in Figure 2.3, the results are mostly supportive. Firms benefit from having human resource practices that support their overall strategy. For instance, law firms with a competitive strategy of expanding into new markets, which is consistent with a strategy of differentiation, have been shown to perform better when they hire and retain highly skilled lawyers.[71] Call centers with a competitive strategy of customizing responses to customers—also consistent with differentiation—perform better when their human resource practices ensure good training and high pay.[72] Compared to hotels where customers' service expectations are not as high, hotels providing higher levels of service benefit more from good hiring, training, and compensation practices.[73] Overall, this line of research confirms that organizations perform better when they use human resource practices that help them secure and motivate employees who have skills that match their approaches for providing value to customers.[74]

The final question is whether organizations with a cost leadership or differentiation strategy perform better when they have matching human resource strategies. Research in this area is generally supportive. For instance, a study of manufacturing firms found that plants with a differentiation strategy have higher performance when their human resource practices include selective staffing, comprehensive technical training, and group incentives to ensure that employees are well paid. These practices fit with the Committed Expert HR strategy. As described in the "How Do We Know?" feature, banks focusing on differentiation similarly benefitted from human resource practices that empowered employees to deliver high-quality service. As additional evidence supporting alignment of strategies and practices, manufacturing plants using a cost leadership strategy have been found to have higher performance when their practices focused on ensuring compliance with policies and procedures, consistent with the Loyal Soldier HR strategy.[75] In still another study, organizations in both service and manufacturing performed best when they combined a cost leadership competitive strategy with a Loyal Soldier HR strategy rather than a human resource strategy focused on differentiation. Also, organizations following a competitive strategy of differentiation performed best with a Committed Expert HR strategy rather than human resource practices associated with a cost focus. Employees working in firms with matching competitive and human resource strategies were also found to have higher morale.[76]

How Do We Know?

DO HUMAN RESOURCE PRACTICES INFLUENCE CUSTOMER SERVICE?

Why is the customer service at some banks better than others? Is it by chance, or do successful banks encourage specific actions to ensure that employees meet the needs of customers? Samuel Aryee, Fred Walumbwa, Emmanuel Seidu, and Lilian Otaye sought answers to this question by obtaining data from 37 branches of two different banks located in Ghana.

Branch managers reported on human resource practices associated with enhancing employee skills and knowledge, empowerment, information sharing, and delivery of high-quality service. Managers also rated the market performance of the bank. Front-line employees completed a similar measure that assessed human resource issues such as training, compensation, job design, and performance appraisal, along with a measure of their personal orientation toward providing superior service. Employees also rated the empowerment climate of the bank, as well as the degree to which they personally felt empowered. More senior customer representatives rated the customer service performance of the front-line employees. Results of the study showed that human resource practices designed to facilitate differentiated customer service helped employees feel that they were empowered to do whatever it took to serve customers. Feelings of empowerment, particularly for individuals predisposed toward helpful customer service behavior, led to higher ratings of individual performance. Increased individual performance further translated into stronger branch-level market performance.

The Bottom Line. Human resource practices that emphasize decentralized decision making, service quality–focused feedback, extensive service training, and performance contingent compensation increase feelings of empowerment. Empowerment results in increased customer service performance for both individuals and bank branches. The authors concluded that effective human resource practices do indeed represent an effective method for pursuing a strategy of providing excellent service.

Source: Samuel Aryee, Fred O. Walumba, Emmanuel Y.M. Seidu, and Lilian E. Otaye, "Impact of High-Performance Work Systems on Individual- and Branch-Level Performance: Test of a Multilevel Model of Intermediate Linkages," *Journal of Applied Psychology* 97 (2012): 287–300.

PUTTING IT ALL TOGETHER

Although research is still developing, the evidence suggests that organizations do better when their human resource strategies fit their competitive strategies. As we have seen, these results support the contingency approach to human resource strategy. At this point, we can also tie in the more general universalistic approach. Recall that this approach suggests that organizations benefit from a commitment strategy. The commitment strategy is similar in many ways to the internal labor orientation of the contingency approach. Thus, we can combine the two approaches and conclude that, although there are important exceptions, many organizations improve their long-term success when they adopt an internal labor orientation. Organizations using an internal orientation develop strong bonds with their employees. People are treated as a valuable resource that helps the organizations meet the needs of customers.

Given the choice of an internal orientation, the remaining choice concerns whether the organization will use a Loyal Soldier or Committed Expert HR strategy. This choice depends on the competitive business strategy of the organization. Organizations seeking cost reduction benefit from the Loyal Soldier HR strategy, whereas those seeking innovation and creativity benefit from the Committed Expert strategy.[77] In the chapters that follow, we will explore how specific human resource practices differ depending on which strategy is chosen. We will also explore practices associated with the external orientation strategies.

CONCEPT CHECK

1. *In what ways does research support the contingency approach to human resource management?*
2. *How does the commitment strategy fit with the contingency approach?*

alynst/iStockphoto

A MANAGER'S PERSPECTIVE REVISITED

IN THE MANAGER'S PERSPECTIVE THAT OPENED THE CHAPTER, ELIZABETH WAS THINKING ABOUT WAYS TO TIE HUMAN RESOURCE STRATEGY TO COMPETITIVE BUSINESS STRATEGY. SHE FELT THAT HER SMALL CHAIN OF CONVENIENCE STORES COULD BENEFIT FROM A BETTER STRATEGY FOR COMPETING WITH OTHER STORES. SHE ALSO WANTED TO FIND WAYS TO USE HUMAN RESOURCE PRACTICES TO HELP THE STORES ACHIEVE A STRATEGY. ELIZABETH WONDERED WHETHER THE PREVIOUS OWNER'S EMPHASIS ON EMPLOYEE LOYALTY WAS THE BEST APPROACH. FOLLOWING ARE ANSWERS TO THE WHAT DO YOU THINK? QUIZ THAT FOLLOWED THE DESCRIPTION OF ELIZABETH'S CIRCUMSTANCES. WERE YOU ABLE TO CORRECTLY IDENTIFY THE TRUE STATEMENTS? COULD YOU DO BETTER NOW?

1. Having good employees is more important than having good production equipment. TRUE. *Good employees are an organizational resource that is rare and difficult to imitate.*

2. Much of the workforce lacks needed skills, so high-quality employees are difficult to find and retain. TRUE. *Quality employees represent a critical internal strength for organizations, but surveys suggest that companies find it difficult to hire and retain enough employees who have not only technical skills but also critical thinking and communication skills.*

3. The most effective way for an organization to compete with other organizations is to produce similar goods and services at lower prices. FALSE. *Organizations can compete through either cost reduction or differentiation. Because only one firm can be the true lowest cost producer, a majority of successful organizations adopt a differentiation strategy.*

4. Organizations are most effective when they develop a highly committed workforce. TRUE. *The commitment strategy, which emphasizes treating employees well and seeking to retain them, has been linked with higher overall productivity for organizations.*

5. An organization seeking to produce the highest-quality products should have different human resource practices from an organization seeking to produce inexpensive products. TRUE. *The contingency perspective focuses on aligning human resource practices with competitive strategies.*

Elizabeth's questions are common to all organizations. Organizational leaders must make decisions about how they will compete with other organizations in their respective industries. The strategy formulation process can help guide their decisions. Focusing on either cost leadership or differentiation provides them with a way to emphasize things that customers value. Organizations also benefit from ensuring that human resource practices match competitive strategies.

SUMMARY

LEARNING OBJECTIVE 1

How is strategy formulated?

A strategy is a set of coordinated choices and actions. The first step in strategy formulation is gathering information from outside and inside the organization. Information about the organization's external environment describes opportunities, which are favorable conditions, and threats, which are unfavorable conditions. Demographic and cultural trends, economic and political conditions, and technological developments represent important threats and opportunities for most organizations. Information is also gathered about the organization's internal resources and capabilities. Areas of high capability are labeled strengths, and areas of low capability are labeled weaknesses. A strategic set of human resource practices can represent a valuable and rare strength.

Once information has been gathered, the next step is to analyze the information and make decisions. Encouraging a group of decision makers to work together can facilitate this process. Members of the group should meet often and develop their collective intuition. They should also make sure that they explore different points of view and numerous alternatives. In addition, they should set flexible timelines that keep them moving forward and making decisions. Minimizing organizational politics also facilitates decision making.

LEARNING OBJECTIVE 2

What are common competitive business strategies?

Business-level strategies determine how an organization will compete with other companies that provide similar goods and services. One common strategy is the cost leadership strategy. Organizations using this strategy strive to produce goods and services at the lowest possible cost. They usually produce basic and standardized products. The key to success for these organizations is having employees who are more efficient than the employees of other organizations.

Another common competitive business-level strategy is differentiation. Organizations using a differentiation strategy strive to produce goods and services that are somehow better than those produced by competitors. They usually strive to produce unique products and to offer exceptional service. The key to success for these organizations is having employees who do things better than the employees of other organizations.

LEARNING OBJECTIVE 3

What are basic approaches to human resource strategy?

Two basic approaches to human resource strategy are the universalistic approach and the contingency approach. The universalistic approach focuses on identifying a set of practices that are beneficial to all organizations. This approach has identified a bundle of practices, labeled the commitment strategy, that appear to be generally beneficial. Practices in the commitment bundle communicate the message that management cares about employees. The commitment strategy also helps ensure that employees have the training and freedom to pursue important job tasks.

The contingency approach seeks to align human resource practices with competitive business practices. One distinction within this approach is a focus on cost leadership versus a focus on differentiation. Organizations mainly concerned with reducing costs emphasize processes and general roles. They carefully prescribe appropriate behaviors for performing work. Organizations that focus on differentiation are more interested in innovation and quality enhancement. They emphasize career development and having good results. Another distinction of interest in the contingency approach is whether an organization has an internal or an external labor orientation. Organizations with an internal labor orientation seek long-term relationships with employees, whereas organizations with

an external labor orientation seek flexibility and do not make long-term commitments to employees.

LEARNING OBJECTIVE 4

What are common human resource strategies?

The dimension of cost versus differentiation can be combined with the dimension of internal versus external labor orientation. The result is four different forms of human resource strategy. Organizations using the Loyal Soldier HR strategy focus on developing long-term relationships with employees and encouraging efficiency by having them contribute in a number of different roles. Organizations using the Bargain Laborer HR strategy also encourage efficiency but do not develop strong relationships with employees. Organizations using the Committed Expert HR strategy develop long-term relationships with employees and encourage them to become experts in a particular area. Finally, organizations using the Free Agent HR strategy seek employees who make short-term contributions in highly specialized roles.

LEARNING OBJECTIVE 5

How do human resource strategies align with competitive business strategies?

Organizations are likely to have human resource practices that fit with their competitive business strategies. Organizations that effectively recruit, select, train, and compensate their employees develop an advantage that is hard for other organizations to copy. This advantage is maximized when the organization has a clear competitive strategy and a matching human resource strategy. Organizations whose human resource strategies match their competitive strategies do indeed perform better. A strategic approach to human resource management sees people as an important resource vital to organizational effectiveness. Research suggests that organizations with a cost leadership competitive strategy excel when they follow a Loyal Soldier HR strategy. Similarly, organizations with a differentiation competitive strategy excel when they use a Committed Expert strategy.

KEY TERMS

DISCUSSION QUESTIONS

1. Why are effective human resource practices often a better competitive resource than equipment and buildings?
2. What are some external opportunities and threats that you think organizations will face in the next 10 years? What types of organizations will benefit most?
3. Why can groups be more effective than individuals for making decisions?
4. What are the primary differences between a cost leadership and a differentiation strategy?
5. What are the key elements of the commitment strategy from the universalistic approach? Why does this approach generally contribute to success for organizations?
6. What human resource practices might be associated with a cost reduction emphasis?

What practices might be associated with a differentiation emphasis?
7. What are the strengths and weaknesses of internal and external labor orientations?
8. Choose a company where you or someone you know works. Which of the four human resource strategies do you think is most common in the company?
9. What are the key elements of the four human resource strategies: Loyal Soldier, Bargain Laborer, Committed Expert, and Free Agent?
10. The chapter text pointed out that a majority of organizations have a human resource strategy that fits their competitive strategy. What should an organization do if the strategies don't match?

EXAMPLE CASE   *United Parcel Service*

Of course, every company wants to attract the best people it can. Equally important at UPS is attracting people who fit the company culture, which encourages high energy, hard work, fairness, inclusiveness, teamwork, and sharing the wealth.

Those who work at UPS are more than employees; they're business partners. Promotions come largely from within the organization. Managers typically will handle assignments in about a half dozen different functional areas of the business during their careers. This employer/employee relationship remains relevant in today's economy, because the nature of UPS's business involves an extraordinary degree of teamwork.

Every business day, UPS moves 13 million packages around the globe. In effect, UPS is the world's conveyor belt for commerce, one that requires 350,000 employees to work in harmony and with precision. Every day, 85,000 drivers take responsibility for roughly 6 percent of the nation's GDP, which is delivered from their package cars.

Every day, thousands of decisions must be made by managers in the field to keep the conveyor belt moving smoothly—decisions about lost packages, transportation schedules, preparations for bad weather, and myriad other details. And every day, logistics and financial services people are creatively exploring ways for customers to streamline their supply chains to improve productivity and service.

Successfully coaching people is also critical to the company's success. Managers must be empathetic to one of the world's largest and most diverse employee workforces. They must be team builders. That takes experience and training; it's not something that can be gotten from a textbook or learned overnight.

How does UPS attract and retain such leaders? The answer lies in *connection*, the way the company connects to the world. This connection begins with the way UPSers connect inside, to each other and, as in any enduring culture, to their roots.

QUESTIONS

1. How do practices such as internal promotion and assignment of broad job duties help UPS achieve its competitive business strategy?
2. How do the human resource practices at UPS help build teamwork?
3. Why are training and experience so important at UPS?

Source: Lea Soupata, "Managing Culture for Competitive Advantage at United Parcel Service," *Journal of Organizational Excellence* 20, no. 3 (2001): 19–26. [Reprinted with permission of John Wiley & Sons, Inc.]

DISCUSSION CASE | *Mountain Bank*

Mountain Bank is located in the northwest United States. The bank has four major business lines: retail banking, consumer lending, real estate and mortgage banking, and corporate banking. Traditionally, Mountain Bank has had a strong presence in the retail banking line, with only a limited presence in the other lines. However, deregulation in the banking industry has led to mergers and acquisitions for Mountain Bank, as well as for several of its competitors.

Retail banking includes traditional banking activities such as providing checking and savings accounts. Mountain Bank currently has about 50 percent of the market for retail accounts in its area. Often, however, these accounts are not very profitable. Consumer lending encompasses a variety of secured and unsecured consumer loans, such as home equity lines of credit, automobile loans, boat loans, and card lines of credit. Mountain Bank currently has about 25 percent of this market. Real estate and mortgage banking involves obtaining and servicing home mortgage loans, which are seen as a stable form of income for most banks. Mountain Bank currently has less than 10 percent of this market. Corporate banking provides services to businesses. Corporate clients are provided with a wide variety of basic services, as well as financing for equipment acquisitions and plant expansions. These services are often seen as very profitable. However, Mountain Bank has a very small presence in the corporate market—less than 5 percent of the market, according to current estimates.

Mountain Bank has established a strategy of leveraging its strong retail banking presence into gains in the real estate and corporate areas. Past experience suggests that one of the best methods for achieving this leverage is cross-selling, which occurs when tellers and customer service representatives convince customers with retail accounts to open corporate accounts or to obtain home mortgages from Mountain Bank.

Recent studies have found that bank tellers are critical to the success of Mountain Bank. In fact, one study found that customers' experiences with tellers is the single most important driver of customer satisfaction. After all, a bank teller is often the only person an individual customer has contact with when visiting a bank branch. Although fewer tellers are needed every year due to technological improvements, tellers are still the heart and soul of a bank.

A typical branch of Mountain Bank has three to seven tellers, depending on size and location. Floating tellers (part-timers) are also used to increase the staff during lunch hours and pay days. Mountain Bank has traditionally approached the teller position as a low-paying, entry-level position. Tellers are frequently part-time employees. Turnover is quite high, and successful tellers are often transferred to customer service positions.

Job Description

Job: Bank Teller

Pay: $14 per hour

Receives and pays out money and keeps records of money and negotiable instruments involved in financial transactions. Receives checks and cash for deposit, verifies amount, and examines checks for endorsements. Cashes checks and pays out money after verification of signatures and customer balances. Enters customers' transactions into a computer to record transactions and issues computer-generated receipts. Places holds on accounts for uncollected funds. Orders daily supply of cash and counts incoming cash. Balances currency, coin, and checks in cash drawer at end of shift, using calculator, and compares totaled amounts with data displayed on computer screen. Explains, promotes, and sells products and services, such as traveler's checks, savings bonds, money orders, and cashier's checks.

QUESTIONS

1. What competitive business strategy do you recommend for Mountain Bank?

2. Based on the universalistic approach and commitment strategy, what types of human resource practices do you recommend for Mountain Bank with respect to its tellers?

3. Which of the four human resource strategies do you recommend for Mountain Bank with respect to its tellers? Why?

EXPERIENTIAL EXERCISE

Explore Company Websites

Explore the websites of several companies. Choose at least two companies from the same industry. See what you can learn about their competitive strategies. Visit the part of their website that links to employment opportunities.

See if you can find answers to the following questions:

1. Does the website clearly identify either a cost or a differentiation strategy?
2. Does the information on the website fit with your general beliefs about the company?
3. Does the website have a portal for selling goods or services? If so, does it seem to emphasize price or quality features?
4. What has happened to the stock price of the company over the past 10 years?

5. What types of jobs are advertised in the employment section of the website?
6. Does the website emphasize long-term relationships between the organization and employees? Does it emphasize training programs?

Based on the information you obtain, do the following:

1. Evaluate how well the websites succeed in communicating information.
2. Determine whether you think each company's competitive strategy and human resource strategy match.
3. Identify any relationships between strategies and stock prices.
4. Compare and contrast the strategies and practices of the companies that are direct competitors.

INTERACTIVE EXPERIENTIAL EXERCISE

HR Strategy in Action: Selling the HR Function at Mega Manufacturing
http://www.wiley.com/college/sc/stewart

Access the companion website to test your knowledge by completing a Mega Manufacturing interactive role-playing exercise.

In this exercise, you meet with senior management at Mega and try to convince other members of the management team that HR needs to have a "seat at the table" and function as a business partner within the company. The CFO, however, expresses the opinion that HR is just a "touchy feely" department that adds no legitimate business value. Your objective is to gain credibility and show that a strategic approach to HR can improve Mega Manufacturing. Based on previous discussions, you have learned that Mega believes that its products are better than those of its competitors. You also know that the company prefers to hire experienced people who won't require much training. How will you defend the HR function to the CFO and others in the meeting who may share the same opinion of HR? •

ENDNOTES

1. Jeffrey Pfeffer, "Competitive Advantage Through People," *California Management Review* 34, no. 2 (1992): 9–28; Jon Birger, "The 30 Best Stocks from 1972 to 2002," *Money* 31, no. 11 (2002): 88.
2. Birger, "The 30 Best Stocks," 88.
3. Daniel Fisher, "Is There Such a Thing as Nonstop Growth?" *Forbes* 170, no. 1 (2002): 82.
4. Wendy Zeller and Michael Arndt, "Holding Steady as Rivals Sputter, Can Southwest Stay on Top?" *BusinessWeek,* Issue 3818 (February 2003): 66.
5. Pfeffer, "Competitive Advantage Through People," 9–28.

6. Birger, "The 30 Best Stocks," 88.

7. Sally B. Donnelly, "One Airline's Magic,' *Time* 160, no. 18 (2002): 45; Melanie Trottman, "Inside Southwest Airlines, Storied Culture Feels Strains," *Wall Street Journal,* July 11, 2003, A1.

8. Company website http://www.southwest.com.

9. Justin Martin, "Balancing Elephants," *Fortune Small Business* 14, no. 8 (2004): 84–90.

10. Melanie Trottman and Scott McCartney, "Southwest's CEO Abruptly Quits a 'Draining Job'; Parker's 3-Year Tenure Saw Labor Woes, Sept. 11 Costs; Airline Gives Upbeat Forecast," *Wall Street Journal,* A1, July 16, 2004.

11. Melanie Trottman, "Southwest Air Profit Rises 12% As Cost-Cutting Shows Results," *Wall Street Journal,* B6, October 15, 2004.

12. Melanie Trottman, "At Southwest, New CEO Sits in a Hot Seat," *Wall Street Journal,* B1, July 19, 2004.

13. Sophie Segal, "Third Consecutive Quarterly Loss for Southwest," *Airfinance Journal* (April 6, 2009): 45.

14. Paulo Prada, Susan Carey, and Mike Esterl, "Corporate News: Southwest Air Turns in a Profit—UAL is Aided by Fuel Hedging, but Continental Posts a Loss Amid Lackluster Demand," *Wall Street Journal,* B2, July 22, 2009.

15. Paul Seidenman and David J. Spanovich, "Synergies Evolve in Southwest—AirTran Integration," Aviation Week and Space Technology, September 17, 2012.

16. R. Duane Ireland and Michael A. Hitt, "Achieving and Maintaining Strategic Competitiveness in the 21st Century: The Role of Strategic Leadership," *The Academy of Management Executive* 13 (1999): 43–57.

17. Robert B. Duncan, "Characteristics of Organizational Environments and Perceived Environmental Uncertainty," *Administrative Science Quarterly* 17 (1972): 313–327.

18. Jane E. Dutton and Susan E. Jackson, "Categorizing Strategic Issues: Links to Organization Action," *Academy of Management Review* 12 (1987): 76–91.

19. Donald C. Hambrick and Phyllis A. Mason, "Upper Echelons: The Organization as a Reflection of Its Top Managers," *Academy of Management Review* 19 (1984): 193–207.

20. Michael A. Hitt, R. Duane Ireland, and Robert E. Hoskisson, *Strategic Management: Competitiveness, and Globalization* 6th ed. (Mason, OH: South-Western, 2005); Michael E. Porter, *Competitive Strategy* (New York: Free Press, 1985).

21. Min-Huei Chien, "The Study of Human Resource Development and Organizational Change in Taiwan," *Journal of American Academy of Business* 11 (2007): 309–314.

22. Susan Meisinger, "Shortage of Skilled Workers Threatens Economy," *HR Magazine* 49, no. 11 (2004): 12.

23. Anonymous, "International Comparisons of Qualifications," *Labor Market Trends* 112 (September 2004): 351.

24. Patrick M. Wright, Gary C. McMahan, and Abigail McWilliams, "Human Resources and Sustained Competitive Advantage: A Resource-Based Perspective," *International Journal of Human Resource Management* 5 (1994): 301–326.

25. Kathleen M. Eisenhardt, "Strategy as Strategic Decision Making," *Sloan Management Review* 40 (1999): 65–72.

26. Karen A. Jehn, "A Multimethod Examination of the Benefits and Detriments of Intragroup Conflict," *Administrative Science Quarterly* 40: 256–282.

27. Michael E. Porter, *Competitive Advantage: Creating and Sustaining Superior Performance* (New York: Free Press, 1985).

28. Jim Edwards, "Sour Tweets Get Sweet Results," *Brandweek* 49, no. 33 (2008): 6.

29. Raymond E. Miles and Charles C. Snow, "Designing Strategic Human Resource Systems," *Organization Dynamic* 13, no. 1 (1984): 36–52.

30. Jonathan Birchall, "Target's Sales Slip Further Behind Walmart," *Financial Times,* May 21, 2009, 15; Kerri Shannon, "Target Corp. Has Dethroned Wal-Mart as Discount King," Money Morning, August 25, 2011.

31. Porter, *Competitive Advantage.*

32. Jay Barney, "Firm Resources and Sustained Competitive Advantage," *Journal of Management,* 17 (1991): 99–120.

33. A Kaifeng Jiang, David P. Lepak, Jia Hu, and Judith C. Baer, "How Does Human Resource Management Influence Organizational Outcomes? A Meta-Analytic Investigation of Mediating Mechanisms," *Academy of Management Journal* 55 (2012): 1264–1294.

34. Patrick Wright and Gary C. McMahan, "Theoretical Perspectives for Strategic Human Resource Management," *Journal of Management* 18 (1992): 295–320.

35. Randall S. Schuler and Susan E. Jackson, "Linking Competitive Strategies with Human Resource Management Practices," *Academy of Management Executive* 1 (1987): 207–219.

36. John E. Delery and D. Harold Doty, "Modes of Theorizing in Strategic Human Resource Management: Tests of Universalistic, Contingency, and Configurational Performance Predictions," *Academy of Management Journal* 39 (1996): 802–835.

37. Brian Becker and Barry Gerhart, "The Impact of Human Resource Management on Organizational Performance: Progress and Prospects," *Academy of Management Journal* 39 (1996): 779–801.

38. John Paul MacDuffie, "Human Resource Bundles and Manufacturing Performance: Organizational Logic and Flexible Production Systems in the World Auto Industry," *Industrial and Labor Relations Review* 48 (1995): 197–221.

39. Richard E. Walton, "From Control to Commitment," *Harvard Business Review* 63 (1985): 77–84; John Paul MacDuffie, "Human Resource Bundles and Manufacturing Performance: Organizational Logic and Flexible Production Systems in the World Auto Industry," *Industrial and Labor Relations Review* 48 (1995): 197–221; Casey Ichinowski, Kathryn Shaw, and Giovanna Prennushi, "The Effects of Human Resource Management Practices on Productivity: A Study of Steel Finishing Lines," *American Economic Review* 87 (1997): 291–313.

40. Jeffrey Pfeffer, *Competitive Advantage through People* (Boston: Harvard Business School Press, 1994).

41. Ichinowski, Shaw, and Prennushi, "The Effects of Human Resource Management Practices on Productivity."

42. MacDuffie, "Human Resource Bundles and Manufacturing Performance."

43. Ichinowski, Shaw, and Prennushi, "The Effects of Human Resource Management Practices on Productivity"; Scott Snell and James W. Dean, Jr., "Integrated Manufacturing and Human Resource Management: A Human Capital Perspective," *Academy of Management Journal* 35 (1992): 467–504.

44. John T. Delaney and Mark A. Huselid, "The Impact of Human Resource Management Practices on Perceptions of Organizational Performance," *Academy of Management Journal* 39 (1996): 949–969.

45. James P. Guthrie, "High-Involvement Work Practices, Turnover, and Productivity: Evidence from New Zealand," *Academy of Management Journal* 44 (2001): 180–190; Johngseok Bae and John J. Lawler, "Organizational and HRM Strategies in Korea: Impact on Firm Performance in an Emerging Economy," *Academy of Management Journal* 43 (2000): 502–517.

46. Nathan Bennett, David J. Ketchen, Jr., and Elyssa Blanton Schultz, "An Examination of Factors Associated with the Integration of Human Resource Management and Strategic Decision Making," *Human Resource Management* 37 (1998): 3–16.

47. Yaping Gond, Kenneth S. Law, Song Chang, and Katherine R. Xin, "Human Resource Management and Firm Performance: The Differential Role of Managerial Affective and Continuance Commitment," *Journal of Applied Psychology* 94 (2009): 263–275.

48. Riki Takeuchi, Gilad Chen, and David P. Lepak, "Through the Looking Glass of a Social System: Cross-Level Effects of High-Performance Work Systems on Employee Attitudes," *Personnel Psychology* 62 (2009): 1–29.

49. Jeffrey B. Arthur, "Effects of Human Resource Systems on Manufacturing Performance and Turnover," *Academy of Management Journal* 3 (1994): 670–687; Guthrie, "High-Involvement Work Practices, Turnover, and Productivity."

50. Lisa H. Nishii, David P. Lepak, and Benjamin Schneider, "Employee Attributions of the 'Why' of HR Practices: Their Effects on Employee Attitudes and Behaviors, and Customer Satisfaction," *Personnel Psychology*, 61 (2009): 503–545.

51. Becker and Gerhart, "The Impact of Human Resource Management."

52. Jeffrey A. Sonnenfeld and Maury A. Peiperl, "Staffing Policy as a Strategic Response: A Typology of Career Systems," *Academy of Management Review* 13 (1988): 588–600.

53. Peter Bamberger and Ilan Meshoulam, *Human Resource Strategy: Formulation, Implementation, and Impact* (Thousand Oaks, CA: Sage Publications, 2000).

54. Sonnenfeld and Peiperl, "Staffing Policy as a Strategic Response."

55. Bamberger and Meshoulam, *Human Resource Strategy*.

56. Safeev Varki and Shirley Wong, "Consumer Involvement in Relationship Marketing of Services," *Journal of Service Research* 6 (2003): 83–91.

57. David Rynecki and Doris Burke, "Morgan Stanley's Man on the Spot," *Fortune*, November 15, 2004, 120; Justin Hibbard, "Morgan Stanley: No Stars—and Lots of Top Tech IPOs," *BusinessWeek*, Issue 3916 (2005): 56.

58. David P. LePak and Scott A. Snell, "The Human Resource Architecture: Toward a Theory of Human Capital Allocation and Development," *Academy of Management Review* 24 (1999): 31–48; Anne S. Tsui, Jone L. Pearce, Lyman W. Porter, and Angela M. Tripoli, "Alternative Approaches to the Employee–Organization Relationship: Does Investment in Employees Pay Off?" *Academy of Management Journal* 40 (1997): 1089–1121.

59. Stanley B. Malos and Michael A. Campion, "Human Resource Strategy and Career Mobility in Professional Service Firms: A Test of an Options-Based Model," *Academy of Management Journal* 43 (2000): 749–760; John K. Masters and Grant Miles, "Predicting the Use of External Labor Arrangements: A Test of the Transaction Costs Perspective," *Academy of Management Journal* 45 (2002): 431–442; Tsui, Pearce, Porter, and Tripoli, "Alternative Approaches to the Employee–Organization Relationship: Does Investment in Employees Pay Off?"

60. Tsui, Pearce, Porter, and Tripoli, "Alternative Approaches to the Employee–Organization Relationship"; Sonnenfeld and Peiperl, "Staffing Policy as a Strategic Response."

61. LePak and Snell, "The Human Resource Architecture." 5

62. Ibid., 31–48; Sonnenfeld and Peiperl, "Staffing Policy as a Strategic Response."

63. Masters and Miles, "Predicting the Use of External Labor Arrangements."

64. Sarah Bloom, Employee Wellness Programs, Professional Safety, 53, no. 8 (2008): 41–42.

65. Anonymous, "UPS versus FedEx," *Financieal Times*, March 26, 2009, page 14.

66. Company website http://www.merck.com.

67. Katherine Spencer Lee, "IT Compensation on the Rise in '05," *Computerworld*, January 18, 2005, http://www.computerworld.com/careertopics/careers.

68. Jeffrey B. Arthur, "The Link Between Business Strategy and Industrial Relations Systems in American Steel Mini-mills," *Industrial and Labor Relations Review* 45 (1992): 488–506.

69. Johngseok Bae and John J. Lawler, "Organizational and HRM Strategies in Korea: Impact on Firm Performance in an Emerging Economy," *Academy of Management Journal* 43 (2000): 502–517; Snell and Dean, "Integrated Manufacturing and Human Resource Management."

70. Soo Min Toh, Frederick P. Morgeson, and Michael A. Campion, "Human Resource Configurations: Investigating Fit with the Organizational Context," *Journal of Applied Psychology* 93 (2008): 864–882.

71. Michael A. Hitt, Leonard Bierman, Katshuhiko Shimizu, and Rahul Kochhar, "Direct and Moderating Effects of Human Capital on Strategy and Performance in Professional Service Firms: A Resource-Based Perspective," *Academy of Management Journal* 44 (2001): 13–28.

72. Rosemary Batt, "Managing Customer Services: Human Resource Practices, Quit Rates, and Sales Growth," *Academy of Management Journal* 45 (2002): 586–597.

73. Li-Yun Sun, Samual Aryee, and Kenneth S. Law, "High Performance Human Resource Practices, Citizenship Behavior, and Organizational Performance: A Relational Perspective," *Academy of Management Journal* 50 (2007): 558–577.

74. Patrick M. Wright, Dennis L. Smart, and Gary C. McMahan, "Matches Between Human Resources and Strategy Among NCAA Basketball Teams," *Academy of Management Journal* 38 (1995): 1052–1074; Mark A. Youndt, Scott A. Snell, James W. Dean, Jr., and David P. LePak, "Human Resource Management, Manufacturing Strategy, and Firm Performance," *Academy of Management Journal* 39 (1996): 836–866.

75. Youndt, Snell, Dean, and LePak, "Human Resource Management, Manufacturing Strategy, and Firm Performance."

76. Allan Bird and Schon Beechler, "Links Between Business Strategy and Human Resource Management Strategy in U.S.-Based Japanese Subsidiaries: An Empirical Investigation," *Journal of International Business Studies* 26 (1995): 23–46.

77. Miles and Snow, "Designing Strategic Human Resource Systems."

Chapter 3
Ensuring Equal Employment Opportunity and Safety

A MANAGER'S PERSPECTIVE

ALEX RETURNS TO HIS OFFICE AFTER MEETING WITH JASMINE, ONE OF HIS MOST VALUED TEAM MEMBERS. JASMINE HAS JUST INFORMED ALEX THAT SHE WILL BE MAKING A FORMAL CLAIM OF SEXUAL HARASSMENT. BOB, A MEMBER OF THE SAME MANUFACTURING TEAM AS JASMINE—THE RED TEAM—HAS REPEATEDLY BEEN MAKING SEXUAL COMMENTS THAT CAUSE JASMINE TO FEEL UNCOMFORTABLE. JASMINE MENTIONED THIS TO ALEX A FEW WEEKS AGO, BUT ALEX HOPED THE ISSUE WOULD JUST GO AWAY. NOW HE IS WORRIED THAT HIS RESPONSE WAS NOT WHAT IT SHOULD HAVE BEEN. TODAY HE ASSURED JASMINE THAT HE WOULD SEE TO IT THAT THERE WAS NO RETALIATION FOR MAKING A HARASSMENT CLAIM. HOWEVER, ALEX WONDERS IF THINGS WOULD HAVE GOTTEN THIS BAD IF HE HAD STEPPED IN SOONER.

Alex knows that he should have tried to help resolve Jasmine's concern. Yet, he is unclear whether the company is responsible for Bob's actions. Does he as a supervisor have a responsibility to reprimand Bob for making sexual comments? Are there laws that protect people from having to work in environments that make them uncomfortable? Is there real harm as long as Bob is not physically touching Jasmine?

As Alex thinks about legal issues, he remembers seeing an accident report for the blue team. Tim, one of the team members, received an injury while cleaning a piece of equipment. He tried a short-cut procedure that was not approved by company policy. In the accident report, however, Tim stated that he did not know there was a specific policy about how the equipment was to be cleaned. Tim will probably not be able to work for the next two weeks. Is the company required to pay him for the work he misses during the two weeks? Is the company responsible for the medical bills? After talking to Jasmine, Alex is now wondering if Tim might also sue the company.

Alex also remembers a story he recently saw on the morning news. A nearby company is having legal difficulties because minority workers are not

Bloomberg/Getty Images

> **THE BIG PICTURE** *A Number of Laws and Court Decisions Protect Workers from Discrimination and Unsafe Working Conditions*

being promoted. Alex thinks about his company and realizes that there are very few employees who are racial minorities. He wonders if having a more diverse workforce would be helpful. Since he personally thinks diversity might be good, Alex also wonders what he could do to better promote diversity. What could he do to better enhance work opportunities for groups of people that have not historically been hired?

Of all the things he has faced as a supervisor, Alex realizes that legal issues are among those he fears most. What are his responsibilities? He remembers receiving some training when he was promoted from the line. It seemed like common sense at the time. But maybe he should review the material now that he has gained experience to help him understand what things are really important.

WHAT DO YOU THINK?

Suppose you are having a conversation with Alex. He is trying to remember the training he received and makes the following statements. Which of the statements do you think are true?

T OR F People who are victims of sexual harassment can sue the person who harassed them but not the company.

T OR F Companies must hire minority workers even when they are not as qualified as other people who are applying for the same job.

T OR F A company can have legal problems when it doesn't hire enough women, even if it treats men and women the same.

T OR F Men and women must be paid the same when they perform the same job.

T OR F Employees have a right to know about any hazardous chemicals they are exposed to at work.

After reading this chapter you should be able to:

LEARNING OBJECTIVE 1 Explain how Title VII of the Civil Rights Act of 1964 and its amendment by the Civil Rights Act of 1991 protect workers against discrimination.

LEARNING OBJECTIVE 2 Describe how major laws such as the Age Discrimination in Employment Act, the Americans with Disabilities Act, the Equal Pay Act, and the Family and Medical Leave Act protect workers.

LEARNING OBJECTIVE 3 Describe different methods for increasing workplace diversity, including opportunity enhancement, equal opportunity, tiebreak, and preferential treatment.

LEARNING OBJECTIVE 4 Explain the laws and practices concerning employee safety, including (a) the Occupational Safety and Health Act and (b) workers' compensation.

LEARNING OBJECTIVE 5 Describe specific practices that can help an organization comply with legal guidelines and promote good health and safety practices.

Why Is It Important to Understand Legal and Safety Issues?

People sometimes criticize human resource departments for being too concerned about following laws. However, a major part of the employee advocate role is ensuring that people are treated fairly. This human resource function provides important guidance for treating employees fairly and helping organizations comply with laws. Complying with laws, in turn, can save organizations a great deal of funds they would have to spend to fight legal accusations or to try to repair damaged reputations.

The importance of fulfilling legal responsibilities often becomes apparent only when things go wrong. Consider that many well-known companies have faced lawsuits over employment discrimination. Most of these cases have been settled outside of legal courts, but a substantial amount of money is usually spent defending and settling claims. Some of the most widely publicized and expensive examples of discrimination settlements include those made by State Farm Insurance, Coca-Cola, Texaco, Shoney's, and Home Depot. Some of these high-profile cases involved alleged sex discrimination. For instance, State Farm paid $240 million to settle a case brought by 800 female employees. Home Depot took a charge of $104 million to settle claims that women were denied jobs and promotions. Other cases involve allegations of racial discrimination. Settling racial lawsuits cost Texaco $176 million, Coca-Cola $192 million, and Shoney's $132 million.[1]

Several years ago, former and current employees filed a large discrimination case against Walmart. These unhappy employees claimed that Walmart denied women equal pay and opportunities for promotion. Judges originally ruled that the case could proceed as a class-action suit. This was an important issue, because class-action status meant that anyone who might have been harmed by Walmart's alleged actions—in this case, women applying for jobs or working at Walmart after December of 1998—could choose to join forces and be represented together in the case. In 2011 the Supreme Court ruled that the women bringing forth the case did not have enough in common to proceed as a group. Yet, a number of smaller, region-focused suits continue to be litigated.

Building Strength Through HR

RESPONDING TO DISCRIMINATION CLAIMS

Walmart, Coca-Cola, State Farm Insurance, and other large employers have learned the importance of preventing and quickly responding to allegations of discrimination. Organizations accomplish these goals by

- Developing and enforcing clear policies against discrimination.
- Adopting programs that provide employment opportunities for groups that have been historically disadvantaged.
- Using advertising and public relations campaigns to improve the image of their company as a desirable place to work.

Walmart spokespersons have denied the allegations. They argued that differences in promotions could be explained by fewer women applying for promotions, and that pay differences are the result of women not performing the same jobs as men. Walmart also embarked on a proactive campaign to address its employment practices. The company established a number of programs to advance the causes of women. It evaluated and restructured its pay scales, and it now posts job openings through an electronic system. In addition, the CEO announced a more affordable health plan, and executives now receive bonuses for meeting diversity goals.[2] These measures to ensure equal treatment for women and better communication of its employment practices have helped Walmart to successfully defend itself, but the cost has been very high. In the end, it seems safe to conclude that Walmart would prefer that the legal action had never begun.[3]

Of course, there are no magic methods for ensuring that at least some employees will not feel they are victims of discrimination. But being familiar with employment laws reduces the likelihood of facing discrimination charges. Thus, an important part of effective human resource management is knowing the laws and then teaching managers and others involved in personnel decisions how to comply with legal requirements.

LEARNING OBJECTIVE 1

What Is the Main Law Relating to Discrimination and Employment?

Who is protected from discrimination? The cases mentioned so far have dealt with racial and sexual discrimination. But what happens if a company has a policy prohibiting employees from having long hair? What about a policy against wearing a nose ring? Can a company have a policy against hiring college students?

Common Protected Classes										
	Race	Sex	National/ Ethnic Origin	Color	Age	Religion	Disability	Political Opinion	Sexual Orientation	Marital/ Family Status
Canada	X	X	X	X	X		X	X	X	X
Chile	X	X	X	X	X	X		X		X
Germany	X	X	X			X	X		X	
India		X					X			
Italy	X	X			X	X	X	X	X	
Japan		X	X		X	X	X	X		
Kenya	X	X	X	X		X	X	X		
Korea	X	X	X	X	X	X	X	X	X	X
South Africa	X	X	X	X	X	X	X	X	X	X
Spain	X	X	X		X	X	X	X	X	X
Taiwan	X	X	X			X	X	X		X
United Kingdom	X	X	X	X	X		X			X
United States	X	X	X	X	X	X	X			

Figure 3.1 Protected Classes of Employees in Various Countries. *Source:* Adapted from Brett Myors et al., "International Perspectives on the Legal Environment for Selection," Industrial and Organizational Psychology 1 (2008): 206–246.

Immutable characteristics
Personal characteristics that cannot reasonably be changed, such as race and sex.

Although there seem to be laws to protect everyone, in reality federal laws in the United States protect only a few specific groups of people. In most cases, people can only claim discrimination based on immutable characteristics, that is, traits they cannot reasonably change if they really want a job. **Immutable characteristics** usually include sex, race, age, and religion. Specific laws have been enacted to protect people in each of these categories from discrimination. Laws to protect people with certain characteristics are not confined to the United States. Figure 3.1 shows protected classes of employees in a number of different countries.

In the United States the Constitution and its amendments provide people with some assurance that they will be treated fairly. However, protection from discrimination comes primarily from specific laws, most of which were enacted in the last 50 years. Table 3.1 presents an overview of major federal laws related to discrimination and employment. States and even cities have

Table 3.1	*Major U.S. Employment Laws*
Law	**Protection Based On**
Title VII of Civil Rights Act of 1964	Race, color, national origin, religion, sex
Civil Rights Act of 1991	Race, color, national origin, religion, sex
Age Discrimination in Employment Act	Age (people over 40)
Americans with Disabilities Act	Physical and mental disability
Equal Pay Act	Sex
Family and Medical Leave Act	Illness and parental status
Executive Order 11246	Race and sex

acts that provide additional protection in many cases. For instance, most states have laws against discrimination based on marital status, and a number of states prohibit discrimination based on sexual orientation.[4] These state laws can provide additional guidelines, but they cannot conflict with the concepts set forth by federal acts. If a state law does conflict with a federal law, the federal law rules.

In the realm of employment and discrimination, one specific law is the basis for a majority of legal issues. That law is Title VII of the Civil Rights Act of 1964. We discuss Title VII in this section, along with an amendment known as the Civil Rights Act of 1991.

TITLE VII OF THE CIVIL RIGHTS ACT OF 1964

The most important law affecting human resource practices, the Civil Rights Act of 1964,[5] was passed by Congress and signed into law as a result of the civil rights movement of the 1960s, which sought to end racial discrimination. Being a law passed by the U.S. Congress, the Civil Rights Act of 1964 is of course a federal law. The part of the act that specifically applies to equal opportunity in employment is **Title VII**. Thus, people working in human resources often refer to the Civil Rights Act of 1964 simply as Title VII.

Title VII
The portion of the Civil Rights Act of 1964 that focuses specifically on employment discrimination.

Given that it was passed as part of a larger effort to end racial discrimination, it seems obvious that Title VII should protect the interests of racial minorities. It does more than that, however. Title VII provides protection to people based on five specific traits: race, color, national origin, religion, and sex. The law is applied for the protection of people who have been historically disadvantaged, including women and members of minority racial groups. These groups are referred to as **protected classes**, because they represent a collection of individuals specifically protected from discrimination by the wording and intent of Title VII.

Protected classes
Groups of people, such as racial minorities and women, who are protected against discrimination by law.

Most, but not all, companies are required to comply with Title VII. When the Civil Rights Act was originally passed in 1964, lawmakers were concerned that it would place an unreasonable burden on small employers who did not have enough resources to make sure they were in compliance. The law was thus limited to companies with 25 or more employees. It has since been amended to exclude only companies with fewer than 15 employees. Another exemption is religious institutions. Churches are not required to comply with the guidelines of Title VII. Even with these exceptions, however, Title VII covers almost all employees who work for either private or public organizations. Furthermore, in cases of exemption, state laws often provide the same protection as Title VII. Thus, a company that has too few employees to come under federal Title VII may still have to comply with a similar state law.

A major part of Title VII was creation of the **Equal Employment Opportunity Commission (EEOC)**. The EEOC is a federal agency in charge of administrative and judicial enforcement of federal civil rights laws. The commission is led by five commissioners who are appointed by the president of the United States. The president also appoints a general counsel who conducts and oversees litigation. A large number of people work under the direction of these leaders in regional offices. An individual who feels that he or she has been the victim of employment discrimination can file a complaint with the EEOC. EEOC staff members research the claim and try to help resolve the complaint. Where the complaint cannot be resolved, the EEOC can sometimes take the case to court, where it proceeds with a lawsuit on behalf of the alleged victim or victims.

Equal Employment Opportunity Commission (EEOC)
A federal agency with responsibility to oversee, investigate, and litigate claims of employment discrimination.

Discrimination
In the context of employment, unfair treatment that occurs when people from particular groups are not given the same employment opportunities as people in other groups.

Equal employment opportunity
Absence of discrimination in the workplace; the condition in which people have an equal chance for desirable employment regardless of belonging to a certain race, gender, or other group.

Disparate treatment
The practice of treating job applicants and employees differently based on race, gender, or some other group characteristic.

Bona fide occupational qualification (BFOQ)
Characteristic of members of a specific group that is necessary to perform a certain job.

In a broad sense, Title VII protects people from discrimination. **Discrimination** in the context of employment occurs when not all people are given the same opportunity for employment and promotions. In this sense, Title VII requires **equal employment opportunity**, meaning that people should be given an equal chance to obtain employment regardless of their race, color, national origin, gender, or religion. Specifically, Title VII offers protection from three distinct types of discrimination: disparate treatment, adverse impact, and harassment.

Disparate Treatment

What happens when a restaurant decides to hire women but not men to serve food? Is it fair to make being female a requirement for doing the job? Does it violate Title VII? What if the restaurant is trying to differentiate itself by providing a certain type of atmosphere? Should the government step in and help men who want to work as servers? These issues were hotly debated a number of years ago when a lawsuit was filed against the Hooters restaurant chain. Hooters has a company policy of having food served by women dressed in shorts and small T-shirts. The company openly denies men the opportunity to apply for server positions. A few men who wanted to work as servers complained to the EEOC, which brought legal action against Hooters. The case was eventually settled out of court, but it illustrates some important legal principles.[6]

Having a policy against hiring men is an example of **disparate treatment**, which is the specific practice of treating certain types of people differently than others. In the Hooters case, men were treated differently from women. A more common example might be asking some people but not others certain interview questions. For instance, suppose that an interviewer asks women applicants if they have childcare arrangements that will enable them to be available to work when scheduled. If the interviewer does not ask the same question of men, disparate treatment has taken place. Holding women to a different standard from men is disparate treatment. Another example is requiring job applicants from a certain racial group to pass a problem-solving test when no such requirement is in place for people from other racial groups. In most cases, Title VII prohibits disparate treatment. There are, however, some instances in which disparate treatment is allowed.

Suppose, for example, that a prison system that houses men wants to hire only male guards. Should the prison be allowed to refuse applications from women? One reason an exclusion might be allowed is that the presence of women to guard convicted rapists could create a dangerous situation for the women guards, the prisoners, and other male guards.[7] In this case, Title VII may allow men and women job applicants to be treated differently. The entertainment industry provides another example. Only males might be given the opportunity to perform male roles in theater productions, and only females might perform female roles. In both cases, being one gender rather than the other is seen as a **bona fide occupational qualification (BFOQ)**. The idea of a BFOQ usually applies to gender—and in some cases religion—and means that it is reasonable to assume that only a person with that particular characteristic can do the job.

Let's return to the Hooters case, which, as noted, was settled before it actually went to court. The settlement required the restaurant to give men an opportunity to work in a different job that was seen as being similar to the waitress position.[8] Had a trial been conducted, a central issue would have been the type of job being performed. If the job was simply to serve food, then the restaurant would most likely be in violation of Title VII. It's difficult to think of a good reason why men could not serve food. In contrast, if the job was to provide a particular form of sex entertainment, then BFOQ would be a possible defense for not hiring men. No man could provide the particular type of entertainment Hooters required. Examples of BFOQ are rare. In most cases as noted, disparate treatment is a violation of Title VII.

What can a company do to protect itself against claims of disparate treatment? In most cases, it must ensure consistent treatment for all employees. Company policies and practices should treat everyone the same. Fair treatment has other benefits as well. Treating people differently because of their race, sex, or religion is not only illegal but also reduces motivation. People are less likely to work hard when they see themselves or others being treated in unfavorable ways.[9]

Adverse Impact

What would happen if your professor decided to base grades on students' height? On average, women would receive lower grades than men. Such an act might seem unfair, but it would not be disparate treatment. Grades for men and women would be based on the same thing: height. Nevertheless, basing grades on height would create unequal results for men and women. Discrimination of this sort is called **adverse impact**. Adverse impact is subtler than disparate treatment and occurs when a company's policies treat all applicants the same but result in different employment opportunities for different groups.

Adverse impact
Discrimination that results from employer practices that are not discriminatory on their face but have a discriminatory effect.

An example of adverse impact occurred years ago when airlines had height requirements for flight attendants. Everyone had to meet a certain standard of height, so all applicants were treated the same. However, using height to make selection decisions had the effect of screening out most Asian applicants. Another example occurred approximately 40 years ago when a power company began to require laborers to have a high school diploma.[10] Educational opportunities were not the same for members of different races. As a result of requiring a diploma, the power company hired a very small number of minority applicants. There was no disparate treatment, as everyone was required to have a diploma. Yet requiring a diploma had the effect of screening out a greater proportion of minority applicants.

Although disparate treatment is normally a violation of Title VII, the legality of adverse impact is less clear. The very purpose of employee selection is to separate people so that those who are less qualified are not hired. Problems arise when certain groups are screened out at a higher rate than others. Still, screening out more people from some groups than others isn't by itself necessarily a violation of Title VII.

An important key is whether the selection method accurately identifies people who can do the job better. Companies do not violate the law when they hire fewer applicants from a protected class if they use appropriate methods to make hiring decisions. A common defense for adverse impact is thus validity. **Validity** is shown when the measures used to select employees provide assessments that accurately identify the people most likely to succeed.

Validity
The quality of being justifiable. To be valid, a method of selecting employees must accurately predict who will perform the job well.

Potential victims of discrimination are usually unable to determine whether a company's selection methods are valid. The courts have thus placed the burden of proof in adverse impact cases on the company. The potential victim of discrimination must simply show that members of the protected class are hired, promoted, or laid off at a different rate than others. For example, the potential victim might show that the company hires a larger percentage of men than women. The burden of proof would then shift to the company to demonstrate that its selection procedures are valid—that is, that the procedures identify the people who are best able to do the job.[11]

Note, too, that the courts have not required companies to employ exactly the same proportion of people from all categories. Rather, they have adopted the **four-fifths rule**. This rule is violated when the percentage of people selected from one group is less than 80 percent of the percentage of people selected from the best-represented group. For instance, suppose a company selects 50 percent of male applicants but selects less than 40 percent (four-fifths of 50 percent) of female applicants. Under the four-fifths rule, a potential victim of adverse impact discrimination would simply need to show that the company selects people from the protected class at this lower rate. That doesn't necessarily mean the company is in violation of Title VII. It does mean that the burden of proof falls to the company, which is required to demonstrate the validity of its selection procedures. The typical legal proceedings in adverse impact cases are shown in Figure 3.2.

The example in the "How Do We Know?" feature describes how companies that use good human resource practices are less likely to be seen as discriminatory. The potential value of effective HR is illustrated by the case mentioned earlier, as in which laborers were required to have a high school diploma. This case clearly illustrates the purposes and procedures associated with adverse impact. The company, Duke Power, established the policy near the time that Title VII was passed into law. Because of the policy, many minority group members were barred from applying for a position they desired. These people believed that requiring a diploma was nothing more than a pretext; in their view, the company's real goal was to avoid hiring members of the minority group. They produced statistics showing that only a small percentage of people from their protected class were hired, even though a large percentage of white applicants were hired. The burden of proof then shifted, and the power company was required to demonstrate that having a diploma was indeed necessary to successfully perform the job. When the company was unable to show an adequate link between having a diploma and performing the job, the case was decided in favor of the minority applicants.

Four-fifths rule
Evidence of adverse impact that occurs when the hiring rate of one group is less than 80 percent of the hiring rate of another group.

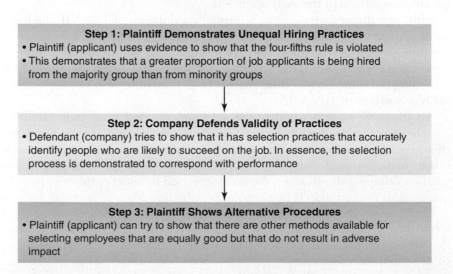

Figure 3.2 Adverse Impact Case Proceedings.

How Do We Know?

DO COURTS GIVE COMPANIES CREDIT FOR GOOD HR PRACTICES?

What can a company do to reduce the chances of being found guilty of discrimination? Does it help to follow good human resource practices? Maury Buster, Philip Roth, and Philip Bobko answer this question in a study that describes a scientific method for ensuring that hiring practices are related to job performance.

The process these researchers describe is used to determine the minimum qualifications for jobs. Minimum qualifications often include certain educational degrees and job experience. Such requirements are common, but an important question is whether they are really necessary. The researchers' process for linking minimum qualifications to job performance involves obtaining expert ratings and includes three steps:

1. People currently doing the job and their supervisors generate statements of minimum qualifications.
2. These statements are placed into a questionnaire, and experts in the field rate each potential statement with respect to whether the qualifications it describes are truly necessary for a minimally acceptable candidate on the first day of the job.
3. The statements rated most favorably are then used in determining minimum qualifications for job applicants.

The three-step procedure was used to develop minimum qualifications for an engineering position. The problem was that use of the qualifications resulted in adverse impact—fewer members of some minority groups were hired. When the case went before a federal court, however, the court accepted the three-step process as an appropriate method for determining whether minimum qualifications for education and experience were necessary.

The Bottom Line. Federal courts do indeed look favorably on the use of scientific practices to show that hiring methods result in choosing the most qualified applicants. Professor Buster and colleagues conclude that scientific principles can be used to develop selection methods that properly screen applicants, even when adverse impact exists.

Source: Maury A. Buster, Philip L. Roth, and Philip Bobko, "A Process for Content Validation of Education and Experienced-Based Minimum Qualifications: An Approach Resulting in Federal Court Approval," *Personnel Psychology* 58 (2005): 771–799.

Duke Power could have benefitted from better development of employee selection practices. The most critical practice is to make sure a company uses valid methods to select employees. The results of tests, interviews, and other measures must be linked to differences in job performance, as described in Chapter 6. Employers with good human resource practices not only treat employees better but also are able to better defend themselves against claims of discrimination.

Fortunately, in many cases the legal requirement of showing a relationship between selection practices and job performance is consistent with actions that increase profitability. Why incur the effort and expense of testing and evaluating job applicants if the measures do not provide information that helps make better selection decisions? A company that doesn't check to make sure its selection procedures accurately identify the applicants most likely to succeed on the job may be wasting its resources as well as unfairly discriminating against applicants from protected classes.

Harassment
In the workplace, improper actions or words of coworkers that cause an employee to feel persistently annoyed or alarmed.

Sexual harassment
In the workplace, improper words or actions that are sexual in nature or that are directed toward workers of a specific sex or sexual orientation.

Quid pro quo
In the context of sexual harassment, a form of harassment that makes continued employment and advancement contingent upon sexual favors.

Harassment

What if you are required to work with someone who says and does things that make you uncomfortable? Do you have the right to ask that person to stop? Can you require the company to create an environment that is less harmful to you? These questions get at the notion of **harassment**, which occurs when an employee is persistently annoyed or alarmed by the improper words or actions of other people in the workplace, such as supervisors or coworkers.

Whether harassment is illegal depends on what the person who bothers you is saying and doing. In terms of Title VII, harassment is illegal if the harassing behavior is related to any of the five protected classes. Most cases of harassment, however, involve behavior directed at an employee because of his or her gender. This kind of harassment is known as **sexual harassment**. According to the EEOC, which monitors compliance with Title VII, "Unwelcome sexual advances, requests for sexual favors, and other verbal or physical conduct of a sexual nature constitute sexual harassment when (1) submission to such conduct is made either explicitly or implicitly a term or condition of an individual's employment, (2) submission to or rejection of such conduct by an individual is used as the basis for employment decisions affecting such individual, or (3) such conduct has the purpose or effect of unreasonably interfering with an individual's work performance or creating an intimidating, hostile, or offensive working environment."[12] Because sexual harassment has received a great deal of attention and is the kind most commonly discussed, we'll focus on it here. Table 3.2 provides a list of specific guidelines for dealing with sexual harassment.

Consistent with the definition we just presented, the courts have defined two types of sexual harassment. One type is **quid pro quo** (literally, "something for something") sexual harassment, which occurs when an employee is told that continued employment or advancement depends on sexual favors. This type of harassment occurs, for example, if a supervisor informs an employee that she will be promoted only if she engages in sexual activities with him. Quid pro quo sexual harassment is fairly straightforward. It is illegal to make employment consequences dependent on sexual favors. Even a single quid pro quo statement by a supervisor is enough to warrant a sexual harassment action under Title VII.

Quid pro quo harassment can also affect employees who are not directly propositioned. For instance, suppose two people are competing for a promotion and one engages in sexual activities with the supervisor in order to obtain the position. Does this constitute harassment for the employee who did not receive the promotion? The courts have ruled that it does. An employee who does not receive a promotion may be a victim of harassment if he or she can

Table 3.2	*Sexual Harassment Guidelines*
Define harassment and affirmatively express company disapproval of harassing actions.	
Clearly define the sanctions and penalties for violation of the harassment policy.	
Inform employees of their legal rights, including how to make an EEOC claim.	
Establish a grievance procedure that is sensitive to the rights of all parties.	
Widely communicate the plan and rapidly investigate and resolve complaints.	

Source: Adapted from Arthur Gutman, *EEO Law and Personnel Practices,* 2nd ed. (Thousand Oaks, CA: Sage, 2000), p. 126. [*Reprinted with permission.*]

show that the person who did receive the promotion received it as the result of a sexual relationship.[13]

The second type of sexual harassment is labeled **hostile environment**. This type of harassment occurs when comments or behavior in the workplace have the purpose or effect of unreasonably interfering with an individual's work performance or creating an intimidating, hostile, or offensive working environment. For example, continually subjecting a woman (or a man) to unwelcome sexual remarks can create a hostile environment. The person making the remarks need not be a supervisor.

An important issue in harassment cases has been whether the company should be liable for the actions of an employee or supervisor who has engaged in harassment. As explained in the "How Do We Know?" feature, not all employees are equally likely to discriminate. Some early court rulings suggested that only the individuals doing the harassing would be accountable. However, a number of harassment cases made their way to the Supreme Court, which clearly established that organizations are indeed liable for the actions of their employees.[14] If the organization knows or should have known about the harassment, then the victim of harassment can look to the company to pay damages.

Most people would agree that continually asking someone for sexual favors or improperly touching someone represents harassment, but the effects of

Hostile environment
In the context of sexual harassment, a form of harassment that occurs when employees create an offensive environment in the workplace that interferes with an individual's ability to perform work duties.

How Do We Know?

WHO IS MOST LIKELY TO UNFAIRLY DISCRIMINATE?

When is unfair discrimination most likely to occur? Most of us think that some people are more likely than others to discriminate against women and minorities. We also think that discrimination is more likely in some circumstances than others. But who is most likely to discriminate, and when? A study by Jonathan Ziegert and Paul Hanges provides answers to these questions.

The researchers asked 103 undergraduate students to complete a number of measurement scales. One scale measured their implicit racial attitudes, which are attitudes and ingrained beliefs about race. Students also provided a measure of their motivation to control prejudice. People with higher motivation seek to hide their prejudices. About a month after completing these measures, students completed an exercise that asked them to evaluate potential job applicants. Some of the fictional applicants were members of racial minorities. Students were also told to assume that they were working for a boss with certain preferences about hiring minority workers.

Students gave lower evaluations to minority job candidates when they were told that their supposed boss preferred not to hire members of the minority group. This negative bias against recommending minority job candidates was highest for people with an implicitly negative attitude toward minorities. Students who were implicitly biased but were also motivated to control their prejudice were not as likely to give lower evaluations to minorities.

The Bottom Line. The organizational climate for prejudice is important. People seem less likely to discriminate when their supervisors establish a clear preference that everyone be treated equally. People who have subtle negative attitudes about minorities are more likely to discriminate than people who are not as biased. Yet these negative attitudes can be controlled when people consciously choose to control them. The authors conclude that in order to understand discrimination we need to assess both people's attitudes and their level of motivation to appear nonprejudiced.

Source: Jonathan C. Ziegert and Paul J. Hanges, "Employment Discrimination: The Role of Implicit Attitudes, Motivation, and Climate for Racial Bias," *Journal of Applied Psychology* 90 (2005): 553–562.

other actions are less clear. What if male workers place pictures of nude women in the workplace? What if men tease women in a way that doesn't seem offensive to them but does seem offensive to the women? In these cases, it is sometimes difficult to determine whether actions represent violations of Title VII. A single isolated comment would not normally be enough to show a pattern of hostility. However, repeated comments and unwelcome requests do constitute harassment. Behavior that makes others feel uncomfortable is generally forbidden. In short, actions and comments become harassment when a reasonable person would interpret them as harassment. Victims need not show that the comments and actions make them completely incapable of performing their jobs, but only that the environment had a negative impact on their psychological well-being.[15]

Sexual harassment has been linked to a number of undesirable outcomes. Individuals who are harassed report decreased physical and mental health. They also have lower job satisfaction and are more likely to avoid tasks, be absent, and quit. Work groups where harassment occurs are also less productive.[16] Individuals and organizations can thus benefit greatly from organizational policies and practices that stop harassment. What can a company do to keep harassment from occurring? Organizations can do several things to reduce discrimination. Sexual harassment is less likely to occur when an organization has a climate of respect. Such a climate can be facilitated by formal procedures that provide guidelines for appropriate behavior, as well as channels for reporting harassment without fear of retaliation. Education can also help prevent harassment.[17] Most organizations have thus outlined specific procedures for making sure that no unwanted sexual and racial comments and behavior occur in the workplace. Formal policies concerning harassment, as well as formal channels to communicate allegations of harassment, are important for demonstrating that the organization is taking reasonable care to eliminate unwanted behavior. Companies must also act aggressively when allegations are made. The accompanying "Technology in HR" feature describes how organizations are working to decrease harassment and other counterproductive actions that can occur with Internet and email use.

THE CIVIL RIGHTS ACT OF 1991

The Civil Rights Act of 1991 created some important extensions of Title VII.[18] One significant issue concerned shifting of the burden of proof to companies accused of adverse impact discrimination. Normally, the burden of proof in a lawsuit is on the plaintiff—the person bringing the suit. That means that it is the plaintiff's responsibility to show that the defendant committed a wrongful act. If the plaintiff can't meet this burden of proof, the defendant is not required to prove anything. However, the burden is somewhat different in employment discrimination cases.

Let's look briefly at the history of this issue to clarify what happened. Following passage of Title VII in 1964, the Supreme Court issued a number of rulings that essentially shifted the burden of proof to companies in discrimination cases. If the plaintiff could show adverse impact, then the company bore the responsibility for demonstrating that its hiring practices were not unfairly discriminatory. However, the makeup of the Court changed over time, and in the years leading up to 1991 the Court decided a number of cases that appeared to signal that the burden of proof should not be shifted to the company.[19]

Technology in HR

LEGAL ISSUES WITH INTERNET AND EMAIL USE

Widespread use of email messaging and the Internet has certainly made it easier to exchange information. This ease of information exchange can, however, create legal problems for organizations. Employees who might know better than to directly make a harassing remark often write inappropriate notes in email messages that get forwarded around the office.

A sense of anonymity might also encourage employees to post inappropriate sexual comments to electronic bulletin boards. Similar problems occur when employees create a hostile work environment by viewing pornographic material on company computers. A number of court decisions have established that organizations are responsible for offensive acts such as inappropriate email messages, sexually derogatory electronic board postings, and viewing of pornographic material.

Another potential legal liability arises when an organization allows employees to use company computers to share copyrighted material such as music and videos. Integrated Information Systems, a software company located in Arizona, paid the Recording Industry Association of America more than $1 million to settle a claim that it had allowed employees to use its equipment to share illegal copies of music. The Motion Picture Association of America has also made it clear that it will prosecute corporations if they do not take steps to discourage and eliminate sharing of illegal video copies.

Of course, an important question is whether an employer has the right to access its employees' private email messages and associated computer content. The clear answer is yes. The courts have consistently ruled that employees have no right to privacy when it comes to communications produced on company time with company equipment. The very act of accepting employment

©Nicklas Blom/Corbis

provides the employer with permission to monitor employee communications. Employees should therefore not assume privacy for email messages and other electronic content created and sent with company equipment.

So what can an organization do to protect itself from problems that occur when employees misuse electronic communication? The first answer is that an organization needs a clear policy that describes acceptable uses of company computers and other equipment. This policy must prohibit messages and communications that are sexually, religiously, and racially offensive. Many companies also have policies that prohibit the use of peer-to-peer (P2P) technology that facilitates the transfer of illegal music and videos. In fact, some organizations are designing their computer systems to prevent the use of P2P software. Although these safeguards might eliminate the use of some helpful electronic tools, they are necessary to limit the liability that organizations assume for the acts of employees.

Sources: Daniel J. Langin, "Employer Liability for Employee Use of Peer-to-Peer Technology," *Journal of Internet Law* 9, no. 5 (2005): 17–20; Chauncey M. DePree, Jr., and Rebecca K. Jude, "Who's Reading Your Office E-mail? Is That Legal?" *Strategic Finance* 87, no. 10 (2006):44–48.

To counter this trend, the 1991 act directly specified that the burden of proof rests with the company once a potential victim establishes that adverse impact exists.

Another question that was repeatedly debated in the courts in the 1980s was whether it was appropriate for companies to use different methods to score tests for people from different protected classes. When this practice, known as **race-norming**, is used, each person receives a score that only tells how he or she did in comparison with others of the same race or gender. The effect is to make some people rank higher than they otherwise would, since scores in their group are lower on average. The Civil Rights Act of 1991 made race-norming illegal. Now an individual's scores must be compared with all other scores, not just with the scores of members of his or her own group.

Race-norming
The practice of evaluating an applicant's score by comparing the score only with scores achieved by people of the same race.

The 1991 act also changed the kind of damages that could be awarded in discrimination cases. Until 1991, companies found guilty of discrimination could only be held liable for the actual damages caused to employees; these actual damages might include such things as lost wages. The 1991 act provides for not only actual damages but also punitive damages. **Punitive damages** are payments designed to punish the company and can be substantially higher than actual damages. Many victims now receive punitive damages. For instance, a woman who brought a sex discrimination case against Merrill Lynch & Company received a $2.2 million settlement that included not only back pay and lost earnings but also punitive damages against the company.[20] The award was given by a board of arbitrators who determined that the company had failed to train and discipline employees who engaged in sexual harassment.

Punitive damages
Payments ordered by courts that exceed actual damages and are designed to punish a defendant—for example, to punish a company for discrimination.

Also, until 1991 judges heard employment cases, and potential victims could not ask for a jury trial. The 1991 act allows jury trials for employment discrimination cases. In many cases juries appear to be more willing than judges to award punitive damages. Allowing jury trials, along with awards of punitive damages, substantially changed the nature of employment law.

APPLICATION OF U.S. LAWS TO INTERNATIONAL EMPLOYERS

The application of Title VII and other employment discrimination laws can be complex for international employers. What laws apply if the employer is based in a foreign country? Do U.S. laws apply to U.S. citizens who are working in foreign countries? The trend toward increased globalization is making issues such as these increasingly important.

Figure 3.3 shows a decision tree that can be used to help determine whether U.S. discrimination laws apply to international employers. The first step is to determine whether the job is located in the United States. If it is, and if the employer is a U.S. company, then U.S. laws protect the employee holding that job against discrimination, as long as the employee is authorized to work in the United States. Protection may be limited if the employee entered the United States illegally or without permission to work. Even if the employer is not a U.S. company, discrimination laws generally apply to jobs located in the United States. An exception arises if a treaty or special status exempts the foreign employer from U.S. law. For example, an individual located in the United States but working for a foreign government may not be protected from discrimination because the employer is granted special diplomatic status.[21] This is a rare exception, so most employees working in the United States are covered by Title VII and other discrimination laws, even if the employer is a foreign-based company.

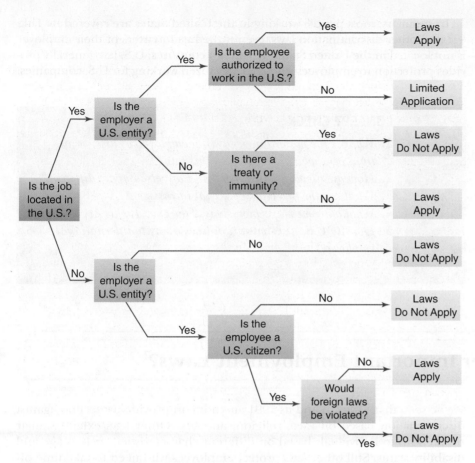

Figure 3.3 Do U.S. Discrimination Laws Apply to International Employers?
Source: Adapted from Richard A. Posthuma, Mark V. Roehling, and Michael A. Campion, "Applying U.S. Employment Discrimination Laws to International Employers: Advice for Scientists and Practitioners," Personnel Psychology 59 (2006): 711. [Reprinted by permission of Wiley-Blackwell.]

If the job is located outside the United States, a different set of rules applies. Of course, Title VII and similar laws do not apply in other countries when the employer is not a U.S. company. This makes sense, as there is no basis for the U.S. government to enforce its laws on foreign companies doing business in their own lands. However, if the employer is a U.S. company, then its employees who are U.S. citizens are protected by U.S. discrimination law, unless such protection would violate the laws of the country where the job is located. We can see an example of this exception in a case involving a non-Muslim who was prevented from working as a helicopter pilot flying into a sacred area in Saudi Arabia. U.S. courts allowed the U.S.-based employer to disqualify the pilot—a U.S. citizen—from employment on religious grounds (a potential violation of Title VII) because the presence of a non-Muslim in this area would have violated the law of Saudi Arabia.[22] We should also point out that U.S. law does not generally protect employees who are citizens of foreign countries from discrimination, even if the employer is a U.S. business. Thus, workers in foreign lands are only protected by U.S. discrimination laws when they are U.S. citizens working for U.S. organizations.

In summary, most people working in the United States are covered by Title VII and other discrimination laws, even if the headquarters of their employer is not located in the United States. In foreign countries, U.S. law generally provides protection to employees who are U.S. citizen working for U.S. companies.

CONCEPT CHECK

1. *What is the major law regarding employment discrimination, and who is protected by this law?*
2. *How are disparate treatment and adverse impact different?*
3. *What are the two types of sexual harassment?*
4. *What are some major provisions of the Civil Rights Act of 1991?*
5. *How do U.S. discrimination laws apply to international employers?*

LEARNING OBJECTIVE 2

What Are Other Important Employment Laws?

We've seen that Title VII and its 1991 amendment provide protection against discrimination based on race, religion, and sex. Other laws extend similar protections to individuals based on different characteristics, such as age and disability status. Still other laws protect employees who need to take time off from work to help family members or deal with medical conditions.

THE AGE DISCRIMINATION IN EMPLOYMENT ACT

Older people constitute a protected class that is not included in Title VII. Lawmakers were uncertain about the right way to address age discrimination, so they decided to study the issue further before passing a specific law. The law that was created from this study is the Age Discrimination in Employment Act of 1967 (ADEA), which essentially provides Title VII protections to older workers.[23] Specifically, the law as amended applies to everyone over 40. Some special occupations, such as police officer and firefighter, have been allowed to require people to retire at a specific age.

An interesting feature of the ADEA is that it doesn't simply classify people as either younger or older than 40. In cases of gender, race, and religion, people can simply be classified as being or not being a member of the protected class. When it comes to age, people are compared against others. Thus, discrimination can occur when a worker who is 50 receives better treatment than a worker who is 60. Companies cannot defend themselves against claims of age discrimination by simply showing that they employ a number of people over 40.

ADEA is similar to Title VII in that small employers are exempt. The difference is that the minimum number of employees is 20 rather than 15. Like Title VII, the ADEA protects people from several types of discrimination, including disparate treatment, adverse impact, and hostile environment discrimination.

Whereas Title VII is usually applied to hiring and promotion decisions, ADEA protection has historically been focused mostly on termination decisions, even though the reach of the law includes hiring and promotion. The most common complaint associated with the ADEA occurs when older employees are laid off or have their job benefits reduced. Disparate treatment is shown when a qualified person older than 40 is terminated and replaced with someone substantially younger. Some cases of disparate treatment are subtler, however. For example, a company might replace a worker with someone slightly younger, and then replace the new person with someone else slightly younger, until finally the person in the position is substantially younger than the original person. Another, sometimes disguised, form of disparate treatment occurs when a company terminates a number of employees in all age categories but then offers younger workers better opportunities for other positions.[24]

Adverse impact operates the same as for Title VII. Statistical patterns are used to show that negative employment decisions harm older workers more than other groups. Companies then bear the burden of showing that their termination policies were based on reasonable factors other than age. In the case of hostile environment, an older employee can claim that derogatory comments and conditions create an abusive workplace. For instance, an older woman going through menopause successfully used the ADEA in her claim that comments related to her age were intimidating and hostile.[25]

Age discrimination is of particular concern to companies when they must reduce their workforces. Unfortunately, many companies face the task of workforce reduction and thereby have the potential of negatively harming older workers more than younger workers. Good human resource practices can help these companies manage layoffs better. For instance, companies should carefully document the need for layoffs. They should then create a written policy that describes the principles that they use to determine who is laid off. Table 3.3 provides important suggestions for things that an organization should take into account when it faces the difficult task of laying off workers.

Organizations' performance can also be enhanced by eliminating age discrimination. Some people have stereotypes of older workers as less effective than younger workers. However, these notions are generally false. Research clearly shows that older workers are just as effective as younger workers when it comes to completing core job tasks. Moreover, older workers are less likely to do things that harm the organization. They engage in more safe work practices, arrive to work on time, take fewer days off, and spend extra effort to improve performance.[26] In fact, the only area where older workers have been shown to be problematic is that they are less likely to engage in training and career development activities.[27]

Table 3.3	*Guidelines for Effective Layoffs*
Conduct a management study to support necessity of a layoff and what principles will guide who is affected.	
Based on the management study, construct a written layoff policy.	
Document alternatives to layoff that were considered and/or used.	
Use length of service as a layoff principle whenever possible.	
Use an internal committee for layoff decisions, not individual department heads.	

Source: Adapted from Arthur Gutman, *EEO Law and Personnel Practices*, 2nd ed. (Thousand Oaks, CA: Sage, 2000), p. 224. [*Reprinted with permission.*]

THE AMERICANS WITH DISABILITIES ACT

What if you were in a skiing accident and lost the use of your legs? Should business organizations bear a burden to help you find work that can be done even with your disability? Should businesses be required to alter some of their work processes so that you can perform certain jobs? What if your eyesight is bad and you need to wear glasses? Are you disabled? These are questions addressed by the Americans with Disabilities Act (ADA), which was passed into law in 1990.[28]

Who Is Covered?

The ADA provides protection for individuals with physical and mental disabilities. **Physical disabilities** include conditions such as loss of an arm or leg, blindness, and chronic illnesses, such as cancer and diabetes. **Mental disabilities** include conditions such as depression, learning disorders, and phobias. Actually determining whether an individual has a disability can, however, be somewhat difficult in practice. In order to be classified as a disability, a condition must impair or limit a major life activity. Major activities include functions such as caring for oneself, walking, hearing, speaking, performing manual tasks, and learning. In essence, the ADA provides protection for individuals who have physical or mental impairments that prevent them from doing normal life activities.

Lawmakers excluded a few specific conditions. People are not protected by ADA if they have sexual behavior disorders or gambling addictions, for example, or if they currently use illegal drugs. In addition, a disability must be something that cannot be easily fixed. For instance, poor vision can normally be fixed with eyeglasses or contact lenses. Someone who has poor vision that can be corrected with glasses is thus not considered disabled.[29]

The ADA provides specific protection to individuals currently suffering from a disability. The law also protects people in two other categories: those who have a record of having a disability in the past and those who are regarded as having a disability, even if they do not. The distinction between being currently disabled and having a record of being disabled is particularly important in the case of illegal drug use. Current drug addicts are specifically exempted from the law. However, people who have a record of drug use in the past may be covered. The condition must have been a true addiction rather than just casual use, and sufficient time must have passed since the last drug use.[30] But a former addict who has not used drugs for at least a number of months can qualify for protection under the ADA.[31]

What Protection Is Offered?

The ADA does not guarantee that people with disabilities will be given any job they want. ADA guidelines apply only when the disabled person has the knowledge, skills, and abilities that are essential for performing the job. The law is thus designed only to assure that qualified individuals have fair employment opportunities. In some cases, a disabled person may not be required to perform functions that are not essential to the job. This means that organizations need to be very specific about the essential and nonessential parts of jobs. They do this through the process of job analysis, which will be discussed in Chapter 4.

Physical disabilities
Body impairments that substantially limit an individual's ability to engage in normal life activities.

Mental disabilities
Impairments of the mind that substantially limit an individual's ability to engage in normal life activities.

The ADA also may require companies to provide disabled individuals with **reasonable accommodation** to help them perform the essential duties of their jobs. Under the law, an accommodation is any change in the work environment or in the way things are customarily done that enables an individual with a disability to enjoy equal employment opportunities. Common accommodations include making facilities accessible to people in wheelchairs, restructuring parts of the job, modifying work schedules, modifying work equipment, reassigning a person to a different job, and providing a helper to read or interpret.[32] An organization is not required to change the job conditions to meet the preferences of the employee, however.[33]

An organization may not have to make reasonable accommodations if doing so would create **undue hardship** for the organization. Whether making an accommodation creates an undue hardship depends on several issues. The courts generally take into account the cost of the accommodation, the overall financial resources of the organization, the size of the business, and the nature of what it produces.[34] In essence, bigger companies with more resources are expected to be capable of making more accommodations. However, even a large company need not make an accommodation that severely harms the company's productivity. For instance, one disabled person brought a lawsuit asking that a company be required to change the assembly-line process so that he could perform a specific job. The court concluded that changing the assembly line placed an undue hardship on the company.[35]

A special case within the ADA is alcoholism. Alcoholism is covered to a degree within the ADA, but that doesn't mean that a person with a drinking problem will be excused from performing his or her work tasks. The law specifically says that a company can prohibit the use of alcohol at the workplace, that it can prohibit employees from being under the influence of alcohol at the workplace, and that alcoholics can be held to the same performance expectations as other employees.[36] Employees who drink at work or are under the influence of alcohol at work can be terminated. The area where reasonable accommodation comes into play is usually reduced performance or absences that come from alcohol use outside of work. One court settlement suggested that a company should strive to help the person deal with alcoholism as a disability. This includes informing the person of available counseling services, offering a choice between treatment and discipline, providing progressive discipline, and allowing sick days to be used for receiving treatment.[37]

How Do Companies Comply?

The ADA places some important limitations on what organizations can ask and measure during the job application process. Asking people whether they have a disability on an application form or in an interview is generally prohibited. Conducting a medical exam to learn of a disability is also prohibited, with one important exception. A medical exam can be required after a conditional job offer has been made, as long as the medical exam is required of all job applicants. In essence, the person is offered the job with the provision that he or she pass a physical exam testing for the abilities necessary to perform job tasks.[38]

The ADA requires employers and employees to work together to find ways to accommodate disabilities. Unless the disability is obvious, the employer cannot ask the employee whether he or she has a condition that limits his or her ability to perform job-related tasks. This means that disabled people bear a responsibility to communicate their needs for reasonable accommodation.

Reasonable accommodation
Under the ADA, an alteration of the work environment that enables a qualified individual with a disability to perform essential tasks.

Undue hardship
Under the ADA, a severe economic or other hardship placed on an employer by the requirement to make accommodations for workers with disabilities; an employer is not required to make accommodations that impose undue hardship.

Similarly, students who are disabled have an obligation to inform their professors and seek help. They cannot simply claim a disability after they have already completed the coursework. The ADA does not offer protection to someone who is disabled but does not make requests for accommodation.

A company can help ensure that it follows the guidelines of the ADA by first clearly describing the content of jobs. Specific lists of the tasks that are part of each job are necessary for determining whether someone who is disabled is capable of performing the job. A company should also develop clear lines of communication so that people with disabilities can comfortably ask for reasonable accommodations. When requests for accommodation are made, the company needs to carefully examine them and thoroughly study whether the accommodation can be made. In many cases, making accommodations can help companies find and keep high-quality employees. For instance, McDonald's specifically recruits workers with disabilities and has found them to be among the company's best and most loyal employees.[39]

THE EQUAL PAY ACT

Suppose a man and woman sit at desks next to each other and perform the same tasks. Is it fair to pay one of them more than the other? Does lower pay for the woman mean that the company discriminates? Can the woman make the company pay her the same as it pays the man? As described earlier, one major complaint in the lawsuit against Walmart was that women were paid less on average than men. The Equal Pay Act, which was passed into law in 1963, addresses the issue of pay differences for men and women. Unlike many other laws, this act applies only to gender.[40] It provides no protection for differences based on race or other factors.

The Equal Pay Act specifically makes it illegal for a company to pay men and women different wages, as long as they are doing equal work. Equal work is defined as tasks that require equal skill, effort, and responsibility and that are performed under similar working conditions. Of course, it is often difficult to determine if all job factors are truly equal. Soon after the Equal Pay Act became law, some organizations tried to get around it by adding a few minor tasks to jobs performed by men. For instance, one firm allowed only men to lift certain objects and then paid them more.[41] A medical firm tried to justify paying male nurses more by saying that they worked harder to lift patients and that men had to use extra skills to perform private duties for male patients.[42] In both cases, the court system found the reason for the differences to be little more than an excuse to pay men more. The court then prescribed keys for determining when jobs are truly different: (1) One job must require extra effort and more time than the other and (2) that job must affect the company's financial results more than the other job.[43]

The Equal Pay Act does recognize nondiscriminatory reasons why people in the same job might be paid differently. One reason is seniority. Paying people according to seniority is acceptable as long as men and women with the same years of service are paid the same. Another acceptable reason for differential pay is merit. The law recognizes differences in performance and allows higher compensation for stronger contributors, as long as accurate performance measures are in place. Paying some people more than others is also acceptable if the employees are paid according to a piece-rate system—that is, when they are paid a certain amount for each part they produce or service they perform. For instance, it would be permissible for men and women working as sewing machine operators to be paid differently if their pay was based on the number of shirts they made each day.

One thing that the Equal Pay Act does not require is basing pay on **comparable worth**. This practice involves determining what each job is worth to the company and paying accordingly, so that people whose jobs make equally important contributions are paid the same, even if the jobs are quite different in nature. Although comparable worth has been advocated at times, no U.S. law requires it. Under the Equal Pay Act, companies are only required to ensure that pay is equal for men and women performing the same job. Comparable worth is, nevertheless, a topic that is often debated.

Complying with the Equal Pay Act requires that the human resource function make a number of important contributions:

- Job analysis provides tools for determining when jobs are equal. We look more closely at job analysis in Chapter 4.
- Job evaluation uses surveys and statistics to determine how much to pay people based on comparisons both within the organization and between the organization and other organizations. These practices are described in Chapter 11.
- Performance measures assess the contribution of each employee and ensure that people who contribute more to the organization can be recognized and paid more. Performance measures are discussed in Chapter 8.

THE FAMILY AND MEDICAL LEAVE ACT

Suppose a woman who is about to give birth to a child decides she would like to take time off work to spend with the new baby. Must the company that she works for grant her request for leave? If so, how long can the leave last? Will she be paid while she is on leave? When she returns to work, will she be able to return to the same job? These important questions are addressed by the Family and Medical Leave Act (FMLA), enacted in 1993.[44] The FMLA provides up to 12 weeks of unpaid leave for people in certain situations. Furthermore, when the employee returns to work, he or she must be restored to the same position or an equivalent position in terms of pay, benefits, and responsibilities.

Under the FMLA, an employee—either male or female—may request a leave of absence for four reasons:

1. The employee is unable to work because he or she has a serious health condition.
2. The employee needs to care for an immediate family member with a serious health condition. Immediate family members are usually limited to spouses, parents, and children who are either under 18 or disabled.
3. The employee needs to care for a newborn child.
4. The employee needs to care for a child just adopted by the employee or placed with the employee for foster care.

Not everyone is covered by FMLA. Only companies with 50 or more employees who live within 75 miles of the workplace are required to grant leave under FMLA. In addition, in order to be covered, an employee must have worked for the company for at least 12 months and must have worked at least 1,250 hours during the previous 12 months. Also, certain key employees may be ineligible for FMLA leave.

Comparable worth
A measure that assumes that each job has an inherent value to the organization and that dissimilar jobs can be compared to determine whether the pay for these jobs reflects this value.

Employees who take leave under FMLA receive no pay while they are not working. The company is, however, required to continue providing health-care coverage under a group plan. Employees who wish to take the leave must usually provide 30 days' advance notice, when possible. The company may also require an employee requesting leave based on a serious health condition to provide certification of the condition. The requirement that employees inform employers before taking leave for medical conditions is an important feature of FMLA. The courts have ruled that an employee who is fired cannot later claim that absences were caused by medical conditions and thus are covered by FMLA.[45] The employee must inform the employer of the condition when the absence occurs and before being terminated.

The goal of FMLA is to help employees balance their work demands with their family needs. Providing time off so that employees can meet their family obligations provides benefits to the company as well as to employees, because employees who are worried about family needs may not be able to focus their attention and effort while at work. Companies can ensure that they comply with FMLA by informing employees of their rights for unpaid leave. When an employee does take a leave of absence, the company should communicate support and caring for the individual. In the end, companies often find that policies that support families are an important tool for retaining a diverse workforce.

CONCEPT CHECK

1. *Who is protected by the ADEA, the ADA, the Equal Pay Act, and the FMLA?*
2. *How do the concepts of reasonable accommodation and undue hardship guide the application of ADA principles?*

LEARNING OBJECTIVE 3

How Can Organizations Increase Diversity?

Organizations need to prevent discrimination and provide equal employ-ment opportunity in order to comply with laws. However, a strong case can be made that preventing discrimination increases employee diversity, which in turn increases organizational performance. Although increased diversity does not automatically improve organizational results, evidence suggests that a more diverse workforce is particularly beneficial when work tasks require creativity and diverse inputs.[46] As described in the "Building Strength Through HR" feature, people from minority racial and ethnic groups are effective at meeting the needs of customers from the same group. Diversity enhancement programs can also increase the available pool of potential employees, which makes it more likely that the best job applicants will be identified and hired. An important question is thus what organizations can

Building Strength Through HR

PEPSICO

PepsiCo is a global food and beverage company with annual revenues of more than $66 billion. The company has over 300,000 employees in nearly 200 different countries and seeks to sell its food and beverage products to consumers in all racial and ethnic groups. Increasing the diversity of employees as a means of increasing sales to minority groups is therefore a critical objective at Pepsi.

PepsiCo actively recruits diverse employees in several ways. First, the company cultivates relationships with African American colleges and universities and has an affirmative action planning process that seeks to increase the percentage of minority workers. Two external advisory boards of academics, politicians, and customers provide guidance on diversity issues. In addition, PepsiCo encourages employees to join *affinity groups* that consist of people of a particular race or gender who get together to discuss issues that affect them. Each group has as its sponsor an executive who is not a member of that race or gender.

Diversity initiatives at PepsiCo have increased the number of its minority workers. People of color now represent 17 percent of managers at midlevel and above, and women represent 34 percent of managers.

Indeed, the current CEO, Indra Krishnamurthy Nooyi, was born in India and is frequently listed among the most influential female leaders in the world. PepsiCo is also routinely rated as one of the best places of employment for minorities, and has been named to the list of Black Enterprise's 40 Best Companies for Diversity. Such awards increase the number of minority job applicants, which further advances diversity initiatives.

Diversity also adds to PepsiCo's profits. Innovation centers on identifying new product flavors to match the unique tastes of diverse customers. Among these products are Guacamole Doritos and Mountain Dew Code Red.

Sources: Information from Irene Chekassky, "Pepsi's for Everybody," *Beverage World* 117 (1998): 248; Carol Hymowitz, "The New Diversity: In a Global Economy," *Wall Street Journal,* November 14, 2005; Chad Terhune, "Pepsi, Vowing Diversity Isn't Just Image Polish, Seeks Inclusive Culture," *Wall Street Journal,* April 19, 2005; http://cdn3.blackenterprise.com/wp-content/blogs.dir/1/files/2012/07/2012-Best-Companies-For-Diversity.pdf; http://www.pepsico.com/PEP_Diversity/commitment/index.cfm.

do to increase diversity. Approaches to diversity enhancement can be classified into four categories:[47]

1. Opportunity enhancement programs focus on identifying and actively recruiting employees from groups that have historically been targets of discrimination, such as women and minorities.
2. Equal opportunity programs emphasize the elimination of biases and forbid unfair treatment of underrepresented groups.
3. Tiebreak programs suggest that minority status be considered a plus when deciding between otherwise equally qualified individuals.
4. Preferential treatment programs give positive weight to being a member of an underrepresented group.

Not surprisingly, people almost universally agree that the first two forms of diversity enhancement are appropriate. But some people harbor negative attitudes about the tiebreak and preferential treatment programs. As might be expected, women and members of racial minority groups tend to have less negative views.[48] Interestingly, white men may develop negative views of diversity enhancement as a way to preserve their self-esteem.[49]

Evidence clearly suggests that attitudes about diversity can be influenced by effective communication. Employees are more accepting of diversity enhancement when they are exposed to logical reasoning about why it is beneficial. Organizations should specifically provide empirical facts about the need for diversity, focus on the economic benefits of diversity, and encourage employees to think deeply about reasons behind diversity enhancement.[50] Diverse groups also perform better when they have been specifically shown how their group's diversity can benefit their processes and outcomes.[51] This often requires an organizational training initiative, which is described in Chapter 10.

EXECUTIVE ORDER 11246

Affirmative action plans
A plan aimed at increasing representation of employees from protected classes who have historically been victims of discrimination.

There is no law requiring organizations to increase diversity. However, practices to increase the representation of women and minority workers are often contained in **affirmative action plans** that are required by Executive Order 11246.[52] Executive orders are not passed by Congress but rather are issued by the president of the United States. Executive Order 11246 was issued by President Lyndon B. Johnson in 1965 and requires any organization doing business with the federal government to have an affirmative action plan. Doing business with the federal government is defined as having government contracts valued at over $10,000.

Executive Order 11246 does not have the force of law and is only indirectly related to private businesses. Nonetheless, it affects any organization that wants to do business with the federal government. Since a large number of organizations contract with the federal government, Executive Order 11246 has a long reach that makes it very similar to law. Most universities are covered by 11246, for example, because they receive federal funding. Construction companies that want to build public roads or buildings are also covered. In essence, the government uses its power as a large business partner to encourage companies to follow the affirmative action guidelines of <u>Executive Order 11246</u>.

Utilization study
An assessment to determine how closely an organization's pool of employees reflects the racial and gender profile of the surrounding community.

An affirmative action plan that complies with Executive Order 11246 requires organizations to submit a number of reports to show their progress in providing work opportunities for minorities and women. One requirement is a **utilization study**, which compares the percentages of women and minorities currently holding jobs in the company with the percentages of minorities and women in the population of the immediate labor area. Once a utilization analysis has been conducted, the next step, if needed, is to use the results of the analysis to develop goals and timetables—specific plans to increase the representation of women and minorities in the company's work force. Plans should not include quotas, which prescribe certain percentages to be hired; rather, they must be flexible objectives. Organizations must then show a good faith effort, or reasonable actions, to achieve the goals and timetables. There is no requirement to hire unqualified workers. Indeed, evidence suggests that organizations pursuing affirmative action plans do not have fewer qualified workers.[53]

Organizations doing business with the federal government that do not follow affirmative action guidelines face a number of possible sanctions. Their contracts with the government can be canceled, and they can be prohibited from doing further business with the government. In rare cases, the Department of Justice or the EEOC may also pursue lawsuits for violations of criminal law or Title VII. In most cases, however, a company cannot be sued for failing to follow an affirmative action plan.

RESTRICTIONS ON AFFIRMATIVE ACTION PLANS

A series of court decisions has placed important restrictions on affirmative action plans. One of the first of these cases concerned medical school admission. The medical school in question set aside a certain number of places in each entering class for members of minority groups. When a white male applicant was denied admission to the school, even though he had higher grades and scores than some minority applicants who were accepted, he brought a lawsuit against the school claiming that its admission policy resulted in reverse discrimination—denying him admission on account of his race. The case was eventually heard by the Supreme Court, which ruled that the school's quota system was unacceptable. However, the Court upheld the principle of affirmative action and stated that race could be used along with other factors in making admission decisions.[54]

Other court cases have focused on the issue of layoffs. In one instance, a fire department was forced to lay off some of its workers. In order to meet its affirmative action goals, the department terminated some white firefighters who had more seniority than some minority employees who were retained. The Supreme Court ruled that the policy was unacceptable because it punished innocent employees to remedy past discrimination. In this particular case, helping minorities procure jobs was seen as coming at too high a cost to others.[55]

More recent cases related to affirmative action include a high-profile case in which a contractor was found guilty of discrimination for giving favorable status to minority subcontractors. The Supreme Court rejected the need for affirmative action in this particular case because the plan seemed too broad and not specifically tailored to correct a particular problem.[56] This decision illustrates the necessity of creating an affirmative action plan that corrects a specific problem.

AFFIRMATIVE ACTION PLANS TODAY

A year seldom passes without a number of hotly debated questions surrounding affirmative action plans. One basic question that is frequently debated is whether affirmative action is contrary to the aims of Title VII. If Title VII is designed to provide equal opportunity for all, then how can Executive Order 11246 require preferential treatment for some? In general, the courts have upheld the legality of Executive Order 11246 by ruling that its practices are consistent with the intent of Title VII. Another frequently debated issue is whether it is appropriate to give preference to people who were not themselves actual victims of discrimination. In most cases, they receive preferential treatment because they are of the same race as others who may have been harmed in the past. People in favor of affirmative action, however, argue that because of past discrimination, some groups of people still have less opportunity than others in terms of education and career preparation.

Issues surrounding affirmative action will likely continue to be argued. Late in 2012 the Supreme Court heard oral arguments in a case filed by a woman claiming discrimination by the University of Texas because of preferences given to others who were members of a racial minority group. In June of 2013 the Supreme Court sent the case back to lower courts for further review and essentially postponed judgment, making it so that affirmative action will continue to be debated and argued in the legal system.

So, what should organizations do about affirmative action and diversity enhancement? First, it is important to remember that discrimination is still felt by many. Women, as well as racial and ethnic minorities, continue to report feelings of discrimination in organizations where they are not well represented. Women from minority racial groups are particularly in jeopardy of being harassed.[57] Research evidence confirms the validity of such perceptions. For example, research findings have shown that many people perceive mothers as less-competent employees.[58] Some of the negative feelings of discrimination decrease when organizations have supervisors who are from underrepresented groups.[59] Organizations can also benefit from creating a work climate that values and encourages differences and communicates caring for all employees. Chapter 5 discusses methods for making the workplace a desirable environment for members of protected classes and provides guidance for helping all employees feel valuable to the company. The chapter also describes recruiting practices that increase minority applications. In many cases, these procedures can help organizations meet affirmative action goals through practices that are widely accepted.

CONCEPT CHECK

1. *What are four approaches to increasing workforce diversity?*
2. *What is Executive Order 11246, and what does it require of companies doing business with the federal government?*

LEARNING OBJECTIVE **4**

What Are the Major Laws Relating to Occupational Safety?

As we've seen, the federal government has passed a number of laws that address discrimination in the workplace, and similar laws have been passed at the state level. Other areas of law are equally important to businesses. One such area is occupational safety.

In early 2006, an explosion in a West Virginia coal mine resulted in the deaths of 12 miners. The mine was relatively new but had received numerous citations for safety violations. During 2005, a total of 208 violations were recorded, and 96 of the violations were considered significant and substantial. Among the violations were problems with ventilation and safety inspections.[60] Could the deaths have been prevented by closer adherence to safety guidelines?

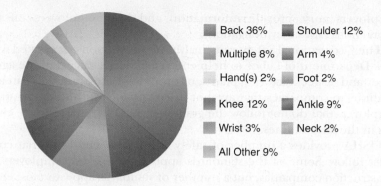

Legend:
- Back 36%
- Shoulder 12%
- Multiple 8%
- Arm 4%
- Hand(s) 2%
- Foot 2%
- Knee 12%
- Ankle 9%
- Wrist 3%
- Neck 2%
- All Other 9%

Figure 3.4 Nonfatal Occupational Injuries and Illnesses with Days Away from Work by the Part of Body Affected, 2011. *Source: Bureau of Labor Statistics, U.S. Department of Labor, Nonfatal Occupational Injuries and Illnesses Requiring Days Away From Work, 2011.* http://www.bls.gov/news.release/pdf/osh.2.pdf.

Although many people think very little about safety in the workplace, a look at a few statistics shows that problems exist. As many as 5,703 people are killed in occupational accidents during a calendar year.[61] Each year there are also as many as 4.3 million workplace injuries and accidents that do not result in death. This translates to approximately five injury cases for every 100 workers. Injuries and illnesses are most common in jobs such as transportation, manufacturing, and agriculture.[62] Figure 3.4 shows that most of the injuries and illnesses involved problems with shoulders and backs.[63]

Two major types of law provide employees with some assurance of safety and protection on the job. The first is a federal law passed in 1970, the Occupational Safety and Health Act. The second is not a specific law but a group of laws at the state level generally labeled workers' compensation laws.

OCCUPATIONAL SAFETY AND HEALTH ACT

Suppose an employee of a construction company works with chemicals that could cause blisters on his feet and hands. Does the company have an obligation to protect him from exposure to such chemicals? Is the company required to provide him with information about the chemicals? What are his rights as a worker who must use these chemicals? Such issues are the focus of the Occupational Safety and Health Act (OSHA), a federal law passed in 1970.[64] Compliance with these laws, and general efforts to promote employee well-being, not only reduce workplace accidents but also improve productivity.

Like most other laws affecting work practices, OSHA requires employers to keep records—in this case, about safety practices and incidents. Companies must have records of the information they provide to teach employees about the health concerns and dangers present in the workplace, they must keep track of all illnesses and injuries that occur at work, and they must also conduct periodic inspections to ensure workplace safety. In these inspections, they examine and test structures, machines, and materials to guarantee proper operation and not place employees in dangerous situations.

Employers must provide information and keep employees informed of protections and safety obligations.

The Occupational Safety and Health Administration was created within the U.S. Department of Labor to help enforce OSHA. Officers of the agency can enter and inspect factories, plants, or other worksites, and they can also issue citations to companies that are not in compliance with safety requirements. Employers that do not follow the guidelines of OSHA may receive civil penalties in the form of fines.

OSHA provides a number of safety and health standards that companies must follow. Some of the standards apply only to a few employers, such as construction companies, but a number of standards apply to most employers. These standards cover such topics as emergency plans, hazardous chemicals, workspace layout, and medical treatment and first aid availability.

Emergency Plans

Emergency action plan standard
The OSHA requirement that organizations develop a plan for dealing with emergencies such as fires or natural disasters.

Plans for dealing with fires and other emergencies are the main subject of the **emergency action plan standard**. Not all companies are required to have formal emergency plans, but many organizations find them helpful for planning ways to prepare for potential disasters. The plan should provide details about reporting fires and other emergencies and should also describe evacuation procedures and escape routes, establishing a process to account for all employees after evacuation. If employees have responsibility to rescue others or provide medical attention, the plan should make these duties clear. In addition, the plan should guide the actions of employees who might need to remain and operate or shut down critical equipment before they evacuate.

Hazardous Chemicals

Hazard communication standard
The OSHA requirement that organizations identify and label chemicals that might harm workers.

Exposure to certain chemicals can create both long-term and short-term problems. Which chemicals are harmful? What should employees do if they accidentally spill a harmful chemical? These concerns are the focus of the **hazard communication standard**, which is aimed at ensuring that employers and employees know about hazardous chemicals in the workplace. Under this standard, organizations must identify any chemicals to which workers might be exposed on the job. All chemical containers must be clearly labeled. Organizations must also provide information about protective measures that reduce the chance of harm from the chemicals. Each workplace must have a written plan that includes a list of the chemicals present at the site, the names of people who are responsible for overseeing the chemicals, and information about where employees can learn more about the chemicals. This information is usually contained in a **material safety data sheet (MSDS)**, a paper that specifically describes the nature of the chemical and how to prevent injury. An example of an MSDS in shown in Figure 3.5.

Material safety data sheet (MSDS)
An OSHA-required document that describes the nature of a hazardous chemical and methods of preventing and treating injuries related to the chemical.

Workspace Layout

Walking/working surfaces standard
The OSHA requirement that an organization maintain a clean and orderly work environment.

The **walking/working surfaces standard** emphasizes the need to keep the workplace clean and orderly in order to prevent slips and falls that may result in injury. Organizations are required to keep floors clean and dry and to keep aisles sufficiently wide and clear of obstructions. The standard also provides guidelines for the proper use of ladders and scaffolding and requires covers and guards for potentially dangerous structures, such as pits, tanks, and ditches.

AMMONIA (ANHYDROUS)

ICSC: 0414

NH$_3$
Molecular mass: 17.03
(cylinder)

ICSC # 0414
CAS # 7664-41-7
RTECS # BO0875000
UN # 1005
EC # 007-001-00-5
March 27, 1998 Peer reviewed

TYPES OF HAZARD/ EXPOSURE	ACUTE HAZARDS/ SYMPTOMS	PREVENTION	FIRST AID/ FIRE FIGHTING
FIRE	Flammable.	NO open flames, NO sparks, and NO smoking.	In case of fire in the surroundings: use appropriate extinguishing media.
EXPLOSION	Gas/air mixtures are explosive.	Closed system, ventilation, explosion–proof electrical equipment and lighting.	In case of fire: keep cylinder cool by spraying with water.
EXPOSURE		AVOID ALL CONTACT!	
•INHALATION	Burning sensation. Cough. Laboured breathing. Shortness of breath. Sore throat. Symptoms may be delayed (see Notes).	Ventilation, local exhaust, or breathing protection.	Fresh air, rest. Half–upright position. Artificial respiration may be needed. Refer for medical attention.
•SKIN	Redness. Skin burns. Pain. Blisters. ON CONTACT WITH LIQUID: FROSTBITE.	Cold–insulating gloves. Protective clothing.	ON FROSTBITE: rinse with plenty of water, do NOT remove clothes. Refer for medical attention.
•EYES	Redness. Pain. Severe deep burns.	Face shield or eye protection in combination with breathing protection.	First rinse with plenty of water for several minutes (remove contact lenses if easily possible), then take to a doctor.
•INGESTION			

SPILLAGE DISPOSAL	STORAGE	PACKAGING & LABELLING
Evacuate danger area! Consult an expert! Ventilation. NEVER direct water jet on liquid. Remove gas with fine water spray. Personal protection: gas–tight chemical protection suit including self-contained breathing apparatus.	Fireproof. Separated from oxidants acids, halogens Cool. Keep in a well-ventilated room.	T symbol N symbol R: 10–23–34–50 S: 1/2–9–16–26–36/37/39–45–61 UN Hazard Class: 2.3 UN Subsidiary Risks: 8

SEE IMPORTANT INFORMATION ON BACK

ICSC: 0414	Prepared in the context of cooperation between the International Programme on Chemical Safety & the Commission of the European Communities (C) IPCS CEC 1994. No modifications to the International version have been made except to add the OSHA PELs, NIOSH RELs and NIOSH IDLH values.

Figure 3.5 Sample Material Safety Data Sheet. *Source: International Occupational Safety and Health Information Centre (CIS), www.ilo.org/public/english/protection/safework/cis/products/icsc/dtasht/a_index.htm. [Copyright © International Labour Organization 2007]*

Medical and First Aid

Even when an employer takes precautionary steps, some accidents are likely to occur. The **medical and first aid standard** requires employers to make medical personnel and first aid supplies available to workers to treat injuries. Employees must also have access to medical personnel and treatment facilities so that they can receive treatment for more serious injuries. This requirement is particularly important for employees who are required to handle dangerous chemicals or to work in potentially dangerous environments.

Medical and first aid standard
The OSHA requirement that an organization make medical and first aid resources available to workers who may become injured.

WORKERS' COMPENSATION

Each state has laws and programs governing workers' compensation. Although some differences exist between states, all these programs have a common purpose, and most are quite similar. **Workers' compensation** provides protection for

Workers' compensation
State programs that provide workers and families with compensation for work-related accidents and injuries.

Building Strength Through HR

UNION PACIFIC CORPORATION

Union Pacific Corporation is a leading transportation company with 32,000 miles of railroad operations covering 23 states. The company employs over 42,000 workers and has assets valued at more than $43 billion. The safety and wellness of employees are particular areas of emphasis for Union Pacific.

Safety initiatives are highly visible throughout the company. Newsletters, job briefings, and safety hotlines provide ways to make sure that everyone talks about how to make the workplace safer. Employees frequently provide input that results in modifications to equipment and work practices. Supervisors are held accountable for achieving safety goals. An industrial hygiene program ensures compliance with regulations related to toxic chemicals, noise, dust, and fumes. Employees receive supplies such as safety glasses, hearing protection, and safety shoes.

Union Pacific also has a wellness program that seeks to reduce illnesses by improving employee health and fitness. Since fatigue and stress can cause accidents, this program also helps to reduce accidents. Employees are encouraged to improve their fitness by exercising in fitness centers. Programs to help people quit smoking have reduced the number of employees who smoke from 40 percent to 23 percent. The company also provides health assessments to identify health risk factors such as obesity, diabetes, and high blood pressure.

Health and safety programs at Union Pacific have had a positive impact on bottom-line results. On-the-job injuries have decreased over the past 10 years, and healthcare claims related to lifestyle problems such as high blood pressure have

©AP/Wide World Photos

dropped from 29 percent to 19 percent. Union Pacific also estimates that reducing the prevalence of excess weight among employees by one percentage point can save the company $1.7 million—and so reducing the prevalence by 10 percent can save nearly $17 million.

Sources: Information from Sandy Smith, "At Union Pacific Safety Is Number One," *Occupational Hazards* 67, no. 10 (2005): 30; Marybeth Luxzak, ". . . with UP Director—Health and Safety Marcy Zauha," *Railway Age* 206, no. 8 (2005): 9.

employees who are injured or disabled while working. In most cases, workers' compensation takes the form of an insurance program. Employers are required to carry workers' compensation insurance, insurance that provides benefits to compensate for injuries suffered during work, no matter how the injuries were caused. Benefits include payment of medical expenses for injured workers, disability benefits to replace income for injured workers unable to return to work, and benefits for family members of workers killed on the job. Most states make workers' compensation a no-fault and exclusive remedy for injury. This means that insurance must compensate an injured employee even if the actions of the employee caused the injury, but the employee cannot bring a lawsuit to try to collect more money than what is provided by the insurance policy.[65]

Workers' compensation programs require employees and employers to record and report workplace accidents. In most states, workers must report an accident or injury within a certain time, such as 90 days after it occurs. Employers also must file an injury report with a state agency within a certain amount of time. An important role of the human resource function is thus to ensure the accuracy of the relevant records. Training workers in how to report injuries is important as well. Human resource professionals in many companies work with medical providers who treat injuries and help determine when employees are ready to return to work.

CONCEPT CHECK

1. *What is OSHA, and how does it affect business organizations?*
2. *What protection is provided by state workers' compensation laws?*

LEARNING OBJECTIVE 5

What Specific Practices Increase Fairness and Safety?

Failure to comply with laws and regulations can be costly to an organization. The "Building Strength Through HR" feature illustrates specific benefits from safety and health initiatives at Union Pacific. What can an organization do to help all its members work safely? Research suggests that employees safety is compromised when employees feel burned out. In contrast, safety is enhanced when employee engagement is increased through a supportive work environment.[66] A few key areas that facilitate a supportive work environment for safety are outlined in Figure 3.6. As shown in the figure, employees need knowledge and motivation; knowledge and motivation, in turn, can be increased by leaders who show commitment, measure progress, and provide rewards.[67]

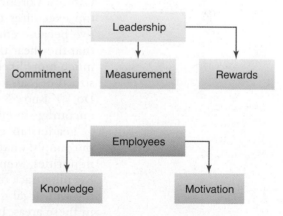

Figure 3.6 Encouraging Legal and Safety Compliance.

EMPLOYEES

Employees cannot follow laws and other guidelines unless they know about them; an important part of the human resource management function is thus to provide information about laws and guidelines. Managers involved in hiring and supervising employees must know about relevant employment laws. Specifically, they need to know what things to avoid, such as asking interview questions about protected issues such as age and disability. They also need to know how to prevent harassment. Employees working in hazardous areas must be trained in procedures to protect them from injuries and illnesses. The more engaging and active the training, the more likely safety is to be improved, particularly in seriously hazardous conditions.[68] Ongoing training programs, which are discussed in Chapter 9, are thus an important aspect of complying with laws and ensuring fair treatment. For instance, Calpine Corporation, a producer and marketer of electrical power, uses video and other materials to train employees in hazard communication, fire prevention, and disciplinary procedures. The training increases knowledge and helps employees understand why certain procedures are required.[69]

Knowledge alone is not enough, however. Members of an organization must also be committed to doing what they know is right. Motivation can be increased when organizational leaders help managers and employees see that they have the skills necessary to do what is being asked. Worker motivation for safe actions is also enhanced when supervisors have personal values that correspond with safety.[70] Individuals who work hard to ensure fairness and safety should be rewarded with higher pay and promotions. Conversely, workers who try to accomplish tasks using shortcuts that compromise safety may need to suffer penalties.

LEADERSHIP

Employees generally follow their leaders. They are therefore much more likely to comply with laws and guidelines when leaders show high commitment to compliance. Leaders make a difference. Leaders must set a good example and clearly communicate their expectations.[71] In the case of Calpine Corporation, mentioned earlier, employees are shown a video of top executives talking about the importance of safety. This video is effective because employees tend to follow directions and engage in behaviors that they hear their leaders emphasize. Compliance with regulations is thus much more likely when leaders develop and carry out programs that emphasize the goals of the regulations, such as diversity and safety. The "How Do We Know?" feature explains how leaders can create work climates that encourage safety.

Leadership can also encourage compliance by measuring key results; put simply, what gets measured gets done. Progress in hiring and recruiting minorities, women, disabled workers, and older workers should be tracked. Keeping track of these numbers not only shows that the company is complying with legal guidelines but also demonstrates that leaders value progress in these areas. In a similar way, efforts to track and reduce injuries and accidents not only comply with laws but also communicate interest on the part of leaders.

Managers who create fair hiring practices should be rewarded for their efforts. Achievement of diversity objectives should result in positive evaluations and bonuses, and supervisors' efforts to communicate the importance of safety should be tracked and rewarded. Groups of employees who follow guidelines and remain accident-free should also receive bonuses.

An example of the value of leadership in encouraging compliance is shown by the results of initiatives undertaken by Catholic Healthcare West (CHW), which operates hospitals in Arizona, Nevada, and California. The company implemented a program designed to reduce workers' compensation claims. The program began with upper management, whose bonuses were tied to reducing costs associated with worker injuries. Organizational leaders carefully measured and monitored the number and severity of injuries and were given clear responsibilities to ensure that information was obtained and communicated throughout the organization. The end result has been a 50 percent decrease in the cost of workers' compensation claims. For CHW, compliance with safety guidelines therefore not only made employees safer but also increased bottom-line profits.

How Do We Know?

WHAT CAN ORGANIZATIONS DO TO PROMOTE SAFETY?

What factors explain safe behavior? Is creation of an organizational climate that encourages safety the key? Are some people just more safety conscious than others? Does emphasizing safety decrease productivity? Craig Wallace and Gilad Chen conducted a study to find the answers to these questions. They collected data from 254 employees organized into 50 work groups. They assessed safety climate by measuring the extent to which supervisors emphasized compliance with safe procedures. They asked employees to report their conscientiousness, which captures the degree to which someone is organized and goal driven. Employees also reported on the extent to which they focused on either accomplishing a lot of work or following rules and regulations. Supervisors rated each employee on both safety performance (carrying out work in a safe manner) and production (completing tasks on time).

Conscientious employees simultaneously emphasized accomplishing work and following rules and regulations. Conscientious employees were thus successful on both performance dimensions; they completed a lot of work and did so in a safe manner. A different pattern of results was observed for safety climate. When supervisors emphasized safety, workers focused on following rules and regulations and were thus rated higher on safety performance. However, an emphasis on safety came at the expense of production. A strong safety climate resulted in less emphasis on accomplishing a lot of work and thereby resulted in decreased production. Safety climate thus exhibits a tradeoff. A work climate that encourages safe behavior does result in employees who focus on rule compliance, yet increased safety comes at the expense of productivity.

The Bottom Line. Creation of a strong safety climate increases safe behavior, but the strong safety climate may also reduce productivity. Professors Wallace and Chen thus suggest that organizations think carefully about the balance between safety and production. Leaders should emphasize safe behavior when accidents and injuries are prevalent or in settings where they are most likely to occur and cause a great deal of damage. The authors also suggest that hiring conscientious workers is one way to increase both safety performance and productivity.

Source: Craig Wallace and Gilad Chen, "A Multilevel Integration of Personality, Climate, Self-Regulation, and Performance," *Personnel Psychology* 59 (2006): 529–557.

CONCEPT CHECK

1. *What can organizational leaders do to encourage compliance with laws and regulations?*

A MANAGER'S PERSPECTIVE REVISITED

©Lava/beyond/Corbis

IN THE MANAGER'S PERSPECTIVE THAT OPENED THE CHAPTER, ALEX WAS THINKING ABOUT LEGAL AND SAFETY ISSUES. HE WAS CONCERNED ABOUT HIS RESPONSE TO A CLAIM OF SEXUAL HARASSMENT, AND HE DIDN'T KNOW IF HE WAS DOING ALL THAT WAS NECESSARY TO PROMOTE WORKFORCE DIVERSITY. HE ALSO WONDERED ABOUT THE CORRECT RESPONSE TO SAFETY VIOLATIONS AND ACCIDENTS. FOLLOWING ARE THE ANSWERS TO THE "WHAT DO YOU THINK?" QUIZ THAT FOLLOWED THE CASE. WERE YOU ABLE TO CORRECTLY IDENTIFY THE TRUE STATEMENTS? COULD YOU DO BETTER NOW?

1. People who are victims of sexual harassment can sue the person who harassed them but not the company. **FALSE.** *Employers can be held accountable for the illegal actions of their employees.*

2. Companies must hire minority workers even when they are not as qualified as other people who are applying for the same job. **FALSE.** *Diversity enhancement and affirmative action require companies to increase their efforts to hire minority workers, but they do not require that preference be given to minority applicants who are less qualified.*

3. A company can have legal problems when it doesn't hire enough women, even if it treats men and women the same. **TRUE.** *Treating people the same can result in adverse impact discrimination, which occurs when employees from one group are hired at a higher rate than employees from other groups, even though the groups are treated the same. When a company's* hiring procedures result in adverse impact discrimination, the company is required to demonstrate that the procedures identify the people most likely to succeed on the job.

4. Men and women must be paid the same when they perform the same job. **TRUE.** *The Equal Pay Act requires them to be paid the same when the job is the same. Exceptions can be made for differences in job tasks, seniority, or performance.*

5. Employees have a right to know about any hazardous chemicals they are exposed to at work. **TRUE.** *The Occupational Safety and Health Act requires employers to inform workers of chemical hazards.*

The questions that Alex faced are common to most managers. Employment and safety laws require organizations to follow certain guidelines. Alex, for example, does have an obligation to stop sexual harassment. He must also comply with a number of laws to eliminate discrimination and provide a safe workplace. Although Alex may have thought company guidelines were common-sense matters, he is wise to review them and see that he and other members of the organization are meeting legal requirements. Fortunately, compliance with the laws and guidelines can also increase productivity and profits in many ways.

SUMMARY

LEARNING OBJECTIVE 1

What is the main law relating to discrimination and employment?

Title VII of the Civil Rights Act of 1964 is the most important law providing protection against employment discrimination. Title VII specifically prohibits discrimination based on race, color, national origin, sex, and religion. Disparate treatment is one generally prohibited form of discrimination that occurs when employees and potential employees are treated differently. Adverse impact occurs when employees are treated the same but the outcome in terms of employment opportunity is different. Adverse impact discrimination can also be illegal unless an organization can show that its methods for hiring people truly identify the people most likely to succeed. Title VII also prohibits sexual harassment in the form of either quid pro quo or hostile environment harassment. The Civil Rights Act of 1991 extended Title VII by clarifying burden of proof, outlawing race-norming, and adding punitive damages. U.S. discrimination laws apply to most people working in the United States and to most U.S. citizens working in foreign countries for U.S. companies.

LEARNING OBJECTIVE 2

What are other important employment laws?

The Age Discrimination in Employment Act makes it illegal to discriminate against people over 40. Age discrimination is frequently observed when organizations lay off workers, and the act states that employees cannot be terminated and replaced by younger workers. The Americans with Disabilities Act protects people who have physical or mental disabilities. Organizations are required to provide reasonable accommodations so that qualified disabled workers can perform essential job tasks. Accommodation is not required when it creates an undue hardship for the organization. The Equal Pay Act requires men and women to be paid the same when they do the same job. People doing the same job can be paid differently based on seniority or merit, however. The Family Medical Leave Act provides employees with the opportunity to take up to 12 weeks of unpaid leave. Acceptable reasons for taking the leave include personal illness, illness of a direct family member, birth of a child, and adoption of a child.

LEARNING OBJECTIVE 3

How can organizations increase diversity?

There are four basic approaches to increasing workforce diversity. Opportunity enhancement programs focus on recruiting minorities and women. Equal opportunity programs ensure that people from underrepresented groups are not victims of discrimination. When applicants are equally qualified, tiebreak programs give an edge for employment or promotion to members of groups that have historically been victims of discrimination. Preferential treatment programs give positive weight to minority status. Executive Order 11246 requires affirmative action plans for organizations that do business with the federal government. A number of court decisions provide guidance for organizations pursuing affirmative action plans. Organizations cannot use quotas to ensure that a specific portion of new hires are from protected classes. Affirmative action plans also are illegal when they unduly harm the interests of individuals who are not members of a protected class.

LEARNING OBJECTIVE 4

What are the major laws pertaining to occupational safety?

The Occupational Safety and Health Act is a federal law that requires organizations to provide a safe work environment. The act requires organizations to provide information and training to employees and to keep records related to accidents and injuries. Some specific OSHA guidelines relate to hazardous chemicals, emergency plans, workspace layout, and medical treatment and first aid.

Workers' compensation laws exist at the state level. These laws require companies to carry insurance that pays medical bills and disability claims for people who are injured while working. Claims are paid even if the injured employee was at fault for causing an accident, but employees cannot generally sue an employer to receive additional compensation.

LEARNING OBJECTIVE 5

What specific practices increase fairness and safety?

Organizations can encourage compliance with laws and guidelines by ensuring that managers and employees have knowledge and motivation. Managers who hire and supervise others need to be familiar with the requirements of major employment laws. Managers and employees need to be aware of safety procedures. Knowledge and motivation increase when organizational leaders demonstrate high commitment to following laws and guidelines. Organizations that measure and reward compliance are also less likely to experience negative results from lawsuits, injuries, and accidents.

KEY TERMS

Adverse impact   83
Affirmative action plan   100
Bona fide occupational qualification (BFOQ)   82
Comparable worth   97
Discrimination   82
Disparate treatment   82
Emergency action plan standard   104
Equal employment opportunity   82
Equal Employment Opportunity Commission   81
Four-fifths rule   84
Harassment   86
Hazard communication standard   104
Hostile environment   87
Immutable characteristics   80
Material safety data sheet (MSDS)   104

Medical and first aid standard   105
Mental disabilities   94
Physical disabilities   94
Protected classes   81
Punitive damages   90
Quid pro quo   86
Race-norming   90
Reasonable accommodation   95
Sexual harassment   86
Title VII   81
Undue hardship   95
Utilization study   100
Validity   83
Walking/working surfaces standard   104
Workers' compensation   106

DISCUSSION QUESTIONS

1. How can human resource professionals reduce employment discrimination?
2. Why do you think the majority of employment and safety laws have been passed in the last 50 years, rather than at an earlier time?
3. How is adverse impact different from disparate treatment?
4. How are Title VII and Executive Order 11246 similar? How are they different?

5. What trends in society do you think encouraged the Americans with Disabilities Act and the Family and Medical Leave Act?
6. What are some reasons employees might engage in unsafe acts even when they know they could be harmed?
7. How do workers' compensation laws protect both employees and employers?

8. How might efforts to hire more minorities and women result in greater productivity and profits?

9. What are some ways organizations can motivate employees to follow safety guidelines?

10. Why are the example and actions of top organizational leaders so important for encouraging employees and supervisors to follow laws and guidelines?

EXAMPLE CASE — *Xerox*

Leslie Varon's boss lived by a simple rule: If he was in the office, she should be, too. In the early 1990s Varon worked in finance at Xerox, and the department's VP was an old-style organization man. "You could set your watch by the hours this man worked," Varon says, recalling 12-hour days that often began at 7 A.M. For Varon and her colleagues, that meant missing family dinners. After much discontent, they called a meeting. Couldn't they take work home in order to get out in time for supper? The boss agreed, slowly growing to believe that an employee's value lies in her work, not the hours spent at her desk. As for Varon, her earlier departures don't seem to have impeded her career: Today she's Xerox's finance VP.

Her status as a female officer would make her a rarity at many companies, but not at Xerox. The $15.7 billion document-management company is one of only nine in the Fortune 500 with a female CEO, but its gender diversity extends far beyond the corner office. Of Xerox's 32 corporate officers, eight are women. So are 800 of its middle managers, more than 30 percent of the total. The company is routinely ranked among the best places for women to work. Inside its Connecticut headquarters, female employees describe a culture where no one hesitates to reschedule a meeting to take a child to the pediatrician. Managers are judged—and compensated—on meeting diversity goals. At Xerox, "people really believe this—this is not cosmetic," says David Nadler, chairman of Mercer Delta Consulting, who worked with Xerox for 20 years. It doesn't see diversity as being somehow in conflict with meritocracy.

It's an attitude that began taking root nearly 40 years ago, when Xerox's top management became concerned about its treatment of black employees. By the 1970s, Xerox was aggressively hiring blacks and supporting a caucus of black employees who met to network and discuss grievances. And as feminism took hold, Xerox's progressive attitudes on race made it especially receptive to changes. But David Kearns, Xerox's CEO from 1982 to 1991, says he moved to promote women not because of fairness or altruism but because drawing from a bigger labor pool would help Xerox compete. "You had to get all of the people [involved] or you weren't going to be able to succeed," he recalls. During the 1980s, female employees formed a Women's Alliance, which lobbied management to promote more women.

Many of today's senior Xerox women directly benefitted from these early moves. Anne Mulcahy began as a sales rep in 1976. Though her numbers were great, she figured her Xerox career would be limited by her refusal to relocate with her husband and two children. But her bosses accommodated her by letting her commute to ever-bigger jobs. "[They said], 'We think you've got a career path here and we want you to take it as far as you can'," she says. She took it far indeed: In 2001, with Xerox mired in financial crisis, Mulcahy became CEO. She cut the workforce from 79,000 to 58,000, refreshed the product line, and strengthened the balance sheet. The result: Its stock price is up 65 percent, and Mulcahy ranked ahead of Oprah Winfrey on Forbes's 2005 list of powerful women.

QUESTIONS

1. How has hiring women and minorities improved Xerox's profitability?
2. What changes did Xerox make to become a more attractive employer for women and minorities?
3. Do you think the emphasis on hiring and promoting women and minorities has been unfair to white men? Why or why not?

Source: With permission. Daniel McGinn, "Women Hold Close to a Third of Top Management Jobs at Xerox. Inside a Kinder Culture," *Newsweek*, October 24, 2005, p. 68.

DISCUSSION CASE | *Jones Feed and Seed*

Jones Feed and Seed is a large regional warehouse that supplies agricultural products to retail stores. These products include pesticides that are used to treat animals and herbicides that are used to improve crops. For its warehouse operations, the company generally hires employees who have just finished high school. These employees work under the supervision of a more senior laborer, who is usually someone with about one year of experience working in the warehouse. The supervisor is in charge of interviewing job candidates and normally makes final hiring decisions.

Job Description

- Receive and count stock items and record data manually or using computer.
- Pack and unpack items to be stocked on shelves in stockrooms, warehouses, or storage yards.
- Verify inventory computations by comparing them to physical counts of stock and investigate discrepancies or adjust errors.
- Store items in an orderly and accessible manner in warehouses, tool rooms, supply rooms, or other areas.
- Mark stock items using identification tags, stamps, electric marking tools, or other labeling equipment.
- Clean and maintain supplies, tools, equipment, and storage areas in order to ensure compliance with safety regulations.
- Determine proper storage methods, identification, and stock location based on turnover, environmental factors, and physical capabilities of facilities.
- Keep records on the use and/or damage of stock or stock-handling equipment.
- Move controls to drive gasoline or electric-powered trucks, cars, or tractors and transport materials between loading, processing, and storage areas.
- Move levers and controls that operate lifting devices, such as forklifts, lift beams and swivel-hooks, hoists, and elevating platforms, in order to load, unload, transport, and stack material.
- Position lifting devices under, over, or around loaded pallets, skids, and boxes, and secure material or products for transport to designated areas.
- Manually load or unload materials onto or off pallets, skids, platforms, cars, or lifting devices.
- Load, unload, and identify building materials, machinery, and tools and distribute them to the appropriate locations, according to project plans and specifications.

QUESTIONS

1. What training would you provide to the supervisors who conduct job interviews?
2. What are some primary safety concerns that the company should have about the warehouse operation?
3. What OSHA guidelines does the company need to follow and communicate to employees?
4. What kind of disabilities do you think could be reasonably accommodated for this job position?

Source: Information for job description from http://online.onetcenter.org/.

EXPERIENTIAL EXERCISE
Locating Government Resources on the Web

Visit the website that describes workers' compensation for your state. Links can be found at http://www.workerscompensation.com/workers_comp_by_state.php.

1. Whom can employees contact if they think they have claims?
2. How would an employee go about filing a workers' compensation claim?
3. How soon after an injury must an employee make a claim?
4. What types of benefits might an injured employee receive?
5. What happens if the employee and employer have a dispute over workers' compensation?

Visit the OSHA website at www.osha.gov. In the compliance assistance section, visit the area called "Quick Start." Look at the modules that describe guidelines for the construction industry.

Based on what you learn, answer the following questions.
1. What kind of records should a construction company keep?
2. What should be included in a jobsite safety program?
3. What type of training should construction companies offer to employees?

What features of the OSHA website do you find most helpful? What would you do to improve the website?

INTERACTIVE EXPERIENTIAL EXERCISE
The Legal Side of HR: Handling Equal Employment Issues at Mega Manufacturing
http://www.wiley.com/college/sc/stewart

Access the companion website to test your knowledge by completing a Mega Manufacturing interactive role-playing exercise.
In this exercise, it's Friday afternoon, and you're looking forward to catching up on some leisure activities this weekend. You accompany the owner of Mega Manufacturing on a tour of the plant to meet some of the hourly employees. A female employee comes up to you and complains that a male coworker has been sexually harassing her. While you are talking with her, the owner receives a phone call. When he hangs up, he tells you that the caller was a former job applicant, who insists that he was not hired because he is member of a minority group. The former applicant plans to file a claim with the EEOC. The owner asks for your advice on how to begin handling these issues. So much for that weekend of relaxation.   •

ENDNOTES

1. Ann Zimmerman, "Judge Certifies Wal-Mart Suit as Class Action; Up to 1.6 Million Could Join Sex-Discrimination Case; Company Plans to Appeal," *Wall Street Journal*, A1, June 23, 2004.

2. Douglas P. Shuit, "People Problems on Every Aisle," *Workforce Management* 83, no. 2 (2004): 26–34; Daniel McGinn, Susanna Schrobsdorff, and Nicole Joseph, "Wal-Mart Hits the Wall," *Newsweek*, November 14, 2005, 42–44.

3. Andy Serwer, Kate Bonamici, and Corey Hajim, "Bruised in Bentonville," *Fortune*, April 18, 2005, 84–89; McGinn, Schrosdorff, and Joseph, "Wal-Mart Hits the Wall."

4. Michael A. Zigarelli, *Can They Do That? A Guide to Your Rights on the Job* (New York: Lexington Books, 1994).

5. www.eeoc.gov/policy/vii.html.

6. Anonymous, "Restaurant Chain to Resist on Hiring Men," *New York Times*, A20, November 16, 1995.

7. *Dothard v. Rawlinson* (1977) 433 U.S. 321.

8. Anonymous, "Hooters Settles Suit by Men Denied Jobs," *New York Times*, A20, October 1, 1997.

9. Jason A. Colquitt, "Does the Justice of the One Interact with the Justice of the Many? Reactions to Procedural Justice in Teams." *Journal of Applied Psychology* 89 (2004): 633–646; Jason A. Colquitt, Donald E. Conlon, Michael J. Wesson, Christopher O. L. H. Porter, and K. Yee Ng, "Justice at the Millennium: A Meta-Analytic Review of 25 Years of Organizational Justice Research," *Journal of Applied Psychology* 86 (2001): 425–445.

10. *Griggs v. Duke Power* (1971) 401 U.S. 424.

11. Arthur Gutman, EEO Law and *Personnel Practices*, 2nd ed. (Thousand Oaks, CA: Sage, 2000).

12. Code of Federal Regulations, from the U.S. Government Printing Office, Title 29, Vol. 4, 29 CFR 1604.11.

13. Gutman, *EEO Law*.

14. *Burlington v. Ellereth* (1988) 524 U.S. 742; *Faragher v. City of Boca Raton* (1998) 139 LED 2d 867 (no. 97-282).

15. *Harris v. Forklift Systems, Inc.* (1993) 510 U.S. 17.

16. Nathan A. Bowling and Terry A. Beehr, "Workplace Harassment from the Victim's Perspective: A Theoretical Model and Meta-Analysis," *Journal of Applied Psychology* 91 (2007): 998–1012; Chelsea R. Willness, Piers Steel, and Kibeom Lee, "A Meta-Analysis of the Antecedents and Consequences of Workplace Sexual Harassment," *Personnel Psychology* 60 (2007): 127–162.

17. Ibid.

18. www.eeoc.gov/policy/cra91.html.

19. *Wards Cove Packing v. Antonio* (1989) 490 U.S. 642.

20. Patrick McGeehan, "Merrill Lynch Firm Is Told It Must Pay in Sexual Bias Case," *New York Times*, A1, April 21, 2004.

21. *Kato v. Ishihara*, *239* F. Supp. 2d 359 (S.D.N.Y).

22. *Kern v. Dynalectron Corp.*, 577 F. Supp 1196 (N.D. Tex. 1983), aff'd, 746 F.2d 810 (5th Cir. 1984).

23. www.eeoc.gov/policy/adea.html.

24. Gutman, *EEO Law*.

25. *EEOC v. Massey* (CA11 1997) 117 F.3d 1244.

26. Thomas W. H. Ng and Daniel C. Feldman, "The Relationship of Age to Ten Dimensions of Job Performance," *Journal of Applied Psychology* 93 (2008): 392–423.

27. Thomas W.H. Ng and Daniel C. Feldman, "Evaluating Six Common Stereotypes About Older Workers with Meta-Analytic Data," *Personnel Psychology* 65 (2012): 821–858.

28. http://www.usdoj.gov/crt/ada/adahom1.htm.

29. *Sutton v. United Airlines* (1999) WL 407488 (No. 97-1943).

30. *Hartman v. Petaluma* (ND Calif. 1994) 841 F. Supp. 946.

31. *EEOC v. Exxon* (ND Texas 1997) 967 F. Supp. 208.

32. http://www.ada.gov/pubs/ada.htm

33. *Stewart v. Happy Herman's Cheshire Bridge* (CA11 1997) 117 F.3d 1278.

34. www.usdoj.gov/crt/ada/pubs/ada.txt.

35. *Dexler v. Tisch* (D Conn 1987) 660 F. Supp. 1418.

36. www.usdoj.gov/crt/ada/pubs/ada.txt.

37. *Rodgers v. Lehman* (CA4 1989) 869 F.2d 253.

38. Gutman, *EEO Law*.

39. Gillian Flynn, "Can't Get This Big Without HR Deluxe," *Personnel Journal*, December 1996, 47–53; Margaret Sheridan, "Difficult Labor," *Restaurants and Institutions*, July 15, 1998, 79.

40. www.eeoc.gov/policy/epa.html.

41. *Schultz v. Wheaton Glass* (CA 3 1970) 421 F.2d 259.

42. *Hodgson v. Brookhaven General Hospital* (CA 5 1970) 423 F.2d 719; 470 F.2d 729.

43. Gutman, *EEO Law*.

44. http://www.dol.gov/whd/fmla/.

45. *Brenneman v. MedCentral Health Sys* (CA 6 2004) 366 F.3d 412.

46. Jurgen Wegge, Carla Roth, Barbara Neubach, Klaus-Helmut Schmidt, and Ruth Kanfer, "Age and Gender Diversity as Determinants of Performance and Health in a Public Organization: The Role of Task Complexity and Group Size," *Journal of Applied Psychology* 93 (2008): 1301–1313.

47. David A. Harrison, David A. Karvitz, David M. Mayer, Lisa M. Leslie, and Dalit Lev-Arey, "Understanding Attitudes Toward Affirmative Action Programs in Employment: Summary and Meta-Analysis of 35 Years of Research," *Journal of Applied Psychology* 91 (2006): 1013–1036.

48. Ibid.

49. Miguel M. Unzueta, Brian S. Lowery, and Eric D. Knowles," *Organizational Behavior and Human Decision Processes* 105 (2008): 1–13.

50. Fiona A. White, Margaret A. Charles, and Jacqueline K. Nelson, "The Role of Persuasive Arguments in Changing Affirmative Action Attitudes and Expressed Behavior in Higher Education," *Journal of Applied Psychology* 93 (2008): 1271–1286.

51. Astrid C. Homan, Daan van Knippenberg, Gerben A. Van Klef, and Carsten K. W. DeDreu, "Bridging Faultlines by Valuing Diversity: Diversity Beliefs, Information Elaboration, and Performance in Diverse Work Groups," *Journal of Applied Psychology* 92 (2007): 1189–1199.

52. http://www.dol.gov/ofccp/regs/statutes/eo11246.htm

53. Harry Holzer and David Neumark, "What Does Affirmative Action Do?" *Industrial and Labor Relations Review* 53 (2000): 240–271.

54. *Regents of University of California v. Bakke* (1978) 438 U.S. 265.

55. *Firefighters of Local Union 1784 v. Stotts* (1984) 467 U.S. 561.

56. *Adarand v. Pena* (CA 10 1999) 169 F.3d 1292.

57. Jennifer L. Berdahl and Celia Moore, "Workplace Harassment: Double Jeopardy for Minority Women," *Journal of Applied Psychology* 91 (2006): 426–436.

58. Madeline E. Heilman and Tyler G. Okimoto, "Motherhood: A Potential Source of Bias in Employment Decisions," *Journal of Applied Psychology* 93 (2008): 189–198.

59. Derek R. Avery, Patrick F. McKay, and David C. Wilson, "What Are the Odds? How Demographic Similarity Affects the Prevalence of Perceived Employment Discrimination," *Journal of Applied Psychology* 93 (2008): 235–249.

60. Alan Levin, Thomas Frank, and Paul Overberg, "Mine Had Hundreds of Violations," *USA Today, A3,* January 5, 2006.

61. www.stats.bls.gov/iif/oshcfoi1.htm#2004.

62. www.bls.gov/iif/oshsum.htm.

63. http://www.bls.gov/news.release/pdf/osh2.pdf.

64. https://www.osha.gov/pls/oshaweb/owadisp.show_document?p_id=2743&p_table=OSHACT.

65. A good overview of different state workers compensation laws can be found at http://www.ic.nc.gov/ncic/pages/wcadmdir.htm.

66. Jennifer D. Nahrgang, Frederick P. Morgeson, and David A. Hofmann, "Safety at Work: A Meta-Analytic Investigation of the Link Between Job Demands, Job Resources, Burnout, Engagement, and Safety Outcomes," *Journal of Applied Psychology* 96 (2011): 71–94.

67. Information in this section is based somewhat on an article by David A. Hofmann, Rick Jacobs, and Frank Landy, "High Reliability Process Industries: Individual, Micro, and Macro Organizational Influences on Safety Performance," *Journal of Safety Research* 26 (1995): 131–149.

68. Michael J. Burke, Rommel O. Salvador, Kristin Smith-Crowe, Suzanne Chan-Serafin, Alexis Smith, and Shirley Sonesh, "The Dread Factor: How Hazards and Safety Training Influence Learning and Performance," *Journal of Applied Psychology* 96 (2011): 46–70.

69. Sandy Smith, "Calpine: Safety Is Personal," *Occupational Hazards,* October 2005, 10.

70. Sharon Newman, Mark A. Griffin, and Claire Mason, "Safety in Work Vehicles: A Multilevel Study Linking Safety Values and Individual Predictors to Work-Related Driving Crashes," *Journal of Applied Psychology* 93 (2006): 632–644.

71. David A. Hofmann and Frederick P. Morgeson, "Safety-Related Behavior as Social Exchange: The Role of Perceived Organizational Support and Leader-Member Exchange," *Journal of Applied Psychology* 84 (1999): 286–296.

Part 2
Securing Effective Employees

George Frey/Getty Images   ©William Perlman/StarLedger/Corbis   Robert Nickelsberg/Getty Images   Jeremy M. Lange/©The New York Times/Redux Pictures

Chapter 4

Designing Productive and Satisfying Work

A MANAGER'S PERSPECTIVE

JANE SITS IN HER CUBICLE WONDERING HOW SHE CAN MAKE WORK MORE ENJOYABLE FOR THE TELEMARKETERS SHE SUPERVISES. SHE PERSONALLY FEELS A SENSE OF ACCOMPLISHMENT WHEN SHE CLOSES A SALE OR RESOLVES A CUSTOMER'S CONCERN. BUT SHE KNOWS THAT SEVERAL MEMBERS OF HER TEAM DON'T GET A GREAT DEAL OF SATISFACTION FROM THEIR WORK. THEY OFTEN INTERACT WITH PEOPLE WHO ARE IRRITATED FOR BEING INTERRUPTED. RECEIVING INBOUND CALLS CAN ALSO BE FRUSTRATING, AS CUSTOMERS OFTEN MAKE UNREALISTIC DEMANDS. ALTHOUGH JANE KNOWS IT IS UNLIKELY THAT SHE CAN CHANGE THE TELEMARKETER JOB SO THAT IT IS FUN, SHE WONDERS IF THERE ARE THINGS SHE CAN DO TO IMPROVE WORKING CONDITIONS AND MOTIVATION.

Amos Morgan/Getty Images

The members of Jane's team sit in private cubicles and take calls. They are given approved scripts that describe what they should say. Jane and other managers often listen to conversations to make sure the telemarketers are following the scripts. Jane knows the scripts were developed with input from some of the most successful telemarketers, but she often thinks that members of her team come across as presenting a memorized speech rather than being genuinely interested in the customer. She wonders if it wouldn't be better to allow members of her team

more freedom to stray from the scripts. Would allowing greater individual freedom improve service and sales, or would too many telemarketers say the wrong thing?

Jane receives reports about things such as the number of calls made to potential customers and average time to resolve a complaint from a current customer. When she shares these reports with employees, they often provide long lists of reasons why they cannot process more calls. They also complain that they feel as if they are being treated as machines rather than people. Jane is sympathetic to their concerns, but she has noticed that team members are completing more calls since she began tracking their efficiency.

As she continues thinking, Jane receives a call from Steve in the human resource department. Steve wants to know if Jane has completed her revision of the telemarketer job description. Last week when she began working on the new job description, Jane actually laughed at what was written 10 years ago. Technology had changed the telemarketer position so much that the old description was totally inaccurate. This makes Jane wonder why the company even needs job descriptions. Why waste her time working on a

George Frey / Getty Images

THE BIG PICTURE *Organizations Maximize Productivity and Employee Satisfaction by Understanding and Effectively Coordinating Work Tasks*

new description, if the company had survived for this long with a description that was this out of date? But Steve was insistent and she promised to work on the revision.

As Jane hangs up the phone and leaves her cubicle, she notices that Erin is just arriving for the afternoon shift. She greets Erin and thinks how grateful she is that Erin is still on her team. Last month Erin gave birth to her first child and was thinking about quitting. However, Jane worked with Erin to find a schedule that could accommodate her needs as a new mother. Erin seems appreciative of Jane's understanding about her family needs. Jane is glad that she has been able to keep one of her top performers. Jane wonders whether there are other ways that she could make the job of telemarketer more attractive to working mothers.

WHAT DO YOU THINK?

Suppose Jane asks her boss, Monica, for guidance about designing employee work. Monica makes the following statements. Which of the statements do you think are true?

T OR F Giving workers more autonomy is a sure way to improve their performance.

T OR F Having updated job descriptions is important to keep the company out of legal trouble.

T OR F The primary objective of good work design is to cluster tasks into jobs that maximize the efficiency of workers.

T OR F People who continuously perform repetitive tasks often find their work to be unsatisfying.

T OR F Employees who have flexibility in deciding when they will work have higher performance.

After reading this chapter you should be able to:

LEARNING OBJECTIVE 1 Describe how the design of work tasks and roles can align with overall HR strategy.

LEARNING OBJECTIVE 2 Explain the steps in the process of job analysis and how to translate results into knowledge, skill, and ability lists that can be used to guide other human resource practices.

LEARNING OBJECTIVE 3 Describe various approaches to job design, including the motivational, biological, mechanistic, and perceptual perspectives.

LEARNING OBJECTIVE 4 Identify practices that make jobs more compatible with family demands.

How Can Strategic Design of Work Tasks Improve an Organization?

Work design
The process of assigning and coordinating work tasks among employees.

Differentiation
The process of dividing work tasks so that employees perform specific pieces of the work process, which allows them to specialize.

Integration
The process of coordinating efforts so that employees work together.

Many of us like to describe what we do at work by telling others about our jobs. Most of the time, we do this without thinking about who decides what tasks should go with which job. Why does an organization have sales representatives who meet with potential customers, while other employees make the actual products? Why do automobile manufacturers organize workers into assembly lines? These questions involve **work design,** the process of assigning and coordinating work tasks. One key principle of work design is differentiation. **Differentiation** suggests that each worker should be assigned a set of similar tasks in order to specialize in doing certain things very well. Another key principle of work design is integration. **Integration** is concerned with coordinating the efforts of employees.[1]

Strategic work design uses both differentiation and integration to determine who does what. Good differentiation and integration of work helps organizations increase productivity and improve customer satisfaction.[2] When work is designed strategically, employees' efforts are coordinated in a way that helps the organization achieve its competitive strategy.

One example of an organization with effective work design is W. L. Gore & Associates. Gore is perhaps best known for manufacturing apparel and camping products that are both water resistant and breathable. The company began in 1958 as a small shop in Bill Gore's basement. Since that time, it has grown into a multinational company with overall sales of $3 billion. Gore employs over 9,000 employees located throughout the world.[3] In addition to manufacturing water-resistant fabric, known as Goretex, the company makes products for use in medicine, electronics, and industry.

The various products made by W. L. Gore are tied together by quality and innovation. People don't normally buy Gore products because they are inexpensive; they buy them because they are excellent products that meet their specific needs. Gore's official statement about its strategy is "Gore's products are designed to be the highest quality in their class and revolutionary in their effect."[4] W. L. Gore clearly competes with other organizations by pursuing a differentiation rather than a cost strategy.

In order to encourage innovation and quality, Gore allows workers a great deal of freedom in deciding what they will do. Workers at Gore don't usually have specific jobs. Nobody is given a job title, and employee business cards don't list specific positions. Employees are simply called associates. New employees negotiate with others to determine "commitments" that define their work role. Commitments take advantage of individual strengths and abilities and are different for every employee. Gore thus replaces top-down planning with a system that allows each employee freedom to determine the specific tasks that he or she will perform. This freedom encourages each individual to find a set of enjoyable tasks. Requiring negotiation with other employees ensures that the chosen tasks will indeed help the organization achieve its goals.[5]

Integration at W. L. Gore is achieved through dynamic teams. Many organizations use a hierarchical structure with bosses and clear channels of authority. In contrast, Gore is organized around a lattice structure, which allows employees to talk to anyone who might have information they need. Instead of having bosses plan and organize tasks, the efforts of individual workers at Gore are coordinated through teamwork.

Gore's practices have created a workplace where employees are highly satisfied. The company has been named one of the best places to work by numerous surveys conducted in a variety of countries including Germany, Italy, South Korea, Sweden, France, and the United Kingdom. And Gore was named for the sixteenth consecutive year as one of the U.S. "100 Best Companies to Work For" by Fortune magazine in 2013.[6]

Of course, not everyone is able to succeed in Gore's structure. Some people are uncomfortable without specific jobs that tell them what to do and leave Gore soon after they join. Positive peer pressure encourages people not to take advantage of the loosely organized system by not working hard.

Replacing formal planning and role assignment with a process in which roles evolve is beneficial for Gore. But would this evolutionary process

Building Strength Through HR

W. L. Gore & Associates

W. L. Gore & Associates is an international company employing over 9,000 people throughout the world. Human resource management at Gore builds competitive strength by encouraging creative innovation through

George Frey / Getty Images

- Creating flexible job descriptions that allow employees freedom to perform work tasks that best fit their skills and abilities.
- Using teams to coordinate the work efforts of individuals.
- Reducing top-down organizational control.

be successful elsewhere? Few other organizations seem willing to try, suggesting that it may not fit their needs as well. In particular, the informal process at Gore is successful because it fits with the overall strategy of differentiation through innovation. Hiring creative employees and then letting them find ways to utilize their unique talents encourages new ideas. The process may not always be efficient, as the contributions of some workers may overlap with the contributions of others. However, small losses in efficiency are acceptable in return for the increased innovation that makes Gore products highly desirable to consumers. In essence, then, W. L. Gore & Associates is a successful company because it has developed an effective human resource system, which includes an untraditional approach for work design, to help carry out its competitive strategy of innovation.

LEARNING OBJECTIVE 1

How Is Work Design Strategic?

The example of W. L. Gore shows that strategic work design can benefit an organization by assigning and coordinating tasks in ways that increase employee productivity. However, what it means to be productive may not be the same for all organizations. Instead of innovation and creativity, other organizations may benefit from speed and efficiency. The key to making work design strategic is therefore to align the methods used for assigning and coordinating tasks with overall HR strategy. Next, we consider two fundamental elements of work design—autonomy and interdependence—and then explain how these elements can be aligned with the HR strategies from Chapter 2.

DEVELOPING AUTONOMY

Take a moment and imagine you are observing the following experience. A family with four small children sits down in a restaurant. The waitress places a glass of water in front of each person. Fearing that the glasses will be broken, the parents ask the waitress to remove the glasses she placed in front of the children. "I'm sorry," the waitress says, "I'll get in trouble if everyone at the table doesn't have a glass of water. It's our policy." Even though the parents beg her to make an exception, the waitress follows standard procedure and leaves the glasses in front of the children. Sure enough, several minutes later, one of the glasses of water is pushed onto the floor and broken. Unlike W. L. Gore, the restaurant in this example gives employees little autonomy.

Autonomy
The extent to which individual workers have freedom to determine how to complete work.

Autonomy concerns the extent to which individual workers are given the freedom and independence to plan and carry out work tasks.[7] Greater autonomy provides two potential benefits to organizations. One benefit concerns information. In many cases, front-line workers are closer to customers and products and so they have information that a manager does not have.[8] The workers can use this information to adapt quickly to change. Employees who are closer to products and customers are often able to make rapid changes if something in the production process shifts or if customers' needs vary. The "How Do We Know?" feature also describes a study that found greater autonomy to result in better coordination for teams, which in turn increased productivity.

A second potential benefit of high autonomy is increased motivation. People with a greater sense of autonomy feel more responsibility for their work.[9] More-autonomous employees are less likely to shirk their responsibilities. Employees who don't feel autonomy often fail to do their share of work tasks. People are also more likely to go beyond minimum expectations without extra pay when autonomy is high. High-level managers with greater autonomy in both the United States and Europe report greater job satisfaction and less chance of leaving their current employer.[10] Managers working in a foreign country also adjust to the new environment better when they experience autonomy.[11]

High autonomy may not be desirable for all workers in all situations, however. High autonomy can create coordination problems. An employee with a great deal of freedom to change the work process might do something that changes processes and outcomes for other employees.[12] Such changes are particularly troublesome when the work process is carefully planned in advance. For instance, high autonomy may not be good for workers in an automobile assembly plant. Production processes are carefully planned, and failure to

How Do We Know?

DO EMPOWERED TEAMS HAVE HIGHER PERFORMANCE?

Do teams perform better when they feel as though they have the responsibility and authority to complete their work independently of a supervisor? If so, what can organizations do to help teams feel a greater sense of being empowered? John Mathieu, Lucy Gilson, and Thomas Ruddy sought to answer these questions in a study designed to examine empowerment in teams.

They gathered and analyzed data from 452 service technicians. The technicians were organized into 121 groups with responsibility for servicing and repairing photocopy machines. Team members reported the degree to which they felt the team was empowered with authority and responsibility. They reported on team processes related to planning, communicating, and cooperation. Teams also reported on ways that their work tasks were designed and the support they received from the larger organization. Team performance was assessed by measures of how quickly teams responded to calls, how well machines operated after service, and expense control. Customer satisfaction measures were also obtained from client surveys.

Teams who felt more empowered worked together more effectively and in turn had higher performance and received better reports of customer satisfaction. The sense of empowerment came from teams having more freedom and responsibility to plan and carry out work tasks, as well as a stronger sense of support from the organization. Teams were thus found to be most effective when organizational practices provided them with support and autonomy that led them to cooperate more and work together effectively. Better team processes in turn resulted in improved service and customer satisfaction.

The Bottom Line. Empowerment can be beneficial for teams. Empowered teams perceive greater authority and responsibility for completing work. Teams that feel empowered do a better job of planning and coordinating their efforts, which in turn results in higher performance. Organizations can thus benefit from empowering teams. However, the study authors point out that empowerment only works when it is supported by the larger organizational context. For empowerment to be effective it needs to be extensive and go beyond a quick fix.

Source: John E. Mathieu, Lucy L. Gilson, and Thomas M. Ruddy, "Empowerment and Team Effectiveness: An Empirical Test of an Integrated Model," *Journal of Applied Psychology* 91 (2006): 97–108.

follow rules and procedures might harm the entire assembly process. In contrast, autonomy can be helpful when tasks are complex and difficult to plan in advance. Workers with high autonomy can adapt to changing conditions and can do whatever is required to better meet the needs of customers.[13]

DEVELOPING INTERDEPENDENCE

Have you ever been assigned to write a group paper with other students? If so, how did your group complete the task? Did everyone write different sections of the paper? Did the group meet together and discuss the content of the paper? Did members of the group work in sequence so that individuals could add to what had already been done? These different processes for coordinating activities relate to interdependence.

Interdependence
The extent to which a worker's actions affect and are affected by the actions of others.

Interdependence is the extent to which an individual's work actions and outcomes are influenced by other people. When interdependence is low, people work mostly by themselves. Each person completes his or her set of tasks without much help from or coordination with others. A good example is a group of sales representatives, each with an individual selling territory. At the other end of the spectrum is high interdependence, which occurs when people work together closely. Perhaps each team member completes a part of the task, and the work flows back and forth between team members. Each person adapts his or her inputs to the inputs of others. An example of high interdependence is found in a strategic planning team. Team members meet together and discuss issues to combine their knowledge and perceptions in order to arrive at shared decisions.

Greater interdependence often corresponds with improved performance. When interdependence is high, people tend to feel greater responsibility for completing their tasks.[14] People also report higher work satisfaction when their goals and tasks are interdependent with those of other workers.[15] However, as with autonomy, the benefits of interdependence are not universal. Some organizations are most effective when there is little interdependence and employees work mostly by themselves. When employees do work together, the type of interdependence that is best for one organization is not necessarily the type that is best for another organization.

Sequential processing
Work organized around an assembly line such that the completed tasks of one employee feed directly into the tasks of another employee.

One common form of interdependence is **sequential processing**, which takes place when work tasks are organized in an assembly line. In a sequential process, tasks must be performed in a certain order. One person completes a certain set of tasks. The work then flows to the next person, who completes a different set of tasks. This flow continues until each member of the team has completed his or her work and the production of the good or service is complete. A computer manufacturing plant uses sequential processing when a number of workers sit at a table and assemble parts. One person places the memory board in the computer, another adds the hard drive, and someone else installs the software. The steps are completed in a specific order, and each of the workers has a clearly defined set of tasks to complete.

Reciprocal processing
Work organized around teams such that workers constantly adjust to the task inputs of others.

Another common form of interdependence, **reciprocal processing**, requires more interaction and coordination among workers. Reciprocal interactions occur when people work together in a team without carefully prescribed plans for completing work tasks. A group of workers is given a broad set of tasks, and the workers decide among themselves who will do what. The work process might be different each time the set of tasks is completed. In this situation, the specific actions of any worker depend a lot on the actions of other workers. Software engineers use reciprocal processing when they work as a team to create application programs. Because each program is different, the design process for one will be different from the design process for another. One person might have the expertise needed to take the lead role for one program, and another person might be the best leader for designing a different program. Someone in the team might make a suggestion that helps other team members think of new ideas. Team members work together, and the value of each engineer's contribution depends on the contributions of others.

The best type of interdependence depends on the work situation. Individuals and teams tend to benefit from sequential processes when work activities can be broken into small tasks that do not change. These tasks are often physical. Reciprocal processes tend to be optimal when activities are complex and require mental rather than physical inputs.[16]

LINKING AUTONOMY AND INTERDEPENDENCE TO HR STRATEGY

Figure 4.1 shows how differences in autonomy and interdependence can be linked to HR strategy. Organizations using cost HR strategies—either Bargain Laborer or Loyal Soldier—focus on efficiency. Efficiency is often created by combining low autonomy and sequential processing.[17] With cost strategies, one objective is to standardize jobs so that employees can quickly learn a set of relatively easy tasks. A cook at a fast-food restaurant, for example, receives an order and follows clearly defined rules to cook the food, which is then delivered to someone who gives it to the customer. Another objective with cost strategies is to provide a way for each worker to become very skilled and efficient at performing certain tasks. Doing something over and over helps workers learn how to eliminate errors. Scientific studies are done to find ways to perform tasks more quickly, and everyone is required to follow best practices.

Figure 4.1 Strategic Framework for Work Design.

Sequential processes and low autonomy thus correspond with improved performance when processes are simple and require mostly physical inputs. Managers overseeing this type of work are able to determine the best methods for accomplishing tasks. Activities are completed most quickly when each person performs a specific set of tasks that are coordinated by managers.

Organizations that use differentiation HR strategies—either Committed Expert or Free Agent—focus on innovation. High autonomy and reciprocal processes encourage creativity. With differentiation, the objective is to create new products and services that are better than those offered by competitors. People within the organization are more likely to meet this objective when they are free to try new approaches. Giving workers the freedom to experiment with new ideas helps companies such as W. L. Gore come up with new products. In addition, the close interaction between workers using reciprocal processes allows them to help each other and learn new things.

(?) **CONCEPT CHECK**

1. *What is autonomy, and how does it influence work performance?*
2. *What are the different forms of interdependence?*
3. *How do autonomy and interdependence link to overall HR strategy?*

LEARNING OBJECTIVE 2

How Are Employee Jobs Determined?

Job
A collection of tasks that define the work duties of an employee.

We wouldn't generally expect all the employees in an organization to perform the same tasks. Employees specialize in certain tasks, and people adopt specific roles. These tasks and roles are usually summarized in terms of jobs. A **job** is a collection of tasks that a person performs at work. The idea of being employed in a job is so common that many people think in terms of jobs when they describe themselves to others. But how are jobs defined? Why are some tasks grouped into a certain job while other tasks are grouped into a different job?

THE JOB ANALYSIS PROCESS

Job analysis
The process of systematically collecting information about the tasks that workers perform.

 Job analysis is the process of systematically collecting information about work tasks. The process involves obtaining information from experts to determine the tasks that workers must perform, the tools and equipment they need to perform the tasks, and the conditions in which they are required to work. For instance, a job analysis of the work a student does might bring together a panel of experienced students and faculty. This panel would develop a list of the tasks that students commonly perform. Accompanying the list might be a description of typical tools, such as computers and textbooks. The analysis would also describe the conditions in which students work, such as lecture halls and study groups.

Job analysis is important because it helps clarify what is expected of workers. In the context of human resource management, knowing what tasks need to be completed helps managers select people with appropriate knowledge and skills. Understanding job tasks also provides important information for planning training programs. In addition, being able to compare the tasks of different workers helps guide decisions about pay. Finally, careful job analysis helps ensure that human resource practices comply with legal guidelines. In fact, good job analysis is often seen as a first step to appropriately recruiting, hiring, training, and compensating workers. A good example of a company that benefits from incorporating effective job analysis procedures is Purolator, which is featured in the "Building Strength Through HR" feature.

Building Strength Through HR

PUROLATOR

Purolator is the largest courier company in Canada, with annual revenue over $1.5 billion. During an average day, Purolator's 12,500 employees move over 1.1 million packages. Employing a large number of people involved in physical labor can be challenging. Each year, the company processes over 2,000 workers' compensation claims and pays over $13 million for workers' compensation insurance. Most of the claims are filed by couriers and sorters, who spend a great deal of time lifting, pushing, and pulling boxes.

Purolator uses job analysis to better understand the physical demands of various jobs. One purpose of job analysis is to provide information about jobs that injured workers can do while they are recovering. Purolator works with medical doctors to assess the tasks that each injured worker can do and then to match workers with temporary assignments that require only inputs they are physically capable of providing. Workers can return to the workplace more quickly, which saves Purolator money. Many injured workers also find being at work in a short-term assignment preferable to staying home alone with nothing to do.

Since implementing the job analysis and assignment program, Purolator has reduced the number

Toronto Star/Getty Images

of work days lost for injury from nearly 10,000 per year to around 6,000. This improved use of workers has helped Purolator become more efficient and thereby compete more successfully with other shipping companies. Human resource management at Purolator builds competitive strength by using job analysis to assess the physical demands of job tasks and then matching job requirements with the capabilities of individual workers.

Sources: www.purolator.com; Uyen Vu, "How Purolator Dealt with Skyrocketing Costs," *Canadian HR Reporter* 19, no. 5 (2006): 910.

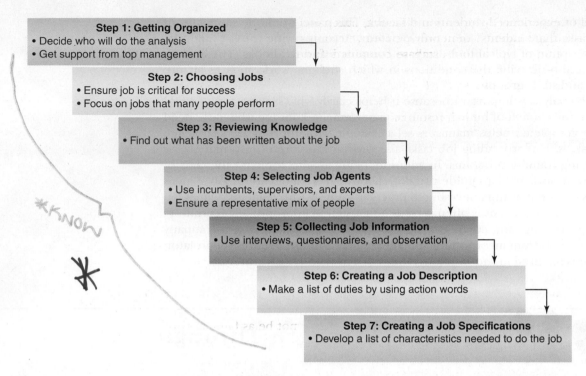

Figure 4.2 Phases of Job Analysis. *Source:* Information from Robert D. Gatewood and Hubert S. Field, *Human Resource Selection*, 5th ed. (Cincinnati, OH: South-Western, 2001).

The steps in the job analysis process, as shown in Figure 4.2, are getting organized, choosing jobs, reviewing knowledge, selecting job agents, collecting job information, creating job descriptions, and creating job specifications.[18]

Step 1. Getting Organized

An important first step is planning. Careful plans describing needed resources, such as staff support and computer assets, can help ensure success. During the organizing phase, it is also necessary to make sure that key decision makers support analysis plans. No matter how carefully procedures are planned, problems will arise, and top-management support will be necessary to make sure that the analysis proceeds successfully.

Step 2. Choosing Jobs

Of course, the goal in any organization is to analyze all jobs, but constraints on budgets and staff time often make it necessary to choose only some of these jobs. As you might expect, high priority should be given to jobs that are important to the success of the organization. Particular emphasis should be placed on jobs in which large numbers of people are employed. Focusing analysis on jobs that are both important and widely held ensures that efforts will be concentrated in areas where improvement can have its largest impact on making the organization successful.

Step 3. Reviewing Knowledge

The next step, reviewing knowledge, involves learning what is already known about similar jobs in other organizations. One important source of information is the **Occupational Information Network**, which was developed by the U.S. Department of Labor. The network, called O*Net, is online at http://online. onetcenter.org. The online database contains information for over a thousand occupations. A visitor to the website simply types in a common job—or occupational—title and is presented with a list of tasks that are normally associated with that position, along with other information. Although developed in the United States, O*Net data have been shown to be applicable in other countries such as New Zealand and China.[19] Other sources of knowledge for job analysts include studies published in research journals such as *Personnel Psychology* and *Journal of Applied Psychology*. The information in these existing sources is not a substitute for a careful analysis but does provide a good starting point for learning about jobs.

Step 4. Selecting Job Agents

Job agents are the people who provide the job information. In many cases, the best people to provide this information are job incumbents—the people currently doing the job. These employees are very familiar with day-to-day tasks. But one potential problem with using current employees is that they may emphasize what is actually done rather than what should be done. Another source of information is supervisors. Supervisors may not be as familiar with the details of the job, but they can often provide clarification about the tasks that they would like to see done. A third source of information is professionally trained analysts who make careers out of studying jobs. Although such specialists can provide an outside perspective, they may not be as familiar with how things are done in a particular organization.

A number of studies have examined differences in job agents. Information provided by job incumbents who are experienced is different from the information provided by incumbents who recently started the job.[20] In addition, differences have been found for ratings from men and women,[21] as well as for ratings from minority and nonminority incumbents.[22] Some differences have also been reported between high- and low-performing employees.[23] Given these differences, it is important that the characteristics of the sample of people who provide information for a job analysis be representative of the characteristics of people who will actually do the job.

Step 5. Collecting Job Information

The next step is to actually collect information about the job. A common method for collecting information is the **job analysis interview**, a face-to-face interaction in which a trained interviewer asks job agents about their duties and responsibilities. Agents can be interviewed individually or in groups. In either case, the interview should be structured so that the same questions are asked of everyone. Job analysis interviews can be useful for learning unique aspects of a particular job. Interviews can, however, be time consuming and costly.

A second common method for collecting information is the **job analysis questionnaire**. Here, agents respond to written questions about the tasks they perform on the job. One type of questionnaire is an off-the-shelf instrument that has been developed to provide information about numerous different jobs. Another type is a tailored questionnaire developed just to obtain information about a specific job in a specific organization. An advantage of job analysis questionnaires is that they are relatively inexpensive; a disadvantage is that they may only provide very general information.

Occupational Information Network
An online source of information about jobs and careers.

Job analysis interview
Face-to-face meeting with the purpose of learning about a worker's duties and responsibilities.

Job analysis questionnaire
A series of written questions that seeks information about a worker's duties and responsibilities.

Job analysis observation
The process of watching workers perform tasks to learn about duties and responsibilities.

A third common method is observation. **Job analysis observation** requires job analysts to watch people as they work and to keep notes about the tasks being performed. This method can provide excellent information about jobs involving frequently repeated tasks. However, observation is difficult for jobs where tasks either are mental or are not done frequently enough to be observed by an outsider.

Given the different strengths and weaknesses of analysis techniques, the best advice is often to use a combination of techniques. Job analysis questionnaires can serve as relatively inexpensive tools to obtain broad information. This information can be supplemented by interviews and observations. The overall goal of this step is to obtain as much information as possible about the work tasks. We will look more closely at some specific job analysis methods in the next section.

Step 6. Creating Job Descriptions

Job description
Task statements that define the work tasks to be done by someone in a particular position.

Next, analysts use the job analysis information to create a job description. A **job descrip**tion is a series of task statements that describes what is to be done by people performing a job. This description focuses on duties and responsibilities and usually consists of a list of actions that employees perform in the job being described. An example of a job description for the job of home health aide is shown in Table 4.1.

Step 7. Creating Job Specifications

Job specifications
Listing of the knowledge, skills, and abilities needed to perform the tasks described in a job description.

The final step uses job analysis information to create job specifications. **Job specifications** identify the knowledge, skills, and abilities that workers need in order to perform the tasks listed in the job description. Of course, job specifications are different from the job description. Job descriptions focus more on what is done, whereas job specifications focus on who is most

Table 4.1	*Job Description for Home Health Aid*

Overview: Provide routine individualized healthcare such as changing bandages and dressing wounds, and applying topical medications to the elderly, convalescents, or persons with disabilities at the patient's home or in a care facility. Monitor or report changes in health status. May also provide personal care such as bathing, dressing, and grooming the patient.

1. Maintain records of patient care, condition, progress, or problems to report and discuss observations with supervisor or case manager.

2. Check patients' pulse, temperature, and respiration.

3. Provide patients with help moving in and out of beds, baths, wheelchairs, or automobiles and with dressing and grooming.

4. Care for patients by changing bed linens, washing and ironing laundry, cleaning, or assisting with their personal care.

5. Entertain, converse with, or read aloud to patients to keep them mentally healthy and alert.

6. Administer prescribed oral medications, under the written direction of physician or as directed by home care nurse or aide, and ensure that patients take their medicine.

7. Plan, purchase, prepare, or serve meals to patients or other family members, according to prescribed diets.

8. Accompany clients to doctors' offices or on other trips outside the home, providing transportation, assistance, and companionship.

9. Direct patients in simple prescribed exercises or in the use of braces and artificial limbs.

10. Provide patients and families with emotional support and instruction in areas such as caring for infants, preparing healthy meals, living independently, or adapting to disability or illness.

Source: Information from the Occupational Information Network O*Net OnLine, http://online.onetcenter.org/.

likely to be able to perform the tasks successfully. An example of job specifications for the position of home health aide is shown in Table 4.2.

SPECIFIC METHODS OF COLLECTING JOB ANALYSIS INFORMATION

Let's look more closely at how information is gathered in Step 5 of the job analysis process. Many methods have been developed for collecting job analysis information. In this section, we examine three representative methods: the task analysis inventory, the critical-incidents technique, and the Position Analysis Questionnaire. The first two are broad techniques that provide a general methodology for analyzing jobs. Although several different consulting firms market applications of these techniques, the principles used are not unique to these firms. A number of common principles underlie specific practices, and we describe these principles rather than the specific practices of a particular consulting firm. The third tool we discuss, the Position Analysis Questionnaire, is a bit different; it is a specific analysis tool that is marketed by a single firm.

Task Analysis Inventory

The **task analysis inventory** asks job agents to provide ratings concerning a large number of tasks. Most analyses require responses for at least 100 different task statements. These task statements usually begin with an action verb that describes a specific activity—for example, "explains company policies to newly hired workers" and "analyzes data to determine the cost of hiring each new employee."

Task analysis inventory
A method of job analysis in which job agents rate the frequency and importance of tasks associated with a specific set of work duties.

Table 4.2	*Job Specifications for Home Health Aide*

Knowledge of
- Psychology including human behavior and performance, individual differences in ability and motivation
- Information and techniques needed to diagnose and treat human injuries, diseases, and deformities
- Structure and content of the English language including the meaning and spelling of words, rules of composition, and grammar
- Principles and processes for providing customer and personal services, including customer needs assessment and evaluation of customer satisfaction

Skills in
- Active listening
- Critical thinking and complex problem solving
- Speaking to convey information effectively
- Social perceptiveness
- Monitoring performance of self and others to make improvements

Ability for
- Vision to see things at close range
- Deductive and inductive reasoning
- Speech recognition
- Information ordering
- Oral and written expression
- Knowing when something is wrong or likely to go wrong

Source: Information from the Occupational Information Network O*Net OnLine, http://online.onetcenter.org/.

Most task analyses require job agents to provide at least two ratings for each task statement; one rating is for frequency or time spent, and the other is for importance. Ratings for *frequency of performing the task* range from "never performed" to "performed most of the time." Ratings might also be made for *time spent on the task.* However, ratings of frequency and time spent essentially measure the same thing.[24] Ratings for *task importance* usually range from "not important" to "extremely important."[25]

Task inventories yield information that is consistent across time, meaning that ratings provided by a specific rater at one point in time are similar to ratings obtained from the same rater at a different point in time.[26] Different groups of raters do, however, sometimes provide different results. The task analysis inventory thus seems to work best when job incumbents who are relatively new to the position provide ratings of frequency and importance.[27]

A task analysis inventory is fairly specific to a particular category of jobs. Thus, an analysis that provides insight into the job of grocery store clerk will provide little information about the job of taxi driver. However, the inventory does provide a good deal of detailed information about the job being studied.

Critical-Incidents Technique

Critical-incidents technique
A method of job analysis in which job agents identify instances of effective and ineffective behavior exhibited by people in a specific position.

The **critical-incidents technique** identifies good and bad on-the-job behaviors. Job agents are asked to generate a number of statements that describe behaviors they consider particularly helpful or harmful for accomplishing work. Each statement includes a description of the situation and the actions that determined whether the outcome was desirable or undesirable.[28] Statements are then analyzed to identify common themes.

Results from an analysis using the critical-incidents technique are shown in Table 4.3. The analysis provides information about nurse behavior that encourages or discourages patients to participate in their own care while hospitalized. In the study, 17 patients were interviewed and asked to describe specific incidents that encouraged or discouraged them from participating in their own care. Interviewers asked additional questions to understand the circumstances leading to the event, nurse actions, and patient responses. Results illustrated that patients participate more when nurses regard them as a person, share information, and acknowledge the patient as competent. Patients withdraw from participating when they feel abandoned, belittled, or ignored. These responses were linked to the nurse behaviors shown in Table 4.3, clarifying specific actions that nurses can take to increase patient participation.[29]

Position Analysis Questionnaire

Position Analysis Questionnaire (PAQ)
A method of job analysis that uses a structured questionnaire to learn about work activities.

The **Position Analysis Questionnaire (PAQ)** is a structured questionnaire that assesses the work behaviors required for a job.[30] This questionnaire collects information not about tasks or duties but rather about the characteristics people must have in order to do the job well. In essence, the PAQ skips Step 6 in the job analysis process and goes right to Step 7.

The PAQ includes 187 items that relate to job activities or the work environment. These items assess characteristics along six dimensions:

1. *Information input*—where and how a worker obtains needed information.
2. *Mental processes*—reasoning and decision-making activities.
3. *Work output*—physical actions required for the job, as well as tools or devices used.

Table 4.3	*Critical Incident Results for Nurse Actions Encouraging Patient Participation*

Incidents Stimulating Patient Participation

  Nurse Actions

    Listens and asks

    Gives necessary explanations

    Gives written materials

    Acts as intermediary of contacts

    Gives tips about self-care

    Discusses and makes agreements

    Hands over responsibilities

  Patient Feels

    Regarded as a person

    Engaged through information

    Acknowledged as competent

Incidents Inhibiting Patient Participation

  Nurse Actions

    Disparages with baby talk

    Makes ironic remarks about an experience

    Decides by self to reject views

    Answers curtly

    Neglects making notes in records

    Hands over responsibilities

  Patient Feels

    Abandoned without backup

    Belittled verbally

    Ignored without influence

Source: Information adapted from Inga E. Larson, Monica J.M. Sahlsten, Kerstin Segesten, and Kaety A.E. Plos, "Patient Perceptions of Nurses' Behavior That Influence Patient Participation in Nursing Care: A Critical Incidents Study," *Nursing Research and Practice*, Article ID 534060 (2011).

4. *Relationships with other persons*—the interactions and social connections that a worker forms with others.

5. *Job context*—the physical and social surroundings where work activities are performed.

6. *Other job characteristics*—activities, conditions, or characteristics that are important but not contained in the other five dimensions.

Questions on the PAQ are rated on scales according to what is being measured. One scale, for example, is based on *extent of use* and ranges from "very infrequently" to "very substantial." Another is based on *importance to the job* and ranges from "very minor" to "extreme." A few items are simply rated as "does not apply" or "does apply."

An advantage of the PAQ is its usefulness across many different jobs. Since the information concerns worker characteristics rather than tasks, results can be compared across jobs that are quite different. For instance, PAQ results might be used to determine whether two very different jobs require similar inputs. The degree of similarity will tell management whether people doing these jobs should be paid the same amount. A disadvantage of the PAQ is its lack of task information, which limits its usefulness for creating job descriptions or guiding performance appraisal practices. The PAQ is nevertheless one of the most commonly used methods of job analysis.

HOW IS JOB DESCRIPTION INFORMATION MADE USEFUL?

A few methods, like the PAQ, develop descriptions of worker characteristics rather than tasks and duties. However, the result of most job analysis techniques is a list of duties. As shown in Figure 4.3, job descriptions focus on tasks and duties, whereas job specifications focus on characteristics of people. Information in job descriptions must therefore be translated into job specifications, which are required for purposes such as employee selection. After all, just knowing what employees do in a certain job isn't very helpful for determining the type of person to hire. The people doing the hiring also need to know what characteristics to look for in job applicants.

Translation into job specifications is usually done by job agents. To make good translations, job agents must be highly familiar with the job and what it takes to perform it well. They look at the list of tasks and make judgments about the knowledge, skills, and abilities needed to complete the tasks. The characteristics are incorporated into the job specifications. For instance, job agents for the position of student might be asked to make judgments about the skills needed to take notes in class. The list of skills would include some obvious characteristics, such as ability to hear and write. Other characteristics

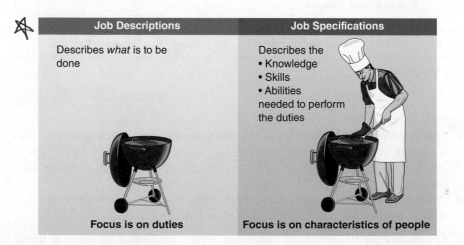

Figure 4.3 Comparing Job Descriptions and Job Specifications.

might be less obvious but more helpful for identifying people who do the tasks well—for example, the ability to simultaneously listen and write, a knowledge of note-organizing techniques, and skill in asking follow-up questions. Good job specifications thus focus attention on knowledge, skills, and abilities that separate high- and low-performing workers.

Job specifications provide information that serves as a foundation for a number of other human resource practices. Managers can use the list of worker characteristics as a "shopping list" when they begin identifying the type of workers they want to hire. Carefully prepared job specifications also guide selection practices so that appropriate tests can be found to identify who actually has the desirable characteristics. In addition, areas in which current employees lack skills necessary for promotion can be established as training priorities.

These priorities serve as important information for designing the training programs discussed in Chapters 9 and 10. Also, as explained in Chapters 11 and 12, knowing the employee characteristics associated with high task performance can also provide important guidance for compensation decisions. People who have more desirable characteristics will likely expect to receive higher pay, particularly if few others have the same characteristics.

JOB ANALYSIS AND LEGAL ISSUES

The process of job analysis is a starting point for many good human resource practices. Practices grounded in good analysis are most likely to result in good decisions about how to hire, evaluate, and pay employees. Legal considerations are another important reason for good job analysis.

A number of court decisions have confirmed the importance of using good job analysis procedures.[31] When an organization makes hiring or promotion decisions that have discriminatory effects, the organization can defend itself successfully by showing that it based its decisions on solid analyses of the jobs involved. In contrast, such decisions appear arbitrary and can be judged illegal if the organization has not used good job analysis procedures. Some procedures that have been identified as critical for conducting a legally defensible job analysis are listed in Table 4.4. Following these procedures helps ensure that an organization thoroughly analyzes jobs and uses the information to develop fair hiring and compensation procedures.[32]

Table 4.4	*Legal Issues and Job Analysis*

1. Analysis results should be in writing.
2. The method used to analyze the job should be clearly described.
3. Expert job analysts should collect data from several up-to-date sources.
4. Data should be collected from enough people to be sure the results are accurate.
5. Tasks, duties, and activities must be identified and included in the job analysis.
6. The relative degree of competency necessary for entry-level performance should be specified.

Source: Information from Duane E. Thompson and Toni A. Thompson, "Court Standards for Job Analysis in Test Validation," *Personnel Psychology* 35 (1982): 865–874.

Job analysis results can also help many organizations determine whether they are complying with requirements of the Americans with Disabilities Act (ADA), which we discussed in Chapter 3. ADA guidelines make an important distinction between essential and nonessential tasks. For a disabled employee to be qualified for a position, he or she must be able to perform all essential tasks (with reasonable accommodations). The employee is not, however, required to be able to perform non-essential tasks. For example, an essential task for a landscape worker might be to identify and remove weeds. A nonessential task might be communicating verbally with other employees. In this case, an applicant with a speech disability might be seen as qualified for the job. The key to qualification is the extent to which verbal communication is necessary. If the job description does not identify verbal communication as an essential task for landscape workers, then the organization cannot appropriately refuse to hire someone who cannot speak.

COMPETENCY MODELING

The process of job analysis has been criticized in recent years, primarily because work today is less structured around specific jobs than it once was.[33] Work activities are more knowledge based. People increasingly work in teams. Task activities are more fluid and are determined through ongoing negotiation among workers.[34] By the time human resource practices based on job analysis can be designed and carried out, the task activities may have changed.[35] Work behavior in modern organizations is thus not easily described.

A recent development designed to adapt to the changing needs of modern organizations is **competency modeling**, which describes jobs in terms of **competencies**—characteristics and capabilities people need in order to succeed at work. Competencies include knowledge, skills, and abilities, but they also seek to capture such things as motivation, values, and interests. Competencies thus include both "can-do" and "will-do" characteristics of people.[36] One area of difference between competency modeling and traditional job analysis is that competency modeling tends to link a broader set of characteristics to work success.

Typical steps for competency modeling are shown in Figure 4.4.[37] Part of data collection is an assessment of competitive strategy. Consistent with the strategic focus of this textbook, competency modeling seeks to develop links between work activities and organizational strategy. The competency approach tailors solutions to purposes and uses. An analysis that will be used for compensation decisions may be different from an analysis that will be used for determining the type of job candidate to recruit. Competencies also tend to be somewhat broader and less specifically defined than the activities assessed in job analysis. Typical competencies might include skill in presenting speeches, ability to follow through on commitments, proficiency in analyzing financial information, and willingness to persist when work becomes difficult. Competencies can be rated in terms of things like current importance, future importance, and frequency.

You can see that job analysis and competency modeling differ in some important respects. Competency modeling is much more likely than job analysis to link work analysis procedures and outcomes to business goals and strategies. However, in most cases, the methods used in competency modeling are seen as being less scientific.[38] Competency modeling procedures are often not documented as clearly as job analysis procedures and may be less rigorous.

Competency modeling
An alternative to traditional job analysis that focuses on a broader set of characteristics that workers need to effectively perform job duties.

Competencies
Characteristics and capabilities that people need to succeed in work assignments.

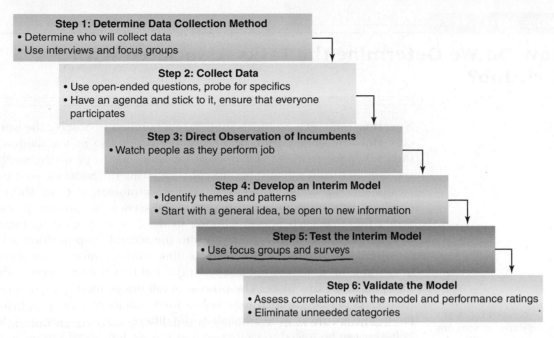

Figure 4.4 Steps in Competency Modeling. *Source:* Information from Antoinette D. Lucia and Richard D. Lepsinger, *The Art and Science of Competency Models: Pinpointing Critical Success Factors in Organizations* (San Francisco: Jossey-Bass/Pfeiffer, 1999).

Comparing the strengths and weaknesses of traditional job analysis and competency modeling, however, obscures the important contribution that is possible by combining the best elements of the two practices. Competency modeling incorporates strategic issues and allows for a broader range of characteristics. From the other side, traditional job analysis provides excellent techniques for scientifically analyzing work activities. Combining the broader, more strategic approach of competency modeling with scientific methods should yield superior results. Indeed, a series of research studies concluded that a combined approach is better than either approach alone.[39] Best practices thus incorporate job analysis along with future-oriented job requirements and organizational goals to analyze competencies. Information is then presented in the common language of organizations, including diagrams and pictures. A final key is that competency information be strategically integrated to ensure that HR practices associated with hiring, performance appraisal, and compensation work in unison to select and motivate employees through consistent policies.[40]

CONCEPT CHECK

1. *What are the seven steps involved in job analysis?*
2. *What can an organization do to make sure its job analysis procedures comply with legal guidelines?*
3. *How is competency modeling different from job analysis?*

How Do We Determine the Tasks Associated with Each Job?

Job design
The process of deciding what tasks will be grouped together to define the duties of someone in a particular work position.

Job redesign
The process of reassessing task groupings to create new sets of duties that workers in particular positions are required to do.

Next time you visit a sandwich shop, take a moment to observe the work process. Does the same person who takes your order also fix the sandwich and then take your payment? Or does one person take your order, another fix the sandwich, and still another accept your payment? Some shops use a process in which a single employee serves each customer. In other shops, each employee specializes in only one part of the service. Job analysis procedures would find that each person working in the first shop must perform a lot of different tasks, whereas employees in the second shop perform a limited set of tasks over and over. Job analysis thus provides information about who does what, but it doesn't tell us anything about how the tasks were combined into jobs in the first place. The process of **job design** focuses on determining what tasks will be grouped together to form employee jobs. This process of job design is critical, as nearly half of the differences in worker attitudes and behavior can be traced to factors such as task design, social interactions, and work conditions.[41]

Job design is important when companies are first created and when existing companies open new plants or stores. However, the principles of job design are also important for existing companies that are looking to improve. Many companies use **job redesign** to reorganize tasks so that jobs are changed. Job redesign often increases the sense of control for workers.[42] Indeed, job redesign that empowers employees is particularly effective for improving performance when managers have not been providing employees with feedback and information.[43] The "Building Strength Through HR" feature describes how such a redesign benefitted a large teaching hospital in England.

Problems arise when work tasks are not organized well. Earlier in this chapter, we discussed the concepts of differentiation and integration. Differentiation allows people to specialize in specific tasks, while integration coordinates actions among employees. Employees feel isolated when there is too much differentiation. Many also feel frustrated when they are unable to easily integrate their actions with the actions of other workers. A major objective of work design is thus to differentiate and integrate work tasks in ways that not only make employees more productive but also increase their satisfaction.

Work tasks that are not properly differentiated and integrated deplete employee mental and physical capacity and create fatigue and burnout.[44] Burned out employees are more likely to leave the organization.[45] Workers with unclear roles, and those who experience constraints such as bad equipment and supplies, are particularly at risk.[46] These exhausted employees have decreased motivation and are less likely to help other workers voluntarily.[47] They are also more prone to abuse alcohol and drugs.[48] Some burnout can be resolved by making sure that people have jobs that fit their capabilities and by treating employees fairly.[49] Workers experience less exhaustion when they receive social support from coworkers.[50] People also seem to be better able to cope with exhaustion when they believe that they are performing at a high level.[51] Taking a vacation can also reduce burnout.[52]

Building Strength Through HR

LEICESTER ROYAL INFIRMARY

Leicester Royal Infirmary National Health Service Trust is a large teaching hospital in England. Each year, the hospital staff of 4,200 people treats 400,000 outpatients, 105,000 inpatients, and 125,000 accident and emergency victims. The hospital used work redesign to reduce waiting time and improve satisfaction for patients. Human resource experts worked with clinical teams to redesign the way services were delivered. The analysis assessed patient needs and determined who should provide care. One common outcome was the streamlining of processes. For example, a review of procedures in one department revealed that five different areas of responsibility and seven transfers of information were required to help a patient make an appointment. These tasks were combined into a single job, resulting in a 15 percent reduction in costs. In some cases, tests that had previously taken hours to complete were delivered in minutes as a result of redesign. Other new processes increased efficiency so that nurses could spend more time with patients. Involving hospital workers in work redesign has improved not only efficiency but

Charles Thatcher/Getty Images

also patient satisfaction. Furthermore, nurses have benefited from redesigning jobs in ways that allow each individual to perform a broader array of tasks. This not only improves patient care but also makes nurses' activities more interesting. Human resource management at Leicester Royal Infirmary builds competitive strength by getting nurses and other workers involved in identifying better ways to complete work tasks.

Source: Information from "HR's Role in Re-engineering at Leicester Royal Infirmary," *Human Resources Management Journal International Digest* 10, no. 4 (2002): 4–7.

Job design and redesign specialists have adopted a number of approaches for attacking the problem of grouping tasks in ways that make jobs more productive and satisfying. The main objective of any work design method is to separate and combine work tasks in ways that make the most sense. What makes sense depends on the overall objective of the organization and is driven by strategic choices. In this section, we describe four general approaches to grouping work tasks: mechanistic, motivational, perceptual, and biological. As you will see, many of the differences in these approaches can be traced to differences among the research areas and disciplines where they originated.

MECHANISTIC APPROACH

In a mechanistic approach, engineers apply concepts from science and mathematics to design efficient methods for creating goods and services. In particular, industrial engineers approach job design from the perspective of creating an efficient machine that transforms labor inputs into goods and services. They use principles of **scientific management** to create jobs that eliminate wasted effort so that organizations can produce goods and services quickly.[53] In creating these jobs, they often use analyses designed to find the work methods that take the least time. For example, in a typical analysis, an

Scientific management
A set of management principles that focus on efficiency and standardization of processes.

observer might use a stopwatch to time different methods for moving boxes from one spot to another. Emphasis is placed on finding the fastest way to lift and carry boxes. The job is then designed so that each employee learns and uses the fastest method.

The basic goal of the mechanistic approach is to simplify work tasks as much as possible. Tasks are automated. Each job is highly specialized, and to the degree possible, tasks are straightforward. Workers focus on carrying out only one task at a time, and a small set of tasks is completed over and over.[54] The mechanistic approach thus tends to reduce worker autonomy and create sequential processing. Having workers specialize and complete simplified tasks has indeed been linked to greater efficiency.[55] Organizations pursuing either Loyal Soldier or Bargain Laborer HR strategies can thus benefit from job design practices that emphasize the mechanistic approach.

United Parcel Service (UPS) uses the mechanistic approach as part of a Loyal Soldier HR strategy. UPS needs to move packages as efficiently as possible. People who work as sorters in package warehouses use carefully planned methods for carrying packages. From time to time, specialists observe sorters and make sure that they are following prescribed practices. Truck drivers at UPS also follow specific procedures for tasks such as planning delivery routes and starting trucks. The entire process is very much like an assembly line. The most efficient methods for completing tasks are determined and then taught to everyone. This standardization creates efficiency, which helps reduce the cost of moving packages and, in turn, creates value for customers.

MOTIVATIONAL APPROACH

Work design can also be approached from the perspective of psychologists. Instead of seeking to build a machine, psychologists study human minds and behavior. A specific branch of study called *organizational psychology* emphasizes designing work to fulfill the needs of workers. This motivational approach is aimed at increasing employees' enjoyment of their work and thus increasing their effort. For example, people given the goal of developing a marketing plan for a cell phone manufacturer might be given a large number of different tasks that allow them to exercise creativity. Jobs are designed not simply to get work done as quickly as possible but also to provide workers with tasks they find meaningful and enjoyable.[56] The "How Do We Know?" feature describes a study that illustrates the benefits of making work tasks meaningful and significant.

Unlike the mechanistic approach, the motivational approach seeks to design work so that it is complex and challenging. One popular model of motivational job design is the **job characteristics model**, which focuses on building intrinsic motivation.[57] Intrinsic motivation exists when employees do work because they enjoy it, not necessarily because they receive pay. According to the job characteristics model, people are intrinsically motivated when they perceive their work to have three characteristics:

Job characteristics model
A form of motivational job design that focuses on creating work that employees enjoy doing.

1. *Meaningfulness.* People see work as meaningful when they are able to use many different skills, when they can see that their inputs lead to the completion of a specific service or product, and when they see their tasks as having an important impact on other people.
2. *Responsibility.* People feel personal responsibility for work outcomes when they have autonomy, which comes from the freedom to make decisions.

Know.

3. *Knowledge of the results.* Knowledge of the results of work activities comes from receiving feedback in the form of information about how effectively the work is being done.

People who feel intrinsic motivation exhibit higher creativity.[58] This suggests that the motivational approach to job design is particularly useful for organizations pursuing Committed Expert or Free Agent HR strategies. Organizations with these strategies can benefit from the greater intrinsic motivation and creativity that comes from experiencing meaningfulness, responsibility, and knowledge of results. Designing work around motivational principles also increases worker satisfaction and enables organizations to retain quality employees.[59] In particular, providing workers with high autonomy provides a means for organizations pursuing differentiation strategies to maximize the benefit of employing highly educated and trained workers who often know more than managers.

W. L. Gore & Associates, which you read about earlier in the chapter, offers a good example of a company that uses the motivational approach as part of a differentiation strategy. Workers are given a great deal of autonomy to determine work tasks. Based on their interests and capabilities, they enter

How Do We Know?

DO EMPLOYEES WORK HARDER WHEN THEY THINK THEIR TASKS MATTER?

Employees are sometimes asked to complete small tasks that they often think are boring. Do employees work harder on these tasks when they believe their actions contribute something valuable to society? Adam Grant sought to answer this question by studying the work outcomes of call center employees and lifeguards.

In one study he conducted an experiment by separating call center employees working at a university into groups. One group of callers developed a greater sense that their work was significant by reading stories about how the funds they were raising had improved the lives of students. Another group read stories from previous employees that described how working as a caller had helped their own personal careers. A third group did not read any stories. The group that read the stories about how much their work could help students obtained more pledges for a higher amount of money than either of the other two groups.

A second study was similar but focused on lifeguards. A sense of the importance of work tasks was communicated to one group of lifeguards by having them read stories about other lifeguards rescuing drowning swimmers. Compared to a control group, the lifeguards who read the life-saving stories had a higher sense that their work was important. They were more dedicated to their jobs, and they helped others more frequently.

The Bottom Line. Employees perform better when they perceive that their work is benefitting others. This sense of making a difference for others is a stronger motivator than a sense that work will benefit oneself. In order to help employees better see the significance of their tasks, Professor Grant recommends that managers share stories with employees about how what they are doing makes a difference for other people.

Source: Adam M. Grant, "The Significance of Task Significance: Job Performance Effects, Relational Mechanisms, and Boundary Conditions," *Journal of Applied Psychology* 93 (2008): 108–124.

agreements that allow them to complete work tasks that they perceive as important. They also have the freedom to engage in a variety of activities. Decreases in efficiency that come from duplication of effort are balanced by high levels of creativity. Intrinsically motivated workers create unique products.

PERCEPTUAL APPROACH

Some psychologists take a perceptual, rather than a motivational, approach. Job designers using this approach group tasks together in ways that help workers to process information better. These experts look at things such as how easily displays and gauges can be read and understood. They design written materials and instructions to be easy to read and interpret. They also examine how much information must be remembered and how much complex problem solving is required.

The basic objective of the perceptual approach is to simplify mental demands on workers and thereby decrease errors. Safety and prevention of accidents are critical. Given its emphasis on simplicity, the perceptual approach to job design usually results in work characterized by sequential processing and low autonomy. Thus, it is most commonly found in organizations pursuing either Loyal Soldier or Bargain Laborer HR strategies. For instance, an oil refinery could use perceptual principles to ensure that gauges and meters are designed to present information clearly so that plant workers do not make mistakes that result in accidents.

BIOLOGICAL APPROACH

People with backgrounds in biology and physiology also provide inputs into work design. They study issues associated with health and physical functioning. Physiologists particularly emphasize the physical stresses and demands placed on workers. Yet physical demands often combine with psychological stress to cause injuries.[60]

Ergonomics
An approach to designing work tasks that focuses on correct posture and movement.

Carpal tunnel

The biological approach is sometimes associated with **ergonomics**, which concerns methods of designing work to prevent physical injury. Task demands are assessed in terms of strength, endurance, and stress put on joints. Work processes are then designed to eliminate movements that can lead to physical injury or excessive fatigue. Workers are often taught principles such as good posture and elimination of excessive wrist movement.

The basic goal of the biological approach is to eliminate discomfort and injury. Fatigue is reduced by incorporating breaks and opportunities to switch tasks. Short-term gains in efficiency are sometimes sacrificed in order to prevent discomfort or injury. Principles associated with the biological approach can therefore be useful in work that is characterized by sequential processing. Unlike the mechanistic and perceptual approaches, which provide guidance for ways to increase efficiency, the biological approach guides work design specialists in making sure that assembly-line processes do not harm workers. Work design from the biological perspective thus helps organizations with Bargain Laborer or Loyal Soldier HR strategies to balance their quest for efficiency with a focus on the physical needs of workers. A good example is seen in automobile plants, where machines and work surfaces are designed to increase employee comfort and reduce repetitive motions that lead to injuries.

COMBINING WORK DESIGN APPROACHES

A potential problem associated with work design is the sometimes conflicting goals of the various approaches. For instance, the mechanistic approach simplifies processes by assigning workers a few specialized tasks that are rapidly repeated. In contrast, the motivational approach emphasizes whole tasks, high variety, and substantial autonomy. Does increased efficiency come at the expense of worker satisfaction and creativity?

Research has indeed found tradeoffs between the motivational and mechanistic approaches. On the one hand, jobs designed around the motivational approach increase job satisfaction, but the price may be reduced efficiency.[61] On the other hand, jobs designed around the mechanistic approach normally improve efficiency, even though job satisfaction may decline.[62] Still, studies show that tradeoffs are not always necessary and that in some cases jobs can be designed simultaneously from the mechanistic and motivational approaches.[63] In fact, a recently developed Work Design Questionnaire successfully includes measures of work context and task knowledge with social characteristics.[64] In this way the combined approach examines tasks in terms of both motivational and mechanistic properties. For instance, someone performing the job of statistical analyst might be given a set of very specialized tasks to improve efficiency but might also have high expertise and autonomy, which would create a sense of responsibility and ownership.[65]

Combining principles from the mechanistic and motivational approaches can thus lead to jobs that are not only efficient but also satisfying.[66] Of course, in many instances the primary consideration will be either efficiency or motivation; the strategic objectives of the organization should be the primary factor that drives work design. The mechanistic approach, incorporating perceptual and biological influences, is most relevant for organizations pursuing cost strategies. The motivational approach provides important guidance when the underlying strategy is differentiation.

CONCEPT CHECK

1. *What are four different approaches to designing jobs in organizations?*
2. *How does the mechanistic approach differ from the motivational approach?*

LEARNING OBJECTIVE 4

How Can Work Be Designed to Improve Family Life?

One area of increasing importance for job design is conflict between work and family. Many employees find it difficult to balance their roles as employees with their roles as parents or spouses. This conflict operates in both directions. Stress from problems at home can have a negative influence on work

Family-to-work conflict
Problems that occur when meeting family obligations negatively influences work behavior and outcomes.

Work-to-family conflict
Problems that occur when meeting work obligations negatively influences behavior and outcomes at home.

performance, resulting in **family-to-work conflict**. At the same time, stress encountered at work can have a negative influence on family life, a situation called **work-to-family conflict**.[67] In essence, employees have spillover of work and family stress.[68] For example, employees who experience dissatisfaction at work are more likely to be in a bad mood, and to have lower marital satisfaction, when they return home.[69] Employees who are more embedded in both their work organizations and surrounding communities seem to experience greater conflict between work and family roles,[70] but such conflict is not restricted to workers in the United States. For example, a survey of Australian construction professionals found that strain in the workplace had a negative influence on family relationships.[71] Nevertheless, compared to workers in areas such as Asia and South America that value groups over individuals, workers in individualistic societies such as the United States are more likely to be dissatisfied and leave when they feel that their work interferes with family.[72]

Creating organizational policies that support families can help alleviate work and family conflict. Specific policies include providing flexible spending accounts for dependent care, elder care resources and referral, and child care resources such as on-site daycare.[73] Having supervisors specifically support employees by showing empathy and helping balance family and career issues is also critical for reducing work and family conflict.[74]

One simple reason why work and family roles can conflict is shortage of time. Studies have shown that spending more hours at work creates more stress at home and that spending more hours with family can create stress at work.[75] Being able to control work scheduling can, however, buffer some of the stress of not having enough time.[76] A second reason for work and family conflict is that the psychological effort required to cope in one area takes away from resources needed to cope in the other.[77] A young mother who engages in a difficult confrontation with a coworker is likely to be emotionally exhausted when she returns to her family.

Conflict between work and family roles presents problems for both organizations and employees. From the organizational perspective, increased conflict between work and family roles is a problem because it increases absenteeism and turnover.[78] Conflict between roles is a problem for employees because it reduces satisfaction, increases alcohol and drug abuse, and results in poor physical health.[79] These problems tend to be particularly difficult for women.[80] Constraints from family duties that inhibit them from accepting international assignments is one particular example of negative family–work conflict for women.[81]

Some organizations are, however, effective in structuring work in ways that help decrease conflict between work and family roles. IBM, which is profiled in the next "Building Strength Through HR" feature, is a good example. One key for IBM and other organizations that minimize work and family conflict is to be seen as fair by employees.[82] People working in these organizations report going beyond minimum expectations by helping coworkers and suggesting ways to improve work processes.[83] This extra effort appears to translate into higher organizational performance. Organizations perform better when they incorporate family-friendly policies and procedures, such as daycare and elder-care assistance, paid parental leave, and flexible scheduling.[84] Some of these policies concern benefits and services, which we discuss in later chapters. But other family-friendly practices, such as flexible scheduling and alternative work locations, relate to job design.

FLEXIBLE WORK SCHEDULING

Dual-career households are common in the United States. Parents in these households can often benefit from flexible work scheduling that allows them to coordinate the many demands on their time. Flexible scheduling practices allow people to coordinate their schedules with a partner and thereby reduce the conflict associated with being both a parent and an employee. The potential benefits are so high that most large organizations provide some form of flexible scheduling.[85] Two of the most common forms of flexible scheduling are flextime and the compressed workweek.

Flextime

Flextime provides employees with the freedom to decide when they will arrive at and leave work. The organization creates a core time period when all employees must be present. For example, a bank may require all tellers to be at work between the busy hours of 11 A.M. and 3 P.M. Outside of this core band, employees can work when they wish. Some may choose to arrive at 7 A.M. so they can go home early. Others may choose to arrive at 11 A.M. and leave at 8 P.M. This flexibility allows employees to better balance work with family and other demands.

Flextime
A scheduling policy that allows employees to determine the exact hours they will work around a specific band of time.

Building Strength Through HR

INTERNATIONAL BUSINESS MACHINES CORPORATION

International Business Machines Corporation (IBM) is an information technology company with over 400,000 employees and annual revenue of $106 billion. Over the last 30 years, IBM has been a leader in helping employees balance work and family issues. Since the 1980s, IBM has offered services such as childcare referral, parental leave, and flexible working arrangements. One innovative program allows full-time employees to move to part-time status; salary and work expectations are reduced, and the company continues to pay full benefits. This practice provides flexibility for workers who may need to spend additional time dealing with family issues, such as caring for a new child or an ailing parent. Flexibility helps IBM retain key employees. In fact, over 70 percent of employees who use flexibility say they would quit working for IBM if the program were not available. IBM has also pioneered programs enabling employees to work where it is most convenient, including at customer sites and in their homes. Analyses suggest

Nick Clements/Getty Images

that such flexible arrangements can result in substantial improvements in productivity for individual workers and workgroups. Human resource management at IBM builds competitive strength by providing flexible job designs, which enable the company to retain workers who are seeking less traditional types of employment.

Sources: www.ibm.com/ibm/us/; E. Jeffrey Hill, Andréa D. Jackson, and Giuseppe Marinengo, "Twenty Years of Work and Family at International Business Machines Corporation," *American Behavioral Scientist* 49 (2006): 1165–1183.

As you can probably imagine, some work design problems can arise with flextime. Employees who must work with others on projects might find it difficult to coordinate their efforts with coworkers who work on different schedules. Supervision can also be a problem if employees are working when no supervisor is present. These work design issues tend to limit flextime to non-manufacturing positions that do not require close supervision or ongoing sequential processing.[86] Flextime is thus most useful for organizations pursuing differentiation strategies.

Even with potential difficulties, many organizations that allow flextime appear to reap substantial benefits. Flextime is associated to some extent with higher productivity, but the primary benefit is increased satisfaction among workers. In turn, workers are absent less frequently and are more likely to remain with the organization.[87] Flextime is thus most consistent with the motivational approach to job design.

Compressed Workweek

Compressed workweek
Working more than eight hours in a shift so that 40 hours of work are completed in fewer than five days.

A **compressed workweek** enables employees to have full-time positions but work fewer than five days a week. Typically, employees with compressed schedules work four 10-hour days. Allowing employees to have three-day weekends can provide them with additional time for family activities. A compressed workweek may make it easier to schedule events such as doctor and dentist appointments, for example. Commuting on four rather than five days can also reduce time and expenses spent traveling.

As with flextime, employees who work a compressed workweek report higher levels of job satisfaction; they also have slightly higher performance. Unlike flextime, the compressed workweek does not appear to decrease absenteeism.[88] It thus appears that providing flexibility each day may be more beneficial for reducing absenteeism than providing a designated day off each week. However, compressed workweeks may be more feasible than flextime in organizations that use assembly lines. Employees can be scheduled to work at the same time each day, and setup costs can be minimized by longer shifts. Using compressed workweeks does not seem to compromise principles associated with the mechanistic approach to job design, but the longer hours may create fatigue, which is at odds with the biological perspective. Because of its compatibility with assembly-line processes, the compressed workweek seems to be best suited for organizations with Loyal Soldier HR strategies.

ALTERNATIVE WORK LOCATIONS

Many organizations allow employees to work at locations other than company facilities. The most common arrangement is for employees to work at home. This practice is often called **telework**, since employees stay connected with the office through voice and data services provided over telephone lines. Over 80 percent of companies report at least some employees doing telework, and 45 million people in the United States spend at least some of their time teleworking.[89] As described in the "Technology in HR" feature, telework is fundamental for many organizations.

Telework
Completion of work through voice and data lines such as telephone and high-speed Internet connections.

Researchers evaluating telework have created a list of suggestions to improve its effectiveness. One critical suggestion is to use care in choosing the employees who are allowed to do telework. Most likely to succeed are employees who are independent and conscientious, and employees should embark

Technology in HR

POTENTIAL PROBLEMS WITH WORKING FROM HOME

Allowing employees to work from home can help employers retain good workers. One company that allows employees to work at alternative locations is AT&T. The company reports that 30 percent of management employees work full-time outside the office, while another 41 percent work away from the office an average of one or two days a week. The move to work away from the office has cut expenses for office space by $30 million. These and other savings have led AT&T to conclude that allowing employees to work at alternative locations saves the company over $180 million each year.

However, difficulties balancing the benefits and difficulties of working from home have caused some companies to curtail telework. For example, Yahoo! CEO Marissa Mayer announced in early 2013 that the company would end policies allowing workers the flexibility to work from home. The stated explanation was that collaboration could be increased by additional face-to-face interaction. Many insiders also claimed that the telework policy was frequently abused by employees who rarely used technology resources. Best Buy similarly announced that employees not working in a store need to specifically coordinate their schedules with supervisors.

Research has indeed identified a number of potential problems that can arise when employees work from home. One such problem is the sense of isolation that some workers experience. These workers feel that they miss out on important social interaction, and in some cases, they also feel that by working at home their contributions are less likely to be noticed and rewarded. Employees often feel less connected. Indeed, research suggests that working from home more than two days per week can harm relationships with coworkers. Supervisors may perceive a decrease in their ability to influence and coach employees. In addition, the security of data stored on home computers presents a growing concern. Home computers may not be as secure from hackers or other potential thieves as office networks.

The effect on individual careers depends somewhat on manager perceptions of reasons behind the work arrangement. Employee careers can be facilitated when their managers perceive that employees

MichaelDeLeon/iStockphoto

are using telework and other flexible scheduling techniques to increase productivity. In contrast, careers can be inhibited if managers perceive benefits to personal life as the primary reason behind employees taking advantage of such arrangements.

Sources: Information from Ann Bednarz, "Telework Thrives at AT&T," *Network World* 22, no. 50 (2005): 29; G. Manochehri and T. Pinkerton, "Managing Telecommuters: Opportunities and Challenges," *American Business Review* 21, no. 1 (2003): 9–16; Ravi S. Gajendran and David S. Harrison, "The Good, the Bad, and the Unknown about Telecommuting: Meta-analysis of Psychological Mediators of Individual Consequences," *Journal of Applied Psychology* 92(2007): 1524–1541; Timothy D. Golden, John F. Veiga, and Zekj Simsek, "Telecommuting's Differential Impact on Work–Family Conflict: Is There No Place Like Home?" *Journal of Applied Psychology* 91(2006): 1340–1350; Timothy D. Golden, John F. Veiga, and Richard N. Dino, "The Impact of Professional Isolation on Teleworker Job Performance and Turnover Intentions: Does Time Spent Teleworking, Interacting Face-to-Face, or Having Access to Communication-Enhancing Technology Matter?" *Journal of Applied Psychology* 93 (2008): 1412–1421; Jessica Guynn, "Yahoo CEO Marissa Mayer Causes Uproar With Telecommuting Ban," Los Angeles Times, February 26, 2013; Anonymous, "First Yahoo, now Best Buy Bans Telework," *Network World*, 30, no. 4 (2013): 8; Lisa M. Leslie, Collen Flaherty Manchester, Tae-Youn Park, and Si Ahn Mehng, "Flexible Work Practices: A Source of Career Premiums or Penalties?" *Academy of Management Journal* 55 (2012): 1407-1426.

on telework only after they have physically worked in the office for some time so that they can develop relationships and prove themselves worthy of the opportunity to work at home. A second critical suggestion is that telework should be limited to jobs where it is most appropriate; these jobs often involve word processing, Web design, sales, and consulting. A common characteristic of these jobs is the existence of clear performance objectives and methods for measuring outputs.[90]

In the end, telework offers substantial autonomy and usually requires employees to work independently to complete meaningful tasks. Telework is thus consistent with the motivational approach to job design. Given the need for workers in most jobs to process substantial amounts of information, principles from the perceptual approach can also be important for properly designing telework. In particular, companies need to focus less on work processes and more on establishing clear goals and performance measures. This means that telework is most likely to occur in organizations that are pursuing differentiation strategies.

CONCEPT CHECK

1. *How do flextime and compressed work weeks make organizations more family friendly?*
2. *What are advantages and disadvantages of allowing employees to complete their work tasks at alternative locations?*

A MANAGER'S PERSPECTIVE REVISITED

Amos Morgan/Getty Images

IN THE MANAGER'S PERSPECTIVE AT THE BEGINNING OF THE CHAPTER, JANE FACED A NUMBER OF ISSUES CONCERNING WORK TASKS. SHE WONDERED HOW TO ORGANIZE WORK TASKS TO MAXIMIZE THE SUCCESS OF HER TEAM MEMBERS. FOLLOWING ARE ANSWERS TO THE "WHAT DO YOU THINK?" QUIZ THAT FOLLOWED THE CASE. WERE YOU ABLE TO CORRECTLY IDENTIFY THE TRUE AND FALSE STATEMENTS? COULD YOU DO BETTER NOW?

1. Giving workers more autonomy is a sure way to improve their performance. FALSE. *Autonomy is most beneficial for organizations that expect creativity. High autonomy can actually cause coordination problems in organizations using efficient processes such as assembly lines.*

2. Having updated job descriptions is important to keep a company out of legal trouble. TRUE. *The courts have ruled that job descriptions are evidence of good human resource practices.*

3. The primary objective of good work design is to cluster tasks into jobs that maximize the efficiency of workers. FALSE. *The primary objective of work design depends on the particular approach being adopted. Efficiency is the primary objective of the mechanistic approach. The motivational approach aims for high satisfaction and intrinsic desire to perform well.*

4. People who continuously perform repetitive tasks often find their work to be unsatisfying. **TRUE.** *People find work to be satisfying when they experience high autonomy, task meaningfulness, and skill variety.*

5. Employees who have flexibility in deciding when they will work have higher performance. **TRUE.** *Employees with flextime have higher productivity and are less likely to leave the organization.*

Almost all managers are faced with issues concerning effective work design. Jane was wise to assess the effects of autonomy. Following the principles outlined in this chapter could help Jane better coordinate the work of her team members. Updating the job description would be a good place for Jane to start. The effort will be worthwhile, for good job descriptions can help improve many other areas of human resource management. The concepts discussed in this chapter can also help Jane balance the need for efficient work processes with the need to continually motivate her team members.

SUMMARY

LEARNING OBJECTIVE 1

How is work design strategic?

Work design practices should align with overall HR strategy. Organizations that pursue either Loyal Soldier or Bargain Laborer HR strategies benefit from efficiency. Efficiency comes from designing work so that employees have relatively little autonomy, meaning that they have little freedom to alter the way tasks are carried out. Efficiency is also increased with sequential processing, which occurs when people use assembly lines to complete work tasks. Competitive strategy that focuses on cost reduction thus aligns with work design practices that limit autonomy and create sequential processing.

Organizations that pursue either Committed Expert or Free Agent HR strategies benefit from innovation and creativity. Innovation comes from designing work so that employees have substantial autonomy, meaning that they have freedom to make decisions and ongoing adjustments to the work process. Reciprocal processing, which occurs when employees work closely together and share tasks, also leads to higher creativity. Competitive strategy that focuses on differentiation thus aligns with work design practices that provide high autonomy and create reciprocal processing.

LEARNING OBJECTIVE 2

How are employee jobs determined?

There are seven steps in the job analysis process. (1) Get organized by determining who will do the analysis and by gaining the support of top management. (2) Choose jobs that are critical for success and have a sufficient number of employees. (3) Review what has already been written about the job. (4) Select job agents, such as incumbents, supervisors, or experts. (5) Collect job information through interviews, questionnaires, and observations. (6) Create a job description that specifies the actions that workers do when performing the job. (7) Create job specifications that list the knowledge, skills, abilities, and other characteristics that workers need in order to successfully perform the job.

In order to guide other human resource practices, job analysis information needs to be translated into a "shopping list" of the characteristics needed by people who perform the job. Some worker-oriented job analysis procedures, such as the Position Analysis Questionnaire, provide a list of characteristics that employees need to succeed at the job. In most cases, the information in a job description needs to be translated into a list of desired worker characteristics. Job agents can do this by examining lists of duties in the job description and determining the knowledge, skills, abilities, and other characteristics that workers need to perform the required tasks. Competency modeling, an alternative to traditional job analysis, seeks to determine a list of desirable worker characteristics linked to the strategic objectives of the organization.

LEARNING OBJECTIVE 3

How do we determine the tasks associated with each job?

In the mechanistic approach to job design, principles of scientific management are used to determine the most efficient methods for completing work tasks. Each employee is expected to learn and follow procedures that result in producing goods and services as quickly as possible. The motivational approach is concerned with designing jobs to increase workers' intrinsic motivation. Intrinsic motivation arises when employees feel that their work provides meaningfulness, responsibility, and knowledge of results. When the perceptual approach is used, jobs are designed so that workers can easily process important information. Equipment is developed to simplify work, and accident prevention is a focus. The biological approach involves designing jobs to prevent physical injury. Equipment is used to reduce fatigue and need for excessive movement. Workers are also taught principles such as maintaining good physical posture.

There are some inherent tradeoffs associated with the various approaches to work design. In many cases, striving for efficiency by adopting the mechanistic approach comes at the expense of the principles of the motivational approach. The job design approach should thus be aligned with the overall HR strategy. The mechanistic approach is most appropriate for cost strategies, whereas the motivational approach is most appropriate for differentiation strategies. Yet, benefits can be obtained from simultaneously incorporating principles from all approaches.

LEARNING OBJECTIVE 4

How can work be designed to improve family life?

Workers experience work-to-family conflict when the stress they feel at work is carried into their family environment. They experience family-to-work conflict when the stress they encounter at home affects their work. One way to reduce conflict between work and family roles is through flexible scheduling, including flextime and compressed workweeks. Another way to reduce work and family conflict is to allow workers to perform their tasks in alternative locations, such as at home or on the premises of clients. This practice is often referred to as telework because employees communicate with others via telephone lines. Employees who can take advantage of flexible work scheduling and working at alternative locations are more satisfied with their jobs, more productive, and less likely to leave the company.

KEY TERMS

Autonomy   124
Competencies   138
Competency modeling   138
Compressed workweek   148
Critical-incidents technique   134
Differentiation   122
Ergonomics   144
Family-to-work conflict   146
Flextime   147
Integration   122
Interdependence   126

Job   128
Job analysis   128
Job analysis interview   131
Job analysis observation   132
Job analysis questionnaire   131
Job characteristics model   142
Job description   132
Job design   140
Job redesign   140
Job specifications   132
Occupational Information Network   131

DISCUSSION QUESTIONS

1. Why is high autonomy beneficial for organizations pursuing differentiation strategies?
2. What are the key differences between sequential and reciprocal processes of interdependence?
3. Why would government officials expend significant resources creating O*Net? What are the benefits of O*Net?
4. Have you ever seen a job description for a work position you have held? If so, do you think the job description was accurate?
5. Are job descriptions more beneficial for some types of organizations than others? Could having specific job descriptions harm an organization?
6. Would you rather work in an organization using mechanistic job design principles or an organization using motivational principles?

7. Do you think any of the four job design approaches (mechanistic, motivational, perceptual, biological) will become more important in the future? Why? Do you think any of the approaches will become less important as organizations change?
8. Would you like to work a compressed workweek? Why or why not?
9. Do you think you would be successful in a job that allowed you to do telework? What challenges do you think you would face?
10. Identify some specific ways strategic work design can guide other human resource practices, such as selecting employees, determining training needs, and making pay decisions.

EXAMPLE CASE   *Coney Island Hospital*

Often, the success of hospital-based nursing depends on its adaptability. Nurses can ensure that success when they think outside of traditional nursing roles and focus on effective ways to deliver care. You'll most likely find our assignment familiar: reduce costs, improve quality and access to care, and improve satisfaction for patients and caregivers. This is no small feat, and it requires caregivers to innovate new ways to care for patients.

To start the work redesign, they created a steering committee to collect and analyze data and create the new design. The committee included nurses from administration, education, middle management, and direct care providers, as well as nurses with differing credentials (RN and LPN) who work all shifts.

The committee agreed that staff satisfaction, leading to increased autonomy and control, would be one of its priorities while developing the new model. The committee had a threefold objective:

1. Develop a nursing model that will more efficiently utilize RNs, LPNs, and unlicensed assistive personnel within quality standards.
2. Give staff attractive and satisfying roles.
3. Stay within the current budget.

The committee collected data through surveys, interviews, onsite observations, and work sampling. Topics for data collection included:

- The efficiency of nursing care delivery (focusing on nursing and non-nursing tasks)
- The impact of managed care on the nurse's role
- Issues that occupy the nurse's time, affect staffing, and create chaos
- Patient management throughout the hospital stay, including ways to decrease length of stay
- Nurse–physician communication
- Working relationships across departments

Each committee member took part in gathering the data and presenting it to the committee. Members defined and redefined roles based on the actual and described job performances of RNs, LPNs, and unlicensed assistive personnel. They also identified problem areas in the delivery system.

Next, they needed to write a work redesign proposal. The committee members wrote wish lists for the nursing model redesign with input from their peers and presented them to the committee.

With the newly designed jobs, certain registered nurses (admission nurses) would work to help transition patients to the units, maintaining the continuum of care. The nurse's primary responsibility would be to minimize admission delay at the point of entry and to make this experience less distressing to patients. Today, the admission RN interviews the patient, develops a care plan, explains procedures, and tries to alleviate the patient's anxiety.

Nurses work at the other end of the continuum as well. Discharge RNs work with other disciplines to plan expedient discharge. Their primary objectives are to ensure that the patient leaves the hospital without any delays in the discharge process and that he or she experiences favorable outcomes. Discharge RNs also emphasize patient education and follow-up appointments. They call the patient the day after discharge to ensure that he or she

- Understood instructions.
- Could obtain medications and is taking them properly.
- Gets an earlier follow-up appointment if necessary
- Was satisfied with hospitalization

Positive results of this new process include the following:

- Decreased time patients spend in the emergency room, which enhances patient satisfaction
- Increased compliance with guidelines for effective healthcare
- Improvement in patient ratings of nurse performance, particularly in the area of time spent doing paperwork

QUESTIONS

1. What are some specific ways the new work design improves the satisfaction of patients?
2. How do you think the new procedures increase autonomy?
3. What lessons can be learned from this case about the way to implement effective work redesign?

Source: Terry Mancher, "A Better Model by Design . . . and It Works," *Nursing Management* 32, no. 5 (2001): 45–47. Reprinted with permission of Lippincott, Williams & Wilkins.

DISCUSSION CASE   *Josh's Toy Manufacturing*

Josh's Toy Manufacturing is a manufacturer of small toys that are included in kids' meals at fast-food restaurants. Josh's uses plastic injection technology to produce toys efficiently. Price is the main criterion restaurant chains use to determine whether they will buy toys from Josh's or some other manufacturer.

One assembly line for toy manufacturing at Josh's has four machines. Each machine requires an operator. Operator skill is important, since an effective operator can often manufacture toys twice as fast as an ineffective operator. The four operators on the assembly line at Josh's were hired a year ago when the new line began operation. Machine 1 is very loud, making its operation the least desirable job. Machines 2 and 3 are very similar and require operators to constantly push a variety of levers. Working on Machine 4 is the easiest job, as the operator does little more than monitor progress and push buttons. The four operators currently rotate every hour so that each operator spends two hours on each machine during an eight-hour workday.

	Machine 1	Machine 2	Machine 3	Machine 4	Units Made
Hour 1	Mary	Bonnie	Tom	Fred	335
Hour 2	Fred	Mary	Bonnie	Tom	200
Hour 3	Tom	Fred	Mary	Bonnie	400
Hour 4	Bonnie	Tom	Fred	Mary	370

Supervisors have noted that production output varies depending on which operator is working on which machine. The chart shows this variance.

Analysis suggests that lower production during Hour 2 mostly results from Fred's having trouble working with Machine 1. The noise bothers him more than the others, and he often takes short breaks to walk away from the machine and regain his composure. The relative high productivity during Hour 3 can be traced to having Bonnie work on Machine 4. Bonnie finds it especially difficult to work on Machines 2 and 3.

Given their current production process, the four operators produce an average of 2,610 units each day. If they worked all day in the Hour 3 configuration they could average 3,200 units each day, which would be a production increase of over 22 percent.

QUESTIONS
1. Do you recommend that the four machine operators continue to switch machines every hour? Would you recommend that the operators be permanently assigned to the machines they currently operate during Hour 3? What do you think would be the consequences of any changes you might recommend?
2. How can the principles of the mechanistic approach to job design inform a decision about how to assign workers to machines? What about the principles of the motivational approach? the perceptual approach? the biological approach?
3. How could job analysis be used to improve this assembly line?

EXPERIENTIAL EXERCISE — *Assessing the Accuracy of Job Descriptions*

Find out the job titles of three friends or acquaintances. Use the O*Net database(http://online.onetcenter.org) to obtain a job description and specifications for each position. Have each friend or acquaintance read the information you obtained for his or her job position. After the friend or acquaintance has looked at the material you obtained, discuss the following questions.

1. Which of the things listed in the job description does the person *not* do as part of his or her job?
2. What important tasks or duties have been left out of the job description?
3. Which of the tasks or duties take up the most time? Which tasks are most important for achieving high performance? Are the tasks that are performed most frequently the same as those that are most important?
4. Given the particular job, how often would this list of tasks and duties need to be revised to make sure that it is up to date?

5. Which of the knowledge, skills, and abilities listed in the description does the person consider most critical for performing this job well?
6. What advice would the person give to a college student who might want to work in the job someday?

Once you have discussed the job descriptions and specifications with three different people, answer the following questions.

1. How are the jobs similar? How are they different?
2. Are there any tasks that seem to be important across all of the jobs?
3. Are there any areas of knowledge, skills, or abilities that seem to be important across the different jobs?
4. Are the tasks that are most frequently done in a job generally the same as the tasks that are most important for success?

INTERACTIVE EXPERIENTIAL EXERCISE — *Job Design: Creating New Positions at Graphics Design, Inc.*
http://www.wiley.com/college/sc/stewart

Access the companion website to test your knowledge by completing a Mega Manufacturing interactive role-playing exercise.

In this exercise, you work with another client, Graphics Design, Inc. (GDI), who produces display boards and signs. The company is in the process of creating several new positions because of growth and a need for more efficiency. You recommend that some form of job analysis be used to design the features of the new jobs. One of the company's managers tells you that job analysis isn't necessary, since the new jobs will be similar to existing jobs. But in view of the company's need for increased efficiency and its preference for employees with high levels of loyalty, you are not sure that the old job descriptions can or should be used. When the CEO asks for your input, how will you respond? •

ENDNOTES

1. Paul R. Lawrence and Jay W. Lorsch, *Organization and Environment* (Boston: Harvard Business School Press, 1986).
2. Michael A. Campion, "Interdisciplinary Approaches to Job Design: A Constructive Replication with Extensions," *Journal of Applied Psychology* 73 (1988): 467–481.
3. www.gore.com.
4. Ibid.
5. Frank Shipper and Charles C. Manz, "Self-Management Without Formal Teams: The Organization as a Team" pp. 131-150 in Charles C. Manz and Henry P. Sims, Jr., *Business Without Bosses: How Self-Managing Teams Are Building High Performing Companies* (New York: John Wiley, 1993).

6. http://www.greatplacetowork.com/best-companies/ browse-international-lists; http://money.cnn.com/ magazines/fortune/best-companies/.

7. Claus Langfred and Neta A. Moye, "Effects of Task Autonomy on Performance: An Extended Model Considering Motivational, Informational, and Structural Mechanisms," *Journal of Applied Psychology* 89 (2004): 934–945.

8. Edwin A. Locke and D. M. Schweiger, "Participation in Decision Making: An Information Exchange Perspective," *Research in Personnel and Human Resource Management* 15 (1998): 293–331.

9. J. Richard Hackman and Greg R. Oldham, "Motivation Through the Design of Work: Test of a Theory," *Organizational Behavior and Human Performance* 16 (1976): 250–279.

10. John B. Bingham, Wendy R. Boswell, and John W. Boudreau, "Job Demands and Job Search among High-Level Managers in the United States and Europe," *Group & Organization Management* 30 (2005): 653–681.

11. Riki Takeuchi, Jeffrey P. Shay, and Li Jiatao, "When Does Decision Autonomy Increase Expatriate Managers' Adjustment? An Empirical Test," *Academy of Management Journal* 51 (2008): 45–60.

12. Brian D. Janz, Jason A. Colquitt, and Raymond A. Noe, "Knowledge Worker Team Effectiveness: The Role of Autonomy, Interdependence, Team Development, and Contextual Support Variables," *Personnel Psychology* 50 (1997): 877–905.

13. Greg L. Stewart and Murray R. Barrick, "Team Structure and Performance: Assessing the Mediating Role of Intrateam Process and the Moderating Role of Task Type," *Academy of Management Journal* 43 (2000): 135–148; Brett M. Wright and John L. Cordery, "Production Uncertainty as a Contextual Moderator of Employee Reactions to Job Design," *Journal of Applied Psychology* 84 (1999): 456–463.

14. Jone L. Pearce and Hal B. Gregersen, "Task Interdependence and Extrarole Behavior: A Test of the Mediating Effects of Felt Responsibility," *Journal of Applied Psychology* 76 (1991): 838–844.

15. Gerben S. Van Der Vegt, Ben J. M. Emans, and Evert Van de Vliert, "Patterns of Interdependence in Work Teams: A Two-Level Investigation of the Relations with Job and Team Satisfaction," *Personnel Psychology* 54 (2001): 51–70.

16. Stewart and Barrick, "Team Structure and Performance"; Richard Saavedra, Christopher P. Earley, and Linn Van Dyne, "Complex Interdependence in Task Performing Groups," *Journal of Applied Psychology* 78 (1993): 61–72; Ruth Wageman, "Interdependence and Group Effectiveness," *Administrative Science Quarterly* 40 (1995): 145–180.

17. Ibid.

18. Robert D. Gatewood and Hubert S. Field, *Human Resource Selection*, 5th ed. (Cincinnati OH: South-Western, 2001).

19. Paul J. Taylor, Wen-Dong Li, Kan Shi, and Walter C. Borman, "The Transportability of Job Information across Countries," *Personnel Psychology*, 61 (2008): 69–111.

20. Thorvald Haerem and Devaki Rau, "The Influence of Expertise and Objective Task Complexity on Perceived Complexity and Performance," *Journal of Applied Psychology* 92 (2007): 1320–1331.

21. Richard D. Arvey, Emily M. Passino, and John W. Lounsbury, "Job Analysis Results as Influenced by Sex of Incumbent and Sex of Analyst," *Journal of Applied Psychology* 62 (1977): 411–416.

22. Neal Schmitt and Scott Cohen, "Internal Analyses of Task Ratings by Job Incumbents, "*Journal of Applied Psychology* 74 (1989): 96–104.

23. Wayman C. Mullins and Wilson W. Kimbrough, "Group Composition as a Determinant of Job Analysis Outcomes," *Journal of Applied Psychology* 73 (1988): 657–664.

24. Lee Friedman, "Degree of Redundancy between Time, Importance, and Frequency of Task Ratings," *Journal of Applied Psychology* 75 (1990): 748–752; Lee Friedman, "Degree of Redundancy between Time, Importance, and Frequency of Task Ratings: Correction," *Journal of Applied Psychology* 76 (1991): 366.

25. Juan I. Sanchez and Scott L. Fraser, "On the Choice of Scales for Task Analysis," *Journal of Applied Psychology* 77 (1992): 545–553.

26. Mark A. Wilson, Robert J. Harvey, and Barry A. Macy, "Repeating Items to Estimate the Test–Retest Reliability of Task Inventory Ratings," *Journal of Applied Psychology* 75 (1990): 158–163.

27. Michael K. Lindell, Catherine S. Clause, Christina J. Brandt, and Ronald S. Landis, "Relationship Between Organizational Context and Job Analysis Task Ratings," *Journal of Applied Psychology* 83 (1998): 769–776; Wendy L. Richman and Miguel A. Quinones, "Task Frequency Rating Accuracy: The Effect of Task Engagement and Experience," *Journal of Applied Psychology* 81 (1996): 512–524.

28. John C. Flanagan, "The Critical Incident Technique," *Psychological Bulletin* 5 (1954): 327–358.

29. Inge E. Larsson, Monika J.M. Sahlsten, Kerstin Segesten, and Kaety A.E. Plos, "Patients' Perceptions of Nurses Behaviour That Influence Patient Participation in Nursing Care: A Critical Incident Study," Nursing Research and Practice, published online 2011 April 27: Article ID 534060.

30. www.paq2.com/.

31. *Griggs v. Duke Co.*, 401 U.S. 424, 436 (1971); *Albemarle Paper Co. v. Moody,* 422 U.S. 405 (1975).

32. Duane E. Thompson and Toni A. Thompson, "Court Standards for Job Analysis in Test Validation," *Personnel Psychology* 35 (1982): 865–874.

33. William Bridges, *Job Shift: How to Prosper in a Workplace without Jobs* (Reading, MA: Addison-Wesley, 1994).

34. Greg L. Stewart and Kenneth P. Carson, "Moving Beyond the Mechanistic Model: An Alternative Approach to Staffing for Contemporary Organizations," *Human Resource Management Review* 7 (1997): 157–184.

35. Benjamin Schneider and A. Konz, "Strategic Job Analysis," *Human Resource Management* 28 (1989): 51–63.

36. Jeffery S. Shippmann, *Strategic Job Modeling: Working at the Core of Integrated Human Resources* (Mahwah, NJ: Lawrence Erlbaum Associates, 1999).

37. Ibid.

38. Jeffrey S. Shippmann, Ronald A. Ash, Mariangela Battista, Linda Carr, Lorraine D. Eyde, Beryl Hesketh, Jerry Kehoe, Kenneth Pearlman, Erich P. Prien, and Juan I. Sanchez, "The Practice of Competency Modeling," *Personnel Psychology* 53 (2000): 703–740.

39. Filip Lievens, Juan I. Sanchez, and Wilfried De Corte, "Easing Inferential Leap in Competency Modeling: The Effects of Task-Related Information and Subject Matter Expertise," *Personnel Psychology* 57 (2004): 881–905.

40. Michael A. Campion, Alexis A Fink, Brian J. Ruggebert, Linda Carr, Geneva M. Phillips, and Ronald B. Odman, "Doing Competencies Well: Best Practices in Competency Modeling," *Personnel Psychology* 64 (2011): 225–262.

41. Stephen E. Humphrey, Jennifer D. Nahrgang, and Frederick P. Morgeson, "Integrating Motivational, Social, and Contextual Work Design Features: A Meta-Analytic Summary and Theoretical Extension of the Work Design Literature," *Journal of Applied Psychology* 92 (2007): 1332–1356.

42. Frank W. Bond, Paul E. Flaxman, and David Bunce, "The Influence of Psychological Flexibility on Work Redesign: Mediated Moderation of a Work Reorganization Intervention," *Journal of Applied Psychology* 93 (2008): 645–654.

43. Frederick P. Morgeson, Michael D. Johnson, Michael A. Campion, Gina J. Medsker, and Troy V. Mumford, "Understanding Reactions to Job Redesign: A Quasi-Experimental Investigation of the Moderating Effects of Organizational Context on Perceptions of Performance Behavior," *Personnel Psychology* 59 (2009): 333–363.

44. Russell Cropanzano, Deborah E. Rupp, and Zinta S. Byrne, "The Relationship of Emotional Exhaustion to Work Attitudes, Job Performance, and Organizational Citizenship Behaviors," *Journal of Applied Psychology* 88 (2003): 160–169.

45. Einer M. De Croon, Judith K. Sluiter, Roland W. B. Blonk, Jake P. J. Broersen, and Monique H. W. FringsDresen, "Stressful Work, Psychological Job Strain, and Turnover: A 2-year Prospective Cohort Study of Truck Drivers," *Journal of Applied Psychology* 89 (2004): 442–454.

46. Simona Gilboa, Arie Shirom, Yitzhak Fried, and Cary Cooper, "A Meta-Analysis of Work Demand Stressors and Job Performance: Examining Main and Moderating Effects," *Personnel Psychology* 61 (2008): 227–271.

47. Russell Cropanzano, Deborah E. Rupp, and Zinta S. Byrne, "The Relationship of Emotional Exhaustion to Work Attitudes, Job Performance, and Organizational Citizenship Behaviors," *Journal of Applied Psychology* 88 (2003): 160–169; Jonathan R.B. Halbesleben and Wm. Matthew Bowler, "Emotional Exhaustion and Job Performance: The Mediating Role of Motivation," *Journal of Applied Psychology* 92 (2007): 93–106.

48. Michael R. Frone, "Are Work Stressors Related to Employee Substance Abuse? The Importance of Temporal Context Assessments of Alcohol and Illicit Drug Use," *Journal of Applied Psychology* 93 (2008): 199–206.

49. Peter Villanova, H. John Bernardin, Dennis L. Johnson, and Sue A. Danmus, "The Validity of a Measure of Job Compatibility in the Prediction of Job Performance and Turnover of Motion Picture Theater Personnel," *Personnel Psychology* 47 (1994): 73–90; Christina Maslach and Michael P. Leiter, "Early Predictors of Job Burnout and Engagement," *Journal of Applied Psychology* 93 (2008): 498–512.

50. Jonathon R. B. Halbesleben, "Sources of Social Support and Burnout: A Meta-Analytic Test of the Conservation of Resources Model," *Journal of Applied Psychology* 91 (2006): 1134–1145.

51. Jason D. Shaw and Nina Gupta, "Job Complexity, Performance, and Well-Being: When Does Supplies–Values Fit Matter?" *Personnel Psychology* (57): 847–880.

52. Charlotte Fritz and Sabine Sonnentag, "Recovery, Well-Being, and Performance-Related Outcomes: The Role of Workload and Vacation Experiences," *Journal of Applied Psychology* 91 (2006): 936–945.

53. Frederick W. Taylor, *The Principles of Scientific Management* (New York: Harper & Brothers, 1911).

54. Campion, "Interdisciplinary Approaches to Job Design."

55. Jeffrey R. Edwards, Judith A. Scully, and Mary D. Brtek, "The Nature and Outcomes of Work: A Replication and Extension of Interdisciplinary Work-Design Research," *Journal of Applied Psychology* 85 (2000): 860–868.

56. Campion, "Interdisciplinary Approaches to Job Design," Michael A. Campion and Paul W. Thayer, "Development and Field Evaluation of an Interdisciplinary Measure of Job Design," *Journal of Applied Psychology* 70 (1985): 29–43.

57. J. Richard Hackman and Greg R. Oldham, *Work Redesign* (Reading, MA: Addison-Wesley, 1980).

58. Richard M. Ryan and Edward L. Deci, "Self-Determination Theory and the Facilitation of Intrinsic Motivation, Social Development, and Well-Being," *American Psychologist* 55 (2000): 68–78; Edward L. Deci, Richard Koestner, and Richard M. Ryan, "A Meta-Analytic Review of Experiments Examining the Effects of Extrinsic Rewards and Intrinsic Motivation," *Psychological Bulletin* 125 (1999): 627–668.

59. Edwards, Scully, and Brtek, "The Nature and Outcomes of Work."

60. Christine A. Sprigg, Christopher B. Stride, Toby D. Wall, David J. Holman, Phoebe R. Smith, "Work Characteristics, Musculoskeletal Disorders, and the Mediating Role of Psychological Strain: A Study of Call Center Employees," *Journal of Applied Psychology* 92 (2007): 1456–1466.

61. Rodger W. Griffeth, "Moderation of the Effects of Job Enrichment by Participation: A Longitudinal Field Experiment," *Organizational Behavior and Human Decision Processes* 35 (1985): 73–93; Ricky W. Griffin, "Objective and Social Sources of Information in Task Redesign: A Field Experiment," *Administrative Science Quarterly* 28 (1983): 184–200.

62. Richard S. Billings, Richard J. Klimoski, and James A. Breaugh, "The Impact of a Change in Technology on Job Characteristics: A Quasi-Experiment," *Administrative Science Quarterly* 22 (1977): 318–339; Greg R. Oldham and Daniel J. Brass, "Employee Reaction to an Open-Office Plan: A Naturally Occurring Quasi-Experiment, *Administrative Science Quarterly* 24 (1979): 267–284.

63. Michael A. Campion and C. L. McClelland, "Follow-up and Extension of the Interdisciplinary Costs and Benefits of Enlarged Jobs," *Journal of Applied Psychology* 78 (1993): 339–351.

64. Frederick P. Morgeson and Stephen E. Humphrey, "The Work Design Questionnaire (WDQ): Developing and Validating a Comprehensive Measure for Assessing Job Design and the Nature of Work," *Journal of Applied Psychology* 91 (2006): 1321–1139.

65. Frederick P. Morgeson and Michael A. Campion, "Minimizing Tradeoffs When Redesigning Work:

Evidence from a Longitudinal Quasi-experiment," *Personnel Psychology* 55 (2002): 589–612.

66. Eric Trist, "The Sociotechnical Perspective," pp. 19–76 in *Perspectives on Organizational Design and Behavior*, edited by A. H. Van de Ven and W. F. Joyce (New York: Wiley, 1981); Morgeson and Campion, "Minimizing Tradeoffs When Redesigning Work."

67. Michael R. Frone, Marcia Russell, and M. Lynne Cooper, "Antecedents and Outcomes of Work-Family Conflict: Testing a Model of the Work–Family Interface," *Journal of Applied Psychology* 77 (1992): 65–78.

68. Michael T. Ford, Beth A. Heinen, and Krista L. Langkamer, "Work and Family Satisfaction and Conflict: A Meta-Analysis of Cross-Domain Relations," *Journal of Applied Psychology* 92 (2007): 57–80.

69. Remus Ilies, Kelly Schwind Wilson, and David T. Wagner, "The Spillover of Daily Satisfaction onto Employees' Family Lives: The Facilitating Role of Work–Family Integration," *Academy of Management Journal* 52(2009): 87–102; Zhaoli Song, Maw-Der Foo, and Marilyn A. Uy, "Mood Spillover and Crossover among Dual-Earner Couples: A Cell Phone Event Sampling Study," *Journal of Applied Psychology* 93(2008): 443–452; Remus Ilies, Kelly M. Schwind, David T. Wagner, Michael D. Johnson, Scott D. DeRue, and Daniel R. Ilgen, "When Can Employees Have a Family Life? The Effects of Daily Workload and Affect on Work–Family Conflict and Social Behaviors at Home," *Journal of Applied Psychology* 92 (2007); 1368–1379.

70. Thomas W.H. Ng and Daniel C. Feldman, "The Effects of Organizational and Community Embeddedness on Work-to-Family and Family-to-Work Conflict," *Journal of Applied Psychology* 97 (2012): 1233–1251.

71. Helen Lingard and Valerie Francis, "'Negative Interference' between Australian Construction Professionals' Work and Family Roles: Evidence of an Asymmetrical Relationship," *Engineering, Construction and Architectural Management* 14 (2007): 79.

72. Paul E. Spector, Tammy D. Allen, Steven A. Y. Poelmans, Laurent M. LaPierre, Cary L. Cooper, Michael O'Driscoll, Juan I. Sanchez, Nureya Abarca, Matilda Alexandrova, Barbara Beham, Paula Brough, Pablo Ferreiro, Guillermo Fraile, Chang-Qin Lu, Luo Lu, Ivonne Moreno-Valezquez, Milan Pagon, Horea Pitariu, Volodymyr Salamatov, Satoru Shima, Alejandra Wuarez Simoni, Oi Ling Siu, and Maria Widerxzal-Bazyl, "Cross-National Differences in Relationships of Work Demands, Job Satisfaction, and Turnover Intentions with Work-Family Conflict," *Personnel Psychology* 60(2007): 805–835.

73. Marcus M. Butts, Wendy J. Casper, and Tae Seok Yang, "How Important are Work–Family Support Policies? A Meta-Analytic Investigation of Their Effects on Employee Outcomes," *Journal of Applied Psychology* 98 (2013): 1–25.

74. Leslie B. Hammer, Ellen Ernst Kossek, W. Kent Anger, Todd Bodner, and Kristi L. Zimmerman, "Clarifying Work–Family Intervention Processes: The Roles of Work–Family Conflict and Family-Supportive Supervisor Behaviors," *Journal of Applied Psychology* 96 (2011): 134-150; Ellen Ernst Kossek, Shaun Pilcher, Todd Bodner, and Leslie B. Hammer, "Workplace Social Support and Work-Family Conflict: A Meta-

Analysis Clarifying the Influence of General and Work–Family-Specific Supervisor and Organizational Support," *Personnel Psychology* 64 (2011): 289–313.

75. Barbara A. Gutek, Sabrina Searl, and Lilian Klepa, "Rational versus Gender Role Explanations for Work–Family Conflict, *Journal of Applied Psychology* 76 (1991): 560–568; Virginia Smith Major, Katherine J. Klein, and Mark G. Ehrhart, "Work Time, Work Interference with Family and Psychological Distress," *Journal of Applied Psychology* 87 (2002): 427–436.

76. Monique Valcour, "Work-Based Resources as Moderators of the Relationship between Work Hours and Satisfaction with Work–Family Balance," *Journal of Applied Psychology* 92(2007): 1512–1523.

77. Frone et al., "Antecedents and Outcomes of Work–Family Conflict."

78. Stephen J. Goff, Michael K. Mount, and Rosemary L. Jamison, "Employer Supported Child Care, Work/Family Conflict, and Absenteeism: A Field Study," *Personnel Psychology* 43 (1990): 793–809; Richard G. Netemeyer, James S. Boles, and Robert McMurrian, "Development and Validation of Work–Family Conflict and Family-Work Conflict Scales," *Journal of Applied Psychology* 81(1996): 400–410.

79. Netemeyer et al., "Development and Validation"; M. R. Frone, "Work-Family Conflict and Employee Psychiatric Disorders: The National Comorbidity Survey, *Journal of Applied Psychology* 85 (2000): 888–895.

80. Luis L. Martins, Kimberly A. Eddleston, and John F. Veiga, "Moderators of the Relationship Between Work–Family Conflict and Career Satisfaction," *Academy of Management Journal* 45 (2002): 399–409.

81. Phyllis Tharenou, "Disruptive Decisions to Leave Home: Gender and Family Differences in Expatriation Choices," *Organizational Behavior and Human Decision Processes* 105 (2008): 183–200.

82. Timothy A. Judge and Jason A. Colquitt, "Organizational Justice and Stress: The Mediating Role of Work–Family Conflict," *Journal of Applied Psychology* 89 (2004): 395–404.

83. Susan J. Lambert, "Added Benefits: The Link Between Work–Life Benefits and Organizational Citizenship Behavior," *Academy of Management Journal* 43 (2000): 801–815.

84. Jill E. Perry-Smith and Terry C. Blum, "Work–Family Resource Bundles and Perceived Organizational Performance," *Academy of Management Journal* 43 (2000): 1107–1117.

85. Anonymous, "Flexibility Has Become a Top Priority for Today's Workers," *HR Focus* 81, no. 7 (2004): 9.

86. Boris B. Baltes, Thomas E. Briggs, Joseph W. Huff, Julie A. Wright, and George A. Neuman, "Flexible and Compressed Workweek Schedules: A Meta-Analysis of Their Effects on Work-Related Criteria," *Journal of Applied Psychology* 84 (1999): 496–513.

87. Ibid.

88. Ibid.

89. William "Rick" Crandall, "An Update on Telecommuting: Review and Prospects for Emerging Issues," S.A.M. *Advanced Management Journal* 70, no. 3 (2005): 30–37; Anonymous, "Get the Most from Teleworkers," *HR Focus* 81, no. 12 (2004): 9.

90. Crandall, "An Update on Telecommuting."

Chapter 5
Recruiting Talented Employees

A MANAGER'S PERSPECTIVE

SANJIV LEAVES HIS SUPERVISOR'S OFFICE FEEL-
ING GOOD ABOUT HIS RECENT ACCOMPLISHMENTS.
WHEN HE GRADUATED FROM COLLEGE TWO YEARS
AGO, HE ACCEPTED A JOB IN THE MARKETING
DEPARTMENT AT A CONSUMER PRODUCTS COM-
PANY. OVER THE PAST YEAR, HE HAS SPENT
MOST OF HIS TIME WORKING ON A TEAM, WHICH
JUST COMPLETED A REPORT ON AREAS OF POTEN-
TIAL GROWTH FOR NEW PRODUCTS. HE IS SORRY
THAT THE PROJECT IS ENDING BECAUSE HE WILL
NO LONGER BE WORKING SO CLOSELY WITH HIS
FRIENDS ON THE TEAM, BUT HE IS EXCITED TO
MOVE ON TO SOMETHING NEW. THE SOMETHING
NEW IS QUITE A SURPRISE. SANJIV HAS JUST
BEEN ASKED TO BE A MEMBER OF A TEAM THAT
WILL RECOMMEND BETTER WAYS TO RECRUIT NEW
EMPLOYEES.

Sanjiv starts to think about why he chose this
company two years ago. A friend introduced him to
the opportunity and connected him with managers
who were making hiring decisions. Being referred
by his friend helped assure Sanjiv that it would be

a good place to work.
His friend even told him
some of the undesir-
able things about the
company. This actually reassured Sanjiv because
he knew that he was getting an accurate picture
of how things would be. Reflecting back, Sanjiv is
sure that having a friend at the company positively
influenced his choice to accept the position.

As he thinks back, Sanjiv also remembers a
conversation he had with his college roommates.
He was surprised to learn that they had very different images of the ideal place to work. One of
his roommates was most interested in working for
a company that allowed a great deal of flexibility
and freedom. Another roommate cared mostly about
promotions and money. Sanjiv realizes that these
differences are also important from the organizational side. Which of his roommates would be most
successful working with him now?

Sanjiv's supervisor made it clear that a major
objective of the committee is to identify specific

THE BIG PICTURE *Effective Organizations Gain the Interest and Commitment of Job Applicants Who Will Become Excellent Employees*

sources for recruiting. Should Sanjiv suggest that the company continue to recruit mostly through university placement centers? What about newspaper advertisements? Should the company use the Internet?

Sanjiv knows there is a lot he doesn't understand about recruiting employees. He is, however, excited about this new opportunity. His two years with the company have been terrific. He highly values his relationships with other employees. Finding ways to help attract more great coworkers could make things even better.

WHAT DO YOU THINK?

Imagine that you are listening to a conversation between Sanjiv and Alicia, who is a full-time recruiter. Alicia makes the following statements. Which of the statements do you think are true?

T OR F Effective organizations do all they can to get as many people as possible to apply for jobs.

T OR F Organizations should be careful to communicate only positive things to job applicants.

T OR F A company should develop strong relationships with professors at universities where it recruits.

T OR F One way of attracting more job applicants is to pay high wages.

T OR F Job applicants referred by current employees seldom work out because employees often refer friends who don't have good work skills.

161

After reading this chapter you should be able to:

LEARNING OBJECTIVE 1 — Explain how overall HR strategy guides recruiting practices.

LEARNING OBJECTIVE 2 — Describe the key elements of human resource planning.

LEARNING OBJECTIVE 3 — Explain important characteristics and search patterns of different types of people looking for jobs.

LEARNING OBJECTIVE 4 — Describe the characteristics of organizations that attract recruits.

LEARNING OBJECTIVE 5 — List various recruiting sources and be able to describe their strengths and weaknesses, as well as their linkage with strategic recruiting practices.

LEARNING OBJECTIVE 6 — Explain various approaches for evaluating the effectiveness of recruiting.

How Can Strategic Recruiting Make an Organization Effective?

Employee recruiting
The process of getting people to apply for work with a specific organization.

Employee recruiting is the process of identifying and attracting people to work for an organization.[1] The basic goals of recruiting are to communicate a positive image of the organization and to identify and gain the interest and commitment of people who will be good employees. Effective recruiting thus entails getting people to apply for positions, keeping applicants interested in joining the organization, and persuading the best applicants to accept job offers.[2]

Organizations that recruit well have more options when it comes to hiring new employees. They are in a position to hire only the best. Good recruiting can also lower employment costs by making sure that new employees know what to expect from the organization, which helps keep employees on board once they are hired. Obtaining sufficient numbers of applicants and using the best recruitment sources have been linked to increased profitability.[3] In short, a strategic approach to recruiting helps an organization become an employer of choice and thereby obtain and keep great employees who produce superior goods and services.

One example of effective recruiting is Google. The Internet search company has frequently been identified as a top place to work. It receives as many as 1,300 résumés a day.[4] Having so many people apply for jobs puts Google in a position to hire only the best. Working at Google is so desirable that 95 percent of job applicants who receive an offer accept it.[5] It takes effective recruiting to convince so many people to apply and to have such a high percentage of offers accepted. What makes Google the kind of place where so many people want to work? And what makes it the kind of place where very few quit?

The first key to successful recruiting at Google is a culture that creates a fun and supportive working environment. Given its competitive emphasis on differentiation and creativity, Google benefits from allowing employees the freedom to be themselves. Engineers are encouraged to dedicate 20 percent of their work time to new and interesting projects that are not part of their formal work assignments. The company also provides a number of benefits that allow employees to focus on completing work. For example, Google provides onsite support for personal tasks such as dry cleaning, haircuts, and oil changes. Yet, the perk that seems to create the most excitement is gourmet food. Employee cafeterias offer free food and cater to unique tastes with dishes like roast quail and black bass with parsley pesto.[6] The supportive environment allows employees to focus their energy on getting work done rather than running personal errands, and the company is rewarded by employees willing to work long hours.

The culture at Google is particularly supportive of parents with family responsibilities. When the company was young and only had two employees with children, founders Larry Page and Sergey Brin suggested that a conference room be converted into an onsite daycare. The family-friendly focus continues today with new mothers getting three months of leave while receiving 75 percent of their salary. New fathers receive two weeks' paid leave. Free meals are also delivered to the homes of new parents.[7] Lactation rooms and company-provided breast pumps help new mothers transition back to the workplace. Google has thus developed a reputation as an employer who helps balance work and family demands. Such efforts help make it so that only about 3 percent of staff members leave the company.[8]

So what does Google do to recruit employees? One effective recruitment source is referrals from current employees. Current employees are given a $2,000 bonus for each new employee they help recruit.[9] Google also works closely with university professors to make sure they refer their best students for jobs. Another innovative recruiting source is contests. For example, Google once hosted an India Code Jam where computer experts competed to earn a prize for writing computer code. The contest drew 14,000 participants trying to win the prize of approximately $7,000. However, the real reason for the contest was to identify top talent, with about 50 finalists eventually being offered positions at Google.[10]

 ## Building Strength Through HR

GOOGLE

© William Perlman/
StarLedger/Corbis

Google is an Internet search company with over 58,000 employees. Human resource management at Google builds competitive strength by:

- Creating a working environment that attracts highly creative and intelligent employees.
- Offering perks and programs that help employees balance work and family demands.
- Targeting highly talented recruits by encouraging employee referrals, building university relationships, and sponsoring contests.

How Is Employee Recruiting Strategic?

As shown in the Google example, employee recruiting is strategic when it focuses on attracting people who will make great employees. Of course, recruiting practices that are successful at Google may not be as successful at other places. Google's business model requires hiring people with very specific skill sets. In such a situation, success in recruiting depends on receiving applications from the best and the brightest people available. Organizations that desire employees with less-specific skill sets may benefit from very different recruiting methods. Recruiting practices are thus best when they align with overall HR strategies.

Figure 5.1 shows how selection decisions can be aligned with the HR strategies from Chapter 2. As the figure shows, two important dimensions underlie strategic recruiting choices: skill scope and source of applicants. We examine these dimensions next.

BROAD VERSUS TARGETED SKILL SCOPE

The horizontal dimension in Figure 5.1 represents differences in skill scope. At one end of the continuum is broad scope, which represents a set of work skills that a lot of people have. At the other end is targeted scope, which represents a set of skills that only a few people have.

Broad Scope

One way to think about differences in skill scope is to think about potential strategies for romantic dating. Suppose you wish to find a romantic partner. How do you go about finding him or her? One approach is to try to meet as many people as possible. You attend lots of different social events, talk with

Figure 5.1 Strategic Framework for Employee Recruiting.

a variety of people, and go on numerous dates with different people. This strategy might work if you aren't that picky when it comes to relationship partners. Casting a wide net also makes sense if you are not sure about the type of person you're looking for. It also helps if you have a lot of time to evaluate potential partners. Such an approach to dating can be summarized as "How do I know what I want until I've seen what's out there?"

Some organizations adopt employee recruiting strategies that are very similar to dating a lot of different people. These organizations cast a wide net and try to get many people to apply for positions. This **broad skill scope** strategy focuses on attracting a large number of applicants. Such an approach makes sense when a lot of people have the characteristics needed to succeed in the job. McDonald's is a good example, since it is constantly working to attract numerous people who do not have highly specialized skills. Successful employees learn skills on the job, and the constant need for new employees requires maintaining a large pool of potential workers. Broad recruiting practices can also be helpful when an organization is recruiting for a new position where the characteristics of a successful worker are unclear or where a number of different characteristics might lead to success.

In terms of the HR strategies discussed in Chapter 2, broad scope recruiting is most often used by organizations with cost leadership strategies. Organizations using the Bargain Laborer HR strategy hire a large number of nonspecialized employees, who often stay with the company for only short periods of time. These organizations are therefore constantly searching for new employees. In many cases, they are not too choosy about whom they hire. Most people have the necessary skills. Of course, organizations using the Loyal Soldier HR strategy seek to keep employees for longer periods, but again, the employees do not need specialized skills to succeed. Most people have what it takes to perform the job tasks, and having a lot of applicants provides the organization with many alternatives. This means that successful recruiting for organizations with Loyal Soldier HR strategies often entails attracting a large number of applicants for each position and then basing hiring decisions on assessments of fit with the culture and values of the organization. Broad scope recruiting is thus optimal for organizations with both internal and external forms of the cost strategy.

Targeted Scope

Although dating a lot of different people is one approach to finding a romantic partner, it certainly isn't the only approach. You might instead establish a very clear set of characteristics desired in a mate and then date only people who are likely to have those characteristics. Instead of going to as many different parties as possible, you might just go to parties where you know certain types of people will be. You would not go on dates with people who clearly don't meet your expectations. Such an approach makes sense if you know exactly what you want and if you don't want to waste time meeting people who are clearly wrong for you. This approach to dating can be summarized as "I know exactly what I want, and all I need to do is find that person."

A number of organizations adopt recruiting strategies that are similar to this targeted approach for dating. The **targeted skill scope** strategy seeks to attract a small group of applicants who have a high probability of possessing the characteristics needed to perform the specific job. Such an approach makes sense when only a select few have what it takes to perform the job successfully. Recruiting a university professor is one example of such a targeted

Broad skill scope
A recruiting strategy that seeks to attract a large number of applicants.

Targeted skill scope
A recruiting strategy that seeks to attract a small number of applicants who have specific characteristics.

approach. Only a small number of people have the education and experience necessary to work as professors. Receiving and reviewing applications from people without the required expertise wastes valuable time and resources. Universities thus benefit from targeting their recruiting to attract only qualified applicants.

As you might expect, targeted scope recruiting is most often pursued by organizations with a competitive strategy of differentiation. Differentiation HR strategies rely on specific contributions from a select group of employees. People are hired because they have rare skills and abilities, and only a small number of people actually have what it takes to succeed. Receiving applications from a large number of people who clearly do not have the characteristics needed to perform the work is wasteful. Targeted scope recruiting is thus optimal for organizations with both Committed Expert and Free Agent HR strategies. These organizations benefit from identifying and attracting only the people who are most likely to be successful.

Skill Scope and Geography

One caution when thinking about targeted and broad approaches is to distinguish skill scope from geographic scope. Broad skill scope recruiting seeks to identify a large number of people. Given that many people have the required skills, this recruiting can usually be done in small geographic areas near where the new employees will work. Most likely, a sufficient number of recruits already living in the area can be identified. For instance, a local grocery store recruits cashiers by looking for people who already live close to the store. In contrast, targeted recruiting seeks to identify a smaller group of people with specialized skills and abilities. The number of qualified people in a particular area often is not large. Thus, targeted skill recruiting frequently covers wide geographic areas. An example is a law firm that conducts a nationwide search to identify a patent attorney. In summary, the terms *broad* and *targeted* refer to the range of applicant skills and not the geographic area of the recruiting search.

INTERNAL VERSUS EXTERNAL SOURCING

Think back to our dating example. What are the chances you are already friends with the person who will become your romantic partner? Should you try and develop deeper relationships with people you already like? Or do you want to identify new and exciting prospects? These questions start to touch on the next aspect of strategic recruiting—internal versus external sourcing. The vertical dimension in Figure 5.1 represents this aspect of recruiting, with internal sourcing at one end of the continuum and external sourcing on the other.

Internal Sourcing

Internal sourcing of recruits seeks to fill job openings with people who are already working for the organization. Positions are filled by current employees who are ready for promotions or for different tasks. These people have performance records and are already committed to a relationship with the organization. Because a lot is known about the motivation and skill of current employees, the risks associated with internal recruiting are relatively low. Of course, internal sourcing is a fundamental part of Loyal Soldier and Committed Expert HR strategies. With the exception of hiring entry-level workers, most organizations with these HR strategies try to fill as many job vacancies as possible by recruiting current employees.

Internal sourcing
A recruiting strategy that fills job openings by transferring people who are already working in the organization.

A common example of internal sourcing is organizations looking at current employees to identify people who can fill international assignments. The people filling these assignments, usually referred to as expatriates, move to a foreign country to take a work assignment that will last for a few years. Such assignments help organizations better take advantage of the skill and expertise of people who are already working for the company. Employees who serve as expatriates also develop new skills that can help them in their future assignments. Historically, expatriate workers have received high wages and benefits to offset the potential pains of relocation. However, foreign assignments are becoming more common, and many expatriates now receive pay similar to what they would receive in their home country.[11]

External Sourcing

External sourcing of recruits seeks to fill job openings with people from outside the organization. Primary sources of recruits are other organizations. The high number of entry-level positions in organizations with a Bargain Laborer HR strategy often necessitates external sourcing. Almost all employees are hired to fill basic jobs, and there are few opportunities for promotion or reassignment. Organizations with a Free Agent HR strategy also use primarily external sourcing. Bringing in a fresh perspective is key for these organizations. Since little training and development is provided, current employees rarely have the specialized skills needed to fill job openings. External sourcing, then, is an essential part of the recruiting practices of organizations with either Bargain Laborer or Free Agent HR strategies.

An extreme example of external sourcing occurs when organizations do not actually hire people to fill positions. For example, positions may be filled by temporary workers, who are people actually employed by an outside staffing agency.[12] Organizations often use such arrangements to avoid long-term employment commitments. This makes it easier to adjust the size of the workforce to meet increasing or decreasing demand for products and services. A potential disadvantage of using temporary workers is that it involves sharing employees with other organizations, which makes it difficult to develop a unique resource that creates a competitive advantage.[13] In some cases, organizations hire successful temporary workers into permanent positions—a practice we revisit later in this chapter when we discuss employment agencies.

Another example of extreme external sourcing is independent contractors, who have a relationship with the organization but technically work for themselves.[14] An example of a company that uses independent contractors is Newton Manufacturing, which sells promotional products such as coffee mugs and caps.[15] Newton products are distributed by approximately 800 independent sales representatives. These representatives set their own hours and make their own decisions about how to sell. Representatives receive a percentage of their sales receipts, but they are not actually employed by Newton.

Temporary workers and independent contractors are examples of contingent workers—people working without either an implicit or an explicit contract for continuing work and who are not required to work a minimum number of hours.[16] Cost savings are often cited as a potential benefit of using contingent workers. A potential problem is that organizations have limited control over the actions of contingent workers. Many experts also believe that contingent workers have weaker commitment and motivation. However, research suggests that contingent workers generally feel high levels of support from their associated organizations.[17] Much of this support seems to come from a

External sourcing
A recruiting strategy that fills job openings by hiring people who are not already employed by the organization.

Temporary workers
Individuals who are employed by an outside staffing agency and assigned to work in an organization for a short period of time.

Independent contractors
Individuals who actually work for themselves but have an ongoing relationship with an organization.

Contingent workers
People working without either an implicit or an explicit contract and who are not required to work a minimum number of hours.

feeling that the contingent worker status allows them to effectively balance their professional career with other life interests.[18] Nevertheless, contingent workers need to proactively learn new skills and develop a progressive career. They can do this by continually demonstrating competence, building relationships to get referred to other projects, and framing their skill sets in terms of new opportunities.[19]

REALISTIC VERSUS IDEALISTIC MESSAGING

Idealistic messaging
The recruiting practice of communicating only positive information to potential employees.

Realistic messaging
The recruiting practice of communicating both good and bad features of jobs to potential employees.

Realistic job previews
Information given to potential employees that provides a complete picture of the job and organization.

Another important aspect of dating is how much you tell others about yourself. One approach is to be on your best behavior and only tell people the good things. This is similar to **idealistic messaging**, wherein an organization conveys positive information when recruiting employees in order to develop and maintain an upbeat image. An opposite approach to dating is to let others see the real you. This necessitates sharing not only positive information but also information about your problems and weaknesses. Such an approach is similar to **realistic messaging**, which occurs when an organization gives potential employees both positive and negative information about the work setting and job. *bargain & free agent*

Realistic Messaging

Realistic messaging is used to increase the likelihood that employees will stay with the organization once they have been hired. Job applicants are given **realistic job previews** designed to share a complete picture of what it is like to work for the organization. These previews usually include written descriptions and audiovisual presentations about both good and bad aspects of the working environment.[20] Negative things such as poor working hours and frequent rejection by customers are specifically included in the recruiting message. That way, new recruits already know that the working environment is less than perfect when they start the job. Their expectations are lower, so they are less likely to become disappointed and dissatisfied. The overall goal of realistic messaging is thus to help new recruits develop accurate expectations about the organization. Lowered expectations are easier to meet, which decreases the chance of employees leaving the organization to accept other jobs.[21] Studies such as the one described in the "How Do We Know?" feature also suggest that realistic job previews increase perceptions of honesty by the organization, which in turn make employees less likely to leave.

In terms of the HR strategies presented in Chapter 2, realistic messaging is most valuable for organizations seeking long-term employees. These organizations benefit from the reduced employee turnover that comes from realistic recruiting. The recruiting process provides an opportunity for people to get a sense of how well they will fit. If the organization does not provide honest and realistic information, then the assessment of the potential for a good long-term relationship is less accurate.

Realistic recruiting thus operates much like being truthful while dating. People make commitments with full knowledge of the strengths and weaknesses of the other party, increasing the likelihood that their expectations will be met in the future. Being honest increases the likelihood of developing a successful long-term relationship. Since maintaining long-term relationships with employees is critical for the success of organizations pursuing either Loyal Soldier or Committed Expert HR strategies, realistic recruiting is most appropriate for these organizations.[22] Of course, internal job applicants

How Do We Know?

WHY DO REALISTIC JOB PREVIEWS REDUCE EMPLOYEE TURNOVER?

Why does providing potentially negative information about an organization make it less likely that employees will leave? Is it because employees better understand their role? Does being honest somehow make the organization seem like a better place to work? David Earnest, David Allen, and Ronald Landis sought to answer this question by combining and analyzing the results of 52 previous studies.

Results of the study found that employees who receive a realistic preview are indeed less likely to voluntarily leave organizations, even though the negative information has virtually no influence on whether or not candidates accept job offers. Some of the effect of the realistic preview operates through better clarification of work roles, but the primary reason for the increased likelihood to remain employed is a perception of organizational honesty. Organizations that provided both positive and negative information about jobs were perceived as being more open and trustworthy, which in turn helped retain workers. Also, realistic information given after a candidate accepts an offer is equally as beneficial as information given before hiring.

The Bottom Line. Organizations can use realistic job previews to reduce employee turnover because employees who receive such information perceive organizations as being more honest. The study authors conclude that the relatively inexpensive practice of providing both positive and negative information about jobs provides a meaningful benefit to organizations.

Source: David R. Earnest, David G. Allen, and Ronald S. Landis, "Mechanisms Linking Realistic Job Previews with Turnover: A Meta-Analytic Path Analysis," *Personnel Psychology* 64 (2011): 865–897.

who are working for the organization already have a realistic picture of the work environment. The key for these organizations is thus to use realistic job previews for new hires. The importance of realistic messaging for new hires with internal labor strategies is shown in Figure 5.1, which suggests that even though most hires come internally, those who do come from outside sources should receive realistic job previews.

Idealistic Messaging

Unlike realistic messaging, idealistic messaging excludes negative information and paints a very positive picture of the organization. This positive emphasis can be helpful because realistic recruiting messages discourage some job applicants and cause them to look for work elsewhere.[23] Unfortunately, in many cases, highly qualified applicants who have many other alternatives are the most likely to be turned off by realistic recruiting.[24]

Let's think about idealistic messaging in terms of our dating situation. Withholding negative information from a partner may work for a while, but when the "honeymoon" is over, faults are seen and satisfaction with the relationship decreases. Clearly, this is not an effective strategy for building a long-term relationship. But maybe a short-term relationship is all you want, so you aren't concerned that your partner will enter the relationship with unrealistic expectations. Once you get to know each other's faults and weaknesses, both of you may be ready to move on to other relationships. You might also be concerned that sharing negative information will scare some potential partners off before they get a chance to really know you.

In recruiting, too, idealistic messaging corresponds best with an emphasis on short-term relationships. This is shown in Figure 5.1 by the use of idealistic messaging for organizations pursuing external HR strategies. In particular, the Bargain Laborer HR strategy is used by organizations seeking to reduce cost through high standardization of work practices. Finding people to work in these lower-skilled jobs for even a short period of time, such as a summer, may be all that can be expected. Training for the job is minimal, so replacing people who quit is not as costly as replacing more-skilled workers. The Free Agent HR strategy requires people with more highly developed work skills, but these individuals are expected to be more committed to careers than to a particular organization. They likely have many choices of where to work, and negative information may push them to take a position elsewhere. In these cases, idealistic messaging may lead to inflated expectations about how good the job will be, but that may not matter a great deal because the new recruit is not expected to become a loyal long-term employee.

CONCEPT CHECK

1. *How does broad scope recruiting differ from narrow scope recruiting?*
2. *Why would an organization tell job applicants negative information about the position?*

How Does Human Resource Planning Facilitate Recruiting?

An important part of recruiting is planning. Organizations fail to take advantage of available talent when they begin recruiting only after a job is vacant. Carefully constructed recruiting plans not only increase the chances of identifying the best workers but also reduce costs associated with finding workers. In this section, we explore specific ways that an organization can plan and maximize recruiting effectiveness. First, we look at the overall planning process. We then describe differences between organizations that hire employees periodically in groups and organizations that have ongoing recruiting efforts. We also explore differences between a recruiting approach that is consistent across the entire organization and an approach that allows different departments and locations to develop their own recruiting plans.

THE PLANNING PROCESS

Human resource planning
The process of forecasting the number and type of employees that will be needed in the future.

Human resource planning is the process of forecasting employment needs. A proactive approach to forecasting can help organizations become more productive. The basic steps of human resource planning are shown in Figure 5.2. The process involves assessing current employment levels, predicting future

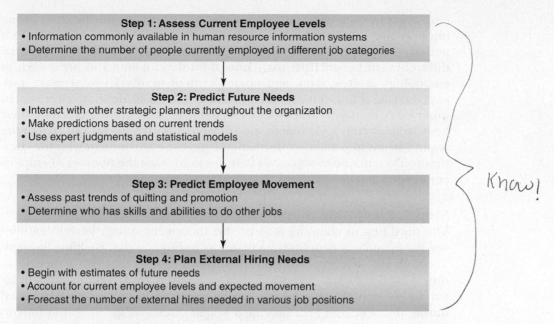

Figure 5.2 Human Resource Planning.

needs, planning for internal movement, and predicting external hiring needs. This planning process is similar to models of inventory control. First, you figure out what you currently have; next, you determine what you expect to need in the future; and then you plan where to obtain additional inventory.

Step 1. Assessing Current Employment Levels

The first step of human resource planning, assessing current employment levels, relies heavily on the organization's information system. Most large corporations have some type of HR information system, with the most common systems being SAP and Oracle's PeopleSoft. These databases track employees and can generate reports showing where people are currently working. This information provides a snapshot summary of the number of people in different positions. The HR information system can also provide details about the qualifications and skills of current employees. This is helpful in planning for internal movement of people during the third planning step.

Step 2. Predicting Future Needs

The second step in human resource planning is to predict future needs. This step requires close collaboration with strategic planners throughout the organization. Predicting future needs begins with assessing environmental trends (changing consumer tastes, demographic shifts, and so forth). Based on these trends, a forecast is made of expected changes in demand for services and goods. Will people buy more or less of what the company produces? Such projections are used to predict the number of employees that might be needed in certain jobs.

One common method for making employment predictions is to assume that human resource needs will match expected trends for services and goods. For instance, an organization may assume that the number of employees in each position will increase by 10 percent during the upcoming year simply because sales are expected to grow by 10 percent in that period. More sophisticated forecasting methods might account for potential differences in productivity that come from developments in areas such as technology, interest rates, and unemployment trends. In some cases, projected changes are entered into statistical models to develop forecasts. In other cases, managers and other experts simply make guesses based on their knowledge of trends. Although specific practices vary, the overall goal of the second step is to combine information from the environment with the organization's competitive objectives in order to forecast the number of employees needed in particular jobs.[25]

✭Step 3. Predicting Employee Movement

The third step in planning is to predict movement among current employees. An example of benefits from planning is shown in the "Building Strength Through HR" feature. Generally, predictions assume that past patterns will repeat in the future. Historical data is assessed to determine how many employees in each job category can be expected to quit or be terminated during the next year. Measures such as quit rates, average length of time in specific jobs, and rates of promotion are used. As mentioned earlier, the organization's information system can be used to determine how many individuals have skills and experiences that qualify them for promotions or lateral moves. Although this information may not be exact, it does provide a rough idea

Building Strength Through HR

WELLPOINT HEALTH NETWORKS

WellPoint Health Networks is a healthcare organization with about 37,000 employees. It has an extensive information system that helps predict when people might leave, as well as identifying current employees who might be promoted into positions that are left vacant. The information system provides a type of "depth chart" that illustrates strengths and weaknesses for each position. Leaders use the information to quickly identify people who might fill job vacancies. The information is also helpful for tracking career development and determining areas where additional training might be helpful. The use of information technology has helped the company reduce the average time positions are open from 60 to 35 days. The system has also reduced turnover and saved WellPoint around $21 million. Human resource management at

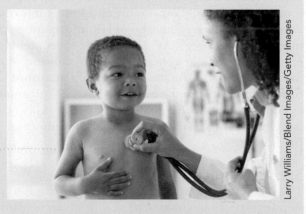

Larry Williams/Blend Images/Getty Images

WellPoint thus builds competitive strength by maintaining a database of current employee skills and abilities, looking internally to fill job openings, and predicting future job vacancies before they occur.

Source: Information from Patrick J. Kiger, "Succession Planning Keeps WellPoint Competitive," *Workforce Management* 81, no. 4 (2002): 50–54.

	Entry-Level Workers	Mid-Level Supervisors	Top-Level Managers
Predicted Future Needs[1]	700	70	14
Current employees			
Currently in position	500	50	10
Expected to quit[2]	250	15	3
Expected to move internally to other jobs[2]	16	2	0
Expected to move internally to this job[2]	0	16	2
Internally available[3]	234	49	9
External hiring need[4]	466	21	5

[1] Based on simple assumption of 40 percent growth beyond current level.
[2] Based on analysis of past trends.
[3] Number currently in position—numbers expected to quit or move out + number expected to move in.
[4] Predicted future needs—internally available.

example

Figure 5.3 Illustration of Human Resource Planning.

of where current employees are likely to move. Information about employee skills can be particularly helpful for multinational organizations. Being able to identify the skills of employees currently residing in other countries helps build consistency across organizations. In all cases, using the information to make decisions and plan for the future gives the organization a competitive edge over firms that begin to fill positions only after someone leaves a job.

Step 4. Planning External Hiring

The final step is to determine the number and types of people to be recruited externally. This is accomplished by combining the information from the first three steps. An example of a spreadsheet illustrating all steps is shown in Figure 5.3. Information from Step 2 is used to forecast the total number of employees needed in each position, and information from Steps 1 and 3 is used to determine how many of the projected positions can be filled by people already in the organization. The difference between the number needed and the number available provides an estimate of the number of new employees who will need to be recruited from outside the organization.

Of course, the information and strategies developed through the HR planning process are only estimates and are usually not totally accurate. Nevertheless, careful planning allows organizations to act strategically rather than simply react to changes. Good planning can eliminate many surprises. It can help to smooth out upward and downward trends in employee count to reduce or eliminate those instances in which an organization terminates good employees because of low need in certain areas only to realize a few months later that it has openings to fill in those same areas. It can also help organizations take advantage of opportunities to hire exceptional employees even before specific positions are open. Overall, HR planning takes a long-term perspective on hiring and develops ongoing tactics to make sure high-quality people are available to fill job vacancies.

BATCH AND FLOW APPROACHES

Human resource planning can help organizations develop consistent approaches to recruiting. Some organizations use a batch approach to recruiting, whereas others use a flow approach. A **batch approach** involves engaging in recruiting activities periodically. A **flow approach** involves sustained recruiting activities to meet the ongoing need for new employees.[26]

The flow approach views recruiting as a never-ending activity. The planning process is used to forecast employment needs. New employees are frequently added even before specific positions are open. An organization using a flow approach continually seeks top recruits and brings them onboard when they are available. This enables the organization to take advantage of opportunities as they arise and helps it to avoid being forced to hire less-desirable applicants because nobody better is available at the time.

Batch recruiting is different in that it operates in cycles. Groups of employees are recruited together. Organizations may adopt a batch approach when new employees are only available at certain times. For instance, organizations that recruit college students usually must adopt a batch approach because students are available only at the end of a semester. Organizations also adopt a batch approach when they need to train new employees in a group or when a specific work project has a clear beginning and end. For example, a biological research organization may hire people to work on specific grants. Employees are hired in a group when a new grant begins.

A flow approach to recruiting is optimal in most cases because it allows organizations to operate strategically. Employment needs can be planned in advance, and ongoing activities can reduce the time between job openings and hiring decisions. Organizations that use a batch approach to recruiting can also benefit from good planning, however. For instance, some employees hired directly from college might be enrolled in short-term training programs until specific positions are open. Accurate human resource forecasting facilitates this type of arrangement and allows the batch approach to reap many of the advantages associated with the flow approach.

CENTRALIZATION OF PROCESSES

An additional aspect of planning and recruiting is the extent to which activities are centralized. In organizations that use *centralized procedures,* the human resource department is responsible for recruiting activities. In organizations that use *decentralized procedures,* individual departments and plants make and carry out their own plans.[27]

A primary benefit of centralized procedures is cost savings. Organizations with centralized processes tend to put more effort into planning ways to recruit employees through inexpensive means. With centralization, recruiting is carried out by members of the human resource department, who don't need to learn new details about the recruiting process and labor environment each time a position opens. These professionals also develop ongoing

---

Batch approach
Recruiting activities that bring new employees into the organization in groups.

Flow approach
Recruiting activities that are ongoing and designed to constantly find new employees.

relationships with other businesses, such as newspaper advertising departments and employment agencies. On the whole, then, organizations with centralized procedures are more likely to benefit from human resource planning through forecasting of overall needs and having full-time professional recruiters on staff.

A potential problem with centralized recruiting is the distance it creates between new recruits and the people with whom they will actually work. Managers often blame the human resource department when new recruits don't become good employees. A primary advantage of decentralized procedures is thus the sense of ownership that they create. Managers and current employees involved in recruiting are more committed to helping recruits succeed when they have selected those recruits.

In practice, many organizations benefit from combining elements of centralized and decentralized procedures. Efficiency is created by using centralized resources to identify a pool of job applicants. Managers and other employees then become involved to make specific decisions. Good human resource planning provides a means of coordinating the actions of different parts of the organization. Planning also helps the various parts of the organization work cooperatively by identifying people who might be promoted or transferred across departments or plants.

CONCEPT CHECK

1. *What are the basic steps in human resource planning?*
2. *How do the batch and flow approaches to recruiting differ?*
3. *What benefits and problems are associated with centralization of employee recruiting?*

Who Searches for Jobs?

An important part of effective recruiting is understanding the needs, goals, and behaviors of people searching for jobs. In general, we can identify three types of people looking for work: people entering the workforce for the first time, people who have been in the workforce but are currently unemployed, and people who are currently employed but seeking a different job. Although these groups differ somewhat, they also have a number of things in common.

One characteristic that job seekers share is their tendency to mostly plan their activities.[28] Thus, the things people do to find a job are rather predictable and can be explained by three processes:

1. The first process, *attitude formation,* concerns feelings and emotions. People make an effort to find employment when they feel confident that they have what it takes to get a new job, when they find the search process interesting, and when others such as spouse and family members think it is a good idea.

2. Attitudes and beliefs lead people to form specific *intentions*, which represent goals and plans for future action.
3. Goals and intentions lead to actual *job search behavior*, which includes any actions aimed at finding employment. Typical job search behavior includes gathering information and visiting organizations.

People engage in job-seeking activities when they have clear goals based on their belief that doing certain things will improve their lives. Organizations can thus influence potential recruits by providing information that helps them form positive attitudes. Actions that communicate strong interest and caring are particularly beneficial. Clearly conveying the benefits of a particular job can also result in forming stronger intentions and goals. The exact nature of attitudes and goals is, however, somewhat different for different types of job seekers.

NEW WORKFORCE ENTRANTS

Most people enter the full-time workforce when they graduate from school—either high school or college. The job search activities of these new workforce entrants typically follow a sequence. The first stage in the sequence is a very intense and broad search of formal sources of information about many different opportunities. At this point, job seekers are looking at aspects such as whether openings exist, what qualifications are necessary, and how to apply. The second stage is more focused as the job seekers begin to search for explicit information about a small number of possibilities. Information in this stage often comes from informal contacts rather than through formal channels. The focus shifts from learning about job openings to finding out specific details about particular jobs. If a job seeker spends considerable time in the second stage but is unable to find a job, he or she will go back to the first stage and conduct another broad search.[29]

Take a moment to consider how knowledge of the job search sequence can guide your own current and future efforts. First, you should currently be working in the first stage and learning a lot about various opportunities, even if graduation is still a few years away. As you get closer to graduation, you will benefit from focusing your efforts and learning details about specific jobs in specific organizations. You should also develop informal channels of information such as relationships with current employees. These relationships provide insights that you cannot gain from sources such as formal recruiting advertisements and websites. As described in the "How Do We Know" feature, you will benefit in each of these stages from taking a proactive approach to finding a job.

How can knowledge about the job search sequence help organizations more effectively recruit? Since people entering the workforce search broadly in the beginning, organizations can benefit from finding ways to share positive messages that set them apart from other potential employers. The objective is to build positive impressions that influence attitudes and thereby guide future goals and actions. Normal marketing channels such as television and newspaper advertisements are helpful in this way. For instance, the Sports Authority chain of sporting goods stores has about 14,000 employees, many of whom became interested in working for them because of their positive brand image. Regular customers who have already developed a favorable view of the store can apply for jobs at in-store kiosks.[30]

How Do We Know?

WHO SUCCEEDS IN A JOB SEARCH?

College graduates are not equally successful at finding jobs. Why do some graduates get more job offers than others? Douglas Brown, Richard Cober, Kevin Kane, Paul Levy, and Jarrett Shalhoop investigated this question by obtaining information from 180 graduating university students. A few months before graduation the students provided information about their personality and their confidence concerning getting job offers. Then a few months after graduation they were asked to provide information about their job search actions and their job search success.

Students with a proactive personality—that is, a tendency to take personal initiative—had more confidence in their work abilities and thus engaged in more job search behaviors such as preparing résumés, contacting employers, and filling out applications. This led these proactive students to receive more follow-up interviews and job offers.

The Bottom Line. Graduating students who engage in more job search behaviors do indeed receive more job offers. The study authors conclude that an individual's success or failure in job searching depends a great deal on his or her level of proactivity. More proactive people succeed in obtaining more job offers.

Source: Douglas J. Brown, Richard T. Cober, Kevin Kane, Paul E. Levy, and Jarrett Shalhoop, "Proactive Personality and the Successful Job Search: A Field Investigation with College Graduates," *Journal of Applied Psychology* 91 (2006): 717–726.

Organizations can also benefit from making sure they provide methods of sharing informal information with people who have entered the second stage of the search process. In this second stage, potential employees benefit from contact with current employees, who can share information that helps potential applicants decide whether a specific job is right. This careful examination of potential fit is most critical for firms pursuing long-term relationships with employees, and so it is most appropriate for organizations using Loyal Soldier and Committed Expert HR strategies. Organizations with these strategies benefit from focusing their efforts on recruiting people who are just entering the workforce and have long careers ahead of them.

UNEMPLOYED WORKERS

Potential job recruits also include people who have previously been in the workforce but are currently unemployed. Much of the research in this area explores the negative attitudes associated with being unemployed. You can relate to the frustrations of these people if you have ever had trouble finding a job. Unemployed workers get depressed easily. They experience decreased mental and physical health, less life satisfaction, and increased marital and family problems.[31]

A consistent finding relating to job search for the unemployed is the importance of social support. People remain more optimistic, engage in more activities to find a job, and obtain better jobs when they feel strong social support from others.[32] Like other types of job seekers, unemployed people are also more successful at locating work when they take a proactive approach, set goals, and actively look for jobs.[33] Yet the strong negative emotions associated with being unemployed suggest that many potential employees become so frustrated that they stop looking for work. Organizations recruiting people from the unemployment ranks therefore benefit from actively seeking out and encouraging people who have been laid off from other jobs. Helping individuals regain a sense of self-worth and confidence can communicate interest and caring. Organizations with a Bargain Laborer HR strategy, which have a constant need for new employees who are willing to work for lower wages, may particularly benefit from recruiting unemployed people.

Another interesting development in the recruitment of unemployed workers is the movement toward internationalization. Organizations in many countries find it difficult to recruit enough workers to fill entry-level positions. For instance, hotel operators in Northern Ireland struggle to find enough people to work in jobs such as housekeeping and guest services. In fact, as many as 19 percent of jobs go unfilled in Northern Ireland hotels. Several hotels are addressing this problem by recruiting workers from other countries. Recruiting has attracted people from countries such as Poland, the Czech Republic, Latvia, and Lithuania. Although these workers are not technically unemployed in their home countries, they can find better work alternatives in Ireland. Taking an international approach to recruiting workers who are not yet employed in a particular country can thus be helpful in finding people willing to do entry-level jobs.[34]

WORKERS CURRENTLY EMPLOYED

The third group of potential job recruits includes individuals currently employed by other organizations. Some are actively seeking a change, and others are open to a move if a good opportunity arises. People who search for alternative jobs while still employed tend to be intelligent, agreeable, open to new experiences, and less prone to worry.[35] Talent Wars

Studies suggest that dissatisfaction with a current job is an important key for understanding why people accept new employment.[36] In many cases, employed workers are open to taking new jobs because they have experienced some kind of undesirable change in their current positions. In other cases, people are willing to move because they have slowly become dissatisfied over time.[37] In either situation, they are likely to move because their attitudes about their current jobs are not as positive as they would like. Changes in work conditions that create negative attitudes and make it more likely for people to leave their current jobs include an increased need to balance career and family demands, dissatisfaction with pay, and feelings that the organization is not moving in the right direction.[38]

So what can an organization do to increase its success in recruiting people who are already employed by other firms? One tactic is to direct recruiting messages to employees who have recently experienced negative changes in their work roles. Common signals of negative change at competitor organizations include announcements of decreased profitability, lower bonuses, and changes in upper management. A primary objective of recruiting in these cases is to help channel negative attitudes into a specific goal to seek a better job. The recruiting organization might help potential employees to form positive attitudes about moving to a new job and can do so by clearly communicating the fact that it will provide a superior work environment. An organization trying to recruit can also take steps to minimize the hassle of changing jobs.[39] A constant need for people with highly specialized skills makes efforts to recruit people who are currently working elsewhere particularly important to organizations with Free Agent HR strategies.

Organizations that seek to hire workers from competitors should be careful to avoid talent wars. **Talent wars** occur when competitors seek to "poach," or steal, employees from one another. An organization that believes a competitor is attempting to raid its talent might respond by working to make things better internally. Or it might instead attempt to retaliate against the competitor—for example, stealing some of the competitor's employees. Unfortunately, back-and-forth negative tactics often result in a war that is dysfunctional for both organizations. To reduce the risk of a talent war, organizations can avoid hiring batches of employees away from a competitor and making sure that employees recruited from competitors receive promotions rather than transfers to the same job.[40]

⚐ Talent wars
Negative competition in which companies attempt to hire one another's employees.

CONCEPT CHECK

1. *What are three types of job seekers, and how does each type differ from the others?*
2. *What can an organization do to attract new workforce entrants?*

LEARNING OBJECTIVE **4**

What Characteristics Make an Organization Attractive?

Of course, not all organizations are equally attractive employers. One way to think about differences in organizational attractiveness is to reflect on your choice of a school. Why did you choose to study at your current college or university? Was it because it was close to where you wanted to live? Was it because of a great academic program in an area you wanted to study? Was it because it was the least expensive alternative? Was it because you wanted to be with certain friends? Maybe it was because it provided you with a way to balance other aspects of your life, such as work and family. Or perhaps you just didn't have any other choice.

In a similar way, people choose jobs for a variety of reasons. Potential employees are often attracted to an organization because it provides a work opportunity in a place where they want to live.[41] Why people choose to work for certain organizations is, however, complicated. Factors that influence an applicant's decision about whether to continue applying vary across the job search. Perceptions of fit with the position are critical at the time of application, recruiter behavior and organizational characteristics have a strong influence in the middle of the process, and characteristics of the specific job are given the most weight in the final job choice decision.[42]

Complicating the issue is the fact that what matters to one person may not matter to others. Look around your classes. Do you believe everyone chose the university for the same reasons? It is true that some qualities were probably important to most people, such as the ability to get a good education.

Beyond that, however, different features were likely to be important to different people. Some might have based their choice on the location or on the social atmosphere. Once again, the choice of a work organization is similar. People with certain characteristics are more strongly attracted to some types of organizations than others. Obtaining enough high-quality employees is an increasingly difficult task for most organizations. This means that organizations can develop a competitive advantage by creating a place where people want to work. In order to better understand what makes organizations attractive places to work, let's first look at some of the general characteristics that people desire in their places of employment. We then further explore how certain types of people are attracted to certain types of organizations.

GENERALLY ATTRACTIVE CHARACTERISTICS

What organizations come to mind when you think about places where you will likely look for a job in the future? Job applicants often base their choices on characteristics such as familiarity, compensation, certain organizational traits, and recruiting activities.

Familiarity

Odds are pretty high that you would prefer searching for jobs in companies that are already somewhat familiar.[43] Much of this familiarity comes from corporate advertising that showcases the organizations' products and services. Familiar firms have better reputations because people tend to remember positive things about them.[44] People actively respond to recruiting efforts by companies with strong reputations. Job seekers are more likely to obtain additional information about these organizations and make formal job applications.

Familiar organizations don't benefit much from image-enhancing activities such as sponsoring events or placing advertisements that provide general information about working for them. Because people already have a generally positive image of familiar organizations, such activities are not necessary. In contrast, less well-known organizations can benefit from sponsorships, general advertising, and the like. These organizations must create positive attitudes before they can get people to take actions such as applying for positions. In short, companies with low product awareness benefit from image-enhancing activities like general advertisements and sponsorships, whereas companies with high product awareness benefit most from practices that provide specific information such as detailed job postings and discussions with actual employees.[45]

Organizations with a strong brand image thus have an overall advantage in recruiting. Their efforts to advertise their products and services provide them with a good reputation that helps them attract potential employees. They don't need to spend time and resources helping people become familiar with them. In contrast, the less well-known company needs to create an image as a generally desirable place to work.[46]

Compensation and Similar Job Features

Not surprisingly, compensation affects people's attitudes about an organization. People want to work for organizations that pay more.[47] In general, people prefer their pay to be based primarily on their own work outcomes rather than on the efforts of other people. Most people also prefer organizations that offer better and more flexible benefits.[48] Greater opportunities for advancement and higher job security are also beneficial.[49]

Organizational Traits

Organizations, like people, have certain traits that make them more desirable employers.[50] Desirable organizations have an image of sincerity, kindness, and trust and have a family-like atmosphere that demonstrates concern for employees. Walt Disney, for example, is often seen as desirable employer. Another desirable organizational trait is innovativeness. People want to work for innovative organizations because they think their work will be interesting. Many job seekers see this trait in shoe manufacturers Nike and Reebok. Competence is also a desirable trait. People want to work for an organization that is successful. Microsoft, for example, is widely seen as highly competent. Organizations are better able to recruit when they are seen as trustworthy and friendly, as innovative, and as successful.[51]

Recruiting Activities

What an organization does during the recruiting process also matters. Particularly helpful is obtaining endorsements from people that job recruits trust. For instance, organizations are most successful recruiting on college campuses when faculty and alumni recommend them as good places to work.[52] The interpersonal skill of recruiters also influences attitudes about an organization. Recruits enjoy the process more and are more likely to accept job offers when recruiters develop positive interactions with them.[53] In contrast, as discussed in the "How Do We Know?" feature, long delays tend to decrease organizational attractiveness. Recruits, particularly those who are most qualified, develop an unfavorable impression when organizations take

How Do We Know?

ARE EARLY JOB OFFERS BETTER?

Does it really matter how long after the job interview the organization makes a job offer? This question was examined in a study by William Becker, Terry Connolly, and Jerel Slaughter, who collected data from 3,012 job candidates at a Fortune 500 engineering technology firm. They tracked the time between final interviews and the company's formal offer of a job, as well as the number of days it took the candidate to respond to the offer. They also collected data about subsequent performance for those candidates who joined the company.

The average time for the company to offer positions to applicants was 23 days for students and 15 days for experienced candidates. On average, students took 21 days to respond, whereas experienced candidates took only 3 days. Quicker offers were more likely to be accepted by both students and experienced employees. Speed of the offer

was not clearly associated with speed of candidate responses. There was also no evidence that speed of the offer had an impact on subsequent job performance or leaving the organization after being hired.

The Bottom Line. Job candidates are more likely to accept a job offer when it comes soon after the final interview. Individuals who receive speedy job offers are not more likely to leave once hired, and their performance is the same as people who take longer to receive an offer. The authors conclude that an organization can benefit from extending early offers to job candidates whom they want to hire.

Source: William J. Becker, Terry Connolly, and Jerel E. Slaughter, "The Effect of Job Offer Timing on Offer Acceptance, Performance, and Turnover," *Personnel Psychology* 63 (2010): 223–241.

Table 5.1	*Factors That Influence Job Recruits*
Positive	**Negative**
Meeting with high-ranking leaders	Disorganized interviewers
Meeting with people actually in the position	Rude, condescending, and uninterested interviewers
Meeting with people similar to themselves	Unorganized meeting schedules and arrangements
Flexibility in accommodating scheduling needs	Being required to pay travel expenses in advance
Impressive hotel and dinner arrangements	Cheap hotels and meals
Frequent contact	Lack of prompt follow-up

Source: Information from Wendy R. Boswell, Mark V. Roehling, Marcie A. LePine, and Lisa M. Moynihan, "Individual Job-Choice Decisions and the Impact of Job Attributes and Recruitment Practices: A Longitudinal Field Study," *Human Resource Management* 42 (2003): 23–37.

a long time to make decisions and fail to keep them informed about what is happening.[54] In short, organizations are constantly making an impression on recruits as they carry out the recruiting process. Table 5.1 lists factors that influence job recruits.[55]

FIT BETWEEN PEOPLE AND ORGANIZATIONS

The world would be a boring place if everyone wanted to work for the same type of organization. A number of studies suggest that people with different characteristics are likely to be attracted to different types of organizations. One example concerns the organization's size. Some job seekers prefer to work for large firms, while others prefer small firms.[56] Another example relates to money. Even though people generally want to work for organizations that pay well, some people care more about money than others. In particular, people who describe themselves as having a strong desire for material goods are attracted to organizations with high pay.[57] People who have a high need for achievement prefer organizations where pay is based on performance.[58] Individuals who have high confidence in their own abilities also prefer to work in organizations that base rewards on individual rather than group performance.[59]

Some differences have been found between men and women. Men are more likely to be attracted to organizations described as innovative and decisive, whereas women tend to prefer organizations that are detail-oriented.[60] People also like organizations whose characteristics are similar to their own personality traits. For instance, conscientious people seek to work in organizations that are outcome oriented, and agreeable people like organizations that are supportive and team-oriented. Individuals characterized by openness to experience prefer organizations that are innovative.[61] The same desire for similarity is found in the realm of values. People who place a great deal of value on fairness seek out organizations that are seen as fair, people who have a high concern for others want to work for organizations that show concern, and people who value high achievement prefer a place with an air of success.[62] The bottom line is that people feel they better fit in organizations whose characteristics and values are similar to their own. During the process of recruiting, potential employees also develop more positive perceptions of organizations whose recruiters appear similar to them.[63]

CONCEPT CHECK

1. *What characteristics make some organizations more attractive workplaces than others?*
2. *What are some ways that organizations differ, and what type of person prefers which type of organization?*

LEARNING OBJECTIVE **5**

What Are Common Recruiting Sources?

Organizations use a variety of sources to find job applicants. Sources such as referrals from current employees are relatively informal, whereas sources such as professional recruiters are more formal. In this section, we consider the use of job posting, employee referrals, print advertising, electronic recruiting, employment agencies, and campus recruiting. Each method has its strengths and weaknesses, and certain methods also align better with particular HR strategies.

JOB POSTING

Recruiting people who already work for the organization is relatively easy. Internal recruiting is normally done through **job posting,** which uses company communication channels to share information about job vacancies with current employees. Historically, posting has used such tools as bulletin boards and announcements in meetings; today, most modern organizations use some form of electronic communication, such as websites and email messages. An effective job posting clearly describes both the nature of the duties associated with the position and the necessary qualifications.

    As you would expect, job posting is most appropriate for organizations adopting internal recruiting strategies. When the strategy is a Loyal Soldier HR strategy, job postings should be shared with a large number of people to facilitate movement among a variety of positions. For a Committed Expert HR strategy, the posting should be targeted specifically to those who have the expertise needed to move into relatively specialized roles.

Job posting
Using company communication channels to communicate job vacancies.

move within organization

EMPLOYEE REFERRALS

Employee referrals occur when current employees get their friends and acquaintances to apply for positions. Almost all organizations and job seekers rely on referrals to some extent. In many organizations, up to one third of new employees come through the referral process.[64] A majority of human resource professionals also believe that employee referrals are the most effective method of recruiting.[65] Referrals are thought to have at least four primary strengths: (1) Referrals represent a relatively inexpensive method of recruiting, (2) they are quicker than many other forms of recruiting, (3) people hired through referrals tend to become better employees who are less likely to leave the organization, and (4) current employees become more committed to the organization when they successfully refer someone.[66]

The first benefit, low cost, is sometimes questioned because organizations often pay bonuses to employees who make successful referrals. As described for Google, a typical bonus ranges from $1,000 to $2,000. This amount is, however, usually less than the cost of other recruiting methods, such as advertising and using recruitment agencies.[67] Current employees are also in continuous contact with friends and acquaintances, which eliminates much of the time needed to plan and develop more formal recruiting processes. They also are in a better position to identify people who are ready to make job changes.

The informal nature of the referral process also makes it an effective method for identifying the best candidates. Current employees generally have accurate first-hand knowledge of the potential applicant's skills and motivation. This information can improve hiring decisions. Feelings of responsibility make it likely that employees will only refer people they are confident will succeed; they don't of course want to refer someone who will make them look bad. The informal information that employees share with the people whom they are referring can also serve as a realistic job preview, which helps reduce employee turnover.[68]

A study of call-center employees illustrates the benefits of finding employees through referrals. Highly successful call centers found 21 percent of their employees through referrals, whereas less-successful centers found only 4 percent of employees through this method.[69] In addition, call centers that found more new employees through referrals had lower turnover.

As mentioned earlier, providing a referral also strengthens an employee's commitment to the organization. Some of this increased commitment derives from the current employee's feeling that his or her input is valued. The feeling of being appreciated is strengthened when a reward is offered for helping the organization.[70] Employees also find it more difficult to say and believe bad things about the organization after they have convinced a friend to join them.[71]

Referrals are effective for organizations pursuing any HR strategy. For organizations pursuing a Bargain Laborer HR strategy, referrals help the organization inexpensively identify job candidates. Referrals help decrease turnover for organizations with either a Loyal Soldier or Committed Expert HR strategy. They can also be an effective part of a Free Agent HR strategy, because professional employees often have strong networks of acquaintances who have rare but needed skills. Table 5.2 lists ways to make employee

Table 5.2	*How to Increase Employee Referrals*
Publicize success	Use luncheons, meetings, and email messages to recognize referrals
Provide rewards	Publicly use T-shirts, coffee mugs, etc., to reward employees giving referrals
Use bonuses	The average bonus for a referral is around $1,000—up to $10,000 for top jobs
Make it fun	Use eye-catching flyers and email messages to increase excitement
Make it easy	Provide job vacancy information that can be forwarded easily; minimize rules
Build momentum	Pay bonuses quickly, use motivational posters, have an annual recruiting day

Source: Information from Michelle Neely Martinez, "The Headhunter Within: Turn Your Employees into Recruiters with a High-Impact Referral Program," *HR Magazine* 46, no. 8 (2001): 48–55; Carroll Lachnit, "Employee Referral Saves Time, Saves Money, Delivers Quality," *Workforce* 80, no. 6 (2001): 66–72.

referral programs more effective.[72] Other keys to success include keeping things simple and communicating continuously.

PRINT ADVERTISING

Employment advertisements have historically been a major part of almost all newspapers. Newspaper advertising has the potential to reach a large number of people for a relatively low cost, making it potentially desirable for the Bargain Laborer HR strategy. General advertising in newspapers can also help build a positive reputation for the organization as a desirable place to work.[73] Employment advertising in newspapers has, however, become less frequent as more people gain their information from online sources, and human resource professionals predict that use of newspaper advertising will decrease by as much as 40 percent in the near future.[74]

Focused recruiting messages can also be placed in more specialized publications. For instance, openings in technical fields such as engineering can be advertised in trade journals. This more focused approach helps reduce the costs associated with sending recruiting messages to people who are obviously unsuitable for the job. Advertising in specialized journals is potentially most helpful for organizations that pursue a Free Agent HR strategy.

ELECTRONIC ADVERTISING

Electronic advertising uses modern technology, particularly the Internet, to send recruiting messages. Although electronic communication is seen by applicants as somewhat less informative than face-to-face contact,[75] organizations are rapidly increasing its use. Popular websites, such as Monster.com and Careerbuilder.com, include thousands of job postings that can be sorted in a variety of ways. Website visitors can look for jobs in certain geographic areas, for example, or can search for specific types of jobs regardless of location. Job seekers can post their résumés online. These websites also provide a number of helpful services, such as guidance in building a good résumé.

Company websites are yet another avenue for electronic advertising. Almost all large companies have a career website. Using the company website to recruit employees is relatively inexpensive and can be carefully controlled to provide information that conveys a clear recruiting message. Effective messaging occurs when organizations include racially diverse examples in their recruiting messages, which has been shown to be especially helpful for increasing minority perceptions of organizational attraction.[76]

Of course, not all websites are equally effective. Some are very basic and provide only a list of job openings. More advanced websites include search engines for locating particular types of jobs, as well as services that send email messages notifying users when certain types of jobs appear. An analysis of career websites for Fortune 100 companies found that most support online submission of résumés. A majority of sites also provides information about the work environment, benefits, and employee diversity.[77]

Decreased cost is the most frequently identified benefit of electronic recruiting. Electronic advertising is also much faster than most other forms of recruiting. Job announcements can be posted almost immediately on many sites, and information can be changed and updated easily. Another potential advantage of electronic advertising is the identification of better job candidates. Many organizations report that the applicants they find through online

Electronic advertising
Using electronic forms of communication such as the Internet and email to recruit new employees.

sources are better than the applicants they find through newspaper advertising. Responding through electronic means almost guarantees some level of familiarity with modern technology. In particular, applicants for midlevel positions seem to favor online resources over newspapers.[78]

Perhaps the biggest problem associated with electronic advertising is its tendency to yield a large number of applicants who are not qualified for the advertised jobs. Clicking a button on a computer screen and submitting an online résumé is such an easy process that people may do it even when they know they are not qualified for the job. In fact, one survey found that less than 20 percent of online applicants meet minimum qualifications. A potential solution is to use software that evaluates and eliminates résumés that do not include certain words clearly suggesting a fit with the job.[79] This computer screening could, however, eliminate some applicants who might actually be able to do the job. Another recently advocated strategy is thus to customize recruiting by providing applicants clear information about their potential fit with a specific job. Applicants who learn through electronic communication that their characteristics don't fit a job or organization are less likely to waste time and effort by applying, suggesting that interactive technology may be a key to decreasing the number of unqualified applicants.[80] In particular, websites that combine customization with nice-looking features (color, font size, spacing) are effective at screening out weak applicants.[81] Table 5.3 lists tips for increasing the effectiveness of online recruiting.[82]

In the end, electronic recruiting can be effective for organizations pursuing any HR strategy. Targeted recruiting strategies should provide clear descriptions of job qualifications and should be placed on sites visited primarily by people likely to have the needed skills and abilities. Broad recruiting strategies should cast a wider net and can benefit from the large number of people who visit commercial recruiting sites. As shown in the "Technology in HR" feature, companies can also use electronic communication to stay in touch with recruits.

EMPLOYMENT AGENCIES

Public employment agency
Government-sponsored agency that helps people find jobs.

Each state in the United States, has a **public employment agency**, which is a government bureau that helps match job seekers with employers. These agencies have local offices that normally post information about local job vacancies on bulletin boards and provide testing and other services to help people

Table 5.3	*Effective Online Recruiting*	
Post Information in Multiple Places	Job seekers visit different Internet sites; Target likely applicants
Create an Exciting Job Description	Tell an interesting story; Sell the company but be realistic about positives and negatives
Use Cascading Links to More Information	Keep the design simple; Provide easy access to additional information
Communicate Key Reasons Employees Stay	Focus on company culture; Identify things that make current employees happy
Ensure Data Security	Only obtain necessary information; Prevent spyware and malicious links

Sources: Information from V. Michael Prencipe, "Online Recruiting Simplified," *Sales and Marketing Management* 160, no. 4 (2008): 15–16; Rita Zeidner, "Making Online Recruiting More Secure," *HR Magazine* 52, no. 12 (2007): 75–77; Anonymous, "Ideas for Improving Your Corporate Web Recruiting Site," *HR Focus* 83, no. 5 (2006): 9.

learn about their strengths and weaknesses, as well as different careers that might fit their interests. Many offices help employers screen job applicants. State agencies also maintain websites for electronic recruiting. Links to the various state job banks can be found at CareerOneStop (careeronestop.org), which is sponsored by the U.S. Department of Labor and also offers career exploration information.

Many state employment agencies seek to help people transition from unemployment. They also focus on helping young people move from high school into the workforce. These agencies are therefore particularly helpful for recruiting employees into entry-level positions. Almost all services of public employment agencies are free to both organizations and job seekers. Since

Technology in HR

STAYING IN TOUCH WITH RECRUITS

Electronic forms of communication, such as email messaging, can sometimes cause problems because people get so many messages that they are unable to keep track of them all. But email messaging can also be critical in helping organizations to effectively recruit job applicants. In particular, this relatively quick and easy method of communicating can help organizations keep in touch with individuals they are recruiting.

One company that uses email messages during recruiting is Shell Oil, an international energy company that produces oil and natural gas. The Shell Group is a global employer of more than 90,000 people, with about 24,000 employees in the United States. Human resource management at Shell Oil sends the Shell Careers Newsletter via email to subscribers who might be interested in working for the company. Message content includes information about job market trends and customized content for fields such as marketing and engineering. A major objective of the newsletter is to build emotional connections and relationships with potential future employees. The newsletter costs Shell only about $12,000 a year. Tracking reports suggest that 60 to 70 percent of the people who receive the newsletter open it.

Another organization that benefits from electronic communication is the New York City Police Department (NYPD), which uses email communication to reduce dropouts among people applying to

© viewpress/Demotix/Corbis

take the police exam. Messages are designed to sustain interest by providing career information and linking readers to the NYPD website. One emphasis is on salary and benefits. Email messages cost only about 7 cents each, making them an inexpensive method for communicating with people interested in working for the NYPD. Visits to the NYPD website are up 74 percent since the email program began, and the dropout rate for the police exam is lower.

Technology is helping these two organizations build competitive strength by proactively using ongoing communication to build relationships with people who have shown interest in working for them. These methods are generally more cost effective than alternative channels of communication.

Source: Information from *Workforce Management Online,* May 2005.

most people who seek employment through public agencies do not have specialized education and skills, these agencies are most helpful for companies engaged in broad skill recruiting.

Private employment agency
A business that exists for the purpose of helping organizations find workers.

A **private employment agency** is a professional recruiting firm that helps organizations identify recruits for specific job positions in return for a fee. Kelly Services, for example, provides placement services for approximately 560,000 people annually in areas including office services, accounting, engineering, information technology, law, science, marketing, light industrial, education, healthcare, and home care.[83] Another private agency is Korn/Ferry, which specializes in recruiting top-level executives. Such firms are sometimes referred to as *headhunters*, because they normally target specific individuals who are employed at other organizations.

Private recruiting firms provide direct help to organizations by identifying and screening potential employees for particular positions. They also serve as temporary staffing agencies by maintaining a group of workers who can quickly fill short-term positions in client organizations. In many cases, these temporary workers are eventually hired as full-time employees. The temporary staffing assignment works as a tryout for the job, which helps eliminate costs associated with hiring workers who then perform poorly.

Private employment agencies are frequently able to recruit people who are not actively seeking new positions. Executive recruiters, in particular, are known for their efforts to develop and maintain broad networks of people who are not actively seeking new jobs but who might be willing to move for the right opportunity. In addition, private agencies target people who have the specific skills for the job. Client organizations are presented with a short list of high-quality applicants, which makes the search process more efficient for them. Another advantage of using private agencies is the ability to remain anonymous. The name of the hiring firm is often not disclosed during early stages of recruiting. Such anonymity can be helpful if a high-profile employee's intention to leave has not been publicly announced or if the organization does not want competitors to know its staffing needs.

Because of their targeted approach, private employment agencies can be particularly helpful for organizations pursuing a Free Agent HR strategy. These firms require specific skills that are often rare and in high demand. In these circumstances, qualified applicants are most likely already employed.

A disadvantage of private employment agencies is cost. Most executive recruiters work on a contingency basis; that is, they are only paid when they find someone who accepts the position. The recruiting fee is usually based on the salary that will be paid to the new employee. Typical fees amount to more than 30 percent of the first year's salary; the normal fee for finding an executive is thus at least $50,000.

Because of the expense associated with private employment agencies, most organizations develop written contracts that carefully describe the relationship between the agency and the client firm. A good contract should cover a number of issues, such as a guarantee of confidentiality and amount of fees. The contract should also include an *off-limits statement*, which formalizes an agreement that the agency will not try to recruit the new employee for another organization within a specified amount of time (usually at least a year). Most contracts also contain clauses that clarify that the fee is paid only if the individual stays with the new organization for a minimum period of time.[84]

CAMPUS RECRUITING

The pharmaceutical firm Eli Lilly recruits many of its employees as they graduate from universities. In order to focus its efforts, Lilly targets specific universities for hiring in specific functional areas. A university that is particularly strong in accounting might thus be targeted only for accounting recruits. A different university might be a target only for human resource recruits. Focusing on a few key schools allows Lilly to build relationships that provide important advantages for obtaining the best possible employees. In many cases, Lilly also offers promising students summer internships.[85]

Campus recruiting usually involves a number of activities. Organizations that recruit successfully work hard to build a strong reputation among students, faculty, and alumni. Relationships are built through activities such as giving talks to student organizations and participating in job fairs. Although studies question the benefits, campus recruiting often includes hosting receptions that provide an informal setting where information about the organization can be shared. Managers and current employees attend these events and network with students.[86]

The most widely recognized aspect of campus recruiting is job posting and interviewing. Employers use campus career centers to advertise specific job openings. At the centers, students provide résumés and apply for jobs that interest them. Firms identify students who best match their needs and arrange on-campus interviews. Full-time recruiters and line managers (often alumni) then spend a day or two on campus conducting preliminary interviews. Students who are evaluated positively during the on-campus interview are usually invited to a second interview, which takes place at the organization's offices.

Internships also represent a major component of most campus recruiting programs, giving students an opportunity to gain important work experience while they are enrolled in school. Students who have been interns take less time to find a first position, receive higher pay, and generally have greater job satisfaction.[87] Internships also help organizations develop relationships with potential recruits. Working over a number of months provides a realistic preview of the job, which helps both the individual and the organization to determine whether there is a good fit.

Campus recruiting is well suited for organizations pursuing a Committed Expert HR strategy. These organizations adopt a targeted approach to recruiting that helps them identify people with the skills necessary to perform specialized tasks, such as engineering and accounting. Campus recruiting also helps them meet their strategic objective of identifying people who are just beginning their careers. While campus recruiting can be expensive, cost is not a serious problem for organizations that are seeking to identify people who will spend long careers working for them.

> **(?) CONCEPT CHECK**
> 1. *What are different sources that organizations can use to find job applicants?*
> 2. *What are some advantages and disadvantages of using electronic communication to recruit employees?*

How Is Recruiting Effectiveness Determined?

Some organizations are better at attracting excellent job candidates than their competitors are. These organizations use recruiting as a tool for ensuring that they have the best possible employees, which in turn improves their bottom-line profitability.[88] Effective recruiting is thus an essential part of good human resource management. Unfortunately, many organizations do not measure and track how well they are doing with regard to recruiting. These organizations are at a strategic disadvantage because they do not use readily available information to help them learn about areas where they can improve.

COMMON MEASURES

Cost measures
Methods of assessing recruiting effectiveness that focus on expenses incurred.

Time measures
Methods of assessing recruiting effectiveness that focus on the length of time it takes to fill positions.

Quantity measures
Methods of assessing recruiting effectiveness that focus on the number of applicants and hires found by each source.

Quality measures
Methods of assessing recruiting effectiveness that focus on the extent to which sources provide applicants who are actually qualified for jobs.

Cost per hire
The measure of recruiting effectiveness that determines the expense incurred to find each person who is eventually hired.

Common measures of recruiting effectiveness include assessments of cost, time, quantity, and quality.[89] **Cost measures** include the money paid for advertising, agency fees, and referral bonuses, and should also include travel expenses for both recruiters and recruits, as well as salary costs for people who spend time and effort on recruiting activities. Failure to include the salary expenses of both full-time recruiters and managers who spend time doing recruiting often leads to substantial underestimates of true cost.

Time measures assess the length of the period between the time recruiting begins and the time the new employee is in the position. Estimates suggest that the average time to fill a position is 52 days.[90] During this period, the position is often open, and important tasks are not being done. In many cases, the performance of other employees also suffers because they spend time on activities that the new employee would perform if the position were filled. These factors suggest that an important objective of recruiting is to fill positions as quickly as possible.

Quantity measures focus on the number of applicants or hires generated through various recruiting activities. Common measures include number of inquiries generated, number of job applicants, and number of job acceptances. These are measures of efficiency, and they provide information about the reach of recruiting practices. Recruiting is generally seen as more effective when it reaches a lot of potential applicants.

Quality measures concern the extent to which recruiting activities locate and gain the interest of people who are actually capable of performing the job. In most cases, measuring quality is more important than measuring quantity. Typical measures include assessments of how many applicants are qualified for the job, as well as measures of turnover and performance of the people hired.

The most frequently used measures of recruiting success combine assessments of cost and quantity. One measure is **cost per hire**, which is calculated by dividing the total cost of a particular search by the number of hires it provides. For instance, in one cost-per-hire analysis, Valero Energy Corporation found the cost for candidates from niche-focused Internet sources to be $1,100, from major job boards $1,600, and from employment agencies nearly $22,000. These figures helped the company shift some of its recruiting resources and reduce overall cost-per-hire amounts by 60 percent.[91]

Yet another measure is **cost per applicant**, which is calculated by dividing the cost of a recruiting method, such as a newspaper advertisement, by the number of people who respond. These measures allow organizational leaders to assess the relative value of different methods. For instance, cost-per-applicant analyses may show that placing an advertisement in the local newspaper is more cost effective than placing an ad in a specialized trade journal.

Since cost per hire and cost per applicant are based in part on quantity, they, too, are efficiency measures, which do not include assessments of quality. Cost per applicant, for instance, does not tell the organization how many applicants were qualified for the position. Of course, it does little good to receive a lot of applications from people who are not qualified. More advanced methods of evaluation incorporate assessments of quality.

In assessing quality, it is helpful to provide scores of acceptability for each applicant at various points during the recruiting process.[92] For instance, an initial analysis might compare the cost of an Internet advertisement with the number of applicants considered worthy of an interview. Subsequent measures might look at the proportion of interviewees who were offered a job or the proportion who accepted a job that was offered. Such quality measures do a better job of determining whether the right kinds of people are being identified through recruiting.

Cost per applicant
The measure of recruiting effectiveness that assesses how much it costs to entice each person to submit an application for employment.

DIFFERENCES AMONG RECRUITING SOURCES

Over the years, researchers have tried to determine whether some methods of recruiting are generally better than others. Common questions concern the relative value of different methods: Is the Internet a better method than the employment agency? Do employees found through campus recruiting stay with an organization longer than those found through newspaper advertisements? Do people identified through referrals have higher job performance than people who apply through a company website?

One reason some methods are considered to be better than others is that different methods attract different people. People who respond to an employment agency, for example, may have different skills and attributes from people who read the employment section of the local newspaper. In addition, some methods may provide better information about the job and organization. Hearing a friend describe a job may provide more accurate information than reading about that same job on an Internet site. On the whole, research does not support the idea that methods other than referrals are superior to others. A number of studies have concluded that there are not consistent differences in job performance for people identified through different sources.[93] Each method, of course, has its own potential strengths and weaknesses, and each is more appropriate in some situations than in others.

Recruiting practices are most successful when they are aligned with the organization's HR strategy. The goal of an organization pursuing a Bargain Laborer HR strategy is to identify a large number of job candidates. An organization using a Loyal Soldier HR strategy seeks to recruit people who will fit the organization's culture and will stay for a long time. An organization using a Committed Expert HR strategy also wants to recruit people who will stay over time, but this organization needs people with specialized skills. Finally, an organization pursuing a Free Agent HR strategy seeks employees who have specialized skills but is not especially concerned with how long these employees stay with the organization. Each of these organizations should pursue the recruiting practices that will best meet its needs.

CONCEPT CHECK

1. *How can an organization assess the effectiveness of recruiting sources?*
2. *Why might using the least expensive recruiting sources actually cost an organization money?*

A MANAGER'S PERSPECTIVE REVISITED

IN THE MANAGER'S PERSPECTIVE THAT OPENED THIS CHAPTER, SANJIV WAS ASSIGNED TO BE A MEMBER OF A TEAM CHARGED WITH IMPROVING RECRUITING PRACTICES AT THE CONSUMER PRODUCTS COMPANY WHERE HE WORKS. FOLLOWING ARE ANSWERS TO THE "WHAT DO YOU THINK?" QUIZ AT THE END OF THE MANAGER'S PERSPECTIVE. WERE YOU ABLE TO CORRECTLY IDENTIFY THE TRUE STATEMENTS? CAN YOU DO BETTER NOW?

1. Effective organizations do all they can to get as many people as possible to apply for jobs. FALSE. *Organizations with targeted recruiting strategies generally do not wish to attract a large number of applications.*
2. Organizations should be careful to communicate only positive things to job applicants. FALSE. *Employees who receive realistic job information are more likely to remain with the organization once they are hired.*
3. A company should develop strong relationships with professors at universities where it recruits. TRUE. *An important element of recruiting new workforce entrants is to develop relationships with people who provide advice to job seekers.*
4. One way of attracting more job applicants is to pay high wages. TRUE. *Organizations that pay higher*

wages are more attractive to job seekers.

5. Job applicants referred by current employees seldom work out because employees often refer friends who don't have good work skills. FALSE. *Employee referrals are a high-quality source of recruits. Employees feel personal responsibility and usually only refer people they know will be successful.*

BijoyVerghese/iStockphoto

Sanjiv's thoughts about what attracted him to the consumer goods company were an important step in identifying effective methods for recruiting. Identifying the things that are important to desirable workers can help an organization become an employer of choice. Sanjiv also wondered about different recruiting sources that might be most effective. Finding recruiting sources that are inexpensive yet locate desirable candidates can help an organization achieve a competitive advantage. The principles of recruiting discussed in this chapter can aid in this process.

SUMMARY

LEARNING OBJECTIVE 1

How is employee recruiting strategic?

Employee recruiting practices are most effective when they align with overall HR strategy. In the area of skill scope, a targeted approach seeks to recruit people with specialized skills and abilities. Targeted scope recruiting focuses on communicating with a select group of people and is appropriate when the number of people who can successfully perform the job is limited. In contrast, broad scope recruiting seeks a large number of potential job applicants. Many people have the characteristics necessary to perform the job, and the goal is to cast a wide net and develop a large pool of applicants. Targeted recruiting fits with differentiation strategies (Committed Expert, Free Agent), whereas broad recruiting aligns with cost strategies (Loyal Soldier, Bargain Laborer).

Another strategic element of recruiting is source. Internal recruiting is helpful when the organization seeks to form long-term relationships with employees. People are promoted from within, and existing employees are moved to fill vacancies. External recruiting is necessary when the organization does not have long-term employment relationships. Internal recruiting fits with an internal HR strategy (Loyal Soldier, Committed Expert), and external recruiting fits with an external HR strategy (Bargain Laborer, Free Agent).

Recruiting can also vary in terms of the message sent to potential employees. A realistic approach shares both positive and negative information about the organization and job. An idealistic approach shares only positive information. Realistic messages help employees develop accurate expectations and thereby reduce employee turnover. The realistic approach is most appropriate when an organization seeks to retain employees for extended periods of time, making it most suitable for obtaining new hires in firms with an internal HR strategy.

LEARNING OBJECTIVE 2

How does human resource planning facilitate recruiting?

Human resource planning is the process of forecasting future employment needs. The planning process involves four steps: assessing current employment levels, predicting future needs, predicting employee movement, and planning external hiring. Effective planning can help organizations become more proactive and ensure that high-quality people are available to fill job vacancies. Planning is helpful whether organizations adopt a batch approach to recruiting or a flow approach. Planning provides information that makes flow processes more strategic and makes batch processes more like flow processes. Effective planning can also help organizations strike an effective balance concerning centralization of recruiting procedures.

LEARNING OBJECTIVE 3

Who searches for jobs?

The behavior of people searching for jobs is mostly planned and can be explained in terms of attitudes, intentions, and behaviors. Organizations can influence job seekers by creating positive attitudes and intentions. The three primary types of job seeker are new workforce entrant, unemployed worker, and currently employed worker. The job search behavior of new workforce entrants follows a sequence: first a broad search using formal sources, then a focused search seeking information about specific jobs, and finally a return to a broad search if a position is not found. Unemployed workers struggle with negative emotions. Their behavior can be influenced by actions that help them regain self-esteem and confidence. Currently employed workers are most likely to accept an offer for a new job when they feel a sense of dissatisfaction with their current jobs.

LEARNING OBJECTIVE 4

What characteristics make an organization attractive?

In general, job seekers prefer organizations that are familiar to them. Organizations that are unfamiliar can benefit from general advertising that shows them as desirable places to work. People also prefer to work for organizations that pay more, have better benefits, and offer greater opportunity for advancement. In addition, organizations are more attractive if they are seen as trustworthy and friendly, innovative, and successful. More specifically, recruits are attracted to organizations that have traits and values similar to their personal traits and values.

LEARNING OBJECTIVE 5

What are common recruiting sources?

Job posting, which uses company communication channels to share information about job vacancies, is the primary form of internal recruiting. Employee referrals are a particularly valuable recruiting source and occur when current employees get friends and acquaintances to apply. Print advertising uses newspapers and trade magazines to solicit recruits. Print advertising has historically been widely used but is currently being replaced by electronic advertising, which includes both popular commercial job sites and company websites. Websites are most effective when they include information about the work environment, benefits, and company diversity. Public employment agencies provide free resources that match job seekers and employers. Private employment agencies are professional recruiters with extensive networks that help identify job candidates with specific skills. Campus recruiting involves working with colleges and universities to recruit graduating students.

LEARNING OBJECTIVE 6

How is recruiting effectiveness determined?

Common measures of recruiting effectiveness focus on cost, time, quantity, and quality. Recruiting practices are best when they reach a large number of recruits at a low cost and when they quickly fill positions with high-quality employees. In general, research evidence has not found some recruiting sources to be better than others. Recruiting practices and sources are most effective when they are aligned with overall HR strategy. The Bargain Laborer HR strategy seeks a large pool of applicants, the Loyal Soldier and Committed Expert HR strategies seek employees likely to remain with the organization for long periods of time, and the Free Agent HR strategy seeks employees who already have specialized skills.

KEY TERMS

Batch approach   174
Broad skill scope   165
Contingent workers   167
Cost measures   190
Cost per applicant   191
Cost per hire   190
Electronic advertising   185
Employee recruiting   162
External sourcing   167
Flow approach   174
Human resource planning   170
Idealistic messaging   168
Independent contractors   167

Internal sourcing   166
Job posting   183
Private employment agency   188
Public employment agency   186
Quality measures   190
Quantity measures   190
Realistic job previews   168
Realistic messaging   168
Talent wars   179
Targeted skill scope   165
Temporary workers   167
Time measures   190

DISCUSSION QUESTIONS

1. Why do organizations with differentiation strategies benefit from targeted recruiting approaches?
2. What makes people react positively when organizations share negative information during the recruiting process?
3. What can organizations do to improve their human resource planning process? What types of information improve forecasts?
4. What are some primary differences between new workforce entrants, unemployed workers, and currently employed workers? How can organizations best recruit these different types of job seekers?
5. What characteristics make an organization attractive to you? List some specific companies that you think have those characteristics. What factors have influenced your perceptions about these companies?
6. Why are employee referrals a good recruiting source? What might keep you from referring friends and acquaintances for a position at an organization where you work?
7. What features increase the attractiveness of company websites?
8. For what positions might a company want to recruit through private employment agencies? Why are the services of a private agency worth their high cost for these positions?
9. Which companies do a good job of recruiting students from your college or university? List some of their recruiting activities on your campus.
10. What are some recruiting sources and practices that might be seen as effective in terms of quantity but not in terms of quality?

EXAMPLE CASE   *MITRE*

The MITRE Corporation, founded in 1958, is one of eleven nonprofit U.S. corporations that manage Federally Funded Research and Development Centers (FFRDCs) for the government. Of our workforce of nearly 6,000 employees, most are in our two principal locations in Bedford, Massachusetts, and McLean, Virginia, and the rest at remote sites in the United States and around the world. MITRE's mission is to assist the federal government with scientific research and analysis, development and acquisition, and systems engineering and integration.

MITRE's excellent reputation in operating its FFRDCs is very attractive to many mid- and late-career people, who view our employees as respected subject matter experts. Older engineers and scientists appreciate the kind and quality of work done at MITRE and how it affects at an early stage the high-level decisions made at the government agencies we support. Of the more than 500 new hires who join MITRE annually, nearly half (48 percent) are 40 years of age or older. Drawn heavily from industry, they are seasoned experts with knowledge of the latest technical developments, which enables MITRE to blend long-term domain knowledge and maturity with continuously updated expertise to benefit our sponsors.

In the past, MITRE depended heavily on advertising and employment agencies for the majority of our hires. As those methods became increasingly expensive, MITRE asked employees to become more actively involved in the identification and attraction of appropriately qualified new workers. MITRE employees are motivated to refer high-quality people like themselves because of their desire to fulfill our sponsors' mission expectations and to work in collaboration with other equally talented individuals. In this case it is true that "birds of a feather flock together." To further motivate such referrals, we implemented a referral program that pays employees a bonus of $2,000 for technical staff hires, $1,000 for nontechnical staff hires, and $500 for non-exempt hires. Employee referrals now provide more than half our new hires and assure us of high-quality candidates who are likely to be a good fit with MITRE's culture.

Additionally, our data show that employee referrals significantly lower recruiting costs. In 2001, when 34 percent of new hires were through employee referrals, the average cost for all hires was about $14,200, which included agency and advertising fees, labor costs, relocation and interview expenses, and employee referral bonuses. In 2004, employee referrals accounted for 52 percent for our hires, and our cost per hire had decreased by nearly 40 percent to $8,700.

We use other methods as well to encourage employees to refer suitable candidates:

- We actively and frequently communicate our most urgent recruiting needs to employees by distributing "Hot Jobs" fliers throughout the corporation and posting hiring notices on the company's intranet.
- Staff members attending conferences are encouraged to collect business cards of people who they think would be good team members.
- Potential candidates are also attracted to MITRE when they attend technical symposia or technology transfer meetings on MITRE property. They talk with an engaged cadre of MITRE attendees who are more than happy to respond to questions and inquiries.
- Employees can hand out networking, or "handshake," cards to people who express an interest in MITRE so that they can nominate themselves in the future for a position with us.
- We bring our HR business partners into organizational meetings to alert our technical staff members about the importance of constantly being on the lookout for other subject matter experts.

We attribute the cost effectiveness of our process to several factors, including the following:

- More than two thirds (roughly 70 percent) of our hires come from referrals, website postings, and rehires, which helps maintain our high standards. Thus, we rely very little on print advertising, employment agencies, or other broad-based recruiting channels that are costly and tend to generate less-suitable candidates.
- We focus on certain niches for skilled and experienced workers, targeting organizations that employ people with relevant skills and experiences and certifications that represent a required level of expertise.
- Our recruiting teams are attuned to older workers, those who have demonstrated high levels of competency through past performance. Recruiters are coached so they can focus on relevant skill sets and criteria. Candidates who are subject matter experts (SME) are interviewed and evaluated by employees in the same area, a process we call SME-to-SME—again, birds of a feather.

QUESTIONS

1. What overall HR strategy do you think MITRE is pursuing? Is its recruiting focus broad or targeted? Does it primarily use internal or external sources?

2. What characteristics of MITRE make it particularly attractive to older workers?

3. Why is the referral program at MITRE so successful? What are some elements of success that could be copied by other organizations? What success factors do you think would be hard to duplicate elsewhere?

Source: William D. Albright, Jr., and Gary A. Cluff, "Ahead of the Curve: How MITRE Recruits and Retains Older Workers," *Journal of Organizational Excellence* 25, no. 1 (2005): 53–63. Reprinted with permission of John Wiley & Sons, Inc.

DISCUSSION CASE | *Friendly Financial Works*

Friendly Financial Works is a fictional provider that sells accounting, payroll, and financial services to small businesses. The company uses an integrated software platform to help small businesses better manage their financial assets. Based on the assumption that small business owners often lack the expertise and time to manage financial assets effectively, Friendly Financial seeks to provide a relatively inexpensive "one-stop solution" for financial planning and control.

Friendly Financial's business model calls for providing services at the lowest cost rather than giving customized service to each client. To be successful, Friendly Financial needs to lower its costs by continually increasing the number of small businesses that use its services. The success of Friendly Financial thus depends largely on its sales force.

The sales force is divided into geographic territories, with a territory manager having exclusive responsibility for all sales activity within a specific area. Territories are organized into sales districts. The average number of territories in each district is 20. Each district is led by a district sales manager who oversees all personnel activities, such as hiring and training, in the territories within his or her district.

Territory managers are paid on a commission basis. They generate most of their sales by cold calling on potential businesses. A typical day consists of 10 to 15 unannounced visits to small businesses. The territory manager seeks an appointment with the owner or manager of each firm he or she visits. When an appointment is granted, the territory manager makes a presentation and tries to develop a contract between the small business and Friendly Financial. As with most unannounced sales calls, a large majority of visits end without a contract to provide services.

A major concern for Friendly Financial Works is identifying and keeping enough territory managers. The turnover rate is approximately 200 percent each year. This means that a district sales manager must usually hire about 40 new employees in a given year. In most cases, when a job vacancy occurs, the district sales manager travels to the sales territory to begin recruiting. The district sales manager places an advertisement in the local newspaper and includes a telephone number for potential recruits to call. The manager then spends three to four days at a local hotel answering phone inquiries and conducting interviews. The territory manager position is usually offered to the best available candidate on the final day that the district sales manager is in the territory.

District sales managers pride themselves on being able to land the sales representatives they like best. Many district sales managers boast that they can sell anything to anybody, and this is how they approach employee recruiting activities. Because they are talented sales representatives, district sales managers generally do a great job of touting the benefits of the position.

QUESTIONS

1. What aspects of the recruiting process increase the likelihood that territory managers will leave once they have been hired?
2. Should Friendly Financial use other methods to recruit territory managers? Which methods?
3. Is the recruiting process at Friendly Financial efficient? What are some things that might be done to reduce recruiting costs?

EXPERIENTIAL EXERCISE

Learning about Your Career Center

Visit the career center at your school. Meet with a career counselor. As you learn about the services offered through the career center, try to find answers to the following questions:

1. What services does the career center offer?
2. How can the career center help you find a job? When should you start working with the career center? Are there things you can do long before graduation to improve the effectiveness of your job search?
3. What companies have good relationships with your school? Which of these companies hire people in your field of study? What characteristics do they look for in employees?
4. How do you go about using the career center to locate job openings? Does the career center support a website? Can you apply for as many jobs as you want?
5. Does the career center maintain a list of alumni who currently work for specific companies? Can you use this list to network with potential employers?
6. What other services, such as interview training, are provided through the career center?

INTERACTIVE EXPERIENTIAL EXERCISE

Strategic Recruitment: Finding the Right People for Graphics Design, Inc.
http://www.wiley.com/college/sc/stewart

Access the companion website to test your knowledge by completing a Graphics Design, Inc. interactive role play.

In this exercise it's time to start trying to attract potential employees to fill the newly created positions at GDI. You have many decisions to consider, including which recruiting sources to use, what skill scope is needed, and what type of message to convey to applicants. You also need to consider the HR planning process and the fact that the basic HR strategy of GDI is that of Loyal Soldier. What will be your first recommendation to the GDI management team when you meet with them in the next several days? •

ENDNOTES

1. Alison E. Barber, *Recruiting Employees: Individual and Organizational Perspectives* (Thousand Oaks, CA: Sage, 1998).
2. Ibid.; Kevin D. Carlson, Mary L. Connerley, and Ross L. Mecham III, "Recruitment Evaluation: The Case for Assessing the Quality of Applicants Attracted," *Personnel Psychology* 55 (2002): 461–490.
3. David E. Terpstra and Elizabeth J. Rozell, "The Relationship of Staffing Practices to Organizational Level Measures of Performance," *Personnel Psychology* 46 (1993): 27–48; John T. Delaney and Mark A. Huselid, "The Impact of Human Resource Practices on Perceptions of Organizational Performance," *Academy of Management Journal* 39 (1996): 949–969.
4. Robert Levering and Milton Moskowitz, "In Good Company," *Fortune* 155, no. 1 (2007): 94.
5. Todd Raphael, "At Google, the Proof Is in the People," *Workforce* 82, no. 3 (2003): 50–51.
6. Adam Lashinsky, "Search and Enjoy," *Fortune* 155, no. 1 (2007): 70.
7. Todd Raphael, "At Google, the Proof Is in the People."
8. Rob Willock, "Google Makes the Mind Boggle with Its Recruitment Challenges," *Personnel Today*, February 6, 2007, 6.
9. Adam Lashinsky, "Search and Enjoy."
10. Joseph Puliyenthuruthel, "How Google Searches—For Talent," *BusinessWeek* 3928, April 11, 2005, 52.
11. Anonymous, "Special Report: Travelling More Lightly—Staffing Globalisation," *The Economist* 8483, June 24, 2006, 99.
12. Catherine E. Connelly and Daniel G. Gallagher, "Emerging Trends in Contingent Work Research," *Journal of Management* 30 (2004): 959–983.
13. Jeffrey Pfeffer, *The Human Equation: Building Profits by Putting People First* (Boston: Harvard Business School Press, 1998).
14. Connelly and Gallagher, "Emerging Trends in Contingent Work Research."
15. www.newtonmfg.com.
16. Anne E. Polivka and Thomas Nardone, "On the Definition of Contingent Work," *Monthly Labor Review* 112, no. 12 (1989): 9–16.
17. Soon Ang and Sandra A. Slaughter, "Work Outcomes and Job Design for Contract Versus Permanent Information Systems Professionals on Software Development Teams," *MIS Quarterly* 25 (2001): 321–350.
18. Linn Van Dyne and Soon Ang, "Organizational Citizenship Behavior of Contingent Workers in Singapore," *Academy of Management Journal* 41 (1998): 692–703.
19. Siobhan O'Mahony and Beth A. Bechky, "Stretchwork: Managing the Career Progression Paradox in External Labor Markets," *Academy of Management Journal* 49 (2006): 918–941.
20. Steven L. Premack and John P. Wanous, "A Meta-Analysis of Realistic Job Preview Experiments," *Journal of Applied Psychology* 70 (1985): 706–719.
21. John P. Wanous, Timothy D. Poland, Stephen L. Premack, and K. Sharon Davis, "The Effects of Met Expectations on Newcomer Attitudes and Behaviors: A Review and Meta-Analysis," *Journal of Applied Psychology* 77(1992): 288–297.
22. Glenn M. McEvoy and Wayne F. Cascio, "Strategies for Reducing Employee Turnover: A Meta-Analysis," *Journal of Applied Psychology* 70 (1985): 342–353; Premack and Wanous, "A Meta-Analysis of Realistic Job Preview Experiments"; Peter W. Hom, Rodger W. Griffeth, Leslie E. Palich, and Jeffrey S. Bracker. "An Exploratory Investigation into Theoretical Mechanisms Underlying Realistic Job Previews," *Personnel Psychology* 51 (1998): 421–451.
23. Premack and Wanous, "A Meta-Analysis"; Robert D. Bretz and Timothy A. Judge, "Realistic Job Previews: A Test of the Adverse Self-Selection Hypothesis," *Journal of Applied Psychology* 83 (1998): 330–337.
24. Bretz and Judge, "Realistic Job Previews."
25. Bill Macaller and Shannon Jones, "Does HR Planning Improve Business Performance," *Industrial Management* 45, no. 1 (2003): 14–20.
26. Carlson, Connerly, and Mecham, "Recruitment Evaluation."
27. Michelle Neely Martinez, "Recruiting Here and There," *HR Magazine* 47, no. 2 (2002): 95–100.
28. Brian K. Griepentrog, Crystal M. Harold, Brian C. Holtz, Richard J. Klimoski, and Sean M. Marsh, "Integrating Social Identity and the Theory of Planned Behavior: Predicting Withdrawal from an Organizational Recruitment Process," *Personnel Psychology* 65 (2012): 723-752; Edwin A. J. Van Hooft, Marise Ph. Born, Toon W. Taris, Jenk van der Flier, and Roland W. B. Blonk, "Predictors of Job Search Behavior Among Employed and Unemployed People," *Personnel Psychology* 57 (2004): 25–59.
29. Alison E. Barber, Christina L. Daly, Cristina M. Giannontonio, and Jean M. Phillips, "Job Search Activities: An Examination of Changes over Time," *Personnel Psychology* 47 (1994): 739–766.
30. Allison Stein Wellner, "Shop Our Store! Or Better Yet, Why Not Work Here?" *Workforce Management Online*, October 2004.
31. Frances McKee-Ryan, Zhaoli Song, Connie R. Wanberg, and Angelo J. Kinicki, "Psychological and Physical Well-Being During Unemployment: A Meta-Analytic Study," *Journal of Applied Psychology* 90 (2005): 53–76.
32. Connie R. Wanberg, John D. Watt, and Deborah J. Rumsey, "Individuals Without Jobs: An Empirical Study of Job-Seeking Behavior and Reemployment," *Journal of Applied Psychology* 81 (1996): 76–87.
33. Connie R. Wanberg, Jing Zhu, Ruth Kanfer, and Zhen Zhang, "After the Pink Slip: Applying Dynamic Motivation Frameworks to the Job Search Experience," *Academy of Management Journal* 55 (2012): 261-284; Connie R. Wanberg, "Antecedents and Outcomes of Coping Behaviors Among Unemployed and Reemployed Individuals," *Journal of Applied Psychology* 82 (1997): 731–744; Connie R. Wanberg, Ruth Kanfer, and Maria Rotundo, "Unemployed Individuals: Motives, Job-Search Competencies, and Job-search Constraints as Predictors of Job Seeking and Reemployment," *Journal of Applied Psychology* 84 (1999): 897–910.

34. Frances Devine, Tom Baum, Niamh Hearns, and Adrian Devine, "Managing Cultural Diversity: Opportunities and Challenges for Northern Ireland Hoteliers," *International Journal of Contemporary Hospitality Management* 19 (2007): 120–132.

35. John W. Boudreau, Wendy R. Boswell, Timothy A. Judge, and Robert D. Bretz, Jr., "Personality and Cognitive Ability as Predictors of Job Search Among Employed Managers," *Personnel Psychology* 54 (2001): 25–50.

36. Robert D. Bretz, John W. Boudreau, and Timothy A. Judge, "Job Search Behavior of Employed Managers," *Personnel Psychology* 47 (1994): 275–301.

37. Thomas W. Lee, Terence R. Mitchell, Lowell Wise, and Steven Fireman, "An Unfolding Model of Voluntary Employee Turnover," *Academy of Management Journal* 39 (1996): 5–36.

38. Robert D. Bretz, John W. Boudreau, and Timothy A. Judge, "Job Search Behavior of Employed Managers," *Personnel Psychology* 47 (1994): 275–301.

39. Gary Blau, "Further Exploring the Relationship Between Job Search and Voluntary Individual Turnover," *Personnel Psychology* 46 (1993): 313–330.

40. Timothy M. Gardner, "In the Trenches at the Talent Wars: Competitive Interaction for Scarce Human Resources," *Human Resource Management* 41 (2002): 225–237.

41. Alison E. Barber and Mark V. Roehling, "Job Postings and the Decision to Interview: A Verbal Protocol Analysis," *Journal of Applied Psychology* 78 (1993): 845–856.

42. Krista l. Uggerslev, Neir E. Fassina, and David Kraichy, "Recruiting Through the Stages: A Meta-Analytic Test of Predictors of Applicant Attraction at Different Stages of the Recruiting Process," Personnel Psychology 65 (2012): 597–660.

43. Daniel B. Turban, Chung-Ming Lau, Hang-Yue Ngo, Irene H. S. Chow, and Steven X. Si, "Organizational Attractiveness of Firms in the People's Republic of China: A Person–Organization Fit Perspective," *Journal of Applied Psychology* 86 (2001): 194–206.

44. Margaret E. Brooks, Scott Highhouse, Steven S. Russell, and David C. Mohr, "Familiarity, Ambivalence, and Firm Reputation: Is Corporate Fame a Double-Edged Sword?" *Journal of Applied Psychology* 88 (2003): 904–914.

45. Christopher J. Collins, "The Interactive Effects of Recruitment Practices and Product Awareness on Job Seekers' Employer Knowledge and Application Behaviors," *Journal of Applied Psychology* 92 (2007): 180–190.

46. Christopher J. Collins and Jian Han, "Exploring Applicant Pool Quantity and Quality: The Effects of Early Recruitment Practice Strategies, Corporate Advertising, and Firm Reputation," *Personnel Psychology* 57 (2004): 685–717.

47. Barber and Roehling, "Job Postings and the Decision to Interview."

48. Daniel M. Cable and Timothy A. Judge, "Pay Preferences and Job Search Decisions: A Person–Organization Fit Perspective," *Personnel Psychology* 47 (1994): 317–348.

49. Filip Lievens and Scott Highhouse, "The Relation of Instrumental and Symbolic Attributes to a Company's Attractiveness as an Employer," *Personnel Psychology* 56 (2003): 75–102

50. Jerel E. Slaughter, Michael J. Zichar, Scott Highhouse, and David C. Mohr, "Personality Trait Inferences about Organizations: Development of a Measure and Assessment of Construct Validity," *Journal of Applied Psychology* 89 (2004): 85–103.

51. Ibid.; Timothy A. Judge and Robert D. Bretz, "Effects of Work Values on Job Choice Decisions," *Journal of Applied Psychology* 77 (1992): 261–271; Lievens and Highhouse, "The Relation of Instrumental and Symbolic Attributes."

52. Christopher J. Collins and Cynthia Kay Stevens, "The Relationship Between Early Recruitment-Related Activities and the Application Decisions of New Labor-Market Entrants: A Brand Equity Approach to Recruitment," *Journal of Applied Psychology* 87 (2002): 1121–1133.

53. Steven D. Maurer, Vince Howe, and Thomas W. Lee, "Organizational Recruiting as Marketing Management: An Interdisciplinary Study of Engineering Graduates," *Personnel Psychology* 45 (1992): 807–834.

54. Sara L. Rynes, Robert D. Bretz, Jr., and Barry A. Gerhart, "The Importance of Recruitment in Job Choice," *Personnel Psychology* 44 (1991): 487–521.

55. Taken from Wendy R. Boswell, Mark V. Roehling, Marcie A. LePine, and Lisa M. Moynihan, "Individual Job Choice Decisions and the Impact of Job Attributes and Recruitment Practices: A Longitudinal Field Study," *Human Resource Management* 42 (2003): 23–37.

56. Allison E. Barber, Michael J. Wesson, Quinetta M. Roberson, and M. Susan Taylor, "A Tale of Two Job Markets: Organizational Size and Its Effects on Hiring Practices and Job Search Behavior," *Personnel Psychology* 52 (1999): 841–867.

57. Cable and Judge, "Pay Preferences and Job Search Decisions."

58. Daniel B. Turban and Thomas L. Keon, "Organizational Attractiveness: An Interactionist Perspective," *Journal of Applied Psychology* 78 (1993): 184–193.

59. Cable and Judge, "Pay Preferences and Job Search Decisions."

60. Timothy A. Judge and Daniel M. Cable, "Applicant Personality, Organizational Culture, and Organization Attraction," *Personnel Psychology* 50 (1997): 359–394.

61. Ibid.

62. Judge and Bretz, "Effects of Work Values on Job Choice Decisions."

63. Maurer et al., "Organizational Recruiting as Marketing Management."

64. Jessica Mintz, "Large Firms Increasingly Rely on Employees for Job Referrals," *Wall Street Journal*, March 1, 2005, B4.

65. Mary-Lane Kamberg, "Personal Networking Key in Finding a Job," *Women in Business*, September/October 2001, 11.

66. Carroll Lachnit, "Employee Referral Saves Time, Saves Money, Delivers Quality," *Workforce Management* 80, no. 6 (2001): 66–70.

67. Ibid.; Michelle Neely Martinez, "The Headhunter Within: Turn Your Employees into Recruiters with a High-Impact Referral Program," *HR Magazine* 46, no. 8 (2001): 48–55; Alison Coleman, "Should You Phone a Friend?" *Director*, May 2002, 30.

68. Mark Laurie, "Employee Referral Programs: Highly Qualified New Hires Who Stick Around," *Canadian HR Reporter*, June 4, 2001, 21.

69. Malcolm McCulloch, "The Best Recruiting Sources for Call Centers," *Call Center Magazine*, April 2003, 8.

70. Lachnit, "Employee Referral Saves Time."

71. Rachel S. Shinnar, Cheri A. Young, and Marta Meena, "The Motivations for and Outcomes of Employee Referrals," *Journal of Business and Psychology* 19 (2004): 271.

72. Table content adapted from Michelle Neely Martinez, Lachnit, "Employee Referral Saves Time."

73. Vanessa Peters, "Don't Bury the Newspaper Quite Yet," *Canadian HR Reporter*, December 6, 2004, G9.

74. Rob Willock, "Employer Branding Is Key in Fight for Talent," *Personnel Today*, May 17, 2005, 4.

75. Daniel M. Cable and Kang Yang Trevor Yu, "Managing Job Seekers' Organizational Image Beliefs: The Role of Media Richness and Media Credibility," *Journal of Applied Psychology* 91 (2006): 828–840.

76. H. Jack Walker, Hubert S. Feild, Jeremy B. Bernerth, and J. Bret Becton, "Diversity Cues on Recruitment Websites: Investigating the Effects of Job Seekers' Information Processing," *Journal of Applied Psychology* 97 (2012): 214-224.

77. In Lee, "The Evolution of E-Recruiting: A Content Analysis of Fortune 100 Career Web Sites," *Journal of Electronic Commerce in Organizations*, July/September 2005, 57–68.

78. Ibid.; Anonymous, "The Pros and Cons of Online Recruiting," *HR Focus*, April 2004, 52.

79. David Brown, "Unwanted Online Jobseekers Swamp HR Staff," *Canadian HR Reporter*, April 5, 2004, 1.

80. Brian R. Dineen and Raymond A. Noe, "Effects of Customization on Application Decisions and Applicant Pool Characteristics in a Web-Based Recruitment Context," *Journal of Applied Psychology* 94 (2009): 224–234.

81. Brian R. Dineen, Juan Ling, Steven R. Ash, and Devon DelVecchio, "Aesthetic Properties and Message Customization: Navigating the Dark Side of Web Recruitment," *Journal of Applied Psychology* 92 (2007): 356–372.

82. Jeff Stimson, "Recruiting Via the Web," *The Practical Accountant* 37, no. 7 (2004): 26–30.

83. www.kellyservices.us

84. Martinez, "Employee Referral Saves Time," 66.

85. http://www.lilly.com/careers/

86. James Bailey, Gary Heesacker, Karen Martinis, and Connie Nott, "Student Recruitment Strategies," *CPA Journal* 72 (2002): 58–59.

87. Jack Gault, John Redington, and Tammy Schlager, "Undergraduate Business Internships and Career Success: Are They Related?" *Journal of Marketing Education* 22 (2000): 45–53.

88. Mary L. Connerly, Kevin D. Carlson, and Ross L. Mecham III, "Evidence of Differences in Applicant Pool Quality," *Personnel Review*, 32 (2003): 22–39.

89. Jac Fitz-Enz, "HR Measurement: Formulas for Success," *Personnel Journal* 64, no. 10 (1985): 53–60.

90. Barbara Davison, "The Importance of Cost per Hire," *Workforce* 80, no. 1 (2001): 32–34.

91. Eilene Zimmerman, "Complexity Squashes Ethics—Fight Back with Simplicity," *Workforce Management*, online September 19, 2011; http://www.workforce.com/blogs/1-the-ethical-workplace/post/complexity-squashes-ethics-fight-back-with-simplicity

92. Carlson, Connerly, and Mecham III, "Recruitment Evaluation."

93. Philip G. Swaroff, Lizabeth A. Barclay, and Allan R. Bass, "Recruiting Sources: Another Look," *Journal of Applied Psychology* 70 (1985): 720–728; Charles R. Williams, Chalmer E. Labis, and Thomas H. Stone, "Recruitment Sources and Posthire Outcomes for Job Applicants and New Hires: A Test of Two Hypotheses," *Journal of Applied Psychology* 78 (1993): 163–172; G. Stephen Taylor, "The Relationship Between Source of New Employees and Attitudes Toward the Job," *Journal of Social Psychology* 134 (2001): 99–110.

Chapter 6

Selecting Employees Who Fit

valeriy-davidenko/iStockphoto

A MANAGER'S PERSPECTIVE

JAVIER'S MESSAGE FROM THE HUMAN RESOURCE DEPARTMENT FILLS HIM WITH BOTH ANXIETY AND EXCITEMENT. HE JUST RECEIVED AUTHORIZATION TO HIRE AN ADDITIONAL MEMBER FOR HIS CUSTOMER SERVICE TEAM. JAVIER IS EXCITED BECAUSE HIRING THE RIGHT PERSON COULD REALLY BOOST THE TEAM'S PERFORMANCE; HE IS ANXIOUS BECAUSE THIS WILL BE HIS FIRST HIRING DECISION.

Javier has total freedom to hire anybody he wants. What should he focus on when he makes his hiring decision? Should he hire someone who is likely to stay with the company for a long time? Should he look for someone who already has the skills to do the job? Is it more important to hire someone with the potential to be a high performer in several different jobs? Should he try to find someone who is similar to current team members, or should he bring in new ideas by hiring someone very different?

One reason for Javier's anxiety is a story he recently heard where a manager in a different department asked a number of illegal questions during an interview. He has also heard a number of stories about managers being evaluated negatively because they spent too much money searching for employees. Javier has a general idea

of the questions that should be avoided when conducting interviews, but he makes himself a note to be sure to ask someone from the human resource department to remind him of potentially problematic questions. He also wants to get some help identifying the most cost-effective hiring methods.

Javier also thinks about the specific methods he might use to evaluate people. He has participated in several job interviews, and he knows that interviews are important. But what questions should he ask? Should he ask everyone the same questions? Will he be able to judge whether an answer is good or bad? Should he have someone else interview a group of finalists for the job?

Javier knows he won't have time to interview everyone who will apply. How should he screen applicants? A friend recently told him about using personality tests for hiring. Javier also remembers taking some type of intelligence test when he applied for a different job a number of years ago. He thought the intelligence test was kind of interesting, but he wonders if such tests really help

THE BIG PICTURE   *Effective Organizations Develop Employee Selection Strategies That Include Tests and Assessments to Help Them Hire the Right People*

organizations identify successful employees. Would using tests help him make a better hiring decision? If so, how can he identify the tests that he should use? What about reference checking? He would like to talk to previous employers, but he knows that the policy of his own company is not to give references. Would it be worth the effort to try checking references?

As he continues to reflect, Javier wonders how the results of several different assessments should be combined to arrive at a final hiring decision if he uses tests, reference checking, and interviewing? Would it be best to give scores on all of the measures the same emphasis? Should he give more weight to the interview? The hiring decision is an important one for Javier, as he well knows. He can prove himself as an emerging leader if he makes a good choice. Not only that, his job as team leader will become easier if he hires a new team member who is a real contributor.

WHAT DO YOU THINK?

Suppose you are listening to a conversation between Javier and another manager, Elena. Elena makes the following statements. Which of the statements do you think are true?

T OR F You should hire people who already have the skills and knowledge they will need on the job.

T OR F The benefits of making good hiring decisions are highest when the organization has a lot of job applicants.

T OR F Intelligence tests are very helpful for predicting who will be effective in almost any job.

T OR F Reference checking provides valuable information about prospective employees.

T OR F You need to ask each job applicant individualized questions to determine his or her true strengths and weaknesses.

After reading this chapter you should be able to:

LEARNING OBJECTIVE 1   Describe how employee selection practices can strategically align with overall HR strategy.

LEARNING OBJECTIVE 2   Explain what makes a selection method good; be able to apply the concepts of reliability, validity, utility, legality and fairness, and acceptability to appropriately evaluate different employee selection methods.

LEARNING OBJECTIVE 3   Describe several commonly used selection methods, evaluate their strengths and weaknesses, and explain how they link with particular employee selection strategies.

LEARNING OBJECTIVE 4   Explain how to combine scores from several different selection methods to arrive at a final selection decision.

How Can Strategic Employee Selection Improve an Organization?

Employee selection
The process of testing and gathering information to decide whom to hire.

Employee selection is the process of choosing people to bring into an organization. Effective selection provides many benefits. Selecting the right employees can improve the effectiveness of other human resource practices and prevent numerous problems. For instance, hiring highly motivated employees who fit with the organizational culture can reduce disciplinary problems and diminish costs related to replacing employees who quit. Such benefits help explain why organizations that use effective staffing practices have higher annual profit and faster growth of profit.[1] In short, a strategic approach to selecting employees can help an organization obtain and keep the talent necessary to produce goods and services that exceed the expectations of customers.

One organization that expends a lot of effort on selection is the military. Each year, the United States Marine Corps selects and trains over 38,000 people. Of course, not everyone who wants to become a marine is accepted into the Corps. Before being accepted and enduring training at either the San Diego, California, or Parris Island, South Carolina, location, recruits must pass both mental and physical examinations.[2]

Because marines are required to make sound decisions quickly, the Marine Corps bases part of its selection decisions on scores for a mental ability test. This examination is known as Armed Services Vocational Aptitude Battery (ASVAB). The test consists of 225 multiple-choice questions in the areas of General Science, Arithmetic Reasoning, Word Knowledge, Paragraph Comprehension, Mathematics Knowledge, Electronic Information, Auto and Shop Information, Mechanical Comprehension, and Assembling Objects. Test results determine not only whether someone will be admitted to the Marine Corps but also what type of occupations can be pursued once basic training is complete. For example, it takes a higher score to become an aerial navigator than it does to become a combat photographer.[3]

Building Strength Through HR

UNITED STATES MARINE CORPS

The United States Marine Corps thus uses testing to evaluate not only its 38,000 new recruits each year but also the physical abilities of continuing marines. Testing practices include

- Using a minimum score on a mental ability test to determine who is accepted, as well as cutoff scores to place marines into specific positions.
- Requiring a minimum score on a physical fitness test measuring basic strength and endurance.
- Ongoing assessment of physical ability not only to ensure a minimum level of fitness but also to determine promotions.

Given that the job also requires physical fitness, recruits must additionally pass an assessment known as the Initial Strength Test (IST). The test for men requires pull-ups, crunches, and a timed run. For women the test has historically required a flex armed hang in place of pull-ups, but test administrators are discussing whether they should require female recruits to demonstrate pull-ups the same as male recruits. This shift parallels the recent change to allow female marines into combat units.[4]

Physical testing does not, however, end once someone is accepted into the Marine Corps. Each year a marine must complete an evaluation known as the Physical Fitness Test (PFT), which is similar to the IST. Each marine must also complete an annual Combat Fitness Test (CFT), which includes completing a timed endurance test, a lifting exercise, and an obstacle course requiring activities such as crawling, carrying, and throwing.[5]

LEARNING OBJECTIVE 1

How Is Employee Selection Strategic?

As we can see from the Marine Corps example, hiring the right employees often takes a great deal of planning. An organization's employee selection practices are strategic when they ensure that the right people are in the right places at the right times. This means that good selection practices must fit with an organization's overall HR strategy. As described in Chapter 2, HR strategies vary along two dimensions: whether they have an internal or an external labor orientation and whether they compete through cost or differentiation. These overall HR strategies provide important guidance about the type of employee selection practices that will be most effective for a particular organization.

ALIGNING TALENT AND HR STRATEGY

Consistent with the overall HR strategies, strategic selection decisions are based on two important dimensions. One dimension represents differences in the type of talent sought. At one end of the continuum is *generalist talent*—employees who may be excellent workers but who do not have particular areas of expertise or specialization. At the other end of the continuum is *specialist talent*—employees with specific and somewhat rare skills and abilities.[6]

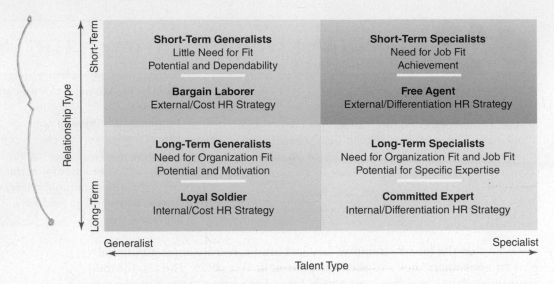

Figure 6.1 Strategic Framework for Employee Selection.

Another dimension represents the type of relationship between the employees and the organization. At one end of the continuum is *long-term talent*. Employees in this category stay with the organization for a long time and develop a deep understanding of company practices and operations. At the other end of the continuum is *short-term talent*. These employees move from organization to organization without developing expertise in how things are done at any particular place.[7] Combining the two dimensions yields four general categories shown in Figure 6.1: short-term generalist talent, long-term generalist talent, long-term specialist talent, and short-term specialist talent. Next, we look at each of these categories in turn and consider how they fit with the HR strategies introduced in Chapter 2.

Short-Term Generalists

Short-term generalists
Workers hired to produce general labor inputs for a relatively short period of time.

If you were hired to work at a drive-in restaurant, you would not need specialized skills, you would not earn high wages, and you probably would not keep the job for a very long time. Fast-food workers are **short-term generalists**, who provide a variety of different inputs but do not have areas of special skill or ability. Other examples include some retail sales clerks and hotel housekeepers. Short-term generalist talent is associated with the Bargain Laborer HR strategy.[8] Organizations with this HR strategy fill most positions by hiring people just entering the workforce or people already working in similar jobs at other companies. Selection has the objective of identifying and hiring employees to produce low-cost goods and services, and selection decisions are based on identifying people who can perform simple tasks that require little specialized skill.

Hiring generalists can be beneficial because people without specialized skills do not generally demand high compensation, which keeps payroll costs as low as possible. Because generalists lack specific expertise, they also are usually more willing to work in routine jobs and do whatever they are asked.

Long-Term Generalists

If you were to take a job working for an electricity provider, you might not need specialized skills, but you would most likely plan to remain with the organization for a long career. People working for utility companies are often **long-term generalists** who do not have technical expertise but who develop skills and knowledge concerning how things are done in a specific organization. Other common examples of long-term generalists are people who work for government agencies and for some package delivery companies. These workers contribute in a number of areas but do not need specific technical skills and abilities. Long-term generalists are beneficial for organizations using the Loyal Soldier HR strategy.[9] Organizations with this HR strategy focus on keeping employees once they are hired. Staffing still has the objective of hiring employees to produce low-cost goods and services, but a stronger commitment is formed, and efforts are made to identify people who will remain with the organization for a long time.

The generalist's lack of specific expertise allows firms to reduce payroll costs. However, over time employees develop skills and abilities that are only valuable to the specific organization, which reduces the likelihood that they will move to another employer. People develop relationships and form a strong sense of commitment to the organization.

Long-term generalists
Workers hired to perform a variety of different jobs over a relatively long period of time.

Long-Term Specialists

Suppose you took a job as an accountant with a large firm that makes and sells consumer goods such as diapers and cleaning products. People doing this job are most often **long-term specialists** who develop deep expertise in a particular area. Pharmaceutical sales representatives and research scientists are commonly employed as long-term specialists. People in these jobs are expected to develop specialized skills and stay with the organization for a long time. The use of long-term specialists fits the Committed Expert HR strategy.[10] Organizations that use this HR strategy develop their own talent. Selection has the objective of identifying people capable of developing expertise in a particular area so they can innovate and produce superior goods and services over time.

Hiring people who can develop specialized skills over time enables organizations to create and keep a unique resource of talent that other organizations do not have. Employees are given the time and assets to develop the skills they need to be the best at what they do.

Long-term specialists
Workers hired to develop specific expertise and establish a lengthy career within an organization.

Short-Term Specialists

Information technology specialists often work as **short-term specialists**—employees who provide specific inputs for relatively short periods of time. These workers are valuable for organizations using the Free Agent HR strategy.[11] Organizations with this HR strategy hire people away from other organizations. Staffing is aimed at hiring people who will bring new skills and produce innovative goods and top-quality service. Selection decisions focus on identifying people who have already developed specific skills. Other examples of this type of talent include investment bankers and advertising executives.

Hiring short-term specialists allows firms to quickly acquire needed expertise. New hires bring unique knowledge and skills to the organization. The organization pays a relatively high price for such knowledge and skills but makes no long-term commitments.

Short-term specialists
Workers hired to provide specific labor inputs for a relatively short period of time.

MAKING STRATEGIC SELECTION DECISIONS

Another way to examine how organizations make employee selection decisions focuses on two primary factors: the balance between job-based fit and organization-based fit and the balance between achievement and potential. As you can see in Figure 6.1, both factors relate clearly to the talent categories just discussed.

Balancing Job Fit and Organization Fit

Job-based fit
Matching an employee's knowledge and skills to the tasks associated with a specific job.

Organization-based fit
Matching an employee's characteristics to the general culture of the organization.

The first area of balance concerns whether employees should be chosen to fit in specific jobs or to fit more generally with the organization. When **job-based fit** is the goal, the organization seeks to match an individual's abilities and interests with the demands of a specific job. This type of fit is highly dependent on a person's technical skills. For instance, high ability in mathematics results in fit for a job such as financial analyst or accountant. In contrast, **organization-based fit** is concerned with how well the individual's characteristics match the broader culture, values, and norms of the firm. Organization-based fit depends less on technical skills than on an individual's personality, values, and goals.[12] A person with conservative values, for example, might fit well in a company culture of caution and tradition. Employees who fit with their organizations have higher job satisfaction, and better fit with the organization has been shown to lead to higher performance in many settings.[13] As described in the "How Do We Know?" feature, the HR strategy has an impact on how job and organization fit are weighted.

As suggested earlier, we can combine the concept of fit with the talent-based categories discussed earlier. In general, job-based fit is more important in organizations that seek to hire specialists than in those that seek generalists. Similarly, organization-based fit is more important for long-term than for short-term employees. These differences provide strategic direction for employee selection practices.

Organizations pursuing Bargain Laborer HR strategies are not highly concerned about either form of fit. Employees do not generally bring specific skills to the organization. Neither are they expected to stay long enough to necessitate close organizational fit. Thus, for firms pursuing a Bargain Laborer HR strategy, fit is not strategically critical, and hiring decisions tend to focus on obtaining the least expensive labor regardless of fit.

Organizations pursuing the Loyal Soldier HR strategy benefit from hiring employees who fit with the overall organization. Job-based fit is not critical. Employees rotate through a number of jobs, and success comes more from loyalty and high motivation than from specific skills. In contrast, lengthy expected careers make fit with the organization very important. Employee selection decisions in organizations with a Loyal Soldier HR strategy should thus focus primarily on assessing personality, values, and goals.

Organizations pursuing a Committed Expert HR strategy require both job-based fit and organization-based fit. Organization-based fit is necessary because employees need to work closely with other members of the organization throughout long careers. Job-based fit is necessary because employees are expected to develop expertise in a specific area. Even though new employees may not yet have developed specific job skills, general aptitude

How Do We Know?

WHICH TYPE OF FIT IS MOST IMPORTANT?

Do managers making selection decisions pay more attention to job fit or organization fit? Are candidates who have average fit on both dimensions preferred to candidates who are high on one and low on the other? Does it depend on the nature of the job? Tomoki Sekiguchi and Vandra Huber conducted two studies to answer these questions. In one study of 120 and a second study of 92 middle- and senior-level executives, participants completed evaluations of candidate profiles that assessed how they would evaluate the credentials of potential job applicants for positions such as management, attorney, nurse, and nurse assistant.

The executives were most likely to reject applicants who had very poor job fit. They were more tolerant of poor organization fit. However, individuals with very poor fit for either the organization or the job were more likely to be rejected than individuals with average fit in both areas. Consistent with the contingency approach to human resource management, organization fit was given more weight for permanent compared to temporary positions, whereas job fit was more important for short-term and knowledge-intensive positions. Managers thus seem to take into account characteristics of the position being filled and adjust their fit assessments to match the situation.

The Bottom Line. Poor fit with a job is the most likely reason why an individual might not be selected for a position, but being really low on either job or organizational fit is likely to result in rejection. Organization fit is more likely to be taken into account when positions are long-term in nature, which suggests that managers do indeed make strategic hiring decisions. Professors Sekiguchi and Huber thus concluded that characteristics of the position do indeed influence the balance between job and organization fit.

Source: Tomoki Sekiguchi and Vandra L. Huber, "The Use of Person–Organization Fit and Person–Job Fit Information in Making Selection Decisions," *Organizational Behavior and Human Decision Processes* 116 (2011): 203–216.

in the specialized field, such as accounting or engineering, is important. Selection decisions in firms pursuing Committed Expert HR strategies should thus be based on a combination of technical skills and personality, values, and goals.

Job-based fit is critical for organizations pursuing a Free Agent HR strategy. These organizations hire employees specifically to perform specialized tasks and expect them to bring required knowledge and skills with them. An employee's stay with the organization is expected to be relatively short, which means that fit with the organization is not critical. Selection decisions in organizations with a Free Agent HR strategy should thus focus primarily on assessing technical skills and abilities.

Balancing Achievement and Potential

The second area of balance concerns whether employees should be chosen because of what they have already achieved or because of their potential for future accomplishments. Assessments aimed at measuring **achievement** focus on history and past accomplishments that reveal information about acquired abilities and skills. For instance, a job applicant for an elementary school teaching position might have graduate degrees and years of experience that demonstrate teaching skills. In contrast, assessments aimed at measuring

Achievement
A selection approach emphasizing existing skills and past accomplishments.

Potential
A selection approach emphasizing broad characteristics that foreshadow capability to develop future knowledge and skill.

potential are future-oriented and seek to predict how a person will learn and develop knowledge and skill over time.[14] In this case, an applicant for an elementary teaching position may just have graduated with high honors from a prestigious university, demonstrating high potential.

Again, we can relate the choice between achievement and potential to the framework in Figure 6.1. Organizations that use Bargain Laborer HR strategies do not require highly developed skills.[15] Measures of achievement are not required. For these organizations, selection methods assess potential by predicting whether applicants will be dependable and willing to carry out assigned tasks.

Hiring people based on potential is critical for organizations with long-term staffing strategies. These organizations provide a great deal of training, which suggests that people learn many skills after they are hired. With a Loyal Soldier HR strategy, selection measures should focus on ability, motivation, and willingness to work in a large variety of jobs. For a Committed Expert HR strategy, the focus is on assessing potential to become highly skilled in a particular area.

Organizations seeking short-term specialists focus on measuring achievement, because they seek employees who already have specific skills. Required skills change frequently, and a general lack of training by the organization makes it very difficult for these employees to keep up with new technologies. Hiring practices for organizations with Free Agent HR strategies thus focus on identifying individuals who have already obtained the necessary skills and who have demonstrated success in similar positions.

Gaining Competitive Advantage from Alignment

Of course, not all organizations have selection practices that are perfectly aligned with overall HR strategies. Some firms hire long-term generalists even though they have a Free Agent HR strategy. Other firms hire short-term specialists even though they have a Bargain Laborer HR strategy. The selection practices in such organizations are not strategic, and these organizations often fail to hire employees who can really help them achieve their goals. In short, organizations with closer alignment between their overall HR strategies and their specific selection practices tend to be more effective. They are successful because they develop a competitive advantage by identifying and hiring employees who fit their needs and strategic plans.[16] What works for one organization may not work for another organization with a different competitive strategy. A key for effective staffing is thus to balance job fit and organization fit, as well as achievement and potential, in ways that align staffing practices with HR strategy.

CONCEPT CHECK

1. *What are the four types of talent, and how do they fit with the four approaches to overall HR strategy?*
2. *What is the difference between organization fit and job fit, and which is most critical for each of the HR strategies?*
3. *How do achievement and potential fit with strategic selection?*

LEARNING OBJECTIVE **2**

What Makes a Selection Method Good?

We have considered strategic concerns in employee selection. The next step is to evaluate specific methods that help accomplish strategy. How can an organization go about identifying tests or measures that will identify people who fit or who have the appropriate mix of potential and achievement? Should prospective employees be given some type of paper-and-pencil test? Is a background check necessary? Will an interview be helpful? If so, what type of interview is best? Answers to the questions provide insights about the accuracy, cost effectiveness, fairness, and acceptability of various selection methods. Next, we examine a few principles related to each question. These principles include reliability, validity, utility, legality and fairness, and acceptability. Figure 6.2 illustrates basic questions associated with each principle.

RELIABILITY

Reliability is concerned with consistency of measurement. An example that illustrates this concept can be made by examining the selection of university athletes.

Imagine that two coaches for a football team have just returned from separate recruiting trips. They are meeting to discuss the recruits they visited. The first coach describes a great recruit who weighs 300 pounds. The second coach reports about someone able to bench press 500 pounds. Which player should the coaches select? It is impossible to compare the recruits, since different information was obtained about each person. The measures are not reliable.

The football example may seem a bit ridiculous, but it is not much different from what happens in many organizations. Just think of the interview process. Suppose five different people interview a person for a job. In many organizations, the interviewers' judgments would not be consistent.

How, then, can we determine whether a selection method is reliable? One way to evaluate reliability is to test a person on two different occasions and then determine whether scores are similar across the two times. We call this the **test-retest method** of estimating reliability. Another way to evaluate

> **Reliability**
> An assessment of the degree to which a selection method yields consistent results.
>
> *essay question*
>
> **Test-retest method**
> A process of estimating reliability that compares scores on a single selection assessment obtained at different times.
>
> *elements for an essay Q on exam*

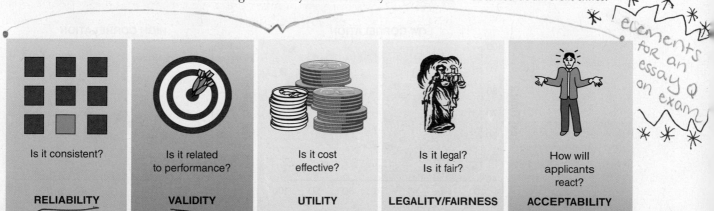

Is it consistent?	Is it related to performance?	Is it cost effective?	Is it legal? Is it fair?	How will applicants react?
RELIABILITY	**VALIDITY**	**UTILITY**	**LEGALITY/FAIRNESS**	**ACCEPTABILITY**

Figure 6.2 What Makes a Selection Method Good?

Alternate-forms method
A process of estimating reliability that compares scores on different versions of a selection assessment.

Split-halves method
A process of estimating reliability that compares scores on two parts of a selection assessment.

Inter-rater method
A process of estimating reliability that compares assessment scores provided by different raters.

Correlation coefficient
A statistical measure that describes the strength of the relationship between two measures.

reliability is to give two different forms of a test. Since both tests were designed to measure the same thing, we would expect people's scores to be similar. This is the **alternate-forms method** of estimating reliability. A similar method involves the use of a single test that is designed to be split into two halves that measure the same thing. The odd- and even-numbered questions might be written so that they are equivalent. We call this the **split-halves method** of estimating reliability. A final method, called the **inter-rater method**, involves having different raters provide evaluations and then determining whether the raters agree.

Each method of estimating reliability has its own strengths and weaknesses. However, all four methods rely on the **correlation coefficient**, a numerical indicator of the strength of the relationship between two sets of scores. Correlation coefficients range from a low of 0, which indicates no relationship, to a high of 1, which indicates a perfect relationship. Figure 6.3 provides an illustration of correlation coefficients. Two scores for each person are represented in the graph. The first score is plotted on the horizontal axis, and the second score is plotted on the vertical axis. Each person's two scores are thus represented by a dot. In the graph representing a low correlation, you can see that some people who did very well the first time did not do well the second time. Others improved a lot the second time. The scores are quite scattered, and it would be difficult to predict anyone's second score based on his or her first score. In the graph representing a high correlation, the scores begin to follow a straight line. In fact, scores with a correlation of 1 would plot as a single line where each person's second score could be predicted perfectly by his or her first score.

Correlation coefficients can also be negative (indicating that high scores on one measure are related to low scores on the other measure), but we do not generally observe negative correlations when assessing reliability. When it comes to reliability estimates, a higher correlation is always better. A correlation coefficient approaching 1 tells us that people who did well on one of the assessments generally did well on the other.

Just how high should a reliability estimate be? Of course, this depends on many different aspects of the assessment situation. Nevertheless, a good guideline is that a correlation coefficient of .85 or higher suggests adequate reliability for test-retest, alternate-forms, and split-halves estimates.[17] Inter-rater

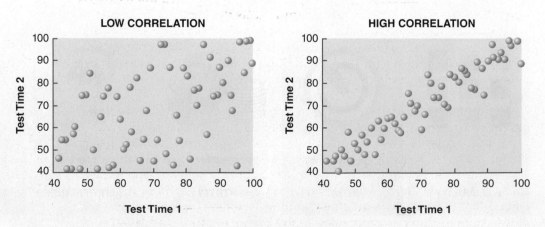

Figure 6.3 Graphical Illustration of Correlations.

reliability estimates are often lower because they incorporate subjective judgment, yet high estimates are still desirable.

Knowing in general how high reliability estimates should be makes managers and human resource specialists better consumers of selection procedures. Consulting firms and people within an organization often propose many different selection methods. Important decisions must be made about which of the many possible methods to use. The first question to ask about any selection procedure is whether it is reliable. Information about reliability should be available from vendors who advocate and sell specific tests and interview methods.

VALIDITY

Once reliability has been established, we can turn to a selection method's validity. Suppose the football coaches in the earlier example have been taught about reliability. They go back to visit the recruits again and obtain more information. This time they specifically plan to obtain consistent information. When they report back, one of the coaches states that his recruit drives a blue car. The second coach says that his recruit drives a green car. The problem of reliability has been resolved. The coaches are now providing the same information about the two recruits. However, this information most likely has nothing to do with performance on the football field. We thus conclude that the information does not have **validity**, which means that it is not relevant for job performance.

How do we know if a test is valid? Evidence of validity can come in many forms, and assessments of validity should take into account all evidence supporting a relationship between the assessment technique and job performance.[18] Nevertheless, as with reliability, certain methods for determining validity are most commonly used.

One method, called the **content validation strategy**, involves determining whether the content of the assessment method is representative of the job situation. For instance, a group of computer programmers might be asked to look at a computer programming test to determine whether the test measures knowledge needed to program successfully. The experts match tasks from the job description with skills and abilities measured by the test. Analyses are done to learn if the experts agree. The content validation strategy thus relies on expert judgments, and validity is supported when experts agree that the content of the assessment reflects the knowledge needed to perform well on the job. Content validation is a particularly important step for developing new tests and assessments. As a student, you see content validation each time you take an exam. The course instructor acts as an expert who determines whether the questions on the exam are representative of the course material.

A second method for determining validity is known as the **criterion-related validation strategy**. This method differs from the content validation strategy in that it uses correlation coefficients to show that test or interview scores are related to measures of job performance. For example, a correlation coefficient could be calculated to measure the relationship between a personality trait and the dollars of business that sales representatives generate. A positive correlation coefficient can indicate that those who have high scores on a test of assertiveness generate more sales. In this case, a negative correlation coefficient might also be instructive, as it would indicate that people who have

Validity
The quality of being justifiable. To be valid, a method of selecting employees must accurately predict who will perform the job well.

Content validation strategy
A process of estimating validity that uses expert raters to determine if a test assesses skills needed to perform a certain job.

Criterion-related validation strategy
A process of estimating validity that uses a correlation coefficient to determine whether scores on tests predict job performance.

Predictive validation strategy
A form of criterion-related validity estimation in which selection assessments are obtained from applicants before they are hired.

Concurrent validation strategy
A form of criterion-related validity estimation in which selection assessments are obtained from people who are already employees.

lower scores on a particular trait, such as anxiety, have higher sales figures. Either way, the test scores will be helpful for making hiring decisions and predicting who will do well in the sales position.

In practice, two methods can be used to calculate criterion-related validity coefficients. One method uses the **predictive validation strategy**. Here, an organization obtains assessment scores from people when they apply for jobs and then later measures their job performance. A correlation coefficient is calculated to determine the relationship between the assessment scores and performance. This method is normally considered the optimal one for estimating validity. However, its use in actual organizations presents certain problems. One problem is that it requires measures from a large number of people. If an organization hires only one or two people a month, it might take several years to obtain enough information to calculate a proper correlation coefficient. Another problem is that organizations may also be reluctant to pay for ongoing measurement before they have evidence that the assessments are really useful for predicting performance.

A second method for calculating validity coefficients uses the **concurrent validation strategy**. Here, the organization obtains assessment scores from people who are already doing the job and then calculates a correlation coefficient relating those scores to performance measures that already exist. In this case, for example, a personality test could be given to the sales representatives already working for the organization. A correlation coefficient could be calculated to determine whether sales representatives who score high on the test also have high sales figures. This method is somewhat easier to use, but it too has drawbacks. One problem is that the existing sales representatives do not complete the personality assessment under the same conditions as job applicants. Applicants may be more motivated to obtain high scores and may also inflate their responses to make themselves look better. Existing sales representatives may have also learned things and changed in ways that make them different from applicants, which might reduce the accuracy of the test for predicting who will perform best when first hired.

Neither the predictive nor the concurrent strategy is optimal in all conditions. However, both yield important information, and this information comes in the form of a correlation coefficient. How high should this correlation coefficient be? Validity coefficients are lower than reliability coefficients. This is because a reliability coefficient represents the relationship between two things that should be nearly identical. In contrast, a validity coefficient represents a relationship between two different things: the test or interview and job performance. Correlation coefficients representing validity rarely exceed .50. Many commonly used assessment techniques are associated with correlation coefficients that range from .25 to .50, and a few that are useful range from .15 to .25. This suggests that, as a guideline for assessing validity, a coefficient above .50 indicates a very strong relationship, coefficients between .25 and .50 indicate somewhat strong relationships, and correlations between .15 and .25 weaker but often important relationships.[19] Once again, this information can help managers and human resource specialists become better consumers of assessment techniques. As with reliability, information about validity should be available for properly developed selection methods.

One additional concept related to validity is generalizability, which concerns the extent to which the validity of an assessment method in one context can be used as evidence of validity in another context. In some cases, differences in the job requirements across organizations might result in an assessment that is valid in one context but not in another. For instance, a test that measures sociability may predict high performance for food servers in a sports bar but not for servers in an exclusive restaurant. This variability is known as **situational specificity**. In other cases, differences across contexts do not matter, and evidence supporting validity in one context can be used as evidence of validity in another context, a condition known as **validity generalization**. A common example of a personality trait that exhibits generalization is conscientiousness. Being organized and goal oriented seems to lead to high performance regardless of the work context. We return to this subject later in discussions about different forms of assessment.

UTILITY

The third principle associated with employee selection methods is **utility**, which concerns the method's cost effectiveness. Think back to the football example. Suppose the university has decided to give all possible recruits a one-year scholarship, see how they do during the year, and then make a selection decision about which players to keep on the team. (For the moment, we will ignore NCAA regulations.) Given an entire year to assess the recruits, the university would likely be able to make very good selection decisions, but the cost of the scholarships and the time spent making assessments would be extremely high. Would decisions be improved enough to warrant the extra cost?

Several factors influence the cost effectiveness, or utility, of a selection method. The first issue concerns validity. All other things being equal, selection methods with higher validity also have higher utility. This is because valid selection methods result in more accurate predictions. In turn, more accurate predictions result in higher work performance, which leads to greater organizational profitability.

A second issue concerns the number of people selected into a position. An organization can generate more money when it improves its hiring procedures for jobs it fills frequently. After all, a good selection procedure increases the chances of making a better decision each time it is used. Even though each decision may only be slightly better than a decision made randomly or with a different procedure, the value of all the decisions combined becomes substantial. This explains why even selection decisions with moderate to low validity may have high utility.

A third issue concerns the length of time that people stay employed. Utility is higher when people remain in their jobs for long periods of time. This principle is clear when we compare the probable monetary return of making a good selection decision for someone in a summer job versus someone in a 40-year career. Hiring a great employee for a few months can be very helpful. Hiring a great employee for an entire career, however, can yield a much greater financial benefit.

A fourth issue that influences utility is performance variability. To understand this concept, think about the difference in performance of good and bad cooks at a fast-food restaurant versus the difference in performance of cooks at an elite restaurant. The fast-food cooking process is so standardized that it usually does not matter who cooks the food. In this case, making a great selection decision has only limited value. In contrast, the cooking process at an elite restaurant requires the cook to make many decisions that directly influence the quality of the food. Selecting a good cook in this situation is

Situational specificity
The condition in which evidence of validity in one setting does not support validity in other settings.

Validity generalization
The condition in which evidence of validity in one setting can be seen as evidence of validity in other settings.

Utility
A characteristic of selection methods that reflects their cost effectiveness.

often the difference between a restaurant's success and failure. Measuring performance variability for specific jobs can be somewhat difficult. Just what is the dollar value associated with hiring a good candidate versus a bad one? A number of studies suggest that salary provides a good approximation of this value.[20] Variability in performance increases as salary increases. The dollar value of hiring a good company president is greater than the dollar value of hiring a good receptionist, and this difference is reflected in the higher compensation provided to the company president.

A fifth issue involves the ratio of applicants to hires for a particular position and concerns how choosy an organization can be. An organization that must hire three out of every four applicants is much less choosy than an organization that hires one out of every ten. If an organization hires almost everyone who applies, then it will be required to hire people even when the selection method suggests that they will not be high performers. Because people are hired regardless of the assessment results, very little value comes from developing quality selection procedures. In contrast, an organization that receives a large number of applications for each position can benefit from good selection techniques that help accurately predict which of the applicants will be the highest performer.

Still another issue related to utility is cost. Cost issues associated with selection methods can be broken into two components: fixed costs associated with developing an assessment method and variable costs that occur each time the method is used. For example, an organization may decide to use a cognitive ability test to select computer programmers. The organization will incur some expenses in identifying an appropriate test and training assessors to use it. This cost is incurred when the test is first adopted. Most likely, the organization will also pay a fee to the test developer each time it gives the test to a job applicant. In sum, utility increases when both fixed and variable costs are low. In general, less-expensive tests create more utility, as long as their validity is similar to that of more-expensive tests.

Let's look more closely at the variable costs of the assessment. Because it costs money for each person to take an assessment, utility decreases as the number of people tested or interviewed increases. However, there is a tradeoff between the number of people being assessed and selectivity. Unless a test has low validity and is very expensive, the tradeoff usually works out such that the costs associated with giving the test to a large number of people are outweighed by the advantages of being choosy and hiring only the very best applicants.

Table 6.1 summarizes factors that influence utility. Of course, dollar estimates associated with utility are based on a number of assumptions and represent predictions rather than sure bets. Just like predictions associated with financial investments, marketing predictions, and weather forecasting, these estimates will often be wrong. Some research even suggests that providing managers with detailed, complex cost information does not help persuade them to adopt the best selection methods.[21] This does not, however, mean that cost analyses are worthless. Utility estimates can be used to compare human resource investments with other investments such as buying machines or expanding market reach. Estimates are also more likely to be accepted by managers when they are presented in a less complex manner and when they are framed as opportunity costs.[22] Managers can use utility concepts to guide their decisions. For instance, managers should look for selection procedures that have high validity and relatively low cost. They should focus their

Table 6.1	*Factors Influencing Utility of Selection Methods*	
Factor	**Utility**	**When . . .**
Validity	↑	selection test accuracy increases
Number	↑	more people are hired into that position
Tenure	↑	people who are hired stay with the organization for longer time periods
Performance variation	↑	there is a lot of variation in how well people do the job
Selectivity	↑	a smaller proportion of applicants are hired
Fixed cost	↓	it is expensive to establish procedures to use the test
Variable cost	↓	the cost of each test that is given is high
Number	↓	you give the test to a lot of people

attention on improving selection decisions for jobs involving a large number of people who stay for long periods of time. They should also focus on jobs in which performance of good and bad employees varies a great deal and in which there are many applicants for each open position.

LEGALITY AND FAIRNESS

The fourth principle associated with selection decisions concerns legality and fairness. Think back to the football example again. Suppose the coaches decided to select only recruits who could pass a lie detector test. Is this legal? Chapter 3 specifically described a number of legal issues associated with human resource management.

Validity plays an important role in the legality of a selection method. As we discussed in Chapter 3, if a method results in lower hiring rates for members of a protected subgroup of people—such as people of a certain race—then adverse impact occurs. In this case, the company carries the burden of proof for demonstrating that its selection methods actually link with higher job performance. Because adverse impact exists in many organizations, being able to demonstrate validity is a legal necessity.

High validity may make it legal for an organization to use a test that screens out some subgroups at a higher rate than others, but this does not necessarily mean that everyone agrees that the test is fair and should be used. **Fairness** goes beyond legality and includes an assessment of potential bias or discrimination associated with a given selection method. Fairness concerns the probability that people will be able to perform satisfactorily in the job, even though the test predicted that they would not.

From the applicants' perspective, selection procedures are seen as more fair if they believe they are given an opportunity to demonstrate their skills and qualifications.[23] Because of this and other factors, assessments of fairness often depend a great deal on personal values. The very purpose of employee selection is to make decisions that discriminate against some people. Under optimal conditions, this discrimination is related only to differences in job performance. Yet no selection procedure has perfect validity. All techniques screen out some people who would actually perform well if given the opportunity. For example, some research has found that tests can unfairly screen out individuals who believe that people like them don't

Fairness
A characteristic of selection methods that reflects individuals' perceptions concerning potential bias and discrimination in the selection methods.

perform well on the specific test.[24] For instance, a woman may not perform well on a mathematics test if she believes that women aren't good at math. Simply seeing the test as biased can result in decreased motivation to try hard and thereby lower scores, even though these people have the skills necessary to do the job.

Even tests with relatively high validity screen out a number of people who could perform the job. Thus, some employee selection procedures may provide economic value to organizations at the expense of individuals who are screened out even though they would perform well. This situation creates a tradeoff between a firm's desire to be profitable and society's desire for everyone with an equal chance to obtain quality employment. Perceptions of the proper balance between these values differ depending on personal values, making fairness a social rather than scientific concept.

ACCEPTABILITY

Acceptability
A characteristic of selection methods that reflects applicants' beliefs about the appropriateness of the selection methods.

• How applicant's accept method of selection

A final principle for determining the merit of selection techniques is **acceptability**, which concerns how applicants perceive the technique. Can a selection method make people see the organization as a less-desirable place to work? Think back to the football coaches. Suppose they came up with a test of mental toughness that subjected recruits to intense physical pain. Would completing the test make some recruits see the school less favorably? Would some potential players choose to go to other schools that did not require such a test?

The football example shows that selection is a two-way process. As an organization is busy assessing people, those same people are making judgments about whether they really want to work for the organization. Applicants see selection methods as indicators of an organization's culture, which can influence not only their decisions to join the organization but also subsequent feelings of job satisfaction and commitment.[25] Organizations should thus be careful about the messages that their selection techniques are sending to applicants.

In general, applicants have negative reactions to assessment techniques when they believe that the organization does not need the information being gathered—that the information is not job related. For instance, applicants tend to believe that family and childhood experiences are private and unrelated to work performance. Applicants also tend to be skeptical when they do not think the information from a selection assessment can be evaluated correctly. In this sense, many applicants react negatively to handwriting analysis and psychological assessment because they do not believe these techniques yield information that can be accurately scored.[26]

One interesting finding is that perceptions of fairness differ among countries. For instance, people in France see handwriting analysis and personality testing as more acceptable than do people in the United States. At the same time, people in the United States see interviews, résumés, and biographical data as more acceptable than do people in France.[27]

There is also some evidence that applicants react more positively to a particular assessment when they believe they will do well on it. One study, for example, found people who use illegal drugs to be less favorable about drug testing.[28] Although this is hardly surprising, it does illustrate the complexity of understanding individual reactions to employee selection techniques.

CONCEPT CHECK

1. *What criteria are used to determine whether employee selection methods are good?*
2. *What are ways to assess selection method validity?*
3. *What influences the cost effectiveness of a selection method?*

LEARNING OBJECTIVE **3**

What Selection Methods Are Commonly Used?

Methods for selecting employees include testing, gathering information, and interviewing. We discuss particular practices associated with each of these categories in the sections that follow.

TESTING

Employment testing provides a method for assessing individual characteristics that help some people be more effective employees than others. Tests provide a common set of questions or tasks to be completed by each job applicant. Different types of tests measure knowledge, skill, and ability, as well as other characteristics, such as personality traits.

Cognitive Ability Testing

Being smart is often measured through **cognitive ability testing**, which assesses learning, understanding, and ability to solve problems.[29] Cognitive ability tests are sometimes referred to as "intelligence" or "mental ability" tests. Some measure ability in a number of specific areas, such as verbal reasoning and quantitative problem solving. However, research suggests that general mental ability, which is represented by a summation of the specific measures, is the best predictor of performance in work contexts.[30] Of course, cognitive ability is somewhat related to education, but actual test scores have been shown to predict job performance better than measures of educational attainment.[31]

In general, cognitive ability tests are very effective selection tools. Specifically, they have high reliability; people tend to score similarly at different times and on different test forms.[32] In addition, these tests are difficult to fake, and people are generally unable to substantially improve their scores by simply taking courses that teach approaches to taking the test.[33] Validity is higher for cognitive ability tests than for any other selection method.[34] This high validity, combined with relatively low cost, results in substantial utility. Cognitive ability tests are good, inexpensive predictors of job performance.

A particularly impressive feature of cognitive ability tests is their validity generalization. They predict performance across jobs and across cultures.[35] Everything else being equal, people with higher cognitive ability perform better regardless of the type of work they do.[36] Nevertheless, the benefits of high

Cognitive ability testing
Assessment of a person's capability to learn and solve problems.

Table 6.2	*Wonderlic Personnel Test Sample Questions*

1. Which of the following is the earliest date?

   A) Jan. 16, 1898   B) Feb. 21, 1889   C) Feb. 2, 1898   D) Jan. 7, 1898   E) Jan. 30, 1889

2. LOW is to **HIGH** as **EASY** is to ___?___

   J) **SUCCESSFUL**   K) **PURE**   L) **TALL**   M) **INTERESTING**   N) **DIFFICULT**

3. What is the next number in the series?   29   41   53   65   77   ___?___

   J) 75   K) 88   L) 89   M) 98   N) 99

4. *One word below appears in color. What is OPPOSITE of that word?*

   She gave a complex answer to the question and we all agreed with her.

   A) long   B) better   C) simple   D) wrong   E) kind

5. Jose's monthly parking fee for April was $150; for May it was $10 more than April; and for June $40 more than May. His average monthly parking fee was ___?___ for these 3 months.

   J) $66   K) $160   L) $166   M) $170   N) $200

6. *If the first two statements are true, is the final statement true?*
   Sandra is responsible for ordering all office supplies.
   Notebooks are office supplies.

   Sandra is responsible for ordering notebooks.

   A) yes   B) no   C) uncertain

7. Which THREE of the following words have similar meanings?

   A) observable   B) manifest   C) hypothetical   D) indefinite   E) theoretical

8. Last year, 12 out of 600 employees at a service organization were rewarded for their excellence in customer service, which was ___?___ of the employees.

   J) 1%   K) 2%   L) 3%   M) 4%   N) 6%

Correct Answers: 1. E, 2. N, 3. L, 4. C, 5. M, 6. A, 7. CDE, 8. K

Source: Sample items for Wonderlic Personnel Test-Revised (WPT-R). Reprinted with permission from Wonderlic, Inc.

cognitive ability are greater for more complex jobs, such as computer programmer or physician.[37] One explanation is the link between cognitive ability and problem solving. People with higher cognitive ability obtain more knowledge.[38] Example items from a widely used cognitive ability test are shown in Table 6.2. Can you see why these tests predict performance better in complex jobs? Researchers have also posited that people with higher cognitive ability adapt to change more quickly, although the actual evidence supporting better adaptation is inconsistent.[39]

A concern about cognitive ability tests is that people from different racial groups tend to score differently.[40] This does not mean that every individual from a lower-scoring group will score low. Some individuals from each group will score better and some will score worse, but on average, some groups do worse than others. The result is adverse impact, wherein cognitive ability tests screen out a higher percentage of applicants from some minority groups. Because of their strong link with job performance, cognitive tests can be used legally in most settings. However, a frequent social consequence of using cognitive ability tests is the hiring of fewer minority workers.

In terms of acceptability, managers see cognitive ability as one of the most important predictors of work performance.[41] Human resource professionals and researchers strongly believe in the validity of cognitive ability tests, even though some express concern about the societal consequences of their use.[42] In contrast, job applicants often perceive other selection methods as being more effective.[43] Not surprisingly, negative beliefs about cognitive ability tests are stronger for people who do not perform well on the tests.[44]

In summary, cognitive ability tests are a useful tool for determining whom to hire. As discussed in the "How Do We Know?" feature, these tests can predict long-term success. They predict potential more than achievement, making them best suited for organizations pursuing long-term staffing strategies. High cognitive ability is particularly important for success in organizations with long-term staffing strategies, as employees must learn and adapt during long careers. Using cognitive ability tests is thus beneficial for organizations seeking long-term generalists and specialists. Organizations seeking short-term generalists can also benefit by using these tests to inexpensively assess basic math and language ability.

Personality Testing

Personality testing measures patterns of thought, emotion, and behavior.[45] Researchers have identified five broad dimensions of personality: agreeableness, conscientiousness, emotional stability, extraversion, and openness to experience.[46] The five broad personality dimensions can be accurately measured in numerous languages and cultures, making the tests useful for global firms.

Personality testing
Assessment of traits that show consistency in behavior.

How Do We Know?

IS IT BETTER TO BE SMART OR BEAUTIFUL?

Do smart people have a better chance of getting rich? How about people who are physically attractive? Are they more likely to be rich? Timothy Judge, Charlice Hurst, and Lauren Simon sought to answer these questions with a study of 191 randomly selected people between the ages of 25 and 74. Participants completed a cognitive ability measure and reported on their level of education attainment and their core self-evaluations (levels of confidence, self-esteem, sense of internal control, and lack of anxiety). They also provided a photograph that was rated for physical attractiveness. At a later time, participants also reported their income.

Results showed a positive effect on income for both intelligence and beauty. Smarter people had higher income, as did people who were rated higher on physical attractiveness. Smarter people attained more education and had more positive perceptions about themselves, which in turn translated into higher income. The effect was similar for physical attractiveness. Better-looking people similarly attained more education and had more positive self-perceptions, which corresponded with increased income.

Bottom Line. Being either smart or good looking makes someone more likely to be rich. But if you had to choose one or the other, choose being smart, as the effect of being smart was twice as large as the effect of being beautiful. Nevertheless, the authors conclude that being beautiful does indeed provide people with a seemingly unfair advantage.

Source: Timothy A. Judge, Charlice Hurst, and Lauren S. Simon, "Does It Pay to Be Smart, Attractive, or Confident (or All Three)? Relationships Among General Mental Ability, Physical Attractiveness, Core Self-Evaluations, and Income," *Journal of Applied Psychology* 94 (2009): 742–755.

Table 6.3	*Summary of Personality Testing Research*		
		Average Correlation with Job Performance	**Average Correlation with Job Satisfaction**
Openness to Experience—High scorers are imaginative, idealistic, unconventional, not cautious, and inventive		.07	.02
Extraversion—High scorers are sociable, aggressive, not shy, enthusiastic, cheerful, and forceful		.15	.25
Emotional Stability—High scorers are not anxious, contented, confident, not moody, not irritable, and not fearful		.15	.29
Conscientiousness—High scorers are efficient, organized, goal-driven, ambitious, and thorough		.24	.20
Agreeableness—High scorers are forgiving, trusting, friendly, not stubborn, warm, and sympathetic		.11	.17

Sources: Information from Timothy A. Judge, Daniel Heller, and Michael K. Mount, "Five-Factor Model of Personality and Job Satisfaction: A Meta-Analysis," *Journal of Applied Psychology* 87 (2002): 530–541; Murray R. Barrick, Michael K. Mount, and Timothy A. Judge, "Personality and Performance at the Beginning of the Millennium," *International Journal of Selection and Assessment* 9 (2001): 9–30.

Patterns of relationships with work performance are similar across national boundaries.[47] A description of each dimension and a summary of its general relationships to job performance and job satisfaction are presented in Table 6.3.

Looking at personality tests in general, we find that measures for the five personality dimensions demonstrate adequate reliability.[48] Different forms and parts of the test correlate highly with each other.

Personality tests with items that specifically ask about typical actions in employment settings tend to yield consistent measures of behaviors that are important at work.[49] Specifically, relationships between personality dimensions and performance, which represent validity, are highest when tests specifically instruct people to respond in relation their work behavior, rather than in relation to their actions across different settings.[50] Personality traits are generally good predictors of citizenship behavior such as helping others and going beyond minimum expectations.[51] Yet, strength of validity often differs depending on the personality dimension being measured. In general, personality dimensions associated with motivation are good predictors of performance. One such dimension is conscientiousness.

Conscientious employees are motivated—they set goals and work hard to accomplish tasks.[52] Conscientious people also tend to be absent from work less frequently.[53] Conscientious workers are more satisfied with their jobs and are more likely to go beyond minimum expectations to make the organization successful.[54] Conscientiousness thus exhibits validity generalization in that it predicts work performance regardless of the type of work. Research evidence suggests that emotional stability does not relate as strongly to performance as conscientiousness, yet, it too captures aspects of motivation and demonstrates validity generalization. People high on emotional stability are more confident in their capabilities, which in turn increases persistence and effort.[55] Yet, people who are highly anxious can actually perform better in some contexts, such as air traffic controller, that require workers to pay very close attention to detail in a busy environment.[56]

Relationships with the other three personality dimensions depend on the work situation, meaning that these measures have situational specificity.

Extraversion corresponds with a desire to get ahead and receive rewards, making it a useful predictor for performance in sales and leadership positions.[57] More extraverted employees who are also more emotionally stable—think happy and bubbly personalities—have also been found to excel in customer-service jobs such as those found in a health and fitness center. Agreeableness is important for interpersonal relationships and corresponds with high performance in teams and service jobs that require frequent interaction with customers.[58] Much of this effect occurs because agreeable employees are more likely to go beyond minimum expectations and help their coworkers.[59] Openness to experience is seldom related to work performance, but recent research suggests that it can increase performance in jobs that require creativity and adaptation to change.[60] One setting requiring adaptation is working in a foreign country, and people more open to experience do indeed perform better in such assignments.[61] People who are more open to experience are also more likely to be entrepreneurs.[62]

A notable feature of personality tests is their helpfulness in predicting the performance of entire teams. Teams that include just one person who is low on agreeableness or conscientiousness have lower performance.[63] This means that personality tests predict not only individual performance but also how an individual's characteristics will influence the performance of other people. This feature increases the utility of personality testing, because hiring someone with desirable traits yields benefits related not just to the performance of that individual but also to the performance of others.

As shown in Table 6.4, a survey of selection practices around the world suggests that personality testing is used more frequently in countries other than the U.S. Within the U.S a few states have laws that prohibit personality testing. However, in most cases, the use of personality tests does not present problems as long as organizations use well-developed tests that do not ask outwardly

Table 6.4	*Use of Selection Methods Around the World*				

Values are based on average ratings with 5 = Always and 1 = Never; Higher scores represent more widespread use

| Selection Method | Scores | | | | |
	United States	Portugal	France	Hong Kong	South Africa
Cognitive ability test	2.09	3.27	2.29	1.83	3.25
Personality test	1.62	3.00	3.42	2.50	3.66
Physical ability test	1.21	1.69	1.29	1.17	1.26
Integrity test	1.09	1.92	1.00	1.33	1.62
Drug test	2.21	1.93	1.18	1.17	1.58
Application form	4.12	3.40	4.09	4.75	4.20
Biodata	1.21	2.29	1.20	1.62	1.41
Work sample	1.40	1.69	1.50	1.83	1.71
Reference check	4.02	3.14	3.32	3.75	4.09
Individual interview	4.78	4.77	4.85	3.38	4.72
Panel interview	3.27	3.29	2.06	3.63	3.63
Handwriting analysis	1.09	1.00	3.26	1.00	1.45

Source: Information from Ann Marie Ryan, Lynn McFarland, Helen Baron, and Ron Page, "An International Look at Selection Practices: Nation and Culture as Explanations for Variability in Practice," *Personnel Psychology* 52 (1999): 359–391.

discriminatory questions.[64] Personality tests do have some adverse impact for women and minorities. For minorities the negative effect is less than that for cognitive ability tests.[65]

With regard to acceptability, a common concern about the use of personality tests is the potential for people to fake their responses. Indeed, research has shown that people are capable of faking and obtaining higher scores when instructed to do so. Moreover, people do inflate their scores when they are being evaluated for selection.[66] Although faking does have the potential to make personality tests less valid predictors of job performance,[67] the overall relationship between personality measures and job performance remains,[68] meaning that even with faking, personality tests can be valid selection measures. Using statistical procedures to try correcting for faking does little to improve the validity of tests.[69] However, faking does involve issues of fairness. Some people fake more than others, and people who do not inflate their scores may be unfairly eliminated from jobs.[70] Faking can thus lead to decisions that are unfair for some individuals, even though it has little negative consequence for the organization. To reduce the potentially negative impact on individuals, organizations can use personality tests in early stages of the selection process to screen out low scorers rather than in later stages to make final decisions about a few individuals.[71] Obtaining personality scores from ratings provided by friends and coworkers rather than applicants themselves is also helpful, and current research is exploring the usefulness of techniques such as eye-tracking technology to identify when applicants are faking.[72]

Another method for reducing faking is to create personality tests with items that have less obvious answers. An example of this approach is a conditional reasoning test. Conditional reasoning tests are designed to assess unconscious biases and motives. With this approach, job applicants are asked to solve reasoning problems which do not have answers that are obviously right or wrong. People with certain tendencies base their decisions on particular forms of reasoning.[73] For example, a person prone to aggression is more likely to attribute actions of others as hostile. What appears to be the most reasonable answer to the aggressive person (that other people do things because they are mean) is different from what less-aggressive people see as the most reasonable answer. Because they tap into unconscious beliefs, these tests are more difficult to fake.[74] Unfortunately, conditional reasoning tests are somewhat difficult to create and as of yet do not measure the full array of personality traits.

Personality testing, then, is another generally effective tool for determining whom to hire. These tests are increasingly available on the Internet, as explained in the accompanying "Technology in HR" feature. This makes personality tests relatively simple to administer. Yet, personality tests often relate more to organization fit than to job fit, suggesting that personality measures are most appropriate in organizations that adopt long-term staffing strategies. People with personality traits that fit an organization's culture and work demands are more likely to remain with the organization.[75] Personality testing is thus especially beneficial for organizations adopting Committed Expert and Loyal Soldier HR Strategies.

Situational Judgment Tests

Situational judgment tests are a relatively new development. These tests place job applicants in a hypothetical situation and then ask them to choose the most appropriate response. Items can be written to assess job knowledge, general cognitive ability, or practical savvy. Indeed, a potential strength of these

Situational judgment test
Assessment that asks job applicants what they would do, or should do, in a hypothetical situation.

Technology in HR

ADMINISTERING TESTS ON THE INTERNET

Widespread access to computers and the Internet provides a potentially improved method for administering employment tests. Using the Internet, people can take tests whenever and wherever they want. Testing can also be individualized so that responses to early questions are used to choose additional questions. Perhaps more important, scoring can be done quickly and accurately. These potential benefits are accompanied by a number of concerns, however.

One source of concern is test security. If someone takes a test at home, can the organization be sure that the test was actually completed by the applicant? Are scores from a computer version of a test equivalent to scores from a paper-and-pencil version of the test? Do people fake their scores more when using a computer? Will people from racial subgroups score higher or lower on a computerized test?

Given the potential benefits of computer-administered tests, researchers have conducted a great deal of research in this area. One large study compared responses from 2,544 people completing a paper-and-pencil version of a personality and biographical data test with responses from 2,356 people completing the same test in a Web-based format. The computer test had higher reliability and less evidence of faking. Other studies have generally concluded that computer-administered tests are just as reliable and valid as traditional tests. In addition, in many instances, computer-based tests have less adverse impact and are seen as more fair by applicants from minority groups. Overall, the results suggest that increased use of technology can result in improved employment testing.

Concerns about faking do, nevertheless, continue to be discussed, and evidence suggests that

©Jeff Morgan Education/Alamy

applicants who take a test multiple times do indeed raise their scores on subsequent tests. Providing a warning that faking will be assessed and detected does, however, appear to reduce instances of distortion.

Sources: Information from Richard N. Landers, Paul R. Sackett, and Kathy A. Tuzinski, "Retesting after Initial Failure, Coaching Rumors, and Warnings Against Faking in Online Personality Measures for Selection," *Journal of Applied Psychology* 96 (2011): 202–210; Robert E. Ployhart, Jeff A. Weekley, Brian C. Holtz, and Cary Kemp, "Web-Based and Paper and Pencil Testing of Applicants in a Proctored Setting: Are Personality, Biodata, and Situational Judgment Tests Comparable?" *Personnel Psychology* 56 (2003): 733–752; Wendy L. Richman, Sara Keisler, Suzanne Weisband, and Fritz Drasgow, "A Meta-Analytic Study of Social Desirability Distortion in Computer-Administered Questionnaires, Traditional Questionnaires, and Interviews," *Journal of Applied Psychology* 84 (1999): 754–775.

tests is their ability to assess interpersonal skills, which are difficult to measure.[76] Situational judgment tests also tend to capture broad personality traits such as conscientiousness and agreeableness, as well as tendencies toward certain behavior (like taking initiative) in more specific situations.[77]

Some situational judgment tests use a knowledge format that asks respondents to pick the answer that is most correct. Other tests use a behavioral tendency format that asks respondents to report what they would actually do in the situation. Although the questions are framed a bit differently, the end result seems to be the same.[78] Situational judgment tests have been found to have good reliability and validity. They predict job performance in most jobs, and they provide information that goes beyond cognitive ability and personality tests.[79] Situational judgment tests thus appear to represent an extension of other tests. They closely parallel structured interviews, which we will discuss shortly. Questions can be framed to measure either potential in organizations with long-term orientations or achievement and knowledge in organizations with short-term labor strategies. They can also be designed to emphasize either general traits or specific skills. This makes them useful for organizations pursuing any of the human resource strategies.

Physical Ability Testing

Physical ability testing assesses muscular strength, cardiovascular endurance, and coordination.[80] These tests are useful for predicting performance in many manual labor positions and in jobs that require physical strength. Physical ability tests can be particularly important in relation to the Americans with Disabilities Act, as organizations can be held liable for discrimination against disabled applicants. Managers making selection decisions should thus test individuals with physical disabilities and not automatically assume that they cannot do the job.

Physical ability tests have high reliability; people score similarly when the same test is given at different times. Validity and utility are also high for positions that require physical inputs, such as police officer, firefighter, utility repair operator, and construction worker.[81] Validity generalization is supported for positions where job analysis has shown work requirements to be physically demanding.[82]

As long as job analysis has identified the need for physical inputs, physical ability testing presents few legal problems. However, men and women do score very differently on physical ability tests. Women score higher on tests of coordination and dexterity, whereas men score higher on tests of muscular strength.[83] Physical ability tests thus demonstrate adverse impact. In particular, selection decisions based on physical ability tests often result in exclusion of women from jobs that require heavy lifting and carrying.

The usefulness of physical ability testing is not limited to a particular HR strategy. Physical tests can be useful for organizations seeking any form of talent, as long as the talent relates to physical dimensions of work.

Integrity Testing

In the past, some employers used polygraph—or lie detector—tests to screen out job applicants who might steal from them. However, the Employee Polygraph Protection Act of 1988 generally made it illegal to use polygraph tests for hiring decisions. Since then, organizations have increasingly turned to paper-and-pencil tests for **integrity testing**. Such tests are designed to assess the likelihood that applicants will be dishonest or engage in illegal activity.

There are two types of integrity test: overt and covert. Overt tests ask questions about attitudes toward theft and other illegal activities. Covert tests are more personality-based and seek to predict dishonesty by assessing attitudes

Integrity testing
Assessment of the likelihood that an individual will be dishonest.

and tendencies toward antisocial behaviors such as violence and substance abuse.[84]

Research evidence generally supports the reliability and validity of integrity tests. These tests predict absenteeism and overall performance, but they most strongly correspond with counterproductive work behavior such as theft, property destruction, unsafe actions, poor attendance, and intentional poor performance.[85] Most often, such tests are used in contexts that involve the handling of money, such as banking and retail sales.

In many ways, integrity tests are similar to personality tests. In fact, strong correlations exist between integrity test scores and personality test scores, particularly for conscientiousness.[86] As with personality tests, a concern is that people may fake their responses when jobs are on the line. The evidence suggests that people can and do respond differently when they know they are being evaluated for a job. Even so, links remain between test scores and subsequent measures of ethical behavior.[87] Furthermore, integrity tests show no adverse impact for minorities[88] and appear to predict performance consistently across national cultures.[89]

Integrity tests can be useful for organizations with Bargain Labor HR strategies. These firms hire many entry-level workers to fill positions in which they handle substantial amounts of money. In such cases, integrity tests can provide a relatively inexpensive method for screening applicants. This explains why organizations like grocery stores, fast-food chains, and convenience stores make extensive use of integrity testing to select cashiers.[90]

Drug Testing

Drug testing normally requires applicants to provide a urine sample that is tested for illegal substances. It is quite common in the United States, perhaps because, according to some estimates as much as 14 percent of the workforce uses illegal drugs, with as many as 3 percent of workers actually using drugs while at work.[91] Illegal drug use has been linked to absenteeism, accidents, and likelihood of quitting.[92] Drug testing, which is both reliable and valid, appears to be a useful selection method for decreasing such nonproductive activities. Even though administration costs can be high, basic tests are modestly priced, supporting at least moderate utility for drug testing.

Research related to drug testing has looked at how people react to being tested. In general, people see drug testing as most appropriate for safety-sensitive jobs such as pilot, heart surgeon, and truck driver.[93] Not surprisingly, people who use illicit drugs are more likely to think negatively about drug testing.[94]

Drug testing can be useful for firms that hire most types of talent. Organizations seeking short-term generalists use drug testing in much the same way as integrity testing. Organizations with long-term employees frequently do work that requires safe operational procedures. In these organizations, drug testing is useful in selecting people for positions such as forklift operator, truck driver, and medical care provider.

Work Sample Testing

One way of assessing specific skills is **work sample testing**, which directly measures performance on some element of the job. Common examples include typing tests, computer programming tests, driving simulator tests, and electronics repair tests. In most cases, these tests have excellent reliability and validity.[95] Many work sample tests are relatively inexpensive as well, which

Work sample testing
Assessment of performance on tasks that represent specific job actions.

translates into high utility. Because they measure actual on-the-job activities, work sample tests also involve few legal problems. However, in some cases work test scores are lower for members of minority groups.[96]

A problem with work sample tests is that not all jobs lend themselves to this sort of testing. What type of work sample test would you use for a medical doctor or an attorney, for example? The complexity of these jobs makes the creation of work sample tests very difficult. However, human resource specialists have spent a great deal of time and effort developing a work sample test for the complex job of manager. The common label for this tool is **assessment center**.

Assessment center
A complex selection method that includes multiple measures obtained from multiple applicants across multiple days.

Assessment center participants spend a number of days with other managerial candidates. Several raters observe and evaluate the participants' behavior across a variety of exercises. In one typical assessment center exercise, the leaderless group discussion, for example, managerial candidates work together in a group to solve a problem in the absence of a formal leader. For the in-basket exercise, participants write a number of letters and memos that simulate managerial decision making and communication. Managers and recruiters from the organization serve as observers who rate the participants in areas such as consideration and awareness of others, communication, motivation, ability to influence others, organization and planning, and problem solving.[97]

Assessment centers have good reliability and validity, which suggests that they can be excellent selection tools in many contexts.[98] Validity improves when assessment center evaluators are trained and when exercises are specifically tailored to fit the job activities of the participants.[99] Minority racial groups have been found to score lower in assessment centers, but women often score higher.[100] Creating and operating an assessment center can be very expensive, which substantially decreases utility for many organizations. Because of their high cost, assessment centers are normally found only in very large organizations.

Assessment centers are most common in organizations with long-term staffing strategies, particularly those adopting Committed Expert HR strategies. Proper placement of individuals is extremely critical for these organizations, and the value of selecting someone for a long career offsets the high initial cost of assessment. Other types of work sample tests are useful for organizations pursuing any of the staffing strategies. A typing test can be a valuable aid for hiring a temporary employee as part of a Bargain Laborer HR strategy, for example. Similarly, a computer programming test can be helpful when hiring someone as part of a Free Agent HR strategy.

INFORMATION GATHERING

In addition to tests, organizations use a variety of methods to directly gather information about the work experiences and qualifications of potential employees. In fact, as illustrated in the "Building Strength Through HR" feature, most organizations combine multiple methods of testing and information gathering. Common methods for gathering information include application forms and résumés, biographical data, and reference checking.

Application Forms and Résumés
Many entry-level jobs require potential employees to complete an application form. Application forms ask for information such as address and phone number, education, work experience, and special training. For professional-level jobs, similar information is generally presented in résumés. The reliability

Building Strength Through HR

TARGET

Target has over 1,700 retail stores that employ 365,000 people. Achieving the overall corporate goal of "friendly service from team members ready to assist with your list, fully stocked shelves and a speedy checkout process" necessitates effective employee selection. Target thus uses a variety of selection tools to help identify job candidates who are friendly and have an upbeat attitude. Specific methods include the following:

- Personality test
- Behavioral interview
- Drug test
- Background check

Using such selection tools has helped Target develop a reputation as having excellent customer service. The process also seems to be acceptable to most candidates, as two stores opening in Los Angeles recently reported having over 4,000 applicants for 250 positions.

The selection tools do, however, sometimes generate controversy from people believing the tests and information gathering discriminate unfairly. For example, a number of years ago Target's use of a specific personality test was challenged because some of the questions asked about sexual practices and religious beliefs. Keeping up with advances in test development, Target settled the claims and replaced the test with an improved personality assessment that does not contain problematic

inquiries. A more recent controversy focuses on background checks that are being challenged because they screen out workers with criminal records. A group called TakeAction Minnesota filed complaints with the Equal Employment Opportunity Commission claiming that the practice is unfair and potentially creates adverse impact for some minority groups. Target's response is that the background check is necessary to provide a safe and secure environment, and that the process is not designed to screen out everyone with a criminal background but only those who present an unreasonable risk to safety.

Sources: Information from target.com; Anonymous, "Complaints Filed Against Target Hiring Policies, *St. Cloud Times,* February 21, 2013; Clair Gordon, jobs. aol.com, August 31, 2012. Accessed online at http://jobs.aol.com/articles/2012/08/31/ target-is-hiring-the-inside-scoop-on-getting-a-job/.

and validity of these selection methods depends a great deal on the information being collected and evaluated. Measures of things such as work experience and education have at least moderately strong relationships with job performance.[101]

With regard to education, the evidence shows that what you do in college really does matter. Employees with more education are absent less, show more creativity, and demonstrate higher task performance.[102] People who complete higher levels of education and participate in extracurricular activities are more effective managers. Those who study humanities and social sciences tend to have better interpersonal and leadership skills than engineers and science majors.[103] Grades received, particularly in a major, also have a moderate relationship with job performance, even though managers do not always use grades for making selection decisions.[104]

Application forms and résumés also provide valuable information about work experience. People with more work experience have usually held more different positions, been in those positions for longer periods, and more often done important tasks.[105] Because they have been exposed to many different tasks, and because they have learned by doing, people with greater experience are more valuable contributors. In addition, success in previous jobs demonstrates high motivation, and executives with more experience are better at strategic thinking.[106] Work experience thus correlates positively with performance, particularly when performance is determined by output measures such as production or amount of sales.[107]

One special advantage of application forms and résumés is their utility. Because these measures are generally inexpensive, they are frequently used as early screening devices. In terms of legality and fairness, measures of education and experience do have some adverse impact.[108] Information being obtained from application forms and résumés should therefore be related to job performance to ensure validity.

Application forms and résumés can provide important information about past achievements, which makes them most valuable for organizations seeking people with specific skills. However, these selection tools can also capture potential and fit, so many organizations seeking long-term employees find them useful as well. Application forms are used mostly in organizations hiring generalists. They provide good measures of work experience and education that help identify people who have been dependable in jobs and school. Résumés are more commonly used in organizations that hire specialists. In particular, résumés provide information about experience and education relevant to a particular position.

Biographical Data

Biographical data
Assessment focusing on previous events and experiences in an applicant's life.

Organizations also collect **biographical data**, or biodata, about applicants. Collecting biodata involves asking questions about historical events that have shaped a person's behavior and identity.[109] Some questions seek information about early life experiences that are assumed to affect personality and values. Other questions focus on an individual's prior achievements based on the idea that past behavior is the best predictor of future behavior. Common categories for biographical questions include family relationships, childhood interests, school performance, club memberships, and time spent in various leisure activities. Specific questions might include the following:

How much time did you spend with your father when you were a teenager?
What activities did you most enjoy when you were growing up?
How many jobs have you held in the past five years?

Job recruiters frequently see these measures as indicators of not only physical and mental ability but also interpersonal skill and leadership.[110] The information provided by biodata measures does not duplicate information from other measures, such as personality measures, however.[111]

Biodata measures have been around for a long time, and they are generally useful for selecting employees. Scoring keys can be developed so that biodata responses can be scored objectively, just like a test. Objective scoring methods improve the reliability and validity of biodata. With such procedures, biodata has adequate reliability.[112] Validity is also good, as studies show relatively strong relationships with job performance and employee turnover.[113] In particular, biodata measures appear to have high validity for predicting sales performance.[114] One common concern has been the validity generalizability of biodata. Questions that link with performance in one setting may not be useful in other settings. However, some recent research suggests that carefully constructed biographical measures can predict performance across work settings.[115] Identifying measures that predict work performance across settings can help overcome a weakness of biodata, which is the high initial cost of creating measures. Finding items that separate high and low performers can take substantial time and effort, making items that predict performance across settings highly desirable.

Some human resource specialists express concern about legality and fairness issues with biodata. Much of the information collected involves things beyond the control of the person being evaluated for the job and is likely to have adverse impact for some. For instance, children from less wealthy homes may not have had as many opportunities to read books. Applicants' responses may also be difficult to verify, making it likely that they will fake. Using questions that are objective, verifiable, and job-related can minimize these concerns.[116]

Biodata measures can benefit organizations, whatever their staffing strategies. Organizations seeking long-term employees want to measure applicants' potential and should therefore use biodata measures that assess core traits and values. In contrast, organizations seeking short-term employees want to measure achievement and can benefit most from measures that assess verifiable achievements.

Reference Checking

Reference checking involves contacting an applicant's previous employers, teachers, or friends to learn more about the applicant. Reference checking is one of the most common selection methods, but available information suggests that it is not generally a valid selection method.[117]

The primary reason reference checking may not be valid relates to a legal issue. Organizations can be held accountable for what they say about current or past employees. A bad reference can become the basis for a lawsuit claiming **defamation of character**, which occurs when something untrue and harmful is said about someone. Many organizations thus adopt policies that prevent managers and human resource specialists from providing more than dates of employment and position. Such information is, of course, of little value. Even when organizations allow managers to give more information, the applicant has normally provided the names only of people who will give positive recommendations.

Nevertheless, a second legal issue makes reference checks critical in certain situations. This issue is **negligent hiring**, which can occur when an organization hires someone who harms another person and the organization could reasonably have determined that the employee was unfit.[118] For instance, suppose an organization has hired someone to be a daycare provider. Further suppose that the organization did not conduct a thorough background investigation and that, if it had investigated, it could easily have discovered that the person had been previously convicted of child abuse. If this person abuses children in the employment setting, the organization can be held liable.

The competing legal issues of defamation of character and negligent hiring make reference checking particularly troublesome. On the one hand, most organizations are not willing to risk providing reference information. On the other hand, safety concerns make a background check mandatory for many jobs, such as daycare provider, transportation worker, and security

Defamation of character
Information that causes injury to another's reputation or character; can arise as a legal issue when an organization provides negative information about a current or former employee.

Negligent hiring
A legal issue that can arise when an organization does not thoroughly evaluate the background of an applicant who is hired and then harms someone.

retention - they didn't get him out of the air fast enough guard. One result has been the growth of professional firms that use public information sources, such as criminal records and motor vehicle registrations, to learn about an applicant's history. Such investigations should be conducted only after initial screening tools have been used and only if the applicant signs an authorization release.

INTERVIEWING

The most frequently used selection method is interviewing, which occurs when applicants respond to questions posed by a manager or some other organizational representative. Most interviews incorporate conversation between the interviewer and the applicant. The interview is useful not only for evaluating applicants but also for providing information to applicants and selling the organization as a desirable place to work.

Assessing Interview Effectiveness

Depending on the questions, an interview can be used to measure a variety of characteristics. Typical areas include knowledge of job procedures, mental ability, personality, communication ability, and social skills. The interview also provides an effective format for obtaining information about background credentials, such as education and experience.[119] People who are more conscientious and extraverted tend to do better in interviews, partly because they tend to spend more time learning about the company and position before the interview actually occurs.[120] Applicants who present themselves well and build rapport with the interviewer also excel in interviews.[121] As described in the "How Do We Know?" feature, even how someone shakes hands can make a difference.

Although the research is somewhat mixed, it appears that applicants who receive training in how to act in interviews do indeed perform better.[122] One concern about the interview is that candidates seek to impress interviewers, which means that the interviewer is not seeing and evaluating the true person. Evidence does indeed show that job applicants seek to manage impressions in job interviews, and that people who excel at making a good impression are not necessarily higher performers.[123]

Although researchers have historically argued that the interview is not a reliable and valid selection method, managers have continued to use this method. Recent research suggests that the conclusions of early studies were overly pessimistic and that managers are right in believing that the interview is a useful tool.

The reliability of interviews depends on the type of interview being conducted. We discuss some particularly reliable types of interviews shortly. For these types, reliability can be as high as for other measures, such as personality testing and assessment centers.[124] The overall validity of the interview is in the moderate range. However, again, validity varies for different types of interviews, with some types showing validity that is as high as that for any selection method.[125] The interview also provides unique information that cannot be obtained through other methods.[126]

The interview is also valuable in determining whether people "fit" with the job, workgroup, or organization. Interviewers often assess the likelihood that applicants will excel in the particular organization. These judgments are not based on typical qualifications, such as knowledge and experience, but rather on characteristics such as goals, interpersonal skills, and even physical attractiveness.[127]

How Do We Know?

DOES IT MATTER HOW YOU SHAKE HANDS IN AN INTERVIEW?

Can a good handshake really help you get a job? A search of the Internet yields over a million sites that provide information about the proper way to shake hands in an employment interview. Yet, little scientific research has been done to determine if the handshake really matters. So Greg Stewart, Susan Dustin, Murray Barrick, and Todd Darnold designed a study to learn more about the handshake. Students who were seeking jobs participated in practice interviews. During the interview process six different people secretly evaluated each student's handshake. Neither the students nor the interviewers were aware that handshakes were being evaluated. Students shook hands with interviewers before a 30-minute interview. At the end of the interview, interviewers provided ratings of how likely they were to hire students. Ratings of the handshake were then correlated with final interview ratings to determine if the handshake was related to assessments of hirability.

Results showed that people with a better handshake (firm and complete grip, eye contact) were indeed more likely to receive job offers. Women were found to have less firm handshakes than men. However, women with a good handshake got more benefit out of it than did men with a firm handshake. Women may therefore not be as good as men at shaking hands, but those who do it well get extra credit from interviewers.

The Bottom Line. Little things like having a good handshake can indeed make a difference in an interview setting. Job candidates can benefit from a good handshake, which includes a complete grip of the hand, a firm grasp, moderate up-and-down movement, comfortable duration, and eye contact.

Source: Greg L. Stewart, Susan L. Dustin, Murray R. Barrick, Todd C. Darnold, "Exploring the Handshake in Employment Interviews," *Journal of Applied Psychology* 93 (2008): 1139–1146.

One concern about the interview is its expense: The time managers spend conducting interviews can be costly. The interview thus has relatively low utility, and generally, only applicants who have been screened with less-expensive selection methods should be interviewed. Another potential concern is discrimination. Interviewers make a number of subjective judgments, bringing up questions of possible bias. Indeed, research does suggest that interviewers can be biased in their judgments.[128] Yet, the general conclusion is that bias is relatively low as long as the structuring techniques described below are used.[129] Of course, interviewers must be careful not to ask questions that violate the laws discussed in Chapter 3. In particular, interviewers should avoid questions about family and marital relationships, age, disability, and religion.

Using Structured Interviews

We have seen that reliability and validity vary with the type of interview conducted. What makes some interviews better than others? The biggest difference between types of interviews concerns the amount of structure. The typical interview is an unstructured interview in which a single rater asks a series of questions and then provides an overall recommendation on whether the person interviewed should be hired. The questions asked usually vary from interviewer to interviewer, and interviewers can base their evaluations on anything that they think is important. Managers tend to prefer this type of interview. Research has

Structured interview
Employment interview that incorporates multiple raters, common questions, and standardized evaluation procedures.

Situational interview
Type of structured interview that uses questions based on hypothetical situations.

Behavioral interview
Type of structured interview that uses questions concerning behavior in past situations.

traditionally shown that this type of unstructured assessment is not as reliable and valid as more-structured interviews.[130] According to some newly emerging research, however, the unstructured interview can be a reliable tool when several people conduct interviews and then combine their individual evaluations.[131]

A different type of interview, generally seen as superior, is the **structured interview**, which uses a list of predetermined questions based on knowledge and skills identified as being critical for success. This ensures that the questions are appropriate and that all applicants are asked the same questions. The structured interview is conducted by a panel of interviewers rather than by a single person. Members of the rating panel use formal scoring procedures that require them to provide numerical scores for a number of predetermined categories. The basic goal of the structured interview is to make sure that everyone who is interviewed is treated the same. This consistency across interviews improves reliability, which in turn improves validity. More-structured interviews are also more effective in reducing the biasing effect of applicant impression management.[132] A method for creating structured interview questions and responses is outlined in Figure 6.4.

Most structured interviews fit into two types: (1) the **situational interview**, in which the interviewer asks questions about what the applicant would do in a hypothetical situation, and (2) the **behavioral interview**, in which the questions focus on the applicant's behavior in past situations. Researchers disagree about which type is better, with some research supporting each type.[133] In general, both types seek to have people discuss actions in a specific context and thus tend to generate responses that are good predictors of job performance. Examples of both types of interview questions are shown in Table 6.5. The table also shows scoring for sample responses; one reason these interview formats work is that they provide raters with clear examples for determining how a response should be scored.

Linking Interviews to Strategy

Interviews are used by organizations with all of the HR strategies. The focus of the interview questions, however, depends on strategy. Organizations seeking Free Agents focus on assessing achievement. Typical questions relate to job experience and certification in specific skills. In contrast, organizations seeking Loyal Soldiers focus on assessing fit. Specific questions measure

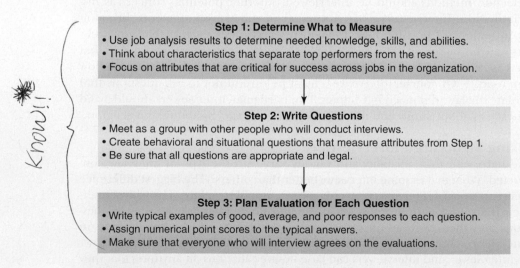

Step 1: Determine What to Measure
• Use job analysis results to determine needed knowledge, skills, and abilities.
• Think about characteristics that separate top performers from the rest.
• Focus on attributes that are critical for success across jobs in the organization.

Step 2: Write Questions
• Meet as a group with other people who will conduct interviews.
• Create behavioral and situational questions that measure attributes from Step 1.
• Be sure that all questions are appropriate and legal.

Step 3: Plan Evaluation for Each Question
• Write typical examples of good, average, and poor responses to each question.
• Assign numerical point scores to the typical answers.
• Make sure that everyone who will interview agrees on the evaluations.

Figure 6.4 Creating Structured Interview Questions.

Table 6.5		Types of Employment Interview Question	
	Format	**Example Question**	**Possible Response**
Behavioral Questions	Ask the applicant to describe actions in a particular past situation.	It is often necessary to work together in a group to accomplish a task. Please tell me about the most recent experience you had working as part of a group.	*Poor Response:* Lots of conflict. The other members were ineffective. *Average Response:* I did all the work myself. *Superior Response:* We worked together. I helped involve everyone.
Situational Questions	Put the applicant in a particular situation and then ask for a description of behavior.	A customer comes into a store where you work to pick up a watch he left for repair. The repair was supposed to have been completed a week ago, but the watch is not yet back from the repair shop. The customer is very angry. How would you handle this situation?	*Poor Response:* Tell him he should check back later. *Average Response:* Apologize and tell him I will call him later. *Superior Response:* Listen, put him at ease, call the repair shop while he waits.

personality characteristics, motivation, and social skills. Organizations seeking Committed Experts use a combination approach that assesses both potential and fit. Typical questions measure problem-solving ability and aptitude in a particular field, such as sales or engineering.

Effective organizations thus begin the interview process by thinking carefully about their HR strategy. After clearly determining their strategy, they begin to develop questions that help them identify individuals with the characteristics they most desire. Using the interview to properly identify and hire employees who are most likely to engage in the behaviors that facilitate either a low cost or differentiation strategy is thus a very effective method for using human resource management to create competitive advantage. Having the right employees develops an organizational culture that helps organizations meet the needs of customers.

CONCEPT CHECK

1. *What are common methods of testing?*
2. *What information can be obtained from application blanks and résumés?*
3. *How can the reliability and validity of employment interviews be improved?*

LEARNING OBJECTIVE **4**

How Are Final Selection Decisions Made?

What happens after an organization tests, interviews, and gathers information about job applicants? In most cases, the organization ends up with several different scores from several different methods. How should it combine these bits of information to arrive at a final hiring decision?

One possibility is that decision makers will simply look at the scores from each method and then make a judgment about who should be hired. This is what frequently happens, but it does not usually lead to the best decision.[134] A better method is to use a set of decision rules and statistical tactics. Here, decision makers first obtain a numerical score for the outcome of each selection method and then apply decision strategies to the numerical scores. Common decision strategies include weighting the predictors, using minimum cutoffs, establishing multiple hurdles, and banding.[135]

PREDICTOR WEIGHTING APPROACH

Predictor weighting
Multiplying scores on selection assessments by different values to give more important means greater weight.

In **predictor weighting**, we combine a set of selection scores into an overall score in which some measures count more than others. For instance, suppose a manager has three applicants for an engineering position. Each candidate has a cognitive ability score, an interview score, and a biographical test score. One applicant has a high cognitive ability score and a low interview score; the second applicant has a low cognitive ability score and a high biographical test score; and the third applicant has an average score on all three tests. How can the manager use these scores to predict which applicant will perform best?

Of course, one approach is to take a simple average of all three test scores, but this procedure ignores the fact that one type of test might provide better information than another. The alternative is to establish a weight for each test, so that the method that provides the most valuable information has a higher influence on the overall decision. For instance, the cognitive ability test and interview might both be weighted as 40 percent of the overall score, with the biodata being weighted as 20 percent. Each score is multiplied by its assigned weight, and final selection decisions are based on an overall score.

How should the weights be determined? Experts who have a thorough knowledge of what it takes to succeed in the job might set the weights. However, an even better method is to use statistical methods for determining the best set of weights. Regardless of how the weights are determined, the process of predictor weighting is helpful for ensuring that managers and human resource specialists give appropriate attention to the information obtained from each selection method.

MINIMUM CUTOFFS APPROACH

Predictor weighting allows an applicant's strength in one area to compensate for weakness in another area. Someone with a low cognitive ability score might still be hired if interview and biodata scores are high, for example. This makes sense in many contexts but not in every case. For instance, consider an organization that is hiring people to work in self-managing teams. These teams succeed only if team members are able to cooperate and work together. Suppose an applicant for a position on the team has a high cognitive ability score but a very low score on an interview measuring interpersonal skills. In the team setting, high cognitive ability will not make up for problems created by low interpersonal skills, and the organization will need to take this fact into consideration.

Minimum cutoffs approach
The process of eliminating applicants who do not achieve an acceptable score on each selection assessment.

In such a situation, the organization can take a **minimum cutoffs approach**, requiring each applicant to have at least a minimum score on each selection method. An applicant who is very weak on any of the measures will not be hired.

In practice, many organizations use minimum cutoffs to identify a pool of people who meet at least minimum requirements in a number of areas. Once this pool of people is identified, then weighted predictors are used to make the final hiring decision.

MULTIPLE HURDLES APPROACH

As we have seen, some selection methods are much more expensive than others. Using minimum cutoffs in a number of areas in progressive order can thus increase the utility of the overall selection process. A relatively inexpensive test, such as a cognitive ability test, is given first. Those who achieve at least the minimum score then go on to the next selection method. This second method might be more expensive, such as an interview. The **multiple hurdles approach** thus involves multiple cutoffs applied in order, and applicants must meet the minimum requirement of one selection method before they can proceed to the next. One advantage of the multiple hurdles approach is that fewer minority candidates may be eliminated because they meet the acceptable criteria even if they are not the highest scorer on a particular test.[136] A potential problem with this approach is that decision makers eliminate applicants without knowing how they would score on all the tests. The process makes sense, though, when organizations use expensive selection tests and wish to limit the number of applicants who take those tests.

Multiple hurdles approach
The process of obtaining scores on a selection method and only allowing those who achieve a minimum score to take the next assessment.

BANDING APPROACH

Because few employment tests are totally reliable, two people with slightly different scores may not really differ on the characteristic being measured. The difference in the scores is caused by poor measurement. This possibility has led some experts to create a process called banding. The **banding approach** uses statistical analysis to identify scores that may not be meaningfully different. People with such scores are placed in a common category, or band, and managers and selection specialists are then free to choose any one of the applicants within the band.[137]

Banding approach
The process of treating people as doing equally well when they have similar scores on a selection assessment.

The practice of banding is somewhat controversial. Some people argue that banding can help organizations meet affirmative action goals. If the band of applicants includes a member of a minority group, this person can be hired even if someone else had a slightly higher score. Others, however, argue that banding can lead to decreased utility because people with lower scores, and thus lower potential to succeed, are often hired.[138]

CONCEPT CHECK
1. *How can scores from different selection measures be combined to make a final hiring decision?*
2. *How is the multiple hurdles method different from the minimum cutoffs method?*

A MANAGER'S PERSPECTIVE REVISITED

IN THE MANAGER'S PERSPECTIVE AT THE BEGINNING OF THE CHAPTER, JAVIER WAS RESPONSIBLE FOR HIRING A NEW MEMBER OF HIS CUSTOMER SERVICE TEAM. HE FACED A NUMBER OF ISSUES CONCERNING WHAT KIND OF PERSON TO HIRE, WHAT SELECTION METHODS TO USE, AND HOW TO MAKE HIS FINAL DECISION. FOLLOWING ARE THE ANSWERS TO THE "WHAT DO YOU THINK?" QUIZ THAT FOLLOWED THE CASE. WERE YOU ABLE TO CORRECTLY IDENTIFY THE TRUE STATEMENTS? COULD YOU DO BETTER NOW?

1. You should hire people who already have the skills and knowledge they will need on the job. **FALSE.** *Although organizations using short-term employment strategies may prefer to hire employees who already have the necessary skills, the potential of new employees is often more important for organizations using long-term employment strategies.*

2. The benefits of making good hiring decisions are highest when the organization has a lot of job applicants. **TRUE.** *Organizations with numerous applicants can be choosier about whom they hire, which increases the utility, or dollar value, of selection methods.*

3. Intelligence tests are very helpful for predicting who will be effective in almost any job. **TRUE.** *Intelligence tests are good predictors of work performance, and they demonstrate generalizability across settings.*

4. Reference checking provides valuable information about prospective employees. **FALSE.** *Unfortunately, because of problems with defamation of character, reference checking provides very little useful information.*

5. You need to ask each applicant individualized questions to determine his or her true strengths and weaknesses. **FALSE.** *Asking applicants individualized questions creates problems with reliability. Structured interviews in which each applicant is asked the same questions are generally better than unstructured interviews.*

Javier's situation is one that almost all managers eventually face. When managers make good hiring decisions, they help the organization secure high-performing employees. These employees, in turn, help produce goods and services of high quality and low cost, resulting in competitive advantage for the organization. The principles discussed in this chapter can help improve hiring decisions.

valeriy-davidenko/iStockphoto

SUMMARY

LEARNING OBJECTIVE 1

How is employee selection strategic?

Employee selection practices should align with overall HR strategy. Employees provide short-term talent when the organization hires from outside sources and long-term talent when the organization promotes from within. Employees offer specialist talent when they possess highly developed expertise in a particular area and generalist talent when they operate in a variety of positions. Combinations of talent can be linked to overall HR strategies. Short-term generalist talent corresponds with a Bargain Laborer HR strategy, long-term generalist talent with a Loyal Soldier HR strategy, long-term specialist talent with a Committed Expert HR strategy, and short-term specialist talent with a Free Agent HR strategy.

Organizations need to achieve a strategic balance between job-based fit and organization-based fit. Fit is not critical for organizations with short-term generalist talent. Organization-based fit is critical for organizations with long-term generalist talent. Job-based fit is critical for organizations with long-term specialist talent. Organization-based fit and job-based fit are both critical for organizations with long-term specialist talent.

Another staffing characteristic that underlies strategic employee selection decisions is the balance between potential and achievement. Organizations with long-term employees who are either generalists or specialists hire based on potential. Organizations with short-term specialist talent hire based on achievement.

LEARNING OBJECTIVE 2

What makes a selection method good?

Reliability, validity, utility, fairness, and acceptability represent five principles that are helpful for determining whether a selection method is good. Reliability concerns the consistency of the method. Validity represents the relationship between what the method measures and job performance. Utility focuses on the cost effectiveness of the method. Fairness concerns the effect of the method on individuals and minority groups. Acceptability focuses on how applicants react when they complete the selection method.

LEARNING OBJECTIVE 3

What selection methods are commonly used?

The usefulness of a particular selection method often differs depending on the context of the organization and job. However, a number of selection methods generally satisfy the five principles for being effective. Common selection tests include cognitive ability testing, personality testing, physical ability testing, integrity testing, drug testing, and work sample testing. Cognitive ability and personality tests can be very useful for assessing potential to succeed. Other methods of information gathering include application forms and résumés, biographical data, and reference checking. Application forms and résumés are generally inexpensive methods for obtaining information about job applicants. The interview is another commonly used method of gathering information. Interviews are more reliable and valid when they are structured to ensure consistent treatment of each person being interviewed.

LEARNING OBJECTIVE 4

How are final selection decisions made?

Managers and human resource specialists should use good decision-making procedures to combine information from different selection methods. One procedure is predictor weighting, which allows more-important selection methods to have a stronger influence on the final decision. Another procedure, labeled minimum cutoffs, requires successful applicants to achieve at least a minimum score on each method. A third procedure is multiple hurdles, where applicants must achieve a minimum score on one selection method before they can advance to the next method. A final procedure is banding, wherein employees with similar scores on a selection method are grouped into categories. People in a given category are seen as having the same score, even though their scores are slightly different.

KEY TERMS

DISCUSSION QUESTIONS

1. How do the concepts of long- and short-term talent and generalist and specialist talent fit with overall HR strategy?

2. For what type of HR strategy is organization fit most important? When is job fit most needed? What type of organization should base hiring on achievement? What type should hire based on potential?

3. What is reliability? How is it estimated?

4. What is validity? How is it estimated?

5. What factors affect the utility of selection methods?

6. What is the difference between fairness and legality?

7. Why do people sometimes react negatively to certain selection methods?

8. What are the strengths and weakness associated with the following selection methods: cognitive ability testing, personality testing, physical ability testing, integrity testing, drug testing, application forms and résumés, biodata, work sample testing, reference checking, and interviewing?

9. Which selection methods are best for organizations with the various employee selection strategies?

10. What are the methods for combining scores from different selection methods?

EXAMPLE CASE   *Outback Steakhouse*

✳ Outback Steakhouse, Inc., now a $3.25 billion company with 65,000 employees and 1,100 restaurants worldwide, began modestly in the spring of 1988. A key to making Outback a great place to work is hiring the right people. One of the things we recognized early on is that you cannot send turkeys to eagle school: Smart leaders do not hire marginal employees and expect them to be able to keep the commitments of the company to customers or to remain very long with the company. If you start with the right people and provide a positive employee experience, turnover stays low. Thus, a rigorous employee selection process was developed in the early years of the company that is rooted in the Principles and Beliefs.

Outback's selection process for hourly and management Outbackers is proprietary; however, we can share some of the details here about the steps involved in the hiring process:

- All applicants are given a realistic job preview that shares both the benefits and the responsibilities of working for Outback. We explain to applicants that being an Outbacker means taking care of others, and we tell them how they will be held accountable for that.
- We share a document, called a Dimension of Performance, which provides detailed examples of the kinds of behavior expected of Outbackers and how those behaviors are tied to the vision of Outback. This is a candidate's first exposure to our vision. (At this point, some candidates have withdrawn from the process because these dimensions set a very high standard.)
- When candidates agree to move forward in the process, they are asked to complete an application. The information they provide is reviewed with an eye toward determining if the candidate can perform the job, fit into the Outback culture, and stay with the company.
- Successful applicants are assessed for their cognitive ability, personality, and judgment through a series of tests that have been validated against existing Outbackers who have been successful in the company.
- Applicants who pass these tests are interviewed using questions that probe not only their experience but also their orientation toward aspects of the Outback culture, including service mindedness, hospitality, teamwork, and ability to think on their feet.

QUESTIONS

1. How do the employee-selection methods at Outback Steakhouse help achieve competitive advantage?

2. How important is organization fit for Outback Steakhouse?

3. Why does Outback Steakhouse order the selection methods such that applicants first complete an application, then complete tests, and then participate in an interview?

4. Why do you think these selection methods are valid?

Source: Tom DeCotiss, Chris Sullivan, David Hyatt, and Paul Avery, "How Outback Steakhouse Created a Great Place to Work, Have Fun, and Make Money," *Journal of Organizational Excellence* (Autumn 2004): 23–33. Reprinted with permission of John Wiley & Sons, Inc.

DISCUSSION CASE   *Stringtown Iron Works*

Stringtown Iron Works is a small fictional shipyard on the East Coast dedicated to ship overhaul. It focuses on obtaining government contracts for overhauling naval ships. These overhauls require Stringtown to maintain a quality workforce that is capable of rapid production. The position of pipe fitter is particularly critical for success.

Pipe fitters are responsible for repairing and installing the piping systems on board the vessels. Employees in the pipe fitter classification may also be called on to work in the shop, building pipe pieces that are ultimately installed on the ships. Like most union jobs in the yard, pipe fitters are predominantly white men between the ages of 30 and 45. As part of the most recent bargaining agreement, work is primarily done in cross-functional teams.

Job Description

Job: Pipe fitter
Pay: $12.00 to $20.00 per hour

A pipe fitter must:

1. Read and interpret blueprints and/or sketches to fabricate and install pipe in accordance with specifications.
2. Perform joint preparation and fit-up to fabricate and install brazed and welded piping systems.
3. Perform layout and calculations to fabricate and install pipe.
4. Fabricate pipe pieces up to 10″ in diameter and up to 10′ long to support shipboard pipe installation.
5. Install ship's piping, such as water, drains, hydraulics, lube oil, fuel oil, high temperature air, etc. on location and within tolerances per design.
6. Inspect and hydro test completed piping systems to ensure compliance with ship's specifications.
7. Use a variety of hand and power tools to perform joint preparation, assembly bolt-up, and positioning during fabrication and installation.
8. Utilize welding equipment to tack-weld pipe joints and to secure pipe supports to ship's structure.

Completion of the above tasks requires pipe fiT1tters to do the following:
* Frequent lifting and carrying of 25–50 pounds
* Occasional lifting and carrying of over 50 pounds
* Occasional to frequent crawling, kneeling, and stair climbing
* Frequent pushing, pulling, hammering, and reaching
* Frequent bending, stooping, squatting, and crouching
* Occasional twisting in awkward positions
* Occasional fume exposure

QUESTIONS

1. Which of the overall HR strategies would be best for Stringtown Iron Works?
2. Should Stringtown focus on job fit or organization fit?
3. Should Stringtown hire based on achievement or potential?
4. What selection methods would you recommend for Stringtown? Why?

EXPERIENTIAL EXERCISE — *Learning through Interviewing*

Interview a family member, friend, or someone else who has a job you would like to someday have. Learn about the hiring practices of the organization where this person works. Ask questions like the following:

1. What makes the company different from its competitors? Does it focus mostly on reducing costs, or does it try to provide goods and services that are somehow better than what competitors offer?
2. What tasks do you do on the job? What knowledge, skills, and abilities do you need in order to do this job effectively?
3. How long do most people stay at the company? Is this a place where most people work for their entire career? How long do you think you will continue working with the company?
4. What did you have to do to get hired at the company? Did you take any tests? Did they ask for a résumé? What was the interview like?
5. What type of qualifications do you think are most important for someone who wants to work at your company? If you were making a decision to hire someone to work with you, what characteristics would you want that person to have? How would you measure those characteristics?

Using the information obtained from the interview, do the following:

1. Identify the competitive business strategy of the organization.
2. Identify the human resource strategy of the organization.
3. Evaluate whether the competitive business strategy and the human resource strategy fit.

4. Evaluate the effectiveness of the organization's selection methods for achieving its human resource strategy.
5. Make recommendations about the selection methods that you think would be most appropriate for the position of the person you interviewed.

INTERACTIVE EXPERIENTIAL EXERCISE

Employee Selection: Choosing the Best of the Best for Graphics Design, Inc.
http://www.wiley.com/college/sc/stewart

Access the companion website to test your knowledge by completing a Graphics Design, Inc., interactive role play.

In this exercise you have identified several potential candidates for the new positions at GDI, and it is now time to begin the selection process. In designing the appropriate selection system for the company, you must consider reliability, validity, utility, legality, and acceptability, along with common testing methods, information-gathering sources, and interview types. Whatever system you choose, you know that you'll need to gain buy-in from the managers who need these new employees. You know, too, that the system must support GDI's basic HR strategy, the Loyal Soldier strategy. Your recommendations on the appropriate selection system are due this afternoon. What will it look like? •

ENDNOTES

1. Chad H. Van Iddekinge, Gerald R. Ferris, Pamela L. Perrewe, Fre R. Blass, Thomas D. Heetderks, and Alexa A. Perryman, "Effects of Selection and Training on Unit-Level Performance Over Time: A Latent Growth Modeling Approach," *Journal of Applied Psychology* 94 (2009): 829–843; David E. Terpstra and Elizabeth J. Rozell, "The Relationship of Staffing Practices to Organizational Level Measures of Performance," *Personnel Psychology* 46 (1993): 27–48.
2. Rod Powers, "Surviving Marine Corps Basic Training," accessed online at http://usmilitary.about.com/od/marinejoin/a/marinebasic.htm.
3. http://www.marines.com/eligibility/prep-test; http://www.instantasvab.com/score/requirements-for-marine-corps-jobs.html.
4. http://www.marines.com/becoming-a-marine/how-to-prepare; Elizabeth Bumiller, "First Pull-Ups, Then Combat, Marines Say," *New York Times,* February 1, 2013.
5. Lance Cpl. John Robbart III, "Tips on Training for Marine Corps' Physical Tests," available online at http://thevillagenews.com/story/50903; http://www.marines.com/becoming-a-marine/how-to-prepare.
6. Paul Osterman, "Choice of Employment Systems in Internal Labor Markets," *Industrial Relations* 26 (1987): 46–67; Randall S. Schuler and Susan E. Jackson,

"Linking Competitive Strategies with Human Resource Practices," *Academy of Management Executive* 9 (1987): 207–219.
7. John E. Delery and D. Harold Doty, "Modes of Theorizing in Strategic Human Resource Management: Tests of Universalistic, Contingency, and Configurational Performance Predictions," *Academy of Management Journal* 3 (1996): 802–835; Schuler and Jackson, "Linking Competitive Strategies," 207.
8. Judy D. Olian and Sara L. Rynes, "Organizational Staffing: Integrating Practice with Strategy," *Industrial Relations* 23 (1984): 170–183; Jeffrey A. Sonnenfeld and Maury A. Peiperl, "Staffing Policy as a Strategic Response: A Typology of Career Systems," *Academy of Management Review* 13 (1988): 588–601; Peter Bamberger and Ilan Meshoulam, *Human Resource Strategy: Formulation, Implementation, and Impact* (Thousand Oaks, CA: Sage Publications, 2000).
9. Olian and Rynes, "Organizational Staffing," 170–183; Sonnenfeld and Peiperl, "Staffing Policy," 588–601; Bamberger and Meshoulam, *Human Resource Strategy*.
10. Olian and Rynes, "Organizational Staffing," 170–183; Sonnenfeld and Peiperl, "Staffing Policy," 588–601; Bamberger and Meshoulam, *Human Resource Strategy*.
11. Ibid.
12. Jeffrey R. Edwards, "Person-Job Fit: A Conceptual Integration, Literature Review and Methodological

Critique," in Vol. 6 of *International Review of Industrial/Organizational Psychology* (London: Wiley, 1991), 283–357; Amy L. Kristof, "Person–Organization Fit: An Integrative Review of Its Conceptualizations, Measurement, and Implications," *Personnel Psychology* 49 (1996): 1–49.

13. Winfred Arthur, Jr., Suzanne T. Bell, Anton J. Villado, and Dennis Doverspike, "The Use of Person-Organization Fit in Employment Decision Making: An Assessment of Its Criterion-Related Validity," *Journal of Applied Psychology* 91 (2006): 786–801.

14. Olian and Rynes, "Organizational Staffing," 170–183.

15. Ibid.

16. Delery and Doty, "Modes of Theorizing," 802–835; Mark A. Youndt, Scott A. Snell, James W. Dean, Jr., and David P. Lepak, "Human Resource Management, Manufacturing Strategy, and Firm Performance," *Academy of Management Journal* 39 (1996): 836–866.

17. Robert Gatewood and Hubert S. Field, *Human Resource Selection*, 5th ed. (Mason, OH: South-Western, 2000).

18. Frank J. Landy, "Stamp Collecting Versus Science: Validation as Hypothesis Testing," *American Psychologist* 41 (1986): 1183–1192.

19. Gatewood and Field, *Human Resource Selection*.

20. Frank L. Schmidt, John E. Hunter, R. McKenzie, and T. Muldrow, "The Impact of Valid Selection Procedures on Workforce Productivity," *Journal of Applied Psychology* 64 (1979): 609–626.

21. Gary P. Latham and Glen Whyte, "The Futility of Utility Analysis," *Personnel Psychology* 47 (1994): 31–47; Glen Whyte and Gary Latham, "The Futility of Utility Analysis Revisited: When Even an Expert Fails," *Personnel Psychology* 50 (1997): 601–611.

22. Kenneth P. Carson, John S. Becker, and John A. Henderson. "Is Utility Really Futile? A Failure to Replicate and an Extension," *Journal of Applied Psychology* 88 (1998): 84–96; John T. Hazer and Scott Highhouse, "Factors Influencing Managers' Reactions to Utility Analysis: Effects of SD-Sub(U) Method, Information Frame, and Focal Intervention," *Journal of Applied Psychology* 82 (1997): 104–112.

23. Deidra J. Schleicher, Vijaya Venkataramani, Frederick P. Morgeson, and Michael A. Campion, "So You Didn't Get the Job . . . Now What Do You Think? Examining Opportunity-to-Performa Fairness Perceptions," *Personnel Psychology* 59 (2006); 559–590.

24. Hannah-Hanh D. Nguyen and Ann Marie Ryan, "Does Stereotype Threat Affect Test Performance of Minorities and Women? A Meta-Analysis of Experimental Evidence," *Journal of Applied Psychology* 93 (2008): 1314–1334; Ryan P. Brown and Eric Anthony Day, "The Difference Isn't Black and White: Stereotype Threat and the Race Gap on Raven's Advanced Progressive Matrices," *Journal of Applied Psychology* 91 (2006): 979–985.

25. I.T. Robertson, P.A. Hes, L. Gratton, and D. Sharpley "The Impact of Personnel Selection and Assessment Methods on Candidates," *Human Relations* 44 (1991): 963–982; Bradford S. Bell, Darin Wiechmann, and Ann Marie Ryan, "Consequences of Organizational Justice Expectations in a Selection System," *Journal of Applied Psychology* 91 (2006): 455–466.

26. Sara L. Rynes, "Who's Selecting Whom? Effects of Selection Practices on Applicant Attitudes and Behavior," in N. Schmitt, W.C. Borman, and Associates, eds., *Personnel Selection in Organizations* (San Francisco: Jossey-Bass, 1993); Stephen W. Gilliland, "Effects of Procedural and Distributive Justice on Reactions to a Selection System," *Journal of Applied Psychology* 79 (1994): 691–701.

27. Dirk D. Steiner and Stephen W. Gilliland, "Fairness Reactions to Personnel Selection Techniques in France and the United States," *Journal of Applied Psychology* 81 (1996): 134–141.

28. Kevin R. Murphy, George C. Thornton III, and Douglas H. Reynolds, "College Students' Attitudes Toward Employee Drug Testing Programs," *Personnel Psychology* 43 (1990): 615–631.

29. *Wonderlic Personnel Test & Scholastic Level Exam: User's Manual* (Libertyville, IL: Wonderlic Personnel Test, 1992).

30. Malcolm J. Ree, James A. Earles, and Mark S. Teachout, "Predicting Job Performance: Not Much More Than g," *Journal of Applied Psychology* 79 (1997): 518–524.

31. Christopher M. Berry, Melissa L. Gruys, and Paul R. Sackett, "Educational Attainment as a Proxy for Cognitive Ability in Selection: Effects on Levels of Cognitive Ability and Adverse Impact," *Journal of Applied Psychology* 91 (2006): 696–705.

32. Anne Anastasi, *Psychological Testing*, 6th ed. (New York: Macmillan, 1988).

33. Ann Marie Ryan, Robert E. Ployhart, Gary J. Greguras, and Mark J. Schmit. "Test Preparation Programs in Selection Contexts: Self-Selection and Program Effectiveness," *Personnel Psychology* 51 (1998): 599–622.

34. John E. Hunter and Ronda F. Hunter, "Validity and Utility of Alternative Predictors of Job Performance," *Psychological Bulletin* 96 (1984): 72–98.

35. Jesus F. Salgado, Neil Anderson, Silvia Moscoso, Cristina Bertua, and Filip de Fruyt, "International Validity Generalization of GMA and Cognitive Abilities: A European Community Meta-Analysis," *Personnel Psychology* 56 (2003): 573–606.

36. Mark W. Coward and Paul R. Sackett. "Linearity of Ability–Performance Relationships: A Reconfirmation," *Journal of Applied Psychology* 75 (1990): 297–300.

37. John E. Hunter, Frank L. Schmidt, and Michael K. Judiesch, "Individual Differences in Output Variability as a Function of Job Complexity," *Journal of Applied Psychology* 75 (1990): 28–42.

38. John E. Hunter, "Cognitive Ability, Cognitive Aptitudes, Job Knowledge, and Job Performance," *Journal of Vocational Behavior* 29 (1986): 340–362.

39. Jeffrey A. LePine, Jason A. Colquitt, and Amir Erez, "Adaptability to Changing Task Contexts: Effects of General Cognitive Ability, Conscientiousness, and Openness to Experience," *Personnel Psychology* 53 (2000): 563–594; Jonas W.B. Lang and Paul D. Bliese, "General Mental Ability and Two Types of Adaptation to Unforeseen Change: Applying Discontinuous Growth Models to the Task-Change Paradigm," *Journal of Applied Psychology* 94 (2009): 411–428.

40. Christopher M. Berry, Malissa A. Clark, and Tara K. McClure, "Racial/Ethnic Differences in the Criterion-Related Validity of Cognitive Ability Tests: A Qualitative and Quantitative Review, *Journal of Applied Psychology* 96 (2011): 881–906.

41. Wendy S. Dunn, Michael K. Mount, and Murray R. Barrick, "Relative Importance of Personality and General Mental Ability in Managers' Judgments of Applicant Qualifications," *Journal of Applied Psychology* 80 (1995): 500–509.

42. Kevin R. Murphy, Brian E. Cronin, and Anita P. Tam, "Controversy and Consensus Regarding the Use of Cognitive Ability Testing in Organizations," *Journal of Applied Psychology* 88 (2003): 660–671.

43. Therese Hoff Macan, Marcia J. Avedon, Matthew Paese, and David E. Smith, "The Effects of Applicants' Reactions to Cognitive Ability Tests and an Assessment Center," *Personnel Psychology* 47 (1994): 715–738.

44. David Chan, "Racial Subgroup Differences in Predictive Validity Perceptions on Personality and Cognitive Ability Tests," *Journal of Applied Psychology* 82 (1997): 311–320; David Chan, Neal Schmitt, Joshua M. Sacco, and Richard P. DeShon, "Understanding Pretest and Posttest Reactions to Cognitive Ability and Personality Tests," *Journal of Applied Psychology* 83 (1998): 471–485.

45. David C. Funder, *The Personality Puzzle*, 2nd ed. (New York: Norton, 2001).

46. Murray R. Barrick and Michael K. Mount, "The Big Five Personality Dimensions and Job Performance," *Personnel Psychology* 44 (1991): 1–26; Gregory M. Hurtz and John J. Donovan, "Personality and Job Performance: The Big Five Revisited," *Journal of Applied Psychology* 85 (2000): 869–879.

47. Mark J. Schmit, Jenifer A. Kihm, and Chet Robie, "Development of a Global Measure of Personality," *Personnel Psychology* 53 (2000): 153–194; Jcsus F. Salgado, "The Five Factor Model of Personality and Job Performance in the European Community," *Journal of Applied Psychology* 82 (1997): 30–43.

48. Robert Hogan and Joyce Hogan, *Hogan Personality Inventory Manual* (Tulsa, OK: Hogan Assessment Systems, 1992); Paul T. Costa and Robert R. McCrae, *NEO PI-R Professional Manual* (Odessa, FL: Psychological Assessment Resources, 1992).

49. Mark J. Schmit, Ann Marie Ryan, Sandra L. Stierwalt, and Amy B. Powell, "Frame-of-Reference Effects on Personality Scale Scores and Criterion-Related Validity," *Journal of Applied Psychology* 80 (1995): 607–620; Mark N. Bing, James C. Whanger, H. Kristi Davison, and Jayson B. VanHook, "Incremental Validity of the Frame-of-Reference Effect in Personality Scale Scores: A Replication and Extension," *Journal of Applied Psychology* 89 (2004): 150–157; John M. Hunthausen, Donald M. Truxillo, Talya N. Bauer, and Leslie B. Hammer, "A Field Study of Frame-of-Reference Effects on Personality Test Validity," *Journal of Applied Psychology* 88 (2003): 545–551; Filip Lievens, Wilfried DeCorte, and Eveline Schollaert, "A Closer Look at the Frame-of-Reference Effect in Personality Scales and Validity," *Journal of Applied Psychology* 93 (2008): 268–279.

50. Jonathan A. Shaffer and Bennett E. Postlethwaite, "A Matter of Context: A Meta-Analytic Investigation of the Relative Validity of Contextualized and Noncontextualized Personality Measures," *Personnel Psychology* 65 (2012): 445–493.

51. Dan S. Chiaburu, In-Sue Oh, Christopher M. Berry, Li Ning, and Richard G. Gardner, "The Five-Factor Model of Personality Traits and Organizational Citizenship Behaviors: A Meta-Analysis," *Journal of Applied Psychology* 96 (2011): 1140–1166.

52. Ian R. Gellatly, "Conscientiousness and Task Performance: Test of Cognitive Process Model," *Journal of Applied Psychology* 81 (1996): 474–482; Murray R. Barrick, Michael K. Mount, and Judy P. Strauss, "Conscientiousness and Performance of Sales Representatives: Test of the Mediating Effects of Goal Setting," *Journal of Applied Psychology* 78 (1993): 715–722; Greg L. Stewart, Kenneth P. Carson, and Robert L. Cardy, "The Joint Effects of Conscientiousness and Self-Leadership Training on Employee Self-Directed Behavior in a Service Setting," *Personnel Psychology* 49 (1996): 143–164; Timothy A. Judge and Remus Ilies, "Relationship of Personality to Performance Motivation: A Meta-Analytic Review," *Journal of Applied Psychology* 87 (2002): 797–807.

53. Timothy A. Judge, Joseph J. Martocchio, and Carl J. Thoresen, "Five-Factor Model of Personality and Employee Absence," *Journal of Applied Psychology* 82 (1997): 745–755.

54. Remus Ilies, Ingrid Smithey Fulmer, Matthias Spitzmuller, and Michael D Johnson, "Personality and Citizenship Behavior: The Mediating Role of Job Satisfaction," *Journal of Applied Psychology* 94 (2009): 945–959.

55. Judge and Ilies, "Relationship of Personality to Performance Motivation," 797–807.

56. Luke D. Smillie, Gilliam B. Yeo, Adrian F. Furnham, and Chris J. Jackson, "Benefits of All Work and No Play: The Relationship Between Neuroticism and Performance as a Function of Resource Allocation," *Journal of Applied Psychology* 91 (2006): 139–155.

57. Murray R. Barrick, Greg L. Stewart, and Mike Piotrowski, "Personality and Job Performance: Test of the Mediating Effects of Motivation Among Sales Representatives," *Journal of Applied Psychology* 87: 43–51; Greg L. Stewart, "Reward Structure as a Moderator of the Relationship Between Extraversion and Sales Performance," *Journal of Applied Psychology* 81 (1996): 619–627. Timothy A. Judge, Joyce E. Bono, Remus Ilies, and Megan W. Gerhardt, "Personality and Leadership: A Qualitative and Quantitative Review," *Journal of Applied Psychology* 87 (2002): 765–780.

58. Michael K. Mount, Murray R. Barrick, and Greg L. Stewart, "Five-Factor Model of Personality and Job Performance in Jobs Involving Interpersonal Interactions," *Human Performance* 2/3 (1998): 145–166.

59. Remus Ilies, "Personality and Citizenship Behavior," 945–959.

60. Jeffrey A. LePine, Jason A. Colquitt, and Amir Erez, "Adaptability and Changing Task Contexts: Effects of General Cognitive Ability, Conscientiousness, and Openness to Experience," *Personnel Psychology*

53 (2000): 563–593; Jennifer M. George and Jing Zhou, "When Openness to Experience and Conscientiousness Are Related to Creative Behavior: An Interactional Approach," *Journal of Applied Psychology* 86 (2001): 513–524.

61. Margaret A. Shaffer, David A. Harrison, Hal Gregersen, Stewart J. Black, and Lori A. Fezandi, "You Can Take It with You: Individual Differences and Expatriate Effectiveness," *Journal of Applied Psychology* 91 (2006): 109–125.

62. Hao Zhao, and Scott E. Seibert, "The Big Five Personality Dimensions and Entrepreneurial Status: A Meta-Analytical Review," *Journal of Applied Psychology* 91 (2006): 259–271.

63. Murray R. Barrick, Greg L. Stewart, Mitchell J. Neubert, and Michael K. Mount, "Relating Member Ability and Personality to Work-Team Processes and Team Effectiveness," *Journal of Applied Psychology* 83 (1998): 377–391; George A. Neuman and Julie Wright, "Team Effectiveness: Beyond Skills and Cognitive Ability," *Journal of Applied Psychology* 84 (1999): 376–389; Jeffrey A. LePine, John R. Hollenbeck, Daniel R. Ilgen, and Jennifer Hedlund, "Effects of Individual Differences on the Performance of Hierarchical Decision-Making Teams: Much More Than g," *Journal of Applied Psychology* 82 (1997): 803–811.

64. Daniel P. O'Meara, "Personality Tests Raise Questions of Legality and Effectiveness," *HRMagazine* 39 (1994): 97–100.

65. Hanna J. Foldes, Emily E. Duehr, and Deniz S. Ones, "Group Differences in Personality: A Meta-Analysis Comparing Five U.S. Racial Groups," *Personnel Psychology* 61 (2008): 579–616; Ann Marie Ryan, Robert E. Ployhart, and Lisa A. Friedel, "Using Personality Testing to Reduce Adverse Impact: A Cautionary Note," *Journal of Applied Psychology* 83 (1998): 298–307.

66. Jill E. Ellingson, Paul R. Sackett, and Leatta M. Hough, "Social Desirability Corrections in Personality Measurement: Issues of Applicant Comparison and Construct Validity," *Journal of Applied Psychology* 84 (1999): 155–166; Leatta M. Hough, Newell K. Eaton, Marvin D. Dunnette, John D. Kamp, et al., "Criterion-Related Validities of Personality Constructs and the Effect of Response Distortion on Those Validities," *Journal of Applied Psychology* 75 (1990): 581–595; Rose Mueller-Hanson, Eric D. Heggestad, and George C. Thornton III, "Faking and Selection: Considering the Use of Personality from Select-In and Select-Out Perspectives," *Journal of Applied Psychology* 88 (2003): 348–355.

67. Shawn Komar, Douglas J. Brown, Jennifer A. Komar, and Chet Robie, "Faking and the Validity of Conscientiousness: A Monte Carlo Investigation," *Journal of Applied Psychology* 93 (2008): 140–154.

68. Hough et al., "Criterion-Related Validities," 581–595; Murray R. Barrick and Michael K. Mount, "Effects of Impression Management and Self-Deception on the Predictive Validity of Personality Constructs," *Journal of Applied Psychology* 81 (1996): 261–272.

69. Neal Schmitt and Frederick L. Oswald, "The Impact of Corrections for Faking on the Validity of Noncognitive Measures in Selection Settings," *Journal of Applied Psychology* 91 (2006): 613–621.

70. Lynn A. McFarland and Ann Marie Ryan, "Variance in Faking Across Noncognitive Measures," *Journal of Applied Psychology* 85 (2000): 812–821; Joseph G. Rosse, Mary D. Stecher, Janice L. Miller, and Robert A. Levin, "The Impact of Response Distortion of Preemployment Personality Testing and Hiring Decisions," *Journal of Applied Psychology* 83 (1998): 634–644.

71. Mueller-Hanson, Heggestad, and Thornton, "Faking and Selection," 348–355.

72. In-Sue Oh, Gang Wang, and Michael K. Mount, "Validity of Observer Ratings of the Five-Factor Model of Personality Traits: A Meta-Analysis," *Journal of Applied Psychology* 96 (2011): 762–773; Edwin A.J. van Hooft and Marise Ph. Born, "Intentional Response Distortion of Personality Tests: Using Eye-Tracking to Understand Response Distortion When Faking," *Journal of Applied Psychology* 97 (2012): 287–300.

73. L.R. James, M.D. McIntyre, C.A. Glisson, J.L. Bowler and T.R. Mitchell, "The Conditional Reasoning Measurement System for Aggression: An Overview," *Human Performance* 17 (2004): 271–295.

74. James M. LeBreton, Cheryl D. Barksdale, Jennifer Robin, and Lawrence R. James, "Measurement Issues Associated with Conditional Reasoning Tests: Indirect Measurement and Test Faking," *Journal of Applied Psychology* 92 (2007): 1–16.

75. Benjamin Schneider, "The People Make the Place," *Personnel Psychology* 40 (1987): 437–453.

76. Filip Lievens and Paul R. Sackett, "The Validity of Interpersonal Skills Assessment Via Situational Judgment Tests for Predicting Academic Success and Job Performance," *Journal of Applied Psychology* 97 (2012): 460–468.

77. Ronald Bledow and Michael Frese, "A Situational Judgment Test of Personal Initiative and Its Relationship to Performance," *Personnel Psychology* 62 (2009): 229–258; Michael A. McDaniel, Nathan S. Hartman, Deborah L. Whetzel, and W. Lee Grubb III, "Situational Judgment Tests, Response Instructions, and Validity: A Meta-Analysis," *Personnel Psychology* 60 (2007): 63–91.

78. Filip Lievens, Paul R. Sackett, and Tine Buyse, "The Effects of Response Instructions on Situational Judgment Test Performance and Validity in a High-Stakes Context," *Journal of Applied Psychology* 94 (2009): 1095–1101.

79. Stephan J. Motowidlo, Amy C. Hooper, and Hannah L. Jackson, "Implicit Policies about Relations between Personality Traits and Behavioral Effectiveness in Situational Judgment Items," *Journal of Applied Psychology* 91 (2006): 749–761; Michael A. McDaniel, "Situational Judgment Tests," 63–91.

80. Joyce Hogan, "Structure of Physical Performance in Occupational Tasks," *Journal of Applied Psychology* 76 (1991): 495–507.

81. Barry R. Blakley, Miguel A. Quinones, Marnie Swerdlin Crawford, and I. AnnJago, "The Validity of Isometric Strength Tests," *Personnel Psychology* 47 (1994): 47–274.

82. Calvin C. Hoffman, "Generalizing Physical Ability Test Validity: A Case Study Using Test Transportability,

Validity Generalization, and Construct-Related Validation Evidence," *Personnel Psychology* 52 (1999): 1019–1043.

83. Michael Peters, Philip Servos, and Russell Day, "Marked Sex Differences on a Fine Motor Skill Task Disappear When Finger Size Is Used as Covariate," *Journal of Applied Psychology* 75 (1990): 87–90; Richard D. Arvey, Timothy E. Landon, Steven M. Nutting, and Scott E. Maxwell, "Development of Physical Ability Tests for Police Officers: A Construct Validation Approach," *Journal of Applied Psychology* 77 (1992): 996–1009.

84. Paul R. Sackett, Laura R. Burris, and Christine Callahan, "Integrity Testing for Personnel Selection: An Update," *Personnel Psychology* 42 (1989): 491–530.

85. Chad H. Van Iddekinge, Philip L. Roth, Patrick H. Raymark, and Heather N. Odle-Dusseau, "The Criterion-Related Validity of Integrity Tests: An Updated Meta-Analysis," *Journal of Applied Psychology* 97 (2012): 499–530; William G. Harris, John W. Jones, Reid Klion, David W. Arnold, Wayne Camara, and Michael R. Cunningham, "Test Publishers' Perspective on "An Updated Meta-Analysis": Comments on Van Iddekinge Roth, Raymark, and Odle-Dusseau (2012)," *Journal of Applied Psychology* 97 (2012): 531–536; Deniz S. Ones, Chockalingam Viswesvaran, and Frank L. Schmidt, "Integrity Tests Predict Counterproductive Work Behaviors and Job Performance Well: Comment on Van Iddekinge, Roth, Raymark, and Odle-Dusseau," *Journal of Applied Psychology* 97 (2012): 537–542.

86. Joyce Hogan and Kimberly Brinkmeyer, "Bridging the Gap Between Overt and Personality-Based Integrity Tests," *Personnel Psychology* 50 (1997): 587–600; James E. Wanek, Paul R. Sackett, and Deniz S. Ones, "Towards an Understanding of Integrity Test Similarities and Differences: An Item-Level Analysis of Seven Tests," *Personnel Psychology* 56 (2003): 873–894.

87. Ones, Viswesvaran, and Schmidt, "Comprehensive Meta-Analysis of Integrity," 679–703; Cunningham, Wong, and Barbee, "Self-Presentation Dynamics," 643–658.

88. Deniz S. Ones and Chockalingam Viswesvaran, "Gender, Age, and Race Differences on Overt Integrity Tests: Results Across Four Large-Scale Job Applicant Datasets," *Journal of Applied Psychology* 83 (1998): 35–42; Bernardin and Cooke, "Validity of an Honesty Test," 1097–1108.

89. Bernd Marcus, Kibeom Lee, and Michael C. Ashton, "Personality Dimensions Explaining Relationships Between Integrity Tests and Counterproductive Behavior: Big Five, or One in Addition?" *Personnel Psychology* 60 (2007): 1–34.

90. Sackett, Burris, and Callahan, "Integrity Testing for Personnel Selection," 491–530.

91. Michael R. Frone, "Prevalence of Illicit Drug Use in the Workforce and in the Workplace: Findings and Implications from a U.S. National Survey," *Journal of Applied Psychology* 91 (2006): 856–869.

92. Jacques Normand, Stephen D. Salyards, and John J. Mahone, "An Evaluation of Preemployment Drug Testing," *Journal of Applied Psychology* 75 (1990): 629–639.

93. Bennett Tepper, "Investigation of General and Program-Specific Attitudes Toward Corporate Drug-Testing Policies," *Journal of Applied Psychology* 79 (1994): 392–401; Paronto et al., "Drug Testing," 1159–1166; Kevin R. Murphy, George C. Thornton III, and Kristin Prue, "Influence of Job Characteristics on the Acceptability of Employee Drug Testing," *Journal of Applied Psychology* 76 (1991): 447–453.

94. Kevin R. Murphy, George C. Thornton III, and Douglas H. Reynolds, "College Students' Attitudes Toward Employee Drug Testing Programs," *Personnel Psychology* 43 (1990): 615–632.

95. Hunter and Hunter, "Validity and Utility," 72–98; Jerry W. Hedge and Mark S. Teachout, "An Interview Approach to Work Sample Criterion Measurement," *Journal of Applied Psychology* 77 (1992): 453–461; Winfred Arthur Jr., Gerald V Barrett, and Dennis Doverspike, "Validation of an Information-Processing-Based Test Battery for the Prediction of Handling Accidents Among Petroleum-Product Transport Drivers," *Journal of Applied Psychology* 75 (1990): 621–628.

96. Philip Roth, Philip Bobko, Lynn McFarland, and Maury Buster, "Work Sample Tests in Personnel Selection: A Meta-Analysis of Black–White Differences in Overall and Exercise Scores," *Personnel Psychology* 61 (2008): 637–661.

97. Winfred Arthur Jr., Eric Anthony Day, Theresa L. McNelly, and Pamela Edens, "A Meta-Analysis of the Criterion-Related Validity of Assessment Center Dimensions," *Personnel Psychology* 56 (2003): 125–154.

98. Ibid.; Kobi Dayan, Ronen Kastan, and Shaul Fox, "Entry-Level Police Candidate Assessment Center: An Efficient Tool or a Hammer to Kill A Fly?" *Personnel Psychology* 55 (2002): 827–850; Filip Lievens and Fiona Patterson, "The Validity and Incremental Validity of Knowledge Tests, Low-Fidelity Simulations, and High-Fidelity Simulations for Predicting Job Performance in Advanced-Level High-Stakes Selection," *Journal of Applied Psychology* 96 (2011): 927–940.

99. Mark C. Bowler and David J. Woehr, "A Meta-Analytic Evaluation of the Impact of Dimension and Exercise Factors on Assessment Center Ratings," *Journal of Applied Psychology* 91 (2006): 1114–1124; Neal Schmitt and Jeffrey R. Schneider, "Factors Affecting Validity of a Regionally Administered Assessment Center," *Personnel Psychology* 43 (1990): 1–13; Annette C. Spychalski, Miguel A. Quinones, Barbara B. Gaugler, and Katja Pohley, "A Survey of Assessment Center Practices in Organizations in the United States," *Personnel Psychology* 50 (1997): 71–90; Deidra J. Schleicher, David V Day, Bronston T. Mayes, and Ronald E. Riggio, "A New Frame for Frame-of-Reference Training: Enhancing the Construct Validity of Assessment Centers," *Journal of Applied Psychology* 87 (2002): 735–746.

100. Neil Anderson, Filip Lievens, Karen van Dam, and Marise Born, "A Construct-Driven Investigation of Gender Differences in a Leadership-Role Assessment Center," *Journal of Applied Psychology* 91 (2006): 555–566; Michelle A. Dean, Philip L. Roth, and Philip Bobko, "Ethnic and Gender Subgroup Differences in

Assessment Center Ratings: A Meta-Analysis," *Journal of Applied Psychology* 93 (2008): 685–691.

101. Miguel A. Quinones, J. Kevin Ford, and Mark S. Teachout, "The Relationship Between Work Experience and Job Performance: A Conceptual and Meta-Analytic Review," *Personnel Psychology* 48 (1995): 887–910; Philip L. Roth, Craig A. BeVier, Fred S. Switzer III, and Jeffrey S. Schippmann, "Meta-Analyzing the Relationship Between Grades and Job Performance," *Journal of Applied Psychology* 81 (1996): 548–556.

102. Thomas W. H. Ng and Daniel C. Feldman, "How Broadly Does Education Contribute to Job Performance?" *Personnel Psychology* 62 (2009): 89–134.

103. Ann Howard, "College Experiences and Managerial Performance," *Journal of Applied Psychology* 71 (1986): 530–552.

104. Arlise P. McKinney, Kevin D. Carlson, Ross L. Mecham III, Nicolas C. D'Angelo, and Mary L. Connerley, "Recruiters' Use of GPA in Initial Screening Decisions: Higher GPAs Don't Always Make the Cut," *Personnel Psychology* 56 (2003): 823–846; Roth et al., "Meta-analyzing the Relationship."

105. Quinones, Ford, and Teachout, "The Relationship Between Work Experience."

106. Lisa Dragoni, In-Sue Oh, Paul Vankatwyk, and Paul E. Tesluk, "Developing Executive Leaders: The Relative Contribution of Cognitive Ability, Personality, and the Accumulation of Work Experience in Predicting Strategic Thinking Competency," *Personnel Psychology* 64 (2011): 829–864; Paul E. Tesluk and Rick R. Jacobs, "Toward an Integrated Model of Work Experience," *Personnel Psychology* 51 (1998): 321–356.

107. Quinones, Ford, and Teachout, "The Relationship Between Work Experience."

108. Philip L. Roth and Philip Bobko, "College Grade Point Average as a Personnel Selection Device: Ethnic Group Differences and Potential Adverse Impact," *Journal of Applied Psychology* 85 (2000): 399–406.

109. Fred A. Mael, "A Conceptual Rationale for the Domain and Attributes of Biodata," *Personnel Psychology* 44 (1991): 763–792.

110. Barbara K. Brown and Michael A. Campion, "Biodata Phenomenology: Recruiters' Perceptions and Use of Biographical Information in Resume Screening," *Journal of Applied Psychology* 79 (1994): 897–908.

111. Michael K. Mount, L. A. Witt, and Murray R. Barrick, "Incremental Validity of Empirically Keyed Biodata Scales over Gma and the Five Factor Personality Constructs," *Personnel Psychology* 53 (2000): 299–323; Anthony T. Dalessio and Todd A. Silverhart, "Combining Biodata Test and Interview Information: Predicting Decisions and Performance Criteria," *Personnel Psychology* 47 (1994): 303–316.

112. Garnett Stokes Shaffer, Vickie Saunders, and William A. Owens, "Additional Evidence for the Accuracy of Biographical Data: Long-Term Retest and Observer Ratings," *Personnel Psychology* 39 (1986): 791–810.

113. Hunter and Hunter, "Validity and Utility," 72–98; Neal Schmitt, Richard Z. Gooding, Raymond A. Noe, and Michael Kirsch, "Meta-Analyses of Validity Studies Published Between 1964 and 1982 and the Investigation of Study Characteristics," *Personnel Psychology* 37 (1984): 407–423; Fred A. Mael and Blake E. Ashforth, "Loyal from Day One: Biodata, Organizational Identification, and Turnover Among Newcomers," *Personnel Psychology* 48 (1995): 309–334.

114. Margaret A. McManus and Mary L. Kelly, "Personality Measures and Biodata: Evidence Regarding Their Incremental Predictive Value in the Life Insurance Industry," *Personnel Psychology* 52 (1999): 137–148; Andrew J. Vinchur, Jeffery S. Schippmann, Fred S. Swizer III, and Philip L. Roth, "A Meta-Analytic Review of Predictors of Job Performance for Salespeople," *Journal of Applied Psychology* 83 (1998): 586–597.

115. Hannah R. Rothstein, Frank L. Schmidt, Frank W. Erwin, William Owens, et al., "Biographical Data in Employment Selection: Can Validities Be Made Generalizable?" *Journal of Applied Psychology* 75 (1990): 175–184; Kevin D. Carlson, Steven E. Scullen, Frank L. Schmidt, Hannah Rothstein, and Frank Erwin, "Generalizable Biographical Data Validity Can Be Achieved Without Multi-Organizational Development and Keying," *Personnel Psychology* 52 (1999): 731–756.

116. Julia Levashina, Frederick P. Morgeson, and Michael A. Campion, "Tell Me More: Exploring How Verbal Ability and Item Verifiability Influence Responses to Biodata Questions in a High Stakes Selection Context," *Personnel Psychology* 65 (2012): 359–383; Thomas E. Becker and Alan L. Colquitt, "Potential Versus Actual Faking of a Biodata Form: An Analysis Along Several Dimensions of Item Type," *Personnel Psychology* 45 (1992): 389–406.

117. Hunter and Hunter, "Validity and Utility," 72–98.

118. Ann Marie Ryan and Marja Lasek, "Negligent Hiring and Defamation: Areas of Liability Related to Pre-Employment Inquiries," *Personnel Psychology* 44 (1991): 293–319.

119. Richard A. Posthuma, Frederick P. Morgeson, and Michael A. Campion, "Beyond Employment Interview Validity: A Comprehensive Narrative Review of Recent Research and Trends over Time," *Personnel Psychology* 55 (2002): 1–82; Allen I. Huffcutt, James M. Conway, Philip L. Roth, and Nancy J. Stone, "Identification and Meta-Analytic Assessment of Psychological Constructs Measured in Employment Interviews," *Journal of Applied Psychology* 86 (2001): 897–913.

120. David F. Caldwell and Jerry M. Burger, "Personality Characteristics of Job Applicants and Success in Screening Interviews," *Personnel Psychology* 51 (1998): 119–136.

121. Brian W. Swider, Murray R. Barrick, Brad T. Harris, and Adam C. Stoverink, "Managing and Creating an Image in the Interview: The Role of Interviewee Initial Impressions," *Journal of Applied Psychology* 96 (2011): 1275–1288; Murray R. Barrick, Brin W. Swider, and Greg L. Stewart, "Initial Evaluations in the Interview: Relationships with Subsequent Interviewer Evaluations and Employment Offers," *Journal of Applied Psychology* 95 (2010): 1163–1172.

122. Todd J. Maurer and Jerry M. Solamon, "The Science and Practice of a Structured Employment Interview Coaching Program," *Personnel Psychology* 59 (2006): 433–456; Todd Maurer, Jerry Solamon, and Deborah

Troxtel, "Relationship of Coaching with Performance in Situational Employment Interviews," *Journal of Applied Psychology* 83 (1998): 128–136; Posthuma, Morgeson, and Campion, "Beyond Employment Interview Validity."

123. Murray R. Barrick, Jonathan A. Shaffer, and Sandra W. DeGrassi, "What You See May Not Be What You Get: Relationships Among Self-Presentation Tactics and Ratings of Interview and Job Performance," *Journal of Applied Psychology* 94 (2009): 1394–1411.

124. James M. Conway, Robert A. Jako, and Deborah F. Goodman, "A Meta-Analysis of Interrater and Internal Consistency Reliability of Selection Interviews," *Journal of Applied Psychology* 80 (1995): 565–579.

125. Michael A. McDaniel, Deborah L. Whetzel, Frank L. Schmidt, and Steven D. Maurer, "The Validity of Employment Interviews: A Comprehensive Review and Meta-Analysis," *Journal of Applied Psychology* 79 (1994): 599–616; Allen I. Huffcutt and Winfred Arthur Jr., "Hunter and Hunter (1984) Revisited: Interview Validity for Entry-Level Jobs," *Journal of Applied Psychology* 79 (1994): 184–190.

126. Jose M. Cortina, Nancy B. Goldstein, Stephanie C. Payne, H. Kristl Davison, and Stephen W. Gilliland, "The Incremental Validity of Interview Scores over and above Cognitive Ability and Conscientiousness Scores," *Personnel Psychology* 53 (2000): 325–352; Michael A. Campion, James E. Campion, and J. Peter Hudson, "Structured Interviewing: A Note on Incremental Validity and Alternative Question Types," *Journal of Applied Psychology* 79 (1994): 998–1102.

127. Sara L. Rynes and Barry Gerhart, "Interviewer Assessments of Applicant 'Fit': An Exploratory Investigation," *Personnel Psychology* 43 (1990): 13–36.

128. Sharon L. Segrest Purkiss, Pamela L. Perrewe, Treena L. Gillespie, Bronston T. Mayes, and Gerald R. Ferris, "Implicit Sources of Bias in Employment Interview Judgments and Decisions," *Organizational Behavior and Human Decision Processing* 101 (2006): 152–167.

129. M. Ronald Buckley, Katherine A. Jackson, Mark C. Bolino, John G. Veres, III, and Hubert S. Field, "The Influence of Relational Demography on Panel Interview Ratings: A Field Experiment," *Personnel Psychology* 60 (2007): 627–646; Joshua M. Sacco, Christine R. Scheu, Ann Marie Ryan, and Neal Schmitt, "An Investigation of Race and Sex Similarity Effects in Interviews: A Multilevel Approach to Relational Demography," *Journal of Applied Psychology* 88 (2003): 852–865; Philip L. Roth, Chad H. Van Iddekinge, Allen I. Huffcutt, Carl E. Eidson, Jr., and

Philip Bobko, "Corrections for Range Restriction in Structured Interview Ethnic Group Differences: The Values May Be Larger Than Researchers Thought," *Journal of Applied Psychology* 87 (2002): 369–376; Allen I. Huffcutt and Philip L. Roth, "Racial Group Differences in Employment Interview Evaluations," *Journal of Applied Psychology* 83 (1998): 179–189.

130. Klaus G. Melchers, Nadja Lienhardt, Miriam Von Aarburg, and Martin Kleinmann, "Is More Structure Really Better? A Comparison of Frame-of-Reference Training and Descriptively Anchored Rating Scales to Improve Interviewers' Rating Quality, *Personnel Psychology* 64 (2011): 53–87; Karen I. van der Zee, Arnold B. Bakker, and Paulien Bakker, "Why Are Structured Interviews So Rarely Used in Personnel Selection?" *Journal of Applied Psychology* 87 (2002): 176–184.

131. Frank L. Schmidt and Ryan D. Zimmerman, "A Counterintuitive Hypothesis about Employment Interview Validity and Some Supporting Evidence," *Journal of Applied Psychology* 89 (2004): 553–561.

132. Murray R. Barrick, "What You See May Not Be What You Get," 1394–1411.

133. Steven D. Maurer, "A Practitioner-Based Analysis of Interviewer Job Expertise and Scale Format as Contextual Factors in Situational Interviews," *Personnel Psychology* 55 (2002): 307–328; Allen I. Huffcutt, Jeff Weekley, Willi H. Wiesner, Timothy G. DeGroot, and Casey Jones, "Comparison of Situational and Behavior Description Interview Questions for Higher-Level Positions," *Personnel Psychology* 54 (2001): 619–644; Elaine D. Pulakos and Neal Schmitt, "Experience-Based and Situational Interview Questions: Studies of Validity," *Personnel Psychology* 48 (1995): 289–308.

134. Yarv Ganzach, Avraham N. Kluger, and Nimrod Kayman, "Making Decisions from an Interview: Expert Measurement and Mechanical Combination," *Personnel Psychology* 53 (2000): 1–21.

135. Gatewood and Field, *Human Resource Selection*.

136. David M. Finch, Bryan D. Edwards, and Craig J. Wallace, "Multistage Selection Strategies: Simulating the Effects on Adverse Impact and Expected Performance for Various Predictor Combinations," *Journal of Applied Psychology* 94 (2009): 318–340.

137. Michael A. Campion, James L. Outtz, Sheldon Zedeck, Frank L. Schmidt, Jerard F. Kehoe, Kevin R. Murphy, and Robert M. Guion, "The Controversy over Score Banding in Personnel Selection: Answers to 10 Key Questions," *Personnel Psychology* 54 (2001): 149–185.

138. Ibid.

Chapter 7

Managing Employee Retention and Separation

A MANAGER'S PERSPECTIVE

ANGELA CLOSES HER CELL PHONE AND TAKES A DEEP BREATH. WAS IT REALLY A GOOD IDEA TO ACCEPT THE JOB AS RESTAURANT MANAGER? IT SOUNDED LIKE SUCH A GOOD IDEA WHEN MARK, THE REGIONAL MANAGER, OFFERED HER THE POSITION TWO MONTHS AGO. SHE WON'T GRADUATE WITH HER DEGREE IN ELEMENTARY EDUCATION FOR TWO MORE YEARS. BEING THE MANAGER PROVIDES HER WITH FLEXIBILITY TO TAKE CLASSES WHEN SHE WANTS, BUT TRYING TO SCHEDULE OTHER EMPLOYEES IS MUCH MORE STRESSFUL THAN SHE EXPECTED.

©Jamie Grill/Corbis

Just now Barbara—a new cook hired last month—called to tell Angela that she is quitting and will not work the hours scheduled during the upcoming week. This is the third time in two months that someone has quit with little or no advance notice. It will be difficult to schedule other employees to cover for Barbara during the upcoming week, let alone quickly find someone to hire as a new cook.

From experience, Angela knows that cooks and food servers are unlikely to stay with the same restaurant for long. Yet surely it should be possible to create a fun working atmosphere that would make employees less likely to leave. Might it help to pay higher wages? Would older workers and people with family responsibilities be more likely to stay than the college students she currently hires?

Angela's thoughts quickly shift to the other disagreeable task she faces today. The very thought of meeting with Simon is enough to make Angela want to quit, herself. Yesterday Simon was late for work the second time this week. Once he arrived, he spent much of his shift wasting time. Working with first graders will surely be easier than supervising Simon. Should she just fire him?

Thinking about firing someone scares Angela. Would Simon become emotional? When should she meet with him if she decides to deliver the bad news? What should she say? As questions about

THE BIG PICTURE *Effective Organizations Retain their Best Employees While Helping People Who Are Not Productive Find Alternative Employment*

firing Simon race through her head, Angela remembers a section of the restaurant operations manual that provides guidance for dealing with problem employees. She read the manual when she began working as manager, and she vaguely remembers a series of steps that she should use to discipline problem employees. Perhaps the operations manual is more useful than she thought.

Angela enters her small manager's office and begins searching for the manual. As she searches, she asks herself why personnel issues have to be so hard. Her life would be so much easier if she could get employees like Barbara to stay and those like Simon to leave. She knows she will need a plan if she is going to survive the next two years.

WHAT DO YOU THINK?

Suppose you are listening to a conversation between Angela and her boss, Mark. Mark makes the following statements. Which of the statements do you think are true?

T OR F Workers are less likely to quit when they feel the organization cares about their personal needs.

T OR F Decisions to quit often begin with a specific event that causes employees to evaluate their work situation.

T OR F It doesn't really matter how you fire people, as long as you make it clear that their employment is being terminated.

T OR F In order to defend against potential lawsuits, an organization should carefully document methods of disciplining problem employees.

T OR F Employees who see coworkers losing their jobs become more committed to staying with the organization.

After reading this chapter you should be able to:

LEARNING OBJECTIVE 1 Explain how employee retention and separation align with overall HR strategy.

LEARNING OBJECTIVE 2 Explain the employee turnover process and describe methods that an organization can use to reduce undesirable turnover.

LEARNING OBJECTIVE 3 Discuss the potential benefits and problems associated with employee layoffs.

LEARNING OBJECTIVE 4 Describe effective methods of employee discipline, including the principles of due process and the actions of progressive discipline.

LEARNING OBJECTIVE 5 Describe effective methods for dismissing employees from an organization.

How Can Strategic Employee Retention and Separation Make an Organization Effective?

Employees are a primary asset of almost every organization, but identifying, hiring, and training good employees can be costly. Replacing an employee who quits costs an organization between one and two times the annual salary of the position.[1] This means, for example, that replacing an accountant with an annual salary of $75,000 costs the firm between $75,000 and $150,000. The company loses money not only from the costs associated with hiring a replacement but also from lower productivity and decreased customer satisfaction.[2] Such costs were illustrated by a study which found that Burger King restaurants with higher employee turnover have longer wait times that translate into decreased customer satisfaction.[3] Employee turnover, then, is very expensive, harms customer service, and relates negatively to organizational performance.[4] Good employees leaving to work for competitors can also be a problem in that it increases the effectiveness of a rival.[5] The expense and negative consequences of replacing workers requires most organizations to focus effort on **employee retention**, a set of actions designed to keep good employees once they have been hired.

Employee retention
The act of keeping employees; retaining good workers is particularly important.

Whereas retaining good employees is beneficial, organizations lose money when they retain poor employees. Ensuring that nonproductive employees don't continue with the organization is often just as important as retaining productive workers. Furthermore, changes in economic conditions and product demand sometimes force organizations to reduce the size of their workforce. **Employee separation** is the process of efficiently and fairly terminating workers.

Employee separation
The act of terminating the employment of workers.

SAS Institute, Inc., is a successful organization that benefits from concerted efforts to retain productive workers. CEO Jim Goodnight summarizes his views about employee retention when he says, "My chief assets drive out the gate every day. My job is to make sure they come back."[6]

SAS is the world's largest privately owned software company, with revenues exceeding $2.7 billion each year. Organizations such as American Express, Chrysler, Pfizer, and the U.S. Department of Defense use SAS products to help them gather and analyze large amounts of information. Many college students also use SAS products to conduct statistical analyses for class projects.[7]

An important key to success for SAS is high customer satisfaction: Its customer retention rate is above 98 percent. One reason for this success is a relentless drive to create innovative products. SAS reinvests 30 percent of its revenue in research and development each year. Another reason for success is its emphasis on building long-term relationships with clients. Each year, the company conducts a survey to determine how well customer needs are being met. Rather than spend money on marketing and advertising, SAS spends money satisfying customer needs.

Having a stable workforce made up of highly intelligent knowledge workers is critical for providing outstanding customer service.[8] Jim Goodnight sums up the human resource philosophy he has practiced over the years by stating, "I think our history has shown that taking care of employees has made the difference in how employees take care of our customers."[9] The average tenure at SAS is 10 years, and 300 employees have worked there for at least 25 years, which is unusual in the software industry. SAS develops long-term relationships with employees, who in turn build long-term relationships with customers. Employees treat customers with the same respect and care that they receive from SAS.[10]

A good indication of successful human resource practices is the low percentage of employees who leave SAS each year. The annual turnover rate at SAS has never been higher than 5 percent, a rate that is much lower than that at competing software firms. The lower turnover saves SAS up to $80 million each year.[11]

What does SAS do to keep employee turnover so low? One answer is that it has created a great work environment. The great environment was recognized by *Fortune* magazine, which has included SAS among the top three places to work for the past four years. Its work sites, located in beautiful areas where people want to live, have a campus atmosphere.[12] SAS employs a resident artist who coordinates sculptures and art decorations.[13] In addition, all professional workers have private offices.[14] Yet, perhaps the most important aspect of the work environment is the expectation that employees leave the office between 5 and 6 o'clock each evening. The corporate philosophy is that working too many hours in a day leads to decreased productivity for creative workers. Employees are encouraged to spend dinnertime at home with their families.[15]

Another reason SAS excels at employee retention is its exceptional benefits. Back in its startup days, SAS faced the possibility of losing some key personnel who were going on maternity leave and unlikely to return to work. Goodnight and other leaders solved the problem by creating an onsite daycare center. In the ensuing 25 years, SAS has become a leader in offering family-friendly benefits. Employees are often seen in the cafeteria eating lunch with their young children who attend onsite daycare. Vacation and sick leave policies are generous, and most workers have the option of flexible scheduling.[16] The company also has excellent fitness facilities, which even launder gym clothes.[17] Pay is rarely more than what is offered by other software firms, but SAS does offer competitive compensation packages that include profit sharing.

SAS is also good at identifying and retaining employees who are compatible with its organizational culture. People who fit with the family-friendly environment are recruited across industries and not just from the software sector. Not being located in Silicon Valley helps SAS recruit workers who are less likely to move to other companies. SAS also takes advantage of poor economic conditions by hiring the best workers who have been laid off from

Building Strength Through HR

SAS INSTITUTE, INC.

SAS Institute, Inc., is a software developer that employs over 11,000 people. Human resource management at SAS builds competitive strength by

- Providing a great work atmosphere that encourages employees to stay with the company.
- Offering family-friendly benefits such as onsite daycare and flexible scheduling.
- Hiring high-performing employees who are motivated not only to make money but also to balance work life with outside interests.

competitors.[18] For each open position, the company receives up to 200 applications.[19] To retain good employees who want to pursue different jobs, the company works hard to facilitate internal transfers.[20] Those who are hired but don't fit the organizational culture are encouraged to leave SAS and find other employment.[21]

LEARNING OBJECTIVE 1

How Are Employee Retention and Separation Strategic?

The SAS Institute example shows how an organization can benefit from placing a strong emphasis on retaining workers. As we have seen with other human resource practices, however, such a strong emphasis on retaining workers may not be as beneficial for other organizations. Strategies for retaining employees are most effective when they fit with an organization's strategy. Figure 7.1 illustrates how employee retention and separation fit with competitive business strategy and overall HR strategy.

STRATEGIC EMPHASIS ON EMPLOYEE RETENTION

Retaining good employees is the very essence of an internal labor orientation. The competitive advantage here comes from developing a loyal workforce that consistently excels at satisfying customer demands. For organizations that use the Loyal Soldier HR strategy, retaining employees reduces recruiting expenses and provides workers with a sense of security that persuades them to work for slightly lower wages than they might be able to earn at competing firms. For instance, people employed at a state government office might be able to earn more money elsewhere but prefer to continue working as public servants because government agencies are less likely to replace workers.

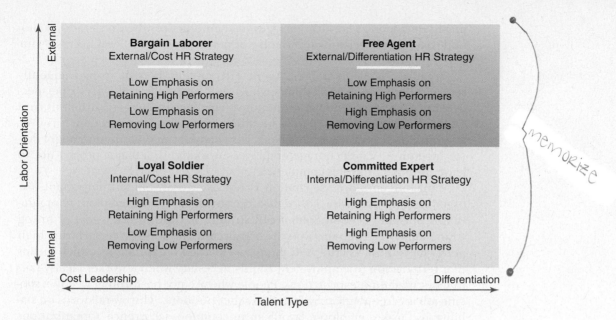

Figure 7.1 Strategic Retention and Separation of Employees.

With the Committed Expert HR strategy, employee retention helps build a workforce with unique skills that employees of other organizations do not have. These skills are critical for producing exceptional products and services that cannot be easily duplicated by competitors. SAS Institute uses a Committed Expert strategy of this kind. Employees with specialized skills develop long-term relationships with customers, who continue to purchase SAS products because of the excellent service they receive.

Employee retention is not as critical for organizations with an external labor orientation. Employees are expected to leave the organization to pursue other opportunities. For organizations pursuing a Bargain Laborer HR strategy, separations are seen as a necessary consequence of combining entry-level work with relatively low wages. Indeed, a moderate amount of employee turnover has been found to be beneficial with the Bargain Laborer HR strategy.[22] For organizations with a Free Agent HR strategy, some employee turnover is desirable, since those who leave can often be replaced by individuals with more up-to-date knowledge and skills.

STRATEGIC EMPHASIS ON EMPLOYEE SEPARATION

When it comes to pursuing a differentiation strategy, employee separation can be just as important as employee retention. Innovative organizations rely on highly skilled employees who have specialized knowledge and ability. An employee who is not capable of providing skilled inputs does not contribute, making termination of nonperforming employees critical for organizations that seek to produce premium goods and services.

Organizations pursuing a Committed Expert HR strategy focus on terminating the employment of low performers soon after they are hired. Quickly identifying individuals who do not fit the organizational culture, or who appear unable to develop needed skill and motivation, reduces the cost of bad hiring decisions. A law firm engages in such practice when it denies promotion to a junior-level attorney who is not performing at the level necessary for making partner.

Organizations with a Free Agent HR strategy benefit from frequently replacing employees with others who bring new skills and a fresh perspective. Employee separation is a common occurrence in such organizations, and ongoing efforts are needed to ensure that disruptions from frequent turnover are minimized as much as possible.[23] For example, an organization might create incentives that encourage employees working on a major project not to leave until the project is completed.

Managing employee separation is not as critical, but still important, for organizations that have cost-reduction strategies. For example, an organization pursuing a Loyal Soldier HR strategy has the primary goal of hiring young employees who stay with the organization for long careers. Having high performers is not as critical in these cost-focused organizations, which means that termination of employment is only necessary when a worker clearly fails to meet minimum expectations. People who are not performing well in a specific job are frequently transferred to other positions. The overall focus on stability also makes employee layoffs an uncommon occurrence. Organizations with Loyal Soldier HR strategies thus expend little effort on developing employee separation practices.

Similarly, effective management of employee separation is not critical for an organization with a Bargain Laborer HR strategy. Because of their relatively low wage rates and repetitive jobs, such organizations expect many of their employees to move on. Furthermore, the basic nature of the work and the emphasis on close supervision mean that identifying and terminating low performers need not be a major focus. A good example is fast-food restaurants that rarely have policies to actively identify and terminate low-performing workers. Employees are allowed to continue working as long as their performance meets minimum standards.

CONCEPT CHECK

1. *Retaining good employees is most critical for which of the HR strategies?*
2. *Which of the HR strategies might encourage some employee separation?*

LEARNING OBJECTIVE 2

How Can Undesirable Employee Turnover Be Reduced?

Who is most likely to remain with an organization? As shown in Figure 7.2, the answer is that employees with average performance are most likely to remain with an organization. High performers are at risk of being recruited away by other organizations to work in more-fulfilling and better-paying jobs. Low performers likely perceive lack of fit with their current position and resent the relatively low compensation they receive. Interestingly, this effect for low performers has been shown to occur predominantly when organizations are located in countries such as the United States that value high individual achievement and greater separation between people of varying status.[24]

Of course, organizations are most concerned about losing high performers. From the organization's perspective, losing low performers is of little concern and is usually seen as a desirable outcome. From the employee's point of view, much of the effect of leaving depends on whether we're dealing with **voluntary turnover**, in which the employee makes the decision to leave, or **involuntary turnover**, in which the organization terminates the employment relationship. Not surprisingly, involuntary turnover has a much more negative effect on the employee.

One way of thinking about turnover is thus to categorize it along two dimensions. One dimension is whether the person leaving is a high or low performer. The second dimension is whether the person plans to voluntarily leave. Combining the two dimensions results in four possible types of turnover:[25]

1. *Functional retention*, which occurs when high-performing employees remain employed, can benefit both the individual and the organization.
2. *Functional turnover*, which occurs when low-performing employees voluntarily quit, can also benefit both parties.
3. *Dysfunctional retention* occurs when low-performing employees remain with the organization. Later in the chapter, we deal with situations in which the organization must terminate low performers who do not leave voluntarily.
4. *Dysfunctional turnover* occurs when an employee whose performance is at least adequate voluntarily quits. We focus on this situation in the remainder of this section.

When a good employee chooses to leave, the organization usually must identify and hire another worker to fill the position. This process can be highly disruptive. Just think of a product development team with high turnover among members. Frequent personnel changes make it difficult for the team to coordinate efforts. A lot of time and energy are spent on finding new team members and teaching them the necessary skills. All this energy and time is wasted if people leave just as they are becoming integrated into the team. Frequently replacing employees consumes many resources and makes it difficult for organizations to develop a competitive advantage. In general, organizations are thus more effective when they have programs and practices that proactively work to reduce employee turnover.

Voluntary turnover
Employee separation that occurs because the employee chooses to leave.

Involuntary turnover
Employee separation that occurs because the employer chooses to terminate the employment relationship.

Dysfunctional turnover
Undesirable employee turnover that occurs when good employees quit.

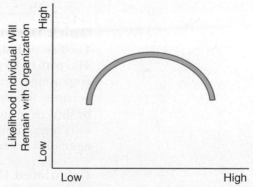

Figure 7.2 Relationship Between Employee Performance and Turn. *Source:* Based on information from Michael C. Sturman, Lian Shao, and Jan H. Katz, "The Effect of Culture on the Curvilinear Relationship Between Performance and Turnover," *Journal of Applied Psychology* 97 (2012): 46–62.

RECOGNIZING PATHS TO VOLUNTARY TURNOVER

We've seen that dysfunctional turnover causes problems for organizations. What, then, can they do to prevent or reduce it? A starting point is to understand why employees choose to leave.[26] Observations of actual decisions suggest specific processes explain how turnover unfolds over time.[27] One difference is the amount of thought that goes into the decision. Since moving from one organization to another is a radical life change for most people, we might expect a person to put a great deal of thought into a

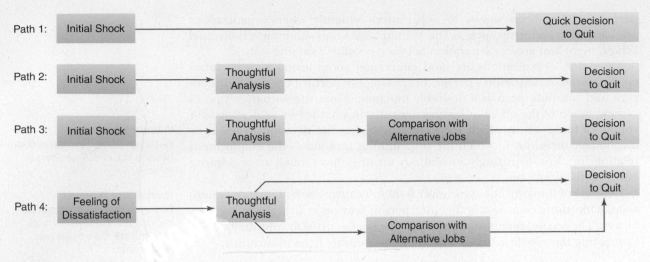

Figure 7.3 Paths to Decisions to Quit. *Source:* Information taken from Thomas W. Lee and Terence R. Mitchell, "An Alternative Approach: The Unfolding Model of Voluntary Employee Turnover," *Academy of Management Review* 19 (1994); 51–90.

decision to move. Yet sometimes people make hasty decisions without carefully thinking about the consequences. Another difference concerns whether a single event can be identified as the beginning of the decision to leave an organization. Figure 7.3 uses these differences to capture four paths to quitting. Next, we examine each of the four paths in more detail.

Quick Decision to Leave

The first path shown in Figure 7.3 is a quick decision to leave the organization. This path begins with some external event that causes an employee to rethink the employment relationship. The employee might be asked to engage in unethical behavior, for example, or might be denied a promotion. The event may not even be directly related to work. For instance, the employee might become pregnant or receive an inheritance. Regardless of what the event is, the result is a highly emotional reaction that leads the employee to quit without much thought.

Calculated Decision to Leave

Like the first path, the second path shown in the figure begins with an event that causes an individual to begin thinking about leaving the organization. Here, however, the individual does not make a quick decision. Alternatives are weighed, and the benefits of staying are compared with the benefits of leaving. For instance, an employee may learn that others in the organization are making more money even though they have less experience on the job. The employee who hears this news might carefully analyze the benefits and drawbacks associated with staying with the present employer. As explained in the "Building Strength Through HR" feature, companies can intervene at this point to communicate potential benefits of staying. Such effort is helpful because a decision to leave the organization occurs only after careful thought. Note, however, that the decision for this path is not influenced by alternative job opportunities. The decision is simply whether to stay or leave.

Comparison with Other Alternatives

The third path in the figure involves a comparison between the current job and other alternatives. Once again, some external event initiates thoughts

Building Strength Through HR

CONVERGYS CORPORATION

Convergys Corporation, which provides various business services, is a global leader, with annual revenues of more than $2.8 billion. The 74,000 employees at Convergys help companies manage customer and employee relationships through activities such as billing, customer inquiry management, and employee benefit management. Convergys uses an "early warning system" to help identify employees who might quit. Team leaders provide a weekly assessment of each employee's probability of leaving the company. Employees unlikely to leave receive a green rating, and employees likely to leave receive a red rating. Organizational leaders meet with red-rated employees to encourage them to stay. These employees are offered alternative work schedules, and many are referred to health and benefit programs. These practices show employees that the organization cares about them. Employees stay with the organization, and 80 percent of managers are promoted from within. Growth and expansion require frequent hiring of new employees, which is much easier than

endless replacing of employees who quit. By emphasizing employee retention, Convergys has been consistently recognized by *Fortune* magazine as one of America's most admired companies.

Sources: www.convergys.com/company_overview.html; Philip Quinn, "Colour Coding for Early Warning: Keeping Employees Is Becoming More Important in Today's Tighter Labour Market," *Ottawa Citizen*, October 7, 2006; Andrew Dunn, "Convergys to add 1,600 jobs at Charlotte Call Centers," *Charlotte Observer*, February 21, 2013; http://money.cnn.com/_magazines/fortune/mostadmired.

about leaving the organization. For example, research has established that receiving a job offer from a different company is a critical event that often leads an employee to quit.[28] Once the event has occurred, the employee begins to look at alternative opportunities. The benefits of jobs with other organizations are carefully compared with the benefits of the current job. A decision to leave becomes a conscious choice between the present job and specific alternatives. This path appears to be the most common course that leads an employee to leave an organization.

Sense of Dissatisfaction

In the final path shown in Figure 7.3, the employee develops a general sense of dissatisfaction over time. This sense of dissatisfaction leads to either a calculated decision to leave or a search and comparison with other job opportunities. This path is different from the other paths in that no specific event can be identified as causing the employee to begin thinking about quitting.

UNDERSTANDING DECISIONS TO QUIT

An important part of each path to turnover is a lack of satisfaction with the current work situation. It is easy to see how a lack of satisfaction can lead to a decision to leave. Most of us can recall a time when we have been part of a team, club, or other organization that we wanted to leave as fast as possible. Perhaps it was a sports team where teammates fought among themselves and seldom won games. Maybe it was a student work team that included several individuals who didn't do their share of the work. Being stuck in such a team can have a negative impact on personal happiness. Working in an organization with an undesirable environment can also lead to feelings of dissatisfaction. Employees who are more dissatisfied are more likely to quit than are employees who experience a positive work environment.[29] In particular, environments that are plagued by constraints, hassles, dysfunctional politics, and uncertainty about what to do increase the likelihood that employees will be less satisfied and quit.[30]

A basic model illustrating how lack of satisfaction leads to quitting is shown in Figure 7.4. The employee's decision to leave begins with a sense of low job satisfaction. Consistent with the paths described above, this sense may be created by a specific event or as part of a global feeling that builds over time. Individuals who are not satisfied with their work arrangements begin to withdraw from the organization and think about quitting. Thoughts translate into action as individuals begin searching for alternative employment, which often leads to turnover.[31] Other factors—such as the availability of other jobs and individual personality characteristics—also influence whether thoughts of withdrawal are acted upon so that an individual actually leaves. Let's explore each aspect of the model in order to better understand why people quit jobs.

Low Job Satisfaction

Job satisfaction
Employees' feelings and beliefs about the quality of their jobs.

Job satisfaction represents a person's emotional feelings about his or her work. When work is consistent with employees' values and needs, job satisfaction is likely to be high.[32] Satisfaction increases when employees are able

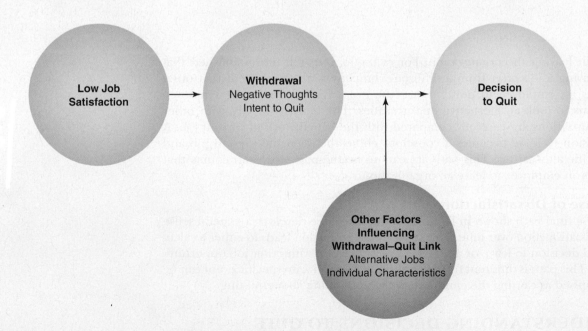

Figure 7.4 How Job Satisfaction Leads to Quitting. *Source:* Adapted from Peter W. Hom, Fanny Caranikas-Walker, Gregory E. Prussia, and Rodger W. Griffeth, "A Meta-Analytical Structural Equations Analysis of a Model of Employee Turnover," *Journal of Applied Psychology* 77 (1992): 905. Adapted with permission.

to pursue goals and activities that are truly important to them.[33] Employees are also happier when they are able to do work that fits with their interests and life plans.[34] For example, a high school mathematics teacher is likely to experience high job satisfaction when she perceives that she is helping others develop critical life skills.

Employees often make an overall assessment of their job satisfaction, but job satisfaction can also be divided into different dimensions, as shown in Table 7.1.[35] An employee who is satisfied with one aspect of the job may not be satisfied with others. Someone may have high satisfaction in the area of job fulfillment because he enjoys the work he does, for instance, but have little satisfaction with how much pay he receives. Also, not every aspect of job satisfaction is equally important to every employee. Some people value empowerment more than security, whereas others will place greater value on security.[36] These different values and perceptions mean that job satisfaction represents a complicated mix of feelings. Nevertheless, satisfaction with compensation is often the dimension that is most strongly related to overall perceptions of job satisfaction.

Overall job satisfaction varies among organizations as well as among individuals. On average, some organizations have happier employees. Those with happier employees tend to be more productive.[37] Yet even organizations with high overall levels of job satisfaction likely have individual employees who are not happy with their jobs.

Withdrawal from the Organization

Employees who are unhappy with their work tend to withdraw from the organization. **Withdrawal** occurs when employees put less effort into their work activities and become less committed to the organization. As their sense of attachment to the organization decreases, they feel less obligated to work toward ensuring the organization's success.

Withdrawal
The process that occurs when employees begin to distance themselves from the organization by working less hard and planning to quit.

Table 7.1	*Dimensions of Job Satisfaction*
Dimension	**Examples**
Satisfaction with empowerment	• Involvement in decisions • Information from management
Satisfaction with job fulfillment	• Sense of personal accomplishment • Good use of skills and abilities
Satisfaction with pay	• Pay relative to others • Pay for type of job
Satisfaction with work group	• Quality of work done by group • Cooperation among people
Satisfaction with security	• Good job security • Good total benefits program
Satisfaction with work facilitation	• Company efforts to make competitive changes • Conditions for employees to be productive

Source: Information from Benjamin Schneider, Paul J. Hanges, D. Brent Smith, and Amy Nicole Salvaggio, "Which Comes First: Employee Attitudes or Organizational Financial and Market Performance?" *Journal of Applied Psychology* 88 (2003): 836–851.

Withdrawal is a progressive process whereby an employee who is dissatisfied pulls away from the organization over time.[38] Dissatisfied employees begin to provide less input[39] and become less helpful toward coworkers.[40] Early signs of withdrawal include increased lateness and in many cases absenteeism, and decreasing commitment, as well as a low sense of empowerment, turn into a decision to quit.[41]

Exit from the Organization

Many dissatisfied workers do not go on to the final step of the turnover process. Instead, they continue in their jobs. What explains why some dissatisfied workers leave while others stay?

As you might expect, one important factor that determines whether workers continue in undesirable jobs is the availability and desirability of alternative jobs. In spite of low job satisfaction, employees are likely to stay with an organization when they perceive that it will be difficult to find another job. People are also more likely to stay with their current jobs when they perceive that switching will have high economic and psychological costs. In essence, dissatisfied employees are more likely to leave when they expect it to be easy to find alternative work with pay that is equal to or higher than what they are receiving.[42]

Substantial evidence suggests that some people are simply more likely than others to leave organizations. Part of the reason is that some people are predisposed toward either high or low levels of satisfaction regardless of the work environment.[43] A small number of employees are likely unsatisfied no matter how good a job is. People with chronically low job satisfaction tend to experience negative moods in all aspects of their lives.[44] They also tend to have dysfunctional characteristics such as perfectionism that undermine their feelings of self-worth.[45] A lower level of general satisfaction makes these people likely to leave jobs, but moving to a new job may not increase their long-term satisfaction with life.

Evidence also suggests that people with certain characteristics are more likely to leave an organization regardless of their level of job satisfaction. Individuals who are low on agreeableness often leave a job because they like doing things their own way. Individuals who are highly open to experience tend to leave to seek out new adventures. In contrast, conscientious employees tend to feel a higher sense of obligation, which makes them less likely to quit.[46] Employees who are more averse to risk, as well as those who care less about what others think of them, are also less likely to actually quit.[47]

ORGANIZATIONAL PRACTICES THAT REDUCE TURNOVER

We have already seen that organizations pursuing internal labor strategies would prefer to retain employees, especially high-performing ones. Once an employee has decided to quit, it is often too late to do anything to change that individual's mind about leaving. Thus, organizations that want to reduce turnover must work to ensure that employees' needs are being met continuously. Good human resource management practices related to staffing, career planning, training, compensation, and workforce governance can help. Table 7.2 provides an overview of practices in each area that have been identified as helping to reduce turnover.

Table 7.2	*Human Resource Practices that Reduce Turnover*
HR Practice	**Example of Effective Tactics**
Staffing	• Use realistic job previews • Provide growth and promotion opportunities • Select employees who fit with the organization
Training and development	• Offer reimbursement for educational programs such as MBA • Provide sabbaticals and other learning opportunities
Career planning	• Specify clear career paths
Compensation	• Maintain competitive pay • Develop fair pay practices • Pay for learning new skills
Labor relations	• Establish quick and fair grievance procedures • Facilitate conflict resolution among employees

know!! (handwritten margin note)

Source: Information from Thomas W. Lee and Steven D. Maurer, "The Retention of Knowledge Workers with the Unfolding Model of Voluntary Turnover," *Human Resource Management Review* 7 (1997): 247–275.

Effective organizations develop ongoing procedures to find out why individuals leave. Each employee who leaves has an **exit interview** in which the interviewer tries to determine why the employee decided to quit. Information gained during exit interviews is used to improve organizational procedures and reduce turnover of other employees. In the rest of this section, we explore organizational procedures that can help to decrease turnover.

Exit interview
Face-to-face discussion conducted by an organization to learn why an employee is quitting.

Assessing Employee Satisfaction

Organizations seeking to reduce employee turnover frequently measure their employees' job satisfaction. Such assessments are done through surveys that ask employees about various facets of their work experience. Generally, employees can fill out the surveys anonymously. A common survey is the Job Descriptive Index, which assesses satisfaction with work tasks themselves, pay, promotions, coworkers, and supervision.[48] Research has shown this index to be an accurate indicator of employee perceptions.[49]

Along with employees' responses, the organization collects general information about demographic characteristics, work positions, and locations. Results are then analyzed to determine average levels of satisfaction, as well as differences between departments and worksites. Analysis provides insight into areas of concern and helps organizations determine which facets of the work experience might need improvement. Business Development Bank of Canada, for example, conducts surveys to obtain assessments about employee benefits. As a result of employees' responses, the bank has offered monetary gifts, extra vacation days, and flexible work hours, increasing employee satisfaction and helping to reduce employee turnover.[50]

Job satisfaction surveys are best when they quickly engage employees by asking interesting questions. Topics expected to be most important to employees should be placed at the beginning of the survey. Routine questions such as length of time worked and department should be placed at the end.[51] The value of employee surveys can also be increased by including items measuring how well the organization is meeting strategic objectives. For example, the survey might ask employees how well they think customer needs are being met or whether they believe the company is truly providing differentiated products and services.[52]

The organization's climate for diversity is something that can be particularly important to assess. People are more likely to leave groups when they perceive that they are very different from others.[53] Women and racial minorities thus tend to quit more frequently than white men.[54] Retention of women and minorities is higher in organizations that value and support diversity.[55] But the benefits don't stop with retention; a supportive climate for diversity can also reduce absenteeism and increase performance.[56] Organizations thus benefit a great deal from measuring and improving their diversity climates.

Yet, one problem with job satisfaction surveys is that the least satisfied employees are not likely to respond to the survey. These employees have already started to withdraw from the organization, so they see little personal benefit in completing the survey. They see things as too negative to fix, and they no longer care about the work environment of the company they are planning to leave. Organizational leaders are thus wise to remember that job satisfaction results will likely make things appear more positive than they really are.[57]

Socializing New Employees

Efforts to retain employees should begin when they are hired, as there is a tendency for new employees to feel a lack of support within a few months of joining an organization.[58] An important process for new employees is **socialization**, the process of acquiring the knowledge and behaviors needed to be a member of an organization.[59] Effective socialization occurs when employees are given critical information that helps them understand the organization. Finding out things such as how to process travel reimbursements and whom to ask for guidance helps to make employees feel welcome in the organization. As employees acquire information during the socialization process, their feelings of fit with the organization increase,[60] and employees who perceive that they fit are more likely to stay with an organization.[61] A key to effective socialization is the opportunity for new employees to develop social relationships by interacting with coworkers and leaders. Orientation meetings, mentoring programs, and social events are thus important tools for reducing employee turnover.[62] As explained in the "Technology in HR" feature, much of the benefit of these programs comes from interactions with others that build a sense of social support.

Building Perceptions of Organizational Support

Another factor that influences employee turnover is **perceived organizational support**—employees' beliefs about the extent to which an organization values their contribution and cares about their well-being. Employees who feel supported by the organization reciprocate with a feeling of obligation toward the organization.[63] Employees who perceive greater support are more committed to sticking with the organization and feel a stronger desire to help the organization succeed.[64] This sense of obligation reduces absenteeism and turnover.[65] For instance, Fraser's Hospitality, a hotel organization in Singapore, has achieved below-average turnover by creating a work culture that encourages a sense of personal worth and dignity. Treating service workers such as housekeepers and technicians with respect, as well as spending substantial amounts of money on training and development, has helped Fraser's generate higher profits by increasing occupancy at its hotels.[66]

Socialization
The process in which a new employee learns about an organization and develops social relationships with other organizational members.

Perceived organizational support
Employees' beliefs about how much their employer values their contributions and cares about their personal well-being.

Technology in HR

COMPUTERIZED ORIENTATION PROGRAMS

Orientation training is often used to help newcomers adjust to an organization. Because this training can be costly, many organizations have explored alternative methods for delivering orientation training. One alternative is self-paced computerized training. An interesting question is whether computerized orientation training is as effective as face-to-face meetings.

A study by Michael Wesson and Celile Gogus compared a traditional newcomer orientation program with a computer-based program. A technology-based consulting firm had been using an orientation program that involved flying all new employees to a central location and providing a week of orientation training. The training included videos, question-and-answer sessions, and team-building activities. In order to reduce costs and make it easier to deliver the training, the company developed a multimedia orientation program that was computer-based. The computer-based training took two to three days to complete and included the same information as the face-to-face training.

The computer-based orientation was similar to face-to-face orientation in terms of teaching the language (such as acronyms and abbreviations) and traditions of the organization and giving instruction on how to efficiently complete work tasks. However, the computer-based training was not as effective for conveying information about the organization's goals, politics, and people. The end result was that employees who received the computer-based orientation were found later to have lower job satisfaction and organizational commitment than employees who received face-to-face training.

snapphoto/iStockphoto

It seems that although computer-based orientation training can be helpful in some areas, interacting with a computer does not help new employees to develop important social relationships or understand other social aspects of the organization. Effective human resource management thus requires that orientation training include the human touch.

Source: Information from Michael J. Wesson and Celile Itir Gogus, "Shaking Hands with a Computer: An Examination of Two Methods of Organizational Newcomer Orientation," *Journal of Applied Psychology* 90 (2005): 1018–1026.

A number of organizational characteristics and practices increase perceptions of organizational support. Actions of organizational leaders are particularly important. Employees feel greater support from the organization and are less likely to quit when they feel that their supervisor cares about them and values their contributions.[67] Better compensation practices, better-designed jobs, fairness of procedures, and absence of politics are also critical for building perceptions of organizational support.[68] In the end, businesses that employees view as having fairer human resource practices have higher employee commitment and lower rates of employee turnover.[69] Organizations can therefore improve employee retention through effective human resource practices related to leadership, work design, compensation, and performance appraisal.

Selecting Employees Who Are Likely to Stay

One way to reduce employee turnover is to avoid hiring people who are likely to quit. An example of a company that does this effectively is FreshDirect, which is profiled in the accompanying "Building Strength Through HR" section. Recognizing and selecting employees who are likely to stay is critical for organizations. Realistic job previews, which we discussed in Chapter 5, offer one method of screening out people who are likely to quit. Realistic previews provide job applicants with both positive and negative information

Building Strength Through HR

FRESHDIRECT

FreshDirect, an online grocer in the New York City area, delivers food daily to homes and businesses. A source of competitive advantage is purchasing food directly from farms, dairies, and fisheries. Delivering rather than stocking food in a store also reduces costs and improves freshness because each type of food can be kept in its optimal climate.

Each day's orders are assembled between 11 P.M. and 11 A.M. A few years back, FreshDirect, which employs over 2,000 people, realized that it was experiencing turnover rates of over 200 percent. Since then, it has reduced turnover to 75 percent, with a goal of 50 percent. Specific methods that have helped reduce turnover include the following:

- Focusing recruitment efforts in neighborhoods that allow easy commutes.
- Providing support to new employees who are adjusting to working at night and in the cold.
- Offering better benefits, such as an upgraded break room, better meals, and improved medical coverage.
- Tying a portion of managers' pay to turnover rates in each department.

Sources: Chana Schoenberger, "Will Work with Food," Forbes.com, September 18, 2006; Laura Demars, "Finders Keepers," *CFO* 22, no. 3 (2006): 8–9.

about the position. A clearer understanding of the job and the organization can help employees better determine whether the position is right for them. Employees who have more realistic expectations about the job are less likely to quit.

Another method of reducing turnover is to directly assess individual differences. We have already seen that some people have characteristics that make them more likely to quit than others. People who spent less time in their last job are more likely to quit, for example. Specific scales that directly ask how long an applicant plans to stay with the organization or that assess certain specific characteristics have also been found to predict who quits.[70] A good example of using selection practices to reduce employee turnover is Via Christi Senior Services, which operates a number of health centers for older people in Kansas and Oklahoma. Via Christi uses an online screening tool that assesses individual characteristics, such as personality. Use of the screening tool helps Via Christi reduce employee turnover and save approximately $250,000 each year.[71]

How Do We Know?

ARE COWORKERS CONTAGIOUS?

Are employees affected by the attitudes and behaviors of their coworkers? In the specific case of employee turnover, the question is whether having other embedded coworkers makes it more likely that a given worker is also embedded and whether working with people who are looking for other jobs is contagious in that it influences an employee to also look for a new job. Will Felps, Terence Mitchell, David Hekman, Thomas Lee, Brooks Holtom, and Wendy Harman conducted two studies to answer these questions.

In the first study they obtained data from 8,663 employees working at 1,037 different golf clubs, country clubs, and resorts. They measured the job embeddedness of each employee and then assessed whether the embeddedness of others working at the club was correlated with an individual voluntarily quitting. They found that an individual employee was less likely to quit if his coworkers were embedded in their jobs. This effect was independent of the employee's own embeddedness, job satisfaction, and commitment to the organization.

In a second study, the authors obtained data from 486 employees working in 45 branches of a retail bank. In addition to measures of embedded-ness, they measured the job search behaviors of coworkers. Their results found that coworkers who were less embedded were more active in searching for other jobs. Having coworkers search for alternative jobs in turn resulted in a greater likelihood that an employee would quit. This suggests that the effect of coworker embeddedness on employee quitting operates through coworker job searching. Less-embedded coworkers spend more time searching for a different job, which in turn makes it more likely that an employee will quit.

Bottom Line. Coworkers' attitudes and behaviors are indeed contagious. Working with people who are not embedded in their jobs and therefore looking for alternative work increases the chance that an employee will quit. Professor Felps and his colleagues thus conclude that organizations should actively strive to increase the embeddedness of all employees.

Source: Will Felps, Terence R. Mitchell, David R. Hekman, Thomas W. Lee, Brooks C. Holtom, and Wendy S. Harman, "Turnover Contagion: How Coworkers' Job Embeddedness and Job Search Behaviors Influence Quitting," *Academy of Management Journal* 52 (2009): 545–561.

Embeddedness
The extent to which an employee is tied to an organization and to the surrounding community.

Promoting Employee Embeddedness

The paths to turnover shown in Figure 7.3 suggest that an employee's decision to quit is often set in motion by an initial shock. Organizations can thus reduce dysfunctional turnover by insulating employees against such shocks. One method of insulating against shocks is to encourage **embeddedness**, which represents the web of factors that ties the individual to the organization. Not surprisingly, organizations with Loyal Soldier and Committed Expert HR strategies tend to have employees who are more embedded.[72] People are more embedded when they have strong connections to others, when they have values and goals that fit with their environment, and when they feel that leaving would result in monetary or psychological losses.[73] People become embedded not only in organizations but also in the communities where they live. People, particularly women, are less likely to leave when they are embedded in either the specific organization or the surrounding community.[74]

Some organizations are better than others at promoting embeddedness. To promote embeddedness, organizations can provide enjoyable work, desirable work schedules, strong promotional opportunities, and good benefits, as well as encouraging employees to build positive social relationships with coworkers. Organizations use a number of specific approaches to do this. Encouraging employees to work in teams helps develop strong social relationships within the organization. Company-sponsored service projects and athletic teams build similar relationships in the community. To increase the sacrifice associated with leaving, compensation packages can reward employees for continuing with the organization for several years. Providing desirable perks such as tickets to athletic events and company vehicles can also reduce turnover by increasing embeddedness.[75] As explained on the previous page in the "How Do We Know?" feature, an individual is also less likely to quit when coworkers are embedded.

Helping employees balance their work and family responsibilities is a particularly strong method of increasing embeddedness. As discussed in Chapter 4, employees with family roles that conflict with work roles experience less job satisfaction.[76] In addition, job satisfaction and general life satisfaction are related, so conflict between work and family roles reduces happiness both on and off the job.[77] Indeed, mental health concerns are greater for people who experience conflict between work and family responsibilities.[78] Organizational policies and programs such as onsite daycare and flexible work scheduling thus increase embeddedness by reducing conflict between work and other aspects of life.

CONCEPT CHECK

1. *What are four common paths to voluntary employee turnover?*
2. *What perceptions and choices explain the process whereby low job satisfaction translates into a specific action of quitting?*
3. *What can an organization do to reduce voluntary employee turnover?*

How Do Layoffs Affect Individuals and Organizations?

Large-scale terminations of employment, which are not a response to individual employees performing poorly, are known as **layoffs**.

Unfortunately, layoffs happen fairly frequently. Almost everyone has a friend or family member who has lost a job in a layoff, and newspaper stories about companies laying off employees are common. This section discusses the effects of layoffs on both organizations and workers. It also describes steps that organizations can take to reduce the negative consequences of layoffs.

Layoffs
Large-scale terminations of employment that are unrelated to job performance.

THE EFFECT OF LAYOFFS ON ORGANIZATIONS

Many organizations lay off employees as part of an overall change effort. In some cases, the need for change comes from shifting demand for products and services. People no longer want to buy as much of what the organization produces. In other cases, competition from rival organizations forces the organization to develop more efficient processes. When an organization engages in widespread layoffs intended to permanently reduce the size of its workforce, it is said to be **downsizing**.

Downsizing has been promoted as a practice that can help an organization shift direction and reorient itself in relation to its customers. An important question, then, is whether downsizing and the associated employee layoffs are actually helpful for organizations. What happens to organizations that lay off workers? Do they really change for the better? Does downsizing help the organization become more efficient and more profitable?

Downsizing
Widespread layoffs with the objective of permanently reducing the number of employees.

The fact is, the effects of downsizing on organizations are not altogether clear. An organization's reputation is usually harmed by downsizing.[79] Yet, research suggests that the financial performance of organizations that have downsized is similar to the performance of organizations that have not downsized. This finding both supports and challenges the effectiveness of downsizing. Firms are usually not performing well when they pursue downsizing, so finding that their performance is similar to that of competitors after downsizing suggests that layoffs may initially improve profitability. Yet, firms that use downsizing do not have higher performance in subsequent years. This suggests that downsizing may not help an organization become more efficient and increase long-term productivity.[80]

Furthermore, the effect of downsizing is not the same for all organizations. Some organizations appear to benefit more than others. About half the firms that downsize report some benefit, whereas half report no improvement in profits or quality.[81] Downsizing is most harmful to organizations with long-term employment relationships: those pursuing Loyal Soldier and Committed Expert HR strategies.[82] Downsizing also seems to present the most problems when an organization reduces its workforce by more than 10 percent and makes numerous announcements of additional layoffs.[83] Moreover, reasons behind downsizing seem critical. Firms that downsize as part of a larger strategy to change before problems become serious are generally valued more by investors than firms that downsize after problems have already occurred.[84] In the end, then, downsizing alone is not as effective as downsizing combined with strategic efforts to change.[85] For example, downsizing that eliminates supervisory positions and reduces hierarchy seems to be particularly beneficial.[86]

THE EFFECTS OF LAYOFFS ON INDIVIDUALS

Being laid off from a job is a traumatic experience. Work provides not only an income but also a sense of security and identity, which are critical for psychological health. But the impact of downsizing goes beyond those who lose their jobs. Widespread layoffs can also have a negative effect on employees who remain with the organization.

Consequences for Layoff Victims

Layoff victims
Individuals whose employment is terminated in a layoff.

Layoff victims—the individuals who actually lose their jobs—experience a number of problems. Job loss begins a chain of negative feelings and events, including worry, uncertainty, and financial difficulties. Layoff victims are likely to suffer declines in mental health and psychological well-being, as well as physical health. They also experience less satisfaction with other aspects of life, such as marriage and family life.[87]

As we might expect, people who spend more effort on finding a new job are more likely to be reemployed quickly.[88] Unfortunately, those who work the hardest to find a new job often suffer the most negative consequences to their physical and mental well-being, as efforts to obtain a new job often result in rejection and frustration.

Figure 7.5 illustrates how individuals cope with job loss:

Work-role centrality
The degree to which a person's life revolves around his or her job.

- Individuals with high **work-role centrality**, which is the extent to which work is a central aspect of life, derive much of their life satisfaction from having a good job. These individuals suffer more from job loss than do individuals for whom work is less important.
- Individuals who have more resources cope better. Common resources include financial savings and support from close friends and family members.
- Mental perceptions are also critical. Individuals who have positive perceptions of their abilities to obtain a new job, and who perceive that the job loss did not result from something they did wrong, cope better than others.[89]
- Strategies for coping with job loss can also affect individual well-being. People who focus their efforts on solving problems and who deal constructively with their emotions have fewer health problems. People who feel that they can control the situation and obtain a new job are less harmed than those who perceive that they have little personal control.[90] Setting goals, proactively managing emotions, and being committed to getting back to work also facilitate reemployment.[91]

The quality of the job the victim finds to replace the one lost is another important factor in determining the long-term consequences of a layoff. Individuals who find new jobs that they enjoy, and that pay well, are less traumatized by the experience of job loss.[92] Perceptions of fairness surrounding the layoff process also have a critical impact on how victims experience a layoff.[93] Organizations should thus strive for fairness during the layoff process.

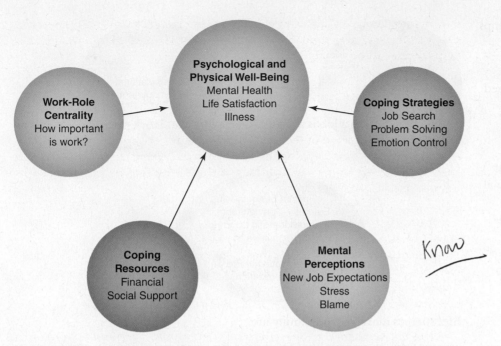

Figure 7.5 Coping with Job Loss and Unemployment. *Source:* Adapted from Frances M. McKee Ryan, Zhaoli Song, Connie Wanberg, and Angelo J. Kinicki, "Psychological and Physical Well-Being During Unemployment: A Meta-Analytic Study," *Journal of Applied Psychology* 90 (2005): 56. Adapted with permission.

Consequences for Layoff Survivors

Layoff survivors are employees who continue to work for the downsizing organization. It seems better to be a survivor than a victim. However, even those whose jobs are not eliminated often react negatively to downsizing.

In many ways, survivors' reactions are similar to victims' reactions. Like victims, survivors can have negative reactions, including anger at the loss experienced by coworkers and insecurity concerning the future of their own jobs. Survivors may also experience some positive emotions, however. They might feel relief that their own jobs were spared. These feelings result in a number of possible outcomes related to job satisfaction, commitment to the organization, and work performance.[94]

One possible reaction of employees who survive a layoff is increased motivation and performance. In some cases, individuals who remain employed feel an obligation to work harder to show that their contributions are indeed more valuable than the workers who were let go.[95] However, this effect does not occur for all survivors. Effort increases the most for survivors who perceive a moderate threat to their own jobs. If people feel that their jobs are completely insulated from future layoffs, or if they believe it is only a matter of time before their own jobs are eliminated, they are unlikely to increase their efforts. Employees who are the primary wage earners in their households are also more likely to increase their efforts after observing coworker layoffs.[96]

Even if they increase their performance, many survivors suffer in terms of psychological and emotional health. Anxiety, anger, and fear lead some individuals to withdraw from the organization. In addition, fewer workers mean

Layoff survivors
Individuals who continue to work for an organization when their coworkers are laid off.

Figure 7.6 Relationships Between Fairness, Reasons for Downsizing, and Organizational Commitment. *Source:* Based on information from Dirk van Dierendock and Gabriele Jacobs, "Survivors and Victims, a Meta-Analytical Review Of Fairness and Organizational Commitment after Downsizing," *British Journal of Management* 23 (2012): 96–109.

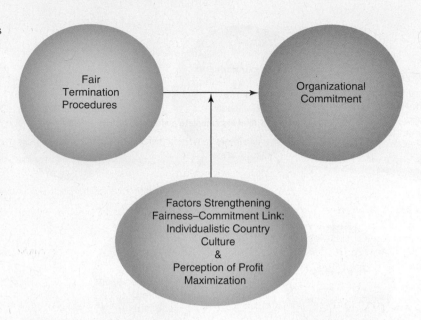

greater work responsibilities for those who remain, resulting in greater stress among workers.[97] Many who were not laid off begin to search voluntarily for new jobs.[98]

Similar to victims, an important factor in determining whether survivors will react positively or negatively is the fairness that they perceive in the layoff procedures. Survivor commitment is highest when employees who remain perceive that terminations were carried out with fair procedures. For example, survivors react more positively when they feel that victims received adequate compensation.[99] As shown in Figure 7.6, fair procedures are particularly important when organizations are located in countries with cultures of individual achievement and when the motive behind a layoff is seen as profit maximization. Effective human resource management practices that ensure fair treatment and provide surviving employees with opportunities for personal development are therefore critical for reducing the negative impact of downsizing.[100]

REDUCING THE NEGATIVE IMPACT OF LAYOFFS

The best method for reducing the negative impact of layoffs is to avoid them. The value of avoiding layoffs was illustrated in the U.S. airline industry following the terrorist attacks of September 11, 2001. The attacks reduced demand for air travel and forced airlines to explore methods of reducing costs and increasing efficiency. Some airlines included downsizing as part of these efforts. Other airlines with financial reserves and good strategic plans did not need to downsize. Those that did not downsize were more effective in the long run.[101] Having a clear plan and accurately forecasting labor needs can help reduce the need for layoffs.

Of course, maintaining employee count isn't always possible. Table 7.3 presents a summary of alternatives to layoffs. When layoffs are unavoidable, laying off low performers is generally more effective than laying off employees across the board. Not hiring new workers when current employees voluntarily quit or are terminated for cause can effectively reduce the employee count. Many organizations also encourage early retirement. The natural process of

Table 7.3	Alternatives to Layoffs
Alternative	**Description**
Reduce Working Hours	Cut the working time and associated pay for every employee rather than totally eliminating the jobs of some.
Reassign Workers	Have employees complete maintenance tasks or other work that is usually outsourced.
Lend Employees	Assign employees to work for neighbor organizations that need seasonal labor; directly bill the neighbor for labor costs.
Reduce Hiring	Stop hiring new employees and reassign existing workers into those positions.
Cut Costs	Ask employees to help identify alternative savings such as travel expense reduction.
Encourage Voluntary Separation	Provide incentives for early retirement or quitting to pursue alternative jobs.

Sources: Information from Matthew Boyle, "Cutting Work Hours Without Cutting Staff," *BusinessWeek* 4122 March 9, 2009, p. 55; Beth Mirza, "Looking for Alternatives to Layoffs," Society for Human Resource Management, available online at http://www.shrm.org/hrdisciplines/businessleadership/articles/pages/alternativestolayoffs.aspx.

not replacing people who leave is less painful than layoffs, but this strategy can take a long time if employees don't leave the organization very often.

Another solution is to reduce or eliminate overtime. Yet another is to ask employees to share jobs, so that each works fewer hours than a normal work-week. Although working fewer hours will reduce employees' pay, total job loss would reduce it much more. Employees might also be transferred to other parts of the organization that are experiencing growth. Such transfers often allow an organization to change while retaining high-quality workers. Finally, organizations can have their employees perform tasks that were previously contracted to outside firms.[102]

When layoffs are necessary, effective communication of downsizing decisions and plans is particularly critical. Table 7.4 provides specific guidelines for making announcements about layoffs.[103] Too often, organizations make

Table 7.4	Minimizing the Negative Effects of Layoffs
Action	**Description**
Identify the Business Need	Look first for other alternatives, examine likely long-term effects of laying off workers
Communicate with Employees	Explain the reasons for downsizing; be honest and open
Identify Future Work	Assess employee inputs that are most likely to be needed in the future; ensure that employees who are retained are likely to have future-oriented skills and abilities
Determine Evaluation Criteria	Determine the factors that will be used to decide layoffs; focus on objective measures of past performance and seniority
Establish Fair Evaluation Procedures	Ensure the appropriateness of measures used to determine who is laid off; use multiple trained evaluators, be sure information is accurate and documented, be fair and establish mechanisms for appeal
Analyze Adverse Impact	Analyze data to see how terminations are related to employee age; take corrective action if older workers are more frequently targeted for layoffs.
Evaluate Processes and Outcomes	Continually monitor what is happening to make corrections and improvements
Involve HR Staff	Include human resource staff in decisions and implementation; empower staff to give inputs from an employee advocate perspective

Source: Information from Michael A. Campion, Laura Guerrero, and Richard Posthuma, "Reasonable Human Resource Practices for Making Employee Downsizing Decisions," *Organizational Dynamics* 40 (2011): 174–180.

the mistake of not involving employees in the decision process. Being honest and giving employees access to information can help alleviate many of the negative consequences of downsizing.[104] Organizational leaders who carefully plan the announcement process are more likely to be perceived as fair and to retain the support of both layoff victims and survivors.

Understanding legal issues is also important for successful downsizing. Layoffs must be completed without discrimination. Analyses should be conducted to determine the impact of layoffs on women, members of minority groups, and older workers. As mentioned in Chapter 3, layoffs often have more impact on older workers. Replacing older workers with younger workers is illegal in many cases and may open the organization to allegations of discrimination. Once again, the fairness with which employees are treated is an important predictor of legal actions. Layoff victims perceive less discrimination when their supervisors communicate with them honestly.[105]

CONCEPT CHECK
1. *How does downsizing affect organizations in the short term? in the long term?*
2. *What are the common reactions of downsizing victims?*
3. *How do employees who remain with an organization react when they see their coworkers being laid off?*

LEARNING OBJECTIVE 4

What Are Common Steps in Disciplining Employees?

Discipline
Organizational efforts to correct improper behavior of employees.

Unfortunately, sometimes employees fail to carry out their duties in an acceptable manner. We have already seen that retaining employees who do not perform at an adequate level is harmful to an organization, particularly when the organization is pursuing a differentiation strategy. Of course, it is usually wrong to terminate problem employees without giving them a chance to improve. The process whereby management takes steps to help an employee overcome problem behavior is known as **discipline**. In essence, discipline is instruction with the purpose of correcting misbehavior.

The world of sports provides some high-profile examples of discipline. Almost every college football team has suspended players for violating team rules. Professional athletes are frequently suspended from practice and games for violating substance-abuse policies. Each instance of drug use results in a greater penalty, and players who continue to violate the rules may be expelled from the team and the league. Athletes, whether at the college or professional level, are representatives of their organizations who are expected to follow a certain code of conduct. Discipline is the corrective action that occurs when the code is not followed. The ultimate goal of discipline is to change behavior and help the individual become a contributing member of the team.

Most organizations and workplace leaders face similar discipline problems with employees, although these problems are less public. Employees who are not meeting organizational expectations are disciplined as part of a process aimed at changing undesirable behavior. Organizations whose employees belong to labor unions generally work with union officials to administer discipline. We will discuss this process in Chapter 13. Most other organizations adopt formal discipline procedures based on the notion of providing due process.

PRINCIPLES OF DUE PROCESS

Due process represents a set of procedures carried out in accordance with established rules and principles. The underlying intent of due process is to make sure employees are treated fairly. A number of court cases and decisions by labor arbitrators have established a set of principles, summarized here, that organizations should follow to provide due process for employees.[106]

1. Employees have a right to know what is expected of them and what will happen if they fail to meet expectations. A production employee should not be punished for failing to clean a machine if she is not aware that the machine needs cleaning. Effective discipline requires that organizations communicate clear expectations for acceptable behavior.
2. Discipline must be based on facts. Reducing a steel worker's pay for being consistently late to work is improper unless evidence shows that he has actually been late a specific number of times. Disciplinary actions should be carried out only after a careful investigation of the facts and circumstances. Fair investigations involve obtaining testimonial evidence from witnesses and those involved. Documents and physical evidence can also provide key details to either support or refute allegations against employees.[107]
3. Employees should also have a right to present their side of the story. A sales representative accused of falsifying expense reports must be given a chance to explain his financial records. Employees should also have the right to appeal decisions. Providing the opportunity for another person to evaluate the facts of the case and the decision of the supervisor is important for ensuring fair and consistent treatment.
4. Any punishment should be consistent with the nature of the offense. Perhaps an employee who becomes angry with a single customer should not be fired. The procedures used to investigate the alleged offense and the nature of the punishment should also be consistent with common practices in the organization. Disciplining an individual for doing something that is routinely done by others who go unpunished can be evidence of discrimination against the person receiving the discipline.

Due process
A set of procedures carried out in accordance with established rules and principles and aimed at ensuring fairness.

THE PROCESS OF PROGRESSIVE DISCIPLINE

Some forms of misconduct are so serious that they result in immediate termination of an employee. For instance, it might be appropriate to fire an employee who physically attacks a client. Stealing from the company might also be grounds for immediate dismissal. In such cases, due process generally allows termination of employment once the facts have been discovered. However, most offenses are not serious enough to warrant immediate dismissal, and in these cases, due process requires the organization to allow employees to correct their misbehavior. In the interest of giving employees an opportunity for improvement, as well as clearly conveying expectations for behavior, most organizations have adopted a process of **progressive discipline**.

Progressive discipline
Discipline involving successively more severe consequences for employees who continue to engage in undesirable behavior.

In the progressive discipline process, management provides successively more severe punishment for each occurrence of negative behavior. A supervisor meets and discusses company policy with an employee the first time an unacceptable behavior occurs. No further action is taken if the misbehavior is not repeated. The employee is punished if the misbehavior is repeated. Subsequent instances of the misbehavior are met with harsher punishment that eventually results in termination of employment.

Although the number of steps and actions differ by organization, most progressive discipline systems include at least four steps.[108] Figure 7.7 presents the four basic steps.

The first step is a *verbal warning*. The supervisor clearly communicates what the employee did wrong and informs the employee of what will happen if the behavior occurs again. If the behavior is repeated, the employee receives a *written warning*. This warning is usually placed in the employee's personnel file for a period of time. A repeat of the behavior after the written warning leads to *suspension*. The employee cannot come to work for a period of time and in most cases will not be paid. A suspension is usually accompanied by a final written warning that clearly states the employee will be dismissed if the behavior occurs again. The final step is *discharge* from the organization.

The concept of progressive discipline thus emphasizes the need for organizations to allow employees an opportunity to correct inappropriate behavior. This is a time when human resource professionals can help mediate potential conflicts if the employee does not respond to the manager's requests for changes in behavior.

Essay Q

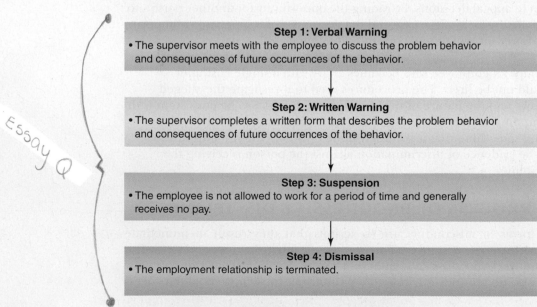

Step 1: Verbal Warning
• The supervisor meets with the employee to discuss the problem behavior and consequences of future occurrences of the behavior.

Step 2: Written Warning
• The supervisor completes a written form that describes the problem behavior and consequences of future occurrences of the behavior.

Step 3: Suspension
• The employee is not allowed to work for a period of time and generally receives no pay.

Step 4: Dismissal
• The employment relationship is terminated.

Figure 7.7 Steps for Progressive Discipline.

How Do We Know?

Do Managers Think Discipline Is Fair?

Are discipline procedures fair? The answer might depend on whom you ask. Perhaps managers perceive discipline as fair, even when employees receiving the discipline think it is unfair. But are there times when managers also believe that discipline is unfair? Kenneth Butterfield, Linda Trevino, Kim Wade, and Gail Ball sought to find out. They asked 62 experienced human resource managers to report on instances of discipline and then rate the instances in terms of fairness.

The results suggested that managers perceive discipline as fair when they believe that the employee knew the offending behavior was wrong and expected to be punished for it. Ratings of fairness were also higher when the managers felt that the

consequence was appropriate given the seriousness of the misbehavior and when there was a clear link between the misbehavior and the consequence.

The Bottom Line. Discipline is perceived as fair when it follows the principles of due process. The authors conclude that perceptions of fairness are important to managers and that managers feel better about carrying out discipline when employees accept some blame for the misconduct.

Source: Information from Kenneth D. Butterfield, Linda Klebe Trevino, Kim J. Wade, and Gail A. Ball, "Organizational Punishment from the Manager's Perspective: An Exploratory Study," *Journal of Managerial Issues* 17 (2005): 363–382.

A common problem associated with progressive discipline is that supervisors are sometimes unwilling to take the first step in the process. Most supervisors, like the rest of us, seek to avoid conflict. As a result, they often ignore instances of misbehavior. (If you don't believe this, just think of group projects you complete as part of your university classes. A low-performing group member is seldom confronted by teammates.) Managers are also reluctant to discipline employees when they perceive unfairness in the disciplinary process, as explained in the "How Do We Know?" feature. Developing fair procedures is thus critical. Managers are also more likely to discipline employees when they know they will be supported by leaders above them in the organization, when they have been trained to deliver discipline properly, and when there is a pattern of constructive discipline within the organization.[109]

CONCEPT CHECK
1. *What are the four principles of due process?*
2. *What are the steps for progressive discipline?*

LEARNING OBJECTIVE 5

How Should Employee Dismissals Be Carried Out?

Having to dismiss employees is one of the most difficult tasks that a manager faces. Just think how much people's lives change when their employment is terminated. Suddenly, they don't have scheduled activities that fill their time; they no longer interact frequently with some of their closest social contacts; and of course, their source of financial security is gone. When employees are terminated, organizations often use outplacement services to help them both cope with emotional struggles and obtain new employment. Nevertheless, the actual dismissal of an employee is usually done by the employee's manager with help from the human resources department.

OUTPLACEMENT SERVICES

Outplacement services
Professional assistance provided to help employees who have been dismissed to cope with job loss and find new positions.

Outplacement services provide employees who have been dismissed from an organization with assistance in finding new jobs. In many cases, outplacement services are provided by outside firms. An outside firm is often in a better position to work with dismissed employees, since these employees may feel some resentment toward the organization that dismissed them. Indeed, displaced workers who receive outplacement assistance from an outside source generally experience more positive reactions and are more likely to find a position that is comparable to the job that was lost.[110]

Outplacement services normally include testing and assessments to help displaced workers understand the type of work for which they are most qualified. Employment counselors provide guidance to improve job search skills in areas such as résumé preparation and interviewing. Many outplacement firms offer financial planning advice. Psychological counseling to deal with grief, anger, and anxiety is also frequently provided not only to displaced workers but also to their spouses. Finally, some outplacement firms provide actual job leads.

THE DISMISSAL MEETING

Outplacement services can help alleviate some of the anxiety associated with job loss. Nevertheless, the actual event in which a person is told that his or her employment is being terminated is highly stressful. Managing this event in the right way is critical if the organization is to show respect for employees and maintain a good reputation.

An example from Radio Shack a few years back illustrates how *not* to fire employees. One day, 400 employees opened their email accounts to learn that they had been dismissed from the company. The messages reportedly read, "The workforce reduction notification is currently in progress. Unfortunately, your position is one that has been eliminated." Sending such traumatic news via email is insensitive to the needs of employees and has been widely criticized.[111]

Because of the emotional nature of dismissal, face-to-face meetings are usually best. Most experts also agree that employees should not be dismissed on a Friday. A late-week dismissal leaves the terminated employee with two days of time before actions can be taken to recover from the bad news. Dismissals early in the week allow the individual an opportunity to get right to work at finding a new job and reduce the amount of time thinking about how bad things might get.

A few key principles should guide communication during the dismissal meeting.[112] In most cases, it is best to have a third person present to serve as a witness. It is important to tell the employee directly that he or she is being dismissed. Although many managers find it difficult to convey the news, an effective dismissal requires a clear statement that the person's employment is being terminated. In addition, the meeting should be brief. If principles of due process have been followed, the employee should already know why he is being fired. The dismissal meeting is not a time for a lengthy discussion of how things might have been different.

Once the bad news has been delivered, the manager should listen to the employee who is being dismissed. There is no need for the manager to argue or to defend the action. This is an emotional moment, and some individuals will simply need to vent their frustration. Finally, it is usually best to present a written summary of the meeting to the employee being dismissed. The summary should include information like when the last day of employment will be, how to return company equipment such as keys and computers, and what will happen to health insurance and other benefits.

The dismissal meeting should include a discussion of severance compensation if it is being offered. **Severance compensation** provides money to help cover living expenses during the upcoming period of unemployment. In many cases, severance compensation is given only if the dismissed worker agrees in a contract not to pursue legal action against the company for discrimination or other reasons.

The safety of the supervisor and other workers has become an increasingly important consideration. When possible, security personnel should be alerted before a dismissal takes place. They can plan to provide assistance if the person becomes violent or makes threatening statements. Security personnel should be close at hand if past behavior suggests that the person being terminated will react in a violent manner. The dismissed employee may also need to be escorted from the work site if the organization works with highly sensitive information or if the employee is being terminated for offenses such as theft or violence with coworkers.

Severance compensation
Money provided to an employee as part of a dismissal package.

CONCEPT CHECK

1. *How can an outplacement firm help an organization manage employee dismissals?*
2. *What should a manager do and say when she tells an employee he is being fired?*

A MANAGER'S PERSPECTIVE REVISITED

IN THE MANAGER'S PERSPECTIVE THAT OPENED THE CHAPTER, ANGELA FELT CONCERN ABOUT AN EMPLOYEE WHO HAD JUST QUIT. SHE WAS ALSO THINKING ABOUT CONFRONTING AN EMPLOYEE WHOSE PERFORMANCE WAS UNACCEPTABLE. FOLLOWING ARE THE ANSWERS TO THE "WHAT DO YOU THINK?" QUIZ THAT FOLLOWED THE MANAGER'S PERSPECTIVE. WERE YOU ABLE TO CORRECTLY IDENTIFY THE TRUE STATEMENTS? CAN YOU DO BETTER NOW?

©Jamie Grill/Corbis

1. Workers are less likely to quit when they feel the organization cares about their personal needs. **TRUE.** *Individuals who feel they receive support from the organization are more likely to remain with the organization, even if they have experiences that cause them to think about leaving.*

2. Decisions to quit often begin with a specific event that causes employees to evaluate their work situation. **TRUE.** *In most cases, a specific event can be identified as the point where the employee begins to think about leaving the organization.*

3. It doesn't really matter how you fire people, as long as you make it clear that their employment is being terminated. **FALSE.** *It is important for the person doing the firing to make it clear that the person is being dismissed, but a number of other issues should be addressed to minimize the trauma of firing someone.*

4. In order to defend against potential lawsuits, an organization should carefully document methods of disciplining problem employees. **TRUE.** *Principles of due process and progressive discipline suggest that employees should receive clear written warnings as part of the disciplinary process.*

5. Employees who see coworkers losing their jobs become more committed to staying with the organization. **FALSE.** *In many cases, layoff survivors begin to look for jobs at other organizations.*

Angela's frustration with employees who quit and employees who perform poorly is not uncommon. High employee turnover is costly. Angela is therefore wise to consider ways to increase the chances of good employees staying with the restaurant. She is also being an effective leader when she takes actions to help low performers such as Simon improve. The principles of due process and the steps of progressive discipline can guide Angela's efforts. These and other concepts in this chapter provide information about effective methods of retaining employees, as well as effective ways to discipline and dismiss employees whose performance is inadequate.

SUMMARY

LEARNING OBJECTIVE 1

How are employee retention and separation strategic?

Employee retention is critical for organizations pursuing internal labor strategies. Competitive advantage for an organization with a Committed Expert HR strategy comes from retaining employees who develop specialized skills that allow them to be more productive than employees working for competitors. Organizations with a Loyal Soldier HR strategy save money by offering job security in place of high wages.

Effective employee separation is important for organizations with differentiation strategies. A Committed Expert HR strategy involves quickly identifying low performers and encouraging them to leave rather than pursue a career with the organization. For organizations with a Free Agent HR strategy, frequent turnover of employees is expected and is often helpful for ensuring that employee skills are up-to-date.

LEARNING OBJECTIVE 2

How can undesirable turnover of employees be reduced?

Employee turnover usually begins with a specific event that causes the individual to think about leaving the organization. Sometimes, however, employees develop a general sense of dissatisfaction that eventually causes them to leave. Low job satisfaction is strongly related to employee turnover. Employees who are not satisfied with their jobs begin to withdraw from the organization and may eventually quit. Organizations can reduce turnover by conducting satisfaction surveys to identify employee concerns and needs. Socialization processes help new employees become more comfortable with the organization, and building perceptions of organizational support among employees increases their sense of commitment to the organization. Selection practices that identify individuals who are less likely to leave can reduce turnover, as can encouraging employees to build social relationships within the organization and the community.

LEARNING OBJECTIVE 3

How do layoffs affect individuals and organizations?

The organizational benefits of downsizing are unclear. Downsizing is most common in organizations struggling with profitability. There is, however, little evidence of long-term improvement in organizational performance after downsizing. Individuals who lose their jobs experience a number of negative effects, including decreased psychological and physical health. Some layoff survivors may increase their individual performance, but most suffer negative psychological consequences. Organizations can reduce the negative consequences of downsizing by being fair and communicating honestly with both victims and survivors.

LEARNING OBJECTIVE 4

What are the common steps in disciplining employees?

Employee discipline is most effective when it follows principles of due process. Due process requires that employees be clearly informed about what is expected of them. Any punishment for misbehavior should follow careful examination of facts, and the offending employee should have an opportunity to defend himself. Punishment should also be consistent with the nature of the misbehavior. Progressive discipline procedures help ensure due process. Progressive discipline moves from verbal warning to written warning, to suspension, and finally to discharge.

LEARNING OBJECTIVE 5

How should employee dismissals be carried out?

Having to fire someone is a difficult part of the management job. Outplacement services alleviate some of the negative effects of dismissal by helping displaced employees improve their job skills, providing emotional support, and sometimes supplying information about alternative jobs. An employee dismissal meeting can be stressful, but following proper procedures helps preserve both the dignity of individuals and the reputation of the organization. Dismissal should take place in a brief face-to-face meeting. Important facts and information about the dismissal should be written down and presented to the person being dismissed. Planning should also address the safety of other employees and the manager conducting the dismissal meeting.

KEY TERMS

Discipline 274
Downsizing 269
Due process 275
Dysfunctional turnover 257
Embeddedness 268
Employee retention 252

Employee separation 252
Exit interview 263
Involuntary turnover 257
Job satisfaction 260
Layoffs 269
Layoff survivors 271

DISCUSSION QUESTIONS

1. How can SAS compete with other software firms when its employees appear to work less than the employees at competing firms?
2. Do you think a fast-food restaurant such as Arby's would benefit from reducing turnover of cooks and cashiers? What could the company reasonably do to encourage employees to stay? What problems might occur if employees stayed for longer periods of time?
3. Do you think the university you attend makes a concerted effort to dismiss low-performing workers? How does the university's approach to dismissing low performers affect overall services for students?
4. What are some specific events that might cause you to leave an organization without having found a different job?
5. Which dimensions of job satisfaction are most important to you? Would you accept less pay to work in a job with better coworkers? How important is doing work that you find enjoyable?

6. What things keep you embedded in your current situation? Are there personal and family factors that encourage you to keep your life as it is? Can you identify social relationships that might influence you to avoid moving to another university or a different job?
7. Why do you think organizations that lay off workers frequently fail to improve their long-term performance?
8. Some people who have been layoff victims look back on the experience as one of the best things in their lives. Why might a victim say such a thing several years after the layoff?
9. Can you identify a time when a low-performing individual has not been disciplined by a leader? How did the lack of discipline affect the poor performer? How did it affect other workers or team members?
10. As a manager, what would you say to a person whom you were firing?

EXAMPLE CASE *Apparel Inc.*

To better understand the challenges that managers on the front lines of downsizing efforts face in delivering messages with dignity and respect, we conducted a study of a Fortune 500 company that we call Apparel Inc. (we disguised the corporation's real name to preserve confidentiality). Both line managers and HR managers at Apparel Inc. reported difficulty handling lay-off conversations. For line managers, the experience was challenging for two reasons: their limited experience with dire personnel situations and their existing relationships with the affected employees. Many managers had genuine friendships with their direct reports and knew or had met their employees' families. Although HR managers tended to have more experience with terminations than line managers, they nonetheless found downsizing conversations to be difficult and emotionally unwieldy. An HR manager with years of experience handling layoff conversations made this point: "It's a pretty horrific event, frankly. It's not easy and it's never easy to get used to." HR managers and line managers alike reported experiencing a range of negative emotions, often at a high level of intensity. Emotions ranged from anxiety and fear to sympathy and guilt—sometimes, even shame. One manager described the physical effects of anxiety both before and during the event:

> Internally there is a nervous stomach, you feel on edge. Sometimes you get physically nauseous or headache. Very often the night before or after you have very bad dreams that are not necessarily related to the downsizing itself, but from the stress. There is a degree of nervousness that almost makes you have to step back and say, "I have to be calm, I can't show that I am nervous about delivering this message."

Alongside anxiety, managers conducting layoffs experience sympathy and sadness. One manager explained: "It is very difficult from an emotional standpoint knowing you are dealing with somebody's livelihood, dealing with somebody's ego, dealing with somebody's ability to provide for their family." Another manager concurred, emphasizing how distressing it can be to deliver the negative news:

> If I am about to cry because this is upsetting me as much as it is upsetting the other individual, I am definitely going to try not to cry. But the emotion that I feel is genuine in terms of the unhappiness or the sorrow that I am feeling that I have to deliver this message to someone.

QUESTIONS

1. What are some ways that managers might cope with negative emotions when they are forced to lay off employees?
2. Why might someone argue that it is a good thing for managers to feel such negative emotions?
3. How do you think you would personally react to the task of laying off workers?

Source: Andrew Molinsky and Joshua Margolis, "The Emotional Tightrope of Downsizing: Hidden Challenges for Leaders and Their Organizations," *Organizational Dynamics* 35 (2006): 145–159. Copyright Elsevier 2006.

 **DISCUSSION CASE**   *County General Hospital*

County General Hospital is a 200-bed facility located approximately 150 miles outside Chicago. It is a regional hospital that draws patients from surrounding farm communities. Like most hospitals, County General faces the difficult task of providing high-quality care at a reasonable cost.

One of the most difficult obstacles encountered by the hospital is finding and retaining qualified nurses. The annual turnover rate among nurses is nearly 100 percent. A few of the nurses are long-term employees who are either committed to County General or attached to the community. Employment patterns suggest that many of the nurses who are hired stay for only about six months. In fact, County General often appears to be a quick stop between graduation from college and a better job.

Many who leave acknowledge that they were contacted by another hospital that offered them more money. Exit interviews with nurses who are leaving similarly suggest that low pay is a concern. Another concern is the lack of social atmosphere for young nurses. Nurses just finishing college, who are usually not married, complain that the community does not provide them enough opportunity to meet and socialize with others their age.

Hospital administrators are afraid that paying higher wages will cause financial disaster. Big insurance companies and Medicaid make it difficult for them to increase the amount they charge patients. However, the lack of stability in the nursing staff has caused some noticeable problems. Nurses sometimes appear to be ignorant of important hospital procedures. Doctors also complain that they spend a great deal of time training nurses to perform procedures, only to see those nurses take their new skills someplace else.

QUESTIONS

1. Turnover is high at almost every facility where nurses are employed. What aspects of nursing make turnover for nurses higher than for many other jobs?
2. What programs do you suggest County General might implement to decrease nurse turnover? Be specific.
3. How might County General work with other hospitals to reduce nurse turnover?

EXPERIENTIAL EXERCISE

Learning about Discipline Procedures

Examine the website for your university to locate information that guides the disciplinary actions of supervisors. If you can't locate this information for your university, visit a few websites for other universities. Examine the supervisor guidelines and answer the following questions:

1. What does the university do to ensure due process?
2. How many steps are in the university plan for progressive discipline? Are the steps similar to the four steps outlined in this chapter?
3. What involvement does the human resource department have in cases of employee discipline?
4. Does the site offer guidance for how to deal with specific instances of employee misbehavior?
5. What steps can an employee take to appeal a disciplinary action?
6. Are any unions involved in disciplinary procedures?
7. Based on your experiences with the university, do you think supervisors actually follow the steps of progressive discipline?

INTERACTIVE EXPERIENTIAL EXERCISE

Turnover: Dealing with the Good, the Bad, and the Ugly at Global Telecommunications
http://www.wiley.com/college/sc/stewart

Access the companion website to test your knowledge by completing a Global Telecommunications interactive role-playing exercise.
In this exercise you work with another client, Global Telecommunications. Global has adopted a Committed Expert HR strategy. Unfortunately, it has some potential turnover problems. In a few minutes, you will meet with a key member of senior management who has posted her résumé online and is actively looking for a new job. How will you handle this discussion? Another problem concerns an employee who, in management's view, is a detriment to his department and truly needs to be fired. He can be very emotional and is viewed as having a bad temper. Before this person can be fired, you will need to make sure all appropriate steps have been taken. This will be a challenging assignment. As you begin reviewing his file, the senior management member arrives for her meeting with you. Good luck—she doesn't look happy to be here. •

ENDNOTES

1. Charles Fishman, "Sanity Inc.," *Fast Company* 21 (December 1998): 84.
2. John P. Hausknecht, Charlie O. Trevor, and Michael J. Howard, "Unit-Level Turnover Rates and Customer Service Quality: Implications of Group Cohesiveness, Newcomer Concentration, and Size," *Journal of Applied Psychology* 94 (2009): 1068–1075.
3. K. Michele Kacmar, Martha C. Andrews, David L. Van Rooy, R. Chris Steilberg, and Stephen Cerrone, "Sure Everyone Can be Replaced … But at What Cost? Turnover as a Predictor of Unit-Level Performance," *Academy of Management Journal* 49 (2006): 133–144.
4. Tae-Youn Park and Jason D. Shaw, "Turnover Rates and Organizational Performance: A Meta-Analysis," *Journal of Applied Psychology* 98 (2013): 268–309; Rosemary Batt and Alexander J. S. Colvin, "An Employment Systems Approach to Turnover: Human Resource Practices, Quits, Dismissals, and Performance," *Academy of Management Journal* 54 (2011): 695–711.
5. Somaya Deepak, Ian O. Williamson, and Natalia Lorinkova, "Gone But Not Lost: The Different Performance Impacts of Employee Mobility Between Cooperators Versus Competitors," *Academy of Management Journal* 51 (2008): 936–953.
6. David A. Kaplan, "SAS: A New No. 1 Best Employer," *Fortune,* January 2010.
7. www.sas.com/corporate/
8. Richard Florida and Jim Goodnight, "Managing for Creativity," *Harvard Business Review* 83, no. 7/8 (2005): 125–131.
9. Jennifer Schu, "Even in Hard Times, SAS Keeps Its Culture Intact," *Workforce* 80, no. 10 (2001): 21.
10. Gerald D. Klein, "Creating Cultures that Lead to Success: Lincoln Electric, Southwest Airlines, and SAS Institute," Organizational Dynamics 41 (2012): 32–43; Simon London, "Profit Machines that Put People First," *Financial Times*, September 26, 2003, p. 16.
11. Janet Wiscombe, "CEO Takes HR to Prime Time," *Workforce* 81, no. 13 (2002): 10.
12. Anonymous, "Case Study: SAS Institute. In a Sector Where the Competition for Talent Is Fierce, One Company Believes that Creating a Good Working Environment Is the Key to Success," *Financial Times*, April 29, 2004, p. 5.
13. Wiscombe, "CEO Takes HR to Prime Time."
14. Charles Fishman, "Moving Toward a Balanced Work Life," *Workforce* 79, no. 3 (2000): 38–42.
15. Michelle Conson and Kathy Moore, "Dr. Goodnight's Company Town," *BusinessWeek* 3686 (2000): 192.
16. Fishman, "Moving Toward a Balanced Work Life."
17. Fishman, "Sanity Inc."
18. John S. McClenahen, "Educating for the Future," *Industry Week* 253, no. 12 (2004): 46.
19. Fishman, "Moving Toward a Balanced Work Life."
20. Kenneth Hein, "Success Secrets," *Incentive* 173, no. 8 (1999): 48–49.
21. Joanne Cole, "Case Study: SAS Institute Inc. Uses Sanity as Strategy," *HR Focus* 76, no. 5 (1999): 6.
22. W. Stanley Seibert and Nikolay Zubanov, "Searching for the Optimal Level of Employee Turnover: A Study of a Large U.K. Retail Organization," *Academy of Management Journal* 52 (2009): 294–313.
23. Jeffrey A. Sonnenfeld and Maury A. Peiperl, "Staffing Policy as a Strategic Response: A Typology of Career Systems," *Academy of Management Review* 13 (1988): 588–600.

24. Michael C. Sturman, Lian Shao, and Jan H. Katz, "The Effect of Culture on the Curvilinear Relationship Between Performance and Turnover," *Journal of Applied Psychology* 97 (2012): 46–62; Charlie O. Trevor, Barry Gerhart, and John W. Boudreau, "Voluntary Turnover and Job Performance: Curvilinearity and the Moderating Influences of Salary Growth and Promotions," *Journal of Applied Psychology* 82 (1997): 44–61.

25. Taken from Peter W. Hom and Rodger W. Griffeth, *Employee Turnover* (Cincinnati, OH: South-Western College Publishing, 1995), 7.

26. Thomas W. Lee and Terence R. Mitchell, "An Alternative Approach: The Unfolding Model of Voluntary Employee Turnover," *Academy of Management Review* 19 (1994): 51–89.

27. Thomas W. Lee, Terence R. Mitchell, Lowell Wise, and Steven Fireman, "An Unfolding Model of Voluntary Employee Turnover," *Academy of Management Journal* 39 (1996): 5–36; Thomas W. Lee, Terence R. Mitchell, Brooks C. Holtom, Linda S. McDaniel, and John W. Hill, "The Unfolding Model of Voluntary Turnover: A Replication and Extension," *Academy of Management Journal* 42 (1999): 450–462.

28. Tae Heon Lee, Barry Gerhart, Ingo Weller, and Charlie O. Trevor, "Understanding Voluntary Turnover: Path Specific Job Satisfaction Effects and the Importance of Unsolicited Job Offers," *Academy of Management Journal* 51 (2008): 651–671.

29. Peter W. Hom and Rodger W. Griffeth, "Structural Equations Modeling Test of a Turnover Theory," *Journal of Applied Psychology* 76 (1991): 350–366; Robert P. Tett and John P. Meyer, "Job Satisfaction, Organizational Commitment, Turnover Intention, and Turnover: Path Analyses Based on Meta-Analytic Findings," *Personnel Psychology* 46 (1993): 259–283.

30. Nathan P. Podsakoff, Jeffrey A. LePine, and Marcie A. LePine, "Differential Challenge Stressor–Hindrance Stressor Relationships with Job Attitudes, Turnover Intentions, Turnover, and Withdrawal Behavior: A Meta-Analysis," *Journal of Applied Psychology* 92 (2007): 438–454.

31. Peter W. Hom, Fanny Caranikas-Walker, Gregory E. Prussia, and Rodger W. Griffeth, "A Meta-Analytical Structural Equations Analysis of a Model of Employee Turnover," *Journal of Applied Psychology* 77 (1992): 890–909.

32. Edwin A. Locke, "What Is Job Satisfaction?" *Organizational Behavior and Human Performance* 4 (1969): 309–336.

33. Timothy A. Judge, Joyce E. Bono, Amir Erez, and Edwin A. Locke, "Core Self-Evaluations and Job and Life Satisfaction: The Role of Self-Concordance and Goal Attainment," *Journal of Applied Psychology* 90 (2005): 257–268.

34. Mary Ann M. Fricko and Terry A. Beehr, "A Longitudinal Investigation of Interest Congruence and Gender Concentration as Predictors of Job Satisfaction," *Personnel Psychology* 45 (1992): 99–117.

35. Benjamin Schneider, Paul J. Hanges, D. Brent Smith, and Amy Nicole Salvaggio, "Which Comes First: Employee Attitudes or Organizational Financial and Market Performance?" *Journal of Applied Psychology* 88 (2003): 836–851.

36. Robert W. Rice, Douglas A. Gentile, and Dean B. McFarlin, "Facet Importance and Job Satisfaction," *Journal of Applied Psychology* 76 (1991): 31–39.

37. James K. Harter, Frank L. Schmidt, and Theodore L. Hayes, "Business-Unit-Level Relationships Between Employee Satisfaction, Employee Engagement, and Business Outcomes: A Meta-Analysis," *Journal of Applied Psychology* 87 (2002): 268–279; Cheri Ostroff, "The Relationship between Satisfaction, Attitudes, and Performance: An Organizational Level Analysis," *Journal of Applied Psychology* 77 (1992): 963–974.

38. Meni Koslowsky, Abraham Sagie, Moshe Krausz, and Ahuva Dolman Singer, "Correlates of Employee Lateness: Some Theoretical Considerations," *Journal of Applied Psychology* 82 (1997): 79–88.

39. Michael C. Sturman, "The Implications of Linking the Dynamic Performance and Turnover Literatures," *Journal of Applied Psychology* 86 (2001): 684–696.

40. Xio-Ping Chen, Chun Hui, and Douglas J. Sego, "The Role of Organizational Citizenship Behavior in Turnover: Conceptualization and Preliminary Tests of Key Hypotheses," *Journal of Applied Psychology* 83 (1998): 922–931.

41. Timothy M. Gardner, Patrick M. Wright, and Lisa M. Moynihan, "The Impact of Motivation, Empowerment, and Skill Enhancing Practices on Aggregate Voluntary Turnover: The Mediating Effect of Collective Affective Commitment," *Personnel Psychology* 64 (2011): 315–350; Liu Dong, Shu Zhang, Lei Wang, and Thomas W. Lee, "The Effects of Autonomy and Empowerment on Employee Turnover: Test of a Multilevel Model in Teams," *Journal of Applied Psychology* 96 (2011): 1305–1316; Kathleen Bentein, Robert Vandenberg, Christian Vandenberghe, and Florence Stinglhamber, "The Role of Change in the Relationship Between Commitment and Turnover: A Latent Growth Modeling Approach," *Journal of Applied Psychology* 90 (2005): 468–482.

42. John D. Kammeyer-Mueller, Connie R. Wanberg, Theresa M. Glomb, and Dennis Ahlburg, "The Role of Temporal Shifts in Turnover Processes: It's about Time," *Journal of Applied Psychology* 90 (2005): 644–658.

43. Robert P. Steel and Joan R. Rentsch, "The Dispositional Model of Job Attitudes Revisited: Findings of a 10-year Study," *Journal of Applied Psychology* 82 (1997): 873–879; Richard D. Arvey, Thomas J. Bouchard, Nancy L. Segal, and Lauren M. Abraham, "Job Satisfaction: Environmental and Genetic Components," *Journal of Applied Psychology* 74 (1989): 187–192.

44. Remus Ilies and Timothy A. Judge, "On the Heritability of Job Satisfaction: The Mediating Role of Personality," *Journal of Applied Psychology* 88 (2003): 750–759.

45. Timothy A. Judge and Edwin A. Locke, "Effect of Dysfunctional Thought Processes on Subjective Well-Being and Job Satisfaction," *Journal of Applied Psychology* 78 (1993): 475–490.

46. Ryan D. Zimmerman, "Understanding the Impact of Personality Traits on Individuals' Turnover Decisions: A Meta-Analytic Path Model," *Personnel Psychology* 61 (2008): 309–348.

47. David G. Allen, Kelly P. Weeks, and Karen R. Moffitt, "Turnover Intentions and Voluntary Turnover: The Moderating Roles of Self-Monitoring, Locus of Control, Proactive Personality, and Risk Aversion," *Journal of Applied Psychology* 90 (2005): 980–990.

48. For information about the Job Descriptive Index see the website located at: http://www.bgsu.edu/departments/psych/io/jdi/

49. Angelo J. Kinicki, Frances M. McKee-Ryan, Chester A. Schriesheim, and Kenneth P. Carson, "Assessing the Construct Validity of the Job Descriptive Index: A Review and Meta-Analysis," *Journal of Applied Psychology* 87 (2002): 14–32.

50. Stephanie Whittaker, "Employees Are Proud to Work Here," *The Gazette (Montreal)*, October 14, 2006, G3.

51. Michael T. Roberson and Eric Sundstrom, "Questionnaire Design, Return Rates, and Response Favorableness in an Employee Attitude Questionnaire," *Journal of Applied Psychology* 75 (1990): 354–357.

52. Benjamin Schneider, Steven D. Ashworth, A. Catherine Higgs, and Linda Carr, "Design, Validity, and Use of Strategically Focused Employee Attitude Surveys," *Personnel Psychology* 49 (1996): 695–705.

53. Hui Liao, Aichia Chuang, and Aparna Joshi, "Perceived Deep-Level Dissimilarity: Personality Antecedents and Impact on Overall Job Attitude, Helping, Work Withdrawal, and Turnover," *Organizational Behavior and Human Decision Processes* 106 (2008): 106–124.

54. Peter W. Hom, Loriann Roberson, and Aimee D. Ellis, "Challenging Conventional Wisdom About Who Quits: Revelations from Corporate America," *Journal of Applied Psychology* 93 (2008): 1–34.

55. Patrick F. McKay, Derek A. Avery, Scott Tonidandel, Mark A. Morris, Morela Hernandez, and Michelle R. Hebl, "Racial Differences in Employee Retention: Are Diversity Climate Perceptions the Key?" *Personnel Psychology* 60 (2007): 35–62.

56. Derek R. Avery, Patrick F. McKay, David C. Wilson, and Scott Tonidandel, "Unequal Attendance: The Relationships Between Race, Organizational Diversity Cues, and Absenteeism," *Personnel Psychology* 60 (2007): 875–902; Patrick F. McKay, Derek R. Avery, and Mark A. Morris, "Mean Racial-Ethnic Differences in Employee Sales Performance: The Moderating Role of Diversity Climate," *Personnel Psychology* 61 (2008): 349–374.

57. Steven G. Rogelberg, Alexandra Luong, Matthew E. Sederburg, and Dean S. Cristol, "Employee Attitude Surveys: Examining the Attitudes of Noncompliant Employees," *Journal of Applied Psychology* 85 (2000): 284–293.

58. Markku Jokisaari and Jari-Erik Nurmi, "Change in Newcomers' Supervisor Support and Socialization Outcomes after Organizational Entry," *Academy of Management Journal* 52 (2009): 527–544; Wendy R. Boswell, Abbie J. Shipp, Stephanie C. Payne, and Satoris S. Culbertson, "Changes in Newcomer Job Satisfaction Over Time: Examining the Pattern of Honeymoons and Hangovers," *Journal of Applied Psychology* 94 (2009): 844–858.

59. Talya N. Bauer and Stephen G. Green, "Testing the Combined Effects of Newcomer Information Seeking and Manager Behavior on Socialization," *Journal of Applied Psychology* 83 (1998): 72–83.

60. Tae-Yeol Kim, Daniel M. Cable, and Sang-Pyo Kim, "Socialization Tactics, Employee Proactivity, and Person–Organization Fit," *Journal of Applied Psychology* 90 (2005): 232–241.

61. Amy L. Kristof, "Person–Organization Fit: An Integrative Review of Its Conceptualizations, Measurement, and Implications," *Personnel Psychology* 49 (1996): 1–49.

62. Connie R. Wanberg and John D. Kammeyer-Mueller, "Predictors and Outcomes of Proactivity in the Socialization Process," *Journal of Applied Psychology* 85 (2000): 373–385.

63. Linda Rhoades and Robert Eisenberger, "Perceived Organizational Support: A Review of the Literature," *Journal of Applied Psychology* 87 (2002): 698–714.

64. Randall P. Settoon, Nathan Bennett, and Robert C. Liden, "Social Exchange in Organizations: Perceived Organizational Support, Leader-Member Exchange, and Employee Reciprocity," *Journal of Applied Psychology* 81 (1996): 219–227; Lynn M. Shore and Sandy J. Wayne, "Commitment and Employee Behavior: Comparison of Affective Commitment and Continuance Commitment with Perceived Organizational Support," *Journal of Applied Psychology* 78 (1993): 774–780.

65. Robert Eisenberger, Peter Fasolo, and Valerie Davis-LaMastro, "Perceived Organizational Support and Employee Diligence, Commitment, and Innovation," *Journal of Applied Psychology* 75 (1990): 51–59; Sandy J. Wayne, Lynne M. Shore, and Robert C. Liden, "Perceived Organizational Support and Leader–Member Exchange: A Social Exchange Perspective," *Academy of Management Journal* 40 (1997): 82–111.

66. Uma Shankari, "The Human Capital Factor: Investing in People Development Has Paid Off Handsomely for Fraser's Hospitality," *The Business Times Singapore*, October 17, 2006.

67. Robert Eisenberger, Florence Stinglhamber, Christian Vandenberghe, Ivan L. Sucharski, and Linda Rhoades, "Perceived Supervisor Support: Contributions to Perceived Organizational Support and Employee Retention," *Journal of Applied Psychology* 87 (2002): 565–573.

68. Rhoades and Eisenberger, "Perceived Organizational Support."

69. Tony Simons and Quinetta Roberson, "Why Managers Should Care about Fairness: The Effects of Aggregate

Justice Perceptions on Organizational Outcomes," *Journal of Applied Psychology* 88 (2003): 432–443.

70. Murray R. Barrick and Ryan D. Zimmerman, "Reducing Voluntary, Avoidable Turnover Through Selection," *Journal of Applied Psychology* 90 (2005): 159–166.

71. Andi Atwater, "Screening Program Reduces Worker Turnover: A Pre-Employment Tool Has Saved Via Christi Senior Services Thousands of Dollars This Year," *Wichita Eagle (Kansas)*, October 21, 2006, 6B.

72. Peter W. Hom, Anne S. Tsui, Joshua B. Wu, Thomas W. Lee, Ann Yan Zhang, Ping Ping Fu, and Lan Li, "Explaining Employment Relationships with Social Exchange and Job Embeddedness," *Journal of Applied Psychology* 94 (2009): 277–297.

73. Terence R. Mitchell, Brooks C. Holtom, Thomas W. Lee, Chris J. Sablynski, and Miriam Erez, "Why People Stay: Using Job Embeddedness to Predict Voluntary Turnover," *Academy of Management Journal* 44 (2001): 1102–1121.

74. Kaifeng Jiang, Dong Liu, Patrick F. McKay, Thomas W. Lee, and Terence R. Mitchell, "When and How Is Job Emeddedness Predictive of Turnover? A Meta-Analytic Investigation," *Journal of Applied Psychology* 97 (2012): 1077–1096; Craig D. Crossley, Rebecca J. Bennett, Steve M. Jex, and Jennifer L. Burnfield, "Development of a Global Measure of Job Embeddedness and Integration into a Traditional Model of Voluntary Turnover," *Journal of Applied Psychology* 92 (2007): 1031–1042; Thomas W. Lee, Terence R. Mitchell, Chris J. Sablynski, James P. Burton, and Brooks Holtom, "The Effects of Job Embeddedness on Organizational Citizenship, Job Performance, Volitional Absences, and Voluntary Turnover," *Academy of Management Journal* 47 (2004): 711–722.

75. Terence R. Mitchell, Brooks C. Holtom, and Thomas W. Lee, "How to Keep Your Best Employees: Developing an Effective Retention Policy," *Academy of Management Executive* 15 (2001): 96–108.

76. Samuel Aryee, E. S. Srinivas, and Hwee Hoon Tan, "Rhythms of Life: Antecedents and Outcomes of Work–Family Balance in Employed Parents," *Journal of Applied Psychology* 90 (2005): 132–146.

77. Timothy A. Judge and Shinichiro Watanabe, "Another Look at the Job Satisfaction–Life Satisfaction Relationship," *Journal of Applied Psychology* 78 (1993): 939–948.

78. Michael R. Frone, "Work–Family Conflict and Employee Psychiatric Disorders: The National Comorbidity Survey," *Journal of Applied Psychology* 85 (2000): 888–895.

79. Geoffrey E. Love and Matthew Kraatz, "Character, Conformity, or the Bottom Line? How and Why Downsizing Affected Corporate Reputation," *Academy of Management Journal* 52 (2009): 314–335.

80. Wayne F. Cascio, Clifford E. Young, and James R. Morris, "Financial Consequences of Employment-Change Decisions in Major U.S. Corporations," *Academy of Management Journal* 40 (1997): 1175–1189.

81. Anonymous, "The Futility of Downsizing," *Industry Week* 242 (1993): 27–28.

82. Christopher D. Zatzick and Roderick D. Iverson, "High-Involvement Management and Workforce Reduction: Competitive Advantage or Disadvantage?" *Academy of Management Journal* 49 (2006): 999–1015.

83. Kenneth P. DeMeuse, Thomas J. Bergmann, Paul A. Vanderheiden, and Catherine E. Roraff, "New Evidence Regarding Organizational Downsizing and a Firm's Financial Performance: A Long-Term Analysis," *Journal of Managerial Issues* 16 (2004): 155–177.

84. Javad Kashefi and Gilbert J. McKee, "Stock Prices' Reactions to Layoff Announcements," *Journal of Business and Management* 8, no. 2 (2002): 99–107.

85. Peter Chalos and Charles J. P. Chen, "Employee Downsizing Strategies: Market Reaction and Post Announcement Financial Performance," *Journal of Business Finance and Accounting* 29 (2002): 847–871.

86. D. Scott DeRue, John R. Hollenbeck, Michael D. Johnson, Daniel R. Ilgen, and Dustin K. Jundt, "How Different Team Downsizing Approaches Influence Team-Level Adaptation and Performance," *Academy of Management Journal* 51 (2008): 182–196.

87. Frances M. McKee Ryan, Zhaoli Song, Connie Wanberg, and Angelo J. Kinicki, "Psychological and Physical Well-Being During Unemployment: A Meta-Analytic Study," *Journal of Applied Psychology* 90 (2005): 53–76.

88. Ruth Kanfer, Connie R. Wanberg, and Tracy M. Kantrowitz, "Job Search and Employment: A Personality-Motivational Analysis and Meta-Analytic Review," *Journal of Applied Psychology* 86 (2001): 837–855.

89. Gregory E. Prussia, Angelo J. Kinicki, and Jeffrey S. Bracker, "Psychological and Behavioral Consequences of Job Loss: A Covariance Structure Analysis Using Weiner's (1985) Attribution Model," *Journal of Applied Psychology* 78 (1993): 382–394.

90. Peter A. Creed, Vivien King, Michelle Hood, and Robert McKenzie, "Goal Orientation, Self-Regulation Strategies, and Job Seeking Intensity in Unemployed Adults, "*Journal of Applied Psychology* 94 (2009): 806–813.

91. Connie Wanberg, "Antecedents and Outcomes of Coping Behaviors Among Unemployed and Reemployed Individuals," *Journal of Applied Psychology* 82 (1997): 731–744.

92. Angelo J. Kinicki, Gregory E. Prussia, and Frances M. McKee-Ryan, "A Panel Study of Coping with Involuntary Job Loss," *Academy of Management Journal* 43 (2000): 90–100.

93. Joel Brockner, Mary Konovsky, Rochelle Cooper-Schneider, Robert Folger, Christopher Martin, and Robert J. Bies, "Interactive Effects of Procedural Justice and Outcome Negativity on Victims and Survivors of Job Loss," *Academy of Management Journal* 37 (1994): 397–409.

94. Joel Brockner, "The Effects of Work Layoffs on Survivors: Research, Theory, and Practice," *Research in Organizational Behavior* 10 (1988): 213–255.

95. Joel Brockner, Jeanette Davy, and Carolyn Carter, "Layoffs, Self-Esteem, and Survivor Guilt: Motivational, Affective, and Attitudinal Consequences," *Organizational Behavior and Human Decision Processes* 36 (1985): 229–244.

96. Joel Brockner, Steven Grover, Thomas F. Reed, and Rocki Lee DeWitt, "Layoffs, Job Insecurity, and Survivors Work Effort: Evidence of an Inverted-U Relationship," *Academy of Management Journal* 35 (1992): 413–425.

97. Aneil K. Mishra and Gretchen M. Spreitzer, "Explaining How Survivors Respond to Downsizing: The Roles of Trust, Empowerment, Justice, and Work Redesign," *Academy of Management Review* 23 (1998): 567–588; Joel Brockner, Steven L. Grover, and Maritz D. Blonder, "Predictors of Survivors' Job Involvement Following Layoffs: A Field Study," *Journal of Applied Psychology* 73 (1988): 436–442.

98. Gretchen M. Spreitzer and Aneil K. Mishra, "To Stay or Go: Voluntary Survivor Turnover Following an Organizational Downsizing," *Journal of Organizational Behavior* 23 (2002): 707.

99. Joel Brockner, Steven Grover, Thomas Reed, Rocki DeWitt, and Michael O'Malley, "Survivors' Reactions to Layoffs: We Get by with a Little Help for Our Friends," *Administrative Science Quarterly* 32 (1987): 526–541.

100. Charlie O. Trevor and Anthony J. Nyberg, Keeping Your Headcount When All About You Are Losing Theirs: Downsizing, Voluntary Turnover Rates, and the Moderating Role of HR Practices," *Academy of Management Journal* 51 (2008): 259–276.

101. Jody Hoffer Gittell, Kim Cameron, Sandy Lim, and Victor Rivas, "Relationships, Layoffs, and Organizational Resilience: Airline Industry Responses to September 11," *Journal of Applied Behavioral Science* 42 (2006): 300–329.

102. Peter Allan, "Minimizing Employee Layoffs While Downsizing: Employer Practices that Work," *International Journal of Manpower* 18 (1997): 576.

103. Larry R. Smeltzer and Marie F. Zener, "Minimizing the Negative Effects of Employee Layoffs Through Effective Announcements," *Employee Counseling Today* 6, no. 4 (1994): 3–9.

104. Wayne F. Cascio and Peg Wynn, "Managing a Downsizing Process," *Human Resource Management* 43 (2004): 425–436.

105. Scott David Williams, William M. Slonaker, and Ann C. Wendt, "An Analysis of Employment Discrimination Claims Associated with Layoffs," *S.A.M. Advanced Management Journal* 68 (2003): 49–55.

106. David S. Dhanoa and Brian H. Kleiner, "How to Conduct Due Process Discipline," *Management Research News* 23, no. 7/8 (2000): 89–94.

107. Antone Aboud, "Conducting a Fair Investigation," *Dispute Resolution Journal* 59, no. 4 (2004–2005): 16–21.

108. Dhanoa and Kleiner, "How to Conduct Due Process Discipline."

109. Peggy Anderson and Marcia Pulich, "A Positive Look at Progressive Discipline," *Health Care Manager* 20, no. 1 (2001): 1–9.

110. Jeanette A. Davy, Joe S. Anderson, and Nicholas DiMarco, "Outcome Comparisons of Formal Outplacement Services and Informal Support," *Human Resource Development Quarterly* 6 (1995): 275–288.

111. Joe Hobel, "Virtually Letting Go Is the Wrong Way to Say Goodbye," *Canadian HR Reporter,* September 25, 2006, 26.

112. Cliff Ennico, "The Right Way to Fire Someone," *Entrepreneur.com,* September 11, 2006, www.entrepreneur.com/humanresources/managingemployees/discipliningandfiring/article166644.html; Michael Bryant, "How to Fire Someone," *Maryland Bar Bulletin,* February 2005, http://www.msba.org/departments/commpubl/publications/bar_bult/2005/feb05/solo.asp.

Part 3
Improving Employee Performance

©AP/Wide World Photos   ©Ingo Schulz/Imagebroker/Corbis   Spencer Platt/Getty Images

Chapter 8

Measuring Performance and Providing Feedback

A MANAGER'S PERSPECTIVE

TYRONE FEELS EXHAUSTED. AS MANAGER OF THE LOCAL HARDWARE STORE, HE JUST COMPLETED AN ANNUAL PERFORMANCE REVIEW FOR EACH OF HIS EMPLOYEES. HE STRUGGLED TO SEPARATE THE GOOD AND BAD EMPLOYEES. WAS HE RIGHT TO CAREFULLY IDENTIFY THE TOP PERFORMERS, OR SHOULD HE HAVE JUST RATED EVERYONE THE SAME?

One of the things that Tyrone found most difficult was how to account for different aspects of performance. One of the sales representatives—Joe—had the highest sales volume, but often refused to help other less-experienced coworkers. Because of Joe's lack of cooperation, Tyrone gave him a much lower rating than might be suggested by the objective sales figures. Was this a good idea?

Another employee, Logan, became upset last week and actually threatened violence against two coworkers. At first Tyrone gave him a very low rating, but then he thought back about Logan's performance over the entire rating period. Up until last week Logan's work had been exemplary. Tyrone thus decided that it would not be fair to penalize Logan with an extremely low rating. On the other hand,

Tyrone wants to communicate that threats of violence will not be tolerated. He wonders what he should say when he meets with Logan.

Tyrone also worries about any potential biases that he might have. When he looked over his ratings he saw that the two lowest scores were given to women. He wondered if this was a problem and spent a great deal of time listing good and bad things that he had seen both women do. In the end he concluded that his initial ratings were accurate, but he continues to worry that he is somehow biased.

In order to prepare for performance discussions, Tyrone asked each employee to provide self-ratings. He was a little shocked when he looked at these ratings last night. Almost everyone had a self-rating that was higher than the rating he gave them. Curiously, Ed and Janice, two of the lowest performers, actually gave themselves some of the highest self-ratings. How could this be? Didn't they know that they were not performing up to standard?

©AP/Wide World Photos

THE BIG PICTURE *Performance Management Evaluates Employees' Contributions and Provides Feedback So That Employees Can Improve.*

Thinking about sitting down with the employees and sharing his evaluations makes Tyrone nervous. Would it be best to provide general comments, or should he describe very specific behaviors that he would like to see? He is sure that Ed and Janice will complain about their low ratings. What if they become defensive and emotional? Will he be able to have a constructive discussion with Logan?

Tyrone realizes that mixed with his uncertainty about how people might react to the ratings is a sense of excitement. Perhaps completing ratings and sharing feedback will give him an opportunity to address some of the performance issues he has been avoiding. This just might be an important key to making the store more profitable. This is important as recently he has been feeling pressure from corporate headquarters to increase sales and customer satisfaction ratings.

WHAT DO YOU THINK?

Suppose Tyrone asks his boss, Monica, for guidance about performance management. Monica makes the following statements. Which of the statements do you think are true?

T OR F Employee rating systems are of no value unless at least some employees receive low ratings.

T OR F When completing performance ratings, it is best to focus only on whether an employee completes tasks and not on how well he or she works with others.

T OR F Objective measures of performance, which are represented by things that can be counted, are better than subjective measures such as supervisor judgments.

T OR F Self-ratings of performance are usually higher than ratings provided by others.

T OR F Employee performance increases when supervisors communicate high expectations.

293

After reading this chapter you should be able to:

LEARNING OBJECTIVE 1   Describe how merit-based and parity-based performance management systems relate to overall HR and competitive strategy.

LEARNING OBJECTIVE 2   Describe the three dimensions of job performance.

LEARNING OBJECTIVE 3   Explain differences among, and common problems with, various types of performance measures.

LEARNING OBJECTIVE 4   Explain the value of using multiple sources to obtain performance appraisal ratings.

LEARNING OBJECTIVE 5   Describe effective methods for providing feedback to employees.

How Can Performance Management Make an Organization Effective?

Performance management
The process of measuring and providing feedback about employee contributions to the organization.

Grades are an important part of almost every university class. What would happen if grades were eliminated? Would your individual performance improve or decline? Would the reputation of your university rise or fall? Similar issues are at the heart of **performance management**, which involves assessing and communicating employee contributions. Rating employees' performance is similar to giving them grades. In the employment context, important questions include the following: Do employees improve their performance when their contributions to the organization are measured? Is it helpful to give feedback so that employees know how they are doing? Does effective measurement of individual contributions lead to improved organizational performance?

Measuring performance and providing feedback does indeed improve employee performance. And improvements in individual performance translate into better organizational performance. Organizations have higher productivity when top management encourages supervisors to set goals, assess performance, and provide feedback to employees.[1] One reason is that trust in management increases when performance is accurately measured and adequately rewarded.[2] Effective appraisals, particularly appraisals that allow employee participation, have also been linked to higher levels of job satisfaction.[3]

An example of a company that practices effective performance management is General Electric (GE). GE is consistently ranked as one of the world's most admired corporations.[4] Much of the admiration comes from GE's ability to attract and retain superior employees. This ability comes from a culture that sees human resource management as a strategic activity. The human resource department is not seen as a support function but rather as a business partner. CEO Jeff Immelt puts it this way: "HR people need to work for companies where people are valued. There's not a day that goes by that I don't talk to our senior HR leader." In fact, Immelt considers the triangle formed by himself, the CFO, and the senior HR leader to be "absolutely central to how the business is led."[5] Within this strategic orientation, one area that most sets GE apart is the successful use of performance management to identify and reward excellent employees, who make up a workforce that is difficult for competitors to imitate.[6]

GE's performance management system is best known for its emphasis on clearly identifying high and low performers. Historically, the company asked managers to follow a rating distribution that placed 20 percent of employees in the top category, 70 percent in a middle category, and 10 percent in a category of low performance.[7] These strict percentages have been relaxed over the past few years, but most managers continue to place about this percentage of employees in each category. One effect of forcing managers to use such categories is clear identification of low performers. The objective of identifying low performers was summarized by the head of human resources, William Conaty, when he stated, "We want to create angst in the system … you have to know who are the least effective people on your team and then you have to do something about them."[8] Either replacing low-performing employees with higher performers or taking specific steps to improve the productivity of low performers increases the likelihood that the company will be successful. Another effect of the forced categories is clear identification of high performers. Only 20 percent of employees receive a top rating, so employees feel a special sense of accomplishment when they are rated in the top category. Employees come to see exceptional performance, rather than politics or favoritism, as the key to promotion and advancement.

Clear goals that encourage employees to stretch and improve are another important aspect of the GE performance system. In the process of measuring and discussing performance, managers work with employees to establish difficult goals. Focusing on goals provides clear direction for improvement. Accomplishing stretch goals requires a great deal of effort and often necessitates working in radically different ways.[9] The performance appraisal process at GE helps ensure that an individual's goals are aligned with company goals. This is done through a process of cascading, wherein goals and performance assessments begin at the top and flow downward. Top-level goals and assessments become critical input for goals and assessments at lower levels.[10]

Performance management at GE also adapts to the changing needs of the organization. The behaviors encouraged in the rating process are behaviors that link to the company's competitive strategy. For example, the performance appraisal system was recently updated to provide ratings for things such as imagination and understanding of market trends.[11] These traits are consistent with GE's strategic focus on innovation and growth.

Performance management at GE is a critical component of the overall human resource system that encourages innovation and quality. Top performers are clearly identified and encouraged to stay with the company. The performance appraisal system also provides a merit-based foundation for compensation decisions. Low performance is likewise identified in order to encourage weaker contributors to improve or to leave the company. With this emphasis, the performance management process at GE creates a culture of excellence that brings out the best in employees.

Building Strength Through HR

GENERAL ELECTRIC

General Electric is a multinational company that employs over 301,000 people. Human resource management at GE builds competitive strength by

- Clearly identifying people who are high and low performers, so that high performers can be rewarded and low performers can be encouraged to improve or leave.
- Establishing stretch goals that focus employee efforts on areas where they can improve their performance.
- Aligning the behaviors assessed in the performance appraisal process with strategic objectives.

LEARNING OBJECTIVE 1

How Is Performance Management Strategic?

Although identifying high and low performers is an important part of performance management at General Electric, it might not be the best approach for other organizations. In some cases, encouraging people to stand out from the crowd may discourage teamwork and harm employee motivation. Like other HR practices, then, performance management practices are most effective when aligned with an organization's competitive strategy.

EMPHASIZING EITHER MERIT OR PARITY

Organizations tend to follow one of two approaches in measuring performance. Some organizations create a merit-based climate that emphasizes performance differences among employees. In other organizations, the system encourages parity, or a sense of equality, among employees.

Merit-based system
A performance management system that specifically seeks to identify and recognize the contributions of high performers.

Relative measures
Performance ratings that assess an employee's contributions through comparison with the contributions of other employees.

Merit-Based Systems
The basic objective of a **merit-based system** is to create and recognize high performance in order to achieve superior outcomes. This is the approach adopted by GE with the underlying purpose of performance management being encouragement to perform at the highest possible level. Employees who produce the highest outcomes, or results, are given high marks. As at GE, this is usually done through the use of **relative measures** that compare employees with each other. Success at work is defined not just as meeting a certain standard but as doing better than others. With a merit-based system, managers are also frequently required to place a certain percentage

of employees in each rating category, which is called a **forced distribution**. Only a few can be given the highest rating, and at least some must be given the lowest rating. In summary, merit-based systems focus on bottom-line results and use relative measures and forced distributions to ensure that high and low performers are clearly identified.[12]

Students who have been in a class with a grading curve have experienced a merit-based performance system. In such classes, a student's grade is determined to some extent by how well other students perform. Even if you have never experienced such a grading scheme, just thinking about it can help identify possible outcomes. Students who want a top grade tend to work very hard because they know the teacher will give only a few As. Students who do receive an A feel a strong sense of accomplishment because they know that they performed better than most others. Students who are not performing well are also clearly identified. In some cases, students resist helping their peers, since doing so may result in their own grade being lower. The class climate is competitive, but individual performance is usually very high.

Parity-Based Systems

The basic objective of a **parity-based system** is to encourage cooperation and allow everyone who meets a certain standard to be classified as a high performer. Parity-based performance measures frequently focus on processes rather than outcomes. High performance is defined as following guidelines and performing behaviors assigned by supervisors. This usually involves **absolute measures** that compare employees with an established benchmark rather than with each other. Most parity-based systems also adopt a **free distribution**, which allows any percentage of employees to be placed in a particular category. For example, any employee who assembles a certain number of cell phones without error can be given a top performance rating, regardless of how many cell phones others assemble. In general, parity-based performance systems do not separate people into categories of high and low performance but rather encourage all employees to perform above a certain standard.

The underlying principle of a parity-based system is communicated whenever a professor announces that every student in a class can achieve an A. More students usually receive As and Bs in such classes than in classes graded on a curve. Without a curve, teachers are less likely to give failing grades. However, receiving a high grade in such classes may not be especially meaningful. If almost everyone receives an A, it is impossible to identify the best students. In fact, it is often the top performers who are most unhappy with a parity-based performance system. They may resent receiving the same grade as others, although they performed better, or they may reduce their effort and perform just above the cutoff for the highest grade. The class climate is thus more cooperative, but fewer students really stretch and perform at their highest level.

LINKING MERIT AND PARITY SYSTEMS TO HR STRATEGY

In general, merit-based approaches are best suited to organizations pursuing differentiation strategies, while parity-based systems make sense for organizations using cost strategies. Organizations with internal and external

Forced distribution
Performance ratings that spread out ratings by requiring raters to place a certain percentage of employees in each category.

Parity-based system
A performance management system that seeks to recognize contributions from all employees without elevating some above others.

Absolute measures
Performance ratings that assess an employee's contribution in comparison to a fixed standard or benchmark.

Free distribution
Performance ratings that allow raters to place as many employees as they wish into each rating category.

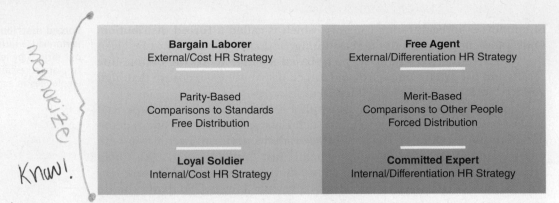

memorize *Know!*

Bargain Laborer External/Cost HR Strategy	**Free Agent** External/Differentiation HR Strategy
Parity-Based Comparisons to Standards Free Distribution	Merit-Based Comparisons to Other People Forced Distribution
Loyal Soldier Internal/Cost HR Strategy	**Committed Expert** Internal/Differentiation HR Strategy

Figure 8.1 Strategic Framework for Performance Management.

labor systems do not differ in terms of their approaches to merit and parity. Linkages between merit and parity approaches to performance management are shown in Figure 8.1.

Merit Systems and Differentiation Strategies

The merit-based approach is most beneficial for organizations pursuing a Free Agent HR strategy. Producing truly exceptional products and services is the key to success and is best accomplished by employees who are stretching to accomplish high goals. This sense of stretching and competition is enhanced by ratings that communicate how the employee is performing relative to others.[13] Employees performing poorly are identified and encouraged to leave the organization so that they can be replaced with others who have greater skill and motivation. Organizations pursuing a Committed Expert HR strategy also tend to adopt merit-based approaches. Promotions and advancement in these organizations depend largely on achieving results and performing better than others. As we saw in the GE example, a merit-based approach to performance management that recognizes truly excellent performance is a key feature of effective differentiation strategies.

Parity Systems and Cost Strategies

For an organization using a Loyal Soldier HR strategy, success comes from cooperative employees who work with maximum efficiency. The contribution of an exceptional performer is often of little more benefit than the contribution of others who simply do what they are asked. In these cases, a performance appraisal system that creates competition among employees may actually harm the group's overall performance. Employees are usually more satisfied with evaluation systems that compare them to standards rather than to other employees.[14] Evaluating most employees as high performers encourages long-term employee relationships and a strong sense of loyalty.

Like organizations that use a Loyal Soldier HR strategy, organizations pursuing a Bargain Laborer HR strategy are not concerned with identifying top performers. In this case, the reason is that these individuals are unlikely to stay employed with the organization for long periods. In addition, placing employees in different performance categories is time consuming and difficult. For an organization requiring only that employees meet expectations, such classification may not be worth the effort.

CONCEPT CHECK

1. *How does a merit-based performance system differ from a parity-based performance system?*
2. *Which HR strategies best align with a merit-based system? Which are best for a parity-based system?*

What Is Performance?

In the simplest sense, **job performance** represents the contribution that individuals make to the organization that employs them.

Figure 8.2 shows a diagram of important elements of job performance. At the top of the figure is a **general performance factor** that represents overall contribution to the organization. This general factor is important because all specific measures of job performance tend to be positively related, meaning that people who do well at one aspect of performance tend to do well at other aspects. Some people are simply better performers than others. Because they have positive traits, such as intelligence and motivation, these individuals excel no matter which aspect of performance is being measured.[15]

Under the general performance factor you will see three main performance dimensions: task, citizenship, and counterproductive performance. We examine each of these dimensions in the following sections.[16]

TASK PERFORMANCE

Task performance is behavior that contributes directly to the production of goods or services. Some actions may be job-specific, as when a secretary

Job performance
The contribution that individuals make to the organization that employs them.

General performance factor
A broad factor of performance that represents an employee's overall contribution to the organization.

Task performance
Employee behavior that directly contributes to producing goods or services.

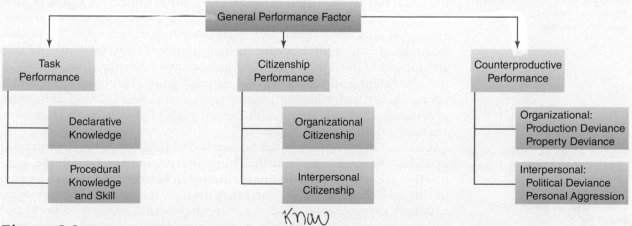

Know

Figure 8.2 Elements of Job Performance.

prepares a document, a home builder lays the foundation for a house, or a waiter fills beverage glasses. Administrative tasks, such as planning and delegating, are important aspects of task performance for people working as managers.[17] Other actions are less specific to a particular job and include things like following safety regulations, making decisions, and keeping the workspace clean.[18] In order to perform tasks in most jobs, employees must also communicate with others by either writing or speaking.[19]

Because it represents behaviors that directly produce goods and services, task performance is the most obvious form of contribution to an organization. In most organizations, a very large proportion of employee effort is spent on task performance. The result is that supervisors see task performance as the most important contribution that an employee makes.[20]

When it comes to task performance, employees are most likely to make significant contributions when they have appropriate knowledge, skill, and motivation.[21] They must first have **declarative knowledge,** which is an understanding of what needs to be done to perform certain tasks. For instance, declarative knowledge for a carpenter might include knowing that constructing a cabinet involves obtaining accurate measurements, cutting boards to appropriate lengths, and then fastening the boards together in the proper sequence. Employees must also have **procedural knowledge and skill**, which concerns the ability to perform the prescribed tasks. Thus, the carpenter must be able to measure accurately, make straight cuts with a power saw, and drive nails without damaging the wood. However, knowing what to do and how to do it is not enough to ensure that the carpenter will actually build the cabinets. The third important factor is motivation. Employees show motivation when they choose to expend effort by engaging and persisting in production tasks. Motivation increases when workers feel supported by supervisors and coworkers, which in turn leads them to higher task performance.[22]

CITIZENSHIP PERFORMANCE

Whereas task performance contributes by directly creating goods and services, citizenship behavior contributes by building a positive organizational environment. **Citizenship performance** is thus behavior that contributes to the social and psychological environment of the organization. Going beyond minimum expectations and helping out is seen as particularly beneficial when employees must work closely with each other to complete tasks.[23] Common examples of citizenship behavior include volunteering to take on tasks that are not part of one's job, following organizational procedures even when it is not convenient, and supporting and defending the organization.[24] Willingly taking charge and initiating positive change also demonstrates citizenship performance.[25] Work groups with higher levels of citizenship performance are more productive and profitable.[26]

Citizenship performance can be pursued to help either the organization as a whole or specific individuals. Things that are done to benefit the organization are labeled **organizational citizenship behavior.** Employees engage in this type of performance when they do such things as protect the organization's property, give advance notice when unable to come to work, and follow informal rules that help maintain order. Another set of actions—labeled **interpersonal citizenship behavior**—has the effect of benefiting specific people. Such behaviors include taking time to listen to coworkers'

Declarative knowledge
An employee's understanding of the tasks that need to be done to perform job duties.

Procedural knowledge and skill
Information and expertise that an employee needs to have in order to carry out specific actions.

Citizenship performance
Employee behavior that helps others and creates a positive work environment.

Organizational citizenship behavior
Positive employee actions aimed at helping the organization as a whole to succeed.

Interpersonal citizenship behavior
Positive employee actions aimed at helping specific coworkers succeed.

problems, passing along information to peers, and helping people who have been absent. Coworkers who are confident and who are the center of communication networks, which makes them popular among coworkers, are most likely to receive helping behavior.[27]

The distinction between organizational and interpersonal citizenship is important because the likelihood that employees will engage in helpful behavior differs depending on whether the behavior is intended to aid the overall organization or some individual. Employees engage in more organizational citizenship behavior when they feel that they receive reasonable pay, are praised for doing a good job, and have pleasant working conditions.[28] Interpersonal citizenship behavior is more likely to occur when employees have close relationships with coworkers and supervisors.[29] Thus, for example, employees who are unwilling to expend extra effort to help the organization may be willing to do extra things that benefit others whom they like.

Even though it may not be part of formal job requirements, citizenship performance represents a critical contribution to the organization. In fact, in many instances citizenship performance is what separates top performers from everyone else. Perhaps this is because citizenship performance primarily represents voluntary action. Given its voluntary nature, citizenship behavior depends not on specific knowledge and skills but on motivation. This means that employees with motivational personality traits such as dependability, cooperativeness, empathy, and being proactive are generally more likely to go beyond minimum expectations and help both the organization and other individuals.[30] Workers who feel they are treated fairly by their supervisors and the organization are also more likely to engage in citizenship behavior.[31] The role of the leader is particularly critical, as citizenship performance often depends on the supervisor's being seen as trustworthy and acting with integrity.[32]

Employees are most likely to engage in citizenship performance when they perceive a long-term work relationship,[33] suggesting that citizenship contributions are higher in organizations with Loyal Soldier and Committed Expert HR strategies. This makes sense because developing cooperation among workers is at the heart of these labor strategies.

COUNTERPRODUCTIVE PERFORMANCE

In addition to engaging in helpful behavior, employees can consciously choose to engage in counterproductive performance. Specifically, **counterproductive performance** is voluntary behavior that harms the organization. Organizations whose employees engage in more counterproductive behavior have been found to have lower productivity.[34] Interestingly, self-reports of counterproductive behavior are very similar to reports provided by others such as supervisors and coworkers.[35] Moreover, although individuals who engage in counterproductive behavior are somewhat less likely to excel at citizenship performance, these two measures are not the two ends of a single dimension.[36] An employee who contributes with high task and citizenship performance in some cases also causes harm by engaging in counterproductive behavior.

Like citizenship performance, counterproductive behavior can be directed toward either the organization or specific individuals. Negative actions directed toward the organization include production and property deviance. **Production deviance** occurs when employees do things that reduce the speed and accuracy with which goods and services are produced. Employees

Counterproductive performance
Employee behavior that is harmful to the organization.

Production deviance
Harmful employee actions aimed at reducing the speed and accuracy of production processes.

Property deviance
Harmful employee actions aimed at destroying assets of the organization.

frequently do this by taking unauthorized breaks, intentionally working slowly, and wasting company resources. Perhaps more serious is **property deviance**, which includes actions that destroy the assets of an organization. Employees who do this sabotage equipment, misuse expense accounts, or steal materials and products.[37]

Counterproductive behaviors can also be targeted toward specific individuals. These actions fall into the categories of political deviance and personal aggression. **Political deviance** occurs when an employee does things that put other employees at a disadvantage. Examples include showing favoritism, gossiping about coworkers, and competing with others in nonbeneficial ways. The more serious form of counterproductive behavior directed toward individuals is **personal aggression**, which is represented by hostile acts such as violence and sexual harassment.[38] Employees working in groups lacking civility and respect are particularly prone to act aggressively.[39]

Political deviance
Harmful employee actions designed to harm the performance and careers of other employees.

Personal aggression
Harmful employee actions that seek to personally harm coworkers.

As described in the "Technology in HR" feature, organizations use a number of tactics to reduce counterproductive behavior. Motivation that comes from a sense of being treated fairly is a very important factor influencing counterproductive performance. Employees are more prone to engage in counterproductive performance when they perceive that the organization treats them unfairly.[40] Having a leader who is ethical, fair, and not abusive is a critical deterrent of counterproductive behavior.[41] Thus, organizations and leaders can reduce counterproductive behavior by communicating an interest in the well-being of employees, providing developmental opportunities, and acting in an ethical manner themselves. In addition, employees who are more conscientious, more agreeable, higher in self-mastery, less anxious, and less driven by a desire to obtain rewards indulge in less counterproductive behavior, even when they do not feel support from the organization.[42]

CONCEPT CHECK

1. *What are three different types of performance that fall directly under the general performance factor?*
2. *How is citizenship performance different from task performance?*
3. *What are four types of counterproductive performance behavior?*

LEARNING OBJECTIVE **3**

How Is Performance Measured?

Performance appraisal
The process of measuring what employees contribute to the organization.

The process of measuring what each employee contributes, called **performance appraisal,** is a necessary but difficult part of managing others. Indeed, for many managers, performance appraisal is near the bottom of the list of things they want to do. Perhaps more troublesome is that a majority of workers say that performance reviews do nothing to improve their future effectiveness.[43] What makes assessing performance so tough? One reason managers dislike

Technology in HR

MONITORING ELECTRONIC ACTIVITY

Increased use of computers and other technology has the potential to make workers more productive. But it is also possible that workers will become less efficient if they use the technology in counterproductive ways. The use of company computers for purposes other than work completion is sometimes referred to as cyberloafing, and it is not unusual. Over 60 percent of workers report surfing the Web at least once a day for personal purposes. Workers themselves report spending about 1.5 hours per week visiting websites unrelated to work, whereas human resource managers suggest the actual time is closer to 8 hours. Such problems have prompted as many as 76 percent of organizations to monitor employees' Internet connections.

One way of monitoring employees' computer usage is through the use of special software. The software is able not only to block access to websites but also to provide supervisors with reports listing the websites visited. Using such software can, however, communicate lack of trust. Research thus suggests that companies need to be careful when monitoring electronic activities.

Employees are more accepting of electronic monitoring when they are given advance notice that it will be used. Monitoring is also less threatening if employees feel general support from the organization. Using monitoring to show employees how they can improve rather than to wield punishment is one way to increase the acceptance of electronic monitoring. On the whole, evidence suggests

qingwa/iStockphoto

that electronic monitoring can deter counterproductive actions, but it is most effective when used in ways that do not violate employee perceptions of trust and fairness.

Sources: G. Stoney Alder, Terry W. Noel, and Maureen L. Ambrose, "Clarifying the Effects of Internet Monitoring on Job Attitudes: The Mediating Role of Employee Trust," *Information & Management* 43 (2006): 894–903; Deborah L. Wells, Robert Moorman, and Jon M. Werner, "The Impact of the Perceived Purpose of Electronic Performance on an Array of Attitudinal Variables," *Human Resource Development Quarterly* 18, no. 1 (2007): 121–138.

performance appraisal is the difficulty of capturing all areas of contribution. Employees contribute in a number of different ways, and it is often hard to accurately evaluate their efforts with a numerical score. Another reason is that many employees seem to feel that performance ratings are biased. They see the process as sometimes unfair. A starting point for thinking about performance measures is thus to consider ways evaluations can be inaccurate. After examining general sources of inaccuracy in performance measures, we will explore various types of performance measures. We will also discuss problems that these specific measures have, and the formats—or specific types of questions—used to provide performance ratings.

CONTAMINATION AND DEFICIENCY AS SOURCES OF INACCURACY

Basic problems with performance appraisal are shown in Figure 8.3. One circle in the figure represents the employee's true contribution to the organization. The other circle represents contribution as it is measured. Of course, the objective of performance appraisal is to have the two circles overlap as much as possible. However, two types of error often interfere with achieving this objective.

One error is **contamination,** which occurs when things that should not be measured are included in an employee's performance evaluation. For instance, a supervisor who is racially biased might give lower ratings to an employee from a minority group. A measure of the number of computer circuits that an employee assembles might be contaminated if the employee must use machinery that frequently breaks down.

The second type of error is **deficiency**, which occurs when things that should be included in an employee's performance evaluation are not measured. A measure that fails to include citizenship behavior is deficient because it does not recognize actions that aid coworkers. A monthly measure of insurance sales might also be deficient if it fails to include an assessment of effort expended to build relationships that will result in future sales.

A good appraisal system minimizes contamination and deficiency. The concepts of deficiency and contamination can also help guide our assessment of different types of performance measures.

GENERAL TYPES OF PERFORMANCE MEASURES

Organizations use a number of different methods for appraising performance. In general, performance appraisal methods vary in two important ways: whether they are subjective or objective and whether they focus on process or outcome.

Contamination
A problem with performance appraisal that occurs when things that should not be included in the measurement are included.

Deficiency
A problem with performance appraisal that occurs when things that should be included in the measurement are not included.

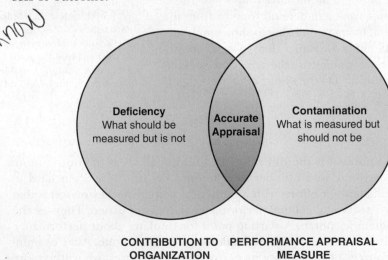

Figure 8.3 Sources of Inaccuracy in Performance Measurement.

Objective Versus Subjective Measures

Beginning in elementary school, students encounter differences between objective and subjective measures of performance. Teachers grade math tests objectively by identifying how many of the problems were solved correctly. Such **objective performance measures** are based on counts of either behavior or outcomes. In contrast, writing assignments are given subjective grades that reflect the teacher's evaluation of quality. These **subjective performance measures** are based on judgments from raters such as teachers and supervisors.

When it comes to job performance, objective and subjective measures often don't agree.[44] An important question thus concerns which type of measure is best. Most people believe the answer is that objective measures are best. It is easy to see how raters could have biases that may reduce the accuracy of subjective measures. For example, workers who have a more positive attitude receive higher evaluations from supervisors but do not generally perform better on objective measures.[45] To many people, objective measures thus seem more consistent and fair. However, objective measures also have problems. In the case of employees with a positive attitude, it may be that their cooperation with others represents a contribution that the objective measure fails to capture. Indeed, subjective ratings have been shown to capture not only task performance but also citizenship performance,[46] making them less deficient than objective measures in many contexts.

Another problem with objective measures can be seen in a common example involving employee productivity. Suppose a supervisor has two employees working on a production line with two machines that manufacture cell phone components. One employee produces 20 components every hour. The other produces only 15. The objective indicator of performance suggests that the first employee contributes more to the organization. However, the supervisor may know that one production machine frequently breaks down. Knowing that the employee who only produces 15 components frequently stops to repair the machine may cause the supervisor to provide a higher subjective rating for that person. In such a case, the objective rating is deficient because it does not capture an important part of overall contribution: repairing the machine.

An example that is closer to home for most college students concerns grading on an accounting exam. A purely objective measure will not give credit for a problem unless the final answer is correct. However, students often ask for and receive partial credit based on the grader's judgment that certain parts of the problem were done correctly. The end result is a combination of objective and subjective measurement. The part of performance where the objective measure is deficient is captured in the subjective measure. In summary, then, objective measures are not necessarily foolproof. It is usually desirable for assessments of job performance to include both objective and subjective measures.

Outcome Versus Behavioral Measures

Performance measures also differ in whether they focus on outcomes or behaviors. Outcome measures assess end results such as number of automobiles repaired or success of an advertising campaign. Behavioral measures place more emphasis on the actions of employees. Typical behavioral measures

Objective performance measures
Performance measures that are numerical and based on counts of behaviors or outcomes.

Subjective performance measures
Performance measures that represent judgments made by raters.

include following company procedures for reacting to customer complaints and using appropriate processes to move and store goods in a warehouse.

We can see some of the differences in outcome and behavioral measures by looking at organizations that employ sales representatives. One approach to managing sales representatives focuses on outcome measures. Organizations adopting this approach identify top performers as the individuals who sell the most products and services. Bottom-line results are most important, and methods of obtaining sales are not specifically evaluated as part of performance appraisal. This approach provides sales representatives with a great deal of autonomy. Individual representatives are expected to use their own knowledge and skills to determine the best way to meet the needs of individual customers.

A different approach to managing sales representatives focuses on behavioral measures. Organizations using this approach have preferred ways of interacting with customers and obtaining sales, and they provide sales representatives with very specific descriptions of appropriate selling behavior. Top performers simply carry out the actions specified by the organization. It is assumed that desirable outcomes will result when representatives engage in the desired actions. Following company procedures is thus emphasized more than simply making a high number of sales.

Outcome and behavioral measures can each suffer from deficiency and contamination, suggesting that both should be assessed in most situations. However, which type of measure dominates often depends on the organization's competitive strategy. Organizations pursuing cost-focused strategies tend to have production processes that are clearly established. In these organizations, research and experience have determined the most efficient production methods, and the objective of low-cost production is best accomplished by having employees follow prescribed procedures. Behavioral measures are thus most often linked with Loyal Soldier and Bargain Laborer HR strategies.

In contrast, outcome measures are most common for organizations pursuing Committed Expert and Free Agent HR strategies. These organizations rely on creativity and innovation. Optimal methods for producing goods and services are often unknown. High-performing employees are expected to use their unique knowledge and skills to produce the desired outcome of delivering superior goods and services. In these cases, the outcome, or end result, is what matters most.

COMMON PROBLEMS WITH PERFORMANCE MEASURES

Objective and subjective measures, as well as outcome and behavioral measures, suffer from several potential problems. For subjective measures, bias can be introduced when humans provide ratings. People are not perfect information processors, and subjective ratings based on human judgments are often both contaminated and deficient. Objective and outcome measures are also imperfect, as they sometimes hold employees accountable for things they cannot control. Finally, all types of performance ratings can suffer from inconsistency, because performance at one point in time is likely different from performance at another time. We can thus identify the following common problems with performance appraisal measures: rater errors and bias, situational influences, and changes over time.

How Do We Know?

WHO IS MOST LIKELY TO PROVIDE ERROR-FREE RATINGS?

Do some people provide better performance measures than others? If so, who are the best raters? Kok-Yee Ng, Christine Koh, Soon Any, Jeffrey Kennedy, and Kim-Yan Chan explored ratings in the Singapore Armed Forces to answer such questions.

Military officers received ratings from supervisors, peers, and subordinates. The ratings were then examined for differences in halo and leniency (giving everyone a high score). Subordinates were more likely than peers or superiors to provide ratings with halo and leniency, and peers were more likely than supervisors to demonstrate leniency. These errors for subordinates were most pronounced when the rater held stronger beliefs in the need for hierarchy and respect for authority.

Subordinates and peers with a stronger sense of harmony and avoiding embarrassing others were also more likely to provide lenient ratings.

The Bottom Line. Some raters are more prone to errors than others. In particular, subordinates and peers appear to provide ratings with error. The authors thus conclude that organizations need to ensure that raters are trained to reduce their idiosyncratic tendencies.

Source: Kok-Yee Ng, Christine Koh, Soon Ang, Jeffrey C. Kennedy, and Kim-Yin Chan, "Rating Leniency and Halo in Multisource Feedback Ratings: Testing Cultural Assumptions of Power Distance and Individualism–Collectivism," *Journal of Applied Psychology* 96 (2011): 1033-1044.

Rater Errors

Research suggests that raters commit a number of errors when they rate employee performance. Rating errors occur when raters provide assessments that follow an undesirable pattern or when the rater does not properly account for factors that might influence assessments. As explained in the "How Do We Know?" feature, some raters are more prone to errors than others. One common error involves the pattern of results that arises when a rater dislikes separating people into categories. This leads to **central tendency error,** which is the pattern of placing almost everyone in the middle of the scale.

Another common problem occurs when a rater unintentionally compares people with one another. Suppose a rater is evaluating three employees and one of them is an outstanding performer. Observing the high performer may raise the rater's expectations so that he gives the other two employees low ratings even though their performance is above average. This type of error is called **contrast error.**

A different sort of error occurs when a rater bases an assessment on a general impression of an employee rather than on the employee's specific contributions.[47] Over an extended period, the rater observes a number of different behaviors and forms an overall judgment of the contribution of the employee. The rater may then judge specific aspects of performance—such as quality of work, quantity of work, and cooperation with others—in terms of this overall perception of the employee, rather than judging each aspect of performance separately. For instance, a rater may be quite accurate in identifying a truck driver as a good employee but may not really be aware of whether the driver is

Central tendency error
A rating error that occurs when raters give almost all employees scores in the middle of the scale.

Contrast error
A rating error that occurs when raters unknowingly allow comparisons among employees to influence ratings.

Halo error
A rating error that occurs when raters allow a general impression to influence ratings on specific dimensions of performance.

Recency error
A rating error that occurs when raters place too much emphasis on performance observed right before the measure is taken.

Primacy error
A rating error that occurs when raters place too much emphasis on performance observed at the beginning of the measurement period.

Frame-of-reference training
Training that focuses on building consistency in the way different raters observe and evaluate employee behaviors and outcomes.

Rater bias
Bias that occurs when a rater unfairly provides lower ratings to certain groups of people, such as women and minorities.

consistently on time with deliveries. When a rater provides similar ratings for all the different dimensions of performance based on a general impression, the result is **halo error.** As might be expected, some raters are more affected by halo error than others.

Yet another type of error is **recency error**, which arises when raters place too much emphasis on recent behaviors and outcomes. Here, an employee who demonstrated outstanding performance during most weeks of the performance period may receive a lower rating if performance was not as high during the week right before the ratings were obtained. It is easier for the rater to recall recent actions and outcomes, so the rater places greater emphasis on more recent data.

A related but opposite problem, **primacy error**, occurs when a rater places too much emphasis on the behavior that is first observed. For example, a sales representative who loses an important account at the beginning of the year may be given a low rating even though her performance is excellent the rest of the year. In this case, the rater makes an initial judgment and fails to adequately account for later contributions that warrant an adjustment to the initial rating. Primacy can be particularly problematic when initial performance is very high, as raters don't sufficiently adjust their ratings downward.[48]

Rater errors result in contamination and deficiency and are difficult to prevent. Rating accuracy can be improved somewhat by making raters aware of the kinds of errors that can arise. Various rating formats, which are discussed below, can also be used to reduce errors. But the most effective method for increasing rating accuracy is to help raters develop a consistent view of what represents good and bad performance.[49] This approach, often labeled **frame-of-reference training**, provides instruction and practice to help raters see different performance episodes in the same way.

An example of effective rater training for restaurant managers might go as follows. A group of raters meet to discuss descriptions of performance for a hostess in a restaurant. At the beginning of the training, one rater believes that a hostess who smiles and greets customers in a pleasant manner should be rated 4 on a 5-point scale. Another rater thinks that really connecting with the customer is important and that being pleasant and smiling represents only a 3 on the scale. Other raters have other views. The raters then discuss various aspects of performance until they arrive at a common frame of reference—an agreement on what constitutes each level of performance. This is beneficial because it makes ratings more consistent. The process also makes individual raters more aware of the behaviors and outcomes they are assessing and tends to result in appraisals that more accurately reflect actual contribution.

Rater Bias

Substantial problems occur when rater errors operate in such a way that people with certain characteristics are consistently rated lower than others. Consistently providing lower ratings to people with certain characteristics is known as **rater bias.**

A frequently asked question is whether raters give lower ratings to employees who are members of minority groups. The simple answer is yes. Ratings tend to differ depending on the race of the person being rated.[50] The reasons for these differences are, however, difficult to determine. One possible explanation is that raters give higher ratings to employees whose race is the same as theirs, but the available data do not support this simple explanation.[51] The pattern is more complex. White raters sometimes give higher ratings to white employees.

Black raters tend to give higher ratings to everyone.[52] Differences in ratings for racial groups are also greater in some occupations than others. For example, ratings for members of racial groups differ more for technical plant operations than for service or healthcare jobs.[53] The reasons behind these racial differences are unclear. However, it is not all rater bias, as racial differences are also observed for objective performance measures.[54] More research is needed to better understand the role of race in performance management.

Performance ratings can also vary for men and women. Women tend to receive lower ratings in jobs done mostly by men, such as construction.[55] Here, stereotypes about who should perform the job seem to sway rater evaluations. Citizenship performance also has different effects for men and women. When women engage in citizenship behavior by helping others, their performance ratings don't necessarily improve as a result, but their ratings go down when they withhold help. In contrast, men don't get lower ratings when they withhold help, but they get higher ratings when they engage in citizenship behavior. The likely explanation is stereotyping. Raters assume that women should be more helpful and cooperative than men. Women are punished when they don't behave in accordance with the stereotype.

Ratings thus may be biased because of both race and sex. One way to overcome bias is simply to make raters aware of it. Another solution is to ask raters to generate lists of instances where they have observed both positive and negative behaviors, and then review the list before completing ratings. Writing lists of each type of behavior seems to reduce unconscious bias from negative stereotypes.[56] Obtaining ratings from multiple sources, since it is unlikely that all the raters will have the same prejudices, is also helpful for reducing the negative impact of rater biases.

Situational Influences

Table 8.1 lists some common situational influences that can either facilitate or inhibit performance outcomes.[57] To understand such influences, suppose you have been given the task of mowing the grass at an exclusive golf resort. Strong thunderstorms roll in every day for a week and prevent you from being able to mow. At the end of the week, your supervisor, who has been away at a golf tournament, calls you and asks why the lawn has not been mowed as

Table 8.1	*Situational Factors Influencing Performance*
1. Job-Related Information—Rules, Policies, Informal Procedures	
2. Tools and Equipment—Machinery and Instruments	
3. Materials and Supplies—Ingredients and Components	
4. Budgetary Support—Financial Resources	
5. Required Services and Help from Others	
6. Task Preparation—Education and Training from Organization	
7. Time Availability—Interruptions and Alternative Obligations	
8. Work Environment—Noise, Temperature, Space, Lighting	

Source: Information from Lawrence H. Peters and Edward J. O'Connor, "Situational Constraints and Work Outcomes: The Influences of a Frequently Overlooked Construct," *Academy of Management Review* 5 (1980): 391–397.

Situational influences
Factors that affect performance but that are outside the control of the employee being rated.

requested. Of course, your answer is that the thunderstorms prevented you from completing your assigned work tasks. The thunderstorms are an example of **situational influences,** which are factors outside the control of workers that influence performance.

In the golf example, it is fairly easy to identify the situational influence that led to lower work performance. Situational factors are not always so easy to identify, but certain factors are fairly common. Another common situational factor is the actions of other people such as coworkers.[58] Clearly, these situational factors can influence the contribution an employee makes to the organization.

Research suggests that subjective ratings are frequently contaminated and deficient because raters fail to account for situational influences.[59] However, it is at least possible for raters to adjust subjective evaluations to control for situational factors.[60] Situational influences present a greater problem for objective, outcome-oriented performance measures.[61] Factors outside the control of the employee often influence production, which is the primary basis for outcome-oriented measures. For instance, one study found great variation in the amount of sales dollars taken in each week by sales representatives. Changes from week to week were largely explained by the number of referrals that the sales representative received from the central office at the beginning of the week. In this case, the measure of sales income is contaminated by the number of referrals.[62]

Although it is impossible to identify all possible situational influences, a few steps can be taken to minimize the biases they create. First, raters can be trained to take situational influences into account. Second, consistent biases, such as difficulty of a sales territory, can be identified and assessed to get a clearer picture of their impact on objective, outcome-oriented measures. Finally, a variety of different measures can be used. Combining information from a number of different measures reduces the contamination present in any single measure.

Changes over Time

Another problem with measurement is that performance may not be consistent across time. A commonly identified source of variation in behaviors and outcomes at various points in time is difference in motivation. For example, an incentive such as a special bonus may motivate employees to achieve high performance for a short period. Measuring this short-term achievement may result in an assessment that is quite different from an assessment that reflects typical performance on most days.[63] Changes in performance may also follow specific patterns of increasing or decreasing contribution.[64] The most common pattern for someone new to a job is a period of rapidly increasing performance followed by a fairly stable plateau.[65] Not everyone follows the same pattern, however. Performance for people with certain characteristics, such as conscientiousness, tends to increase more rapidly than the performance of others.[66]

Unfortunately, differences in performance across time have the potential to decrease the accuracy of the appraisal process, which causes problems in other areas of human resource management. For instance, a number of researchers have suggested that changes in performance across time may reduce the effectiveness of selection measures.[67] This might occur if cognitive ability is critical for high performance in early stages of the job, but conscientiousness is more critical once the job tasks have been mastered. The benefits of hiring people with high cognitive ability might go away after people have been on the job for a certain period of time. In this case, using performance measures taken soon after someone begins a job may result in the organization's not having a good idea about who performs well over time, which in turn may result in hiring the wrong type of employee. Another example involves using appraisal results to determine training needs. Poor decisions about training may be made if the performance measure fails to capture aspects of performance that change over time.

How can organizations deal with appraisal issues related to variability of performance over time? Some evidence shows that supervisor ratings can account for variance over time by capturing trends, suggesting that subjective assessments may present a somewhat acceptable approach.[68] A specific solution to the time problem is to obtain performance measures at many different points in time. Another possibility is to use a measure that reflects what is most important to the organization. For some tasks, such as working on an assembly line, typical performance may be most relevant. For other tasks, such as developing a marketing plan, maximum performance may be more important. The key is to base the timing of performance measurement on the nature of the desired contribution.

RATING FORMATS

Rating format concerns the type of instrument used to obtain ratings. Several different formats, most of which are probably familiar to you, exist for assessing performance. Each of the formats has strengths and weaknesses, and no method is always better than the others. The key to a successful appraisal is to choose the format that best accomplishes the purpose of the appraisal.

Narrative Ratings

One format is the narrative rating. Organizations that use **narrative ratings** ask supervisors or other raters to simply provide a written description of performance. You have experienced such a rating if a professor has written a note evaluating a paper you have turned in. A benefit of narrative ratings is that they can be tailored to describe specific, and perhaps unique, aspects of performance. A stock analyst may have a specific set of goals and circumstances that does not apply to other analysts. In this case, the narrative rating allows the analyst's supervisor to make comments and evaluations that apply only to that analyst. Such comments can also be very helpful for improving future performance.

Personalized ratings can, however, create problems when it comes to comparing the performance of different individuals. The lack of consistent measurement makes it difficult to determine which employees are high and low performers, which in turn creates problems for training and compensation. Narrative ratings are thus best for providing feedback in organizations where decisions related to training, promotions, and compensation are not based on comparisons with other employees.

Graphic Ratings

Perhaps the most common rating format uses graphic scales. With **graphic ratings,** raters are asked to provide a numerical rating for a number of different dimensions of work performance.

Narrative ratings
A rating format that asks raters to provide a written description of an employee's performance.

Graphic ratings
A rating format that asks raters to provide a numerical score for an employee on each of several dimensions of performance.

Graphical ratings can be designed to measure either outcomes or behaviors. Common dimensions of performance include quality of output, quantity of output, cooperation with others, and skill development. For each performance dimension, the rater is asked to place the employee in a specific rating category. Most scales have between three and seven rating categories, each represented by a number. For example, a scale with three categories may include a rating of 1 for unsatisfactory performance, 2 for average performance, and 3 for outstanding performance.

One benefit of graphic ratings is that all employees are rated on a common set of dimensions, which makes it easy to compare employees with one another. A problem is that some performance dimensions may not apply to some employees. Raters who use graphical scales are also prone to rater errors, as described earlier. In many cases, raters who use graphical ratings end up giving most employees a similar score—the central tendency error. This tendency to rate people similarly makes graphical ratings best suited for organizations that are pursuing cost-reduction strategies and encouraging employee parity. Figure 8.4 shows an example of a graphic rating scale.

Forced Rankings

Forced ranking
A rating format that asks raters to directly compare the contribution of an employee with the contribution of other employees.

Another rating format is **forced ranking,** which occurs when a rater is required to rank all employees. For example, an office manager might be asked to rank the office's five secretaries in order from highest performer to lowest performer. A class ranking in which all students are ordered from highest GPA to lowest GPA is another example of such a measure.

The forced ranking technique eliminates central tendency error and provides clear guidance for organizations that want to give promotions and pay raises to top performers. Many supervisors are uncomfortable with rankings, however, because a high proportion of their employees perform at essentially the same level. Forced ranking formats are thus best for organizations that encourage competition among employees, which makes them most suitable for organizations that use merit-based performance management to pursue differentiation strategies.

Directions: Please circle the number that you feel best describes this worker's performance for each work dimension.

Worker's Name _____

	Unsatisfactory	Marginal	Satisfactory	Good	Outstanding	
Quality of Work Performed	☹ 1	2	3	4	5	☺
Quantity of Work Performed	☹ 1	2	3	4	5	☺
Timeliness of Completing Work	☹ 1	2	3	4	5	☺
Cooperation with Others	☹ 1	2	3	4	5	☺
Innovation and Creativity	☹ 1	2	3	4	5	☺

Figure 8.4 Graphic Rating Scale.

Forced Distributions

A rating format that combines the graphic rating with the forced rating is a forced distribution. As mentioned earlier, this format requires that a certain percentage of employees be placed in each rating category. A supervisor of computer programmers, for instance, may be required to rate 50 percent of them as average, 30 percent as outstanding, and 20 percent as unsatisfactory. Raters tend not to like forced distributions because they perceive them as less fair and more difficult to complete.[69] Yet, this format represents a compromise between the graphical format, which allows everyone to receive the same ranking, and the forced ranking format, which requires a different score for each person being rated. Because they encourage competition, forced distribution formats emphasize merit and are most suitable for organizations pursuing differentiation strategies.

CONCEPT CHECK

1. *How do contamination and deficiency affect performance ratings?*
2. *What is the difference between objective and subjective measures? How do outcome and behavioral measures differ?*
3. *What are three common problems that affect performance ratings?*
4. *What are the strengths and weaknesses of various rating formats?*

LEARNING OBJECTIVE 4

Who Should Measure Performance?

Students' performance is usually measured by a professor. What would happen if students rated their own performance? Would their grades be higher than the grades given by the professor? What about having other members of the class determine each student's grade? Would that be fair? Would everyone's grade be the same? If students received ratings from the professor, other students, and themselves, how similar would those different types of ratings be? These are important issues related to who should carry out performance appraisals. As you will see, it's a good idea to have more than one source of performance measurement.

MULTISOURCE PERFORMANCE RATINGS

Just as grades usually come from professors, employee ratings usually come from supervisors. Most organizations place the primary responsibility for managing employees with supervisors, making performance appraisal one of their most important tasks. In a majority of cases, this makes sense, because supervisors are in a good position to evaluate what tasks need to be done, whether the employee is performing the right tasks, and how well the tasks are being performed. However, a supervisor may not see the complete picture, and supervisors have biases that can unfairly influence the ratings. In other words, ratings from supervisors suffer from both deficiency and contamination. Gathering information and ratings from multiple sources is thus a key to effective performance appraisal.

The process of obtaining performance ratings from multiple sources is known as multisource ratings, or sometimes as 360-degree appraisal, based on the notion that a completed circle has 360 degrees. **multisource performance ratings** seek to evaluate performance by obtaining information from multiple raters who have different perspectives. Figure 8.5 shows a typical 360-degree rating approach. Ratings are usually obtained not only from supervisors but also from coworkers and the employees themselves. If the person being rated is a supervisor, ratings are also obtained from the subordinates he or she supervises. Some organizations obtain ratings from customers and suppliers as well. As discussed in the accompanying "How Do We Know?" feature, multisource ratings are more commonly adopted in countries such as Denmark and Israel, where hierarchy and power differences between people are minimized.

In summary, ratings from multiple sources give a more complete picture of performance and usually provide better guidance about what the employee can do to improve.[70] These benefits can be enhanced by having the various raters meet together and discuss their evaluations.[71] Employees also report higher satisfaction with the performance management process when multisource ratings are used.[72]

Multisource performance ratings
Performance ratings obtained from a variety of raters such as customers, coworkers, supervisors, and self.

RATING SOURCE DIFFERENCES

One concern about multisource ratings is that the measures from different sources often do not agree.[73] In particular, researchers have found that self-assessments tend to differ from ratings provided by others.[74] In some cases,

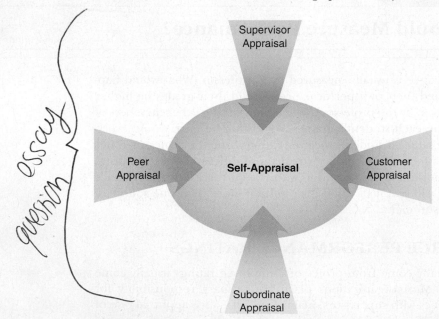

essay question

Figure 8.5 360-Degree Performance Appraisal. This is an example of multisource performance ratings.

How Do We Know?

IS PERFORMANCE MANAGEMENT THE SAME AROUND THE WORLD?

Are methods of managing employee performance the same everywhere? Are companies located in different countries likely to have the same processes? Do these processes have the same effect on outcomes such as employee attendance and turnover? Hilla Peretz and Yizhak Fried sought to answer these questions by exploring the performance management practices with two samples of companies. One set of responses came from 5,991 organizations located in 21 different countries, and the other sample came from 4,878 organizations located in 16 countries.

The most senior human resource manager in each company was asked to complete a questionnaire focused on issues such as whether a formal performance management system was being used, what percentage of employees was evaluated, the number of raters who provided ratings, and whether the appraisal was used to make decisions about individuals (e.g., compensation decisions) or the broader organization (e.g., broad training needs). Managers also provided ratings of annual turnover and absenteeism. These ratings were then linked to data that captured differences in country culture such as power distance (acceptance of inequality and hierarchy), future orientation (planning and delayed gratification),

individualism/collectivism (individual rights verses group loyalty), and uncertainty avoidance (desire for predictability and rules).

The desire for planning and control results in greater use of formal performance assessments in countries with higher future orientation and uncertainty avoidance. Companies are most likely to use multisource ratings when they are located in countries with lower power distance, higher future orientation, and a greater sense of individualism. Moreover, multisource ratings help decrease absenteeism and turnover when operating in these countries.

The Bottom Line. Societal culture practices influence how companies manage the performance of employees. Practices are not the same around the world, and companies with practices more congruent with the culture of their countries reported lower absenteeism and turnover. Professors Peretz and Fried thus conclude that human resource practices should be aligned with broader cultural and strategic objectives.

Source: Hilla Peretz and Yitzhak Fried, "National Cultures, Performance Appraisal Practices, and Organizational Absenteeism and Turnover: A Study Across 21 Countries," *Journal of Applied Psychology* 97 (2012): 448-459.

particularly in cultures that value modesty, self-ratings can be lower than ratings by others.[75] But in most cases, self-ratings are higher than ratings provided by supervisors and peers.[76] Interestingly, self-ratings are still high but more similar to ratings provided by others for women, as well as for employees who are younger, less experienced, more educated, and white. Part of this effect occurs because experienced, nonwhite men seem to overrate their own performance more than others. In addition, ratings from others tend to be lower for people who are older and less educated, contributing to a larger difference between self-ratings and ratings from others for older, less-educated employees.[77] These issues reflect potential biases in self-ratings. Another problem is that people with lower performance are the very ones who are less accurate in their self-appraisals. Lack of perception that keeps some employees from performing well also makes them less accurate in their self-assessments.[78]

Self-ratings and ratings from others differ for several reasons. One reason is that people generally have a self-serving bias—that is, they want to see themselves in the best possible light. People may also rate themselves higher because they have more opportunities than anyone else to observe their own work contributions. Finally, there may be disagreement over standards.[79] For this reason, self-ratings and ratings from others become more similar when organizations establish clear standards to describe high performance and when the employees being rated have more knowledge about the performance appraisal system.[80] Perceptions of performance also tend to be more similar when the person being rated and the other rater are both highly conscientious. This similarity may arise because both raters focus mostly on task contributions, leading to increased objectivity.[81]

Whereas self-ratings and ratings from others often differ, ratings from peers and supervisors tend to be quite similar.[82] The one exception occurs when the person being rated performs very poorly; peer ratings in this case are not as low as ratings from supervisors.[83] Evidently, many peers are not willing to give low ratings to people with whom they work closely, even when those people might deserve low ratings. Regardless of whether peer ratings are consistent with supervisor ratings, simply obtaining peer ratings can be beneficial. In workgroups that use peer ratings, group members have better relationships with each other and focus more on task completion.[84]

Even though ratings from supervisors and peers are similar, they are not identical, suggesting that perceptions of performance may not always be consistent. Indeed, even assessments from raters representing the same source—such as ratings from a number of different peers—tend to disagree somewhat.[85] Furthermore, ratings from any individual are likely to suffer from various biases, as explained earlier. Fortunately, many of the biases of one rater can be offset by different biases of another rater. Each of the ratings can focus on a somewhat different aspect of performance and thereby provide unique information about how well an employee is performing.[86] Obtaining ratings from multiple sources and raters thus provides the best picture of overall contribution to the organization.

CONCEPT CHECK

1. *Who usually provides evaluations for multisource performance ratings?*
2. *How are self-ratings of performance different from ratings provided by others?*

LEARNING OBJECTIVE 5

How Should Feedback Be Provided?

Effective performance management requires more than simply measuring employee contributions. If such measurements are to result in improved performance, employees must receive information about how well they are

Technology in HR

FEEDBACK THROUGH TWITTER AND FACEBOOK

Many employees do not want to wait until their formal performance appraisal interview to receive feedback. They get this information in real time from the people in their online networks. For example, after making a presentation, an employee may tweet to ask others in the room how he or she did. The immediate response from friends is often helpful for improving future behavior. Of course, the accuracy of the feedback depends on who receives the initial tweet and how willing they are to be honest with the presenter.

Wiki technology provides another mechanism for receiving feedback. A manager posts feedback and then allows others to add their perceptions.

Some employees might be uncomfortable receiving feedback in such a public way, but online discussion can open communication channels.

For years managers and trainers have wondered about ways to provide employees with more ongoing feedback. Although social networking sites such as Twitter and Facebook were not developed for this specific purpose, they do provide an easy means for providing rapid, ongoing information. Of course, businesses are also developing dedicated software that can be tailored to the specific task of providing employees with feedback.

Source: Pat Galagan, "Dude, How'd I Do?" *T+D* 63, no. 7 (2009): 26.

---

performing. That is, they must be given **feedback.** Trying to improve performance without feedback can be highly frustrating. Just imagine taking an algebra test and never finding out which problems you solved correctly. You might become aggravated and unwilling to continue working problems. You would also be unlikely to get much better at algebra until you learned what you might be doing wrong. In the same way, employees who do not receive feedback tend to become dissatisfied and perform at suboptimal levels. Feedback is thus desired by most employees. In fact, the accompanying "Technology in HR" feature describes how many younger employees are using Twitter and Facebook to ask for feedback.

Several hundred studies have examined the effect of feedback on performance and have found that people who receive feedback generally perform better than people who do not. Before discussing specific ways to make feedback more effective, it is thus important to note that feedback can have a lasting positive influence on performance. Effective feedback reduces perceptions of negative workplace politics and thereby increases worker morale.[87] Improvement from feedback is greatest when the person receiving the information feedback perceives a real need to change and believes that he or she has the skill and ability to do what is needed to perform at a higher level.[88] Formal feedback meetings, usually held once or twice a year, provide a setting for communicating these matters. Much of the benefit of feedback comes from two-way discussions between supervisors and employees that is created during feedback meetings. Employees who meet with their evaluators gain more from feedback than do employees who are only given written appraisals.[89] However, in some cases, receiving feedback actually decreases performance.[90] It is thus important to pay attention to how feedback is provided.

Feedback
Information given to employees to communicate how well they are performing.

PROVIDING POSITIVE AND NEGATIVE FEEDBACK

Positive feedback
Information that communicates things that an employee is doing well.

Negative feedback
Information that communicates things an employee needs to change in order to improve.

The "Building Strength Through HR" feature illustrates benefits from providing feedback. Of course, feedback can be classified as either positive or negative. Messages communicating high performance convey **positive feedback**. A sales representative who exceeds her sales quota receives positive feedback when her supervisor congratulates her for doing so well. Messages communicating low performance and a need to improve convey **negative feedback.** A parts assembler receives negative feedback when a supervisor tells him that one-half of the components he produced failed the quality test.

The model shown in Figure 8.6 explains how positive and negative feedback relate to motivation. Positive feedback leads to higher motivation when it is linked by employees and supervisors with ongoing expectations for continued high performance. Positive feedback, then, creates a sense of accomplishment that encourages sustained effort as long as employees have goals that provide them with the opportunity to further excel.

Building Strength Through HR

WHIRLPOOL CORPORATION

Whirlpool Corporation is an international manufacturer of household appliances that employs 71,000 people and has annual sales over $18 billion. Performance management is an important part of the overall effort to increase productivity at Whirlpool. A number of years ago, the company streamlined its performance management process to help managers save time. Most feedback was provided through email exchanges. Unfortunately, the streamlined process was ineffective. Whirlpool thus revised its feedback process to include more face-to-face interaction. Specific features of the new appraisal and feedback process include the following:

- Managers are required to meet with each employee at least four times during the year to discuss performance and provide feedback.
- Employees write personal objectives that they share with supervisors. At least one objective must focus on a stretch goal for exceptional performance.
- Managers now spend a significant amount of time coaching and developing employees, which organizational leaders identify as the true role of a manager.

Sources: Bill Stopper, "Innovation at Whirlpool: Embedment and Sustainability," *Human Resource Planning* 29, no. 3 (2006): 28; Erin White, "For Relevance, Firms Revamp Worker Reviews," *Wall Street Journal,* July 17, 2006, p. B1; CEC Council, *CIO* 23, no. 6 (2010).

Ethan Miller/Getty Images

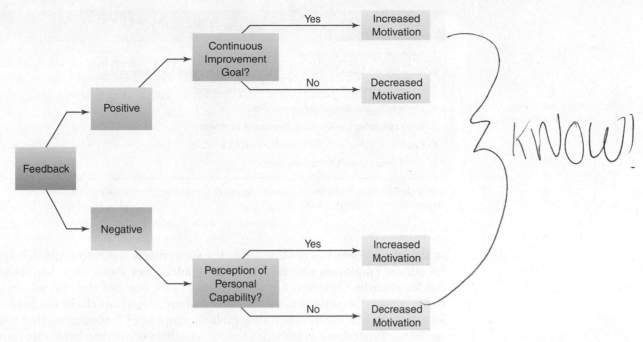

Figure 8.6 Effects of Positive and Negative Feedback. *Source:* Information from Avraham N. Kluger and Angelo DeNisi, "The Effects of Feedback Interventions on Performance: A Historical Review, A Meta-Analysis, and a Preliminary Feedback Intervention Theory," *Psychological Bulletin* 119(1996): 254–284.

The influence of negative feedback on performance is somewhat less clear. Employees who perceive negative feedback as criticism become less motivated and more likely to experience conflict with others.[91] The basic problem is that people become defensive when they hear that they are not performing as well as expected. As shown in Figure 8.6, the initial reaction of employees who have received negative feedback is to increase their effort. But they will continue to put forth greater effort only if they experience success or believe that success is likely. In other words, negative feedback only improves performance when people are confident that they can do what is necessary to improve.[92] Building confidence and helping people see that they have the skills necessary to improve is therefore one important consideration in making sure that negative feedback improves performance.

EFFECTIVELY COMMUNICATING METHODS FOR IMPROVEMENT

Of course feedback is helpful only if it results in employees doing things differently. Feedback should thus be communicated in ways that increase the likelihood that employees will actually change their behavior. People are most likely to accept and act on feedback when they perceive that it is accurate, suggesting that the person giving the feedback must be seen as credible.[93] The first key to effectively communicating feedback is thus to build a relationship

Table 8.2	*Conducting Appraisal Interviews*
1. Place the employee at ease with small talk.	
2. Allow the employee to share his or her perspective before you share yours.	
3. Be positive and use action-oriented behavioral terms.	
4. Use specific and measurable expressions.	
5. Avoid comparing the employee to yourself or others.	
6. Balance negatives with positives; start with a positive.	
7. Spend time planning for improvement.	

Source: Information from David Javitch, "Appraising Employee Performance," *Management Services* 50, no. 3 (2006): 19–20.

so that the receiver has confidence in the supervisor's ability to provide helpful advice. Employees who feel that their leader cares about them and looks out for their best interests are more likely to seek out and respond to negative feedback.[94] Feedback is also improved when supervisors clarify the behaviors they are looking for when they evaluate employees,[95] suggesting that it is useful for supervisors to provide clear descriptions of specific behaviors they hope to observe. For example, a sales supervisor who wants an employee to be more proactive in preparing for meetings with clients might describe specific behaviors, such as gathering relevant sales figures and preparing potential responses to clients' excuses for not making a purchase. Supervisors also communicate effectively when they continue to build relationships by treating employees as individuals and taking into account personal circumstances. In the end, then, feedback is more likely to be accepted when the person giving it has a good relationship with the receiver and when the message is clear enough that the receiver knows exactly what to do to improve.[96] Table 8.2 provides several keys for successfully communicating feedback.

The importance of providing clear direction is captured in the principle of **feedback specificity,** which concerns the level of detail in the message. Specific feedback provides detailed descriptions of actions and outcomes and is good for communicating what someone has done to achieve success. In addition, specific feedback facilitates quick learning of skills when the skills are clearly defined and carried out in environments that do not change.[97] Providing a very detailed description of the optimal steps for bolting a bumper on a car is an example. Carefully describing each and every detail is helpful because the process has been thoroughly studied and optimal methods of performance have been identified. Furthermore, bolting car bumpers onto cars is a process that doesn't vary much from environment to environment.

Specific feedback is not always optimal, however. Less-specific feedback encourages people to explore and try alternative methods for accomplishing tasks. In some cases, giving very specific feedback can inhibit learning. An example might involve giving specific feedback about how to operate a properly functioning machine. The feedback is helpful as long as the machine operates as it should. However, the specific feedback may inhibit the machine operator from exploring different methods of interacting with the machine. This may prevent the operator from learning more about how the machine operates.[98]

We can conclude, then, that specific feedback is best for communicating how to do clearly defined tasks that do not change. However, specific feedback

Feedback specificity
The level of detail in communication, which can range from broad information about overall performance to specific information about certain actions.

may discourage employees from learning that extends beyond knowing how to follow prescribed procedures. To improve performance in such instances, it may be better to provide feedback that is not so specific that it suggests that there is only one best way of doing something.

Another factor that influences whether someone benefits from feedback is the extent to which the receiver can do what is necessary to improve. Feedback is more likely to be accepted when it focuses on things that an individual can actually change.[99] Focusing on factors outside the control of the employee increases frustration and does not provide a path for improving future performance. A store clerk who receives negative feedback because of low sales figures during a snow storm, for example, is left with a sense of confusion and little guidance for how to improve future performance. Supervisors are thus most effective when they separate out situational influences and communicate about issues the employee can control.

REDUCING NEGATIVE EMOTIONAL RESPONSES

Think of a time when you received a very poor grade on an assignment or exam. What was your initial reaction? Were you angry? Disappointed? Did you feel like a failure? Perhaps you wanted to quit trying. Were you upset with the professor who wrote and graded the exam? Did you commit yourself to work harder and make sure you received a better grade the next time?

People who receive feedback, particularly negative feedback, experience a wide range of emotions. These emotions have a lot to do with the effect of feedback on performance. Feedback that is channeled through positive emotions generally improves performance, whereas feedback that is channeled through negative emotions often causes performance to become worse.[100]

Negative emotions such as fear, anger, sadness, and guilt harm performance because they focus attention away from future tasks. Feedback is thus most likely to lead to better performance when it is presented in ways that do not bring out negative emotions.[101] Effective leaders who have good relationships with employees are able to give feedback that doesn't make recipients feel negative.[102] Ideas for presenting feedback in ways that reduce negative emotion are shown in Table 8.3.

Positive emotions that accompany feedback generally focus on learning and skill development. In addition, feedback that specifically teaches new skills can be effective for showing employees what they can do to improve future performance.[103] Organizations that develop a culture of providing ongoing feedback that emphasizes improvement rather than criticism are thus most effective in communicating methods for enhancing performance.[104]

Table 8.3	*Giving Employee Feedback*
1. Focus comments on the task rather than the person.	
2. Combine feedback with goals for improvement.	
3. Describe behaviors in an unemotional manner.	
4. Focus on what is observed rather than underlying causes.	
5. Remain nonjudgmental.	
6. Provide clear examples to support points.	

Individuals who approach life with an orientation toward learning and improving themselves benefit most from receiving feedback.[105] People with positive self-concepts are also more likely to react positively to feedback. When employees have a strong sense of self-worth and confidence in their abilities, they generally perceive negative feedback as intended to improve performance rather than to criticize and tear down.[106] Hiring skilled workers who have a desire to continuously improve is thus one way to ensure successful performance management.

BUILDING HIGH EXPECTATIONS

Pygmalion effect
A process whereby performance increases when leaders have high expectations about the skills and capabilities of followers.

One interesting aspect of feedback is its potential to communicate high expectations. Performance often rises to the level of expectations that leaders have for their followers. The effect by which high expectations lead to better performance is often labeled the **Pygmalion effect**. A number of studies have shown that the Pygmalion effect operates in work organizations where high expectations translate into improved job performance.[107] Supervisors who perceive their employees as having exceptional ability communicate greater confidence, which in turn raises the employees' performance.[108] Supervisors can therefore improve their feedback by clearly communicating high expectations for future performance. How do supervisors communicate high expectations? By telling employees that they have confidence in their abilities and by providing models so that employees can see that others have succeeded.[109]

CONCEPT CHECK

1. *What are keys to effectively giving positive feedback? How should negative feedback be given?*
2. *What can be done to reduce negative emotional reactions to feedback?*

A MANAGER'S PERSPECTIVE REVISITED

IN THE MANAGER'S PERSPECTIVE THAT OPENED THE CHAPTER, TYRONE WAS CONCERNED ABOUT PERFORMANCE RATINGS AND FEEDBACK. HE WONDERED WHETHER HIS RATINGS WERE ACCURATE, AND HE FELT ANXIOUS ABOUT THE NEED TO COMMUNICATE LOW RATINGS TO SOME EMPLOYEES. FOLLOWING ARE THE ANSWERS TO THE "WHAT DO YOU THINK?" QUIZ THAT FOLLOWED THE MANAGER'S PERSPECTIVE. WERE YOU ABLE TO CORRECTLY IDENTIFY THE TRUE STATEMENTS? CAN YOU DO BETTER NOW ?

1. Employee rating systems are of no value unless at least some employees receive low ratings. FALSE. *Parity-based rating systems are helpful for organizations with strategies that do not benefit from identifying differences among employees whose performance is adequate.*

2. When completing performance ratings, it is best to focus only on whether an employee completes tasks and not on how well he or she works with others. FALSE. *Citizenship performance and counterproductive performance are important aspects of contribution that should be reflected in ratings.*

3. Objective measures of performance, which are represented by things that can be counted, are better than subjective measures such as supervisor judgments. FALSE. *Like subjective measures, objective measures can suffer from contamination and deficiency.*

4. Self-ratings of performance are usually higher than ratings provided by others. TRUE. *Because of self-serving biases, people usually give themselves ratings that are higher than the ratings others give them.*

5. Employee performance increases when supervisors communicate high expectations. TRUE. *Performance in organizational settings is higher when leaders believe employees are capable and communicate their high expectations to the employees.*

Although conducting performance appraisals is a difficult task, Tyrone's effort is likely to pay off. Tyrone should take into account all aspects of performance. Given his need to improve store performance, he should also differentiate employees so that the individuals who are not performing at an adequate level can be identified. As explained in this chapter, carefully appraising performance and giving feedback to employees are key methods for improving organizational productivity.

SUMMARY

LEARNING OBJECTIVE 1

How is performance management strategic?

Merit-based systems use relative measures and forced distributions to recognize high performance. Because they encourage competition and stretch goals to foster innovation and high quality, merit-based systems are usually adopted in organizations that pursue either Free Agent or Committed Expert HR strategies. Parity-based systems incorporate absolute measures and free distributions to encourage cooperation. These systems are usually less costly and can recognize most employees as high performers, which aligns them most closely with Bargain Laborer and Loyal Soldier HR strategies.

LEARNING OBJECTIVE 2

What is performance?

Job performance represents the contribution individuals make to an organization. Most specific measures of job performance are related to one another and combine to create a general performance factor that represents overall contribution to the organization. Task performance, citizenship performance, and counterproductive performance represent three main dimensions of the general performance factor. Task performance contributes to the actual production of goods and services. Employees who excel at task performance need both declarative knowledge (an understanding of what needs to be done) and procedural knowledge and skill (the ability to perform the necessary actions). Citizenship performance contributes to the social and psychological environment of the organization. Organizational citizenship behavior benefits the entire organization, whereas interpersonal citizenship behavior is directed toward specific individuals. Counterproductive performance harms the organization. Production and property deviance are forms of counterproductive performance directed toward the entire organization. Political deviance and personal aggression are forms of counterproductive performance that are directed toward specific individuals.

LEARNING OBJECTIVE 3

How is performance measured?

The goal of performance appraisal is accurate portrayal of each employee's contribution to an organization. Appraisal measures that measure things unrelated to contribution suffer from contamination. Measures that fail to capture things that do relate to contribution suffer from deficiency.

Organizations use a variety of methods to appraise performance. Objective performance measures are based on counts of behaviors and outcomes, while subjective measures are based on judgments from raters. Outcome measures focus on end results, whereas behavior measures assess employees' actions. Each type of measure may suffer from contamination and deficiency.

Performance ratings suffer from a number of problems. Raters may commit various errors, including central tendency error, contrast error, halo error, recency error, and primacy error. Rating errors that result in consistently lower scores for people with certain characteristics suffer from rater bias. Objective ratings are particularly susceptible to situational influences, which are factors outside the control of employees. In addition, performance frequently changes across time, so an assessment at a given time may not accurately reflect overall performance. Various rating formats have strengths and weaknesses. Because of these problems, organizations tend to adopt a combination of measures that operate together to provide a more accurate picture of overall contribution.

LEARNING OBJECTIVE 4

Who should measure performance?

Performance ratings should be obtained from multiple sources. An example of an effective measurement of this sort is the multisource performance rating, which includes information not only from supervisors but also from coworkers, subordinates, customers, and employees themselves. Each of these sources can provide information about different aspects of an employee's contribution to the organization.

LEARNING OBJECTIVE 5

How should feedback be provided?

Feedback provides information to employees so that they know how well they are performing. Feedback is most effective when the employee receiving it perceives a need to change and believes in his or her ability to do what is needed for improvement. Positive feedback increases performance when it is linked to goals for continued improvement. Negative feedback increases performance when the individuals receiving the feedback are confident in their abilities. Specific feedback is good for communicating how to accomplish well-defined tasks. However, providing very specific feedback can stifle learning and exploration. Feedback should be presented in a way that reduces negative emotions. An organization can nurture positive emotions by developing a culture of ongoing feedback that encourages continuous learning and development. Leaders can also improve performance by communicating high expectations for followers.

KEY TERMS

DISCUSSION QUESTIONS

1. Would you prefer working under a merit-based or parity-based performance management system?
2. How do you think employees might react to a change from a parity system to a merit system? How about a change from a merit system to a parity system?
3. Which do you think is most important: task performance, citizenship performance, or counterproductive performance? Why?
4. Have you ever observed an employee with high task performance but low citizenship performance? If so, describe that situation. If not, describe a scenario in which you think such performance might occur.
5. Why do you think instances of counterproductive performance are rising? What do you think should be done to decrease counterproductive performance? Is teaching ethics in management classes a good solution?
6. What are typical sources of contamination and deficiency in objective measures of job performance?
7. What are some situational influences that affect your performance as a student? Would it be fair for professors to take into account situational influences when assigning grades?
8. What factors might explain differences between coworker and supervisor ratings?
9. How do you react to negative feedback? What might you do to help yourself and others benefit more from negative feedback?
10. Why do we treat people we think have high ability differently from people we think have low ability?

EXAMPLE CASE | *Medical Center*

This healthcare organization provides a wide array of services including inpatient services, transitional care services, and outpatient treatment and testing.

A few years ago, the facility changed its performance appraisal methodology. It shifted from a subjective performance appraisal system to a more objective rating system that focused on the actions and behaviors of the employee. This shift can be considered a good move because the use of behavior-based scales tends to overcome evaluation errors that plague more subjective evaluations. Employee evaluations in this organization were performed once a year.

The performance appraisal system was instituted in this healthcare organization as a four-step process:

Step 1: The employee performs a self-appraisal first by completing an appraisal sheet and then submitting it to his or her supervisor. Employees generally welcome use of self-appraisal, and it tends to decrease defensiveness about the process.

Step 2: The supervisor then responds to the same questions the employee had previously answered based on his or her perceptions and observations of the employee's performance.

Step 3: Finally, the supervisor and employee meet and discuss the ratings on the evaluation.

Step 4: The results of the evaluation are intended to then be used as a guiding tool to determine the annual raise of the employee.

The questions in the performance evaluation questionnaire were divided into two sections. The first section was based on the overall organizational standards that had been set for the entire hospital. Areas addressed in this section include professionalism, efficiency, quality of work, respect, and service. Every employee, full-time and part-time, has to complete this section of the performance appraisal. The second section of the appraisal consisted of various competencies for each individual position. These competencies were specific to the tasks required to fulfill the duties of the individual in their respective positions. The competencies, varying greatly from position to position, were based strictly on duties required for that position. This is important, as having similarly situated employees evaluated on like criteria improves the consistency of the appraisal process.

In this healthcare organization, both the employee and the supervisor were instructed on the evaluation instrument to rate the employee on each of the areas on the following scale:

0 = Not Applicable
1 = Does Not Meet Expectations
2 = Meets Expectations
3 = Exceeds Expectations

This system was implemented to improve performance appraisals and make them more objective. The use of the same evaluation form throughout the organization improved the consistency in the evaluation process.

The healthcare organization also used some guidelines regarding what should be done if an employee obtained a certain score. Here is a brief description of the organization's policies. If the person being rated received a mark of 1 or 3, then documentation had to be provided to justify that rating. Also, if the employee was given a rating of 1 by the supervisor, then some method of learning was to be designed to help the employee to achieve a level of meeting expectations. Following this, the employee was to be reevaluated in this area and was required to demonstrate abilities to meet expectations.

QUESTIONS

1. Do you think the new system is really more objective?
2. Why do you think the organization requires documentation for certain ratings?
3. What strengths do you see in the new system? What weaknesses do you see in the process?

Source: Ashish Chandra and Zachary D. Frank, "Utilization of Performance Appraisal Systems in Health Care Organizations and Improvement Strategies for Supervisors," *The Health Care Manager* 23, no. 1 (2004): 25–40. [Used with permission.]

DISCUSSION CASE   *Reliable Underwriters*

Reliable Underwriters is a risk management firm that provides insurance services to large organizations. Part of its operation is a claims-processing center that employs 156 clerical workers. These workers interact with clients to answer questions and provide information about the status of claims. Reliable has a corporate objective of obtaining the highest possible customer satisfaction ratings. However, recent customer satisfaction surveys suggest that some of the clerical workers are not adequately meeting clients' needs.

As part of an initiative to increase customer satisfaction, the management team of the claims processing center has decided to change the performance appraisal process. In the past, ratings have been made on a 5-point scale. A score of 5 represented outstanding performance, a score of 1 represented unacceptable performance, and a score of 3 represented average performance. Last year, 135 employees received a score of 4. Only 3 received a score of 5, and only 2 received the lowest rating. Since almost everyone receives the same rating, employees in the claims-processing center have little concern about being evaluated. For the most part, they see performance appraisal simply as a nuisance. However, the newly proposed process will create major changes.

The main change will be the use of a forced distribution. Each supervisor must rate at least 20 percent of employees as outstanding and at least 10 percent as unacceptable. This forced distribution is expected to clearly identify top performers. Low performers will also be identified and encouraged to either improve or seek employment elsewhere.

QUESTIONS

1. Do you predict that the forced distribution will increase customer satisfaction? Why or why not?
2. Which clerical workers do you think will most strongly oppose the change?
3. How do you think supervisors will react to the proposed change?
4. What problems with contamination and deficiency could occur with the forced distribution ratings?

EXPERIENTIAL EXERCISE — *Assessing Performance in Sports*

Visit an Internet site containing performance data for professional athletes. Examples include the following:

National Football League: www.nfl.com/stats
Major League Baseball: http://sports.espn.go.com/mlb/statistics
National Hockey League: www.nhl.com/ice/statshome.htm#?navid=nav-sts-main
National Basketball Association: www.nba.com/statistics

Examine the statistics for individual players and teams, and answer the following questions.

1. How are these measures of performance deficient and contaminated?
2. Do the statistical measures capture behaviors or outcomes?
3. What statistics might you add to measure citizenship performance?
4. Choose five players and look at their statistics across multiple years. How stable is their performance?
5. Does high individual performance equate with high team performance? Can you identify individual players with good personal statistics whose teams are unsuccessful?

INTERACTIVE EXPERIENTIAL EXERCISE

Performance Appraisal: Delivering Positive and Negative Feedback at Global Telecommunications
http://www.wiley.com/college/sc/stewart

Access the companion website to test your knowledge by completing a Global Telecommunications interactive role-playing exercise.

In this exercise it is performance appraisal time for Global Telecommunications. In the past, the company has had problems with several managers who have either failed to complete appraisals of their employees, failed to distinguish among employees in any meaningful way, or failed to evaluate the appropriate information. The company has asked you to modify its appraisal program and to train managers on the benefits and techniques of good performance management programs. In particular, top management wants you to help the company better achieve its Committed Expert HR strategy. How will you modify the program and gain the needed buy-in from individual managers? •

ENDNOTES

1. Robert Rodgers and John E. Hunter, "Impact of Management by Objectives on Organizational Productivity," *Journal of Applied Psychology* 76 (1991): 323–336.
2. Roger C. Mayer and James H. Davis, "The Effect of Performance Appraisal System on Trust for Management: A Field Quasi-Experiment," *Journal of Applied Psychology* 84 (1999): 123–136.
3. Brian D. Cawley, Lisa M. Keeping, and Paul E. Levy, "Participation in the Performance Appraisal Process and Employee Reactions: A Meta-Analytic Review of Field Investigations," *Journal of Applied Psychology* 83 (1998): 615–633.
4. Geoffrey Colvin, "What Makes GE Great," *Fortune* 153, Issue 4 (2006): 90–96.
5. Ann Pomeroy, "CEO of GE Values People, HR," *HR Magazine* 52 (2007): 12.
6. Betsy Morris and Geoffrey Colvin, "The GE Mystique," *Fortune* 153, Issue 4 (2006): 98–102.
7. Jena McGregor, "The Struggle to Measure Performance," *BusinessWeek* 3966, January 9, 2006, 26–28.
8. Diane Brady, "Secrets of an HR Superstar: On the Eve of Retiring, GE's Bill Conaty Offers Tips on Nurturing Leaders in Your Organization," *BusinessWeek*, April 9, 2007, 66.
9. Steven Kerr and Steffen Landauer, "Using Stretch Goals to Promote Organizational Performance and

Personal Growth: General Electric and Goldman Sachs," *Academy of Management Executive* 18 (2004): 134–138.

10. Thomas D. Cairns, "Talent Management at Homeland Security: A Corporate Model Suggests a Recipe for Success," *Employee Relations Today,* Fall 2009, 19–26.

11. McGregor, "The Struggle to Measure Performance."

12. Peter Bamberger and Ilan Meshoulam, *Human Resource Strategy: Formulation, Implementation, and Impact* (Thousand Oaks, CA: Sage, 2000).

13. Don A. Moore and William M.P. Klein, "Use of Absolute and Comparative Performance Feedback in Absolute and Comparative Judgments and Decisions," *Organizational Behavior and Human Decision Processes* 107 (2008): 60–74.

14. Stephen M. Garcia and Avishalom Tor, "Rankings, Standards, and Competition: Task vs. Scale Comparisons," *Organizational Behavior and Human Decision Processes* 102 (2007): 95–108.

15. Chockalingam Viswesvaran, Frank L. Schmidt, and Deniz S. Ones, "Is There a General Factor in Ratings of Job Performance? A Meta-Analytic Framework for Disentangling Substantive and Error Influences," *Journal of Applied Psychology* 90 (2005): 108–131.

16. Maria Rotundo and Paul R. Sackett, "The Relative Importance of Task, Citizenship, and Counterproductive Performance to Global Ratings of Job Performance: A Policy-Capturing Approach," *Journal of Applied Psychology* 87 (2002): 66–80; Stephen J. Motowidlo and James R. Van Scotter, "Evidence that Task Performance Should Be Distinguished from Contextual Performance," *Journal of Applied Psychology* 79 (1994): 475–480.

17. Steven E. Scullen, Michael K. Mount, and Timothy A. Judge, "Evidence of the Construct Validity of Developmental Ratings of Managerial Performance," *Journal of Applied Psychology* 88 (2003): 50–66.

18. John P. Campbell, Rodney A. McCloy, Scott H. Oppler, and Christopher E. Sager, "A Theory of Performance," in *Personnel Selection in Organizations*, ed. Neal Schmitt, Walter C. Borman, and Associates, 35–70 (San Francisco: Jossey-Bass, 1993); Motowidlo and Van Scotter, "Evidence That Task Performance."

19. Jeff W. Johnson, "The Relative Importance of Task and Contextual Performance Dimensions to Supervisor Judgments of Overall Performance," *Journal of Applied Psychology* 86 (2001): 984–996.

20. Walter C. Borman, Leonard A. White, and David W. Dorsey, "Effects of Ratee Task Performance and Interpersonal Factors on Supervisor and Peer Performance Ratings," *Journal of Applied Psychology* 80 (1995): 168–177; Rotundo and Sackett, "The Relative Importance of Task."

21. Rodney A. McCloy, John P. Campbell, and Robert Cudeck, "A Confirmatory Test of a Model of Performance Determinants," *Journal of Applied Psychology* 79 (1994): 493–505.

22. Laura Rhoades Shanock and Robert Eisenberger, "When Supervisors Feel Supported: Relationships with Subordinates' Perceived Supervisor Support, Perceived Organizational Support, and Performance," *Journal of Applied Psychology* 91 (2006): 689–695; Dishan Kamdar and Linn Van Dyne, "The Joint Effects of Personality and Workplace Social Exchange Relationships in Predicting Task Performance and Citizenship Behavior," *Journal of Applied Psychology* 92 (2007): 1286–1298.

23. Daniel G. Bachrach, Benjamin C. Powell, Elliot Bendoly, and R. Glenn Richey, "Organizational Citizenship Behavior and Performance Evaluations: Exploring the Impact of Task Interdependence," *Journal of Applied Psychology* 91 (2006): 193–201.

24. Motowidlo and Van Scotter, "Evidence that Task Performance."

25. Henry Moon, Dishan Kamdar, David M. Mayer, and Riki Takeuchi, "Me or We? The Role of Personality and Justice as Other-Centered Antecedents to Innovative Citizenship Behaviors Within Organizations," *Journal of Applied Psychology* 93 (2008): 84–94.

26. Nathan P. Podsakoff, Steven W. Whiting, Philip M. Podsakoff, and Brian D. Blume, "Individual- and Organizational-Level Consequences of Organizational Citizenship Behaviors: A Meta-Analysis," *Journal of Applied Psychology* 94 (2009): 122–141.

27. Brent A. Scott and Timothy A. Judge, "The Popularity Contest at Work: Who Wins, Why, and What Do They Receive?" *Journal of Applied Psychology* 94 (2009): 20–33.

28. Larry J. Williams and Stella E. Anderson, "Job Satisfaction and Organizational Commitment as Predictors of Organizational Citizenship and In-Role Behaviors," *Journal of Management* 17 (1991): 601–617.

29. Wm. Matthew Bowler and Daniel J. Brass, "Relational Correlates of Interpersonal Citizenship Behavior: A Social Network Perspective," *Journal of Applied Psychology* 91 (2006): 70–82; Remus Ilies, Jennifer D. Nahrgang, and Frederick P. Morgeson, "Leader-Member Exchange and Citizenship Behaviors: A Meta-Analysis," *Journal of Applied Psychology* 92 (2007): 269–277; Vijaya Venkataramani and Reeshad S. Dalal, "Who Helps and Harms Whom? Relational Antecedents of Interpersonal Helping and Harming in Organizations," *Journal of Applied Psychology* 92 (2007): 952–966.

30. Remus Ilies, Brent A. Scott, and Timothy A. Judge, "The Interactive Effects of Personal Traits and Experienced States on Intraindividual Patterns of Citizenship Behavior," *Academy of Management Journal* 49 (2006): 561–575; Randall Settoon and Kevin W. Mossholder, "Relationship Quality and Relationship Context as Antecedents of Person and Task-Focused Interpersonal Citizenship Behavior," *Journal of Applied Psychology* 87 (2002): 255–267; Motowidlo and Van Scotter, "Evidence That Task Performance."

31. Dishan Kamdar, Daniel J. McAllister, and Daniel B. Turban, "All in a Day's Work: How Follower Individual Differences and Justice Perceptions Predict OCB Role Definitions and Behavior," *Journal of Applied Psychology* 91 (2006): 841–855; Brian J. Hoffman, Carrie A. Blair, Hohn P. Meriac, and David J. Woehr, "Expanding the Criterion Domain? A

Quantitative Review of the OCB Literature," *Journal of Applied Psychology* 92 (2007): 555–566.

32. Brian R. Dineen, Roy J. Lewicki, and Edward C. Tomlinson, "Supervisory Guidance and Behavioral Integrity: Relationships with Employee Citizenship and Deviant Behavior," *Journal of Applied Psychology* 91 (2006): 622–635; Adam Grant and John J. Sumanth, "Mission Possible? The Performance of Prosocially Motivated Employees Depends on Manager Trustworthiness," *Journal of Applied Psychology* 94 (2009): 927–944.

33. Jeff Joireman, Dishan Kamdar, Denise Daniels, and Blythe Duell, "Good Citizens to the End? It Depends: Empathy and Concern with Future Consequences Moderate the Impact of a Short-Term Time Horizon on Organizational Citizenship Behaviors," *Journal of Applied Psychology* 91 (2006): 1307–1320.

34. P. D. Dunlop and K. Lee, "Workplace Deviance, Organizational Citizenship Behavior, and Business Unit Performance: The Bad Apples Do Spoil the Whole Barrel," *Journal of Organizational Behavior* 25 (2004): 67–80.

35. Christopher M. Berry, Nichelle C. Carpenter, and Clare L. Barratt, "Do Other-Reports of Counterproductive Work Behavior Provide an Incremental Contribution Over Self-Reports? A Meta-Analytic Comparison," *Journal of Applied Psychology* 97 (2012): 613–636.

36. Reeshad S. Dalal, "A Meta-Analysis of the Relationship Between Organizational Citizenship Behavior and Counterproductive Work Behavior," *Journal of Applied Psychology* 90 (2005): 1241–1255.

37. Sandra L. Robinson and Rebecca J. Bennett, "A Typology of Deviant Workplace Behaviors: A Multidimensional Scaling Study," *Academy of Management Journal* 38 (1995): 555–572.

38. Ibid.

39. M. Sandy Hershcovis, Nick Turner, Julian Barling, Kara A. Arnold, Kathryne E. Dupre, Michelle Inness, Manon Mireille LeBlanc, and Nior Sivanathan, "Predicting Workplace Aggression: A Meta-Analysis," *Journal of Applied Psychology* 92 (2007): 228–238.

40. Timothy A. Judge, Brent A. Scott, and Remus Ilies, "Hostility, Job Attitudes, and Workplace Deviance: Test of a Multilevel Model," *Journal of Applied Psychology* 91 (2006): 126–138; Yochi Cohen-Charash and Jennifer S. Mueller, "Does Perceived Unfairness Exacerbate or Mitigate Interpersonal Counterproductive Work Behaviors Related to Envy?" *Journal of Applied Psychology* 92 (2007): 666–680.

41. Michael E. Brown and Linda K. Trevino, "Socialized Charismatic Leadership, Values Congruence, and Deviance in Work Groups," *Journal of Applied Psychology* 91 (2006): 954–962; Brian R. Dineen, Roy J. Lewicki, and Edward C. Tomlinson, "Supervisory Guidance and Behavioral Integrity: Relationships with Employee Citizenship and Deviant Behavior," *Journal of Applied Psychology* 91 (2006): 622–635; Marie S. Mitchell and Maureen L. Ambrose, "Abusive Supervision and Workplace Deviance and the Moderating Effects of Negative Reciprocity Beliefs,"

Journal of Applied Psychology 92 (2007): 1159–1168; Bennett J. Tepper, Jon C. Carr, Denise M. Breaux, Sharon Geider, Changya Hu, and Wei Hua, "Abusive Supervision, Intentions to Quit, and Employees' Workplace Deviance: A Power/Dependence Analysis," *Organizational Behavior and Human Decision Processes* 109 (2009): 156–167.

42. Amy E. Colbert, Michael K. Mount, James K. Harter, L.A. Witt, and Murray R. Barrick, "Interactive Effects of Personality and Perceptions of the Work Situation on Workplace Deviance," *Journal of Applied Psychology* 89 (2004): 599–609; James M. Diefendorff and Kajal Mehta, "The Relations of Motivational Traits with Workplace Deviance," *Journal of Applied Psychology* 92 (2007): 967–997; Christopher M. Berry, Deniz S. Ones, and Paul R. Sackett, "Interpersonal Deviance, Organizational Deviance, and Their Common Correlates: A Review and Meta-Analysis," *Journal of Applied Psychology* 92 (2007): 410–424.

43. Adrienne Fox, "Curing What Ails Performance Appraisal," *HR Magazine* 54, no. 1, 52.

44. William H. Bommer, Jonathan L. Johnson, Gregory A. Rich, Philip M. Podsakoff, and Scott B. MacKenzie, "On the Interchangeability of Objective and Subjective Measures of Employee Performance: A Meta-Analysis," *Personnel Psychology* 48 (1995): 587–605.

45. Seth Kaplan, Jill C. Bradley, Joseph N. Luchman, and Douglas Haynes, "On the Role of Positive and Negative Affectivity in Job Performance: A Meta-Analytic Investigation," *Journal of Applied Psychology* 94 (2009): 162–176.

46. Steven W. Whiting, Philip M. Podsakoff, and Jason R. Pierce, "Effects of Task Performance, Helping, Voice, and Organizational Loyalty on Performance Appraisal Ratings," *Journal of Applied Psychology* 93 (2008): 125–139.

47. Ian Dennis, "Halo Effects in Grading Student Projects," *Journal of Applied Psychology* 92 (2007): 1169–1176.

48. Todd J. Thorsteinson, Jennifer Breier, Anna Atwell, Catherine Hamilton, and Monica Privette, "Anchoring Effects on Performance Judgments," *Organizational Behavior and Human Decision Processes* 107 (2008): 29–40.

49. Krista L. Uggerslev and Lorne M. Sulsky, "Using Frame-of-Reference Training to Understand the Implications of Rater Idiosyncrasy for Rating Accuracy," *Journal of Applied* Psychology 93 (2007): 711–719. Elaine D. Pulakos, "The Development of Training Programs to Increase Accuracy in Different Tasks," *Organizational Behavior and Human Decision Processes* 38 (1986): 76–91.

50. Joseph M. Staugger and Ronald M. Buckley, "The Existence and Nature of Racial Bias in Supervisory Ratings," *Journal of Applied Psychology* 90 (2005): 586–591.

51. Paul R. Sackett and Cathy L. DuBois, "Rater–Ratee Race Effects on Performance Evaluation: Challenging Meta-Analytic Conclusions," *Journal of Applied Psychology* 76 (1991): 873–877.

52. Michael K. Mount, Marcia R. Sytsma, Joy Fisher Hazucha, and Katherine E. Holt, "Rater–Ratee Race Effects in Developmental Performance Ratings of Managers," *Personnel Psychology* 50 (1997): 51–70.

53. David A. Waldman and Bruce J. Avolio, "Race Effects in Performance Evaluations: Controlling for Ability, Education, and Experience," *Journal of Applied Psychology* 76 (1991): 897–901.

54. Philip L. Roth, Allen I. Huffcutt, and Philip Bobko, "Ethnic Group Differences in Measures of Job Performance: A New Meta-Analysis," *Journal of Applied Psychology* 88 (2003): 694–706.

55. Paul R. Sackett, Cathy L. DuBois, and Ann W. Noe, "Tokenism in Performance Evaluation: The Effects of Work Group Representation on Male–Female and White–Black Differences in Performance Ratings," *Journal of Applied Psychology* 76 (1991): 263–267.

56. Boris B. Baltes, Cara B. Bauer, and Peter A. Frensch, "Does a Structured Free Recall Intervention Reduce the Effect of Stereotypes on Performance Ratings and by What Mechanism?" *Journal of Applied Psychology* 92 (2007): 151–164.

57. Lawrence H. Peters and Edward J. O'Connor, "Situational Constraints and Work Outcomes: The Influences of a Frequently Overlooked Construct," *Academy of Management Review* 5 (1980): 391–397.

58. Greg L. Stewart and Amit Nandkeolyar, "Exploring How Constraints Created by Other People Influence Intraindividual Variation in Objective Performance Measures," *Journal of Applied Psychology* 92 (2007): 1149–1158.

59. Robert L. Cardy and Gregory H. Dobbins, *Performance Appraisal: Alternative Perspectives* (Cincinnati, OH: South-Western, 1994).

60. Erich C. Dierdorff and Eric A. Surface, "Placing Peer Ratings in Context: Systematic Influences Beyond Ratee Performance," *Personnel Psychology* 60 (2007): 93–126.

61. Michael C. Sturman, Robin A. Charamie, and Luke H. Cashen, "The Impact of Job Complexity and Performance Measurement on the Temporal Consistency, Stability, and Test-Retest Reliability of Employee Performance Ratings," *Journal of Applied Psychology* 90 (2005): 269–283.

62. Greg L. Stewart and Amit K. Nandkeolyar, "Adaptation and Intraindividual Variation in Sales Outcomes: Exploring the Interactive Effects of Personality and Environmental Opportunity," *Personnel Psychology* 59 (2006): 307–332.

63. Paul R. Sackett, Sheldon Zedeck, and L. Folgi, "Relations Between Measures of Typical and Maximum Performance," *Journal of Applied Psychology* 73 (1988): 482–486.

64. David A. Hofmann, Rick Jacobs, and Steve J. Gerras, "Mapping Individual Performance over Time," *Journal of Applied Psychology* 77 (1992): 185–195.

65. Robert E. Ployhart and Milton D. Hakel, "The Substantive Nature of Performance Variability: Predicting Interindividual Differences in Intraindividual Performance," *Personnel Psychology* 51

66. (1998): 859–901; David A. Hofmann, Rick Jacobs, and Joseph Baratta, "Dynamic Criteria and the Measurement of Change," *Journal of Applied Psychology* 78 (1993): 194–204.

66. Carl J. Thoresen, Jill C. Bradley, Paul D. Bliese, and Joseph D. Thoresen, "The Big Five Personality Traits and Individual Job Performance Growth Trajectories in Maintenance and Transitional Job Stages," *Journal of Applied Psychology* 89 (2004): 835–853.

67. Rebecca A. Henry and Charles L. Hulin, "Stability of Skilled Performance Across Time: Some Generalizations and Limitations on Utilities," *Journal of Applied Psychology* 72 (1987): 457–462; Kevin R. Murphy, "Is the Relationship Between Cognitive Ability and Job Performance Stable over Time?" *Human Performance* 2 (1989): 83–200.

68. Joachen Reb and Russell Cropanzano, "Evaluating Dynamic Performance: The Influence of Salient Gestalt Characteristics on Performance Ratings," *Journal of Applied Psychology* 92 (2007): 490–499.

69. Deidra J. Schleicher, Rebecca A. Bull, and Stephen G. Green, "Rater Reactions to Forced Distribution Rating Systems," *Journal of Management* 35 (2009): 899.

70. Michael K. Mount, Timothy A. Judge, Steven E. Scullen, Marcia R. Sytsma, and Sarah A. Hezlett, "Trait, Rater and Level Effects in 360-Degree Performance Ratings," *Personnel Psychology* 51 (1988): 557–576.

71. Syvia G. Roch, "Why Convene Rater Teams: An Investigation of the Benefits of Anticipated Discussion, Consensus, and Rater Motivation," *Organizational Behavior and Human Decision Processes* 104 (2007): 14–29.

72. Nihal Mamatoglu, "Effects on Organizational Context (Culture and Climate) from Implementing a 360-Degree Feedback System: The Case of Arcelik," *European Journal of Work and Organizational Psychology* 17 (2008): 426–449.

73. David J. Woehr, Kathleen M. Sheehan, and Winston Bennett, "Assessing Measurement Equivalence Across Rating Sources: A Multitrait–Multirater Approach," *Journal of Applied Psychology* 90 (2005): 592–600; Gary J. Greguras and Chet Robie, "A New Look at Within-Source Interrater Reliability of 360-Degree Feedback Ratings," *Journal of Applied Psychology* 83 (1998): 960–968.

74. M. M. Harris and J. Schaubroeck, "A Meta-Analysis of Self–Boss, Self–Peer, and Peer–Boss Ratings," *Personnel Psychology* 41 (1988): 43–62.

75. Jing-Lih Farh, Gregory H. Dobbins, and Bor-Shiuan Cheng, "Cultural Relativity in Action: A Comparison of Self-Ratings," *Personnel Psychology* 44 (1991): 129–148.

76. Jiayuan Yu and Kevin R. Murphy, "Modesty Bias in Self-Ratings of Performance: A Test of the Cultural Relativity Hypothesis," *Personnel Psychology* 46 (1993): 357–364; Heike Heidemeier and Klaus Moser, "Self–Other Agreement in Job Performance Ratings: A Meta-Analytic Test of a Process Model," *Journal of Applied Psychology* 94 (2009): 353–370.

77. Cheri Ostroff, Leanne E. Atwater, and Barbara Feinberg, "Understanding Self–Other Agreement: A Look at Rater and Ratee Characteristics, Context, and Outcomes," *Personnel Psychology* 57 (2004): 333–375; Manuel London and Arthur J. Wohlers, "Agreement Between Subordinate and Self-Ratings of Upward Feedback," *Personnel Psychology* 44 (1991): 375–391.

78. Joyce Ehrlinger, Kerri Johnson, Matthew Banner, David Dunning, and Justin Kruger, "Why the Unskilled Are Unaware: Further Explorations of (Absent) Self-Insight Among the Incompetent," *Organizational Behavior and Human Decision Processes* 105 (2008): 98–121.

79. Gordon W. Cheung, "Multifaceted Conceptions of Self-Other Ratings Disagreement," *Personnel Psychology* 52 (1999): 1–36.

80. Brian Schrader and Dirk D. Steiner, "Common Comparison Standards: An Approach to Improving Agreement Between Self and Supervisory Performance Ratings," *Journal of Applied Psychology* 81 (1996): 813–820; Jane R. Williams and Paul E. Levy, "The Effects of Perceived System Knowledge on the Agreement Between Self-Ratings and Supervisor Ratings," *Personnel Psychology* 45 (1992): 835–848.

81. David Antonioni and Heejoon Park, "The Effects of Personality Similarity on Peer Ratings of Contextual Work Behaviors," *Personnel Psychology* 54 (2001): 331–360.

82. Todd J. Mauer, Nambury S. Raju, and William C. Collins, "Peer and Subordinate Performance Appraisal Measurement Equivalence," *Journal of Applied Psychology* 83 (1998): 693–702.

83. Paul W.B. Atkins and Robert E. Wood, "Self- Versus Others' Ratings as Predictors of Assessment Center Ratings: Validation Evidence for 360-Degree Feedback Programs," *Personnel Psychology* 55 (2002): 871–905.

84. Vanessa Urch Druskat and Steven B. Wolff, "Effects and Timing of Developmental Peer Appraisals in Self-Managing Work Groups," *Journal of Applied Psychology* 84 (1999): 58–74.

85. Mount, Judge, Scullen, Sytsma, and Hezlett, "Trait, Rater and Level Effects in 360-Degree Performance Ratings."

86. Leanne E. Atwater, Cheri Ostroff, Francis J. Yammarino, and John W. Fleenor, "Self–Other Agreement: Does It Really Matter?" *Personnel Psychology* 51 (1998): 577–599.

87. Christopher C. Rosen, Paul E. Levy, and Rosalie J. Hall, "Placing Perceptions of Politics in the Context of the Feedback Environment, Employee Attitudes, and Job Performance," *Journal of Applied Psychology* 91 (2006): 211–220.

88. James W. Smither, Manuel London, and Richard Reilly, "Does Performance Improve Following Multisource Feedback? A Theoretical Model, Meta-analysis, and Review of Empirical Findings," *Personnel Psychology* 58 (2005): 33–66.

89. Alan G. Walker and James W. Smither, "A Five-Year Study of Upward Feedback: What Managers Do with Their Results Matters," *Personnel Psychology* 52 (1999): 393–423.

90. Avraham N. Kluger and Angelo DeNisi, "The Effects of Feedback Interventions on Performance: A Historical Review, a Meta-Analysis, and a Preliminary Feedback Intervention Theory," *Psychological Bulletin* 119 (1996): 254–284.

91. Robert A. Baron, "Countering the Effects of Destructive Criticism: The Relative Efficacy of Four Interventions," *Journal of Applied Psychology* 75 (1990): 235–245.

92. Adam P. Tolli and Aaron M. Schmidt, "The Role of Feedback, Causal Attribution, and Self-Efficacy in Goal Revision," *Journal of Applied Psychology* 93 (2008): 692–701; AnJanette A. Nease, Brad O. Mudgett, and Miguel A. Quinones, "Relationships Among Feedback Sign, Self-Efficacy, and Acceptance of Performance Feedback," *Journal of Applied Psychology* 84(1999): 806–814.

93. Angelo J. Kinicki, Gregory E. Prussia, Bin (Joshua) Wu, and Frances M. McKee-Ryan, "A Covariance Structure Analysis of Employees' Response to Performance Feedback," *Journal of Applied Psychology* 89 (2004): 1057–1069.

94. Ziguang Chen, Wing Lam, and Jian An Zhong, "Leader–Member Exchange and Member Performance: A New Look at Individual-Level Negative Feedback-Seeking Behavior and Team-Level Empowerment Climate," *Journal of Applied Psychology* 92 (2007): 202–212.

95. R. Blake Jelley and Richard D. Goffin, "Can Performance-Feedback Accuracy Be Improved? Effects of Rater Priming and Rating-Scale Format on Rating Accuracy," *Journal of Applied Psychology* 86 (2001): 134–144.

96. Wing Lam, Xu Huang, and Ed Snape, "Feedback-Seeking Behavior and Leader–Member Exchange: Do Supervisor-Attributed Motives Matter?" *Academy of Management Journal* 50 (2007): 348–363.

97. Jodi S. Goodman, Robert E. Wood, and Margaretha Hendrickx, "Feedback Specificity, Exploration, and Learning," *Journal of Applied Psychology* 89 (2004): 248–262.

98. Jodi S. Goodman and Robert E. Wood, "Feedback Specificity, Learning Opportunities, and Learning," *Journal of Applied Psychology* 89 (2004): 809–821.

99. Joseph J. Martocchio and James Dulebohn, "Performance Feedback Effects in Training: The Role of Perceived Controllability," *Personnel Psychology* 47 (1994): 357–373.

100. Remus Ilies and Timothy A. Judge, "Goal Regulation Across Time: The Effects of Feedback and Affect," *Journal of Applied Psychology* 90 (2005): 453–467; Simon S.K. Lam, Michelle S. Yik, and John Schaubroeck, "Responses to Formal Performance Appraisal Feedback: The Role of Negative Affectivity," *Journal of Applied Psychology* 87 (2002): 192–201.

101. Steven P. Brown, Robert A. Westbrook, and Goutam Challagalla, "Good Cope, Bad Cope: Adaptive and Maladaptive Coping Strategies Following a Critical Negative Work Event," *Journal of Applied Psychology* 90 (2005): 792–798.

102. Don VandeWalle, Shankar Ganesan, Goutam N. Challagalla, and Steven P. Brown, "An Integrated

Model of Feedback-Seeking Behavior: Disposition, Context, and Cognition," *Journal of Applied Psychology* 85 (2000): 996–1003.

103. Don VandeWalle, Steven P. Brown, William L. Cron, and John W. Slocum, "The Influence of Goal Orientation and Self-Regulation Tactics on Sales Performance: A Longitudinal Field Test," *Journal of Applied Psychology* 84 (1999): 249–259.

104. Angelo J. Kinicki, Gregory E. Prussia, Bin (Joshua) Wu, and Frances M. McKee-Ryan, "A Covariance Structure Analysis of Employees' Response to Performance Feedback," *Journal of Applied Psychology* 89 (2004): 1057–1069.

105. Don VandeWalle and Larry L. Cummings, "A Test of the Influence of Goal Orientation on the Feedback-Seeking Process," *Journal of Applied Psychology* 82 (1997): 390–400.

106. Joyce E. Bono and Amy E. Colbert, "Understanding Responses to Multi-Source Feedback: The Role of Core Self-Evaluations," *Personnel Psychology* 58 (2005): 171–204.

107. Brian D. McNatt, "Ancient Pygmalion Joins Contemporary Management: A Meta-Analysis of the Result," *Journal of Applied Psychology* 85 (2000): 314–322.

108. Oranit B. Davidson and Dov Eden, "Remedial Self-Fulfilling Prophecy: Two Field Experiments to Prevent Golem Effects Among Disadvantaged Women," *Journal of Applied Psychology* 85 (2000): 386–398.

109. Dov Eden and Joseph Kinnar, "Modeling Galatea: Boosting Self-Efficacy to Increase Volunteering," *Journal of Applied Psychology* 76 (1991): 770–780.

Chapter 9

Training for Improved Performance

A MANAGER'S PERSPECTIVE

CHARLOTTE WALKED OUT OF THE TRAINING ROOM MORE EXCITED THAN SHE HAD BEEN IN QUITE A WHILE. SHE HAD JUST LEARNED ABOUT A PROJECT MANAGEMENT SOFTWARE PROGRAM THAT SHE'D READ ABOUT A YEAR AGO. WHEN SHE HEARD THAT HER COMPANY WAS OFFERING A PROJECT MANAGEMENT WORKSHOP, SHE HAD CALLED TO SEE WHETHER THE SOFTWARE SHE HOPED TO LEARN WAS COVERED. IT WAS. SO SHE REARRANGED TWO IMPORTANT MEETINGS AND BOOKED THE TRAINING.

The training had gone even better than she had hoped. The trainer opened with a story of a project just like the one Charlotte was managing. The trainer told another short story as a preview to the day's agenda and then asked participants what they hoped to accomplish that day. Charlotte had practically jumped out of her seat to explain how she had long wanted to improve her project management skills, and in particular, use software to track her employees' tasks and, of course, due dates. The trainer had listened to Charlotte, and to the other participants' comments, and offered to make some adjustments to the workshop schedule to allow for more hands-on practice with the project management software.

Charlotte was grateful for the time to actually use the software. She was able to practice and ask

nyul/iStockphoto

questions, and the trainer listened to each question and answered what she could. When Charlotte had a detailed question that the trainer couldn't answer, the trainer had admitted she wasn't sure. After a short break, though, the trainer came over to Charlotte and provided her business card with an Internet address written on the back. "I called technical support, and they said that this web page should have the answer to your question. If it doesn't, my contact information is on the card—give me a call." Charlotte was impressed with how responsive the trainer had been, and how quickly she had found an answer.

As Charlotte left the room, she planned how she would get started. She needed a bit more practice time with the software this week before she would feel comfortable introducing it to her employees. She had the trainer's business card and planned to arrange a few training sessions for her employees and other managers in the department. We should be up and running by the end of the month, she thought.

The bad news began the next morning and continued throughout the day. When she called the trainer, Charlotte found out that she was no longer on contract with her company. She would not be

THE BIG PICTURE *Effective Organizations Systematically Design and Deliver Training to Improve Individual and Organizational Performance.*

able to conduct anymore sessions without a new contract. When she called the HR department to inquire, the Director of Training and Development said, "Our budget has been cut, and we cannot afford any more training by outside vendors." A quick call to her manager confirmed it—Charlotte could go ahead and use the software but there would be no money available to support training. Charlotte hung up the phone dejected.

Charlotte didn't know what to do next. Could she just ask employees to use a new system without training? Was there some other way to get employees to learn the system without formal training? Or was there a way to get them training that would cost less but still be just as effective? Charlotte set about to do some research so she could decide her next move.

WHAT DO YOU THINK?

Imagine you are listening to a conversation between Charlotte and her manager. Her manager makes the following statements. Which do you think are true?

T OR F Training keeps employees happy because it's a break from work, but it has little impact on the organization's bottom line.

T OR F If trainees learn in training, they will transfer that learning back on the job.

T OR F Lecture is a terrible method for delivering training.

T OR F Training presented face to face is always more effective than training presented via computer technology.

T OR F Evaluating training is a waste of everyone's time.

After reading this chapter you should be able to:

LEARNING OBJECTIVE 1 Explain how employee training practices can be aligned with an organization's competitive strategy.

LEARNING OBJECTIVE 2 Describe how partnering and using a systematic process for developing training helps an organization benefit from training.

LEARNING OBJECTIVE 3 Discuss the different ways organizations determine their training needs.

LEARNING OBJECTIVE 4 Describe various training methods and explain how to make each more effective.

LEARNING OBJECTIVE 5 Explain why the purpose of a training evaluation should be used to guide the evaluation process.

How Can Strategic Employee Training Improve an Organization?

Training
A planned effort to help employees learn job-related knowledge, skills, and attitudes.

Nearly everyone who has worked has attended a training program. **Training** is a planned effort by a company to help employees learn job-related knowledge, skills, and attitudes.[1] The vast majority of companies offer training programs, and they come in many shapes and sizes: large group lectures given by an expert, on-the-job training delivered by a supervisor, simulations guided by a computer program, small-group projects coordinated by an executive, or online discussions with colleagues from around the country. The common element that defines training is that employees go through a structured experience that helps them to learn something they can use to improve their performance at work.

Knowledge
Memory of facts and principles.

Skill
Proficiency at performing a particular act.

Attitude
An evaluative reaction to particular categories of people, issues, objects, or events.

Learning
A change in knowledge, skill, or attitude that results from experience.

We usually equate learning with being in school. For example, when we were younger and in primary school, we gained **knowledge**, which includes facts and principles of all kinds. We gained physical and cognitive **skills**, which allow us to perform a wide range of tasks like throwing a ball, using computers, resolving interpersonal conflicts, and solving math problems. We also developed new **attitudes**, such as (hopefully) the belief that school is both fun and beneficial. When our experiences change our knowledge, skills, or attitudes, we call it learning. **Learning**, then, is a change in what we know, what we can do, or what we believe that occurs because of experience.

Of course, the truth is that we don't just learn in school, nor do we ever stop learning. We learn all the time in and out of classes, and we continue to learn throughout our lives. When we start a new job, we must learn about the industry, the company, and the day-to-day details of the position (including where to find the bathroom). To add to this challenge, companies and the jobs in them change over time. A company will get a new computer system, people will quit and new people will join, and products and services will be modified to meet changing customer demands. Most changes require that employees learn something new. So every job requires not only some learning to get started but also continued learning to avoid falling behind.

Most organizations, regardless of size and industry, offer at least some formal training to help employees learn.[2] In a manufacturing setting, for instance, new employees can receive training on how to operate their equipment safely and effectively. Employees can learn in other, less formal ways, such as by watching others, asking for help, experimenting, or studying on their own.[3] These informal methods can be effective and inexpensive, so some firms rely heavily on informal learning. Small firms, in particular, often expect their employees to learn mostly through informal means.[4]

While **informal learning methods** can work, they are not always appropriate. What if new employees at an automotive parts manufacturing facility were asked to learn all about metal stamping on their own? This process involves using large and dangerous equipment to shape metal products such as pipes. If an employee were injured because the company had not prepared him to use the equipment, then the company could be held liable for the injury. Formal training is also useful because it ensures that everyone learns the same things, such as the most efficient and most safe ways to perform a task.

Informal learning methods
Natural learning that is neither planned nor organized.

3 ways

*1

Training, when designed and delivered properly, can improve the overall effectiveness of an organization in three ways.[5] First, it can boost employees' commitment and motivation. Opportunities to learn new skills are important in today's economy, so employees appreciate learning opportunities offered by training. As a result, companies that offer more training foster employee commitment.[6] To be more precise, organizations that offer employees opportunities to learn and grow are seen as having employees' best interests at heart, and as a result, employees feel more committed to the organizations.[7] Employee commitment also can benefit an organization by increasing retention of high-performing employees (see Chapter 7).

*2

Second, training helps employees perform their work more effectively and efficiently, so the organization is able to function better on a day-to-day basis. If you've ever been to a grocery store where the cashier had not been trained to use the cash register efficiently, then you've been a victim of poor training (or, if you were really unlucky, it might have been a combination of poor employee selection and poor training). Research is very clear on this point—employees who receive training know more and are able to do more than employees who do not receive training.[8]

These first two benefits should come as no surprise given research findings about the commitment HR strategy discussed in Chapter 2. Providing employees with formal training is a key element of commitment-based HR.[9] Furthermore, providing training adds value beyond other HR practices. All other things being equal, providing training to a larger percentage of a company's workforce will increase that company's overall productivity.[10] Employees who are trained are more likely to be committed to the organization and have higher levels of knowledge and skill. As a result, they are better individual performers, and this helps the organization to be more productive.

*3

The third way training benefits organizations is by helping them to meet their strategic objectives. It does so by providing employees with the specific knowledge, skills, and attitudes necessary to achieve designated strategic goals. This benefit is more subtle, and it's about alignment of training activities to the organization's overall strategy and specific goals that follow from it. If an organization aligns training effectively, it will have the right people with the right skills necessary to pursue the competitive advantage sought by the strategy.

An example of a company that uses training effectively is Rockwell Collins. A leading supplier of aviation electronics equipment, Rockwell Collins is consistently faced with pressures to reduce design time of new products (in order to keep pace with new technology) and to improve quality of current products (in order to reduce equipment failure). Faced with these challenges, Rockwell Collins continuously examines bottlenecks in moving from initial design to final products, looking for ways to speed up the process and improve quality.

A common bottleneck in the Rockwell Collins product design process was delays caused by electromagnetic interference (EMI), which often results in destruction of electronic parts. The company estimated that it was losing at least $1 million a year because of EMI. A quick investigation into the causes of the problem revealed that many testing engineers lacked a basic understanding of how to avoid EMI. Working with a training company called Strategic Interactive, Rockwell staff developed a 12-hour CD-ROM course that was delivered to 1,300 engineers in about six months. Delivering the training via CD-ROM meant a larger up-front cost for developing the course, but it allowed Rockwell to train engineers more quickly. Engineers could do the training on their own time without taking time away from work to travel to corporate headquarters.

Although the course cost nearly $500,000 to develop, the end result was worth the cost. The EMI problem disappeared, and Rockwell has avoided approximately $1 million in equipment losses every year since the training. The investment in training paid off for Rockwell, and it helped the company to implement its strategy to reduce the time it takes to design new products.

Building Strength Through HR

ROCKWELL COLLINS

©Ingo Schulz/Imagebroker/ Corbis Images

Rockwell Collins is a leading designer and producer of aviation electronics. With approximately 20,000 employees, and nearly $4.5 billion in sales in 2009, it serves government and commercial customers all over the world. Using a strategic approach to training, Rockwell was able to:

- Identify a critical problem for the organization—design delays caused by electromagnetic interference—that could be solved by training.
- Use computer-based training opportunities to deliver a course to over 1,300 engineers in about six months.
- Speed up product design and testing and avoid approximately $1 million in equipment losses.

Sources. Cliff Purington and Chris Butler with Sarah Fister Gale, *Built to Learn: The Inside Story of How Rockwell Collins Became a True Learning Organization* (New York: AMACOM, 2003).

How Is Employee Training Strategic?

As we've just seen, training offers universal benefits for improving employee motivation, commitment, and job performance. Training can also be aligned with strategy to help an organization gain a competitive advantage over other organizations. Training needs and training resources thus vary across firms depending on the business strategy that they pursue.[11] Figure 9.1 summarizes some of these differences.

DIFFERENTIATION VERSUS COST LEADERSHIP STRATEGY

Let's first consider how training efforts should be aligned with the cost and differentiation strategies described in Chapter 2. A cost leadership strategy, including both the Bargain Laborer and Loyal Soldier strategies, requires that employees have knowledge, skills, and attitudes that help reduce costs and improve efficiency. For example, a local restaurant that is trying to compete based on low-cost menu items must have employees who know how to do their work efficiently with little waste. In other words, they must have the knowledge and skill needed to prepare and serve food quickly. Employees should also *believe* in efficiency and cost reduction and have a positive attitude toward working quickly. As a result, training for employees at this restaurant should not only build knowledge and skill so employees can work quickly without creating waste, it should also convince employees it is important to do so. The efforts of this small restaurant are, on a much larger scale, what companies

Figure 9.1 Strategic Framework for Employee Training.

know this

— memorize

like Motorola, General Electric, and Samsung Electronics are trying to accomplish with training programs designed to measure and improve quality. By training their employees on quality control principles and practices, these companies have been able to become more efficient, thereby reducing costs and increasing profits.[12]

A differentiation strategy, including both Free Agent and Committed Expert strategies, requires that employees be able to deliver services or make products that are superior to the services or products offered by competitors.[13] Some companies differentiate via innovation—constantly staying ahead of the competition with new products and services. With this type of differentiation, team-focused creativity training is a useful way to help employees share knowledge and build creative products. Coach, 3M, and General Mills are examples of companies that pursue this type of differentiation strategy and rely on this type of training. Differentiation can also be achieved via excellent customer service. For example, consider a different local restaurant trying to compete based on excellent service. This restaurant will train its employees how to impress customers by being considerate, friendly, and prompt. The efforts of this restaurant are similar to the efforts of companies like Nordstrom, Disney, Ritz-Carlton, and WorldColor.[14] The training efforts that Apple uses at its retail stores are offered as a detailed illustration in the "Building Strength Through HR" feature.

Building Strength Through HR

APPLE

Apple is well known for its revolutionary digital products including the iMac, iPod, iPad, and iPhone. To protect its brand image and expand sales, Apple opened its own retail stores in 2001. The stores include a Genius Bar, where experts answer questions about Apple products. The training for Geniuses ensures not only technical knowledge but also customer service knowledge and skill. Training materials recommend, for example, responding to customer concerns with the three F's: feel, felt, and found. This is a form of empathetic listening aimed at changing the customer's mind without openly disagreeing. When a customer states a concern about the iPad because it does not have a mouse, the training recommends that the Genius respond by saying, "I may know how you feel. I'm a mouse fan and felt as if I'd never get used to the iPad, but I found it becomes very easy with a little practice."

What kind of results does Apple get with their well-trained Geniuses? Industry research suggests

©Albert S. Llop/Demotix/Corbis

that "9 out of every 10 Apple owners are somewhat or much more likely to make another purchase following their tech support experience." They also found that 31 percent had a better perception of Apple after getting help.

Source: Sam Biddle, "How to Be a Genius: This is Apple's Secret Employee Training Manual," Gizmodo (2012) available online at http://www.gizmodo.com; Raz Godelnik, "Apple's Genius Training—Phone 101 or Great Customer Service?" Triplepundit (2012) available online at http://www.triplepundit.com.

INTERNAL VERSUS EXTERNAL LABOR ORIENTATION

Training efforts must also be aligned with the relative emphasis the organization places on internal versus external labor orientations. As you know, a company with an internal labor orientation seeks to make its own talent, whereas a company with an external labor orientation seeks to buy talent that is already developed. These different orientations clearly influence how much time and money a company will spend on training. Companies with an internal labor orientation are willing to spend time and money to train current employees, while companies with an external orientation tend instead to hire new employees to fill their needs.

For example, consider a company with an internal labor orientation that discovers managers are not following appropriate labor laws in their recruiting and hiring (covered in Chapter 3). With an internal labor orientation, the company is likely to see this as a knowledge deficit that should be addressed by training managers on these laws. An alternative approach, and one that might be adopted by a company with an external labor orientation, would be to centralize employee selection and hire a labor attorney to coordinate processes and enforce compliance with laws.

The distinction between internal and external labor orientation can also play out at an organizational level when a company decides whether to train employees for new business opportunities or acquire a new company. As an example of an external orientation, consider Adobe's acquisition of Macromedia in 2005. Adobe was the world leader in static documents on the Internet (you have probably opened and read documents in the Adobe Acrobat PDF file format). However, the company had few employees and no business units with expertise in dynamic content for the Web, such as web pages that automatically update or offer interactive displays. Rather than creating a series of training programs to help employees learn about dynamic documents, and then build that capacity into their products, Adobe chose to buy that expertise. By acquiring Macromedia (which created Flash Player, a commonly used program that runs dynamic content on the Internet), Adobe was able to increase its capacity to compete in the software industry.[15] Adobe acquired this expertise rather than developing it via training.

Do companies with external labor orientations skip training altogether? The answer is clearly no. In such companies, training programs are still offered for a variety of reasons, particularly to help employees learn company-specific knowledge and skills. However, in such firms, HR management must find ways to keep training costs low. One way to do this is to purchase a training course that has already been designed. HR management first should verify that the course is relevant to their organization and potential trainees. If the material is relevant, then purchasing an existing program can be dramatically less expensive than developing a program from scratch. For safety training, for example, the National Safety Council sells self-study books, videos, and DVDs that cover such topics as Defensive Driving, First Aid, Motorcycle Safety, Electrical Safety, and Fire Protection. Most of these courses cost less than $50.[16] Even better from a cost perspective, some government agencies provide free online tools that can be used as instruction, such as the U.S. Department of Labor's programs on eye and face protection, respiratory protection, lockout/tagout, poultry processing, scaffolding, beverage delivery, baggage handling, and grocery warehousing.[17]

Table 9.1	*Costs of Training and Tips for Keeping Training Costs Low*
Type of Cost	**Tips to Reduce Costs**
Visible Costs	
Development Costs	Partner with other organizations to share costs; purchase off-the-shelf training; use free or subsidized training from the government and nonprofits like university extension programs
Delivery Costs	Reduce trainee travel and eliminate facility costs by using self-paced, individualized instruction or technology delivery; reduce number and length of handouts; plan for reuse by laminating and retaining exhibits
Trainer Salary and Benefits	Train current employees to be part-time trainers; use contract trainers for nonrecurring projects
Hidden Costs	
Trainee Compensation and Lost Productivity	Shift training to be readily available at employees' desks; simplify work processes so employees can learn on the job without much training; reduce training time using task analyses to isolate and train only critical knowledge and skills
Wasted Investments	Use needs assessments to ensure that training need exists and is important to address; partner with management to increase transfer

Sources: David Van Adelsberg and Edward A. Trolley, *Running Training Like a Business: Delivering Unmistakable Value* (San Francisco: Berrett-Koehler, 1999); National Court Appointed Special Advocate Association, "Tips to Keep Volunteer Training Costs Down," 2001, retrieved online at http://www.casanet.org on April 4, 2007.

Table 9.1 provides a list of visible and hidden training costs and suggestions for how to reduce them. These tips can also be used by small businesses or any organization that needs training but also has to reduce costs.

CONCEPT CHECK

1. *What is the key focus of training for a company pursuing a differentiation strategy? A cost leadership strategy?*
2. *How does training differ between companies that pursue an internal versus an external labor orientation?*

LEARNING OBJECTIVE **2**

What Are Key Principles for Getting Benefits from Training?

Transfer of training
Application on the job of knowledge, skills, or attitudes learned in training.

Earlier, we identified three benefits an organization can gain from training its employees: Training can increase employees' commitment and motivation, it can enable them to perform better, and it can help the organization to meet its strategic objectives. To achieve these three benefits, training must result not only in learning but also in transfer of training. **Transfer of training** occurs when trainees apply what they have learned in training to their jobs.[18] For transfer to happen, employees must first remember what they learned, or maintain an attitude over time. For example, if a trainer shows a new employee the steps involved in using a piece of manufacturing equipment, the employee must remember those steps after training is complete. Moreover, the employee must actually use those steps back on the job.

Transfer is more complicated than it sounds, and there is considerable evidence that many training programs get employees to learn but not to transfer.[19] In other words, employees seem to understand the training material, but they do not change their behavior on the job. When this happens, investments in training are essentially wasted. Imagine, for example, what would have happened if Rockwell Collins's 1,300 trained engineers had finished training and done nothing differently back at work. A great deal of everyone's time and money would have been wasted, and those responsible might be trying to claim unemployment benefits.

How can training be designed to encourage learning and transfer? Two fundamental practices will help HR professionals to meet this goal: (1) managers, employees, and HR professionals must work in partnership; and (2) organizations must use a systematic process for designing, developing, and delivering training.

PARTNERSHIP

The first fundamental practice for ensuring learning and transfer is to operate training as a partnership among employees, their managers, and HR professionals. A partnership between HR professionals and employees is critical because these professionals cannot determine employees' knowledge and skill levels without their help. In addition, without the support of management, HR professionals are unlikely to be able to change the actual behavior of employees on the job. For example, if managers do not want employees to take the time to work on cost-cutting and quality-control projects, then training employees in how to run these projects is unlikely to change how the employees do their work and even less likely to improve the organization's bottom line.

Another way to think about the need for partnership is to consider that employee performance is determined by many factors that are not under the direct control of a human resource department. Table 9.2 lists six factors that are commonly considered to have a powerful influence on job performance.

The first four factors that affect job performance are primarily the responsibility of the employees' manager. First, managers must set clear expectations about what employees should and should not do on the job. Second, managers must provide necessary support in the form of equipment, supplies, and other

Table 9.2	Factors Affecting Job Performance with Responsible Stakeholders
Factor	**Stakeholder**
1. Clear Expectations	Manager
2. Necessary Support	Manager
3. Useful Feedback	Manager
4. Appropriate Consequences	Manager
5. Individual Capacity	Manager and HR Professional
6. Required Knowledge and Skill	Manager and HR Professional

KNOW!!

Source: Information from Geary A. Rummler and Alan P. Brache, *Improving Performance: How to Manage the White Space on the Organization Chart*, 2nd ed. (San Francisco: Jossey-Bass, 1995).

resources. Third, managers must provide useful feedback indicating whether employees are exceeding, meeting, or failing to meet expectations. The feedback must also guide employees toward better performance. Fourth, managers must set appropriate consequences, which means rewarding effective performance and, if necessary, punishing ineffective performance. The fifth and sixth factors, individual capacity and required knowledge and skill, are the only two factors that HR professionals have much control over. Ineffective performance on the part of any one employee, then, may be largely a function of a manager's failure to ensure that one or more of these factors are in place.

HR professionals can influence employees' job performance by working with managers to ensure that employees have the individual capacity (generally through recruitment and selection) and the required knowledge and skill (generally through training and development) to do the job. So the HR function does play an important role, but even in this role, there must be a partnership. If what HR professionals offer as training seems worthless to managers, then they will tell their employees to disregard training and instead do their work as it should "really be done."

SYSTEMATIC PROCESS

The second fundamental practice used to ensure learning and transfer is to develop training systematically. There are many possible ways to develop training, but almost all have three fundamental components:

1. *Needs assessment* to determine who should be trained and what the training should include.
2. *Design and delivery* to ensure that training maximizes learning and transfer.
3. *Evaluation* to determine how training can be improved, whether it worked as intended, and whether it should be continued.[20]

Traditional model of instructional design
A process used to create training programs in which needs assessment is followed by design and delivery and then by evaluation.

Two different forms of this three-component process are diagrammed in Figure 9.2. Part *a* depicts a circular process. This is the **traditional model of instructional design**, and it suggests beginning with a needs assessment that is followed by design and delivery and then by evaluation. Of course, the process is never complete because training needs are always changing, so after evaluation there will eventually be another needs assessment.

Rapid model of instructional design
A process used to create training programs in which assessment, design and delivery, and evaluation overlap in time.

Part *b* of the figure shows the **rapid model of instructional design**.[21] Organizations may use this version of the process when they need to speed up the time from identified need to delivery of training. In the rapid model,

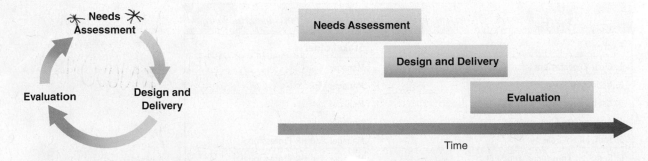

(a) Traditional Model of Instructional Design   (b) Rapid Model of Instructional Design

Figure 9.2 Two Approaches to Designing Training Programs.

training design begins while the needs assessment continues, as indicated by the overlap in the bars. Just as important, training begins before the program design is completely finished, and evaluation is used to modify the training as it is developed.

Whether the traditional or rapid model is appropriate depends on the nature of the training being designed. Training that must be right the first time—either because there is only one opportunity to train particular employees or because the cost of employees doing the wrong thing is too high—should not use the rapid model. For example, training for employees who operate expensive and dangerous equipment (airplanes, cranes, bulldozers, and tanks, for example) should not be delivered to trainees unless it has been examined in great detail for accuracy and safety. Product training for retail sales employees, in contrast, could be delivered before it was perfected, and this would ensure that employees had at least some knowledge of new products as they arrived.

CONCEPT CHECK

1. *What is transfer of training?*
2. *What are the two different systematic approaches to designing training programs? How are they similar, and how are they different?*

LEARNING OBJECTIVE 3

How Are Training Needs Determined?

How does an organization determine what training to offer and who should be trained? This process is called **needs assessment**, and it occurs in two different ways.[22] First, needs assessments may be done on a regular basis as training programs are planned and budgets are set. This planning process requires a proactive approach to determining training needs and developing training plans. Second, needs assessments may also be done in a reactive fashion in response to requests for particular training programs. The reactive and proactive approaches are described in more detail below.

PROACTIVE NEEDS ASSESSMENT

Proactive needs assessment is a systematic process for determining and prioritizing the training programs to be developed and delivered by an organization. It generally has three distinct steps—organization analysis, task analysis, and person analysis.[23] Each step requires different types of data.

Organization Analysis

Organization analysis requires information about the organization's strategic goals, environment, resources, and characteristics. With this information, an organization can determine whether certain types of training would be useful for employees and for the organization as a whole. As noted earlier,

Needs assessment
A process for determining what training to offer and who should be trained.

Proactive needs assessment
A systematic process for determining and prioritizing the training programs to be developed and delivered by an organization.

Organization analysis
A process used to identify characteristics of the organizational environment that will influence the effectiveness of training.

the organization's strategy is relevant to decisions about training because different strategies require different knowledge, skills, and attitudes on the part of employees. Organizations that seek to differentiate themselves from their competitors with excellent service, for example, are more likely to benefit from service-related training courses than organizations with a cost-reduction strategy. The organization's labor orientation helps to determine whether training will be seen as an appropriate way to build employee knowledge and skill.

Organization analysis also requires an understanding of the environment within which the organization functions. Many facets of the environment, including the technical and legal environments, influence the type of training that an organization should offer. The technical environment includes the current and future technologies that employees will use to perform their work. For example, if an organization is planning to upgrade its computer systems, it will need to plan for training to assist in the transition and will also need to change its existing training to be consistent with the new systems.

The legal environment includes both legislative and regulatory mandates. HR professionals should know how training can assist in compliance and reduce the risk of legal problems. As an example, U.S. courts have determined that the degree of an organization's liability for discrimination depends on whether managers were trained in nondiscriminatory hiring practices.[24] Consequently, managerial training covering laws related to discrimination is useful for organizations covered by employment laws like the Civil Rights Act and the Americans with Disabilities Act, discussed in Chapter 3. Organization analysis should determine which laws are applicable.

Organization analysis also measures characteristics of the work environment, such as how much the organization supports its employees in attending training and using what they learned in training back on the job. Such support may take the form of policies, reward systems, management attitudes and actions, and peer support. Organizations that support training are considered to have a positive **training climate**. Thus, they are more likely to have employees who use learned skills back on the job, because employees are much more likely to succeed in transfer if they perceive that their organization has a supportive climate.[25] If trainees will be returning to a work environment that is not supportive, they should be prepared in training with strategies that will help them overcome the lack of support. Alternatively, it may be necessary to change the climate before investing in the training. Of course, this is easier said than done, because changing climate is a difficult process that unfolds over time only with the commitment of top management.[26]

It is important to note that organization analysis need not be repeated every time a proactive needs assessment is conducted, but it should be repeated if the organization or its environment changes. Changes in competitors' practices, in internal management structure, and in labor laws can alter training needs, as can mergers, acquisitions, and alliances. HR professionals should constantly monitor the environment for such changes and conduct a formal organization analysis when changes are noted.

Training climate
Environmental factors that support training, including policies, rewards, and the attitudes and actions of management and coworkers.

Task Analysis

Task analysis is a form of job analysis that involves identifying the work activities performed by trainees and the knowledge and skill necessary to perform the tasks effectively (see Chapter 4). The methods used in task analysis vary

Task analysis
A process used to describe the work activities of employees, including the knowledge and skill required to complete those activities.

depending on the task being analyzed. The most common process used when the task analysis is being done to help design training is the following:

1. Groups of job incumbents develop lists of the tasks performed.
2. HR professionals group tasks into clusters based on similarity.
3. Groups of managers generate knowledge and skill statements for each task cluster.
4. Surveys, given to a new sample of incumbents, verify the task, task cluster, knowledge, and skill lists. Know

To avoid bias in the data collection, it is generally suggested that multiple groups and multiple incumbents be involved.[27] Of course, in smaller organizations or for jobs that don't exist yet, it may be impossible to get information from people already doing the job. In this case, a few of the individuals who will be responsible for the work to be done can participate. Whoever is involved, it is important to use more than one person in order to get high-quality data; any one individual may not have a complete or accurate perspective on the tasks.

There are three common variations of task analysis: competency modeling, cognitive task analysis, and team task analysis.

1. *Competency modeling* is similar to task analysis but results in a broader, more worker-focused (as opposed to work-focused) list of training needs. The process was described in Chapter 4. Competency modeling is most frequently used with managerial jobs. One benefit of using a competency model for needs assessment is lower cost, because this type of analysis does not involve determining specific competencies for a particular job. A related drawback is that the result of competency modeling may not have sufficient detail to guide training for any one particular job.[28]
2. *Cognitive task analysis* examines the goals, decisions, and judgments that employees make on the job.[29] While traditional task analysis focuses on observable tasks and behaviors, cognitive task analysis delves into the thought processes that underlie effective performance of a task. Experts are asked to think out loud while they perform each step of the task. Later, the transcripts of their words are analyzed to identify the knowledge and skills that were necessary at each step.
3. *Team task analysis* involves examining the task and coordination requirements of a group of individuals working together toward a common goal.[30] It is important to use team task analysis in situations where the performance of interest to the organization is largely determined by coordinated efforts. Research on nuclear power plant operations, for example, indicates that operating teams must exchange information and share key tasks in order to perform effectively. Team task analysis will identify the knowledge and skills that underlie these exchanges. Then, training will focus on knowledge and skills identified in the team task analysis as well as the required technical skills.

Person Analysis

Person analysis involves answering three questions:

1. Is training necessary to ensure that employees can perform tasks effectively?
2. If training is needed, who needs the training?
3. Are potential trainees ready for training?

Person analysis
A process used to identify who needs training and what characteristics of those individuals will influence the effectiveness of training.

First, person analysis should determine whether training is necessary by determining whether employees' knowledge and skill are relevant to improving their performance. If employees lack knowledge and skill required for performance, then training is appropriate. There are, however, many other reasons why employees may not perform effectively, including unclear expectations, lack of necessary support in the form of resources and equipment, lack of feedback about performance, inappropriate consequences, and lack of capacity.[31] You may recall this list from Table 9.2.

Second, if training is needed, it is necessary to determine who needs training. A number of different methods can be employed to make this determination. Two of the most common are examining employee records and asking employees whether they think they need training. Both can be useful, but each suffers from potential bias. Employee records may not be sufficiently detailed or may gloss over skill deficiencies because of legal concerns over keeping records of poor performance. As to self-assessments of training needs, employees generally overestimate their skills and thus underestimate the need for training.[32] Another commonly used method is to rely on supervisors to identify those who need or would benefit from training. Because no one method is perfect, multiple methods should be used when possible.

Third, HR professionals must determine if those who need to be trained are ready for training. To do this, they should examine the general mental abilities, basic skills, motivation, and self-efficacy of the potential trainees. Research suggests that individuals with higher levels of general mental ability, necessary basic skills, motivation to learn, and self-efficacy are more likely to benefit from training.[33] That does not mean that training should be offered only to those who fit this profile. Training will, however, be more successful if it is adjusted for particular groups of trainees, as outlined in Table 9.3.

As one example, consider an outsourced call center where employees in another country answer phone calls from the United States. The center might develop two different training programs for employees with different levels of English-language skills. Employees with lower English-language skills may need a course that covers basic terminology and English phone etiquette before being trained on company-specific phone procedures. Assessing the basic

Table 9.3	*Personal Characteristics Relevant to Training Effectiveness and Implications for Design*

Personal Characteristic	Definition	Suggestions for Training Design
General Mental Ability	Overall ability to process information and learn	Trainees with lower general mental ability generally require more time to learn and more structure and guidance in the training environment.
Basic Skills	Ability to perform fundamental tasks like reading, writing, and math	Trainees without basic skills required for a particular training program may need extra assistance during training or remediation prior to training.
Motivation to Learn	Interest in and desire to learn the material in training	Trainees with lower motivation may need to be convinced of the importance of training, either within the training environment or outside the training environment by their managers.
Self-efficacy	Confidence that the skills can be learned and applied on the job	Trainees with lower self-efficacy may need extra practice opportunities and may need to have training framed in a more positive and supportive way.

language skills of employees will be necessary to determine whether language skill differences exist and to help assign employees to the proper training.

REACTIVE NEEDS ASSESSMENT

The analyses we have discussed are useful for proactively determining how an organization should allocate training resources. An alternative model deals with situations that involve a specific performance problem, such as low sales or high turnover. This model, **reactive needs assessment**, is a problem-solving process that begins with defining the problem and then moves to identifying the root cause of the problem and designing an intervention to solve it. Some organizations, like Rockwell Collins, have implemented this problem-solving process by requiring managers who request training to fill out a form. A modified version of the form used at Rockwell Collins is presented in Table 9.4. The questions on this form are designed to help managers think through whether the training requested is relevant to the company's strategy and related goals and whether training is the most efficient solution to the problem.

Reactive needs assessment A problem-solving process used to determine whether training is necessary to fix a specific performance problem and, if training is necessary, what training should be delivered.

Table 9.4	*Reactive Needs Assessment via Training Request Form*

Your Name: _____

Your Position: _____

Your Department: _____

Your Business Unit: _____

Best Way to Reach You: _____

Training Requested: _____

1. What business goals/objectives will this training support?

2. How does it support these goals/objectives?

3. What will the participants know or do differently (that they don't know or can't do now) after training is complete?

4. How critical is this change in knowledge or skill for improving employees' job performance? for your department or business unit's performance?

5. Can you envision benefits to this training beyond an improvement in participants' job performance? Consider, for example, improved teamwork among your employees or retention of high-performing employees.

6. Do any of your current employees have the desired knowledge/skill? If so, please provide information on who these employees are and how they acquired the desired knowledge/skill.

7. Can alternatives to a training course be used to ensure employees get the desired knowledge/skill? Consider, for example, new policies, a performance support tool like a job aid, coaching, or work redesign.

8. Is your department willing to incur the full cost of the training if no other departments are able to be involved?

9. Do you have any preferences for who should deliver this training? If you have an outside vendor in mind, please provide contact information and estimated cost information here.

10. Who needs the desired knowledge/skill? Please describe who they are (positions) and how many. Then answer the following questions about the projected participants:

    a. Approximately what percentage of their working time will be spent on tasks that require this knowledge/skill over the next 12 months?

    b. How soon after training will they make use of the knowledge/skill gained?

    c. In your opinion, are they interested and willing to learn the new knowledge/skill?

11. What is your timeline? When would the training need to start and end?

Source: Information from Cliff Purington and Chris Butler with Sarah Fister Gale, *Built to Learn: The Inside Story of How Rockwell Collins Became a True Learning Organization* (New York: AMACOM, 2003).

Some other organizations follow a three-step process. The steps are (1) problem definition, (2) causal analysis, and (3) solution implementation.[34]

Problem Definition

Problem definition
The gap between desired and actual performance.

Problem definition begins with the identification of a business need. When a request for training comes in, the first question to be asked is whether the problem is important. Companies must prioritize, and it may be that the problem is not sufficiently related to the company's current strategy and goals to warrant the resources required to fix it. If the problem is sufficiently important, then the next question to be asked is, "What should be happening, and how does that vary from what is actually happening?" This means stating the problem as a gap between desired and actual performance. For example, suppose your sales team has been selling primarily inexpensive products (less than $100 per item) but management wants you to increase sales of more-expensive products (more than $1,000 per item) by 50 percent. In this case, the 50 percent difference between current sales and desired sales of expensive products represents a gap between desired and actual performance.

Causal Analysis

Causal analysis
A process used to determine the underlying causes of a performance problem.

Once a problem has been defined as a gap, it is necessary to find out the reasons for the gap. This is done through **causal analysis**. To understand the causes, we ask, "Why does this gap exist?" The gap may result from a lack of knowledge, a lack of motivation, a lack of feedback, or a poor environment. To determine the underlying cause of poor performance, HR professionals explore what employees are doing and why.

In the case of a sales team that should be selling more-expensive products, causal analysis would determine why those products are not being sold. Is it because of a problem with the product itself or with the customers who are currently being targeted? Is it because sales employees are not motivated to make those sales, or perhaps because they are not knowledgeable enough about those products to close sales? Asking the right questions can lead to identifying a set of causes that will help determine whether training will solve the problem. If the cause is a knowledge deficit, then training can help close the gap between desired and actual results. If the cause is most likely the product or employee motivation, then a need has been identified that cannot be resolved through training.

Solution Implementation

The final step involves selecting and implementing the appropriate solution or solutions. This step includes brainstorming possible interventions, examining them for effectiveness and efficiency, and prioritizing them. Table 9.5 gives examples of possible solutions to the sales problem in our example. It is worth noting that many solutions do not involve training; training is not a useful solution to every performance problem. Note also that these solutions are categorized according to the performance factors identified in Table 9.2. Alternative solutions should be considered for their relative effectiveness (how well do we think they will work?) and efficiency (how much will they cost? how long will they take?). People familiar with the job can be asked to rate each potential solution for its anticipated effectiveness and efficiency. The solution that best balances efficiency and effectiveness should be selected for design and implementation.

Table 9.5	*Potential Solutions to Performance Problems*	
Cause	**Category**	**Potential Solutions**
Sales agents expect their *managers* to sell expensive and higher profit margin items.	Clear Expectations	Explain to all sales agents that sales of high-margin items are part of each employee's job duties
Sales agents can't get questions about high-cost products answered from available technical manuals and technical support staff.	Necessary Support	Develop new technical manuals or hire a support person who can answer those questions
Sales agents cannot recall how much they sold that was high-margin and how much was low.	Useful Feedback	Classify products by margin and provide weekly feedback on percent of category sold
Sales agents are rewarded for number of items they sell rather than for total money value of sales.	Appropriate Consequences	Alter rewards so commission is based not on number of sales but on profit from sales
Sales agents do not understand and cannot explain technical details of more-expensive products.	Individual Capacity	Develop technical manuals that customers can access; hire a team of sales agents with this capacity and assign them responsibility for expensive items

PRIORITIZING AND CREATING OBJECTIVES

Once the organization has collected needs assessment information, it must put all that information together to determine what training to offer and whom to train. This part of the assessment process includes prioritizing training needs and setting objectives for training.

Determining Priorities

An organization often identifies a number of different training needs—usually more than can possibly be covered given the training budget and the time that employees can be away from their work. What can be done? Prioritize! There are a few different ways to prioritize, including ratings and interviews, but no one method is best.

Figure 9.3 shows one method for prioritizing training needs based on a task analysis. The figure lists some knowledge and skills necessary for a general manager's human resource responsibilities. A sample of managers and employees familiar with the job can be asked to rate each item on this list along two scales—strategic importance and need for training. Strategic importance is the importance of this particular item for helping the person perform his or her work effectively and in a way that benefits the entire organization. Need for training is the degree to which it is important that the person have this knowledge and skill before beginning work. A low need for training means that performers can learn as they work. Once all the ratings have been collected, they are summed to create a composite rating. Then the list is rank-ordered from highest to lowest scores. The needs that come to the top are those that are most relevant to the organization's strategy and that are required early on the job. The items highest on the list should be the focus of training.

Creating Objectives

Whether proactive or reactive needs assessment techniques are used, if training is required, then an essential output of the assessment process should be a list of training objectives. Here, an objective is simply a desired and intended outcome. Two of the most critical types of objectives are learning objectives and organizational objectives.[35]

Know

Knowledge, Skill, or Attitude	Strategic Importance	Need for Training	Composite
Knowledge of laws, regulations, policies, standards, and procedures for hiring new employees	3	4	7
Knowledge of laws, regulations, policies, standards, and procedures for promoting employees	1	0	1
Knowledge of laws, regulations, policies, standards, and procedures for terminating employees	3	1	4
Skill presenting technical concepts and solutions to nontechnical functional teams	4	2	6
Be passionate about high-quality, high-touch customer service	4	4	8

Strategic Importance

How important is this knowledge, skill, or attitude to the job and the organization as a whole?

Need for Training

How important is it that employees be trained on this before they start work?

Scale

0 = Not Important
1 = Somewhat Important
2 = Important
3 = Very Important
4 = Extremely Important

Figure 9.3 Sample Prioritization Worksheet Using Knowledge, Skill, and Attitude Statements.

Learning objective
The individual learning outcome sought by training.

Learning objectives are the intended individual learning outcomes from training. For a veterinary surgeon, for example, an outcome might be knowledge of the anatomy of a particular animal or skill in using a scalpel to remove cysts. The learning objectives should be used to determine the content, methods, and media used in training (we describe these elements of training in the next section).[36] Learning objectives are useful because they provide a basis for selecting features of training, provide measurable results that can be used to determine if training was effective, offer guidance to learners about what they should be doing, and ensure that, even if multiple trainers or sessions are involved, the same outcomes are achieved.[37]

Effective learning objectives have three components:

1. *Performance* identifies what the trainee is expected to do or produce.
2. *Conditions* describe important circumstances under which performance is to occur.
3. *Criteria* describe acceptable performance in a quantifiable and objective way.

Table 9.6 gives some examples of ineffective learning objectives and the changes necessary to make them effective.

Organizational objective
The organization result sought by training.

Organizational objectives capture the intended results of training for the company. These may include increased productivity, decreased waste, or better customer service. Specifying the intended organizational result of training programs helps to ensure that the training provides value to the organization as a whole and that each program is linked to the strategy of the firm. Setting organizational objectives can thus help in prioritizing. For example, if

Table 9.6	Examples of Ineffective and Effective Learning Objectives	
Ineffective Objective	**Missing Element(s)**	**Effective Objective**
Understand business ethics	Performance Conditions Criteria	*Given videotaped scenes of a manager running a business meeting* (conditions), *be able to identify instances of unethical behavior* (performance). *Identify all instances of unethical behavior as defined by your company's Code of Conduct* (criterion).
Be able to describe the features and benefits of a product	Conditions Criteria	*Given a potential customer, a product, and related literature* (conditions), *describe the features and benefits of the product* (performance). *All key benefits and features in literature are described; all information presented is factual; customer is not insulted, demeaned, embarrassed, or ridiculed* (criteria).
Identify three major varieties of red wine with 100% accuracy	Conditions	*Given three glasses of different varieties of red wine* (conditions), *be able to identify* (performance) *each correctly while blindfolded* (criterion).
On the 15-yard shooting range, be able to draw your revolver and fire five rounds from the hip within three seconds	Criteria	*On the 15-yard shooting range* (conditions), *be able to draw your revolver and fire five rounds* (performance) *from the hip within three seconds. All rounds must hit the standard silhouette target* (criteria).

Source: Information from Robert F. Mager, *Preparing Instructional Objectives,* 3rd ed. (Atlanta: Center for Effective Performance, 1997).

a training program has the objective of increasing customer satisfaction, but reducing costs is the primary strategic direction of the firm, then that program should be considered lower priority than a program intended to help reduce costs.

CONCEPT CHECK

1. *What are the steps in a reactive needs assessment? A proactive needs assessment?*
2. *What components do effective learning objectives include?*

LEARNING OBJECTIVE 4

How Is Effective Training Designed and Delivered?

Once objectives have been written, decisions must be made about content (what to deliver to trainees), methods (how to help trainees learn the content), media (how to deliver content and methods to trainees), and transfer-enhancement techniques (how to help trainees transfer what they learned back to the job).

In terms of content, organizations devote the largest proportion of training time to topics that are specific to the industry, such as computer assembly and testing at computer companies such as Dell and inventory control at clothing companies such as Old Navy. Other types of training that receive considerable time include information technology, managerial and supervisory, mandatory

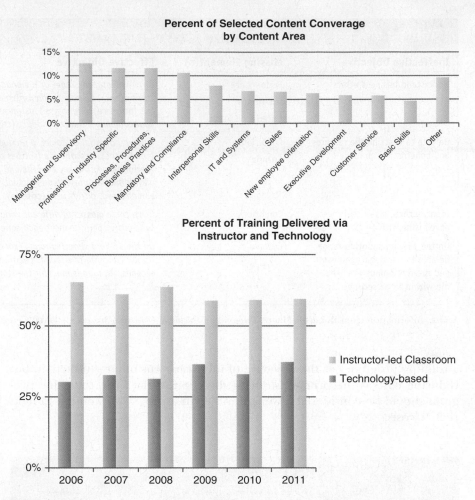

Figure 9.4 Snapshots of Training Practices in the United States.
Source: Laurie Miller, *State of the Industry Report, 2012: ASTD's Annual Review of Workplace Learning and Development Data* (Alexandria, VA: American Society for Training and Development, 2012), 31, 33.

and compliance, business processes and procedures, quality and product knowledge, and sales. Figure 9.4 specifically illustrates the extent to which a variety of content is emphasized by a large sample of organizations in the United States. Part *b* of the figure also captures the type of media used and indicates that training media have changed gradually over the years to include more and more technology-based delivery, including CD-ROM and Internet-based training.

CONTENT

Content is the material that is covered in training. Training objectives are used to determine what content is needed. The person responsible for training can select content in several ways: (1) create it from scratch, (2) consult with subject matter experts, (3) examine theory and research in the literature, (4) purchase off-the-shelf materials, and (5) contract with a training vendor to create the materials.[38] No one way is best, and many training designers combine these techniques. For example, a management training course offered by Ford

Motor Company includes materials created by the company's trainers in consultation with Ford engineers, materials taken from the published literature on management, and some off-the-shelf videos and exercises to help build managerial skills such as delegating and conducting performance reviews.

Because creating materials from scratch or in consultation with local experts is time consuming, many organizations use **training vendors** to create their training. Training vendors are companies whose primary business is to design and deliver training programs. To select a vendor that will provide a strategically relevant and high-quality program, management should ask prospective vendors a series of questions such as the following:[39]

Training vendors
Organizations that sell existing training programs or services to develop and deliver training programs.

- What projects have you completed that are similar to our project in terms of needs, objectives, and situation?
- May we see samples of your work? What evidence do you have that this work was effective? May we contact your references?
- Who will be working on this project, and what are their backgrounds and qualifications?
- Explain your work process. Where will you work? What will you need from us in terms of space, personnel, information, and other resources?
- Explain your evaluation process. How many milestones do you expect? How will you monitor progress? How would you prefer to receive feedback?
- What do you expect that this project, as explained up to this point, will cost? How do you charge? How are expenses handled?
- If we experience overruns in cost or time, how are those handled?
- Who will own the final work—our company, your company, or both?

TRAINING METHODS

The various ways of organizing content and encouraging trainees to learn are referred to as **training methods**. Training methods vary in terms of how active the learner is during training. More-passive methods can be useful, but they should seldom be used without the addition of at least one more-active method.

Training methods
How training content is organized and structured for the learner.

Presentation

Presentation is the primary passive method of instruction. A presentation involves providing content directly to learners in a noninteractive fashion. It is a passive method because learners do little other than read or listen and (hopefully) make sense of the material. The most common type of presentation is a lecture given by an instructor. Lectures have a bad reputation, but research suggests that people can and do learn from them.[40] Lectures are an efficient way for many learners to receive the same content and gain the same knowledge. This means that presentations can be useful when the learning objective of training is for trainees to gain knowledge, such as an understanding of product features. A disadvantage of presentations is that learners are not given any formal opportunity to test or apply what they are learning. For this reason, presentations seldom help trainees gain skills.

Presentations can include various types of information. Some presentations include only verbal information (words), but others also include auditory information (sounds), static visual information (pictures), and dynamic visual information (animation). Presentations can be made more interesting with the addition of these other types of information, but the additional

Table 9.7	*Characteristics of Various Training Methods*					
	Training Objective			**Costs**		**Likelihood of Transfer**
Method	**Knowledge**	**Skill**	**Attitude**	**Development**	**Administration**	
Presentation	Yes	No	No	Low	Low	Low
Discussion	Maybe	Yes	Yes	Low	Low	Low
Case Study	Maybe	Yes	Maybe	Medium	Low	Medium
Discovery	No	Yes	Maybe	Medium	Medium	Medium
Role Play	No	Yes	Yes	Medium	Medium	High
Simulation	Yes	Yes	Maybe	High	Medium	High
Modeling	No	Yes	No	High	High	High

Source: Adapted from Alan M. Saks and Robert R. Haccoun, *Managing Performance through Training and Development,* 3rd ed. (Ontario, Canada: Nelson, 2004), 162.

information should complement rather than distract from the verbal information being conveyed. Trainees can be overwhelmed or confused if confronted with too much information.[41]

To avoid the problem of presenting too much information at once, companies may break training into several units. For example, to prepare its employees for the General Securities Representative Exam (Series 7), Merrill Lynch has a course that combines written text, telephone tutoring, and computer-aided testing. The written text is offered in a series of specially prepared booklets that present information in short paragraphs and use bold print for key concepts.[42] Breaking down material in this way helps to ensure that trainees can learn without being overwhelmed.

Presentations can help employees learn even more if they are combined with active methods. You have probably experienced this in school. Listening to a lecture may help you learn a fact or two, but without an opportunity to do something with that knowledge, you forget it.

Table 9.7 contrasts presentation with other training methods in terms of what works best for particular objectives, as well as relative costs. Methods should be selected primarily based on their usefulness in helping achieve the training method's objectives. The table also indicates whether transfer of training is likely based simply on the nature of the method. These factors, along with preferences of the instructor and of trainees, should all be considered when selecting the training method for a particular program.[43] Methods that directly increase transfer are discussed later in this section.

Discussions

Discussions represent a more-active training method. Discussions increase trainees' involvement by allowing two-way communication between trainer and trainees and among trainees. Discussion can help trainees to accomplish several things:

- Recognize what they do not know but should know.
- Get their questions answered.
- Get advice on matters of concern to them.
- Share ideas and develop a common perspective.
- Learn about one another as people.[44]

Discussions can be used to build knowledge and critical-thinking skills, but they are best used to help improve motivation and change attitudes. Discussions must be facilitated by a trainer in order to allow everyone an opportunity to participate. With larger audiences, discussions often do not work well because not everyone has a chance to contribute.

Case Study

Case analysis is an active training method in which trainees discuss, analyze, and solve problems based on real or hypothetical situations. Cases can be used to help teach basic principles and to improve motivation and change attitudes. Generally, however, the primary objective is to develop skill in analysis, communication, and problem solving.[45] Cases vary in length and complexity. Although long, complex cases are often used in business schools, trainers in businesses shy away from them, preferring to use shorter cases.[46]

Discovery

Discovery is an active method that involves presenting trainees with a task that offers rich opportunities to learn new skills. For example, employees might be given access to a new computer program and asked to figure out for themselves how to do their work tasks using the program. Although this method may sound more like learning by experimentation than training, discovery can be structured so that skills needed for job performance are available to be learned. In effect, discovery is experimentation in a controlled training environment.

Discovery can be highly motivating for trainees, but it has serious drawbacks. Without any guidance from the instructor, it is highly inefficient and can result in people learning the wrong things.[47] A more efficient approach is discovery coupled with guidance, where the instructor is more active in asking questions and providing hints that help learners while they explore. Appropriate guidance can help motivate trainees and ensure that they learn the best way to perform the task.[48]

Role Play

When trainees engage in role playing, each participant acts out a part in a simulated situation. This active method offers an opportunity for trainees to practice new skills in the training environment. It is most often used to help trainees acquire interpersonal and human relations skills. Role playing typically has three phases:[49]

1. *Development* involves preparing and explaining the roles and the situation that will be used in role playing.
2. *Enactment* involves the time that trainees take to become familiar with the details of the role and then act them out. Enactment can be done in small groups, with two actors and an observer, or with larger groups, with a small set of actors and the rest of the audience serving as observers. Of course, for skill building to occur, all trainees must have an opportunity to serve as an actor at some point.
3. *Debriefing*, in which trainees discuss their experiences, is considered the most important phase of role playing. Discussions should address the connections among the role-playing experience, the desired learning outcomes, and the desired organizational outcomes. Trainers must provide feedback to ensure that trainees learn from the role-playing experience. In other words, trainers must offer constructive criticism to trainees, explaining what they did well and where they need more practice.

Simulation

Simulations are active methods that reproduce events, processes, and circumstances that occur in the trainee's job. Participating in a simulation gives trainees the opportunity to experience at least some aspects of their job in a safe and controlled environment and build skills relevant to those aspects of the job. For example, pilots can be trained with mechanical flight simulators. Simulations can also involve role playing with many actors or interactive computer technology, such as in a virtual world like Second Life. To achieve the greatest benefits, simulations should be designed to replicate as closely as possible both the physical and psychological conditions that exist on the job. For instance, to simulate a manager's daily experience, trainees could work on multiple tasks simultaneously and coordinate their efforts with those of other people in order to get their tasks completed.[50] After all, these are the conditions under which managers typically accomplish their work. Related to simulations are educational games, which combine entertaining engagement with attention to user's learning. Computer games are becoming more popular, but they should be used with careful attention to selecting or designing a game that triggers learning of relevant information. [51]

Modeling

Behavior modeling is a powerful method that draws together principles of learning from many different areas. As described in the "How Do We Know?" feature, research has repeatedly found that this method is effective for improving skills.[52] The basic process is simple:

1. The trainer explains key learning points.
2. The trainer or another model performs a task while trainees observe.
3. Trainees practice performance while the trainer observes.
4. The trainer provides feedback to the trainees.

Behavior modeling works particularly well when the model is someone whom the trainees see as credible and when that model shows both positive and negative examples of the task performance.[53]

On-the-Job Methods

With the methods discussed so far, trainees work off the job in a training setting. Training can also occur on the job. One common approach to on-the-job training is also among the least likely to help employees learn. Some companies pair up inexperienced employees with experienced employees and ask the inexperienced employees to watch and learn.[54] This approach can be a useful way to help employees become familiar with the job, but it is not always effective because experienced employees may not do the work properly or may not know how to teach. In fact, because this type of on-the-job training is often poorly planned and ill structured, it seldom fits the definition of training provided at the start of this chapter.

Effective on-the-job training is structured and systematic. Structured on-the-job training is an application of behavior modeling that is carried out in small-group situations on the job. The process is the same as that described in the discussion of behavior modeling: the trainer explains key learning points and then performs the task while trainees observe. The trainees then practice performance while the trainer observes, and the trainer provides feedback.

TRAINING MEDIA

Training media are the means by which content and methods are delivered to trainees. Each passive and active training method we have discussed can be delivered in a number of different ways. For example, the information in a presentation can be transmitted by an instructor face to face (a classic lecture), an instructor via video or Web conference (videoconferencing), a sophisticated computer program, a basic computer presentation or website, an audio presentation (such as with an iPod or other MP3 player), or typed written material. The trend today is toward using some form of technology to deliver training. Indeed, this trend has been heralded as an e-learning revolution. **e-Learning** is training delivered online, and it has both benefits and drawbacks.

With all the possible choices, how can an organization decide which training media to use? There are no powerful research results suggesting that only one or two media work for delivering training. Instead, the choice should be guided by a two-step process. First, the selected training method should be examined to see if it has a media requirement. A media requirement is a characteristic of a training medium that is fundamentally necessary to ensure that a training method is effective. Second, the cost and accessibility of the remaining media should be considered to make the final selection. We next look more closely at each of these steps.

> **Training media**
> How training content and the associated methods are delivered to the learner.

> **e-learning**
> Training delivered through computers and network technology.

How Do We Know?

IS THERE ONE BEST WAY TO TRAIN FOR COMPUTER SKILLS?

One of the most common training challenges organizations face is how to get their employees to use computers effectively and efficiently. Because computers are virtually everywhere, employees who can't use computers can really hurt an organization's ability to produce goods and provide services.

What is the best way to train computer skills? A study conducted by Steven Simon and Jon Werner helped answer this question. These researchers tested four different ways to train computer skills. One method was behavior modeling, another was self-paced study, and a third was lecture. A fourth group of employees did not receive training and was expected to learn on the job. Trainees were novice computer users working in construction for the U.S. Navy in Gulfport, Mississippi.

Measures of knowledge and skill collected immediately after training were highest for employees who received training using behavior modeling.

Results were similar when employees were tested again one month later—those trained with the behavior modeling method still had higher skills. Satisfaction with the computer system, also assessed one month after training, was also highest for behavior modeling.

The Bottom Line. Employees can learn to use computers in many different ways, including simply learning on their own, on the job. However, this study strongly supports the idea that there is one best way to improve computer-related knowledge, skills, and attitudes, at least for novice users. Training using behavior modeling resulted in better outcomes across different measures and over time.

Source: Information from Steven J. Simon and Jon M. Werner, "Computer Training through Behavior Modeling, Self-Paced, and Instructional Approaches: A Field Experiment," *Journal of Applied Psychology* 81 (1996): 648–659.

Technology in HR

BENEFITS AND DRAWBACKS OF E-LEARNING

Widespread access to computers and the Internet provides a cheap, efficient, and customizable means of delivering training. Using the Internet or a corporate intranet, employees can, at least in theory, take training whenever and wherever they want. This benefit can reduce training costs because employees can learn at their workplaces without having to travel to a central training site. Training can also be individualized so that trainees see only the material they need rather than having to sit through a presentation on material they already know. Taken together, these benefits make training more efficient.

Training professionals have some reasonable concerns about e-learning, however. First, the up-front cost can be substantial, particularly for high-quality training that can be accessed by all employees. Second, interaction among peers is constrained, which reduces the enjoyment and networking opportunities offered by traditional face-to-face training. Finally, non-interactive e-learning can bore trainees and can suggest that simply putting written material on a computer makes it training. The truth of the matter is that online material, when all it contains is reading, is no different from a book; it is a source of information rather than training structured to help employees learn. If you have ever taken an online course that consisted of little more than page after page of text, then you have suffered through what some companies offer as e-learning programs.

Research also points to another concern—technology-driven learning often puts control of learning into the hands of learners, and not all learners make choices that help them learn. Learners do not necessarily know what they don't know, so they might skip over material that would benefit them. Employees who are not motivated to learn, and who have many demands placed on their time at work, are more likely to skip over material and thus limit the benefits that training can yield.

Companies can address many of these concerns by (1) taking the time to design e-learning so it requires learners to be active, (2) using e-learning only when the learners are ready and willing to use it, and (3) providing support to learners in the form of time to take the training and, if necessary, a training

Thomas_EyeDesign/iStockphoto

space away from the office. In the end, whether e-learning is appropriate depends on the situation—on whether it is appropriate for this organization, this training, and these trainees. If there is a good fit, then e-learning can be a powerful tool.

Sources: Kenneth G. Brown, Steven D. Charlier, and Abigail Pierotti, "e-Learning in Work Organizations: Contributions of Past Research and Suggestions for the Future," in G.P. Hodgkinson & J.K. Ford (eds.) *International Review of Industrial and Organizational Psychology* 27 (Chichester, UK: Wiley & Sons, 2012): 89-114; Liz T. Welsh, Connie R. Wanberg, Kenneth G. Brown, and Marcia J. Simmering, "e-Learning: Emerging Uses, Best Practices, and Future Directions," *International Journal of Training and Development* 7 (2003): 245–258; Renee E. DeRouin, Barbara Fritzsche, and Eduardo Salas, "Optimizing e-Learning: Research-Based Guidelines for Learner-Controlled Training," *Human Resources Management* 43 (2004): 147–162; Kenneth G. Brown, "A Field Study of Employee e-Learning Activity and Outcomes," *Human Resource Development Quarterly* 16 (2005): 465–480.

Media Requirements

You might wonder whether it is really possible to learn through all of the different media listed above. Occasionally, people ask, "Doesn't training have to be delivered face to face, by an experienced instructor, to be effective?" The answer is clearly no. As described in the "Technology in HR" feature, carefully designed training can be equally effective whether it is presented via technology (like computers or videoconferencing) or face to face by an instructor.[55] In fact, some studies have shown that technology-delivered training can be more effective than traditional face-to-face instruction. Nevertheless, some training methods do require specific media characteristics.[56] Two fundamental media requirements are explained here. Other requirements may arise in the course of developing a training program in a particular organization with a particular set of objectives and methods.

First, if the training uses guided discovery, role playing, simulations, or behavior modeling exercises, then an instructor or sophisticated computer program is required. To be effective, these methods require someone to analyze what the trainees do and provide feedback that helps them gain skills. Therefore, either an instructor must be present, or a computer must be programmed to behave like an instructor.

Second, if a training presentation includes both video and audio, then the training medium must be able to deliver both video and audio. Although somewhat obvious, this requirement suggests that teleconferences, which organizations use to deliver presentations to people scattered all over the country, and podcasts should only be used for presentations that are primarily verbal. If visual materials are an essential part of the presentation, then videoconferencing or some similar medium should be used. Web conferencing, which includes a window to display charts, graphs, video, and animation, has become popular for this type of presentation. A sample screenshot of just such a program is presented in Figure 9.5. This graphic includes a main window for

Figure 9.5 Screenshot of a Web Conference. *Source: Web-ex.* Used with permission.

the display of content, a list of participants in the upper right-hand corner, and a video of the presenter in the bottom right-hand corner.

Cost and Accessibility

Different training media have different costs, and more technologically sophisticated media not only are more expensive but also may create access problems. For example, if you develop a CD-ROM–delivered computer training course, but it only runs on high-end PCs with Windows operating systems, then it's possible that not all employees will be able to use it. Employees who do not have high-end computers, or who work with Apple computers, may be unable to take training conveniently. Both cost and access should be taken into account when finalizing choices about media.

In general, if the audience for training is small, then the organization may choose to save time and money by using media that don't require time-consuming work up front. In such a case, a face-to-face live presentation may be preferable to computer-delivered training. However, if a company already has successful templates for creating computer-delivered training, then it may actually be less expensive than other delivery media.[57]

TRANSFER-ENHANCEMENT TECHNIQUES

As noted earlier, learning does not guarantee that trainees will transfer what they learn to their work back on the job. As a result, transfer will not necessarily happen even if training is designed and delivered in the ways we've just discussed. What can the organization do to foster transfer of training? A number of techniques that can be used before, during, and after training will help.[58]

Before Training

One of the least commonly used but most powerful techniques to enhance transfer, at least according to trainees, is management involvement with trainees prior to training.[59] Managers can work with employees in a number of ways to help them prepare for training. For example, managers can build transfer into employees' performance standards, offer rewards to trainees who demonstrate transfer, involve employees in planning training, brief trainees on the importance of training, send co-workers to training together, and encourage trainees to attend and actively participate in all training sessions. When managers work in partnership with trainers and trainees, transfer is much more likely to occur.

Behavioral contract
An agreement that specifies what the trainee and his or her manager will do to ensure training is effective.

One highly structured way for managers to work with employees is through a **behavioral contract**, which spells out what both the employees and the managers expect to happen during and after training. A behavioral contract would include specific statements about how the employee will use newly acquired knowledge and skill on the job and how the supervisor will support those efforts. The best approach is for employees to work with their managers to create and sign a contract that both agree on.[60] Because it is so formal, the behavioral contract may not be appropriate in all organizations. In organizations whose policies and practices are generally more informal, a simple conversation between manager and employee may be more appropriate. A sample behavioral contract is shown in Figure 9.6.

```
┌─────────────────────────────────────────────────────────────────────────────────┐
│ TRAINEE STATEMENT:                                                                │
│ I, _____, would like to participate  │
│    in the following training program:                                            │
│ _____. If agreed, I will:                                       │
│      * complete all pre-work and other assignment.                               │
│      * attend all portions of the training.                                      │
│      * actively listen and participate throughout the training content.          │
│      * create specific actions detailing how I will apply training content.      │
│                                                        Signed: _____  │
│                                                        Date: _____  │
│ MANAGER STATEMENT:                                                               │
│ I, _____, as the supervisor of the employee identified     │
│    above, agree that I will:                                                     │
│      * release the trainee from sufficient work assignment to allow complete     │
│        preparation for and attendance of all portions of the training.           │
│      * meet with the trainee before and after training  to explore opportunities │
│        for application.                                                          │
│      * provide specific opportunities for the trainee to practice the newly      │
│        acquired behaviors and skills.                                            │
│      * provide encouragement, support, and reinforcement as the trainee applies  │
│        newly acquired behaviors and skills.                                      │
│                                                        Signed:_____  │
│                                                        Date: _____  │
└─────────────────────────────────────────────────────────────────────────────────┘
```

Figure 9.6 Sample Behavior Contract Between Trainee and Manager. *Source:* Information from Mary L. Broad and John W. Newstrom, *Transfer of Training: Action-Packed Strategies to Ensure High Payoff from Training Investments* (Reading, MA: Perseus, 1992).

During Training

During training, the trainer can use at least two different approaches to foster transfer. The first approach is to structure the training in ways that will help trainees to generalize what they learn to situations back on the job. This can be done by focusing training on general principles and varying the situations under which skills are practiced.[61] For example, training managers to conduct performance reviews should provide general guidelines rather than a lock-step process that must be followed every time. General rules provide knowledge that is flexible enough to be applied in a variety of situations. The management trainees can then practice conducting performance reviews in a number of different role-playing situations with characters who react differently. Practice of this type will better prepare them for the uncertainty and variability of the task when it is done back on the job.

The second approach uses an instructional add-on called **relapse prevention training**. This training directly addresses situations in which trainees may have difficulty applying trained skills and provides strategies for overcoming relapses into old patterns of behavior. Relapse prevention programs generally ask trainees to do the following: (1) select a skill from training and set a specific goal to use that skill, (2) anticipate when they might relapse to old behavior instead of using the newly acquired skill, (3) write out the positive and negative consequences of using (or not using) the new skill, (4) review relapse prevention strategies that can be used to prevent or recover from relapses, including recognizing behaviors that might lead to relapse and preparing a support network, (5) describe a few work situations that might contribute to a relapse, and (6) prepare strategies for dealing with these situations. Research has found that relapse prevention programs can be beneficial if the transfer-of-training climate is poor.[62] A downside of relapse prevention is that it requires extra training time.

Relapse prevention training
A transfer enhancement activity that helps prepare trainees to overcome obstacles to using trained behaviors on the job.

After Training

After training, the manager and trainee should work together to ensure transfer. Techniques managers can use include giving positive reinforcement for using trained skills, arranging for practice sessions, supporting trainee reunions, and publicizing successes in the use of trained skills. Managers might also consider reducing job pressures in the first few days that trainees are back from training, to allow the trainees time to test out their new knowledge and skill.

Opportunity to perform
Allowing employees a chance to use the skills they learned in training back on the job.

One other important action that managers must take is to provide trainees with an opportunity to use the skills from training as soon as possible after the training is over. This concept, known as **opportunity to perform**, is essential because without an opportunity to use the new knowledge or skill, it will decay.[63] As you have probably learned in your own lives, knowledge or skill gained and not used is lost over time. For example, you may have memorized the capitals of all the states when you were in elementary school, but you probably don't remember many of them today. If there will be a time delay between when training must be done and when employees need to use it, managers must create opportunities for employees to refresh their knowledge and skill so it is not lost.

In the "How Do We Know" feature, you can learn about two interventions completed after training that helped boost transfer for restaurant managers.

PUTTING IT ALL TOGETHER

When objectives, content, methods, media, and transfer enhancements have all been selected, then training materials must be prepared, reviewed for accuracy and quality, and produced. What training materials will be needed depends on the choices made during design. For example, a course that is instructor-led will require trainees' guides, an instructor's guide, and perhaps audiovisual presentation material.

Effective training can take a long time to develop. It might, for example, take 30 to 80 hours of an HR professional's time to produce one hour of instructor-led training, including the time to conduct a needs assessment, draft a preliminary design, and obtain expert reviews of content. Producing technology-delivered instruction, simulations, and behavior modeling methods can be particularly time consuming. For instance, producing one hour of high-quality computer-delivered simulation may take as many as 400 hours of an HR professional's and a computer programmer's time.[64] Of course, development times vary depending on many factors. The point is that it can take a considerable amount of time to make decisions about training and then act on these decisions to produce the necessary training materials. HR professionals must therefore be effective project managers, taking care to leave enough time to both design and develop all necessary materials.

CONCEPT CHECK

1. *What training methods keep learners active during training?*
2. *What are the benefits and drawbacks of e-learning?*
3. *At what points in time can transfer-enhancement strategies be used?*

How Do We Know?

HOW CAN TRANSFER BE ENHANCED?

All too often, trainees do not use what they learn in training back on the job. One U.S.-wide restaurant chain experimented with ways to make sure that their management training was used on the job. Michael Tews and Bruce Tracey helped the organization design a test to see whether self-coaching, upward feedback, or a combination of both was successful at enhancing transfer. One group of trainees completed self-coaching via a workbook that asked open-ended questions and requested they write down goals and track performance. Another group of trainees received upward feedback in the form of ratings and comments from subordinates regarding the degree to which they used trained behaviors. Yet another group received both, and one group received none of the interventions. In total, 87 new managers participated in this research study. The training was aimed at helping managers clarify expectations, monitor performance, reward performance, provide corrective feedback, and inspire employees. The program was eight hours and included lectures, discussion, video, and role play.

Both interventions worked, but the use of trained behaviors on the job was highest when both interventions were used. Neither intervention was cost free, though, as each requires some post-training administrative work and trainee effort. The restaurant chain that sponsored the research decided to use upward feedback in the future because it required less trainee effort and administrative follow-up.

The Bottom Line. Both self-coaching and upward feedback can be useful for boosting transfer following a training course. The best transfer results occur when both are used, but this requires a good deal of trainee and administrative time. If transfer is a serious concern, and resources are not limited, then using both interventions makes sense. In other situations, the organization should consider which intervention makes the most sense given the nature of the organization, the training, and the trainees.

Source: Information from Michael Tewes and J. Bruce Tracey. "An Empirical Examination of Interventions for Enhancing the Effectiveness of Interpersonal Skills Training," *Personnel Psychology* 61 (2008): 375–401.

LEARNING OBJECTIVE 5

How Do Organizations Determine Whether Training Is Effective?

Training evaluation is the process used to determine the effectiveness of training programs. **Training effectiveness** refers to the extent to which trainees (and their organization) benefit as intended from training. The training evaluation process typically involves four steps: (1) determining the purpose of the evaluation, (2) deciding on relevant outcomes, (3) choosing an evaluation design, and (4) collecting and analyzing the data and reporting the results.[65]

Training effectiveness
The extent to which trainees and their organizations benefit as intended from training.

PURPOSE

The first step in evaluation is to determine the purpose of the evaluation. Most of the reasons to evaluate training fit into three primary categories: (1) provide feedback to designers and trainers that helps improve the training, (2) provide input for decisions about whether to continue or discontinue the training, and (3) provide information that can be used to market the training program.[66]

There are three primary targets of evaluation—that is, three kinds of information that evaluators can collect and analyze: (1) training content and design, which can be assessed to provide feedback to designers and trainers; (2) changes in learners, which can be measured to provide feedback and make decisions about training; and (3) organizational payoffs, which can be collected and used for all three purposes.[67] Each target can be assessed in a number of ways, as discussed in the next section. Figure 9.7 illustrates this perspective on training evaluation.

To provide an example of the connection between purpose and targets, consider a company that offers new supervisors a one-week, face-to-face training course in basic supervisory skills. This training might be evaluated for one, two, or three different reasons. If the training were evaluated to provide feedback that would improve the course in the future, then training experts could be asked to review the training to ensure that the content is accurate and the design choices (methods and media) are appropriate. If the training were evaluated to determine whether it should be continued in the future, then learners could be observed to see if they actually learned the material and used it on the job. Finally, if the training were evaluated to develop marketing materials that would help recruit future trainees, then changes in new supervisor turnover for business units that use the training could be tracked. If turnover rates were lower in business units that used the training, then this result could be crafted into a powerful story about the benefits of training. The story could be distributed widely to encourage other business units to send their

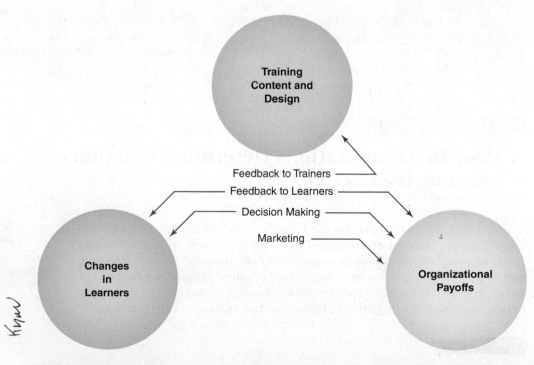

Figure 9.7 The Three Primary Targets of Evaluation. *Source:* Kurt Kraiger, "Decision-Based Evaluation," in Kurt Kraiger (ed.), *Creating, Implementing, and Managing Effective Training and Development* (San Francisco: Jossey-Bass, 2002), 331–376. Used with permission.

supervisors to the training. Of course, an organization might evaluate this training course for all three reasons, in which case it could do all of the above!

Evaluation is not always a single-step activity that only occurs at the end of training. In fact, evaluation efforts may begin while training is being designed. Evaluators may collect information about whether the training objectives and content are aligned with the business strategy and whether the training methods are aligned with the training objectives. This effort might include review by subject matter experts and managers, as well as feedback from trainees following exposure to a course outline or sample materials. Doing evaluation work while training is being developed helps ensure that training is likely to have the desired effects.[68]

OUTCOMES

Training outcomes can be roughly divided into four categories—reactions, learning, transfer, and organizational results.[69] These outcomes provide different types of information about training that are more or less useful, depending on the purpose of the evaluation.

Reactions

Trainee reactions capture how the trainees felt about training: Did they like it? Did they think it was interesting and useful? Reaction measures are similar to the end-of-semester teacher evaluation forms that most colleges have students complete. Evaluations of this sort can be useful for determining how learners react to the training content and design, but they are not good measures of learning. Research shows that reactions do not always relate to how much trainees actually learned.[70] Still, reactions can help evaluators gauge what went well and what did not, which can be useful for providing feedback to training designers and trainers. Reactions can also be useful as overall measures of satisfaction with training courses. High levels of dissatisfaction suggest that something is wrong and that trainers may need to alter the program in some way.

Companies should be careful about making decisions to discontinue courses or to fire trainers based on reaction data alone. Research suggests that there are many determinants of reactions, including factors that are not under the trainer's control. For example, trainees' general tendency to be positive or negative can sway their reactions.[71] If a trainer happens to get a particularly negative set of trainees, then reactions to that course may be lower regardless of what the trainer does. In sum, reaction data should be interpreted cautiously and are probably better used to provide feedback to improve training than to make decisions about discontinuing training.

Learning

As noted earlier, learning is a change that occurs from experience. Learning can involve knowledge, skills, or attitudes, and each of these can be assessed.[72] Knowledge can be assessed with traditional tests, such as multiple-choice, fill-in-the-blank, or open-ended tests. It can also be measured with other techniques, such as asking trainees to explain relationships among key concepts and testing whether trainees' beliefs about relationships are similar to experts' beliefs. Skills can be measured by scoring role plays, simulations, and behavior-modeling exercises for the use of the desired skills. Attitudes can be assessed by asking trainees about their beliefs and their motivation, as well as by watching trainees' behavior for evidence of the desired attitude.

If an objective of training is to have employees believe that promptness is important to customers, for example, then trainees could be scored for their promptness in end-of-training activities.

Learning objectives for a training program should be easily classifiable into these categories and should make clear how to evaluate whether learning has occurred. For example, the learning objective in Table 9.6 concerning wine varieties offers a precise way to determine if a waiter has learned as intended from a wine course. The revised objective was "Given three glasses of different varieties of red wine, be able to identify each correctly while blindfolded." Because this objective was written so effectively, it provides everything necessary to determine whether the training was effective. All that we need is some wine, some glasses, and a blindfold.

Transfer

Transfer, as we have seen, refers to applying learning acquired in training to behavior on the job. To assess transfer, evaluators can ask employees about their own post-training behavior, or they can ask trainees' peers and managers about the trainees' behavior. In some cases, existing records can be used to examine transfer. For example, if sales training encourages trainees to sell items with both high and low profit margins, the records of employees' sales can indicate whether their actual sales move in that direction.

Organizational Results

Organizational results are, of course, outcomes that accrue to a group or the organization as a whole. To assess organizational results, we can use basic measures of effectiveness, such as an increase in sales for the whole company or a decrease in turnover, or we can use efficiency measures, which balance benefits with costs.

Organizational results can be made even more informative by taking into account the resources required to achieve those results. When we analyze the costs of training along with the benefits, we are examining **training efficiency**. An increasingly popular efficiency measure is **return on investment (ROI)**. For a training program, we calculate ROI as follows:

$$\text{Return on Investment} = \frac{\text{Benefits of training}}{\text{Cost of Training}} \times 100$$

Training efficiency
The extent to which the benefits of training exceed the costs of developing and delivering training.

Return on investment (ROI)
An efficiency measure created by dividing the monetary value of training benefits by the costs of delivering training and multiplying the result by 100.

So if a program to train employees in customer service cost a total of $10,000, and the financial benefit was $10,000 from a reduction in returned merchandise, then the ROI is 100 percent; that means the company received benefits equal to the costs of its efforts.

ROI can be negative (if the benefits of training are negative instead of positive), moderate (if the benefits exceed the costs), very large (if the benefits far exceed the costs), and anywhere in between. In one study, a training course resulted in an ROI of nearly 2000 percent, meaning that the company gained back 20 times the money it invested in the training.[73] Of course, few training courses yield a return that large. The same study found that the average ROI for sales/technical training was 156 percent.

Evaluating organizational results requires more resources than evaluating reaction and learning outcomes, because it involves collecting information outside of the training context. Consequently, these outcomes are generally measured less frequently than others. One general rule is to evaluate organizational outcomes only for the most high-profile and expensive programs.[74]

DESIGN

Evaluation designs differ in when data are collected and from whom. Some evaluation designs provide greater certainty about the results of training, but these same designs are more resource intensive. To illustrate this point, we will discuss two of the most common evaluation designs, one on each end of a continuum of certainty.

Post-Test Only

The designs most commonly used in organizations are called *post-test only* designs. This means that training outcomes are measured only at the end of training for the training group. The group is given a survey or test after training, and we examine the results to see if the results are as expected. Post-test-only designs do not offer much certainty about whether training caused the results observed. It is possible, for example, that the trainees knew the training material in advance. It is also possible that they learned it on their own, outside of training. Despite the limited certainty that this design offers, it may still be useful if the evaluator is primarily concerned that trainees reach a certain level of proficiency. For example, if training is intended to ensure that assembly-line employees catch all products with a troublesome manufacturing defect, then knowing for sure whether training was the cause is less critical than having all trainees capable of identifying the defect.

Pre-Test and Post-Test with Control Group

To provide greater certainty about whether training was effective, evaluators can test employees both at the beginning and at the end of training (to look for change) and can compare trained employees with untrained employees with similar characteristics (to verify that training caused the change). To provide the greatest certainty, employees should be randomly selected either to receive training or to be in a control group that does not receive training. When random assignment to training and nontraining conditions is possible, then the pretraining differences between trained and untrained employees are reduced, and we can have greater confidence that differences observed after training are a result of the training and not some other factor.

When is it worth the time and effort to use this particular design, or others that require multiple tests and multiple groups? If a training program is being considered that will be expensive and there are real questions about whether to do it, then this effort will provide decision makers with the information necessary to make the best decision possible. In other words, if the purpose of the evaluation is to determine whether training makes enough of a difference to be continued, then it makes sense to take the time to use a more sophisticated evaluation design. Less sophisticated designs may be sufficient when the purpose of training is to provide feedback to trainers or market the program.

RESULTS

Once the purpose, outcomes, and design of evaluation have been specified, the evaluation can be conducted. Then the data collected must be analyzed and reports generated. Depending on the purpose of the evaluation, the reports may be widely disseminated or simply summarized for the trainer.

Whatever the case, it is important to revisit the purpose of the evaluation and make sure that the right people see the report so that the information gained from the evaluation is used as intended.

CONCEPT CHECK

1. *What are the three purposes for evaluating training?*
2. *What are the four different outcomes that can be used to evaluate training?*
3. *What does ROI stand for?*

A MANAGER'S PERSPECTIVE REVISITED

nyul/iStockphoto

IN THE MANAGER'S PERSPECTIVE THAT OPENED THIS CHAPTER, CHARLOTTE WAS FRUSTRATED THAT SHE COULDN'T GET SUPPORT TO OFFER A TRAINING PROGRAM TO HER EMPLOYEES. SHE WONDERED WHETHER SHE COULD HELP THE EMPLOYEES GAIN THE NECESSARY SKILL WITHOUT A FORMAL TRAINING SESSION. HERE ARE THE ANSWERS TO THE "WHAT DO YOU THINK?" QUIZ THAT FOLLOWED THIS CHAPTER'S MANAGER'S PERSPECTIVE. WERE YOU ABLE TO CORRECTLY IDENTIFY THE TRUE STATEMENTS? CAN YOU DO BETTER NOW?

1. Training keeps employees happy because it's a break from work, but it has little impact on the organization's line. FALSE. *Training can have a big impact on the bottom line if it is created in partnership with management and if it is systematically designed and delivered.*

2. If trainees learn in training, they will transfer that learning back on the job. FALSE. *Learning is a prerequisite for transfer but does not guarantee that transfer will occur.*

3. Lecture is a terrible method for delivering training. FALSE. *When trainees need to acquire basic knowledge, lecture can be an efficient way to help them do so.*

4. Training presented face to face is always more effective than training presented via computer technology. FALSE. *Face-to-face training and computer-based train-*

ing can be equally effective. The choice depends on the requirements of the chosen training method and concerns regarding cost and accessibility.

5. Evaluating training is a waste of time. FALSE. *Evaluation can be used to improve training, make decisions about continuing or discontinuing training, and market training.*

With many organizations facing pressure to keep down costs, Charlotte's experience is a common one. But companies can help to structure informal learning, and they can use cost-effective ways to deliver training such as informal learning among peers or online training. In Charlotte's case, a combination of these approaches would make sense. She could work with a technology expert to build a short online training program about the software program and encourage small groups of employees to meet and exchanges ideas about how to use the software. Regardless of the specific details, when training is linked to organizational strategy, designed and delivered using good practices, and supported by the organization, it can help provide a competitive advantage.

SUMMARY

LEARNING OBJECTIVE 1

How is employee training strategic?

Employee training practices should align with the organization's business strategy. When companies follow a cost strategy, training should help employees solve problems and be more efficient. When companies use a differentiation strategy, training should help employees provide better service or be more creative and innovative. In terms of the overall amount of training, organizations with an internal labor orientation will offer more training than organizations with an external labor orientation. Organizations with an external labor orientation will lean toward acquiring new knowledge and skill by hiring new employees or by merging with or acquiring other organizations. These organizations still offer training programs, though, and they must continually strive to keep costs low.

LEARNING OBJECTIVE 2

What are key principles for getting benefits from training?

Regardless of business strategy, training should be developed according to the same principles: (1) partnership among trainer, employee, and manager and (2) systematic design and development. Design and development should follow a three-phase process that includes needs assessment, design and delivery, and evaluation. Depending on the nature of the training and the setting in which it is developed, these steps can be completed sequentially (traditional design) or almost simultaneously (rapid design).

LEARNING OBJECTIVE 3

How are training needs determined?

Needs assessments can be proactive or reactive. Proactive needs assessment is regular and planned, and it involves collecting information about the organization, the task, and the people. Reactive needs assessment occurs when managers request training, and it follows a problem-solving process of defining the problem, determining the causes, and implementing solutions.

LEARNING OBJECTIVE 4

How is effective training designed and delivered?

Training methods can be categorized as passive, active, and on-the-job. Presentations, the primary method for passive training, can be a useful way to deliver knowledge-based content, but they are limited in that they cannot help trainees gain skills. To develop skills, learners need more active training methods, such as discussion, case analysis, discovery, role playing, simulation, and behavior modeling. For on-the-job training to be effective, it must be structured and systematic.

LEARNING OBJECTIVE 5

How do organizations determine whether training is effective?

The first and most important decision regarding evaluation is deciding its purpose. The purpose of the evaluation influences the outcomes, outcomes measures, evaluation strategy, and final report. Three common purposes for evaluation are (1) providing feedback to designers, trainers, and trainees; (2) providing input for decision making about the value of continuing the training; and (3) providing information that can be used to market the training program. To provide feedback on training, training content and design can be examined before, during, and after training. To provide input to decisions about training, changes in learners and organizational payoffs can be examined to determine if training is effective at producing desired changes. To provide marketing information, information about training design, learners, and organizational payoffs can be crafted into stories about benefits of training.

KEY TERMS

Attitude   336
Behavioral contract   362
Causal analysis   350
e-Learning   359
Informal learning methods   337
Knowledge   336
Learning   336
Learning objective   352
Needs assessment   345
Opportunity to perform   364
Organizational objective   352
Organization analysis   345
Person analysis   347
Proactive needs assessment   345
Problem definition   350

Rapid model of instructional design   344
Reactive needs assessment   349
Relapse prevention training   363
Return on investment (ROI)   368
Skill   336
Task analysis   346
Traditional model of instructional design   344
Training   336
Training climate   346
Training effectiveness   365
Training efficiency   368
Training media   359
Training methods   355
Training vendors   355
Transfer of training   342

DISCUSSION QUESTIONS

1. What kinds of training content are most important for organizations using cost strategies? Differentiation strategies?
2. Why do organizations following an internal labor orientation generally offer more training than organizations with an external labor orientation?
3. What are the key differences between the proactive and reactive needs assessment approaches?
4. How are learning and organizational objectives used in the training design and development process?
5. It is often easy to confuse training methods and training media. Consider the human resources course you are currently taking. What are the methods and what are the media being used?
6. What are the strengths and weakness associated with the following training methods:

presentation, discovery, simulation, and behavior modeling? How can each method be made more effective?

7. Consider the classes you have taken throughout school. Which classes were the most beneficial for you? Do you attribute that to the classes' content, methods, media, or some other factor?
8. Have you ever taken an online course or another form of distance education, such as a correspondence course? How was the experience different from a traditional face-to-face class?
9. Consider the classes you have taken throughout school. How have they been evaluated? What purpose or purposes do you think these evaluations have served?
10. What is transfer enhancement, and why is it helpful for employees?

EXAMPLE CASE   *Northwestern Memorial Hospital*

Many in the Chicagoland region and around the nation would consider Northwestern Memorial Hospital (NMH), a 138-year-old institution, to be among the very best teaching hospitals. It has earned this distinction because of its high-quality patient care, extraordinary physicians and hospital staff, strong financial position, and world-class facilities.

Not one to rest on its laurels, NMH is continually changing and striving for excellence. In 1999, the hospital opened its new, 2 million square foot health-care facility. The 17-story Feinberg Inpatient Pavilion and the 22-story Galter Outpatient Pavilion share an eight-floor base of public areas and diagnostic and therapeutic services. "This was a major accomplishment. When we were finished, we asked ourselves, 'What's the next mountain we should climb?'" says Dean Manheimer, Senior VP, Human Resources.

That mountain turned out to be an ambitious strategic plan with three critical interrelated goals: (1) provide the best patient experience; (2) recruit, develop, and retain the best people; and (3) develop the resources to achieve its mission and vision through exceptional financial performance. Among other things, this strategy strives for a more comprehensive and integrated approach to workforce development. Central to its success is NMH's new Learning Academy, launched in 2002. Seen as the lever to advance its "best people" strategy, the Academy oversees all management development, clinical and other functional education, facilitates the creation of new training and certificate programs, and builds outside workforce development partnerships.

Early in 2000, Human Resources staff conducted an internal audit of its education programs. While the hospital always had an abundance of opportunities for staff development, the audit uncovered unnecessary redundancies within the hospital's education offerings. For example, six courses were being taught six different ways for Body Mechanics—the movement of patients. NMH developed the Academy to establish standardized training policies and solutions, link the education programs closely to the organization's business strategy, provide staff easy access to learning, and utilize the most efficient technologies.

Today, the Academy provides an online catalog and registration system for all the hospital's education programs, which total over 200 courses ranging from communications, project management, information services, and budgeting to an array of healthcare specialties, some of which have been designed by internal instructional staff in cooperation with employees who are subject matter experts. Area community colleges and universities are also brought onsite to deliver high-demand, credit-based courses. Last year, the Academy delivered approximately 55,000 hours of training to 21,000 employees and received a 91 percent satisfaction rate. In addition, the Academy delivered over 3,000 hours of management training to higher level staff, including human resources best practices, diversity education, building collaborative workplaces, and delivering/receiving constructive performance feedback. The Academy also hosts skill development "Lunch and Learn" sessions where managers and employees learn, for example, flexible scheduling strategies, personal development planning, and interviewing techniques.

But what many staff members are most proud of are the three "schools" the Academy developed for Nuclear Medicine, Radiation Therapy, and Diagnostic Medical Sonography. The schools offer onsite programs that are open to both employees and community members. In August 2003, the first class of seven graduated from the school of Nuclear Medicine, an important achievement, given the skill shortage in this area. NMH hired many of the students, eliminating all hospital vacancies for the first time in five years. In addition, NMH eliminated staff overtime and agency usage, resulting in a cost savings of $800,000.

QUESTIONS

1. What is the strategy pursued by NMH? Can it be easily classified as differentiation or cost reduction? As internal or external labor orientation?

2. Describe the various ways NMH is delivering training and other related learning opportunities to its employees.

3. What benefits did NMH gain by developing the Academy and its associated schools?

4. If the NMH School of Nuclear Medicine cost the organization $200,000, what was the return on investment for this particular Academy program?

Source: Excerpted from *Case Study: Northwestern Memorial Hospital,* by Work-Force Chicago and Council for Adult and Experiential Learning. Retrieved online at http://www.workforcechicago2.org on April 5, 2010. Used with permission.

DISCUSSION CASE — *Hypothetical Telecommunications*

Sales at a large telecommunications company were down for the third quarter. Management reviewed several strategies to improve sales and concluded that one solution would be to improve training for the large, dispersed sales force.

For the sake of expediency, the training department began using a needs assessment it conducted several years before as a basis to develop enhanced training. The plan was first to update the original needs analysis, and then to develop new training strategies on the basis of what it found. The department also began investigating new training technologies as a possible means to reduce training delivery costs. However, management was so intent on doing something quickly that the training department was ultimately pressured into purchasing a generic, off-the-shelf package by a local vendor.

One of the features of the package that appealed to management was that the course could be delivered over the Web, saving the time and expense of having the sales force travel to the main office to receive training. Hence, even though the package was costly to purchase, the company believed that it was a bargain compared to the expense of developing a new package in-house and delivering it in person to the sales force.

Six months after the training had been delivered, sales were still declining. Management turned to the training department for answers. Because no measures of training performance had been collected, the training department had little information upon which to base its diagnosis. For lack of a better idea, members of the training department began questioning the sales force to see if they could determine why the training was not working.

Among other things, the salespeople reported that the training was slow and boring and that it did not teach them any new sales techniques. They also complained that, without an instructor, it was impossible to get clarification on things they did not understand. Moreover, they reported that they believed sales were off not because they needed training in basic sales techniques, but because so many new products were being introduced that they could not keep up. In fact, several of the salespeople requested meetings with design engineers just so they could get updated product information.

QUESTIONS

1. Outline the key decisions made from the beginning to the end of this case. Who made each of those decisions, and why?

2. Describe the ideal process for handling the concern about declining sales, ignoring for now the pressure from management.

3. What arguments could be made to convince management that working with an outdated needs assessment is not wise?

4. If you were asked to develop a training program for these sales agents, what content, method, and media would you choose? Explain your answers as best you can given the limited information provided.

Source: Excerpted from Eduardo Salas and Janice A. Cannon-Bowers, "Design Training Systematically," in Edwin A. Locke (ed.), *Handbook of Principles of Organizational Behavior* (Oxford, UK: Blackwell, 2000).

EXPERIENTIAL EXERCISE — *Finding an Off-the-Shelf Training Product*

Imagine that you have been asked to offer a short workshop on stress management to newly promoted supervisors. Because time and money are short, you are going to examine three alternatives: using a training vendor to develop the program as a custom course, purchasing a program as an off-the-shelf product, or building your own barebones training program. To prepare for a meeting on this topic, you must do research on training vendors and off-the-shelf products, including those that help you develop and deliver training.

Write a short report providing descriptions of vendors and products. To get you started, here are some websites called "learning portals" that contain multiple links to courses:

- www.sumtotalsystems.com
- www.myquickcoach.com
- www.skillsoft.com

Here is a website for a company that could help you put your own training online:

- www.gotomeeting.com

You might also consider the trend toward massive open on-line courses (MOOCs). There might a MOOC that fits your needs. Here is a website that aggregates information about MOOCs:

- coursetalk.org.

INTERACTIVE EXPERIENTIAL EXERCISE — *The Art of Training: Finding the Right Program for Global Telecommunications*
http://www.wiley.com/college/sc/stewart

Access the companion website to test your knowledge by completing a Global Telecommunications interactive role play.

In this exercise, Global Communications wants your help in improving its training programs. One of the department managers is complaining that his employees "just don't get it, so they must need more training." It doesn't seem that this manager has very good communication skills, and you can understand why employees may not be learning from him. To make matters more challenging, though, the manager tells you he doesn't have much of a budget for training, and he can't afford to let his employees miss work for more than a few hours anyway. You start thinking about what can be done. Global really wants to use training to support the Committed Expert HR strategy. How should the training program be developed and carried out? •

ENDNOTES

1. Irwin L. Goldstein and J. Kevin Ford, *Training in Organizations*, 4th ed. (Pacific Grove, CA: Wadsworth, 2001); Raymond A. Noe, *Employee Training and Development*, 5th ed. (New York: McGraw Hill, 2009).

2. Ray J. Rivera and Andrew Paradise, *State of the Industry in Leading Enterprises* (Alexandria, VA: American Society for Training & Development, 2006); U.S. Department of Labor. *Reports on the Amount of Employer-Provided Formal Training* (Washington, DC: USDL

96–268, 1996). Retrieved online at http://www.bls. gov/ept on January 8, 2013.

3. Jay Cross, *Informal Learning: Rediscovering the Natural Pathways that Inspire Innovation and Performance* (San Francisco: Pfeiffer, 2007).

4. Rivera and Paradise, *State of the Industry*; U.S. Department of Labor, 1996; John M. Barron, Dan A. Black, and Mark A. Loewenstein, "Employer Size: The Implications for Search, Training, Capital Investment, Starting Wages, and Wage Growth," *Journal of Labor Economics* 5 (1987): 76–89.

5. Phyllis Tharenou, "Do Organizations Get Positive Results from Training? The Big Picture," in P. Holland and H. De Cieri (eds.), *Contemporary Issues in Human Resource Development: An Australian Perspective* (Melbourne, Australia: McGraw Hill, 2006): 153–174.

6. Kenneth R. Bartlett, "The Relationship Between Training and Organizational Commitment: A Study in the Health Care Field," *Human Resource Development Quarterly* 12 (2002): 335–352.

7. David G. Allen, Lynn M. Shore, and Rodger W. Griffeth, "The Role of Perceived Organizational Support and Supportive Human Resource Practices in the Turnover Process," *Journal of Management* 29 (2003): 99–118.

8. Winfred Arthur, Jr., Winston Bennett, Jr., Pamela S. Edens, and Suzanne T. Bell, "Effectiveness of Training in Organizations: A Meta-Analysis of Design and Evaluation Features," *Journal of Applied Psychology* 88 (2003): 234–245.

9. John T. Delaney and Mark A. Huselid, "The Impact of Human Resource Management Practices on Perceptions of Organizational Performance," *Academy of Management Journal* 39 (1996): 949–969; Mark A. Huselid, "The Impact of Human Resource Management Practices on Turnover, Productivity, and Corporate Financial Performance," *Academy of Management Journal* 38 (1995): 635–672; Christopher J. Collins, and Ken G. Smith, "Knowledge Exchange and Combination," *Academy of Management Journal* 49 (2006): 544–560.

10. Thomas Zwick, "The Impact of Training Intensity on Establishment Productivity," *Industrial Relations* 45 (2006): 26–46.

11. P. Nick Blanchard and James W. Thacker, *Effective Training: Systems, Strategic, and Practices,* 2nd ed. (Upper Saddle River, NJ: Pearson, 2004).

12. Ronald D. Snee and Roger W. Hoerl, *Leading Six Sigma: A Step-by-Step Guide Based on Experience with GE and Other Six Sigma Companies* (Upper Saddle River, NJ: Pearson, 2003).

13. Collins and Smith, "Knowledge Exchange and Combination."

14. Michelle Neely Martinez. "Disney Training Works Magic," *HR Magazine* 37 (1992), 53–57.

15. Knowledge@Wharton, "After Acquiring Macromedia, What's Next for Adobe? Ask Bruce Chizen," March 24, 2006. Retrieved online at http://knowledge.wharton. upenn.edu on April 5, 2010.

16. "Products & Training" by the National Safety Council. Retrieved online at http://www.nsc.org on January 8, 2013.

17. "OSHA eTools and Electronic Products for Compliance Assistance." Retrieved online at http:// www.osha.gov/dts/osta/oshasoft on April 5, 2010.

18. Mary L. Broad and John W. Newstrom, *Transfer of Training: Action-Packed Strategies to Ensure High Payoff from Training Investments* (Reading, MA: Perseus, 1992); Timothy T. Baldwin and J. Kevin Ford. "Transfer of Training: A Review and Directions for Future Research," *Personnel Psychology* 41 (1988): 63–103.

19. Brian D. Blume, J. Kevin Ford, Timothy T. Baldwin, and Jason L. Huang. "Transfer of Training: A Meta-Analytic Review," *Journal of Management* 36 (2010): 1065–1105. J. Bruce Tracey, Scott I. Tannenbaum, and Michael J. Kavanagh, "Applying Trained Skills on the Job: The Importance of the Work Environment," *Journal of Applied Psychology* 80 (1995): 239–252; Baldwin and Ford, "Transfer of Training."

20. Eduardo Salas, Scott I. Tannenbaum, Kurt Kraiger, and Kimberly A. Smith-Jentsch, "The science of training and development in organizations: What matters in practice," *Psychological Science in the Public Interest* 13 (2012): 74-101; Goldstein and Ford, *Training in Organizations.*

21. Based on Steven Tripp and Barbara Bichelmeyer, "Rapid Prototyping: An Alternative Instructional Design Strategy," *Educational Technology Research and Development* 38 (1990): 31–44.

22. Blanchard and Thacker, *Effective Training.*

23. Ibid. Goldstein and Ford, *Training in Organizations*; Noe, *Employee Training and Development.*

24. *Mathis v. Phillips Chevrolet Inc.*, 7th Circuit, No. 00–1892, October 15, 2001.

25. Tracey et al., "Applying Trained Skills"; J. Bruce Tracey and Michael J. Tews. "Construct Validity of a General Training Climate Scale," *Organizational Research Methods* 8 (2005): 353–374; Elwood F. Holton III, Reid A. Bates, and Wendy E. A. Ruona, "Development of a Generalized Learning Transfer System Inventory," *Human Resource Development Quarterly* 11 (2000): 333–360.

26. Benjamin Schneider (ed.), *Organizational Climate and Culture* (San Francisco: Jossey-Bass, 1990).

27. Goldstein and Ford, *Training in Organizations*; Noe, *Employee Training and Development.*

28. David J. Edwards, "Models of Management Development: Functional and Competency," *Engineering Management Journal* 4 (1992): 294–297.

29. David A. DuBois, "Leveraging Hidden Expertise: Why, When, and How to Use Cognitive Task Analysis," in Kurt Kraiger (ed.), *Creating, Implementing, and Managing Effective Training and Development* (San Francisco: Jossey-Bass, 2002): 80–115.

30. David P. Baker, Eduardo Salas, and Janice Cannon-Bowers. "Team Task Analysis: Lost but Hopefully not Forgotten," *The Industrial and Organizational Psychologist* 35 (1998): 79–83.

31. Geary A. Rummler and Alan P. Brache, *Improving Performance: How to Manage the White Space on the Organization Chart,* 2nd ed. (San Francisco: Jossey-Bass, 1995).

32. Justin Kruger and David Dunning, "Unskilled and Unaware of It: How Difficulties in Recognizing One's Own Incompetence Lead to Inflated Self-Assessments," *Journal of Personality and Social Psychology* 77 (1999): 1121–1134.

33. Jason A. Colquitt, Jeffrey A. LePine, and Raymond A. Noe, "Toward an Integrative Theory of Training Motivation: A Meta-Analytic Path Analysis of 20 Years of Research," *Journal of Applied Psychology* 85 (2001): 678–707.

34. Jim Fuller and Jeanne Farrington, *From Training to Performance Improvement: Navigating the Transition* (San Francisco: Pfeiffer, 1999).

35. Blanchard and Thacker, *Effective Training.*

36. Steve Yelon, *Powerful Principles of Instruction* (New York: Longman, 1996).

37. Robert F. Mager, *Preparing Instructional Objectives*, 3rd ed. (Atlanta: Center for Effective Performance, 1997).

38. Alan M. Saks and Robert R. Haccoun, *Managing Performance through Training and Development*, 3rd ed. (Ontario, Canada: Nelson, 2004).

39. Nanette Miner, *The Accidental Trainer* (Hoboken, NJ: Pfeiffer, 2006).

40. Arthur et al., "Effectiveness of Training."

41. Ruth Colvin Clark and Richard E. Mayer. *E-Learning and the Science of Instruction: Proven Guidelines for Consumers and Designers of Multimedia Learning* (San Francisco: Jossey-Bass, 2003).

42. James R. Davis and Adelaide B. Davis, *Effective Training Strategies: A Comprehensive Guide to Maximizing Learning in Organizations* (San Francisco: Berrett-Koehler, 1998).

43. Saks and Haccoun, *Managing Performance through Training and Development.*

44. Alvin Zander, *Making Groups Effective*, 2nd ed. (San Francisco: Jossey-Bass, 1994).

45. P. C. Wright, "CEO and the Business School: Is There Potential for Increased Cooperation," *Association of Management Proceedings: Education* 10 (1992): 41–45.

46. Saks and Haccoun. *Managing Performance.*

47. Christine B. McCormick and Michael Pressley, *Educational Psychology: Learning, Instruction, and Assessment* (New York: Longman, 1997).

48. Shelda Debowski, Robert E. Wood, and Albert Bandura, "Impact of Guided Exploration and Enactive Exploration on Self-Regulatory Mechanisms and Information Acquisition Through Electronic Search," *Journal of Applied Psychology* 86 (2001): 1129–1141.

49. Saks and Haccoun, *Managing Performance.*

50. Blanchard and Thacker, *Effective Training.*

51. Jan Cannon-Bowers and Clint Bowers, "Synthetic Learning Environments: On Developing a Science of Simulation, Games, and Virtual Worlds for Training," in S. W. J. Kozlowski and E. Salas (eds.), *Learning, Training, and Development in Organizations* (New York: Taylor & Francis, 2010): 229–262.

52. Paul J. Taylor, Darlene F. Russ-Eft, Daniel W. L. Chan. "A Meta-Analytic Review of Behavior Modeling Training," *Journal of Applied Psychology* 90 (2005): 692–709; Marily E. Gist, C. Schwoerer, and Ben Rosen, "Effects of Alternative Training Methods on Self-Efficacy and Performance in Computer Software Training," *Journal of Applied Psychology* 74 (1989): 884–891; Gary L. May and William M. Kahnweiler, "The Effect of Mastery Practice Design on Learning and Transfer in Behavior Modeling Training," *Personnel Psychology* 53 (2000): 353–373; Phillip J. Decker, and Barry R. Nathan, *Behavior Modeling Training: Principles and Applications* (New York: Praeger, 1985).

53. Decker and Nathan, *Behavior Modeling Training.*

54. Saks and Haccoun, *Managing Performance.*

55. Traci M. Sitzmann, Kurt Kraiger, David W. Stewart, and Robert A. Wisher, "The Comparative Effectiveness of Web-Based and Classroom Instruction: A Meta-Analysis," *Personnel Psychology* 59 (2006): 623–664.

56. Brenda Sugrue and Richard E. Clark, "Media Selection for Training," in Sigmund Tobias and J. D. Fletcher, *Training and Retraining: Handbook for Business, Industry, Government, and the Military* (New York: MacMillan Reference, 2000): 208–234.

57. Ibid.

58. Alan M. Saks and Monica Belcourt, "An Investigation of Training Activities and Transfer of Training in Organizations," *Human Resource Management* 45 (2006): 629–648.

59. Broad and Newstrom, *Transfer of Training.*

60. Ibid.

61. Daniel Druckman and Robert A. Bjork (eds.), *Learning, Remembering, and Believing* (Washington, DC: National Academies Press, 1994).

62. Lisa A. Burke and Timothy T. Baldwin, "Workforce Training Transfer: A Study of the Effects of Relapse Prevention Training and Transfer Climate," *Human Resource Management* 38 (1999): 227–242.

63. J. Kevin Ford, Miguel Quinones, Douglas Sego, and Joann Sorra, "Factors Affecting the Opportunity to Perform Trained Tasks on the Job," *Personnel Psychology* 45 (1992): 511–527.

64. Michael Greer, "Estimating Instructional Development (ID) Time," Retrieved online on May 23, 2010, at http://www.michaelgreer.com.

65. Kenneth G. Brown, "Training Evaluation," in Steven G. Rogelberg (ed.), *The Encyclopedia of Industrial and Organizational Psychology*, vol. 2 (Thousand Oaks, CA: Sage, 2007): 820–823.

66. Kurt Kraiger, "Decision-Based Evaluation," in Kurt Kraiger (ed.), *Creating, Implementing, and Managing Effective Training and Development* (San Francisco: Jossey-Bass, 2002): 331–376.

67. Ibid.

68. Kenneth G. Brown and Megan W. Gerhardt, "Formative Evaluation: An Integrated Practice Model and Case Study," *Personnel Psychology* 55 (2002): 951–983.

69. This is based on a slightly modified version of the classic *Kirkpatrick* framework; see Donald L. Kirkpatrick, *Evaluating Training Programs: The Four Levels* (San Francisco: Berrett-Koehler, 1998).

70. George M. Alliger, Scott I. Tannenbaum, W. Bennett, Holly Traver, and Allison Shotland, "A Meta-Analysis of the Relations among Training Criteria," *Personnel Psychology* 50 (1997): 341–358; Kenneth G. Brown, "Examining the Structure and Nomological Network of Trainee Reactions: A Closer Look at Smile Sheets," *Journal of Applied Psychology* 90 (2005): 991–1001

71. Brown, "Examining the Structure."

72. Kurt Kraiger, J. Kevin Ford, and Eduardo Salas, "Application of Cognitive, Skill-Based, and Affective Theories of Learning Outcomes to New Methods of Training Evaluation," *Journal of Applied Psychology* 78 (1993): 311–328.

73. Charles C. Morrow, M. Quintin Jarrett, and Melvin T. Rupinski, "An Investigation of the Effect and Economic Utility of Corporate-Wide Training," *Personnel Psychology* 50 (1997): 91–119.

74. Jack J. Phillips, "ROI Best Practices," Chief Learning Officer, September 2003.

Chapter 10

Developing Employees and Their Careers

A MANAGER'S PERSPECTIVE

©ColorBlind Images/Corbis

ALEJANDRO SITS AT HIS DESK AND STARES AT THE WALL. HE IS BORED, PLAIN AND SIMPLE, AND THE BOREDOM IS STARTING TO TAKE ON AN EDGE OF DESPAIR. OVER THE LAST MONTH THERE HAD BEEN NOTHING AT WORK THAT CAPTURED HIS ATTENTION IN A MEANINGFUL WAY. HE WASN'T BEING CHALLENGED, HE WASN'T LEARNING ANYTHING NEW, AND IT SEEMED HE WASN'T GOING ANYWHERE WITH HIS CAREER IN THIS COMPANY. HE REFLECTS ON THE LAST CONVERSATION HE HAD WITH HIS BOSS, ERIKA. "WHAT'S WRONG?" SHE HAD ASKED. "YOU LOOK TERRIBLE."

Alejandro had paused before answering. "I'm not completely sure. I used to really enjoy coming to work, but now I find it hard to get out of bed in the morning. It's not that I don't like it, and I do like working for you. But I feel like I'm wasting my time doing the same things over and over again. I feel like there must be something more I could do, something that could really make a difference. The problem is that I don't know what to do." Erika had listened and then offered, "I think you are just depressed. Why don't you take the afternoon off and go see a movie? Then go for a run, and you'll feel better tomorrow." At that point, she had turned back to her computer, ending the conversation. Alejandro waited a moment, and then walked slowly back to his office.

Alejandro continues to sit and mull over the details of the conversation. It was much like previous conversations he had had with Erika. She was convinced that life was simple—do your work, get some exercise, have a little fun, and all will be well. Alejandro used to like this simplicity but today it leaves him feeling cold. He wants more but he doesn't know exactly what, let alone how to go about getting it.

Alejandro picks up the phone to call Matilda, an old friend. They arrange to meet that night for dinner, and already Alejandro feels a little better. Now, at least, I have something to look forward to, he thinks.

That evening with Matilda, the conversation turns quickly to how Alejandro is feeling about his job. Matilda listens carefully and then asks what has changed at work. Alejandro thinks for a minute, and it dawns on him that he has been missing a goal to strive for. He had always wanted to make general manager, and when he did he was elated. That elation diminished some, but stayed around as he learned the job. But now, three years later, the job seems too small for him. Alejandro wonders aloud how his perspective shifted from "I love this job" to "I wonder what I'm doing here."

Matilda tells him about an opening at her company starting up a new division. She explains that

Spencer Platt/Getty Images

THE BIG PICTURE *Effective Organizations Attract, Develop, and Retain Skilled Employees by Helping Them Make Progress Toward Their Career Goals*

this job is not just a general management job, it is an opportunity to build something new. The company offers great support for whoever is willing to take on the challenge, including a budget for personal development and access to an executive coach. Alejandro feels a familiar surge of energy as he thinks about the job. This just might be what he needs.

The next day Alejandro follows Matilda's parting advice and makes a call to the Louis Calderon, Senior Vice President at Matilda's company. Louis is delighted to hear from Alejandro, and excitedly talks about the business opportunity. Most important of all, Louis says warmly, is the opportunity to work with our fantastic leadership team. He acknowledges that the new business is risky and it may not all go as planned, but members of the team are excited by the challenge and will help out the new hire as much or as little as needed.

Alejandro asks a few more questions before hanging up, and sits thoughtfully at his desk. What's my next move, he wonders.

WHAT DO YOU THINK?

Suppose Alejandro hears the following comments during a meeting with some friends who are entrepreneurs. Which of the statements do you think are true?

T OR F In today's economy, companies have no responsibility for helping employees learn and grow.

T OR F The "career ladder" is often not an accurate description of how people progress through their careers.

T OR F Mentoring and coaching are simply buzzwords for networking; those programs don't do much else.

T OR F Multisource feedback systems are too complicated; employees don't learn anything from them.

T OR F To help employees have a successful career, companies should give them challenging work assignments.

After reading this chapter you should be able to:

LEARNING OBJECTIVE 1	Explain why employee development practices are useful for organizations.
LEARNING OBJECTIVE 2	Describe how employee development practices can strategically align with overall HR strategy.
LEARNING OBJECTIVE 3	Explain the typical career pattern in organizations today as well as the various perspectives on career success.
LEARNING OBJECTIVE 4	Describe several commonly used development methods.
LEARNING OBJECTIVE 5	Identify critical career development challenges facing organizations and describe how organizations can meet these challenges.

How Can Strategic Employee Development Make an Organization Effective?

Employee development
Activities that influence personal and professional growth.

Career development
Activities that help people manage the progression of their work experiences across their lives.

Talent management
Processes involved in managing the flow of well-qualified employees into an organization and through various positions within the organization.

Employee development involves activities that influence personal and professional growth. Development activities generally help employees learn skills that will be helpful in future jobs.[1] This differs from employee training, covered in Chapter 9, which focuses on the knowledge and skills employees need to perform their current jobs. Closely related to employee development is **career development**, which includes activities that help people manage the progression of their work experiences across their lives.[2] Employee and career development are both discussed in this chapter under the general label employee development, and they are a substantial component of what some organizations refer to as their talent management process. **Talent management** is a term increasingly used to describe core HR processes of recruiting, selecting, and developing well-qualified employees.[3]

What are the benefits of programs that encourage and support employee development? For employees, benefits include opportunities to acquire new knowledge and skills that are personally satisfying and to grow as individuals. Moreover, as employees gain skill and improve their job performance, they are more likely to be rewarded with promotions involving more responsibility and pay. For organizations, the primary benefit of providing development opportunities is that it enhances their ability to respond to changing environmental forces.[4] It does so in two ways: (1) by increasing the range of skills that employees possess and (2) by increasing the chances that the most capable employees will be attracted and remain committed to the organization. In other words, development practices help a company compete by ensuring a continual supply of employees who are talented and committed.

Employee development is critical today because the amount of change and the degree of uncertainty regarding work has increased dramatically in recent years. From year to year, companies face the uncertainty of changing market conditions, which can necessitate changing what they sell or how they sell it.

Consider the well-known case of a company founded by a merger of paper, rubber, and cable companies. Through divestitures and acquisitions in response to changing technology and market needs, that company has become what we know today as Nokia, which has a major share of the global market in mobile phones.[5] Without efforts to help their employees develop knowledge and skill in the area of digital communications, Nokia would have been unable to make this transition. Of course, uncertainty also arises for individuals in such situations. Nokia employees with considerable expertise in paper production, for example, were not certain of future employment with the company as it moved fully into the mobile phone market. Either those employees had to acquire new knowledge and skills in order to keep their jobs with Nokia, or they had to leave the company to continue working in the paper industry. Today, Nokia is facing tough competition from companies like Apple and Samsung, so it must continue to invest in the development of its employees.

Aflac, perhaps best recognized for the duck in its advertising, also provides a good example of strategic employee development. This insurance giant reported more than $25 billion in global sales in 2012, with markets in both Japan and the United States.[6] Despite its size and global reach, Aflac is consistently named among the best places to work in the United States.[7]

Aflac's reputation as a good employer stems at least in part from its developmental programs, which help employees learn valuable life skills as well as work-related skills. Some of the company's life skill programs include "lunch and learn" sessions on topics such as how to buy your own home, how to have a healthy pregnancy, and how to be a great grandparent. To help employees develop work-related skills, Aflac provides access to online courses and to scholarships for courses at local colleges and universities. These programs are offered in addition to training for industry certification. Taken as a whole, Aflac's development efforts help the company to recruit and retain employees and to keep the skills of those employees attuned to market needs.

Building Strength Through HR

AFLAC

Aflac has a great reputation as an employer that cares about its employees. It offers a number of programs that help attract and retain great employees, including programs that help employees grow and pursue fulfilling careers. Some of these developmental programs include:

Spencer Platt/Getty Images

- Support for industry-wide certification training.
- A two-year rotation for select new hires that blends courses, mentoring, and work experiences.
- A three-phase leadership development program that helps managers as they progress through their careers.
- Learning opportunities available to all employees, including onsite workshops and online courses.
- Scholarships that enable employees to pursue educational opportunities for personal growth.

LEARNING OBJECTIVE 1

How Is Employee Development Strategic?

As you can see from the Aflac example, an organization's employee development practices are strategic when they help the organization maintain a continual supply of talented and committed employees. Research has suggested that most organizations use certain basic development programs, and organizations that do not use them may be at a disadvantage in recruiting and retaining employees.[8] Of course, the specific development practices used by organizations differ depending on their overall HR strategy, as shown in Figure 10.1. Next, we consider these differences.

EXTERNAL VERSUS INTERNAL LABOR ORIENTATION

Organizations that use the Free Agent and Bargain Laborer HR strategies rely heavily on the external labor market for their talent, so they are competing with other organizations for employees. Nevertheless, organizations using the Bargain Laborer strategy are unlikely to invest heavily in employees' long-term development. They may offer development that supports job training to ensure that employees know exactly what they should do on the job. Such development is not extensive, though, as the work done by employees in these organizations is generally not complex.

Organizations using the Free Agent strategy must invest more in development to ensure that their jobs look attractive to employees. These organizations must offer formal education, particularly support for professional licensing and/or certification (discussed later in the chapter), and other

Figure 10.1 Strategic Framework for Employee Development.

long-term development opportunities in order to lure people to change jobs and organizations. Formal education is particularly important because it is valued by nearly everyone, so it will be attractive to employees who are willing to move from organization to organization.

Suppose, for example, that you are graduating with a law degree and have your choice of working for two firms. One firm provides no support to prepare for the state bar exam (which you must pass in order to practice law) and no financial support to take the continuing education courses required to keep your license (so you can continue to practice law). The other firm provides a tutor and time during work to study for the bar exam and will also reimburse your expenses for continuing education. Because passing the bar exam and gaining entry into your state bar association are necessary to conduct most business as an attorney, you will likely favor the firm offering the developmental assistance.

Companies that use the Loyal Soldier and Committed Expert HR strategies rely on internal supplies of labor to fill positions. Such companies must have more extensive development programs because they must create the pool of employees that they will use in the future, even if the industry and the company change. Moreover, they must offer enough development opportunities that employees do not feel compelled to leave in order to learn, grow, and advance in their careers. These companies typically offer support for formal education, but they have additional programs as well, including assessment and feedback, developmental relationships, and job experiences—all of which we discuss later in the chapter.

DIFFERENTIATION VERSUS COST STRATEGY

Employee development is equally important for firms with differentiation and cost strategies. Firms at either end of this continuum must still attract and retain high-performing employees. The difference is that firms pursuing a cost strategy need to focus on keeping development costs low, and firms pursuing a differentiation strategy must use development to foster high-quality service and innovation.

The good news for organizations pursuing a cost strategy is that many development efforts are not expensive. For example, consider the minimal costs of encouraging employees to take inexpensive online career assessment tests and talk with their supervisors about the results. Similarly, many developmental opportunities—for example, job enrichment that challenges employees to learn new skills—arise from the work itself. Using work experiences as a form of development allows organizations to improve their employees' knowledge and skills without pulling them away from work completely, as would occur with formal training and education. For that reason, work experiences as a developmental program should be particularly useful for organizations concerned with costs, such as those using the Loyal Soldier and Bargain Laborer HR strategies.

Organizations pursuing a differentiation strategy are less concerned with controlling costs than with gaining a competitive advantage by offering superior service or products. To ensure that innovation occurs, development in these organizations must be far-reaching and must include opportunities not only for learning from work but also for learning from formal education, feedback from bosses and colleagues, and developmental relationships, such as relationships with mentors.

At General Electric, for example, the strategy of differentiation is supported by rotational leadership programs in different areas of the business. While in rotations, GE trainees are challenged with real work assignments, receive classroom training, and are paired with mentors who guide them along the way.[9] Extensive developmental programs like GE's prepare employees to collaborate and innovate.

CONCEPT CHECK
1. *What are some development programs that fit with internal strategies? With external strategies?*
2. *How should a company adjust its development offerings if it pursues a cost strategy?*
3. *How should a company adjust its development offerings if it pursues a differentiation strategy?*

What Are Careers Like Today?

Career
The pattern of work experiences a person has over his or her lifetime.

Career ladder
A career characterized by step-by-step, hierarchical transitions from jobs with lower pay and responsibility to jobs with higher pay and responsibility.

The importance of employee development in organizations today is best understood in light of changes that have occurred in the pattern of work experiences that people have over their lifetimes. This pattern is called a **career**. In this section, we describe what careers are like today, including fundamental shifts in who is responsible for employee development and how employees define success.

In generations past, the typical career involved going to school, joining a company, and then staying with that company until retirement. Particularly in large companies, workforce needs were predictable, and thus employees could be relatively certain that, given adequate performance, they could stay with the company for a long time. Progression from position to position generally occurred in the form of promotions that involved more pay and more responsibility—what we refer to as moves up the **career ladder**.[10] Today's careers, however, do not typically progress in a hierarchical, step-by-step process implied by the term *career ladder*.

Today, a more typical pattern of work experiences includes lateral as well as hierarchical movement within a company, along with movement from company to company.[11] In addition, it is much more common today for work experiences to include time spent as a contract employee or small business owner.[12] For example, Meg Whitman began her career at Procter & Gamble in Cincinnati, where she worked in brand management from 1979 to 1981. After that, she worked for Bain & Company, Disney Consumer Products Division, Stride Rite Corporation, Florists Transworld Delivery (FTD), and Hasbro Inc. before becoming the CEO of eBay in 2008.[13] After an unsuccessful run to become Governor of California, Whitman was recruited to serve as the President and CEO of Hewlett-Packard. The common theme in her career has been neither predictable movement up the career ladder nor a long stay with any one company in any one industry, but instead movement and change, including jumps across traditional industry boundaries.

Because of the changes we've just described, a new type of career has emerged in the past several decades. It has been called the **Protean career**, named after Proteus, a sea god in Greek mythology who was able to change his shape. *Protean* generally means varied and versatile. Characteristics of the new career, summarized in Table 10.1, include the shift in emphasis toward psychological success just discussed. The Protean career also emphasizes development that is continuous, self-directed, relational, and found in work challenges. This means that employees increasingly expect to learn in ways other than those offered by their organizations. And, fundamentally, it means that employees are increasingly responsible for selecting and pursuing development, while organizations are primarily responsible for making those development opportunities available. As noted earlier, organizations benefit from helping employees manage their careers by providing support in the form of specific developmental programs. Examples of these programs will be covered in the next section.

Another career-related change in recent decades involves a shift in the emphasis that people place on different types of success. Career success can be defined by both objective and subjective measures.[14] Objective measures of career success include promotions and pay. Subjective measures include career satisfaction and personal well-being. For many people, emphasis has shifted from an objective perspective (how much money do you make?) to a subject perspective (how happy are you with your work?). This shift does not mean that people are no longer concerned with money, but it does mean that employees are increasingly concerned with psychological success, such as the quality of their day-to-day work and home life.[14]

Even with all the changes we've just discussed, a number of organizations still communicate expectations about how employees will progress from job to job. This is particularly true for managerial work. Specifically, some companies identify a series of work experiences that are likely to prepare the employee for high-level jobs, such as general manager, vice president, and CEO. This progression, when defined and communicated, is called a **career path**. Organizations that identify internal career paths, communicate this information to employees,

Protean career
A career characterized by personal responsibility, continuous and self-directed development, and an emphasis on psychological success.

Career path
The series of work experiences that prepare an employee for higher-level jobs.

Table 10.1	*Differences Between the Traditional and Protean Career*	
Issue	**Protean Career**	**Traditional Career**
Responsibility	Person	Organization
Core values	Freedom, growth	Advancement, power
Degree of mobility	Higher	Lower
Important performance dimensions	Psychological success	Position level, salary
Important attitude dimensions	Work satisfaction, professional commitment	Organizational commitment
Important identity dimensions	Self-esteem, self-awareness	Esteem from others, organizational awareness
Important adaptability dimensions	Work-related flexibility (measure: marketability)	Organization-related flexibility (measure: organizational survival)

Source: D. T. Hall, *Careers in Organizations* (Glenview, IL: Scott, Foresman 1976), p. 202. Used with permission.

and make opportunities clear can help employees who set career goals achieve them. If the organization uses this process in a sincere attempt to help employees manage their careers and accomplish their personal goals, then employees are likely to reciprocate with greater commitment and job performance.[16]

One company that has increased its use of career paths recently is Toyota, the Japanese car manufacturer. Toyota has developed a set of minimum guidelines for promotion into managerial positions. If an employee wants to become a general manager at a plant, for example, he or she must first work with at least two Toyota manufacturing units. To be president of a Toyota subsidiary, the employee also must have worked in more than one country.[17]

CONCEPT CHECK

1. *What is the difference between a career ladder and a career path? Which is a more accurate description of typical careers today?*
2. *What are the characteristics of a Protean career?*
3. *What dimensions of performance, attitudes, identity, and adaptability are becoming more common today?*

How Can Organizations Help Employees Develop?

We turn next to a description of four types of programs that help employees develop new knowledge and skills that will help them succeed in their careers: formal education, assessments and feedback, work experiences, and developmental relationships. These programs can be run by human resource professionals, but they do not necessarily need to be.

FORMAL EDUCATION

Formal education is a category of development that includes formal learning experiences such as training courses. These courses can be a single event or a series of events, but the key is that they must help employees learn a particular skill or skills that are likely to be relevant in their future work. Courses may be organized around helping the employee gain public recognition for skills in the form of a certificate or license.

Courses

Formal education, as a form of development, includes courses specifically designed for the company's employees; courses offered by consultants, trade organizations, or universities; or courses that are part of degree programs from accredited institutions like community colleges and universities.[18] Such courses may involve lectures, discussions, simulations, or other learning activities, as described in Chapter 9. While some companies provide simple and broad-based tuition assistance programs (that is, they support any courses employees take), others are moving toward focusing employee development efforts on preferred education providers and preferred skills. Specifically, they are offering development through low-cost providers whose programs will help the organization accomplish its goals. For example, Consolidated Edison, an energy company in the New York area, partnered with the Stevens Institute of Technology to design a customized online course called Analytical Capabilities for Business Improvement. As part of the course, Consolidated Edison managers examined real-world business problems in the company and proposed solutions that would benefit the company.[19]

Certification and Licensing

People earn certificates and licenses by demonstrating competence in a particular area of professional practice. **Licenses** are regulated by state governments. In many fields, an individual must obtain a license in order to legally conduct business.[20] For example, doctors, lawyers, and real estate agents must have licenses to practice. In contrast, there is no legal requirement for people to obtain **certification**. Certificates are still valuable, though, because a person who holds a certificate has demonstrated a general knowledge of, and competence to do work in, the area being certified.

There are many examples of certification in various occupations. In the field of human resources, the Human Resources Certification Institute offers a few different certifications: Professional in Human Resources (PHR), Senior Professional in Human Resources (SPHR), Global Professional in Human Resources (GPHR), California Certifications (PHR-CA and SPHR-CA), Human Resource Management Professional (HRMP), and Human Resource Business Professional (HRBP).[21] These certificates are described in the appendices (available online). Some of the many certifications available in the information technology field include Apple Certified System Administrator, Cisco Certified Network Professional, HP Certified IT Professional, IBM Certified Enterprise Developer, Microsoft Certified Systems Administrator, Nortel Networks Certified Network Architect, Oracle Certified Professional Java Developer, Sun Certified Java Programmer, and Symantec Certified Security Engineer.[22] Providing support to gain and maintain certifications is one way organizations can be attractive to both current and prospective employees.

License
A required designation of competence within a professional field.

Certification
An optional designation of competence within a professional field.

ASSESSMENTS AND FEEDBACK

Using assessments and feedback for development involves collecting information and providing feedback to employees about their interests, personality, behaviors, skills, and preferences. The feedback can help employees understand what type of work they should choose so they experience a good fit between their interests, skills, and work demands. Feedback can also help them determine what types of developmental activities they should pursue. A wide variety of assessments are available for purposes of helping employees better understand their strengths and weaknesses, plan their developmental activities, and manage their careers. Some of the tests described in Chapter 6 can be used for this purpose, such as personality tests and work sample tests. In this section, we'll cover two basic types of assessments—career assessments and multisource assessments.

Holland typology
A classification, developed by Dr. John Holland, of people's interests, values, and skills and of job environments; the typology asserts that people will be more satisfied and more successful in jobs that closely match their characteristics.

Career Assessment

In the area of career interests and career fit, the most widely used assessment instruments are based on a typology developed by John L. Holland.[23] The **Holland typology** identifies six different personality types—realistic (R), investigative (I), artistic (A), social (S), enterprising (E), and conventional (C)—which correspond with six different job environments. One instrument based on this typology, the Self-Directed Search (SDS), can help employees gain insight into their interests, skills, and desired working conditions. The instrument is a simple pencil-and-paper measure that can be scored quickly using an answer key. The answer key is provided in a manual that also includes descriptions of careers that match the results of the person taking the assessment. Descriptions of Holland's categories appear in Table 10.2.

Another assessment tool, the World of Work Map, is illustrated in Figure 10.2. It simplifies the Holland typology into two dimensions—whether a person prefers working with data or ideas and whether he or she prefers working with people or things—and links these interests to a wide variety of occupations. The map provides examples of jobs that match peoples' preferences and skills. For example, jobs that require working with data include bank teller, insurance underwriter, and tax accountant; jobs that require working with ideas include criminologist, political scientist, and sociologist. Examples of jobs that require working with people include counselor, lawyer, and social worker; examples of jobs that require working with things include locksmith, millwright, and automotive technician.[24] Encouraging employees to take these types of assessments, and helping them interpret the results, can be useful for providing them with guidance concerning what careers and jobs they are likely to enjoy.

Multisource assessments and feedback
A process in which an employee's managers, peers, and sometimes subordinates and customers answer questions about the employee. Responses are combined and provided as developmental feedback to the employee.

Multisource Assessments

A type of assessment and feedback program that is being used with increasing frequency is **multisource assessments and feedback**. We first discussed these programs in Chapter 8. A typical process involves having an employee's managers, peers, and sometimes subordinates and customers answer questions about the employee. Raters are typically asked to evaluate the person along a number of different dimensions. One example of an instrument used in this sort of assessment is ManagerView360. This instrument measures 20 managerial

Table 10.2	*Holland Typology*

Realistic (R) people enjoy jobs as mechanics, electricians, and farmers. Realistic people have mechanical and athletic abilities and like to work outdoors with tools.

Investigative (I) people enjoy jobs as scientists, laboratory assistants, and technicians. Investigative people have math and science abilities and like to work alone solving problems.

Artistic (A) people enjoy jobs as musicians, dancers, actors, and writers. Artistic people have good imaginations and like to create original work.

Social (S) people enjoy jobs as therapists, counselors, and teachers. Social people have people-related abilities and like to work with and help other people.

Enterprising (E) people enjoy jobs as promoters, producers, salespeople, and executives. Enterprising people have leadership and public speaking abilities and like to influence other people.

Conventional (C) people enjoy jobs as analysts, bankers, and secretaries. Conventional people have clerical and math abilities and like to work indoors to organize things.

Source: Information from John L. Holland, *Making Vocational Choices: A Theory of Careers* (Englewood Cliffs, NJ: Prentice Hall, 1973).

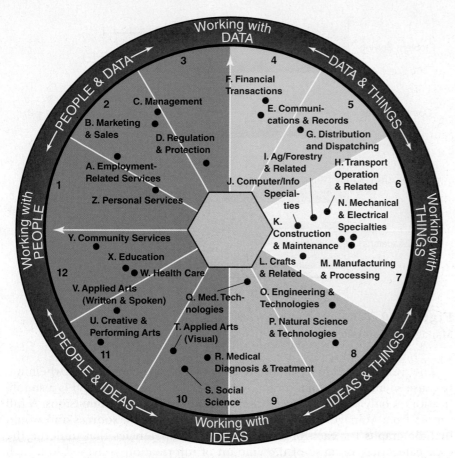

Figure 10.2 The World of Work Map. A service of ACT, Inc. The map is reproduced here with permission, and may be accessed at http://www.act.org/wwm.

competencies clustered into four major areas: task/leadership, interpersonal, communication, and problem solving.[25] As with other assessment tests, the results of these evaluations, along with feedback to the employee, can be used to identify strengths and weaknesses and guide development efforts.

As an illustration, an abbreviated feedback form is presented in Figure 10.3. This particular form uses bar graphs to represent average ratings across a number of descriptive statements about the target employee. The ratings, provided on a seven-point scale, indicate the degree to which the target uses various behaviors grouped into categories (four are shown in this example). For example, raters could be asked to rate the degree to which the target employee "Clearly expresses and requests information from others" and "Uses written communications effectively and appropriately" as indicators of communication skill.

On the graph, each bar represents the average of the responses of a particular group of respondents: a self-rating by the person who is the target of the assessment, ratings by three employees who report to the target (direct reports whose scores are averaged together), and ratings by the target's manager. An average of the direct report and manager ratings is also presented. The lines at the end of each bar indicate the spread of responses that underlie the average response depicted by the bar.

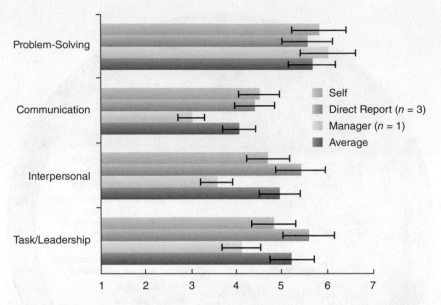

Figure 10.3 Sample Multisource Feedback for Four Categories of Managerial Competence.

The results presented in multisource feedback can be overwhelming because so much information is conveyed. This particular graph is a simplification; it only presents data from three sources for four dimensions. A full report from ManagerView360 might include up to five sources and would include graphs for each of the 20 specific competencies that underlie the four categories. Because of the amount of information conveyed in a such a feedback report, people often need training or guidance in interpreting their reports.

In the example provided, it appears that the manager and direct reports of the employee being rated agree that she is an effective problem solver. However, her manager and direct reports are less consistent in their rating of her other competencies. In particular, the manager of this employee has rated her low on communication and interpersonal competence. This feedback could be used to initiate a conversation about how her communication skills might be improved. As a result of the feedback and conversation, this employee might set a developmental goal, such as increasing the degree to which she clarifies her expectations about how work should be done (a communication behavior). Then she should identify development opportunities that will help her accomplish that goal.

Multisource feedback systems work best when reliable ratings are provided, raters' confidentiality is maintained, the system is easy to use, the behaviors assessed are job-relevant, and managers act on the feedback received.[26] One of the research studies that helped to discover these best practices is presented in the "How Do We Know?" feature.

As the feature shows, providing feedback of this kind does not always result in positive outcomes. Some employees may not change as a result of the feedback, and other employees may be frustrated if the feedback is overly negative and not constructive.[27] To prevent this from happening, the organization should provide clear guidance to people filling out evaluation forms, along with support for people receiving feedback. Support can

How Do We Know?

CAN A FEEDBACK PROGRAM REALLY IMPROVE PERFORMANCE?

Having managers, coworkers, subordinates, or even customers rate employees in your company is a resource-intensive undertaking. Does all that effort have any effect on employee performance? To find an answer to this question, Alan Walker and James Smither tracked 252 bank managers participating in an upward feedback program over a five-year period. In this program, managers' subordinates anonymously rated the behaviors of their managers, and that feedback was collected into five-page reports providing information about average ratings and comparing the ratings to others in the organization. The ratings were provided for developmental purposes only and were not used to make promotion decisions. Managers were strongly encouraged to meet with their subordinates to discuss the results but were not required to do so.

The results indicated that not all managers improved their performance. However, managers initially rated poor or moderate showed significant improvements in upward feedback ratings over the five-year period, and these improvements were beyond what could be expected due to chance alone. The researchers also found that managers who met with direct reports to discuss their upward feedback improved more than other managers.

The Bottom Line. Feedback can improve performance, but what people do with the feedback matters. It is important for an organization to encourage employees to talk with others about the feedback and publicly commit to improving their performance.

Sources: James W. Smither, Manuel London, and Richard R. Reilly, "Does Performance Improve Following Multisource Feedback? A Theoretical Model, Meta-Analysis, and Review of Empirical Findings," *Personnel Psychology* 58 (2005): 33–66; A. G. Walker and James W. Smither, "A Five-Year Study of Upward Feedback: What Managers Do with Their Results Matters," *Personnel Psychology* 52 (1999): 393–423; Jai Ghorpade, "Managing Five Paradoxes of 360-Degree Feedback," *Academy of Management Executive* 14 (2000): 140–150.

include providing a trained professional to help employees interpret the report or training employees so that they have the knowledge and skill to interpret their own reports.

WORK EXPERIENCES

We mentioned earlier that organizations can use a variety of work experiences to help employees develop. These options include enrichment, lateral moves (including rotations and transfers), upward moves, and downward moves. Using work experiences for employee development can be very effective, and as an added advantage to organizations pursuing cost strategies, they are relatively low cost.

Job enrichment involves adding challenges or new responsibilities to employees' jobs. Enrichment may involve a project assignment that is outside an employee's regular duties or a role switch that requires the employee to temporarily take on another employee's responsibilities. Enrichment can have the dual benefit of being motivating because it adds challenge and novelty and being developmental because it requires the employee to develop new skills.

A lateral move involves a change in duties without an increase in pay, responsibility, or status. Lateral moves include job rotations and job transfers.

Job enrichment
The addition of challenges or new responsibilities to jobs.

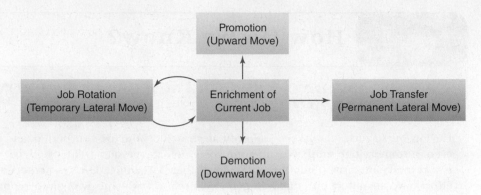

Figure 10.4 Types of Developmental Job Experiences. *Source:* Based on Raymond A. Noe, *Employee Training and Development*, 3rd ed. (New York: McGraw-Hill, 2004), p. 284.

Job rotation
A time-limited lateral work assignment for the purpose of helping employees develop new knowledge and skills.

Job transfer
A permanent lateral work assignment for the purpose of helping employees develop new knowledge and skill.

Job rotations are temporary work assignments in which employees move through multiple jobs within a set period of time. **Job transfers** are permanent lateral moves made for purposes of developing new knowledge and skill. Figure 10.4 depicts these different experiences.

One study of lateral moves found a number of benefits for a job rotation and transfer program at Eli Lilly and Company, a pharmaceutical firm that employs over 38,000 and develops products sold all over the world. Although headquartered in Indianapolis, Indiana, the company has research facilities in eight countries.[28] To help employees develop the breadth of knowledge and skill necessary in this industry, Eli Lilly rotates most of its employees through different jobs in different locations in either short-term rotations or longer-term transfers. The job assignments last anywhere from one to five years. Researchers found that employees who took more frequent rotations had greater salary growth, had more perceived gains in knowledge and skill, and believed their work was more satisfying.[29] Companies are believed to benefit as well, by helping employees to better understand the big picture of what the company does and how, and by encouraging employees to meet people throughout the company so they can collaborate in the future.

Upward move
A career move resulting in an increase in responsibility, pay, and status; also known as a promotion.

Downward move
A career move resulting in a decrease in responsibility, pay, and status; also known as a demotion.

An **upward move** is typically called a promotion; it involves an increase in responsibility, pay, and status. Employees generally welcome promotions as developmental opportunities. When employees are promoted, they receive material rewards as they are being challenged and as they learn. A **downward move** or demotion involves taking a job with less responsibility and authority.[30] Not surprisingly, employees are often resistant to downward moves because moving down often means losing pay as well as responsibility.[31] Employees may be less satisfied with a downward or lateral move than with a promotion and thus be more likely to quit.[32] A downward move may be necessary, though, for an individual to gain knowledge and skill in a new area. For example, a manager who wants to break into product design may have to take a nonmanagerial product design position and work in a lower-paying team role in order to gain the knowledge necessary to manage in that area of the business. So downward moves are likely to work best when they are temporary and when the employees agree to the moves as steps toward long-term career goals.

Of course, not every job experience actually results in learning and growth. Simply adding more work or changing a job title does not promote employee development. Research suggests that the greatest learning occurs when job experiences provide greater authority, require skill at creating change, and call for the use of persuasion rather than authority to get things done. All these factors contribute to a sense of personal growth.[33]

DEVELOPMENTAL RELATIONSHIPS

Developmental relationships are relationships that provide support and encouragement for personal or professional growth. These relationships can involve formally assigned mentors, coaches, supervisors, coworkers, subordinates, or support groups.[34] Table 10.3 lists these different relationships along with a description of their nature and purpose. Young managers are often frustrated that their employers do not provide enough mentoring, coaching, and direct support from their supervisor.[35]

Coaching

An increasingly common form of developmental relationship in organizations is **coaching**. Coaches equip people with the tools, knowledge, and opportunities they need to become more effective.[36] Coaches can be professionals who work outside the company, or they can be employees who have a responsibility for improving other employees' performance. Professional coaching is a big business. The International Coach Federation, the largest association for professional coaches, boasts membership of over 22,000 members.[37]

Professional coaching appears to be most commonly used to remedy problem performance of senior managers and executives.[38] However, it has also come to be considered a positive, proactive practice that should be more broadly used by managers and human resource professionals within their companies. For example, lower-level managers and managers who are not struggling may benefit from meeting with a coach to further improve their performance or to prepare for upcoming challenges. Many supervisors are being asked to take on the role of coach with their subordinates.[39]

What does a good coach do? Good coaches follow a process of contracting, opening, practicing, planning, and evaluating.[40] Contracting and opening are the preliminary phases of coaching, and they involve setting up a clear understanding of the nature and duration of the relationship. These phases also include an initial meeting at which expectations are discussed. Practicing and planning are the core learning processes in which the coach and employee try out new behaviors. Finally, evaluation involves verifying that expectations have been met and that the relationship has worked out as planned.

Coaching
When a person works with others to equip them with the tools, knowledge, and opportunities they need to become more effective at work.

Table 10.3	*Types of Developmental Relationships*
Relationship	**Nature and Purpose**
Coach/Sponsor	Deliberate relationship to develop specific employee skills that improve work performance
Mentor	Deliberate relationship to develop inexperienced employee through personal interaction and discussion
Supervisor/Coworker	Naturally occurring relationship where development is incidental rather than intentional
Role Model	Nonreciprocal relationship where model is observed in order to learn desired traits and behaviors
Support Group/Network	Group of individuals who join around common characteristics or goals and provide meaningful support to one another

Source: Information from Douglas T. Hall, *Careers In and Out of Organizations* (Thousand Oaks, CA: Sage, 2001).

Deloitte & Touche USA, a member of the Deloitte Touche Tohmatsu worldwide professional services organization, uses professional coaches as part of its Career Connections program. Since the program's inception in 2002, Deloitte's full-time coaches have provided one-on-one counseling to about 3,500 partners and employees as well as team coaching to some 1,300 additional employees and clients. The company credits the program for retaining at least 650 people who would have left the organization had there been no access to a coach.[41] Deloitte values this program so much that it has 13 full-time coaches on staff, and it is conducting training to encourage partners and managers to adopt a coaching approach to their management duties.

Mentoring

Another common developmental relationship in organizations is mentoring. **Mentoring** refers to a one-on-one relationship between a less experienced and a more experienced person that is intended to contribute to personal and professional growth.[42] Mentoring can be formal, as when an organization pairs an employee with a more senior manager, or informal, as with a relationship that arises naturally in the course of day-to-day working arrangements. Mentors generally benefit employees in two ways. First, they may provide career benefits by offering challenging work experiences, providing advice, offering political protection, and sponsoring the employee in contests for promotions and other opportunities. Second, they may provide psychological and social benefits, such as by helping the employee build a sense of identity and personal competence.[43]

What makes for a successful mentoring program? A number of studies suggest that it is helpful for mentors and protégés to perceive themselves as similar in some way.[44] This can be accomplished either by helping to match employees and mentors who are similar in their outlook or perspective or by allowing employees and mentors to voluntarily select their own pairings. Other characteristics of good programs include encouraging proximity, providing an orientation, offering guidelines, and encouraging protégés to set goals.[45] For example, one study examined 12 mentoring programs across four different organizations, involving a total of 175 protégés and 110 mentors. The researchers found that providing high-quality training to mentors and protégés and allowing them to have input on the type of person with whom they were matched contributed to participants reporting that the program was effective.[46] Another study, reported in the "How Do We Know?" feature, found that the best performance following a mentoring relationship came from pairing protégés with mentors who were successful in their jobs.

Mentoring
When an experienced person helps a less experienced person learn and grow.

? CONCEPT CHECK

1. *What is the difference between a certificate and a license?*
2. *What distinguishes successful and unsuccessful multisource feedback programs?*
3. *What are some types of job experiences that can help employees learn and grow?*
4. *What are key characteristics of a successful mentoring program?*

How Do We Know?

HOW DO WE MAXIMIZE THE RETURN ON MENTORING?

How can we ensure that the time put into a mentoring program pays off? To answer this question, Scott Tonidandel, Derek Avery, and McKensy Phillips studied NCAA Division 1 head coaches in women's basketball. Seventy-four coaches were asked a series of questions about their interactions with their head coaches when they were assistant coaches. The coaches with the best records were those who had worked for more successful head coaches (more career wins) who had provided mentoring (given support and career advice). When the head coaches had done little by way of mentoring, then their records did not matter. And when the head coaches had provided mentoring but had not been successful themselves, then their mentoring did not seem to make a difference for their protégés' later performance.

The Bottom Line. If you want employees to learn to be winners, then have them mentored by more senior employees who are already winners. It's not enough to simply pair people together. For the greatest chance of future protégé success, mentors should provide both personal and professional support to their protégés. In other words, not just any mentor will do.

Source: Information from Scott Tonidandel, Derek R. Avery, and McKensy G. Phillips, "Maximizing Returns on Mentoring: Factors Affecting Subsequent Protégé Performance," *Journal of Organizational Behavior* 28 (2007): 89–110.

LEARNING OBJECTIVE 4

How Do Organizations Integrate Development Efforts?

Companies with effective human resource practices use their development programs in a systematic as well as a strategic fashion. They use competency models to integrate their development efforts with the company's strategy and goals, encourage employees to follow a thorough process that includes a number of discrete steps, and employ technology to integrate development with other human resource activities.

COMPETENCY MODEL

Rather than choosing programs haphazardly, forward-looking organizations use competency models to design a set of related programs, link them together, and ensure they are congruent with other HR practices. Competency models, as described in Chapter 4, can be developed to indicate what types of knowledge, skills, and behaviors will help the organization accomplish its strategy. Based on this information, the organization can strategically staff important positions with people who have the right characteristics. It can also develop those characteristics in others by first identifying current employees' strengths and weaknesses and then encouraging development using one or more of the types of development presented in this chapter.

One example of a program that uses this approach is a leadership development program at Johnson & Johnson. Johnson & Johnson operates more than 200 companies that employ approximately 122,000 men and women in

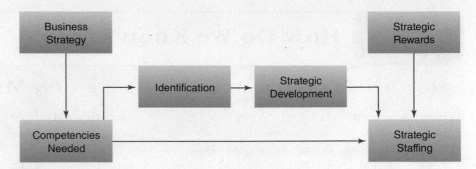

Figure 10.5 Model of Strategic Career Development. *Source:* Adapted from Douglas T. Hall, *Careers In and Out of Organizations* (Thousand Oaks, CA: Sage, 2001), p. 285. Used with permission. Know

57 countries. These companies manufacture healthcare products and provide related services in the consumer, pharmaceutical, and medical devices markets. Johnson & Johnson, which has won many awards for its concern for employee and consumer well-being, works hard to ensure that its emphasis on responsibility and innovation will be supported over time by its next generation of leaders. To accomplish this goal, the company developed a competency model for its leaders, called the standards of leadership (SOL), built around the Johnson & Johnson credo values of responsibility, integrity, and ethical behavior. The SOL competencies are used to guide leadership development programs in many parts of Johnson & Johnson.[47] Figure 10.5 graphically illustrates steps in such an approach.

Another example of a company that takes leadership development seriously, and bases these efforts on core competencies related to their core business, is LG Electronics. This company is described in more detail in the Building Strength Through HR feature.

CAREER DEVELOPMENT PROCESS

Forward-looking companies help employees to manage their development using the career development process. This is a series of steps that helps employees identify and pursue career goals, along with appropriate developmental goals to help them achieve their long-term career goals. The **career development process** includes four steps: self-assessment, reality check, goal setting, and action planning.[48]

Self-assessment is a process in which employees determine their interests, values, personalities, and skills. Self-assessment often involves the use of psychological tests like the SDS, discussed earlier. Assessment can also include exercises that ask employees to consider where they are today and where they want to be in the future. Employees can conduct these activities alone, with the help of a supervisor, or with a specialist in the area of career coaching or counseling. These professionals can be particularly useful for helping administer and interpret the results of psychological tests.

In performing a **reality check**, employees gather information to determine whether their self-assessments are realistic and how those assessments fit with opportunities in the labor market and with their current employer's future labor needs. Employees can talk with their current supervisors as one way to obtain a reality check. Supervisors can often provide information about their

Career development process
A series of steps that people can use to identify and pursue their long-term career goals.

Self-assessment
A process in which employees determine their interests, values, personalities, and skills.

Reality check
A process in which employees determine the accuracy of their self-assessments and how those assessments fit with opportunities in the environment.

Building Strength Through HR

LG ELECTRONICS

LG Electronics is a South Korea–based firm that designs and manufactures a wide variety of consumer electronics including smartphones, refrigerators, air conditioners, and televisions. To help fuel its growth, LG makes substantial investments in leadership development. In recent years they have sought to build a single standard Global Leadership Framework that connects to the company's vision and values and guides leadership development practices. Working with a consulting firm, LG created a list of behaviors needed by leaders at each level in the company. Then they launched a leadership academy that began with a multi-source assessment of participants' leadership behaviors. With data in hand, participants worked through custom-designed learning modules to enhance those skills. To further develop their skills, participants are given work assignments that help

©Andrew Kent/Corbis

improve particular skills. Finally, the consulting firm offered coaching to help participants practice behaviors on the job.

Source: Information from Erin Wilson Burns, Laurence Smith, and Dave Ulrich, "Competency Models with Impact: Research findings from the Top Companies for Leaders," *People & Strategy,* 35 (2012): 16-23.

---

subordinates' strengths and weaknesses and about opportunities within the company. Other sources of information about labor market opportunities include career centers of colleges and universities, trade magazines published by professional associations, computer discussion groups, online resources, and current incumbents.[49] Contacting current incumbents, a process referred to as *information interviewing,* gives an insider view of a job or profession. Meeting someone at his or her work environment can be a great way to test assumptions about what the work is like. If one of your ambitions is to be an executive at your company, for example, then you might try meeting with a current executive and asking questions about her work to discover whether the work is as you imagine it.

Goal setting involves setting milestones or achievements for the future, such as positions to achieve, skills to be gained, and development efforts to pursue. For example, an employee with the long-term goal of being a chief accounting officer should plan to gain skill in financial analysis, auditing, corporate tax planning, and strategic analysis. This employee might also want to seek a degree or certification in this area, such as a master's degree in accountancy or a designation as a Certified Public Accountant.

In **action planning**, employees make plans for how they will accomplish their goals. In most cases, action planning means selecting developmental opportunities appropriate to the goal. An employee who aspires to be a chief accounting officer, for example, should plan for action by selecting one or more developmental activities for each of the areas in which she needs to gain skills in order to meet her goal. For example, to gain auditing skills, she might

Goal setting
A process in which employees set milestones or desired achievements for the future.

Action planning
A process in which employees plan how they will achieve their goals.

plan for the following: Within three months, find a mentor with considerable audit experience (developmental relationship); within a year, take a class from a local university in accounting (formal education); in three years, take a work assignment in internal auditing (work experience).

TECHNOLOGY

Companies with effective human resource practices make use of technology to ensure that employees have ready access to a variety of developmental opportunities. Technology can also be used to integrate various programs so that a common database of competencies and associated learning experiences can be used to make and track development plans.

One example of an integrated employee and career development website is the National Aeronautics and Space Administration (NASA) System for Administration, Training, and Educational Resources for NASA (SATERN). Before 2005, NASA used three different computer systems to coordinate its training and development programs.[50] It operated a registration system

Technology in HR

NATIONAL AERONAUTICS AND SPACE ADMINISTRATION (NASA)

Headquartered in Washington, DC, NASA also has 10 field centers that support its mission to pioneer the future in space exploration, scientific discovery, and aeronautics research. NASA has over 18,000 full-time employees, many with advanced degrees in their fields and an interest in continued learning and education.

To make learning and education opportunities easily available to employees, and easy for supervisors to manage, NASA launched the SATERN website in 2005. A major objective of the system is to provide supervisors with "an integrated system that ties training, IDPs [individual development plans], and competencies into a single system, enabling them to make more informed decisions."

The SATERN website allows employees to do a number of things: search for or simply browse learning opportunities; indicate an interest in opportunities and, if they are qualified, enroll directly; create and modify a learning plan that keeps track of desired, ongoing, and completed learning opportunities; and launch online and mobile learning opportunities.

Source: Information from https://saterninfo.nasa.gov, accessed April 12, 2013.

deslover/iStockphoto

that allowed employees to sort through and select learning opportunities, an administration system that tracked employees' learning and produced reports for supervisors and others, and an online delivery system that provided Internet-based training. Working with an outside partner called Plateau, NASA integrated this system into a single website that performs all of these functions for NASA employees and contractors. This system simplifies learning for employees and is expected to save NASA money by reducing the amount of time required to complete paperwork required by the government. More information on this system is presented in the "Technology in HR" feature.

CONCEPT CHECK

1. *What role do competency models play in career development?*
2. *What are the steps in the career management process?*
3. *What role does technology play in career development?*
4. *What are the major steps in the career development process?*

LEARNING OBJECTIVE 5

What Are Some Important Career Development Challenges?

Organizations in general, and HR departments in particular, face several major challenges in the area of the career development of employees. These challenges include effectively orienting new employees, preventing employee burnout, helping employees to balance their work with their personal lives, developing a diverse workforce, and assisting employees to manage international assignments. Fundamentally, these challenges represent ways organizations can help their employees learn and grow within the organization so that they do not leave in search of opportunities elsewhere. In addition, organizations that have programs to address these challenges are more likely to be attractive to potential hires, so these programs can help attract new employees.

ORIENTING NEW EMPLOYEES

Organizations face a challenge every time they hire a new employee. New employees need to be helped through a transition from being only loosely connected with the organization (an outsider) to being knowledgeable and comfortable in their role within the organization (an insider). **New employee orientation** is the process of bringing people into the organization and helping them adjust so that they can perform their work effectively. This process goes by many other names, including on-boarding, induction, and socialization (see Chapter 7).[51] Although often considered a single event (an orientation program), it is best to think about orientation as an ongoing process that helps employees adjust and ensures their success. Orientation, then, is one way organizations help employees succeed in their careers, because it helps employees to become successful in their jobs and to prepare for future jobs within the organization.

New employee orientation
A process in which organizations help new employees adjust so that they can perform their work effectively.

A typical orientation program might involve lectures and discussions on the mission, values, and history of the firm, as well as specific information about the policies and procedures that employees are expected to follow. Lectures and discussions can be supplemented with a tour of the physical space, team-building activities, and opportunities to practice some skills that are critical to success in the organization. To make orientation an ongoing process, structured meetings between the new employees and their managers, as well as other important employees in the organization, can be arranged. In addition, new employees can meet again informally to share their successes and their challenges.

Research has found that organizations that provide orientations to their new employees help them learn important characteristics of the company.[52] When compared to employees who did not attend an orientation program, employees who attended orientation training had significantly higher levels of affective organizational commitment. So offering new employees orientation programs is a way to increase commitment and reduce turnover of new employees.[53]

An effective orientation program should be guided by five principles:

1. Present realistic information about the company and the new employees' role in it.
2. Provide support and reassurance to alleviate anxiety and fear.
3. Have a successful employee demonstrate how employees can use coping skills to succeed at work, allow discussion, and encourage practice.
4. Teach self-control of thoughts and feelings to help employees manage negative thoughts and feelings that arise because of challenges in adjusting.
5. Give the new employees information specific to their new jobs and new bosses.[54]

To follow these principles, orientation cannot be a one-time event conducted solely by an HR professional. Instead, it should be a series of events that involve not only HR professionals but also other employees of the company, including the new employees' future bosses.

REDUCING BURNOUT

Burnout
A psychological phenomenon involving emotional exhaustion, cynicism, and a decline in feelings of competence about work.

Burnout is a psychological phenomenon involving emotional exhaustion, cynicism, and a decline in feelings of competence about work. We first introduced this concept in Chapter 4 when we discussed work design. Employees who experience burnout exhibit the following symptoms: (1) feelings of being overextended and emotionally drained, (2) indifference or a distant attitude toward work, and (3) reduced expectations of continued effectiveness. These symptoms of burnout are similar across different industries and countries.[55] Organizations must address the challenge of burnout, or their employees may quit. High levels of burnout are associated with low levels of commitment and high turnover intentions.[56]

What causes burnout? Research suggests that burnout is highly related to workload, pressure, stress, conflict, and unmet expectations. This means, for example, that employees who are given a lot of work with tight timelines, and who did not expect these working conditions, are more prone to burnout. What can help to reduce burnout? Research suggests that supervisors can play a key role by being clear about their expectations, offering support, and providing employees with the opportunity to help make decisions about the work.[57]

Organizations that do not keep an eye out for symptoms of burnout may waste their investments in employee development. For example, if an employee who is given multisource feedback, mentors, and an enriched job becomes overwhelmed by the balancing of current work demands and the time required for developing new skills, he may experience burnout and leave the organization. If this employees leaves, then all the learning gains from development will be taken to another organization, possibly even a competitor!

HELPING EMPLOYEES BALANCE WORK WITH PERSONAL LIVES

As we first mentioned in Chapter 1, the U.S. labor force has undergone a number of changes, including an ongoing shift toward a higher proportion of women in the workforce. This shift has created a compelling need for organizations to help employees balance their work and nonwork lives. Figure 10.6 shows that the percentage of families in which both spouses work in the United States has increased by nearly one third since 1970, from 45.7 percent to 59.8 percent. This means that the average family in the United States has to juggle two jobs as well as other life obligations, such as running the household, raising children, and taking care of aging parents.

The strain of balancing the demands of work and personal life can cause dissatisfaction that leads employees to quit their jobs. However, organizations can do something about it. Programs that allow flexible work hours, provide assistance locating services, and offer time off to deal with family needs can help employees meet the demands of their lives outside the workplace. Research reveals an interesting finding about such programs. For nearly all employees, these programs send a message about how much the organization cares about its employees. Having these programs is seen as a positive even by employees who do not use them. More specifically, employees are more committed to organizations that have family-friendly policies, even if they don't make use of the programs.[58]

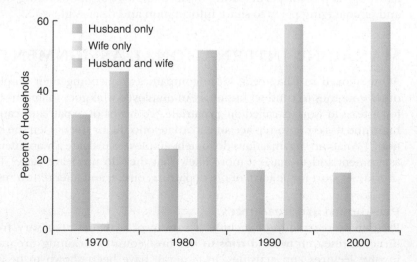

Figure 10.6 Changing Earnings Structure of Families. *Source:* Information from U.S. Bureau of Labor Statistics, "Annual Social and Economic Supplement 1968–2005 Current Population Survey" (Washington, DC: U.S. Department of Labor Bureau of Labor Statistics, 2006). Available online at http://www.bls.gov/cps/wlf-table23-2005.pdf. Percentages do not add up to 100% because no-earner and other multiple-earner households are omitted.

DEVELOPING A DIVERSE WORKFORCE

Increased workforce diversity, as noted in Chapter 1, requires that organizations address the different development needs of different employees. How can organizations provide career support and developmental opportunities to women, ethnic minorities, disabled workers, and older workers, all of which are growing segments of the labor market?

One way to provide career support for members of a diverse workforce is to give these employees access to developmental programs, including work experiences and developmental relationships. At a number of Johnson & Johnson companies, for example, young adults who are members of ethnic minorities are offered key internship and mentoring opportunities. The program helps these employees develop their careers, and it helps to interest them in future opportunities with the company. Since 1999, 100 percent of the job offers to interns in these programs have been accepted.[59] Abbott, a multi-billion-dollar pharmaceutical company, places particular emphasis on its mentoring programs as a way to develop its diverse workforce. Approximately half of Abbott's managers companywide serve as mentors. The program includes formal goals for the mentoring relationship, training, and follow-up.[60]

Affinity group
A group of similar employees that meets to support one another.

Another way to provide career support for members of a diverse workforce is for an organization to organize one or more affinity groups. An **affinity group** can be formed around any of a variety of issues, including ethnicity, age, sexual orientation, and disability. Individuals with similar interests and experiences meet to share information and support one another.[61] In 2013 for example, Texas Instruments Diversity Network includes 38 grassroots diversity initiatives such as the TI Women's Initiative, the Hispanic Employees Initiative Forum, the Chinese Initiative, the Jewish Initiative, Muslim Employees Initiative, and the Deaf Employee Network. Each group is sponsored by senior management, has a budget, and meets on company time.[62]

For older workers, there is an additional challenge. As they get older, employees run the risk of losing confidence in their ability to learn and having their skills become out of date.[63] There are a number of ways to ensure that older employees continue to update their skills, including providing challenging work assignments, emphasizing continuous learning, rewarding learning via pay for participating in development or contributing new ideas, and encouraging peers to share information and discuss ideas.[64]

MANAGING INTERNATIONAL ASSIGNMENTS

As mentioned in Chapter 5, more companies are sending their employees to other countries to conduct business. An employee who goes to another country for a time to work is called an **expatriate**. Turnover of expatriates can be very high, and it is costly to replace an expatriate once he or she has left the organization.[65] What can organizations do to help employees prepare for an international assignment and to make it more likely that they do not leave early? They can provide support in the form of pre-departure, onsite, and after-return resources.

Expatriate
An employee who goes to another country for a time to work.

Pre-departure Resources

Pre-departure resources include a variety of activities that vary from self-directed research to field trips to the host country. Training programs that involve lectures and activities, in general, have been shown to be an effective way to prepare employees.[66] Training should provide expatriates with basic knowledge that they will need upon arrival. For example, expatriates must be aware of what customs they must adopt in the host country (called *cultural imperatives*) and what customs they should not participate in (called *cultural exclusives*). Imperatives often involve behaviors like greetings and meals. In China, for example, business greetings typically involve a handshake with a slight nod of the head. Formal names are used, and business cards are exchanged by offering and receiving them with both hands. To fail to follow these customs is to be seen as impolite. Exclusives, on the other hand, often involve religious customs. For example, a visitor to Indonesia should not participate in Muslim prayer rituals, reserved for members of the religion, unless the expatriate is a Muslim. If necessary, language training also should be included at this point. Basic language training can help employees navigate day-to-day life in their host country.

Another component of pre-departure training involves explaining that, after an initial "honeymoon" stage, expatriate employees may begin to suffer from culture shock. **Culture shock** is stress that stems from the uncertainty and confusion that people sometimes experience when they must deal with an unfamiliar culture. To help manage this stress, expatriates should be instructed to expect it and should be given advice on how to cope with it. Coping mechanisms include maintaining a reasonable fitness schedule, adhering to a sensible diet, and discussing thoughts and feelings with sympathetic others throughout the visit.[67]

Culture shock
Stress caused by uncertainty and confusion that may arise when people must deal with an unfamiliar culture.

Certain assignments may require more preparation than others. If the country where the employee is going is very different, and if the job requires extensive and intensive contacts with the host society, more rigorous preparation should be provided. This preparation might include advance trips and other field experiences.[68]

Onsite Resources

To help employees adjust to the uncertainties of living in a new culture, the organization should provide onsite assistance as well as pre-departure training. Onsite assistance should include the opportunity to have, when needed, conversations with people who understand the culture and the work that the expatriate is doing. These conversations can take a variety of forms. Expatriates could have access to a local mentor—an individual who was born and raised in the host country but understands the challenges of adjusting to its culture. An organization-sponsored coach or a more experienced expatriate could also provide guidance and advice. Whatever the form, onsite assistance can be invaluable for helping the expatriate determine how to behave in specific situations. This approach is useful because it provides the expatriate with individualized information that can be used right away.[69]

After-Return Resources

The third phase of the process of helping employees manage international assignments, called **repatriation**, involves support provided after the employees return home. After living in a new culture for some time, people often have some difficulty readjusting when they return home. Following an international assignment, employees have valuable knowledge and skills that the organization does not want to lose. Organizations can help the expatriate readjust by offering workshops, encouraging meetings between the expatriate and managers in the expatriate's organization, and providing challenging work that allows the repatriate to use the new knowledge and skills gained from living in another country.

Repatriation
The process of adjusting to a home culture after returning from living and working in another culture.

Other Issues

Another important issue for international assignments is the expatriate employee's spouse and family. If the expatriate has a family, family members should be invited to participate in each of the three phases just described. Offering assistance to family members increases the likelihood that they will adjust to the new culture and thus reduces the chances that family dissatisfaction will become a factor for the expatriate. Failure of the family to adjust is a common reason for expatriates' terminating their assignments early.[70]

Finally, we should not forget that organizations should offer the same support to their employees from other countries who come to the United States as they give to their U.S.-based employees working abroad. There are ways to help ensure that employees from other countries working in the United States are successful, including providing accurate information about life in the specific area in which they will be living and assistance with the practical details of finding housing, jobs for spouses, and schools for children.[71]

CONCEPT CHECK

1. *What are some common career-development challenges that organizations face?*
2. *What can an organization do to make sure employees are oriented effectively?*
3. *What can an organization do to help an employee prepare for an international assignment?*

A MANAGER'S PERSPECTIVE REVISITED

IN THE MANAGER'S PERSPECTIVE AT THE BEGINNING OF THE CHAPTER, ALEJANDRO WAS FEELING THAT HIS JOB WAS MISSING SOMETHING. AFTER TALKING WITH A FRIEND, HE REALIZED THAT A POSITION OFFERING NEW CHALLENGES MIGHT BE JUST WHAT HE NEEDS. FOLLOWING ARE THE ANSWERS TO THE "WHAT DO YOU THINK?" QUIZ THAT FOLLOWED THE CASE. WERE YOU ABLE TO CORRECTLY IDENTIFY THE TRUE STATEMENTS? COULD YOU DO BETTER NOW?

1. In today's economy, companies have no responsibility for helping employees learn and grow. FALSE. *Although it is true that today's employees tend to depend less on the*

©ColorBlind Images/Blend Images/Corbis

organization for development opportunities, organizations still have a role to play. More specifically, organizations that want to attract and retain the best employees must provide resources and support for development.

2. The "career ladder" is often not an accurate description of how people progress through their careers. TRUE. *The typical progression from lower to upper levels within a company is much less prevalent today than in prior years. Some firms still have predictable*

internal career progressions, but even those progressions do not often fit the straight upward progress that was more common in the past. A more suitable term today is career path.

3. Mentoring and coaching are buzzwords for networking; those programs don't do much except help people get to know each other. FALSE. *Both mentoring and coaching offer useful development opportunities. In addition, mentoring provides psychological and social support that can help organizations to retain employees by increasing their job satisfaction.*

4. Multisource feedback systems are too complicated; employees don't learn anything from them. FALSE. *Although it is true that not all employees learn from feedback, research suggests that managers with the worst skills do improve after using these systems. Of*

course, the feedback program must be well run, and managers must commit to changing their behavior.

5. To help employees have a successful career, companies should give them challenging work experiences. TRUE. *Challenging work experiences, particularly job enrichment and lateral moves, have been shown to benefit employees in a variety of ways. Employees who have had challenging work experiences tend to have higher pay, and they tend to be more satisfied with their work.*

Alejandro's situation is repeated in many organizations where managers fail to consider the developmental needs of their employees. Erika, his boss, has a lot of work ahead of her to replace Alejandro. And she will face this problem again and again until she realizes that her HR practices fall short of her competitor's HR practices.

SUMMARY

LEARNING OBJECTIVE 1

How is employee development strategic?

Development practices are useful for organizations because they help to increase the knowledge and skills of their employees and to attract and retain talented employees. Both benefits translate into a better ability to adapt and change as the market demands.

Organizations with an external labor orientation must offer programs that prepare people for their work and are valued by the external labor market. This is particularly true for organizations using a Free Agent strategy, as they must lure employees with valued opportunities such as formal education and support for licensing and certifications. Organizations with an internal labor orientation must offer a broader range of programs, including assessments and developmental relationships. With regard to cost and differentiation, development is equally important but with a

different focus. Organizations with a cost strategy can control development costs by making use of work experiences for development. Organizations with a differentiation strategy use a wider variety of developmental opportunities to foster innovation and collaboration.

LEARNING OBJECTIVE 2

What are careers like today?

The typical career pattern has moved away from a predictable sequence of promotions—a career ladder—to a varied array of experiences that may include movements in and out of companies and industries. There has been a shift in emphasis away from objective indicators of career success, such as material wealth, toward more psychological measures of success, such as career satisfaction and work–life balance.

How can organizations help employees develop?

Four major categories of development include formal education, assessment and feedback, work experiences, and developmental feedback. Within each of these categories, organizations can offer more specific programs that help employees learn skills that help them to pursue their career goals.

How do organizations integrate development efforts?

Information gathered through the use of competency models allows organizations to strategically staff important positions with people who have the right characteristics. Employees can identify and pursue career goals through the career development process, a four-step process of self-assessment, reality check, goal setting, and action planning.

What are some important career development challenges?

Five critical issues are (1) orienting new employees, (2) reducing burnout, (3) helping employees manage a work–family balance, (4) developing a diverse workforce, and (5) assisting employees on international assignments. Each is critical to ensuring that employees who are the recipients of development do not leave the organization. Failing to meet these challenges is a sure-fire way to encourage affected employees to quit and take their skills to another organization, possibly a competitor!

KEY TERMS

Action planning   397
Affinity group   402
Burnout   400
Career   384
Career development   380
Career development process   396
Career ladder   384
Career path   385
Certification   387
Coaching   393
Culture shock   403
Downward move   392
Employee development   380
Expatriate   402
Goal setting   397

Holland typology   388
Job enrichment   391
Job rotation   392
Job transfer   392
License   387
Mentoring   394
Multisource assessments
  and feedback   388
New employee orientation   399
Protean career   385
Reality check   396
Repatriation   403
Self-assessment   396
Talent management   380
Upward move   392

DISCUSSION QUESTIONS

1. What types of development efforts are most appropriate for companies with an internal labor orientation? An external labor orientation? Can you think of examples of how companies with these different orientations develop their employees?

2. What impact should differentiation versus cost strategies have on employee development?

3. Consider the difference between a traditional career and a Protean career. Does one sound more appealing to you? If so, why? If you choose a traditional career, can you think of industries and companies where such a career still exists?

4. Choose a particular job in which you are interested. Research the job to see if licenses are required or certificates are offered. If so, why do you think this is the case? If not, what does that tell you about the job?

5. Brainstorm a list of jobs in which you might be interested. Classify these according to the World of Work map. Is there a pattern to these jobs? Does the placement on the map give you other ideas for jobs you might consider?

6. What are the various types of developmental relationships, and when might each be useful for you?

7. What are different types of developmental work experiences, and when might each be useful for you?

8. In multisource assessments, the ratings assigned by supervisors, peers, and employees do not always agree with one another. Why do you think that is the case? What should be done to help the person being rated to reconcile the differences?

9. Have you ever attended an orientation program for work or for school? How useful was the orientation? Did the orientation cover everything it should have covered? What things were left out that you would like to have had included?

10. Would you be interested in working in another country for an extended period of time? Pick a country where you would consider working, and discuss the positives and negatives that you would expect to come from living and working there.

EXAMPLE CASE   *Expanding into Switzerland*

Your company decides to open a business unit in Switzerland, and you are charged with deciding what the HR policies and practices will be in that unit. In general, your firm is innovative and relies on external labor to maintain a steady supply of talented employees. At this point, the company intends to staff the unit with a mix of employees from the United States and Switzerland. Read the following description of the labor market in Switzerland, and answer the questions that follow.

ZURICH—Working women have never had it easy in slow-to-change Switzerland. But that situation could change as the country's tight labor market forces employers to look more closely at the advantages of having satisfied women in the workforce.

The signal came when the Swiss Employers Association, noted for its conservative approach to women's issues, released a report in January 2001 calling on companies to do everything they can to allow women to combine career and family through flexible working hours and support for childcare centers. The association also called for a change in a primary education system where children come home at all hours of the day. It suggested that schools move to fixed hours and make it possible for children to have lunch at school. All-day schools are also desirable, not just fixed hours in the morning or afternoon, the association said.

"The Swiss have stuck to the old ideal of a family where the man works and the wife stays at home," says an association vice director, Hans Rudolf Schuppisser. "There is an expectation that someone is always at home. We now have revised this idea and we are adjusting to a new situation."

"To make it easier for women to have a profession and a family makes good economic sense," says the association's president, Fritz Blaser. Indeed, there are a number of reasons for the new way of thinking.

Topping the list is one of the world's tightest labor markets, with an unemployment rate of only 2 percent.

"There is a shortage of labor across the board," says association vice director Daniel W. Hefti. He explains that Switzerland's gross domestic product—the national output of goods and services—can grow by only 1.5 to 2 percent. If GDP is to grow beyond this rate, manpower shortages need to be satisfied through immigration. This is a tricky political issue, however, as Switzerland already has a million foreign workers, around a quarter of its working population. That is one of the highest percentages of foreign workers in Europe. If women take up the slack, there will be less demand for imported workers, so the thinking goes.

A factor that is taking on greater significance is the high level of education among Swiss women. In 1999, women accounted for 53 percent of the candidates completing the Matura, a diploma that qualifies them for university admission. Although men still lead in university degrees—56 percent compared with 44 percent for women—their female counterparts are catching up fast. In 1999, the number of university diplomas awarded to women increased by 14 percent, compared with 7 percent for men.

"The future depends on women," says Barbara Zuber, head of human resources at Zurich Financial Services. "In Switzerland, there is huge competition for highly qualified people. We have a war for talent."

On paper, a woman's place in the workforce doesn't appear to be that much of a problem. According to data from the Organization for Economic Cooperation and Development, nearly 72 percent of Swiss women between the ages of 15 and 64 were employed outside the home in 1999, compared with an average of 53 percent in the European Union.

However, these figures gloss over the fact that a great number of these women work very few hours, says Mr. Schuppisser of the Swiss Employers Association. In addition, some 60 percent of women temporarily leave the workforce after the birth of their second child, which produces a loss of trained talent for the Swiss economy, according to Mr. Schuppisser.

The reasons for such a trend are obvious: an acute shortage of childcare centers, irregular primary-school hours, and a lingering social belief that mothers should stay at home.

Camilla Leuzinger, a Zurich-based Swedish marketing executive married to a Swiss architect, recently gave birth to her second child and is now ready to return to work. "I go for an interview, and no one is interested in my qualifications, just in how I'm going to manage the children. My sister has four children and she wasn't even asked about them when interviewed in Sweden," Ms. Leuzinger says. "Somehow it's impossible to convince them that having two children is no big deal. But I'm going to keep on trying. I'm determined to work."

QUESTIONS

1. What challenges to employee recruiting, retention, and career management will your company face in Switzerland?
2. What development programs could be put in place to address these challenges?
3. What other human resource policies and programs would support the development programs you intend to offer?

Source: Article by Margaret Studer, "Tight Labor Market Helps Swiss Women," *The Wall Street Journal Online,* http://www.careerjournaleurope.com/myc/workfamily/20010509-studer.html. Used with permission.

DISCUSSION CASE   *First Day on the Job*

Malik's first day as a new manager ended up more challenging than he expected. While having to adjust to a new workplace and new colleagues, he had an interesting management challenge thrown at him. Toward the end of the day, one of his employees came to him, looking frustrated and exhausted. Malik had heard that this employee was going to be one of his best, a high-potential employee who would be a great asset. On this day, the employee did not look to be an asset to anyone.

Without providing much history or detail, this employee explained to Malik that she is planning to quit her job. She is exhausted and frustrated, she explains, because the work seems to be at once too much and too little. She feels overworked, but at the same time, she does not feel any excitement about her work. She doesn't feel she is being challenged to learn skills that will help her to reach the ultimate goal of owning her own business.

Unfortunately, Malik has to leave for the day before you can get more information. What should he do? Answer these questions, and formulate a plan of action.

QUESTIONS

1. What might be the factors that are causing this employee's dissatisfaction?
2. Which of these factors could be addressed with improvements in the way the organization handles development as described in this chapter?
3. What should Malik do tomorrow with regard to this employee?
4. What long-term changes should Malik suggest for this organization, if it appears that this employee is not the only one with these complaints?

EXPERIENTIAL EXERCISE   *Creating a Personal Development Plan*

Create a personal document that will guide your development over the course of the coming year. To create the document, follow these steps.

1. Conduct a self-assessment. Who are you? What are your strengths and weaknesses? What are you best at doing, and what could you use some improvement in doing? To narrow these questions down, you might consider your strengths and weaknesses with respect to a current job or your role as a student.
2. Conduct a reality check. How accurate is your own assessment? To answer this question, interview two or three people who know you and your work well. They should be people who, in addition to knowing you, are willing to be honest. Ask open-ended questions of them without

revealing your own answers. After you have heard their answers, compare your responses with theirs. Did you miss anything useful in your self-assessment?
3. Set some goals. What do you hope to accomplish in the coming year? How might building on your strengths or improving in areas where you have weaknesses help you meet those goals? For this step, you should review your life and career goals and see whether your current set of skills is sufficient. If you identify a skill that needs improvement, then describe a specific goal to improve that skill in some way, such as by interacting with a mentor, taking on an assignment (such as chairing a committee), or simply reading a book.

4. Make a plan for meeting your goals and measuring your progress. Make a timeline that identifies the steps you will need to take to accomplish each goal. Plan in advance the key milestones. For example, if you are going to read a book to improve a particular skill, the milestones may include identifying the book, acquiring a copy, reading the book, discussing it with colleagues or friends, and putting the book's ideas into practice.

INTERACTIVE EXPERIENTIAL EXERCISE

Career Development: Building a Workforce for Long-Term Success at Global Telecommunications
http://www.wiley.com/college/sc/stewart

Access the companion website to test your knowledge by completing a Global Telecommunications interactive role play.

Global has been quite impressed with your work. In this exercise, top management has asked you to help the company with the issue of career development. Members of the top management team have decided to try using a competency model program to align the values and vision of Global's employees with those of the organization. They feel that this will lead to better employee retention and higher commitment. They would like you to evaluate whether this plan aligns with Global's basic HR strategy—that of Committed Expert. You should also be prepared to discuss with them any other critical career management dilemmas that they may encounter.

ENDNOTES

1. Raymond A. Noe, Stephanie L. Wilk, Ellen J. Mullen, and James E. Wanek, "Employee Development: Issues in Construct Definition and Investigation of Antecedents," in J. K. Ford (ed.), *Improving Training Effectiveness in Work Organizations* (Mahwah, NJ: Lawrence Erlbaum, 1997), pp. 153–189.
2. Manuel London, "Organizational Assistance in Career Development," in Daniel C. Feldman (ed.), *Work Careers: A Developmental Perspective* (San Francisco: Jossey-Bass, 2002), 323–345.
3. David G. Collings and Kamel Mellahi, "Strategic Talent Management: A Review and Research Agenda," *Human Resource Management Review,* 19 (2009): 304–313. Robert E. Lewis and Robert J. Heckman, "Talent Management: A Critical Review. *Human Resource Management Review,* 16 (2006): 139–154.
4. London, "Organizational Assistance."
5. Alex Konrad, "In Emerging Markets, Samsung Is King—While Nokia and Blackberry Are Not Dead yet" posted March 28, 2013 at http://www.forbes.com; "Gartner Says Worldwide Mobile Phone Sales Declined 1.7 Percent in 2012" posted February 28, 2013, at http://www.gartner.com/newsroom/id/2335616.
6. "Delivering our Promise: 2012 Year in Review," http://www.aflac.com, accessed April 12, 2013.
7. "Fortune 100 Best Companies to Work For," http://money.cnn.com/magazines/fortune, accessed April 12, 2013; Christopher Hosford, "AFLAC's Advantage," *Incentive* 177 (2003): 26–28.

8. Yehuda Baruch and Maury Peiperl, "Career Management Practices: An Empirical Survey and Implications," *Human Resource Management* 39 (2000): 347–366.
9. "Experienced Leadership Programs," http://www.ge.com/careers, accessed April 12, 2013; Martha Frase-Blunt, "Ready, Set, Rotate!" *HR Magazine* 46 (October 2001): 46–52.
10. James O'Toole and Edward E. Lawler III, *The New American Workplace: The Long Awaited Follow-Up to the Bestselling Work in America* (New York: Palgrave McMillan, 2006).
11. Ibid.; Douglas T. Hall, *Careers In and Out of Organizations* (Thousand Oaks, CA: Sage, 2003).
12. O'Toole and Lawler, *The New American Workplace.*
13. "Meg Whitman," http://topics.wsj.com, accessed May 23, 2010.
14. Thomas W. H. Ng, Lillian T. Eby, Kelly L. Sorenson, and Daniel C. Feldman, "Predictors of Objective and Subjective Career Success: A Meta-Analysis," *Personnel Psychology* 58 (2005): 367–408.
15. Hall, *Careers In and Out of Organizations.*
16. Linda Rhoades and Robert Eisenberger, "Perceived Organizational Support: A Review of the Literature," *Journal of Applied Psychology* 87 (2002): 698–714.
17. Lindsay Chappell, "Toyota Crafts Tool to Develop Managers," *Automotive News* 76, 5965 (2002): 42.
18. Raymond A. Noe, *Employee Training and Development,* 3rd ed. (Boston: McGraw-Hill, 2005).
19. Jeanne C. Meister, "Grading Executive Education," *Workforce Management* (December 11, 2006): 1, 27.

20. William C. McGaghie, "Professional Competence Evaluation," *Educational Researcher* 20 (1991): 3–9.

21. "Our Certifications," http://www.hrci.org, accessed April 12, 2013.

22. For a more exhaustive list of certifications in IT, see http://certcities.com; for a list of careers in which certification may be useful, see Katharine Hansen, "Certifiably Empowering: Hot Field in Which Certification May Boost Your Career," http://www.quintcareers.com, accessed April 12, 2013.

23. John L. Holland, *Making Vocational Choices: A Theory of Careers* (Englewood Cliffs, NJ: Prentice Hall, 1973); T. J. Tracey and J. Rounds, "Evaluating Holland's and Gati's Vocational Interest Models: A Structural Meta-Analysis." *Psychological Bulletin* 113 (1993): 229–246.

24. "About the Map," http://www.act.org/wwm, accessed September 19, 2013.

25. Kenneth M. Nowack, "Manager View/360," in J. Fleenor, and J. Leslie (eds.), *Feedback to Managers: A Review and Comparison of Sixteen Multi-rater Feedback Instruments*, 3rd ed. (Greensboro, NC: Center for Creative Leadership, 1997); Kenneth M. Nowack, "Longitudinal Evaluation of a 360 Feedback Program: Implications for Best Practices," Paper presented at the 20th Annual Conference of the Society for Industrial and Organizational Psychology (Los Angeles, CA: 2005).

26. Kenneth M. Nowack, Jeanne Hartley, and William Bradley, "How to Evaluate Your 360 Feedback Efforts," *Training & Development* 53 (April 1999): 48–53.

27. Scott Wimer, "The Dark Side of 360-Degree Feedback," *T&D* 56 (September 2002): 37–42.

28. "Key Facts," http://lilly.com, accessed April 12, 2013.

29. Michael A. Campion, Lisa Cheraskin, and Michael J. Stevens, "Career-Related Antecedents and Outcomes of Job Rotation," *Academy of Management Journal* 37 (1994): 1518–1542.

30. Douglas T. Hall and L. A. Isabella, "Downward Moves and Career Development," *Organizational Dynamics* 14 (1985): 5–23.

31. Rollin H. Simonds and John N. Orife, "Worker Behavior Versus Enrichment Theory," *Administrative Science Quarterly* 20 (1975): 606–612.

32. Lillian T. Eby and Jacquelyn S. Dematteo, "When the Type of Move Matters: Employee Outcomes under Various Relocation Situations," *Journal of Organizational Behavior* 21 (2000): 677–687.

33. Cynthia D. McCauley, Marian N. Ruderman, Patricia J. Ohlott, and Jane E. Morrow. "Assessing the Developmental Components of Managerial Jobs," *Journal of Applied Psychology* 79 (1994): 544–560.

34. Kathy E. Kram, *Mentoring at Work: Developmental Relationships in Organizational Life* (Glenview, IL: Scott, Foresman, 1985); Tammy D. Allen and Lisa M. Finkelstein, "Beyond Mentoring: Alternative Sources and Functions of Developmental Support," *The Career Development Quarterly* 51 (2003): 346–355.

35. Monika Hamori, Jie Cao, and Burak Koyuncu, "Why Top Young Managers Are in a Nonstop Job Hunt," Harvard Business Review, July–August (2012): 28.

36. David B. Peterson and Mary Dee Hicks, *The Leader as Coach: Strategies for Coaching and Developing Others* (Minneapolis, MN: Personnel Decisions, 1996); David B. Peterson, "Management Development: Coaching and Mentoring Programs," in Kurt Kraiger (ed.), *Creating, Implementing, and Managing Effective Training and Development: State of the Art Lessons for Practice* (San Francisco: Jossey-Bass, 2002), 160–191.

37. Jordan Robertson, "Corporations Using Coach Approach," *The Dallas Morning News*, Wednesday, August 17, 2005; "International Coach Federation," http://www.coachfederation.org, accessed April 12, 2013.

38. Daniel C. Feldman and Melanie J. Lankau, "Executive Coaching: A Review and Agenda for Future Research," *Journal of Management* 31 (2005): 829–848.

39. Peterson, "Management Development."

40. Feldman and Lankau, "Executive Coaching."

41. Jack Gordon, "The Coach Approach," *Training* 43 (2006): 26–30.

42. Connie R. Wanberg, Elizabeth T. Welsh, and Sarah A. Hezlett, "Mentoring Research: A Review and Dynamic Process Model," *Research in Personnel and Human Resource Management* 22 (2003): 39–124.

43. Kram, *Mentoring at Work*.

44. Ellen A. Ensher and Susan E. Murphy, "Effects of Race, Gender, Perceived Similarity, and Contact on Mentor Relationships, *Journal of Vocational Behavior* 50 (1997): 460–481; Wanberg et al., "Mentoring Research."

45. Tammy A. Allen, Lillian T. Eby, and Elizabeth Lentz, "The Relationship between Formal Mentoring Program Characteristics and Perceived Program Characteristics," *Personnel Psychology* 59 (2006): 125–153; Belle Rose Ragins, John L. Cotton, and Janice S. Miller, "Marginal Mentoring: The Effects of Type of Mentor, Quality of Relationship, and Program Design on Work and Career Attitudes," *Academy of Management Journal* 43 (2000): 1177–1194; Wanberg et al., "Mentoring Research."

46. Allen et al., "The Relationship."

47. Kathleen Cavallo and Dottie Breinza, "Emotional Competence and Leadership Excellence at Johnson & Johnson: The Emotional Intelligence and Leadership Study," published online by the Consortium for Research on Emotional Intelligence in Organizations, www.eiconsortium.org.

48. Noe, *Employee Training and Development*.

49. Liz Harris-Tuck, Annette Price, and Marilee Robertson, *Career Patterns: A Kaledeiscope of Possibilities*, 2nd ed. (Upper Saddle River, NJ: Pearson Prentice Hall, 2004).

50. "SATERN," https://saterninfo.nasa.gov, accessed April 12, 2013.

51. John P. Wanous and Arnon E. Reichers, "New Employee Orientation Programs," *Human Resource Management Review* 10 (2000): 435–451.

52. Howard J. Klein and Natasha A. Weaver, "The Effectiveness of an Organizational-Level Orientation Training Program in the Socialization of New Hires," *Personnel Psychology* 53 (2000): 47–66.

53. Ibid.

54. Wanous and Reichers, "New Employee Orientation Programs."

55. Nico Schutte, Salla Toppinen, Raija Kalimo, and Wilmar Schaufeli, "The Factorial Validity of the Maslach Burnout Inventory—General Survey (MBI-GS) across Occupational Groups and Nations," *Journal of Occupational and Organizational Psychology* 73 (2000): 53–66.

56. Raymond T. Lee and Blake E. Ashforth, "A Meta-analytic Examination of the Correlates of the Three Dimensions of Job Burnout," *Journal of Applied Psychology* 81 (1995): 123–133.

57. Ibid.

58. Stephen L. Grover and Karen J. Crooker, "Who Appreciates Family-Friendly Human Resource Policies: The Impact of Family-Friendly Policies on the Organizational Attachment of Parents and Non-Parents," *Personnel Psychology* 48 (1995): 271–288.

59. Jennifer Millman, "Why You Need Diversity to Be Competitive: Case Studies from the 2007 DiversityInc Top 50 Companies for Diversity," *DiversityInc* 6 (June 2007): 24–44.

60. "Profiles of Companies 11–50," *DiversityInc* 6 (June 2007): 82–120.

61. Jennifer Taylor Arnold, "Employee Networks," *HRMagazine* 51 (2006): 145–150.

62. "Diversity Network," http://www.ti.com, accessed April 12, 2013.

63. Todd J. Maurer, "Career-Relevant Learning and Development, Worker Age, and Beliefs about Self-efficacy for Development," *Journal of Management* 27 (2001): 123–140.

64. Sandy L. Willis and Samuel S. Dubin (eds.), *Maintaining Professional Competence: Approaches to Career Enhancement, Vitality, and Success Throughout a Work Life* (San Francisco: Jossey-Bass, 1990); Steve W. J.

Kozlowski and Brian M. Hults, "An Exploration of Climates for Technical Updating and Performance," *Personnel Psychology* 40 (1988): 539–564.

65. Margaret A. Shaffer, David A. Harrison, Hal Gregersen, J. Stewart Black, and Lori A. Ferzandi, "You Can Take It with You: Individual Differences and Expatriate Effectiveness," *Journal of Applied Psychology* 91 (2006): 109–125.

66. Lisa N. Littrell, Eduardo Salas, Kathleen P. Hess, Michael Paley, and Sharon Riedel, "Expatriate Preparation: A Critical Analysis of 25 Years of Cross-Cultural Training Research," *Human Resource Development Review* 5 (2006): 355–389; Regina Hechanova, Terry A. Beehr, and Neil D. Christiansen, "Antecedents and Consequences of Employees' Adjustment to Overseas Assignment: A Meta-analytic Review," *Applied Psychology* 52 (2003): 213–236.

67. Alizee B. Avril and Vincent P. Magnini, "A Holistic Approach to Expatriate Success," *International Journal of Contemporary Hospitality Management* 19 (2007): 53–64.

68. Rosalie L. Tung, "A Contingency Framework of Selection and Training of Expatriates Revisited," *Human Resource Management Review* 8 (1998): 23–37.

69. Mark E. Mendenhall and Gunter K. Stahl, "Expatriate Training and Development: Where Do We Go from Here?" *Human Resources Management* 39 (2000): 251–265.

70. Margaret A. Shaffer and David A. Harrison, "Expatriates' Psychological Withdrawal from International Assignments: Work, Nonwork, and Family Influences," *Personnel Psychology* 51 (1998): 87–118.

71. Carol Lachnit, "Low-Cost Tips for Successful Inpatriation," *Workforce* (August 2000): 42–47.

Part 4
Motivating and Managing Employees

©Kristoffer Tripplaar/Alamy   ©Edmund D.Fountain/
                               ZUMAPRESS.com   ©Felix Adamo/ZUMAPRESS.com   ©Douglas Peebles/Corbis

Chapter 11
Motivating Employees Through Compensation

A MANAGER'S PERSPECTIVE

Robert Daly/Getty Images

LYNETTE LOOKS OVER THE NUMBERS ONE LAST TIME TO MAKE SURE THAT HER CALCULATIONS ARE CORRECT. TOMORROW SHE WILL MEET WITH A HUMAN RESOURCE SPECIALIST TO TALK ABOUT HER COMPENSATION RECOMMENDATIONS. MAKING DECISIONS ABOUT PAY IS ONE OF THE THINGS SHE HAS FOUND MOST DIFFICULT SINCE BECOMING A PARTNER IN THE CONSULTING FIRM. THIS YEAR LYNETTE IS PLANNING TO RECOMMEND THAT HIGH PERFORMERS GET A MUCH LARGER RAISE THAN LOW PERFORMERS. SHE HOPES THIS WILL HELP MOTIVATE ALL EMPLOYEES TO STRETCH AND IMPROVE THEIR PERFORMANCE. YET, SHE ALSO KNOWS THAT HER FIRM HAS FALLEN SOMEWHAT BEHIND COMPETITORS WHEN IT COMES TO COMPENSATION. WILL GIVING HIGHER RAISES TO TOP PERFORMERS MEAN THAT AVERAGE PERFORMERS WILL BE MORE LIKELY TO QUIT AND MOVE TO ANOTHER FIRM? DOES IT REALLY MATTER AS LONG AS THE TOP PERFORMERS STAY? WILL BIGGER DIFFERENCES IN PAY DECREASE COOPERATION AMONG EMPLOYEES?

As she contemplates these questions, Lynette begins to think about her own pay. Since making partner she knows that her compensation is higher than most employees of the firm. However, she feels some frustration knowing that there are other partners who work fewer hours but will make three times more than she will this year. Lynette wonders if it is fair that pay is based largely on number of years with the firm rather than current productivity. Shouldn't pay be tied more closely to contributions that are made now rather than in the past?

Lynette's assistant Wayne interrupts her and asks about preparing a report. Seeing Wayne reminds her that he is deciding whether to accept a new job at a local bank. The new job would actually involve less interesting work but would give Wayne a 20 percent raise. Lynette doesn't want to lose him, and she wonders if she should match his offer. Matching the offer would mean that Wayne would be getting paid more than some administrative assistants with

THE BIG PICTURE *Effective Organizations Design Compensation so that People Are Motivated to Work Hard and Help the Organization Succeed*

10 more years of experience. Wouldn't this be a problem? She also wonders if she needs to raise his salary the whole 20 percent, or whether the fact that his current position offers more interesting work will offset some of the potential salary gain.

As Wayne leaves, Lynette sits at her desk and looks once more at her compensation recommendations. She realizes how unsettling she finds the task of determining compensation. Is she making good decisions? Should she go ahead with the proposal to restructure pay so that a higher percentage is given to top performers? Should she match Wayne's offer from the bank? She looks forward to meeting with the human resource specialist and hopes that she will gain some new insight.

WHAT DO YOU THINK?

Suppose you are talking to Lynette about the changes in pay practice. She makes the following statements. Which of the statements do you think are true?

T OR **F**   If people don't think they are being paid fairly, they often steal things from their employer.

T OR **F**   Increasing employee pay doesn't increase motivation unless workers feel they have the skill and ability needed to increase their performance.

T OR **F**   People who are paid a lot don't worry much about what others are being paid.

T OR **F**   Organizations are more profitable when they pay their employees no more than what competitors are paying.

T OR **F**   Paying some employees substantially more than their peers can decrease teamwork and cooperation.

After reading this chapter you should be able to:

LEARNING OBJECTIVE 1   Describe how employee compensation practices strategically align with overall HR strategy.

LEARNING OBJECTIVE 2   Use the concepts of reinforcement theory, goal-setting theory, equity theory, expectancy theory, and agency theory to explain how people react to compensation practices.

LEARNING OBJECTIVE 3   Describe how pay surveys are conducted and used to create compensation-level strategies.

LEARNING OBJECTIVE 4   Explain job-based pay and skill-based pay approaches to compensation structure.

LEARNING OBJECTIVE 5   Describe the major protections provided by the Fair Labor Standards Act, as well as state and local regulations.

How Can Strategic Employee Compensation Make an Organization Effective?

Employee compensation
The human resource practice of rewarding employees for their contributions.

Employee compensation is the process of paying and rewarding people for the contributions they make to an organization. A major part of compensation, of course, is the amount of money employees take home in their paychecks, but there are other important aspects as well. Compensation includes benefits such as insurance, retirement savings, and paid time off from work. Employees' positive feelings that come from working at a particular place are also sometimes seen as a form of compensation. In a broad sense, compensation thus represents the total package of rewards—both monetary and psychological—that an employee obtains from an organization. However, in practice we usually think of compensation as the economic rewards and benefits that an organization gives to its employees.

Good compensation practices offer many advantages. Companies offering good pay and benefits attract better employees.[1] Once hired, employees are more likely to stay with an organization if they feel they are paid well.[2] A good incentive system communicates expectations and provides guidance so that employees understand what the organization wants from them. Paying people more when they contribute more increases motivation, which in turn leads to higher performance.[3] Linking pay to performance is particularly helpful in encouraging people to produce a higher quantity of goods and services.[4] In short, effective compensation practices motivate employees to do things that help increase an organization's productivity.

The benefits of effective compensation can be seen in the success of Marriott International, Inc. Beginning as a root beer stand in 1927, the company has grown into an international hospitality corporation that operates several hotel chains, including Courtyard, Fairfield Inn, Residence Inn, and Marriott Hotels & Resorts. A basic motto at Marriott is "If we take care of our associates, they'll take care of our guests."[5] Leaders in the company note that workers shopping for a job have choices similar to hotel guests shopping for a place to stay. Attracting and taking care of associates—or employees—is accomplished through compensation practices that build a culture of loyalty and high performance.

A major problem faced by Marriott and others in the hospitality industry is finding people who are willing to work in entry-level jobs such as house-keeping and food service. Education requirements for these jobs are not high, and many of the positions require difficult physical labor. People working in such conditions often find it difficult to feel strong commitment toward a specific employer. Turnover in the hospitality industry is therefore high. This makes it difficult for hotels and restaurants to obtain a stable workforce that creates a competitive advantage.

Marriott develops competitive advantage by taking a systematic approach to compensation that reduces employee turnover. The company obtains and analyzes a great deal of data to determine why employees leave. Human resource professionals then explore changes that can improve the chances of keeping good employees. For instance, by examining when people quit, Marriott learned that people are much less likely to leave once they become eligible for benefits such as health insurance and retirement savings plans. When they recognized this pattern, leaders at Marriott changed their compensation practices so that employees do not have to wait as long before becoming eligible for benefits. Having people wait to become eligible for benefits, which was meant to reduce labor costs, actually cost the company money due to increased employee turnover. Analyzing employee preferences also revealed that workers were most likely to remain loyal when they were given the opportunity to work some overtime each week. Being required to work more than 10 hours overtime per week, however, caused some workers to leave. Marriott thus decided to give employees an opportunity to work a moderate amount of overtime, thereby increasing employee satisfaction and retention.[6]

A systematic review of Marriott practices also revealed that each of the hotel chains operated independently. Compensation practices for employees working at a Courtyard were often different from practices for employees working at a Residence Inn, even though the two hotels were located in the same geographic area. As a result, employees thought of themselves as working for a specific chain rather than for the Marriott Corporation. Employee movement between hotel chains was limited, which reduced opportunities for promotion.

In response to this problem, Marriott adopted a **market-based pay approach,** which seeks to create a wage structure where people are paid fairly in comparison to what they could earn doing a similar job for another company in the specific geographic area. Thus, the pay for someone working in house-keeping at Residence Inn should be similar to the pay for someone working at Fairfield Inn, though the pay level for housekeepers in New York may be quite different from the pay level for housekeepers in Kansas. One benefit of moving to market-based wages has been greater movement of employees between chains. Having more employees who have worked at a variety of different hotel chains within Marriott has increased instances in which employees encourage their current customers to stay at other Marriott hotels.[7]

Another important practice at Marriott has been to move responsibility for compensation away from the human resource department. Individual line managers now have the primary responsibility for determining each employee's pay. Human resource department rules are deemphasized. The pay range for each job is placed in a broad band that provides guidance for different levels of compensation. Managers have a good deal of flexibility to decide where

Market-based pay
A compensation approach that determines how much to pay employees by assessing how much they could make working for other organizations.

Building Strength Through HR

MARRIOTT INTERNATIONAL, INC.

Marriott International is a hospitality provider that employs over 120,000 people. Human resource management at Marriott builds competitive strength by

- Systematically evaluating compensation to make sure pay practices are helping the company achieve its competitive goals.
- Giving line managers rather than a centralized human resource department the primary responsibility for determining how much to pay each employee.

©Kristoffer Tripplaar/Alamy

- Linking pay to performance so that outstanding performers receive higher compensation than average performers.

in the band to locate the pay for each employee. This allows managers to take into account the pay for other work opportunities in the area, as well as the qualifications and performance of the particular employee.[8]

As a whole, Marriott's compensation practices have developed a culture that rewards high performance. Not only does Marriott tend to pay more than its competitors, but it also differentiates more between high and low performers. Fewer people get paid at the top of the scale, but the overall pay is much higher for those who do. Truly exceptional performers thus make more than others and are more likely to continue working at Marriott. The company also recognizes outstanding performance with rewards such as trips and merchandise.[9]

Marriott's systematic approach to compensation, which includes pushing decisions to line managers and emphasizing greater pay for higher performance, plays an important part in the company's success. Simplifying procedures and having managers more involved increases the likelihood that employees believe they are paid fairly. These practices help Marriott continue to be ranked as one of the best places to work.[10] Such a satisfying work experience helps reduce turnover, saving Marriott millions of dollars each year.

LEARNING OBJECTIVE 1

How Is Employee Compensation Strategic?

Similar to other aspects of human resource management, compensation practices are most effective when they fit with an organization's overall HR strategy. In short, pay practices need to fit the broader human resource strategies first described in Chapter 2. As you know by now, these broad HR strategies vary along two dimensions: whether their labor orientation is internal or external and whether the company competes through cost or differentiation.

EXTERNAL VERSUS INTERNAL LABOR

Organizations choosing an external labor orientation frequently hire new employees, and these employees are not expected to form a long-term attachment to the organization. The lack of long-term commitment makes compensation particularly important. In fact, compensation is the primary factor in these employees' decisions about where to work. Current and potential employees frequently compare the organization's compensation packages with packages offered by other employers. Employees' perception of **external equity**—which concerns the fairness of what the company is paying them compared with what they could earn elsewhere—are critical in such employment relationships. People who see a lack of external equity become dissatisfied and choose to work somewhere else. This means that organizations with an external labor orientation must frequently assess how their compensation compares with the compensation offered by other organizations.[11]

> **External equity**
> Employee perceptions of fairness based on how much they are paid relative to people working in other organizations.

Organizations with an internal labor orientation seek to retain employees for long periods of time. These organizations encourage employees to stay by providing security and good working conditions, which are emphasized more than money.[12] Employees become attached to the organization and are less likely to compare their compensation with the compensation they believe they could earn elsewhere. Instead, these employees compare their compensation with that of their coworkers. Employees' perceptions of **internal equity**—their beliefs concerning the fairness of what the organization is paying them compared with what it pays other employees—become critical. Internally oriented organizations also use long-term incentives to reward employees who stay with them for long periods.

> **Internal equity**
> Employee perceptions of fairness based on how much they are paid relative to others working in the same organization.

DIFFERENTIATION VERSUS COST STRATEGY

Organizations following a differentiation strategy seek high-performing employees who create superior goods and services. Compensation is used to encourage risk taking. For example, companies like 3M reward rather than punish employees who pursue uncertain products and ideas, even if they fail. Organizations with differentiation strategies also pay some employees much more than others. Success depends a great deal on outstanding contributions from a few individuals, so these organizations reward high performance by paying excellent performers substantially more than low performers. The result is substantial spread between the pay of high contributors and the pay of low contributors.[13]

In contrast to differentiation, a cost strategy requires organizations to adopt compensation practices that reduce labor expenses. Employees are usually paid fixed salaries that do not increase as performance improves. Thus, there is very little variation in pay between high and low performers. Emphasizing efficiency and tight coordination results in standardization, which is often accomplished by treating all employees the same. The value of a high performer is not substantially greater than the benefit of an average performer, so compensation is used to develop feelings of inclusion and support from the organization.

ALIGNING COMPENSATION WITH HR STRATEGY

Combining differences in internal and external pay with differences in cost and differentiation results in the grid shown as Figure 11.1. The horizontal dimension represents differences associated with cost and differentiation. Here, the major difference concerns the extent to which high performers are rewarded differently than low performers.[14] A differentiation HR strategy is associated with **variable rewards,** which have the overall goal of spreading out compensation so that high performers are paid more than low performers. A cost reduction strategy is associated with **uniform rewards** and is aimed at providing consistent compensation so that employees are treated the same regardless of differences in performance.[15]

The vertical dimension of Figure 11.1 represents the type and length of the desired relationship between employees and the organization. One type of relationship is **relational commitment.** Relational commitments are based primarily on social ties rather than monetary incentives. Employees in this type of relationship work for an organization over time because they feel a sense of belonging. The organization uses compensation to build a sense of camaraderie and support.

Another type of relationship is **transactional commitment.** Transactional commitments are based primarily on financial incentives. In this type of relationship, employees are motivated by the short-term rewards they receive. Management uses compensation to encourage individuals to make outstanding contributions, but no one expects employees to develop a long-term relationship with the organization.[16]

In Chapter 12, we will look at specific pay practices that fit particular human resource strategies. Here, we review broad differences between the goals of the four types of compensation.

Variable rewards
A reward system that pays some employees substantially more than others in order to emphasize differences between high and low performers.

Uniform rewards
A reward system that minimizes differences among workers and offers similar compensation to all employees.

Relational commitment
A sense of loyalty to an organization that is based not only on financial incentives but also on social ties.

Transactional commitment
A sense of obligation to an organization that is created primarily by financial incentives.

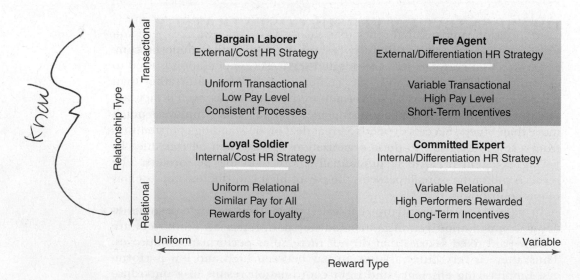

Figure 11.1 Strategic Framework for Employee Selection.

Bargain Laborer Compensation

Perhaps you or a friend of yours has worked as a bagger in a grocery store. Most employees working in this role do not expect a long-term career. There is also little difference in the amount paid to high- and low-performing baggers. This type of compensation is most often associated with the Bargain Laborer HR strategy. As explained in Chapter 4, an extreme cost reduction strategy requires consistent contributions from all employees, which reduces the need to recognize high performance with additional compensation. Pay levels are set at the lowest level that allows the organization to attract enough workers, and there is a clear understanding that employees may leave if they receive better offers. Given that most employees working in these organizations have low-paying jobs, many workers can be expected to believe that their pay is lower than it should be. An important aspect of compensation in these organizations is thus developing fair processes and uniform practices that increase perceptions of fairness.

Loyal Soldier Compensation

The Loyal Soldier HR strategy also seeks to reduce costs, but the emphasis is on building a stable long-term workforce. Emphasizing low labor expenses and encouraging average rather than outstanding performance once again create a setting where high and low performers are treated similarly. However, the long-term orientation requires that compensation be used as a tool to bind employees to the organization. An example might be a community school district that employs a number of teachers and secretaries. Limited funding combined with the desire for stability will often result in the school district providing similar rewards to all employees while building a sense of commitment to the organization.

With the Loyal Soldier strategy pay increases are usually linked to time with the organization. Employees are rewarded for remaining loyal and not leaving to accept positions with competitors. Cooperation among employees, as well as a feeling of solidarity, is enhanced through compensation structured to decrease differences between high and low performers. Procedures that allow employees to express concerns about unfairness are also important. Long-term forms of compensation other than salary, such as health insurance and retirement benefits, are particularly helpful in building the employee commitment that is necessary for success with the Loyal Soldier HR strategy.

Free Agent Compensation

Compensation is the primary source of motivation for employees working in organizations with a Free Agent HR strategy. These organizations provide strong monetary incentives for high performers. A good example is a technology consulting firm. Highly skilled employees join and remain with a firm specifically because they receive high wages. Because organizations pursuing a Free Agent HR strategy need high performers with somewhat rare skills, they must pay more than other employers. Paying top performers within the organization more than low performers also attracts more productive people to apply for jobs.[17] Short-term salary and bonuses are emphasized more than future rewards, such as retirement savings. Top performers are paid well, and individuals who succeed at risky ventures receive substantial rewards.

Employees in Free Agent organizations usually have opportunities to work for many possible employers, so an individual's salary is based primarily on what he or she would be worth to other organizations. The result is highly flexible compensation practices. Often, new employees are paid much more than employees who have been working at the organization for years in a similar position—a situation known as **salary compression**.

Salary compression
A situation created when new employees receive higher pay than employees who have been with the organization for a long time even though they perform the same job.

Committed Expert Compensation

Organizations pursuing a Committed Expert HR strategy also use compensation to reward high performers, but at the same time they strive to build long-term commitment. Management sets high goals for employees, and those who reach the goals are paid more than those who do not. Thus, people doing the same job are often paid very different amounts. An example of such strategy and compensation is a medical research and development laboratory. High performing researchers are paid more than low performers, but the need for long-term inputs also necessitates compensation practices that bind employees to long-term careers.

Overall, compensation in Committed Expert organizations is set at a level that is high enough to attract people with the most desirable skills. Because of their relatively high levels of expertise and skill, employees working for these organizations expect to receive higher wages than people working for other organizations. As long as the organization communicates its policies clearly and fairly, paying the best employees more than others helps retain top performers.[18] Turnover is also reduced by offering long-term incentives such as retirement benefits and stock options. Top performers need to receive immediate rewards that recognize their contributions, but they must also receive long-term incentives that bind them to the organization for a number of years.

CONCEPT CHECK

1. *How are variable rewards different from uniform rewards?*
2. *What is the major emphasis of relational commitment? What is the emphasis of transactional commitment?*
3. *How do compensation differences align with basic HR strategies?*

LEARNING OBJECTIVE 2

How Does Compensation Motivate People?

Underlying the compensation strategies just discussed is the assumption that pay can be used to motivate employees. How does money motivate people? Several theories explain why people react to pay as they do. These theories, which are grounded in psychology and economics, provide principles that can be used to develop effective compensation practices. We discuss several theories in this section, but first we provide some background on the concept of motivation.

Motivation can be defined as a force that causes people to engage in a particular behavior rather than other behaviors. More specifically, motivation is represented by three elements: behavioral choice, intensity, and persistence.[19] Each element, in turn, requires a decision:

- *Behavioral choice* involves deciding whether to perform a particular action.
- *Intensity* concerns deciding how much effort to put into the behavior.
- *Persistence* involves deciding how long to keep working at the behavior.

As a student, you encounter each of these choices every day when you demonstrate whether you are motivated to do homework. The first step in showing motivation is to choose to spend time on schoolwork rather than other activities, such as watching television or playing sports. Once you have decided to spend time doing homework, you must next decide how hard you will focus on the work you are doing. Higher motivation is shown when you work continuously with maximum effort rather than taking frequent breaks and thinking mostly about other things. The final aspect of motivation is persistence, or how long you will keep at the task. You show low motivation if you work only for a few minutes and high motivation if you work for several hours. In sum, you show high motivation when you choose to do your homework rather than something else, when you pursue your homework with high intensity, and when you persist in doing it for a long period of time. Similarly, employees show high motivation by choosing to exert maximum effort to perform critical work tasks for a long period of time.

THEORIES OF MOTIVATION

Every organization wants to motivate its employees. Organizations want employees to engage in behaviors that will lead to success, and they want them to pursue desirable behaviors with intensity and persistence. How can organizations use compensation to meet these goals? Principles from various motivation theories explain how compensation practices can provide motivation. Here, we discuss five theories: reinforcement theory, goal-setting theory, justice theory, expectancy theory, and agency theory.

Reinforcement Theory

Would performance in your human resource class improve if your professor offered cash to the students who scored highest on a test? Although such a motivational tactic might become expensive, the performance of most students—particularly those who considered themselves the smartest and most likely to get the cash reward—would improve.

Using a reward such as money to encourage high performance is consistent with **reinforcement theory.** This theory, which comes from the field of psychology, holds that behavior is caused by chains of antecedents and consequents. *Antecedents* are factors in the environment that cue someone to engage in a specific behavior. For instance, the smell of fresh-baked apple pie might serve as an antecedent that encourages a person to eat. *Consequents* are results associated with specific behaviors. Antecedents and consequents are linked together because the antecedent causes people to think about the consequent. For example, one consequent of eating apple pie is the pleasurable feeling it gives you. Thus, the good smell motivates you to eat

Motivation
The sum of forces that cause an individual to engage in certain behaviors rather than alternative actions.

Reinforcement theory
A psychological theory suggesting that people are motivated by antecedents (environmental cues) and consequents (rewards and punishments).

Contingency
A reinforcement principle requiring that desirable consequences only be given after the occurrence of a desirable behavior.

Pay-for-performance
Compensation practices that use differences in employee performance to determine differences in pay.

the pie because it reminds you of the pleasure associated with the taste. Of course a behavioral consequent can be negative, as when eating too much pie makes you feel sick. When associated with compensation, though, the core idea of reinforcement theory is that people will engage in the behaviors for which they are rewarded. Furthermore, cues in the environment can help focus attention on the rewards that come after the completion of specific behaviors.[20]

One important principle of reinforcement is **contingency**. This principle tells us that a consequent motivates behavior only when it is contingent—that is, when it depends on the occurrence of the behavior. Contingency suggests that a reward should be given if, and only if, the desired behavior occurs. Otherwise, the potential reward loses the ability to motivate. Think about a parent who tells a child that he can have a cookie if he cleans his room. The child fails to clean the room, but the parent gives him the cookie anyway. According to the principle of contingency, the child will not be motivated to clean his room in return for a cookie in the future. The cookie has lost its motivational power.

In a similar way, pay motivates performance only when it is contingent on specific behaviors and outcomes. A key principle from reinforcement theory is thus that compensation should be based on performance so that better performers receive higher pay. The practice of allocating pay so that high performers receive more than low performers is known as **pay-for-performance**. As described in the "How Do We Know?" feature, employees whose pay is contingent generally perform better than employees whose pay is not contingent.[21] Linking pay to performance can be particularly beneficial when it is part of an overall program of performance assessment, goal setting, and feedback.[22]

How Do We Know?

DO CONTINGENT REWARDS REALLY IMPROVE PERFORMANCE?

Can compensation be used as a tool to increase the performance of fast-food workers and thus improve bottom-line profits? Suzanne Peterson and Fred Luthans conducted an experiment to find the answer to this question. They trained managers in fast-food restaurants to use contingent rewards for employees. Once the training was completed, they compared the performance of the restaurants with trained managers to the performance of other restaurants.

Managers who received the training used an incentive system that rewarded all their employees if they observed enough individuals performing critical tasks. The restaurants that used contingent rewards had faster drive-through times and higher profits. Employee turnover was also lower in the restaurants that used contingent rewards.

The Bottom Line. Contingent rewards can improve performance. Peterson and Luthans specifically conclude that contingent rewards have a positive effect that endures over time.

Source: Suzanne J. Peterson and Fred Luthans, "The Impact of Financial and Nonfinancial Incentives on Business-Unit Outcomes over Time," *Journal of Applied Psychology* 91 (2006): 156–165.

Goal-Setting Theory

Does setting a goal to achieve a certain grade in a class help you to perform better in that class? The simple answer is yes. The potential value of setting specific goals is highlighted in many studies showing that people who set goals do indeed perform better.[23] **Goal-setting theory** is grounded in cognitive psychology and holds that behavior is motivated by conscious choices.[24] Goals improve performance through four specific motivational processes:[25]

1. Goals focus attention away from other activities toward the desired behavior. This effect is seen, for example, when a long-distance runner sets herself a goal to run a marathon in a certain time. Because of this goal, the runner is likely to spend more effort on running and less on other activities.

2. Goals get people energized and excited about accomplishing something worthwhile. In our example, the runner's goal provides her with a vision of accomplishing a difficult task. This sense of vision and potential accomplishment builds excitement that increases her intensity during workouts.

3. People work on tasks longer when they have specific goals. The runner's goal encourages her to be more persistent and not give up when facing setbacks such as fatigue or injury.

4. Goals encourage the discovery and use of knowledge. Thus, the runner's goal might encourage her to investigate and learn training tips and race strategies. In sum, having a goal can improve performance by focusing attention, increasing intensity and persistence, and encouraging learning.

If goals are to act as effective motivators, they must be achievable.[26] Suppose the goal of the runner in our earlier example was to run a marathon in under three hours. Running a marathon in this amount of time is beyond the skill of most people, no matter how hard they train. Having a goal that is nearly impossible to reach may actually harm performance by building a sense of frustration. Goals should thus be combined with effective selection and training practices to ensure that employees develop the needed skills.

Goal setting in work organizations can be combined with compensation in a number of ways.[27] One obvious method is to offer a difficult goal and provide a bonus only to those who achieve it. This has the benefit of encouraging employees to really stretch and put forth their best effort. A problem with providing a reward only to individuals who achieve the so-called stretch goal is that many employees will barely miss the goal and will then become frustrated.

Another method of linking goals and compensation is to provide incremental rewards for people who achieve progressively higher goals. In this case, employees who achieve an initial, easy goal receive small rewards. Those who go on to achieve more difficult goals receive somewhat larger rewards, and those who accomplish the stretch goal receive rewards that are still larger. This incremental method can encourage everyone to try harder, even those who don't think they can achieve the highest goal. The problem is that some are satisfied with the small rewards, and fewer people may put forth their maximum effort to achieve the highest level of performance.

A third method of combining goals with compensation is to establish a difficult goal and then decide on the amount of the reward after performance has occurred. This method allows the manager to take into account factors such as how close the employee came to the goal, how hard the employee appeared to work, and whether environmental conditions had an effect on

Goal-setting theory
A psychological theory suggesting that an individual's conscious choices explain motivation.

the employee's ability to meet the goal. Unfortunately, waiting to decide on the amount of the reward until after the performance has occurred can sometimes seem unfair. Accurately determining how much to pay can also be difficult if the manager doesn't know the whole set of circumstances that affected the employee's opportunity to achieve the goal.

Justice Theory

Suppose you studied much harder for an exam than a friend, only to end up getting a lower grade than the friend. Would you consider that outcome unfair? Judgments about the fairness of outcomes in relation to efforts are at the core of **justice theory.** This psychological perspective holds that motivation depends on beliefs about fairness.

An early form of justice theory was equity theory, which is illustrated in Figure 11.2. According to **equity theory**, people compare their inputs and outcomes to the inputs and outcomes of others.[28] Employees are particularly prone to comparing themselves to others whom they perceive as being paid the most, suggesting that comparisons may be biased.[29] Nevertheless, equity theory suggests that a computer programmer is motivated by the comparisons that she makes between herself and other people. She first assesses how much effort and skill she puts into her job relative to how much she is paid. She then compares this with how much effort and skill others put into their jobs relative to how much they are paid. She compares the ratio of her inputs and outcomes with the ratios for others. She feels inequity if she believes that she works harder and contributes more to the organization than another programmer who is paid the same salary.

Employees who perceive inequity might try a number of things to make their pay seem fairer. On the one hand, they may decrease their inputs to the organization—for example, by spending less time at work and putting forth

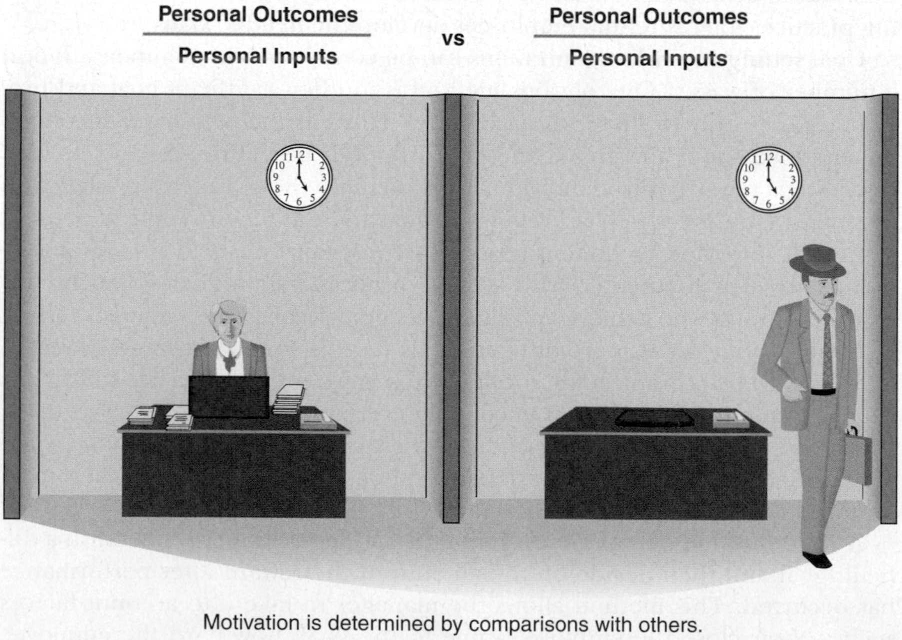

Justice theory
A psychological theory suggesting that motivation is driven by beliefs about fairness.

Equity theory
A justice perspective suggesting that people determine the fairness of their pay by comparing what they give to and receive from the organization with what others give and receive.

Motivation is determined by comparisons with others.

Figure 11.2 Equity Theory.

less effort. On the other hand, they might try to increase the outcomes they receive from the organization. Asking for and receiving a pay raise is one way to increase outcomes. Equity theory has also been used to explain employee theft. People who perceive inequity are more likely to steal from their employers in an attempt to increase their outcomes.[30] People who continue to feel inequity are likely to leave the organization and start working somewhere else.[31]

Equity theory is an example of what is known as distributive justice. **Distributive justice** is concerned with the fairness of outcomes. In terms of compensation, distributive justice focuses on whether people believe the amount of pay they receive is fair. A different form of justice is **procedural justice**, which is concerned with the fairness of the procedures used to allocate outcomes. The focus here is on the process used to decide who gets which rewards.

Although some people are simply prone to see everything as unfair,[32] most people consider a number of issues when judging whether an organization's compensation procedures are fair. Not surprisingly, people with higher wages tend to see pay as more fair.[33] Employees who are near the bottom of the pay scale are concerned about the minimum amount they will make, whereas employees near the top of the scale care more about the maximum they can make.[34] Overall, compensation strategies tend to be seen as more fair when they are free of favoritism, encourage employee participation in decisions about how rewards will be allocated, and allow appeal from people who think they are being mistreated.[35] Compensation procedures are also more likely to be seen as fair when they are based on accurate performance appraisal information.[36] In the end, employees who see the organization as more fair tend to have higher levels of satisfaction and commitment, as well as higher individual performance.[37]

Distributive justice
Perceptions of fairness based on the outcomes (such as pay) received from an organization.

Procedural justice
Perceptions of fairness based on the processes used to allocate outcomes such as pay.

Expectancy Theory
Expectancy theory offers a somewhat complex view of how individuals are motivated. The theory proposes that motivation comes from three beliefs: valence, instrumentality, and expectancy.[38] The overall framework is shown in Figure 11.3

Expectancy theory
A psychological theory suggesting that people are motivated by a combination of three beliefs: valence, instrumentality, and expectancy.

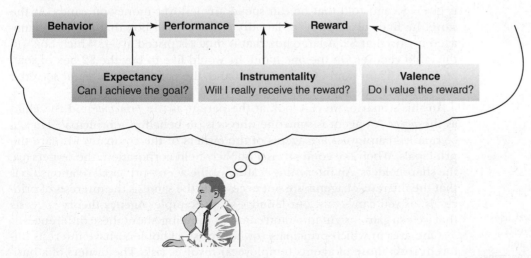

Motivation is a function of beliefs.

Figure 11.3 Expectancy Theory.

Valence
The value that an individual places on a reward being offered.

Instrumentality
The belief in the likelihood that the reward will actually be given contingent on high performance.

Expectancy
An individual's belief that he or she can do what is necessary to achieve high performance.

1. **Valence** is the belief that a certain reward is valuable. The concept of valence is an important reminder that not everyone is motivated by the same thing. Suppose, for example, that a company offers to send its highest performing employees on an all-expenses-paid trip to a Caribbean resort. This reward may be highly valued by some employees but may be undesirable to others. Only those who value the vacation will be motivated to do what is required to earn it.

2. **Instrumentality** is the belief that a reward will really be given if and only if the appropriate behavior or outcome is produced. Obviously, if employees don't believe that they will receive the promised reward even if they perform the required actions, they will not be motivated by the reward.

3. **Expectancy** concerns people's belief that they can actually achieve the desired level of performance. This belief is based in part on people's assessment of their own skills and abilities. Motivation is higher when people believe they are capable of high performance.[39] Expectancy belief may also be based in part on an assessment of whether the environment will create obstacles that limit performance. Motivation is reduced when people believe that things such as lack of materials and equipment will keep them from being able to perform well.[40]

According to expectancy theory, all three desirable beliefs must be present for motivation to occur. For example, a sales representative may value a high commission (valence) and may believe that she will receive it if she closes a specific sale (instrumentality). However, she won't be motivated to pursue the sale unless she really believes she can do something that will influence the client to make the purchase (expectancy). A food server in a restaurant may believe that he is able to provide great service (expectancy), and he may value high tips (valence), but if he doesn't believe a certain customer will leave a tip even if his performance is excellent (instrumentality), he will not be motivated to give that customer great service.

Agency Theory

Imagine that a child is sent to the store to buy laundry soap for his family. He is given $5 and told that he can spend any leftover money on candy. At the store, he finds two cartons of laundry soap. A small box that has been damaged is priced at $2. A large box that is intact is priced at $4. Which box will the child choose? On the one hand, he would like to buy the $2 box of soap and spend $3 on candy. On the other hand, the parent will be better served if the child buys the $4 box of soap.

In this scenario, we can look at the parent as the *principal* and the child as the *agent*. An agent is someone who acts on behalf of a principal. Thus, a company's employees are agents of the owners of the company, who are the principals. When the company is a publicly held corporation, the owners are the shareholders. An interesting feature of the agent–principal relationship is that the interests of agents are not necessarily the same as the interests of principals, as you can see in our laundry soap example. **Agency theory** suggests that we can gain insight into motivation by thinking about these differences.[41]

Agency theory
An economic theory that uses differences in the interests of principals (owners) and agents (employees) to describe reactions to compensation.

One area in which principals (owners or stockholders) have interests different from those of agents (employees) involves risk. The owners of a business might benefit from taking risks that grow the business at a very rapid pace. However, the risk associated with high growth may be undesirable for an employee who perceives that growth may create short-term problems and cause the employee to lose his or her job. In most cases, employees are not willing to share risk unless they can also share the potential for a bigger reward. This idea seems obvious if you think about risk in terms of earning wages. Suppose you agree to work in a sandwich shop for a week, and you get to decide how you will be paid. One choice is to get paid $400 for working 40 hours. The other choice is to get paid a percentage of total sales up to a certain level. With this option you may earn more than $400 if sales are good, but you may also earn less than $400 if sales are poor. Would you take the second option if the most you could possibly earn was $405? You probably would not accept the risk for such a small gain. But what if the most you could earn was $1,000?

If you chose the second option, you—the employee—would be bearing some of the risk for sales being high or low. You would most likely be willing to assume that risk only if you thought there was a chance for you to earn significantly more money. A general principle of agency theory is thus that wage rates should be higher when employees bear risk. For this reason, incentive plans that pay for performance are only effective when they give employees the opportunity to earn more than they could earn with fixed wages, such as hourly pay.[42]

Another important aspect of agency theory is the observation that principals and agents often don't have the same information. For example, think about large corporations. The owners—or stockholders—really know very little about the operations of the company. Agents—or managers—know a lot about the company, but the managers may be afraid to share information. Sometimes the information may make the agents look incompetent, suggesting that agents may not share all the different methods available for increasing profits. Owners may not be made aware of potential courses of action that might benefit them. Because owners can't always observe and effectively monitor the actions of employees, agency theory suggests that compensation practices must be structured so that employees are rewarded when they do the things that would be most desirable from the owners' perspective. A common example is giving stock options to top executives. With stock options, executives are rewarded when the stock price increases, which is assumed to be the preferred outcome of owners. Another example is to pay sales representatives with commissions so that they are rewarded for behavior that is aligned with the selling interests of the owners.[43] A second general principle of agency theory beyond the first principle of risk a risk premium is thus that pay should be structured so that managers and employees receive higher rewards when they do the things that increase value for owners and shareholders.

LINKING MOTIVATION WITH STRATEGY

Each motivational theory has a slightly different focus, and in some cases concepts from one theory may be slightly at odds with concepts from another theory. Nevertheless, we can derive several basic principles from the motivational theories. These principles provide guidance for determining the best ways to motivate employees through the use of compensation practices.

Motivational principles can also be linked to the compensation strategies we discussed earlier in the chapter. (You may want to refer back to Figure 11.1 to review the strategic framework for employee compensation.) Recall that organizations using differentiation strategies tend to use variable compensation, while organizations focusing on cost tend to use uniform compensation. In general, then, organizations with variable compensation systems have a

Table 11.1	*Principles for Increasing Motivation Through Compensation*

Develop pay-for-performance plans.

Link pay with goals that encourage stretch efforts.

Understand the referent groups employees use when assessing the fairness of pay.

Follow principles of procedural fairness, including accurate assessment, lack of bias, and opportunity to have input.

Provide rewards that are large enough to matter.

Coordinate with selection and training to ensure that employees have the skills they need to meet goals.

Align the interests of employees with the interests of owners.

Give higher rewards for employees who assume risk.

greater need for high motivation than organizations with uniform compensation practices. However, organizations with uniform compensation practices can also make use of key motivational principles. Table 11.1 summarizes how these key principles of motivation can guide compensation practices.

Variable Compensation and Motivation

Although some experts have suggested that linking pay to performance can reduce the joy of performing naturally interesting tasks,[44] a majority of evidence shows that performance increases when high performers are paid more than low performers.[45] The importance of pay for performance is therefore particularly high in organizations using variable compensation.

The strategic focus of differentiation makes high performance of employees critical for these organizations, and linking pay with performance is a strong motivator that encourages employees to put forth their best efforts. Organizations using variable compensation also benefit a great deal from making rewards contingent on achieving goals. As part of a Free Agent HR strategy, the organization can encourage exceptionally high performance by rewarding only individuals who reach the highest level of goal achievement. This practice provides a short-term incentive that pushes employees to exert maximum effort. Organizations pursuing a Committed Expert HR strategy can benefit from providing rewards to everyone who attains at least some level of goal achievement. This ensures that long-term employees don't get discouraged and quit if they fail to achieve a particularly high goal. Because employees working under variable compensation tend to assume greater risk, the overall level of compensation should thus be higher in organizations with Free Agent and Committed Expert HR strategies than in organizations with Bargain Laborer and Loyal Soldier strategies.

Understanding what reference group employees use in assessing the fairness of their pay is another important feature of variable compensation strategies. As part of the Committed Expert HR strategy, the primary reference group is people working in the same organization. With a Free Agent HR strategy, the primary reference group is people working in similar jobs at other companies. This distinction is important for understanding how compensation can be used to help an organization achieve a particular competitive strategy.

For instance, a professor who teaches in a medical school will likely believe that she is paid well when she compares her salary with the salaries of, say, professors of literature at her university. She may, however, not feel as good if her comparison group is highly paid medical school professors at other universities. How do these comparisons relate to competitive strategies? Comparisons with other professors at the same university are most critical if the university has a strategy of developing long-term relationships that focus on commitment rather than monetary rewards. Such long-term relationships are likely beneficial if the university is well established and seeking to defend its status. In contrast, comparisons with similar professors at other universities are most critical if the university has a strategy that benefits from short-term relationships. Such short-term relationships may be helpful if the organization is seeking to change, grow, or innovate.

Because organizations with a Committed Expert HR strategy are interested in developing ongoing relationships with employees, procedural fairness is particularly important for these organizations. Employees need to develop trust and feel that the organization supports them. Support often comes from feeling that the organization treats them fairly.[46] Such perceptions are less critical in organizations with a Free Agent HR strategy.

Unfortunately, many variable compensation practices fail to motivate because the size of the potential reward is not large enough to influence behavior. Motivation will not increase, for example, if the organization offers a 2 percent salary increase to low performers and a 2.1 percent increase to high performers. In the terminology of expectancy theory, the amount of extra salary that can be earned doesn't have the valence required. This is a particular problem for many organizations that provide relatively small annual salary increases to a majority of employees. The amount of difference between a raise for a high performer and a raise for a low performer is just too small to motivate behavior.[47]

Uniform Compensation and Motivation

Uniform compensation practices are not as effective as variable compensation practices for encouraging high motivation. The goal with uniform practices is to create a culture of fairness and cooperation. Incentives that encourage high individual performance for some often lead individuals to sabotage and compete with coworkers, which in turn reduces the performance of the group as a whole.[48] Rewards in organizations with uniform compensation are thus structured to reduce the emphasis on extreme individual performance.

In judging whether their pay is fair, employees in an organization with a Loyal Soldier HR strategy tend to compare themselves with employees working in the same organization. Such organizations usually seek competitive advantage through cost reduction, which means that they are unlikely to pay the premium wages required to secure employees who already possess rare skills and abilities. Rather than using high pay to buy talent, these organizations often use training to develop skills. Often, these skills are unique to a particular organization. For example, a consultant may become very skilled at understanding and resolving problems within a framework that is used only within the firm. The common framework increases the efficiency of his efforts, but his knowledge and ability would not be of much value to other firms not using the company-specific framework. For this reason, employees in cost-focused organizations often develop skills that have little value to other organizations, which decreases the likelihood that other organizations will be willing to offer them higher salaries. This has the effect of binding employees to the organization in a way that does not increase overall labor costs.

Organizations with a Bargain Laborer HR strategy seek to pay the lowest possible wages. Employees in these organizations are likely to move from organization to organization depending on which organization is willing to pay the most. Yet the relatively low skill level of these employees suggests that the wage rate will be near the minimum wage that is allowed under the law. We discuss the effect of minimum wage laws later in this chapter.

CONCEPT CHECK

1. *What are the three elements of motivation?*
2. *How do different theories explain motivational processes?*
3. *What compensation guidelines can be derived from motivational theories?*

LEARNING OBJECTIVE 3

How Is Compensation Level Determined?

Pay level
The compensation decision concerning how much to pay employees relative to what they could earn doing the same job elsewhere.

We turn next to the question of how an organization determines its **pay level**—the amount of overall pay that employees earn in that organization relative to what employees earn in other organizations. As with motivational strategies, the pay-level strategy an organization chooses depends largely on its competitive strategy. However, the first step in the process of determining pay level is to gain information to understand the compensation packages being provided by other organizations. This is done through pay surveys.

PAY SURVEYS

Pay survey
Gathering information to learn how much employees are being paid by other organizations.

To determine the appropriate pay level, an organization must identify a comparison group and then obtain data about compensation in the organizations that make up the comparison group. The result of this analysis is a **pay survey** that provides information about how much other organizations are paying employees. Pay surveys are often conducted by consulting firms, which obtain confidential information from numerous organizations and create reports that describe average pay levels without divulging information about specific companies. Professional organizations, such as associations of accountants and engineers, also conduct pay surveys that report wage and salary information for particular positions.

A source of public data about pay level is the Bureau of Labor Statistics, an agency of the U.S. Department of Labor, which collects employment data.[49] For instance, Figure 11.4 shows compensation rates reported by the Bureau of Labor Statistics for three different jobs in three different cities. The data show that in each city, electricians are paid more than fast food workers. Fast food workers were generally paid the same in all three cities during the first two years, but in 2010 they received higher pay in Chicago. Over the three-year period, compensation for human resource managers increased in Los Angeles and New York but decreased in Chicago. This information can be

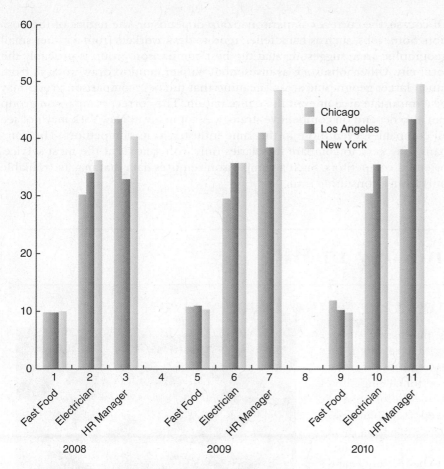

Figure 11.4 Sample BLS Pay Survey Results. *Source:* Information from Bureau of Labor Statistics (http://www.bls.gov/home.htm).

helpful for organizations trying to determine how much to pay employees. However, thinking carefully about the information in Figure 11.4 reveals a number of potential problems with pay surveys.

One problem is choosing the appropriate comparison group. An interesting example is how a major university might conduct a pay survey to determine how much to pay athletic coaches. One potential choice is to use all university coaches as the comparison group. Another choice is to use coaches in the top 20 nationally ranked programs. Since high-performing college coaches often receive offers from professional teams, still another choice may be a comparison group that includes coaches of professional teams. The outcome of a pay survey will likely be very different depending on which of these groups is chosen.

How does an organization choose the right comparison group? Good comparison groups often include organizations that compete in the same product and service markets.[50] As shown by the data in Figure 11.4, choosing the right geographic region for the comparison can also be important. A firm using comparison data from Los Angeles might determine that it is paying human resource managers an above-average wage, but the same firm might determine that it has below-average pay if it uses comparison data from New York.

Of course, the correct comparison group depends on the nature of the position. Some jobs, such as bank teller, tend to draw workers from a rather small geographic area, suggesting that the best comparison group is probably the local city. Other jobs, such as investment banker, tend to draw workers from much larger geographic areas, meaning that the best comparison group may be a multistate area or even the entire nation. The correct comparison group can also depend on competitive strategy. A company in New York may not see all companies, even those in the same industry, as its competitors. The company may want to compare its salaries only with salaries at the most service-oriented competitors. Such a comparison requires data that may be available only from a consulting firm.

Technology in HR

Be Careful When Obtaining Information

A few years ago, companies purchasing survey information received large written reports from consulting firms. The widespread use of the Internet as a convenient method for sharing information has largely put an end to the practice of preparing extensive written reports. Companies now want direct access to databases that allow them to conduct specific analyses. They want to examine a large variety of comparisons to better understand their pay levels. They also want to obtain information for more specific job categories, and they want comparisons within more specific geographic locations. This greater specificity of information can be helpful when the database contains information from enough companies to create reliable and accurate comparisons, but problems can arise when comparisons are based on data from a small number of organizations. In many cases, the amount of data available is simply insufficient for specific comparisons.

Widespread use of the Internet has also increased the amount of information that employees can find. Many employees use the Internet to obtain salary information, which they use to negotiate starting salaries and pay raises. In many cases this is helpful. More information provides the employee with a greater understanding of his or her pay relative to the pay of others in similar positions. But problems arise when an employee obtains information that is not accurate, and the

©William Whitehurst/Corbis

Internet can be a source of inaccurate information. Much of the data available to employees on the Internet does not adequately account for geographic differences, for example. In addition, job categories are so broad that specific comparisons are usually inaccurate. Data provided free of charge on the Internet may not be well suited for the specific comparisons being made by employees.

Source: Information from "Web Access Transforms Compensation Surveys," *Workforce Management* 85, no. 8 (2006): 34.

As illustrated in the "Technology in HR" feature, the Internet creates easy access to data, but not all data are good data. One potential problem with pay surveys concerns the difficulty of obtaining salary information for specific jobs. Identifying jobs that are the same in all organizations may seem relatively simple, but it is actually quite difficult. For example, a secretary in one organization may have a large number of important duties such as planning and maintaining budgets. A secretary in another organization may act primarily as a receptionist who answers telephone calls. In Figure 11.4, the position of human resource manager is the one most likely to suffer from this problem. The duties and responsibilities of managers in one organization may be very different from those of managers in other organizations. Factors that make the human resource manager position different across organizations include the number of people being supervised, the nature of the work assigned, and the education and training of subordinates. To address this problem, high-quality pay surveys obtain information that extends beyond job titles and includes a list of actual duties performed.

Because of the difficulty in creating pay comparisons for every job, a common practice in pay surveys is to obtain comparison data only for key positions. Comparing pay level in these key positions helps the organization picture its overall compensation relative to other organizations. The amount of pay for positions not included in the comparison data is then determined by weighing their value relative to the positions included in the survey.

The data in Figure 11.4 also illustrate that pay levels change over time—and they may change rapidly. For example, notice the rapid upward trend of pay for human resource managers in Los Angeles. An organization in Los Angeles using old comparison data might conclude that it is paying more than competitors when it is actually paying only average. Good pay surveys thus use current data.[51]

It should be clear by now that when it comes to pay surveys, an organization must clearly understand the data it is obtaining from a comparison group in order to know whether it is making an appropriate comparison. Consider one final example. Figure 11.5 illustrates the results of a pay survey for employees

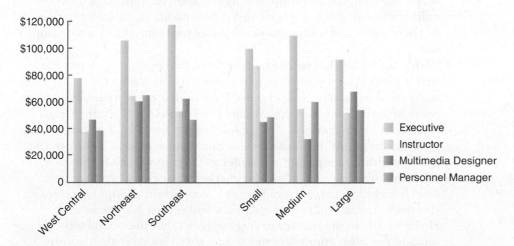

Figure 11.5 Pay Survey Results for Training Professionals. *Source:* Information from Holly Dolezalek, "The 2005 Annual Salary Survey," *Training* 42, no. 10 (2005): 12–23.

who work in the field of training and development.[52] Suppose a small organization located in Colorado pays an executive in that field an annual salary of $90,000. If the organization compares this salary with salaries within its geographic area, then it will conclude that it is paying an above-average wage. However, if it uses small firms for the comparison, it will conclude that it is paying a below-average wage. Of course, a solution is to obtain data from small firms in Colorado. This is, however, somewhat difficult in practice, because the number of organizations fitting such a specific category and willing to provide data may not be large enough to make up a good comparison sample. The organization may need to use a number of different comparison groups and combine the results to arrive at the estimate that best reflects its standing relative to others. No matter the specific approach, it is critical that organizational leaders critically evaluate the usefulness of the data.

PAY-LEVEL STRATEGIES

After obtaining information about compensation in other organizations, the next step is to develop a pay strategy that determines how high pay should be. One possible compensation strategy is to pay employees more than what they can earn elsewhere. For instance, our earlier discussion of Marriott explained how the hotel chain strives to maintain a higher level of pay than other employers. But not all organizations benefit from paying more than their competitors. There are three basic strategies for pay level: meet-the-market, lag-the-market, and lead-the-market.[53] Here "the market" refers to a selected group of organizations, such as organizations in the same industry or in the same geographical area. Data about the pay of these comparative organizations is collected through the pay survey.

Meet-the-market strategy
A compensation decision to pay employees an amount similar to what they can make working for other organizations.

- An organization with a **meet-the-market strategy** establishes pay that is in the middle of the pay range for the selected group of organizations. Some employees in the organization may be paid more than they could earn elsewhere, and some may be paid less. On average, though, the pay level is the same as the average pay level for employees across the comparison group. An organization that adopts a meet-the-market strategy seeks to attract and retain quality employees but does not necessarily use compensation as a tool for maintaining a superior workforce.

Lag-the-market strategy
A compensation decision to pay employees an amount below what they might earn working for another organization.

- With a **lag-the-market strategy,** an organization establishes a pay level that is lower than the average in the comparison group. Of course, some employees may be paid more than similar employees working for other organizations. But the average level of pay for the entire organization is lower than the average level of pay for organizations in the comparison group. In most cases, organizations adopt a lag-the-market pay level strategy as part of a broader strategy to reduce labor costs.

Lead-the-market strategy
A compensation decision to pay employees an amount above what they might earn working for another organization.

- In an organization with a **lead-the-market strategy,** the average pay level is higher than the average in the comparison group. Once again, this doesn't mean that every employee will receive higher wages. However, a lead-the-market strategy suggests that the organization seeks to pay most employees more than they would be able to earn in a similar position in another organization. The labor cost for each employee may be higher in these organizations, but they expect the higher cost to be offset by higher performance and lower turnover.

The Container Store, which is profiled in the "Building Strength Through HR" feature, is one example of an organization that benefits from a lead-the-market strategy.

LINKING COMPENSATION LEVEL AND STRATEGY

Even though wages rise as compensation level increases, profitability can often be increased by better employee performance. Differences in pay level can therefore be linked to strategic decisions. Organizations with Bargain Laborer HR strategies tend to focus on reducing labor costs. These firms most frequently adopt lag-the-market or meet-the market strategies. At the other extreme, organizations with Free Agent HR strategies use compensation to attract top performers. These firms tend to pursue lead-the-market strategies that help them to hire high-quality workers who are highly skilled. Organizations with internal labor strategies emphasize the development of long-term relationships rather than focusing on money. These organizations

Building Strength Through HR

THE CONTAINER STORE

The Container Store is the nation's originator and leading retailer of storage and organization products. The company has consistently grown at an above average rate. More than 58 retail locations in the United States now produce over $750 million in sales each year. The Container Store attributes its success to providing better service than its competitors. Prices are important and are kept at competitive levels. However, what sets the Container Store apart from the competition is the 6,000 employees who provide outstanding service.

In large part, The Container Store attracts and retains great employees by paying above-average wages. The company's objective is to pay store salespeople 50 to 100 percent above the industry average. Generous benefits include health coverage and paid vacations. Many employees are also attracted by flexible scheduling, which helps working mothers and fathers balance work with family demands.

Technology is also an important factor in the company's success. The American Payroll Association Leadership Forum gave The Container Store the PRISM award for best practices in payroll technology. Notable payroll practices include a website that is

available 24 hours a day. Online benefits enrollment, outsourced child-support payments, a dedicated payroll phone line, and payroll tax filings are also included in the technology package. These features supplement the generous pay and benefit programs to create a workplace that has frequently been rated as a desirable place to work.

Sources: Marianne Wilson, "Employer of Choice," *Chain Store Age,* August 2004, p. 156; David Drickhamer, "The Container Store: Thinking Outside of the Box," *Material Handling Management* (June 2005): 16–18; "The Container Store Wins PRISM Award for Best Practices in Payroll Technology," www.ioma.com, October 2006.

generally adopt pay levels somewhere between meet-the-market and lead-the-market. Organizations pursuing a Committed Expert HR strategy tend to have more of a lead-the-market orientation than those pursuing a Loyal Soldier HR strategy.

CONCEPT CHECK
1. *How do organizations use the results of pay surveys?*
2. *What is the key difference between meet-the-market, lag-the-market, and lead-the-market pay level strategies?*

LEARNING OBJECTIVE 4

How Is Compensation Structure Determined?

When you graduate from college and accept a full-time position, do you expect to get paid the same as everyone else who works for the company? The likely answer is no. You might expect to earn less than someone who has been in the same position for several years. However, you might expect to earn more than an employee without a college degree. You might also expect to make more (or less) than a friend who works in a different department and has a degree in a different field. These differences in pay relate to the organization's pay structure. Whereas pay level is concerned with how compensation differs across organizations, pay structure focuses on how compensation differs for people working in the same organization.

There are two major methods for determining pay structure. One method—often referred to as **job-based pay**—focuses on evaluating differences in the tasks and duties associated with various positions that employees have. With this method, it is expected that people who have more difficult jobs will be paid more. The other method focuses on directly evaluating differences in the skills and abilities of employees and is often called skill-based pay. In an organization using **skill-based pay**, an employee might be paid for having a certain set of skills, even if the tasks that the employee normally performs do not require those skills.

JOB-BASED PAY

A job-based pay approach typically uses a **point system** that assigns a numerical value to each job position. The numerical value is designed to capture the overall contribution of the job to the organization. Of course, not everyone performing a certain job will be paid the same amount. Each job is assigned a range of acceptable compensation. Individuals in the job who contribute less are paid near the bottom of the range, and those contributing more are paid near the top. The general trend, however, is for people in jobs worth more points to receive higher compensation.

A simplified example including management accountants is shown in Figure 11.6.[54] These jobs differ on the dimension of accountability and are

Job-based pay
A determination of how much to pay an employee that is based on assessments about the duties performed.

Skill-based pay
A determination of how much to pay an employee that is based on skills, even if those skills are not currently used to perform duties.

Point system
A process of assigning numerical values to each job in order to compare the value of contributions within and across organizations.

ordered so that those with lower accountability appear on the left side of the graph. Moving from left to right, we move to jobs with higher accountability and thus higher point values. The box above each point category represents the range of pay associated with that category. For example, the midpoint of the range for people working in low-accountability positions is $83,000. The bottom of the range is $73,000, and the top of the range is $93,000.

One widely used point system is the Hay System.[55] This system was developed and is marketed by the Hay Group, a worldwide compensation consulting firm. The Hay System evaluates jobs in terms of four characteristics: know-how, problem solving, accountability, and working conditions.[56]

1. *Know-how* concerns the knowledge and skills required for the job. Jobs are given more points when they require an employee to know and use specialized techniques, when they involve a need to coordinate diverse activities, and when they involve extensive interpersonal interaction.

2. *Problem solving* assesses the extent to which the job requires employees to identify and resolve problems. Higher points are assigned to jobs that are less routine, require more thought, and frequently call for adaptation and learning.

3. *Accountability* focuses on how much freedom and responsibility a job affords. Jobs are given higher ratings when the people filling them have substantial freedom to determine how to do things and when the tasks performed have a large impact on the organization's results.

4. *Working conditions* captures the extent to which performing the job is unpleasant. The main idea is that jobs should pay more when they require employees to work in dirty, strenuous, or dangerous conditions.

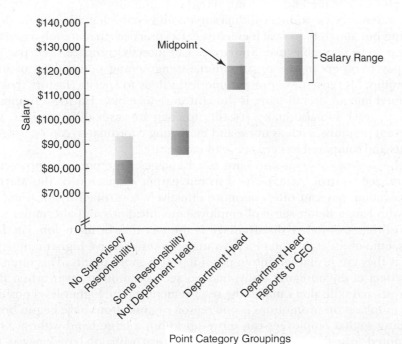

Figure 11.6 Job-Based Pay for Management Accountants.
Source: Some of the data for these ranges are from Karl E. Reichardt and David L. Schroeder, "2005 Salary Survey," *Strategic Finance* 87, no. 12 (2006): 34–50.

The points assigned on each of the four dimensions are added together to create a numerical score that represents the value of the job. Jobs are then arranged along a continuum from positions assigned low point values to positions assigned high point values. Each job within the organization is given a specific point value. Jobs with similar point values are then grouped together into categories. A category that includes jobs within a specific range is known as a pay grade. A midpoint value, which represents a target for average pay of the jobs included in the category, is established for each pay grade. A range is then created around each midpoint so that pay for everyone performing jobs worth a certain number of points falls within the range. An individual's level of compensation within the range is determined by things such as experience and performance level.

An important consideration for job-based pay concerns the range of point totals that are grouped together into a pay grade. Some organizations adopt narrow categories so that each pay grade includes only a few jobs. This process allows clear distinctions among positions. Other organizations use a process known as **broadbanding.** Here, there are fewer categories, and each category includes a broader range of jobs. The practice of broadbanding thus results in fewer pay grades, which are sometimes referred to as pay bands. An organization that uses broadbanding may need to establish and track only three to five pay grades, resulting in improved efficiency. At the same time, each pay grade includes more jobs covering a wider range of points. Thus, the pay range within each pay grade is larger, so that an employee's salary does not hit the top of the range as quickly. Indeed, more flexibility in determining an individual's pay is a primary benefit of broadbanding.

Job-based pay systems have a number of advantages. Use of the point system provides a clear method for controlling and administering pay. Centralized human resource personnel conduct surveys and establish guidelines for determining how much to pay each employee. Pay practices that are job-based also appear to be very objective. Employees can directly compare their pay with the pay of others in the organization, strengthening perceptions of internal equity. Moreover, assigning numerical values to specific factors that are summed into an overall score is thought to reduce bias. Having a numerical value for each job also makes it easier to compare vastly different jobs. Very different positions, such as nurse and marketing coordinator, can be assigned points and compared to get a sense of pay equity.[57]

Job-based pay systems also have disadvantages. One potential problem is centralized control. As explained in our earlier discussion of the Marriott Corporation, pay can often be more effectively controlled by local managers, who have a better sense of employee qualifications and alternative work opportunities. Another disadvantage is the fact that in many job-based systems, employees at the top of a pay range can only receive higher compensation if they are promoted into a position worth more points. This often has the effect of encouraging individuals to seek promotions even when their interests and skills don't match the requirements of the higher-level position. This emphasis on promotions is one reason organizations have begun broadbanding so that employees can move up within a large band without being promoted to a different job. Another concern with job-based pay is that individuals often try to get their current positions reevaluated and valued with higher points, so that they will receive higher pay, even though the tasks they are performing have not really changed. Inflexibility and resistance to change are also common with job-based pay systems, since the major focus is

Broadbanding
The practice of reducing the number of pay categories so that each pay grade contains a large set of different jobs.

on classifying tasks into clear-cut objective categories that can be represented by a numerical score. Job-based compensation makes it difficult to hire new employees who require a wage that is above the established range. Finally, there is little incentive for employees to learn new skills that are not part of their formal job duties.

SKILL-BASED PAY

A skill-based pay system shifts emphasis away from jobs and focuses on the skills that workers possess. In essence, this system pays people relative to their long-term value rather than relative to the value of their current position. Employees are paid more when they develop more skills. The primary objective is to encourage the development of skills linked to the overall strategic direction of the organization.

An application of skill-based pay in a manufacturing plant is shown in Figure 11.7. In this case, Skill Set 1 might include the ability to solve simple math problems, communicate orally, and read and follow written directions. People need this skill set in order to be hired at the starting rate of $11 per hour. Once employees learn Skill Set 2 (operating basic machines and equipment), their pay rises to $15 per hour. Pay increases to $18 per hour when employees learn Skill Set 3 (production planning, equipment repair) and to $21 when they learn Skill Set 4 (ability to interact with vendors and customers). Employees are thus paid for the skills they develop rather than for occupying a specific position.

Skill sets can be defined in a number of ways. Some organizations require employees to learn entirely new skills, as when a salesperson learns accounting skills. Other organizations encourage employees to develop deeper skills in specific areas, as when an accountant learns new tax rules and regulations. In either case, the primary objective is to tie pay increases to the development of skills useful to the organization.

Several different methods can be used to determine whether an employee has learned a skill set. In some cases, written tests are used to assess learning. In other cases, coworkers or supervisors administer tests or observe actions to certify that a skill set has been mastered. Regardless of how the assessment is made, an important feature of most skill-based pay systems is allowing employees to learn new skills at their own pace. Some employees advance quickly under this plan, while a few never advance to higher levels.

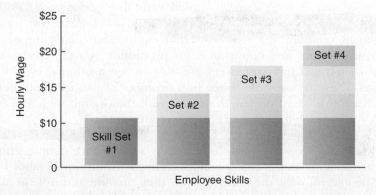

Figure 11.7 Skill-Based Pay.

Skill-based pay plans do have some disadvantages. One problem is that payroll costs tend to be higher with skill-based pay. Employees are paid higher wages when they acquire additional skills, even if they don't use those skills to perform their current duties. Training costs can also be high if classes and other training resources are needed to develop the skills. In addition, problems arise when employees master the highest skill set and perceive that they have no more room for advancement.[58]

Even with the potential disadvantages, skill-based pay appears to offer a number of benefits. For one thing, the increased emphasis on skill development provides a better-trained workforce. A related advantage is greater flexibility in production processes. In most cases, a large number of employees have been trained to perform several different duties. Thus, when someone is ill, or when someone quits, several substitutes are available to fill in. Emphasizing skills rather than jobs also helps to build a culture that supports greater participation and employee self-management.[59] These benefits are substantial enough that skill-based pay has been linked to higher organizational productivity.[60]

LINKING COMPENSATION STRUCTURE TO STRATEGY

Once again, we can link organizations' compensation structure to their overall HR strategies. In organizations pursuing Free Agent HR strategies through variable transactional compensation, pay is used to attract people with specific skills. Skill-based pay that compensates individuals for the specific skills they bring is thus useful for many organizations pursuing this strategy. Internal equity is not critical, and people with better skills are paid substantially more than people with limited skills. Once people are hired in these organizations, little emphasis is placed on the acquisition of new skills, since employees are not expected to stay with the organization for long.

Skill-based pay can also be beneficial for organizations pursuing a Loyal Soldier HR strategy. Organizations pursuing this strategy use uniform relational compensation to bind individuals to the organization and minimize differences between employees. Skill-based pay that is linked to specific training is helpful in promoting these goals. Giving everyone the opportunity to learn new skills and advance to higher pay levels builds a sense of teamwork. Linking pay to the skills needed by the organization also forms stronger ties between employees and the organization, which creates uniformity.

Job-based pay is most closely aligned with the Committed Expert HR strategy and variable relational compensation. The emphasis on long-term employment relationships makes internal equity particularly important in these organizations, and opportunity for promotion is a significant motivator. With job-based pay, employees are able to see a rational basis for pay decisions. They are also able to see how promotions can increase their pay. Compensation is based on length of time with the organization and type of input contributed, but a sense of equity is retained.

Job-based pay is also beneficial for organizations with Bargain Laborer HR strategies. These organizations don't usually seek to hire people who have developed specific skills. The overall objective is to minimize labor cost by paying people only for the contributions they provide and not for skills in other areas.

LEARNING OBJECTIVE 5

How Do Government Regulations Influence Compensation?

We end the chapter with a look at how government regulations affect the decisions organizations make about compensation. First, we describe a major federal law in this area, and then we discuss state and local regulations. Taken together, these laws create some important requirements with which organizations must be familiar.

FAIR LABOR STANDARDS ACT

Have you ever heard people say they don't earn overtime because their jobs are "exempt"? What does it mean to be exempt? Perhaps you have heard statements about how pay in certain jobs compares with the minimum wage. Who decides what the minimum wage is? Both of these questions are related to the **Fair Labor Standards Act (FLSA)**, a federal law that governs many compensation practices. The FLSA, which was passed in 1938, is designed to protect employees. The law establishes a national minimum wage, regulates overtime, requires equal pay for men and women, and establishes guidelines for employing children. Many types of workers, however, are exempt from FLSA regulations.

Exempt and Nonexempt Employees

The FLSA creates two broad categories of workers: exempt and nonexempt. **Exempt employees** are not covered by FLSA regulations. Members of the other group, often referred to as **nonexempt employees**, are covered. Perhaps the most noticeable difference between these groups is how they are paid. Exempt employees can be paid a salary. In most cases, they aren't required to keep track of the actual hours they work. Nonexempt employees are paid an hourly wage. For these employees, the number of hours worked, including the beginning and ending times, must be carefully recorded. This basic difference stems from FLSA regulations. Employees who are covered by the FLSA are required to keep track of their hours and be paid on an hourly basis, whereas employees who are not covered can be paid a set amount that is not directly tied to hours worked.

What determines whether an employee is exempt or nonexempt? As a starting point in understanding these classifications, it is easiest to think of all employees as being covered by the FLSA and then identify which types of workers are exempt. The list of specific types of exempt workers is quite

Fair Labor Standards Act (FLSA)
Federal legislation that governs compensation practices and helps ensure fair treatment of employees.

Exempt employees
Workers, such as executives, administrators, professionals, and sales representatives, who are not covered by the FLSA.

Nonexempt employees
All employees who are not explicitly exempt from the FLSA, sometimes referred to as hourly workers.

lengthy and includes specific types of laborers, such as amusement park employees and farm workers. There are, however, four general classifications that usually underlie the exempt designation.[61]

1. The *executive exemption* applies to workers whose primary duties are managing a business and supervising others.
2. The *administrative exemption* applies to workers who perform office or non-manual work that is directly related to management. They must exercise substantial discretion and judgment in their work.
3. The *professional exemption* applies to employees who perform tasks that require special skills and advanced knowledge learned through special-ized study.
4. Workers may also be exempt from the FLSA through the *outside sales exemption,* which applies to salespeople who work away from the place of business.

In any of these cases, the employees must spend at least 80 percent of their workday doing work activities that qualify them for the exemption. For instance, to qualify for the outside sales exemption, the salesperson must spend at least 80 percent of his or her time selling in locations other than the company prem-ises. Table 11.2 provides a brief summary of the four major exemptions.

Accurately classifying employees as exempt or nonexempt is very impor-tant. One example of potential problems involves Nordstrom Department Stores. Nordstrom's competitive strategy is to provide highly individualized service, which often requires employees to do things such as deliver goods. A number of years ago, Nordstrom ran into difficulties with state regulators when some sales associates failed to record hours they spent making deliveries and doing small tasks to facilitate sales. At the time, Nordstrom associates were paid a high hourly rate for the hours they did record, and they received sub-stantial bonuses for high performance. Their overall pay was more than that of sales associates working for other department stores. However, Nordstrom sales associates were covered by the FLSA, which required them to record and be specifically compensated for every hour they worked. In order to fix the problem, Nordstrom developed procedures to ensure that its practices would comply with FLSA regulations—even though many employees would have preferred a system that did not require them to track each hour.[62] As explained in the "How Do We Know?" feature, employees often have complex reactions to pay changes.

Table 11.2	*Common Exemptions to the Fair Labor Standards Act*
Executive Exemption	**Professional Exemption**
Primarily manages a business or department	Performs tasks that require specialized knowledge
Supervises two or more employees; hires and fires	Produces original and creative work
Exercises discretion	Exercises discretion
Administrative Exemption	**Outside Sales**
Performs office or nonmanual work	Regularly works away from place of business
Performs technical work	Spends at least 80 percent of time selling
Assists executives	

How Do We Know?

DO PEOPLE LOSE SLEEP OVER PAY?

What happens when someone's pay gets cut? Do people who receive a pay cut feel increased stress? Are they less able to sleep at night? Does being treated fairly reduce stress? Jerald Greenberg worked with four private hospitals to answer these questions. The hospitals were in the process of adding responsibilities to the job of nurse and reclassifying the position as exempt. Before the reclassification nurses typically worked 55 hours per week, meaning that they earned overtime pay. However, overtime pay was eliminated when the nurses became exempt employees. The net result was a 10 percent reduction in overall pay.

Because the hospitals did not all change at the same time, and because some of them included a training program for nurse supervisors, the change to exempt status and lower pay created an experiment. One group of 158 nurses received the pay cut and worked for supervisors who had received training in ways to treat the nurses fairly. A second group of 164 nursed had their pay cut, but their supervisors did not receive the training. A third group of 156 had supervisors who received the training but did not have a pay cut. A fourth group of 147 nurses did not receive a pay cut, and their supervisors did not receive training. All nurses reported how well they could go to sleep quickly, stay asleep, and awake rested in the morning.

Before the pay cut all nurses reported similar sleep. Sleep problems increased for the two groups of nurses who had their pay cut but not for the nurses who did not have a pay cut. Over time the sleep of nurses with a pay cut who worked for the supervisors who had fairness training improved. Sleep did not improve for those with a cut who worked for the supervisors who were not trained.

Bottom Line. A reduction in pay can cause stress that leads to undesirable consequences such as poor sleep. However, supervisors who treat employees fairly can eliminate some of the negative effects of a pay cut. Professor Greenberg thus recommends that organizations train supervisors in ways to treat employees more fairly.

Source: Jerald Greenberg, "Losing Sleep Over Organizational Injustice: Attenuating Insomnia Reactions to Underpayment Inequity with Supervisor Training in Interactional Justice," *Journal of Applied Psychology* 91 (2006): 58–69.

Minimum Wage

Perhaps the most widely known aspect of the FLSA is its **minimum wage** requirement, which establishes a minimum hourly wage rate. In July 2009 the minimum wage was increased to $7.25 per hour. One exception is people who work in service jobs and receive tips. These workers must be paid a minimum of $2.13 as an hourly wage, and the company must pay them enough so that their total pay, including hourly wage and tips, is at least the minimum wage. In some cases, organizations can also pay workers under 20 years of age a training wage of $4.25 for the first 90 days they are employed.[63] Pay for some employees who are covered by the FLSA may be based on productivity factors, such as the number of parts produced, as long as the hours worked are tracked and the minimum amount paid equals what would be paid as the minimum wage.

Minimum wage
A compensation rule requiring organizations to pay employees at least a certain amount for each hour they work.

Overtime

As explained at the beginning of this chapter, many employees at Marriott want to work more than 40 hours per week. One reason is that the FLSA requires

Overtime

A compensation rule requiring organizations to pay a higher hourly rate for each hour that a nonexempt employee works beyond 40 hours in a one-week period.

Marriott and other employers to pay employees an overtime rate of 1.5 times the normal wage rate. **Overtime** is defined as the number of hours over 40 during a one-week period. An employee who is paid $8 per hour and who works 50 hours in one week would thus be paid $440—$8 per hour for the basic 40-hour workweek, totaling $320, and $12 per hour for the 10 overtime hours, totaling $120.

Overtime requirements are slightly different for certain classes of employees. For instance, overtime for hospital employees is usually calculated over a 14-day period. In this case, overtime occurs when the number of hours in a two-week period exceeds 80. A hospital worker may therefore work 60 hours one week and not receive overtime compensation if she only works 20 hours the next week. Another major exception is public employees, such as firefighters and police officers. Rather than receive an overtime rate, these public employees can be compensated with additional time off during other weeks. For instance, a firefighter might work 50 hours one week and not be paid overtime if he works 10 hours less in a subsequent week. However, practices such as the use of broader windows of time and using time off to compensate for previous work above 40 hours are not available for most organizations.

Child Labor

Many high school students find it difficult to get a job before they turn 16. This is because the FLSA has child labor provisions that are designed to protect those under the age of 18 from unsafe and excessive work. Children under 14 are limited to a few jobs such as newspaper delivery and farm work. Fourteen-year-olds and 15-year-olds can be hired in some jobs, but there are many restrictions on the hours they can work. They can work no more than three hours on a school day, for example, and no more than 18 hours in a school week. They are also limited to eight hours on nonschool days and can work only between 7 A.M. and 7 P.M. These rules are relaxed somewhat during the summer and for agricultural jobs. Child laborers are also limited in that they cannot perform hazardous work until they turn 18.

Equal Pay

Chapter 3 discussed the Equal Pay Act, which requires employers to pay men and women the same when they perform the same job. The Equal Pay Act is actually an amendment to the FLSA. The equal pay requirement applies to executive, administrative, professional, and sales positions that are exempt from minimum wage and overtime rules. In essence, the Equal Pay Act requires organizations to pay equal wages for equal work. However, male and female employees can be paid at an unequal rate if the basis for the difference is seniority or performance.

Although the intent of the Equal Pay Act is to ensure that men and women receive equal pay for doing similar work, differences in the overall compensation of men and women remain. Women continue to earn less than men, although the magnitude of the difference decreases as women are better represented in a work group. Pay is more equal in work groups where women are less of a minority.[64] Some of this difference may be explained by job choice, in that women tend to track toward occupations that pay less. However, differences persist even after controlling for things like hours worked and job complexity. One explanation is the continued operation of a traditional stereotype that sees women as less fit for work outside the home. Interestingly, men who hold such a stereotype tend to earn more than men who have a perception of women as equal, yet women with a view of themselves as equals only earn slightly more than women who see themselves in a more traditional role.[65] This illustrates how more research is needed to understand how stereotypes affect compensation.

STATE AND LOCAL REGULATIONS

As mentioned in our discussion of minimum wage rates, state and local governments also create regulations that affect compensation. Under federal law, these regulations cannot contradict federal rules, which usually means that they are stricter than the federal regulations. For example, some states such as Arkansas and Minnesota have minimum wage laws that have not been updated since the federal rate was raised in 2009, so that the minimum rate they prescribe is below the federal rate. These state laws are meaningless because employers must pay the higher federal rate. In contrast, other state and local governments such as Alaska and the District of Columbia have minimum wage rates higher than the federal minimum wage. These rules are acceptable, since requiring a wage rate of $8.25 per hour also meets the federal requirement of having an hourly wage rate of at least $7.25.

The large number of state and local regulations can make it difficult for organizations to keep track of all applicable compensation guidelines. Therefore, interpreting compensation regulations is an area in which human resource professionals can provide substantial help to managers. At a minimum, organizations need to conduct research to determine which federal, state, and local regulations apply to them. Much of this research can now be done online at state government sites that provide detailed information about compensation guidelines.

CONCEPT CHECK

1. *What types of workers are exempt from FLSA regulations?*
2. *What compensation issues are covered by the FLSA?*
3. *How do state and local compensation laws relate to federal laws?*

A MANAGER'S PERSPECTIVE REVISITED

Robert Daly/Getty Images

IN THE MANAGER'S PERSPECTIVE THAT OPENED THE CHAPTER, LYNETTE WAS WORRIED ABOUT CHANGING THE PAY PRACTICES AT HER CONSULTING FIRM. SHE WONDERED WHETHER THE NEW PAY POLICIES WOULD BE BENEFICIAL. SHE WAS CONFLICTED ABOUT MATCHING AN OFFER GIVEN TO HER ADMINISTRATIVE ASSISTANT BY A LOCAL BANK. SHE ALSO WONDERED WHETHER HER OWN PAY WAS FAIR. FOLLOWING ARE ANSWERS TO THE "WHAT DO YOU THINK?" QUIZ THAT FOLLOWED THE CASE. WERE YOU ABLE TO CORRECTLY IDENTIFY THE TRUE STATEMENTS? COULD YOU DO BETTER NOW?

1. If people don't think they are being paid fairly, they often steal things from their employer. **TRUE.** *Theft rates have been shown to increase when employees perceive inequity in their pay.*

2. Increasing employee pay doesn't increase motivation unless workers feel they have the skill and ability needed to increase their performance. **TRUE.** *Expectancy theory suggests that compensation is only motivational when employees perceive that they are able to perform the tasks necessary for high performance.*

3. People who are paid a lot don't worry much about how much others are being paid. **FALSE.** *Equity theory makes it clear that all employees compare their pay and contributions with the pay and contributions of others. People who are paid a lot typically compare themselves with others who are paid a lot.*

4. Organizations are more profitable when they pay their employees no more than what their competitors are paying. **FALSE.** *Some organizations choose a lead-the-market pay strategy with the intention of attracting and retaining the best workers.*

5. Paying some employees substantially more than their peers can decrease teamwork and cooperation. **TRUE.** *Paying high performers more than low performers can motivate high individual performance but can also have a negative effect on teamwork.*

Lynette's concerns about changes in compensation are quite typical. In this chapter, we have described a number of motivation theories that help illustrate how people such as Lynette and other employees react to specific types of compensation. We have also described practices for determining pay level and creating pay structures. As discussed throughout this chapter, the key to success is adopting compensation practices that ensure that pay is aligned with strategy so that the employees who are most critical for organizational success are attracted, satisfied, and retained.

SUMMARY

LEARNING OBJECTIVE 1

How is employee compensation strategic?

Compensation differs along two dimensions. One dimension relates to whether compensation is variable or uniform. Uniform compensation seeks to build a sense of teamwork by paying employees similarly regardless of performance level. Variable compensation seeks to pay high performers substantially more than low performers. Another dimension of compensation concerns relational versus transactional commitment. Transactional commitments emphasize short-term pay and bonuses. Relational commitments emphasize long-term incentives and psychological support from the organization.

Compensation practices should align with general HR strategies. A Bargain Laborer HR strategy is supported by reducing labor costs. An emphasis on teamwork and treating everyone the same is best for organizations pursuing a Loyal Soldier HR strategy. The Committed Expert HR strategy is best supported by compensation that rewards high performers and builds commitment to the organization. Short-term monetary incentives are a key feature of the Free Agent HR strategy.

LEARNING OBJECTIVE 2

How does compensation motivate people?

People show motivation at work by choosing to engage in behaviors that promote organizational success and by pursuing those behaviors in an intense and persistent way. Reinforcement theory suggests that people engage in behavior when they receive desirable consequents. However, consequents only motivate behavior when they are contingent. In the context of compensation, this suggests that higher pay should be given if and only if performance is high.

Goal-setting theory suggests that people are motivated when they have specific goals. Goals increase motivation by focusing attention, energizing effort, encouraging persistence, and promoting the discovery of knowledge. Goals can be linked to compensation in a number of ways ranging from rewards only for achieving a high goal to rewards for achieving smaller goals.

Justice theory focuses on perceptions of fairness. Distributive justice concerns whether people think the outcomes they receive are fair. People have a sense of inequity if they believe they are providing more contributions than others but receiving the same or lower wages. Procedural justice concerns the processes that are used to allocate rewards. Compensation practices are perceived to be fairer when they are free of bias, allow employee participation in key decisions, and offer opportunity for appeal to individuals who feel they are being mistreated.

Expectancy theory asserts that people are motivated when they have three beliefs: valence, instrumentality, and expectancy. Valence is the belief that a certain reward is valuable. Instrumentality is the belief that the desirable reward will really be given if the appropriate behavior or outcome is produced. Expectancy concerns people's belief that they can actually achieve the desired level of performance.

Agency theory highlights the fact that principals (owners) and agents (employees) often have different interests. Employees who bear the risk of having their pay linked to performance must have the opportunity to earn more than employees who receive guaranteed wages. In large public corporations, agents (managers) have more information than principals (shareholders), and compensation is most effective when the agents are rewarded for doing the things that are in the best interests of shareholders.

LEARNING OBJECTIVE 3

How is compensation level determined?

Pay surveys are used to determine wage rates in a comparison group of other organizations. Some information for pay surveys can be obtained from public sources such as the Bureau of Labor Statistics, but many surveys are conducted by private consulting firms. Quality pay surveys make sure that the comparison group consists of organizations with the proper geographic and strategic characteristics. Care must also be taken to ensure that the jobs being assessed in the comparison group are similar to the jobs within the focal organization.

Pay level concerns how much an organization pays employees relative to how much other organizations pay. An organization can adopt one of three pay-level strategies. A lag-the-market strategy establishes a pay level that is below the average for other organizations; a meet-the-market strategy pays at the average level for other organizations; and a lead-the-market strategy adopts a pay level that is higher than the average for other organizations. The pay level strategy should match the overall HR strategy.

LEARNING OBJECTIVE 4

How is compensation structure determined?

Pay structure concerns how people in an organization are paid relative to one another. With job-based pay, each job is assigned a point value based on various characteristics of the job, and people working in jobs worth more points receive higher pay. Advantages of job-based pay include objectivity, ease of comparisons across positions, and clear methods for administering pay. Skill-based pay uses differences in employee skills as the basis for determining pay. Employees are given an opportunity to earn more as they develop better skills. Advantages of skill-based pay include increased flexibility, greater emphasis on participation, and a better-trained workforce.

LEARNING OBJECTIVE 5

How do government regulations influence compensation?

The FLSA regulates compensation for many employees. Some employees are exempt from FLSA regulations. Common exemptions include executive, administrative, and professional workers, as well as outside sales representatives. The FLSA establishes a minimum hourly wage and overtime provisions for workers who are not exempt. Children under 18 are limited to certain types of work and hours. Equal pay is required for men and women performing the same job, unless there are differences in tenure or productivity. State and local laws also provide similar guidelines that organizations must follow when paying employees.

KEY TERMS

Agency theory   428
Broadbanding   440
Contingency   424
Distributive justice   427
Employee compensation   416
Equity theory   426
Exempt employees   443
Expectancy   428
Expectancy theory   427
External equity   419
Fair Labor Standards Act (FLSA)   443
Goal-setting theory   425
Instrumentality   428
Internal equity   419
Job-based pay   438
Justice theory   426
Lag-the-market strategy   436
Lead-the-market strategy   436
Market-based pay   417

Meet-the-market strategy   436
Minimum wage   445
Motivation   423
Nonexempt employees   443
Overtime   446
Pay-for-performance   424
Pay level   432
Pay survey   432
Point system   438
Procedural justice   427
Reinforcement theory   423
Relational commitment   420
Salary compression   422
Skill-based pay   438
Transactional commitment   420
Uniform rewards   420
Valence   428
Variable rewards   420

DISCUSSION QUESTIONS

1. Why would an organization such as Marriott choose to pay wages that are higher than the wages paid by competitors?

2. How might you react if you learned that a coworker who is new to the organization makes more money than you, even though you have five years' experience? What theoretical perspectives explain your reactions?

3. In organizations where you work, or will work, would you prefer compensation to be variable or uniform? Why?

4. What things other than compensation might encourage you to have a long career with a specific organization?

5. How would you react if you learned that your professor was going to pay $100 to the two individuals with the highest scores on the next exam? Would your study effort change? Would your enjoyment of the class change?

6. Under what conditions might an organization choose a lag-the-market pay strategy?

7. Which do you think is most fair: job-based pay or skill-based pay? Why?

8. Do you think child labor laws are really necessary in modern countries like the United States?

9. Do minimum wage laws help society? Why or why not? Do you think the current minimum wage is set at the right level? If not, what do you think a fair rate might be?

10. What specific aspects of compensation are most appropriate for an organization with a Loyal Soldier HR strategy? What characteristics are most closely aligned with a Free Agent HR strategy?

Delphi Corporation

The United Auto Workers filed an objection to Delphi Corporation's plan to offer its top executives cash and bonuses potentially valued at more than $500 million, arguing the proposal would impede the ability of the union to reach an agreement with the auto-parts supplier on wage and job cuts for hourly workers.

The UAW, along with other Delphi unions like the United Steel Workers, says the compensation plan "is decidedly the wrong message to Delphi's workers," at a time union members are being asked to accept pay cuts from an average of $26 an hour to about $12.50 an hour.

"It is imperative that the debtor's key personnel are appropriately incentivized to maximize the financial performance of the debtor's operations," says Delphi in its motion supporting the compensation plan. "The alignment of an incentive program that tracks the debtor's goals is crucial to the debtor's ability to navigate through this process and emerge successfully from Chapter 11."

Under its proposed employee-compensation plan, Delphi would allocate $21.8 million for cash bonuses to executives during the first six months of bankruptcy, and then an additional $87.9 million for 486 U.S. executives who would receive 30 to 250 percent of their salaries once Delphi emerges from bankruptcy.

The most potentially lucrative element of the compensation plan is a proposal to give Delphi's top 600 worldwide executives 10 percent of the equity in the reorganized company, a stake the unions estimate could be worth $400 million.

QUESTIONS

1. How does equity theory explain the UAW's reactions to the proposed compensation plan? How does equity theory explain Delphi leadership's defense of the compensation proposal?
2. What type of competitive strategy does the proposed compensation plan best fit? How would the proposal affect pay structure within Delphi?
3. Based on concepts from agency theory and expectancy theory, how might the compensation proposal motivate executives?
4. What procedural justice issues have been violated by Delphi's proposal? What would you recommend for a compensation plan at Delphi?

Source: Jeffrey McCracken, "UAW Files Protest to Delphi Bonuses for Top Executives," *Wall Street Journal*, November 25, 2005, p. A5. Reprinted by permission of *Wall Street Journal*, © 2005 Dow Jones & Company Inc. All Rights Reserved Worldwide. License Number 1753150729784.

Joe's Hamburger Grill

Joe's Hamburger Grill has been doing business in the same location for the past 20 years. The Grill is located in Phoenix, Arizona, and caters to college students by providing some of the world's biggest hamburgers in a fun and casual dining atmosphere. Joe looks back with fondness on the 20 years that have passed since he first opened the grill. His primary motivation for start-ing the business was the opportunity to work for himself. When he graduated from college, Joe took a job as an accountant and worked for a number of different companies. When he turned 40, Joe decided he was tired of working for a boss, so he began looking for an alternative opportunity. Knowing his love for cooking and his flair for providing great customer service, Joe's wife and friends encouraged him to open the hamburger stand. After taking some time to decide what he wanted to do, Joe followed their advice and founded the business. By all accounts his efforts can be seen as a success. He has made a good living doing something that he truly enjoys.

When Joe turned 60 several years ago, he decided it was time to slow down and let someone else deal with the day-to-day hassles of running the business. He hired a manager to oversee operations at the Grill. After three months, the manager quit and started classes at the local university. Joe was then able to hire a manager who stayed for 18 months but left to work at a bigger store in Dallas, Texas. For the last three months, Joe has been trying to hire a new manager. He hasn't been able to find someone he thinks will be a successful manager. Joe wonders if part of the problem is his compensation package.

When Joe hired the first manager, he decided to pay a monthly salary that included full health benefits. He didn't know how much to pay as salary, so he asked the first manager how much she was making. He then offered her a $500 per month increase to work for him. The second manager seemed fine with the amount, but a few recent candidates have told him that he needs to pay more.

One day a customer of Joe's told him that she was taking a human resource management class where they were discussing compensation issues. Joe described his dilemma about trying to decide how much to pay a store man-ager. The customer offered to do some research and learn more about pay lev-els for managers. A few days later she brought Joe a graph that had information about pay practices. She told Joe that she had been unable to locate specific information about pay for restaurant managers. However, she had found some information about food service supervisors. Just looking at the information she felt that the amount for the supervisor position was probably too low for some-one who actually managed the entire restaurant. She thus found some addi-tional information about the wages for general managers. She also looked at compensation figures for people who owned sales-related businesses. Knowing that Joe's had lost one manager to a job in Dallas, she included information about compensation in Dallas and another large city—Los Angeles.

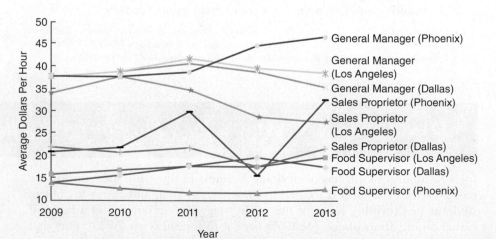

Joe looks at the information in the graph and wonders what to do with it. He wonders how important it is to take into account pay in other cities. Will he need to pay wages similar to what is being paid to managers at larger companies? Joe's goal is to find a manager who will treat the Grill like an owner. He wants the manager to commit to several years of building and maintaining profitability. If things work out, he might even be willing to sell the Grill to a high-performing manager who shows loyalty.

QUESTIONS

1. What are some suggestions that might help Joe as he thinks about changing the way he pays someone to manage the Grill?
2. Do you think Joe's approach to determining how much to pay a manager was successful? Would you recommend that he do something different?
3. How might agency theory guide Joe as he thinks about finding a manager who might someday become the owner of the Grill?
4. How can the concepts of equity theory guide Joe's decisions concerning comparisons with pay in other cities and for other jobs?
5. How might FLSA standards apply to Joe's compensation decisions?

EXPERIENTIAL EXERCISE

Conduct a Pay Survey Using BLS Data

Access the Bureau of Labor Statistics Internet site at www.bls.gov and find out how pay in your geographical area compares with pay in other geographical areas. Within the BLS site choose Occupational Employment Statistics at http://www.bls.gov/oes Locate the section for OES Data and click on Occupational Profiles. First, find a wage survey on the site. This can be done by choosing the tab of "Subject Areas." Once you choose the tab, you will see a list of topics appear along the left of the screen. From this list choose "Occupations." You can then choose from among the more than 400 occupations. Look through the survey results and find pay data for five different jobs. Next, scroll down and see data for the five jobs from different geographic areas.

Compare the pay survey results for the five jobs in three geographic areas. Answer the following questions:

QUESTIONS

1. Which job has pay that is most similar across the geographic areas?
2. Which geographic area has the highest pay level?
3. What do you think accounts for differences in pay level across geographic areas?
4. Why is pay higher in a geographic area for some jobs but not others?
5. What concerns would you have about using these data to actually determine how much to pay employees in the jobs you identified?

INTERACTIVE EXPERIENTIAL EXERCISE

How Much to Pay: Finding the Right Balance at SuperFoods
http://www.wiley.com/college/sc/stewart

Access the comparison website to test your knowledge by completing a SuperFoods interactive role play.

In this exercise, word of your consulting success is spreading rapidly, and SuperFoods has retained your services to help management evaluate the company's compensation strategy and practices. The basic HR strategy of SuperFoods, a producer of dairy products, is to keep pay levels low but to ensure fairness. As you talk with top managers about their beliefs concerning pay, it becomes quite clear to you how you can help them align the company's compensation strategy with its overall competitive strategy. The management team has asked for your input on various aspects of compensation. What will you include in your recommendations that will allow the company to retain its current HR strategy?   •

ENDNOTES

1. Daniel M. Cable and Timothy A. Judge, "Pay Preferences and Job Search Decisions: A Person-Organization Fit Perspective," *Personnel Psychology* 47 (1994): 317–348.

2. Steven C. Currall, Annette J. Towler, Timothy A. Judge, and Laura Kohn, "Pay Satisfaction and Organizational Outcomes," *Personnel Psychology* 58 (2005): 613–641.

3. M. M. Petty, Bart Singleton, and David W. Connell, "An Experimental Evaluation of an Organizational Incentive Plan in the Electric Utility Industry," *Journal of Applied Psychology* 77 (1992): 427–436.

4. Douglas G. Jenkins Jr., Atul Mitra, Nina Gupta, and Jason D. Shaw, "Are Financial Incentives Related to Performance? A Meta-analytic Review of Empirical Research," *Journal of Applied Psychology* 83 (1998): 777–787.

5. J. W. Marriott, Jr., "Competitive Strength," *Executive Excellence* 18, no. 4 (2001): 3–4.

6. Karl Fischer, Steven E. Gross, and Helen M. Friedman, "Marriott Makes the Business Case for an Innovative Total Rewards Strategy," *Journal of Organizational Excellence* 22 (2003): 19–24.

7. Fischer, Gross, and Friedman, "Marriott Makes the Business Case," 19–24; Faye Hansen, "Power to the Line People," *Workforce* 82, no. 6 (2003): 70.

8. Howard Risher, "Planning a 'Next Generation' Salary System," *Compensation and Benefits Review* 34, no. 6, (2002): 13–23; Hansen, "Power to the Line People," 70.

9. Anonymous, "Business: No Prizes for Runners-up: Rewarding Employees," *The Economist* 362, no. 8258 (2002): 57–58; Chad Kaydo, "Marriott's Incentives Strike Gold," *Sales and Marketing Management* 150, no. 12 (1998): 97.

10. http://marriott.com/careers/default.mi

11. Peter Bamberger and Ilan Meshoulam, *Human Resource Strategy* (Thousand Oaks, CA: Sage, 2000).

12. M. Bloom and George T. Milkovich, "Relationships among Risk, Incentive Pay, and Organizational Performance," *Academy of Management Journal* 41 (1998): 283–297.

13. Bamberger and Meshoulam, *Human Resource Strategy*.

14. Barry Gerhart and George T. Milkovich, "Organizational Differences in Managerial Compensation and Financial Performance," *Academy of Management Journal* 33 (1990): 663–691.

15. David B. Balkin and Luis R. Gomez-Mejia, "Toward a Contingency Theory of Compensation Strategy," *Strategic Management Journal* 8 (1987): 169–182; Balkin and Gomez-Mejia, "Matching Compensation and Organizational Strategies."

16. Denise M. Rousseau, *Psychological Contracts in Organizations* (Thousand Oaks, CA: Sage, 1995).

17. Jason D. Shaw and Nina Gupta, "Pay System Characteristics and Quit Patterns of Good, Average, and Poor Performers," *Personnel Psychology* 60 (2007): 903–928.

18. C. Bram Cadsby, Fei Song, and Francis Tapon, "Sorting and Incentive Effects of Pay for Performance: An Experimental Investigation," *Academy of Management Journal* 50 (2007): 387–405.

19. Terence R. Mitchell, "Matching Motivational Strategies with Organizational Contexts," *Research in Organizational Behavior* 19 (1997): 57–149.

20. B. F. Skinner, *Contingencies of Reinforcement* (New York: Appleton-Century-Crofts, 1969); Tim R. V. Davis and Fred Luthans, "A Social Learning Approach to Organizational Behavior," *Academy of Management Review* 5 (1980): 281–291.

21. S. J. Peterson and Fred Luthans, "The Impact of Financial and Nonfinancial Incentives on Business-Unit Outcomes over Time," *Journal of Applied Psychology* 91 (2006): 156–165; Alexander D. Stajkovic and Fred Luthans, "A Meta-Analysis of the Effects of Organizational Behavior Modification on Task Performance, 1975–1995, *Academy of Management Journal* 40 (1997): 1122–1149.

22. Alexander D. Stajkovic and Fred Luthans, "Differential Effects of Incentive Motivators on Work Performance," *Academy of Management Journal* 44 (2001): 580–590; Alexander D. Stajkovic and Fred Luthans, "Behavioral Management and Task Performance in Organizations: Conceptual Background, Meta-Analysis, and Test of Alternative Models," *Personnel Psychology* 56 (2003): 155–194.

23. Edwin A. Locke and Gary P. Latham, *A Theory of Goal Setting and Task Performance* (Englewood Cliffs, NJ: Prentice Hall, 1990).

24. Gary P. Latham and Edwin A. Locke, "Self Regulation through Goal Setting," *Organizational Behavior and Human Decision Processes* 50 (1991): 212–247.

25. Edwin A. Locke and Gary P. Latham, "Building a Practically Useful Theory of Goal Setting and Task Motivation," *American Psychologist* 57 (2002): 707–717.

26. Gary P. Latham, "The Motivational Benefits of Goal Setting," *Academy of Management Executive* 18, no. 4 (2004): 126–129.

27. Edwin A. Locke, "Linking Goals to Monetary Incentives," *Academy of Management Executive* 18, no. 4 (2004): 130–133.

28. J. S. Adams, "Inequity in Social Exchange, in L. Berkowitz (Ed.), *Advances in Experimental Social Psychology*, Vol. 2 (New York: Academic Press, 1965), pp. 267–299.

29. Michael M. Harris, Frederick Anseel, and Filip Lievens, "Keeping Up with the Joneses: A Field Study of the

Relationships among Upward, Lateral, and Downward Comparisons and Pay Level Satisfaction," *Journal of Applied Psychology* 93 (2008): 665–673.

30. Gerald Greenberg, "Employee Theft as a Reaction to Underpayment Inequity: The Hidden Cost of Pay Cuts," *Journal of Applied Psychology* 75 (1990): 561–568.

31. Benjamin Dunford, John Boudreau, and Wendy Boswell, "Out-of-the-Money: The Impact of Underwater Stock Options on Executive Job Search," *Personnel Psychology* 58 (2005): 67–102.

32. Thomas Begley and Cynthia Lee, "The Role of Negative Affectivity in Pay-at-Risk Reactions: A Longitudinal Study," *Journal of Applied Psychology* 90 (2005): 382–388.

33. Margaret L. Williams, Michael A. McDaniel, and Nhung T. Nguyen, "A Meta-Analysis of the Antecedents and Consequences of Pay Level Satisfaction," *Journal of Applied Psychology* 91 (2006): 392–413.

34. Charlie O. Trevor and David L. Wazeter, "A Contingent View of Reactions to Objective Pay Conditions: Interdependence among Pay Structure Characteristics and Pay Relative to Internal and External Referents," *Journal of Applied Psychology* 91 (2006): 1260–1275.

35. G. S. Leventhal, J. Karuza, and W. R. Fry, "Beyond Fairness: A Theory of Social Allocation Preferences," in G. Mikula (Ed.), *Justice and Social Interaction* (New York: Springer-Verlag, 1980), pp. 27–55.

36. Maria P. Miceli, Iljae Jung, Janet P. Near, and David B. Greenberger, "Predictors and Outcomes of Reactions to Pay-for-Performance Plans," *Journal of Applied Psychology* 76 (1991): 508–521.

37. Jason A. Colquitt, Donald E. Conlon, Michael J. Wesson, Christopher O.L.H. Porter, and K. Yee Ng, "Justice at the Millennium: A Meta-Analytic Review of 25 Years of Organizational Justice Research," *Journal of Applied Psychology* 86 (2001): 425–445.

38. Victor H. Vroom, *Work and Motivation* (New York: Wiley 1964).

39. Alexander D. Stajkovic and Fred Luthans, "Self-Efficacy and Work-Related Performance: A Meta-Analysis," *Psychological Bulletin* 124 (1998): 240–261.

40. Greg L. Stewart and Amit K. Nandkeolyar, "Intraindividual Variation in Sales Outcomes: Exploring the Interactive Effects of Personality and Environmental Opportunity," *Personnel Psychology* 59(2006): 307–332; Robert P. Steel and Anthony J. Mento, "Impact of Situational Constraints on Subjective and Objective Criteria of Managerial Job Performance," *Organizational Behavior and Human Decision Processes* 37 (1986): 254–265.

41. E. Fama and M. Jensen, "Separation of Ownership and Control," *Journal of Law and Economics* 26 (1983): 301–325.

42. Kathleen M. Eisenhardt, "Agency Theory: An Assessment and Review," *Academy of Management Review* 14 (1989): 57–73.

43. A. Basu, R. Lai, V. Srinivasan, and R. Staelin, "Salesforce Compensation Plans: An Agency Theoretic Perspective," *Marketing Science* 4 (1985): 267–291.

44. E. L. Deci, R. Koestner, and R. M. Ryan, "A Meta-Analytic Review of Experiments Examining the Effects of Extrinsic Rewards on Intrinsic Motivation," *Psychological Bulletin* 25 (1999): 627–668; Alfie Kohn, "Why Incentive Plans Cannot Work," *Harvard Business Review* (September–October 1993): 54–63.

45. R. Eisenberger and J. Cameron, "Detrimental Effects of Rewards: Reality or Myth?" *American Psychologist* 51 (1996): 1153–1166.

46. Linda Rhoades and Robert Eisenberger, "Perceived Organizational Support: A Review of the Literature," *Journal of Applied Psychology* 87 (2002): 698–714.

47. Edward E. Lawler III, *Strategic Pay: Aligning Organizational Strategies and Pay Systems* (San Francisco: Jossey-Bass, 1990).

48. D. F. Crown and J. G. Rosse, "Yours, Mine, and Ours: Facilitating Group Productivity through the Integration of Individual and Group Goals," *Organizational Behavior and Human Decision Processes* 64 (1995): 138–150; T. R. Mitchell and W. S. Silve, "Individual and Group Goals When Workers Are Interdependent: Effects on Task Strategies and Performance," *Journal of Applied Psychology* 75 (1990): 185–193.

49. www.bls.gov/home.htm

50. Luis R. Gomez-Mejia and David B. Balkin, *Compensation, Organizational Strategy, and Firm Performance* (Cincinnati, OH: South-Western, 1992).

51. Anonymous, "Getting the Most Out of Salary Surveys," *HR Focus* 82, no. 4 (2005): 6–7.

52. Holly Dolezalek, "The 2005 Annual Salary Survey," *Training* 42, no. 10 (2005): 12–23.

53. Gomez-Mejia and Balkin, *Compensation*.

54. www.haygroup.com/ww/Issues/index.asp?id5606

55. Craig Skenes and Brian H. Kleiner, "The Hay System of Compensation," *Management Research News* 26, no. 2–4 (2003): 109–115.

56. Some of the data for these ranges were adapted from Karl E. Reichardt and David L. Schroeder, "2005 Salary Survey," *Strategic Finance* 87, no. 12 (2006): 34–50.

57. Edward E. Lawler III, Strategic Pay: Aligning Organizational *Strategies and Pay Systems* (San Francisco: Jossey-Bass, 1990).

58. Ibid.

59. Ibid.

60. Brian Murray and Barry Gerhart, "An Empirical Analysis of a Skill-Based Pay Program and Plant Performance Outcomes," *Academy of Management Journal* 41 (1998): 68–78.

61. Fred S. Steingold, *The Employer's Legal Handbook* (Berkeley, CA: NOLO, 2000).

62. Susan Faludi, "At Nordstrom Stores, Service Comes First—But at a Big Price," *Wall Street Journal*, February 20, 1990, A1; Stuart Silverstein, "Nordstrom to Change Its Timekeeping Procedures," *Los Angeles Times*, February 24, 1990, D2.

63. http://www.dol.gov/compliance/topics/wages.htm

64. Aparna Joshi, Hui Liao, and Susan E. Jackson, "Cross-level Effects of Workplace Diversity on Sales Performance and Pay," *Academy of Management Journal* 49 (2006): 459–481.

65. Timothy A. Judge and Beth A. Livingston, "Is the Gap More Than Gender? A Longitudinal Analysis of Gender, Gender Role Orientation, and Earnings," *Journal of Applied Psychology* 93 (2008): 994–1012.

Chapter 12
Designing Compensation and Benefit Packages

Garry Wade/Getty Images

A MANAGER'S PERSPECTIVE

TOWANDA DRIVES TOWARD THE CAFÉ WHERE SHE IS MEETING A SMALL GROUP OF SALES REPRESENTATIVES WHOM SHE SUPERVISES. SHOULD SHE ASK THEIR OPINIONS ABOUT THE ISSUES ON HER MIND?

Although Towanda has little experience in human resource management, she has been placed on a task force charged with examining different approaches to compensation. One issue the task force has discussed is employee benefits. Towanda was surprised to learn that almost one third of what the company spends on compensation is used to provide employee benefits such as health insurance. In some ways this doesn't make sense. Why not just pay higher wages and let employees who want things like insurance obtain their own? Towanda thinks that sales representatives might be happier if they received bigger raises and fewer benefits. Most members of the task force, however, feel that the sales representatives place a high value on employee benefits.

Towanda agrees with other members of the task force when it comes to pay for performance.

She feels strongly that sales representatives with higher performance should receive more pay. The problem comes in defining high performance. In the group that she supervises, Towanda can identify two sales representatives who always have top sales numbers. Unfortunately, they also seem to negatively influence the sales figures for other representatives. The top individual performers seldom help others, and they do not service customers unless it is obvious that substantial purchases will result. They have also been accused of stealing clients from other sales representatives.

The task force has discussed a plan to decrease individual incentives and increase team incentives. This plan would place more emphasis on maximizing the overall performance of the sales team and would have the effect of making compensation for all team members more similar. But Towanda wonders whether placing less emphasis on individual compensation will really increase cooperation

> **THE BIG PICTURE** *Effective Organizations Develop Compensation Packages that Align Overall Human Resource Strategy with Incentives*

among team members. If the team-based plan is adopted, will overall sales in her department increase or decrease?

As she reflects on what she has learned about compensation, Towanda is bothered by a proposal to create a service center that helps sales representatives with personal tasks such as dropping off dry cleaning. Should the organization really be expected to take care of personal tasks? Will providing personal services increase motivation or simply create feelings of entitlement?

As she pulls into the parking lot of the café, Towanda sees two of her representatives conversing in the lobby. She trusts both of them, and she definitely wants to make sure they are happy with their compensation. She thus decides to ask their opinions about the benefits and incentives being considered by the task force.

WHAT DO YOU THINK?

Suppose you are in the café and overhear Towanda and the sales representatives discussing compensation. Members of the group make the following statements. Which of the statements do you think are true?

| T or F | Organizations increase the value of over-all compensation by providing benefits such as insurance and retirement plans. |

| T or F | If all members of a team are paid the same amount, some individual team members will not work as hard. |

| T or F | Receiving an annual raise is a key motiva-tor for most employees. |

| T or F | Giving company stock to employees is a poor motivational tool. |

| T or F | Most young people who are just graduat-ing from college are willing to work long hours in boring jobs as long as they receive high wages. |

After reading this chapter you should be able to:

LEARNING OBJECTIVE 1   Describe basic elements of a compensation package.

LEARNING OBJECTIVE 2   Explain different features of base pay and employee benefit plans.

LEARNING OBJECTIVE 3   Explain various types of individual incentives, including the strengths and weaknesses of each form of incentive.

LEARNING OBJECTIVE 4   Explain various types of group and organizational incentives, including the strengths and weaknesses of each form of incentive.

LEARNING OBJECTIVE 5   Create compensation packages that align the mix of individual, group, and organizational incentives with human resource strategy.

How Can a Strategic Compensation Package Make an Organization Effective?

Compensation package
The mix of salary, benefits, and other incentives that employees receive from the organization.

Chapter 11 discussed principles of motivation and described the concepts of pay level and pay structure. In this chapter, we extend these ideas by examining specific components of compensation packages. A **compensation package** represents the mix of rewards employees receive from the organization. Money paid as wages or salary is the largest component of most compensation packages. Some workers are paid a fixed amount for each time period, but for others the amount varies with performance. In these situations, determining the percentage of pay that will depend on performance is an important compensation decision. When pay is linked to performance, another important decision concerns whether the amount paid will depend on individual performance, the performance of a work group, or the performance of the organization as a whole. Still another part of the compensation package is made up of employee benefits such as health insurance and retirement savings, and organizations must decide what proportion of employees' compensation will take this form. In making all these important compensation decisions, as in making decisions about other human resource practices, a key to success is to ensure that the decisions align with organizational strategy.

An example of an organization that aligns compensation practices with competitive business strategy is IKEA, which manufactures and sells Scandinavian furniture at low prices. The company's first showroom opened in Sweden in 1953. Today, IKEA has grown into a global retailer operating in 38 countries. Total sales exceed $35 billion per year.[1]

IKEA's competitive strategy is cost reduction. Ingvar Kamprad, the company founder, was born in a relatively poor province in Sweden. He grew up in a frugal community with limited resources. This upbringing helped shape his entrepreneurial goal to offer functional furniture at very low prices.[2] In fact, the vision for IKEA today is to create a better everyday lifestyle for many by offering a wide range of well-designed, functional products at prices that as many people as possible can afford.[3] The cost-cutting strategy is carried out so effectively that prices on the same products often fall from one year to the next.[4]

IKEA reduces costs by building showrooms where customers serve themselves. Each store is staffed by a limited number of salespeople, who are different from typical furniture salespeople. Instead of using high-pressure sales techniques, associates at IKEA generally stand in the background and seek to be helpful when customers ask them for assistance or when they observe customers needing help. Once they make a purchase, customers are expected to help lift and load furniture, as well as assemble it.[5] These staff reduction practices allow IKEA to hire fewer employees, which reduces payroll costs.

Consistent with the low-cost strategy, most employees at IKEA are paid a relatively low hourly wage. Efforts are made to treat everyone the same. A good example occurred a few years ago when the total dollar value of sales for the entire company on a particular day was split evenly among all employees. All managers and staff members received the same amount.[6] Since employees tend to be treated similarly regardless of performance, few workers make much more than minimum wage. IKEA also minimizes long-term compensation such as stock options. Yet a substantial number of potential workers apply for each open position, and employee turnover is quite low for the industry.[7] So why do employees choose to work at IKEA?

The key to effective compensation at IKEA is benefits. Employees don't generally choose to work at IKEA because they receive high wages. They choose IKEA because they feel that IKEA provides them with an opportunity to balance work with other aspects of life. Employees don't expect to receive cash bonuses. Rather, IKEA retains employees with incentives such as flexible scheduling and generous healthcare plans. Almost the entire expense for health and dental insurance is paid by IKEA. Full medical and dental benefits are offered to part-time employees who work at least 20 hours per week. Once workers have been employed for a year, they become eligible to participate in a retirement savings program where IKEA pays up to 3 percent of salary into a retirement fund.[8] Perhaps most important, employees are allowed to use flextime and job sharing to help them meet family demands.[9] IKEA also tries to provide employees with the opportunity to improve themselves through benefits such as tuition assistance and discounts for weight loss and smoking cessation programs.

Building Strength Through HR

IKEA

Edmund D. Fountain/ ZUMAPRESS.com

IKEA is a global furniture manufacturer and retailer with over 139,000 employees. Human resource management at IKEA builds competitive strength by

- Minimizing labor costs by designing work processes that require fewer employees.
- Developing a compensation package that uses entry-level wages and uniform pay to create a spirit of cooperation.
- Building employee loyalty with employee benefits such as health insurance, retirement savings, and flexible work scheduling.

IKEA thus uses compensation to help attract and retain a specific type of worker. The best employees are not superstar individual performers but rather solid team players. They value frugality and life balance more than high monetary rewards. Interestingly, almost half of IKEA's top earners are women.[10] As a whole, employees appreciate the opportunities offered by IKEA enough that the company is ranked as one of Fortune's "100 Best Companies to Work For." The end result is a workforce of highly committed employees who feel they are valued and treated fairly even though they do not receive extraordinarily high wages. Motivating with benefits rather than high wages is thus a critical aspect of IKEA's strategic effort to reduce cost. The cost reduction strategy has been effective during the recent recession, as IKEA focused on expanding and taking market share from other companies that sell furniture at higher prices.[11]

LEARNING OBJECTIVE 1

How Do Compensation Packages Align with Strategy?

Much of IKEA's success can be traced to alignment between competitive strategy and compensation. Compensation practices help reduce labor costs, which in turn helps IKEA meet its strategy of producing and selling goods at the lowest possible price. However, the practices that best support this low-cost strategy may be very different from the practices that are best for a company pursuing another strategy. A company must carefully consider its strategic objectives when designing a package of wages and benefits. In this section, we discuss elements of strategic design for compensation packages.

AT-RISK COMPENSATION

At-risk pay
Compensation where the amount varies across pay periods depending on performance.

One element of strategic design is the amount of pay to place at risk. **At-risk pay** is compensation that can vary from pay period to pay period. The money is at risk because the employee will not earn it unless performance objectives are met. You can understand the issues associated with at-risk compensation by thinking about two different grading options that a professor might offer students. One option is for students to receive a B grade if they attend all classes and complete all assignments. There is relatively little risk with this option. Simply being in class and doing the work is enough to receive the B grade. The second option is riskier. Students choosing the second option will have all their assignments scored and receive a grade based on performance. Students who perform well will receive a grade higher than B, but those who perform poorly will receive a grade lower than B. Which of the options would you prefer? Would your actions and study habits be the same with both options?

The notion of at-risk pay relates to the motivational theories discussed in Chapter 11. Reinforcement theory and expectancy theory suggest that motivation is higher when at least some pay is at risk. Thus, most students work harder when their assignments are scored and reflected in an overall grade.

Agency theory also suggests that when people bear the risk for outcomes, they want the opportunity to earn higher rewards. In the grading example, students will choose the second option only if there is a chance that they can earn a grade higher than the B that is guaranteed in the first option.

In practice, most compensation packages include some at-risk pay and some guaranteed rewards. The key to aligning compensation and strategy is to determine how much of the compensation to place at risk. On the one hand, organizations pursuing a differentiation strategy generally seek to hire and retain individual high performers. These organizations succeed by encouraging employees to exceed minimum expectations. Organizations can do this, in part, by offering employees strong incentives that place a substantial amount of compensation at risk.[12] Placing a high proportion of pay at risk is thus common for organizations pursuing differentiation strategies. In contrast, organizations with cost leadership strategies, such as IKEA, prefer that employees make consistent contributions. Consistency is encouraged by rewarding employees who loyally complete basic tasks. A relatively low percentage of at-risk pay is thus common for organizations pursuing cost reduction strategies.

LINE OF SIGHT

Another element of strategic compensation packages concerns employees' perceptions of their ability to influence important outcomes. It is important for employees to perceive that their actions truly influence the outcomes used for determining whether they receive a particular reward. In other words, employees' motivation increases when they are rewarded for outcomes that are within their **line of sight**.

Students who have worked on both group and individual assignments have experience with the line of sight concept. Line of sight is clear for individual assignments. Students can see how personal effort on an individual assignment is an important determinant of the grade they receive. The value of working hard is less clear for many group assignments, since the grade is determined by the inputs of many individuals. Students may not be motivated to work hard on group projects unless they feel their inputs will truly influence the overall grade. For any one person, the line of sight is more distant, and therefore less motivating, for group projects.

Like at-risk pay, line of sight has important connections with the motivational theories presented in Chapter 11. Expectancy theory suggests that people are motivated only when they believe their efforts will result in higher performance. Justice theory points out that motivation is higher when people believe that individuals with greater inputs receive better rewards. In the group grade example, these principles suggest that students will not work hard in groups unless they believe that their efforts will influence the final grade and unless they believe that members of the group who contribute more will be recognized with higher individual rewards. Effective compensation packages incorporate the line of sight principle. For example, a consulting firm might offer an accountant a bonus for receiving high ratings from a client where the accountant has been assigned to work. This action makes more sense than offering a bonus for overall corporate sales, as the accountant may be able to do little to influence sales to other clients. We will use the

Line of sight
The extent to which employees can see that their actions influence the outcomes used to determine whether they receive a particular reward.

line of sight concept as we discuss various elements of compensation packages, and particularly as we discuss the relative value of rewarding employees either for individual contributions or for group contributions.

Building Strength Through HR

STRATEGICALLY MANAGING COMPENSATION DURING A RECESSION

A recession forces many companies to rethink their compensation strategies. An increased emphasis on cost reduction increases efforts to reduce labor expense. In the recent past, companies approached the problem of reducing labor cost in different ways. However, the underlying key to making it work was open communication with employees. Here are three specific examples of what small entrepreneurial companies did to alter their compensation practices.

Eight Crossings, a medical and legal transcription company, was pressured into providing services at a lower cost. Historically, the company had paid transcriptionists at an above-the-market rate. However, given that labor cost represents almost the entire operating expenditure, Eight Crossings decided that it needed to reduce the pay of transcriptionists. CEO Patrick Maher determined that even though employees were paid by the amount of work they completed, most transcription jobs included a portion of boilerplate text that did not require as much employee effort. He estimated the boilerplate work to be about 5 percent of each job, which led him to carry out a 5 percent reduction in pay. He carefully explained his reasoning for the change to employees. Employees accepted the pay cut, and many thanked him for preserving their jobs during difficult economic times.

Passageways designs and sells Web-based applications for banks and credit unions. Company owner Paroon Chadha found that many clients were demanding large discounts during the recession. He felt that his sales representatives were too willing to give discounts. When he looked at the compensation plan, he realized that the commission structure made it so that a representative who gave a discount lost much less than the company.

Jetta Productions/David Atkinson/Getty Images

He restructured the plan so that sales representatives earned a higher rate of commission when they did not agree to discounts. The new structure better aligned the representatives' interests with the company's interests. The overall result was significantly fewer discounts, which translated into not only higher company profits but also higher take-home pay for many sales representatives.

Gotham Dream Cars rents luxury sport cars, such as Lamborghinis and Ferraris. As expected, demand for the use of a luxury car decreased when the economy turned bad. CEO Noah Lehmann-Haupt decided that he needed to cut prices and expenses in order to stay in business. To do so he cut his own salary by 40 percent and the salaries of his employees by about 20 percent. Demand for the luxury cars increased a great deal when he offered them at a lower price, and his company was soon back to profitability. Key employees demanded that their pay be returned to where it was before the economic difficulties. They even tendered their resignations unless their pay was restored. After listening carefully to their concerns and considering the cost of hiring new workers, Lehmann-Haupt restored the salaries and looked to other areas for ongoing cost reduction.

Source: Darren Dahl, "The New Rules for Compensation," *Inc.* 31, No. 6 (2009): 91–97.

COMMON ELEMENTS OF COMPENSATION PACKAGES

Compensation packages are best when adapted to fit the unique needs of a specific organization. The "Building Strength Through HR" feature illustrates how three companies altered their pay practices in order to face the challenge of a recession. Each of these approaches was very different depending on the organization's circumstances. Basic elements of compensation, however, are common across organizations. One element is base pay. **Base pay** is a form of compensation that is not at risk and may consist of an hourly wage or an annual salary. As explained in Chapter 11, a certain level of base pay is often required by minimum wage laws. Base pay gives employees a sense of security and provides them with a minimum guaranteed reward for joining an organization. Base pay is not contingent on performance, which makes it relatively ineffective for motivating performance.

Another element of compensation packages that is usually not at risk is the employee benefit package. **Employee benefits**, as we've already seen, are rewards other than salary and wages. Organizations are required by laws and tax regulations to provide similar benefits to all employees. Benefits thus represent an element of compensation that is not at risk. Benefits also represent a form of long-term compensation that builds loyalty and binds employees to an organization. This makes benefits a valuable component of compensation plans for organizations with an internal labor orientation.

One common form of at-risk reward is the individual incentive. An **individual incentive** is a reward that is based on the personal performance of the employee. Individual incentives can easily be linked to performance behaviors and outcomes. These incentives thus have a clear line of sight, which makes them powerful motivators. Yet, individual incentives also have the potential to destroy cooperation among employees. Workers who focus too much on achieving high individual performance often harm the overall performance of the group.[13] Individual incentives must therefore be carefully structured to encourage personal effort without destroying group cooperation. At the individual level, paying people by the hour rather than a salary has also been found to make employees much more conscious of the value of time,[14] which can increase their motivation. Focusing on time can, however, have negative effects such as employees being less willing to volunteer to do tasks for which they are not paid.[15]

Another form of at-risk reward that is common in compensation packages is the group incentive. A **group incentive** is a reward based on the collective performance of a team or organization. Because individual incentives can harm cooperative effort, many organizations use group incentives to focus workers' attention on contributing to the shared goals of the broader group.[16] However, group incentives present their own problems. The main problem occurs when line of sight is so distant that individual workers fail to provide maximum personal effort.[17] Effective group incentives must therefore encourage individuals to contribute maximum personal effort in order to assure the success of the team or organization.

One important decision in constructing the package is how much of overall compensation will be guaranteed and how much will be at risk. Compensation packages with comprehensive benefits and high percentages of base pay place very little of the reward at risk. If a package includes at least some at-risk compensation, then the next critical decision concerns the mix of individual and group

Base pay
Compensation that is consistent across time periods and not directly dependent on performance level.

Employee benefits
Rewards other than salary and wages; typically include things such as retirement savings and insurance.

Individual incentive
A reward that depends on the performance of the individual employee.

Group incentive
A reward that depends on the collective performance of a group of employees.

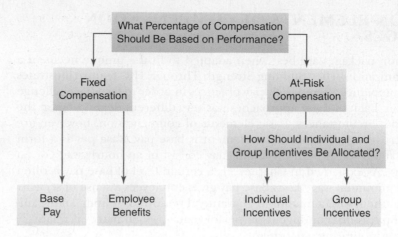

Figure 12.1 Combining Compensation Package Elements.

incentives. Both types of incentive have strengths and weaknesses, and differences in the line of sight must be taken into account to encourage cooperation without diminishing individual motivation. Figure 12.1 captures critical decisions by illustrating how base pay, benefits, individual incentives, and group incentives combine to create an overall compensation package. The following sections describe the four elements of compensation shown in the figure, along with the strengths and weaknesses associated with choices related to each element. Once we have discussed the basic issues associated with each of the four compensation package elements, we will further explore how the elements can be combined to support an overall HR strategy.

CONCEPT CHECK
1. *How do guaranteed and at-risk compensation differ?*
2. *What is meant by the compensation term line of sight?*

LEARNING OBJECTIVE 2

What Are Common Approaches to Base Pay?

As noted earlier, base pay is compensation that is provided for time worked; it is not contingent on performance. Base pay provides employees with stability, because it enables them to plan and budget their personal finances. Some people prefer not to take risks and are therefore attracted to organizations that guarantee them a specific income. From the organization's standpoint, base pay is simple to calculate. In practice, most organizations combine base pay with other incentives. Base pay provides a security net for employees, whereas individual and group incentives provide rewards for high performance.

As explained in our discussion about pay structure in Chapter 11, there are two basic methods for allocating base pay. The first uses job-based analysis.

Each job is evaluated with a point system, and base pay is set at a higher level in jobs worth more points. The second method for allocating base pay uses skill-based analysis. Skill sets are defined in terms of the number of tasks that an employee is capable of performing. Employees who are able to perform more tasks are paid a higher base wage. As explained in Chapter 11, job-based and skill-based methods have different strengths. Job-based methods appear to be less biased and provide employees with higher compensation when the tasks they do require more knowledge and skill. Skill-based methods provide employees incentives to learn new skills.

Regardless which method is chosen, organizations must establish a base pay rate that determines compensation for individual workers. The rate is partially a function of the pay level decision that was discussed in Chapter 11. Organizations with lead-the-market strategies will need to establish a higher compensation level than organizations with lag-the-market strategies. Yet simply establishing a pay level is not the only step in establishing base pay. The overall pay level includes both base pay and incentives. The main question is therefore what percentage of overall pay will be provided as base pay and what percentage as incentive pay. In general, organizations that seek innovation and higher individual performance place a larger percentage of total compensation at risk. Although some companies such as Netflix, which is described in

Building Strength Through HR

NETFLIX

Netflix is a well-known company that rents DVDs through the mail or online. The company has over 2,300 employees and annual revenue of $3.2 billion. Over 26 million people subscribe to Netflix. The company openly advertises that it pays an above average wage. None of the compensation comes in the form of a bonus; it is all guaranteed base pay. The logic behind such a system is that the company only hires top-notch employees who would all earn their bonuses anyway, so why not just fold the bonus into base pay. Employees can take stock options if they desire, but the market value of the options is subtracted from their base pay. There is a health plan, but co-pays are quite high.

Each employee's pay is set according to market, which simply captures what the person could be making elsewhere. An individual's market value is determined by asking (1) what could the employee get elsewhere, (2) what would the company need to pay for someone to replace the employee, and (3) what does the company need to pay to keep the employee? Employees meet with their managers each year and discuss answers to the three questions. The result is a pay level that is not constrained by what others in the company are being paid. Company profits have no immediate effect on an individual's pay.

Consistent with high base pay, the human resource system at Netflix places a great deal of trust in employees. Nobody keeps track of vacation time. Employees frequently refer their friends for positions at Netflix. But what happens when an employee does not meet expectations? Rather than lower his or her pay, the company gives a large severance bonus. CEO Reed Hastings advocates this approach as a way to overcome a manager's guilt for letting someone go. In the end, Netflix has a rather unorthodox approach to employee compensation, but the result is a workforce of highly committed employees who work hard.

Sources: www.netflix.com/jobs; Michelle Conlin, "Netflix: Flex to the Max; Surrounded by Fierce Rivals, Reed Hastings Keeps the Troops Motivated with Hefty Compensation and Luxe Perks, Including Lots of Time Off," *BusinessWeek*, September 24, 2007, p. 72.

the Building Strength Through HR feature go against the grain to use high base pay as part of other strategies, base pay is usually a higher percentage of overall compensation in organizations that pursue Bargain Laborer and Loyal Soldier HR strategies.

CONCEPT CHECK

1. *How do the strategic pay-level concepts of lead-the-market and meet-the-market influence base pay decisions?*
2. *How does the amount of base pay in organizations with a Loyal Soldier HR strategy compare with the amount of base pay in organizations with a Free Agent HR strategy?*

LEARNING OBJECTIVE **3**

What Are Common Employee Benefit Plans?

Common employee benefits include health insurance, retirement savings, and pay without work. Before the 1930s, employee benefits were rare. However, President Franklin D. Roosevelt's New Deal legislation altered tax incentives in ways that encouraged organizations to provide employees with benefits. The overall objective was to increase the likelihood that individuals would receive basic services, such as healthcare. The percentage of total compensation provided through benefits grew steadily until the 1970s, when it reached approximately 25 percent. Over the past 30 years, the growth in benefits has leveled off, and benefits now represent approximately 30 percent of an organization's labor costs.[18]

Favorable tax rules explain most of the trend toward increased employee benefits. Employees must pay taxes on the money they receive as wages and salary, but they are generally not required to pay taxes on the benefits they receive. This means that organizations can use benefits to provide more value to employees. For instance, assume an organization pays an employee a salary of $10,000 per month. If the employee pays a total of 25 percent of this amount in taxes, then the take-home value of the compensation is $7,500. However, suppose the compensation is provided as $3,000 worth of benefits and $7,000 worth of salary. Because benefits are not taxable, the total value of the compensation to the employee increases. With an average tax rate of 25 percent, the additional value for the employee is $750 ($3,000 × 0.25). In addition, the cost of purchasing things like healthcare insurance is usually higher for individuals than for large organizations. Using benefits is thus a way for organizations to provide greater rewards to employees without increasing overall labor costs.

Providing good benefits is an important tool that helps an organization attract and retain high-quality employees.[19] Unfortunately, many organizations fail to obtain the maximum value from employee benefits. Most employees significantly underestimate the amount of money that organizations spend on benefits.[20] Clearly communicating the monetary value of employee benefits is thus an important step toward maximizing the contribution of the benefits package to the overall compensation strategy.

Employee benefits can be placed into two broad categories. One category includes benefits that are required by law. The other category consists of benefits that organizations voluntarily provide to employees.

LEGALLY REQUIRED BENEFITS

Legally required benefits are mandated by government regulations. The regulations are designed to protect people from hardship associated with not being able to work and earn a living. Protection is given to workers who are injured, laid off, or past the age when they might be expected to work. Recent legislation in the form of the Affordable Care Act—often referred to as Obamacare—also requires large organizations to provide healthcare benefits to full-time employees. Because legally required benefits must be given to all workers in specified amounts, it is difficult for an organization to use them to create a workplace that is more attractive than competitors. However, there are ways organizations can use some of these benefits strategically. We explain some of these strategic choices In the following sections as we discuss specific types of benefits.

Social Security

In the early days of the United States, most people lived together in extended families engaged in farming. Families worked together and helped individuals whose age or health prevented them from working. As more people moved into cities, this reliance on families became less common, creating a need for other sources of support for elderly and disabled people. The Great Depression that began in the late 1920s also created severe economic hardship for many people. These needs resulted in the Social Security Act of 1935, which began the establishment of government programs aimed at providing financial security for retired and disabled workers. The Social Security Act created a **social security system** in which workers pay into a fund and then draw from the fund when they retire. With few exceptions, all U.S. workers are required to participate in social security. Approximately 98 percent of U.S. workers are now covered by social security.

Current regulations require both the employee and the organization to contribute 7.65 percent (15.3 percent total) of wages and salary up to a certain amount to the social security fund. Upon retirement, participants in social security receive a monthly payment. The original age of eligibility for receiving social security was 65. A subsequent amendment made people eligible for partial benefits at age 62. Recent changes gradually increased the age of eligibility for full retirement benefits, ending with a full retirement age of 67 for people born in 1960 or later.[21]

Since its creation, social security has been altered so that spouses and dependent children receive benefits if a worker dies before the age of retirement. Spouses and dependent children also continue to receive benefits if the worker dies after beginning to receive social security. A change in 1954 extended benefits to include disability insurance. Individuals who are disabled receive monthly payments similar to those received by retired workers. Other changes during the 1960s created Medicare, which provides health insurance to social security beneficiaries. Social security is thus a mandatory

Social security system
A federal program that requires workers to pay into a retirement fund, from which they will draw when they have reached a certain age.

benefit provided to almost all retired and disabled individuals, as well as to surviving spouses and dependent children. Although the amount of benefit is not adequate to fully support many lifestyles, social security provides many retired workers with at least a minimum level of financial security.

Unemployment Insurance

Unemployment insurance
A network of state-mandated insurance plans that provide monetary assistance to workers who lose their jobs through no fault of their own.

The Social Security Act of 1935 also created incentives for states to provide workers with unemployment insurance. The act created a 3 percent tax on the payroll of organizations with eight or more employees. However, the act allowed the tax to be offset by contributions to state unemployment funds. This resulted in a system wherein each state has an **unemployment insurance** program that provides protection for workers who lose their jobs through no fault of their own.[22]

Although unemployment insurance differs somewhat from state to state, the presence of federal guidelines means that the state programs are highly similar. In general, to qualify for unemployment insurance, an individual must have been employed for a minimum amount of time (usually a year). In addition, the individual must have been discharged from the job for a reason that was outside his or her control. Unemployment insurance is not available to people who quit voluntarily or to people who are fired because of things such as theft or failure to follow organizational rules. In order to continue receiving benefits, individuals must demonstrate that they are actively seeking employment.

People receiving unemployment insurance normally receive a weekly sum equal to half the amount they were paid each week when they were employed. Recipients must file frequent claims that document any earnings or job offers. Unemployment benefits normally last 26 weeks but can be extended when the overall rate of unemployment is high enough to suggest that it is particularly difficult to find a job.[23]

With a few exceptions in states where employees pay a small portion, unemployment insurance is funded entirely by contributions from employers. However, not every employer pays the same percentage. Organizations that have frequent layoffs are assessed a higher rate than organizations that provide stable employment. This provides an incentive that discourages employers from frequently laying off workers. Minimizing employee layoffs is thus one way that an organization can take a strategic approach to legally required benefits.

Workers' Compensation

Workers' compensation
State programs that provide workers and families with compensation for work-related accidents and injuries.

Chapter 3 discussed health and safety issues for workers. As explained in that chapter, all states have **workers' compensation** programs, which provide workers with compensation when they suffer work-related injuries. Because workers' compensation is no-fault insurance, individuals receive benefits even if their own carelessness caused the accident. Workers' compensation provides several specific benefits:

- A percentage of weekly wages is paid to employees during the time when they are unable to work because of the accident.
- Medical expenses and rehabilitation costs are paid to injured workers.
- Money is paid to workers who are permanently disabled, or to families of workers who die because of a work-related accident.

The amount that organizations pay to obtain workers' compensation insurance depends on both the nature of the industry and the accident history of the employer. Organizations engaged in dangerous work, and those that have high accident rates, pay more than those that provide a work environment with little risk of accident or injury. This provides an incentive for organizations to take precautions to protect the safety of workers, which is once again a way for organizations to strategically benefit from legally required benefits.

Healthcare Plans

Until recently healthcare benefits were classified as discretionary. However, in March 2010 the Affordable Care Act was passed to significantly alter healthcare. The overall objective of the legislation was to provide greater access to healthcare. For many employers the effect was to make the provision of a **healthcare plan** legally required. Although healthcare is still not a mandatory benefit for all employees, we will discuss healthcare plans in this section.

Healthcare plan
An insurance plan that provides workers with medical services.

The Affordable Care Act is complex and takes over 2,000 pages to present. There are, nevertheless, a few key issues that affect organizations and employees. For example, beginning in 2010 a benefit that many university students realized is their being able to remain on their parents' health insurance policy until the age of 26. Most of the other provisions phase in over time, with the following benefits being implemented in 2014:

1. All individuals, except those with very low incomes, are required to have health insurance or pay a fine.
2. Companies with more than 50 employees must pay a fine unless they provide health insurance coverage to all full-time employees (implementation of this benefit has been delayed an additional year).
3. Small businesses with fewer than 50 employees receive tax credits when they provide health insurance coverage to their employees.
4. A Health Insurance Marketplace allows individuals and small businesses to purchase health plans through healthcare exchanges.
5. People who are less affluent receive tax credits to help them purchase health insurance, or they receive care through Medicaid.
6. Insurance companies cannot cancel or deny coverage to someone who is ill.

In 2012, approximately 73 percent of workers had access to healthcare benefits through their employer, and over 59 percent were actually enrolled in a health plan. As part of the average benefit plan, the typical organization paid about 80 percent of the cost of healthcare insurance, with the average employee paying about $90 per month for individual coverage and over $350 for family coverage.[24]

Healthcare plans have now become a required benefit, which has benefits in line with those advocated by many companies, given that a majority of company executives believe a good healthcare plan can improve employee health and in turn increases worker productivity.[25] It is instructive, nevertheless, to briefly review the history of health insurance, as well as typical plans that are currently provided.

Many years ago, healthcare plans provided only basic insurance that covered expenses for major medical conditions. For example, healthcare costs might have been paid for an employee with cancer. The purpose of these plans was to protect employees from unexpected costs associated with major medical problems. Over time, these plans evolved to provide coverage not only for major medical conditions but also for routine healthcare. Evolving plans appear to have resulted in increasing healthcare costs. Employees who only pay a portion of the cost often purchase more services than they would if they were required to pay the full cost. Furthermore, patients and doctors have little incentive to control the cost of healthcare, as most of the expense is paid by the insurance company.

Escalating medical costs are a crucial concern of most modern organizations, as healthcare represents the largest benefit cost for most organizations, and recent estimates indicate that the cost of health insurance is growing twice as fast as inflation.[26] Substantial effort has thus gone into finding ways to decrease healthcare costs. One trend to reduce health costs has been the move to **health maintenance organizations (HMOs)**. An HMO is a prepaid health plan with a specific healthcare provider that supplies health services to clients for a fixed rate. Approximately 30 percent of the U.S. population is enrolled in some type of HMO.[27] In most cases, the employer contracts with the HMO to pay a fixed amount per person covered by the plan. Employees who are enrolled in the HMO plan then pay a small fee each time they receive health services. Covered employees must receive their healthcare from providers within the HMO. Because the HMO receives a fixed amount from the organization, it will not benefit from providing extra services. The HMOs thus have an incentive not to recommend or deliver unnecessary care. The downside to such a plan is that employees enrolled in HMOs are required to receive care only from approved providers, resulting in a perception that HMO plans are inflexible. HMOs are also sometimes accused of rationing services so that people do not receive the treatments they need. Many medical providers also refuse to participate in HMOs because they receive a lower rate of reimbursement for services.

A more recent trend in healthcare is to provide employees with **health savings accounts (HSAs)**, which are personal accounts that people use to pay for health services. HSAs represent a new option for funding healthcare that began as part of the Medicare Prescription Drug Improvement and Modernization Act of 2003. Even though the employer may pay into the HSA, it is the employee who establishes and owns the account. An HSA can be set up with a bank, credit union, or insurance company. Money placed into the HSA is not subject to taxes and can be used only to pay for approved medical services. In many ways, HSAs are similar to flexible spending accounts—accounts into which an employer places tax-free money that an employee can use to pay for medical services received. The major difference is that money placed in an employer-sponsored flexible spending account must be spent during the year in which it is saved. With an HSA, the money can be carried over and used in subsequent years.[28]

HSAs are usually combined with high-deductible health insurance plans. A high-deductible insurance plan requires the employee to pay a relatively large sum before the insurance plan pays anything. This helps reduce overspending by providing an incentive to consumers to minimize costs. Government rules allow HSAs to be used when the insurance deductible is between $1,050 and $5,250 for individuals and between $2,100 and $10,500 for families. For example, an organization may provide an individual employee with healthcare insurance that has a deductible of $3,000. Here, the employee must pay the first $3,000 of healthcare expense during a year. The money to pay for these expenses can come from an eligible HSA.[29]

Health maintenance organization (HMO)
A healthcare plan under which the provider receives a fixed amount for providing necessary services to individuals who are enrolled in the plan.

Health savings account (HSA)
A personal savings account that an employee can use to pay healthcare costs.

Some argue that the combination of high-deductible insurance and HSAs could change the way people approach healthcare spending. Employees have an incentive to reduce the amount they spend on healthcare. In a given year, they need not make contributions to their HSAs if the accounts still contain money from the previous year. This means that employees who don't spend their HSA money one year can increase their take-home pay in subsequent years by not having to pay money into the HSA. This helps alleviate the problem of employees paying little attention to the cost of health services. In the end, such plans become more like traditional insurance plans that provide coverage for major medical conditions while individuals pay for routine items such as visits to physicians. Although they are still new, HSA plans are increasing in popularity. Companies such as Walmart and Target are adopting health plans with high-deductible insurance and HSAs.[30] Indeed, recent estimates suggest that over 60 percent of employers are using or planning to use HSAs.[31]

One concern associated with this new trend toward high-deductible insurance plans and HSAs is that people who are generally healthy will move to these plans, leaving only those with severe medical problems in traditional insurance programs. If people who are relatively healthy do not enroll in traditional plans, then the cost per person enrolled in the traditional plan will increase, which in turn is likely to raise the cost of healthcare for people who have severe health problems. In the end, this could make it difficult for people with severe health problems to obtain healthcare.[32]

DISCRETIONARY BENEFITS

Most organizations offer employees a benefit package that extends beyond what is legally required. Offering more than what is legally required provides an opportunity for organizations to use benefits as a tool for attracting and retaining employees. Common discretionary benefits include supplemental insurance, retirement savings, pay without work, and until recently healthcare plans. Figure 12.2 shows the percentage of employees who receive various types of discretionary benefits.

Before discussing the various types of benefits, we should point out that even though they are discretionary, these benefits are subject to government

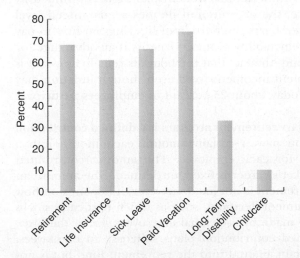

Figure 12.2 Percentage of Workers Receiving Discretionary Benefits.

Qualified benefit plan
A benefit plan that meets federal guidelines so that the organization can provide nontaxable benefits to employees.

Life insurance
A form of insurance that pays benefits to family members or other beneficiaries when an insured person dies.

Disability insurance
A form of insurance that provides benefits to individuals who develop mental or physical conditions that prevent them from working.

Defined benefit plan
A retirement plan under which an organization provides retired individuals with a fixed amount of money each month; the amount is usually based on number of years employed and pay level at retirement.

Vested
Eligible to receive the benefits of a retirement plan; individual employees must often work a certain period of time before such eligibility is granted.

Defined contribution plan
A retirement plan under which the employer and/or the employee contribute to a fund for which only the contributions are defined and benefits vary according to the amount accumulated in the fund at retirement.

regulations. Organizations are not legally required to offer these benefits. However, if they do, they must follow certain guidelines to ensure that good benefits are not being provided only to highly compensated employees. The amount of benefits provided as a percentage of compensation must be the same at the top and bottom of the pay scale.[33] If an organization provides unequal benefits for high-paid and low-paid employees, the benefits will not qualify as tax-exempt compensation, which significantly reduces the value of the benefits. A benefit plan that meets the regulations necessary for tax exemption status is thus known as a **qualified benefit plan**.

Supplemental Insurance

Many employers supplement required benefits with additional types of insurance. The most common supplement is *life insurance*, which is provided to over 50 percent of workers. **Life insurance** pays benefits to families or other beneficiaries when the insured individual dies. Another common supplement is **disability insurance**, which provides benefits to individuals who have physical or mental disabilities that prevent them from being able to work. In most cases, disability insurance pays approximately 60 percent of the person's typical wages.

Retirement Savings

The legally required benefit of social security provides a minimum level of savings for all employees. However, the amount received from social security is not sufficient for most retirees. Many organizations thus supplement the required social security benefit with a discretionary retirement savings plan. Retirement saving programs can be placed into two broad categories: defined benefit plans and defined contribution plans.

A **defined benefit plan** guarantees that when employees retire, they will receive a certain level of income based on factors such as their salary and the number of years they worked for the organization. For instance, an employee who retires after 25 years with the company and who had an average annual salary of $100,000 over the final five years of employment might receive a monthly payment of $2,500. Employees must usually work for the organization for a period of time, such as five years, before they are eligible to participate in the defined benefit program. When they become eligible, they are said to be **vested**. With a defined benefit plan, risk is assumed by the organization. In essence, the organization defines a guaranteed level of monthly payment and then bears the burden of figuring out how to pay it. On the one hand, the predictability of these benefits is an advantage for employees. On the other hand, the fact that the benefits remain constant is also a disadvantage. Retirement income is fixed even though inflation may increase the cost of living. Today, about 25 percent of employees participate in defined benefit plans.[34]

The second type of voluntary retirement program is a **defined contribution plan**. Here, the organization pays a certain amount each month into a retirement savings account for each employee. The amount contributed each month during the worker's career is fixed, or defined. The amount an employee receives upon retirement is not fixed, however; it depends on how the money is invested. Investment decisions, such as which particular stocks and bonds to purchase, are made by individual employees. From the organization's perspective, defined contribution plans shift risk to employees. The organization pays a certain amount into the retirement fund but is not obligated to provide a certain level of income during retirement. Low return rates for investments become the employee's problem. In addition, defined contribution plans require much less paperwork than defined benefit plans. These factors make defined contribution plans more common than defined benefit plans. Nearly 90 percent of organizations with more than 100 employees offer defined contribution plans, and over 40 percent of all employees participate in such plans.[35]

A common form of defined contribution plan is the 401(k), which is named after Section 401(k) of the federal tax code. The 401(k) plan allows employees to set up personal savings accounts to which they make tax-deferred contributions. In most cases, the organization matches employee contributions to the plan. For instance, an employee may invest 3 percent in the savings account, which is matched by the organization providing another 3 percent. The individual decides how to invest the money in the account, and the account grows until retirement. Taxes are paid when money is taken from the account after retirement. As mentioned, this sort of plan places the burden of investment with individual employees. Employees who are willing to put money in riskier investments have the potential to earn higher rates of return. Of course, they also bear the risk of losing a substantial amount of their savings. Thus, employees who participate in defined contribution plans must become more educated about investment decisions. Perhaps the most important lesson for employees is not to invest all their retirement savings in the stock of their employer. Unfortunately, many workers—such as the thousands of Enron employees whose retirement savings were lost when the company went bankrupt—have learned this lesson the hard way.

Young workers often make the mistake of not investing in retirement funds if they are not required to do so. They have a mistaken belief that they can delay retirement savings. However, Figure 12.3 shows that the sooner you start investing in retirement, the better off you will be. Money invested early earns interest for many more years, and the more interest it earns, the faster it grows.

Defined benefit and defined contribution plans result in different perceptions of attachment to an organization. Defined contribution plans are

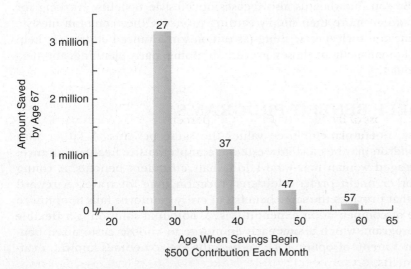

Figure 12.3 Accrual of Retirement Benefits.

highly portable. The employee owns the account, and in most cases leaving an organization has very little impact on the employee's retirement savings. In contrast, defined benefit plans are associated with a particular employer, and savings are not portable. Employees often have to work for a certain period of time before they are eligible for the benefit. These plans are generally structured to reward people who stay with the organization for a long period of time. Although there is a general trend away from defined benefit programs, they make the most sense for organizations with Loyal Soldier and Committed Expert HR strategies.

Pay Without Work

Pay without work Compensation paid for time off, such as holidays.

Pay without work is the most common employee benefit. It involves paying employees as if they worked during a certain period—for example, holidays and vacations—even though they were not actually working. Over 70 percent of employees receive paid holidays and vacations.[36] The number of paid holidays and vacations generally increases with time in the organization, which makes pay without work an important motivator for organizations with Loyal Soldier and Committed Expert HR strategies. Most organizations also provide **sick leave**, which allows employees to receive pay when they cannot work because of illness. In most cases, employees can accrue, or build up, sick leave based on their length of time with the organization. In order to encourage employees not to take sick leave when they do not need it, organizations often allow employees to accrue sick leave over a number of years and to use this accrued sick leave as part of their retirement benefits.

Sick leave Compensation paid to employees who are unable to work because they are ill.

Lifestyle Benefits

Most of the benefits we have discussed so far focus on money. But money is not the most important consideration for many employees. Younger workers in particular are interested in working for organizations that fit their lifestyles. Important lifestyle considerations include being able to do enjoyable work and balancing work responsibilities with other aspects of life, such as family and leisure time. Some organizations emphasize benefits that enhance employees' lifestyles. As described in the "Building Strength Through HR" feature, Burton Snowboards also focuses on lifestyle benefits. Working for Burton is about more than simply earning money. Other common lifestyle benefits include such diverse things as tuition for advanced education, help with weight management classes, grocery shopping, party planning, and flexible schedules.[37]

FLEXIBLE BENEFIT PROGRAMS

Of course, not every employee values the same benefits. A father with young children may be most interested in comprehensive health insurance. A middle-aged woman may want additional retirement benefits. A young single worker might prefer additional vacation time for travel. A reward package that provides the same benefits to every employee fails to optimize the value of compensation expenditures. A potential solution is a **flexible benefit program**, which allows each employee to choose customized benefits from a menu of options. These benefits are sometimes known as cafeteria benefits.

Flexible benefit program, or **cafeteria benefits** A benefit program that allows employees to choose the benefits they want from a list of available benefits.

Most flexible benefit programs provide each employee with an account of dollar credits. A dollar cost is associated with each benefit. Health insurance

Building Strength Through HR

BURTON SNOWBOARDS

Burton Snowboard is a privately held company with 950 global employees with an average age of 30. Burton pursues a competitive strategy of differentiation. Part of this strategy involves hiring top associates to manufacture and sell high-quality snowboards. Young, knowledgeable employees are a valuable asset for satisfying customers. Lifestyle benefits are an important part of the compensation package at Burton. Providing a progressive work atmosphere that allows employees to express their individuality is a key part of Burton's culture—and a feature that attracts workers who know snowboarding. The company philosophy is best captured by a quotation on the company website: "Bringing your dog to the office and skipping work on those epic days when it snows more than two feet are two of the best

benefits of working at Burton. Find your dream job here."

Sources: Jennifer Reingold, "Burton Snowboards," *Fast Company*, September 2006, p. 58; Josh Dean, "It Only Looks Easy," *Inc.*, March 2006, pp. 112–119; Katy Marquardt, "King of the Hill in Snowboards," *US News and World Report*, September 29, 2008; company website at www.burton.com.

might have a value of $400 per month, for example, and dental insurance might have a value of $75. Each employee then uses the allocated dollar credits to purchase benefits he or she wants. Dollars that are not spent cannot be taken as cash, so each employee is encouraged to spend the total allocation. Employees who spend more than their allotment have the extra amount deducted from their wage and salary earnings.

Employees often prefer flexible benefit programs over traditional benefit packages. When the global real estate advisory firm DTZ offered flexible benefits in England, for example, almost half of the 2,000 staff members chose to adjust their benefits. Providing flexible benefits has decreased employee turnover at DTZ.[38] This effect is consistent with other research that shows an increase in employee satisfaction to be associated with flexible benefits.[39] Flexible programs thus provide a strategic method for customizing benefits to maximize the value of benefits for each employee.

CONCEPT CHECK

1. *What are common types of legally required benefits?*
2. *What benefits are provided by workers' compensation?*
3. *How do HMOs and HSAs help control medical care expenses?*
4. *What is the difference between defined contribution and defined benefit retirement plans?*

What Are Common Individual Incentives?

In addition to base pay, most organizations offer at least some incentives to reward high performers. These incentives can be provided to groups or to individuals. In this section, we examine incentives for individual workers. Individual incentives are something almost everyone experiences at a very early age. Clean your room and you can go outside to play. Eat your carrots and you can have a cookie. Don't run in the store and you can get a new toy. These are common incentives that many parents use to motivate the behavior of children.

Rewards in organizations are similar in many ways. Complete the project on time and you will get a bonus. Cooperate with coworkers and you will get a pay raise. Close the sale and you will receive a hefty commission. Each of these incentives is based on personal performance. Individuals who perform the required actions, or obtain the desired outcomes, are rewarded. To be effective, individual incentives should place a portion of compensation at risk and make those rewards dependent on performance, which is consistent with the motivational principle of contingency that we discussed in Chapter 11. Properly designed individual incentives also conform to the notion of line of sight by linking rewards to actions and outcomes that employees believe they can influence. Common individual incentives include piece-rate incentives, commissions, merit pay increases, and merit bonuses.

PIECE-RATE INCENTIVES

Imagine you have been hired to install car stereos. A basic compensation plan might pay you an hourly rate. You would receive the hourly wage regardless of the number of stereos installed. None of your pay would be at risk. Another compensation option is to pay you a set amount for each stereo you install. If you install zero stereos, you earn nothing. All of your pay is at risk. This second option is an example of a **piece-rate incentive**, where employees are paid a fixed amount for each piece of output they produce.

Perhaps the most famous example of an effective piece-rate system is Lincoln Electric. Lincoln manufactures and sells welding equipment. Most employees are paid on a piece-rate system. Each job is rated on skill, required effort, and responsibility. The company then assigns a base wage to each job. The **base wage** is the target compensation for the job, and it is set to be competitive with similar jobs in other organizations located in the same geographic area. Time studies are conducted to determine how many units an average person in each job can produce in an hour. The average number of units produced in an hour is called the **standard rate**. Employees are paid for each unit they produce, so an employee who produces the standard rate of units receives the equivalent of the base wage. An employee who produces more than the standard rate receives the equivalent of a higher hourly wage. An employee who produces fewer units receives the equivalent of a lower hourly wage. Pay is thus contingent on the number of units produced.[40]

Piece-rate incentive systems can be powerful motivators. There is a strong pay-for-performance link. In fact, the strength of motivation with piece-rate

Piece-rate incentive
An individual incentive program in which each employee is paid a certain amount for each piece of output.

Base wage
Target compensation for a job, which is determined in comparison to the wage that similar employees are being paid by other organizations.

Standard rate
The rate of pay that an employee receives for producing an average number of output units.

systems can sometimes create problems. The strong incentive focuses employees' attention and effort on the actions that are rewarded, which means that other important tasks might not get done. Workers may neglect safety practices, for example, and may work so fast that they produce goods of inferior quality. A number of years ago, a national automobile repair chain learned about another potential negative effect of piece-rate incentives. Mechanics were paid a fixed amount for each repair they made. Motivation increased. However, some mechanics also began to recommend repairs that were not really needed. The end result was negative publicity that significantly harmed the repair chain's reputation.

Setting appropriate standards for the base wage rate and standard production rate is difficult. Problems arise when managers and employees disagree about the assumptions used to determine the appropriate standards. In some instances, workers deliberately work slowly when they know the standard rate is being computed. This allows them to easily produce at a rate higher than the standard rate once it has been set. In other instances, companies raise the standard rate when they feel that workers are exceeding the standard rate too much. Such practices destroy trust between managers and employees and often result in decreased motivation.[41]

Piece-rate incentive systems are most effective when the line of sight is such that an individual has sole responsibility for producing a measurable portion of a good or service. This is true at Lincoln Electric, mentioned earlier, where each worker can be given responsibility for a specific component of the overall machine. This clear identification of inputs allows Lincoln not only to clearly establish pay rates but also to track quality defects. Quality problems can be traced to individuals, who must fix the problems without additional pay. These conditions—clearly identifiable work and clear, objective performance measures—are often present in manufacturing facilities that pursue low-cost strategies. Piece-rate incentive systems are therefore most often observed in organizations with either Bargain Laborer or Loyal Solider HR strategies.

COMMISSIONS

Commissions represent a special form of piece-rate compensation that is most often associated with sales. For each sale obtained, a **commission**, or percentage of the total amount received, is paid to the salesperson. Commission rates range from up to 50 percent of the sales total for things like novelty goods to 3 percent for real estate. With a straight commission system, sales representatives are only paid when they generate sales. Alternatively, sales representatives may earn a base salary plus commissions.

From the organization's point of view, commissions offer several advantages. For one thing, they shift some of the risk associated with low sales from the organization to employees. Another advantage comes from the type of person who is attracted to a position with commission pay. People who are aggressive tend to favor commission-based pay, and these are the very people who excel as sales representatives.[42] Commission incentives present potential disadvantages as well. One problem is that people who are paid commissions may tend to think of themselves as free agents with little loyalty to the organization. Turnover can be high if alternative sales jobs are available. Additional problems can arise if the desire to earn commissions drives sales representatives to focus on short-term results. Effort over a number of months to obtain a

Commission
An individual incentive program in which each employee is paid a percentage of the sales revenue that he or she generates.

Technology in HR

ENTERPRISE INCENTIVE MANAGEMENT

Enterprise incentive management (EIM) is a term used to describe computer software that helps organizations manage compensation systems. EIM is configured software, which means that a vendor uses a common platform to develop a partially customized product for each organization. The organization thus gets a customized solution at a relatively reasonable cost.

EIM programs are often Web-based and pull information from a large number of sources. The information is integrated into a series of "dashboard gauges" that summarize performance outcomes for individuals and groups of employees. Individual employees can update their information and obtain real-time summaries of their performance results. The software can be easily updated to change how commission and other incentive forms of compensation are calculated. Organizations can also link incentive systems to strategic goals and objectives.

Substantial resources are being invested in EIM solutions, with expectations of rapid growth. The need for flexible and customer-friendly data management has thus created a new product that is

helping business leaders and human resource professionals make better compensation decisions.

Sources: Ken Sayles, "Enterprise Incentive Management: A Technological Approach," LIMRA's *Market Facts Quarterly* 25, no. 2 (2006): 48–53; Ben Conlin, "Incentive Compensation in the Insurance Industry: Trend and Technologies," *Compensation and Benefits Review* 36, no. 5 (2004): 33–38.

new account may not be immediately rewarded, which may negatively impact long-term results. Sales representatives paid with commissions may also be unwilling to perform activities that do not directly increase sales. From the individual sales representative's perspective, a straight commission system can also present difficulties because income is uneven. Take-home pay can be very high in one month but virtually zero in the next month. Another potential problem is complexity of calculations, which is discussed in the "Technology in HR" feature.

From the employee's point of view, a major advantage of commissions is the fact that the overall level of compensation is usually higher with commissions than with salary. Consistent with agency theory, the employee receives greater rewards for assuming more of the risk of low sales.

One common approach is to combine commissions with a low base salary. The low base salary provides a safety net so that employees such as sales representatives can cover their living expenses when sales are low. This reduces some of the risk. The base compensation is not, however, high enough to sustain their normal standard of living, which provides a strong incentive to perform at a higher level. Because commission-based compensation plans have the effect of creating pay systems where some people receive much higher pay than others, they tend to be most appropriate for organizations that adopt Free Agent and Committed Expert HR strategies.

MERIT PAY INCREASES

Many employees, including university professors, expect an annual pay raise. One purpose of the annual pay raise is to ensure that an individual's salary keeps pace with inflation. The cost of living generally increases each year, and a salary increase is needed so that employees are able to maintain their standard of living. In most organizations, though, employees do not receive equivalent raises. Some receive higher raises than others. Most annual raises contain a **merit pay increase**, which represents an increase in base salary or hourly rate that is linked to performance. Merit pay increases reward employees for ongoing individual contributions. As explained in the "How Do We Know?" feature, there are many potential biases that can create compensation problems.

Merit pay increase
An individual incentive program in which an employee's salary increase is based on performance.

Research suggests that organizations that provide merit pay increases do indeed have higher productivity.[43] Yet, if a reward is going to result in high motivation, it must be seen as being based on performance. This means that merit pay increases work best when there are clear and accurate methods for assessing

How Do We Know?

DOES HOW MUCH YOU MAKE DEPEND ON HOW MUCH YOU WEIGH?

Do people who are overweight make less money than their thinner peers? Is the effect of weight the same for men and women? Timothy Judge and Daniel Cable sought to answer these questions by examining data from two long-term studies. The first study obtained information from 11,340 German workers. The second study captured measures from 12,686 American workers. In both studies workers reported their weight and salaries over a number of years.

The results suggest that wages and salary decline as weight increases for women. The effect is such that additional weight is most harmful for women who were relatively thin. Specifically, a woman 25 pounds below average is expected to make $15,572 more than a woman of average weight, whereas the woman of average weight is predicted to make $13,847 more than a woman 25 pounds

above average. There is thus a wage premium for very thin women. The effect was opposite for men. Men who weighed more had higher salaries.

The Bottom Line. Weight has a negative relationship with earnings for women but a positive relationship for men. The negative effect of additional weight is most pronounced for women who are already below average, meaning that women appear to be rewarded most when they are very thin. Professors Judge and Cable conclude that this effect is consistent with media portrayals of the ideal woman as being unrealistically thin.

Source: Timothy A. Judge and Daniel M. Cable, "When It Comes to Pay, Do the Thin Win? The Effect of Weight on Pay for Men and Women," *Journal of Applied Psychology* 96 (2011): 95-112.

performance. A prerequisite for merit pay is thus a high-quality performance assessment based on the principles discussed in Chapter 8. Performance assessment and compensation are thus specific practices that can work together to create an overall effective approach for human resource management. Indeed, linking raises to performance is critical for merit systems because employees have been found to be happier with their pay raises when they perceive that the raise is a result of their high contribution.[44]

Small differences among merit increases are another concern associated with merit pay increases. The principle of valence, which was discussed in Chapter 11, suggests that people are motivated only if they value the reward being offered. In many organizations, the merit pay increase for a high performer may be only 1 percent higher than the increases for average performers. To be truly motivational, the merit increase needs to be in the 5 to 10 percent range.[45] Unless there is adequate funding to provide meaningful raises, the difference between a high raise and a low raise may simply not have enough valence to motivate higher performance. In the end, small raises can result in little incentive for people receiving a comfortable salary to continue providing maximum contributions to the organization.

An organization's overall human resource strategy is also important in determining the value of merit pay increases. Merit pay increases are designed to recognize ongoing contributions to an organization. Workers become eligible for a pay increase each year they stay employed. Merit pay increases are thus a long-term incentive designed to reward employees who continue to provide quality inputs over extended periods of time. This means that merit pay increase incentives are most common in organizations with a Committed Expert HR strategy.

MERIT BONUSES

Merit bonus
A one-time payment made to an individual for high performance.

A **merit bonus** is a sum of money given to an employee in addition to normal wages. It differs from a merit increase in that a merit pay increase becomes part of the base pay for the next year, whereas a merit bonus does not. In many cases, merit bonuses are given on a fixed schedule, such as at the end of the year. In other cases, bonuses are unplanned and given when high performance is observed. In either case, as you might expect from the discussion of merit pay increases, motivation is maximized when the bonus is clearly tied to specific behaviors and outcomes.

Merit bonuses present a potentially useful alternative to merit pay increases. Think once again of the professor example. Instead of providing an annual salary increase, a university might decide to provide an annual bonus. Now, instead of receiving a salary increase that is guaranteed for future years, the professor will need to earn the bonus again each year. Such an arrangement places more of the salary at risk and clearly communicates an expectation for ongoing high performance.

Current trends suggest that merit bonuses are taking the place of merit raises in more and more organizations. Over the past 10 years, employers have tended to offer slightly lower bonuses, but the number of employees receiving bonuses has increased. For instance, Whirlpool Corporation, which makes household appliances, recently overhauled its entire pay-for-performance system to increase the emphasis on bonuses and decrease the emphasis on raises. Such systems are designed to strengthen perceptions that pay truly depends on performance, which in turn increases motivation.[46]

CONCEPT CHECK

1. *What are some common problems associated with piece-rate incentive systems?*
2. *How is a merit bonus different from a merit pay increase?*

LEARNING OBJECTIVE **5**

What Are Common Group and Organizational Incentives?

Most of us are familiar with group incentives. Think of siblings who are taken out to share a pizza when they work together to clean the house. How about members of a football team who must all run extra sprints because someone makes a mistake? Rewards in many organizations are similarly based on shared behaviors and outcomes.

As described in Chapter 4, work is increasingly being structured around teams rather than individuals. Because providing individual incentives often destroys teamwork, organizations are adopting group-based incentives at an increasing pace. Common group-based incentives include team bonuses and gain-sharing plans. Most businesses also use organizational incentives to encourage employees to develop a sense of ownership in the organization. Common organizational incentives include profit sharing and stock plans.

TEAM BONUSES AND INCENTIVES

In many ways, team incentives are similar to individual incentives. The main difference is that team incentives are linked to the collective performance of groups rather than to the performance of individuals. Rewards are given when the group as a whole demonstrates high performance. Team rewards work best when the size of the group being measured is relatively small, when collective performance can be accurately measured, and when management support for the program is high.[47]

One type of group incentive is the **goal-based team reward**, which provides a payment when a team reaches a specific goal. Following the principles of goal-setting theory that was introduced in Chapter 11, an incentive of this kind provides a team with a specific objective and rewards the team if the objective is achieved. Goal-based team rewards are thus a type of contract in which the organization agrees to provide a reward if the team meets a specific performance objective. Another type of team incentive is the **discretionary team bonus**, which provides payment when high performance is observed. With discretionary rewards, no goal is set to achieve a specific outcome. Managers simply provide a reward whenever they think the team has performed well. The frequency and size of the reward are at the discretion of the manager.[48]

When an award is given to a team, it can be divided among individual team members in two basic ways. One way is to divide it equally among team members. The other is to use some form of individual evaluation and provide higher-performing members with a greater portion of the reward. Each method of division

Goal-based team reward
A group-level incentive provided to members of a team when the team meets or exceeds a specific goal.

Discretionary team bonus
A group-level incentive provided to members of a team when a supervisor observes high collective performance.

Building Strength Through HR

DEERE & COMPANY

Deere & Company—known as John Deere—is an equipment manufacturing and distribution organization with over 55,000 employees and more than $26 billion in annual sales. Until a few years ago, Deere's compensation system focused primarily on individual incentives. Jobs were classified into seven different pay grades, and employees with longer tenure received higher hourly wages. In addition, the company offered piece-rate incentives by paying more to employees who produced above a standard rate. This incentive system discouraged employees from cooperating with each other. The cost of tracking various standards and pay rates was also quite high.

Deere changed its compensation plan to emphasize team rather than individual rewards. Now weekly benchmark standards for output are established for teams rather than individuals. Teams that meet benchmark standards receive a 15 percent bonus. Teams with output below the benchmark are required to absorb two thirds of the efficiency loss, while teams with output

©AP/Wide World Photos

above the benchmark receive two thirds of the cost savings. Products that do not meet quality standards are not included in the output measure used to assess team productivity. This new incentive system helps Deere maximize the collective potential of employees in order to reduce costs and still maintain high quality.

Source: Information from Geoffrey B. Sprinkle and Michael G. Williamson, "The Evolution from Taylorism to Employee Gainsharing: A Case Study Examining John Deere's Continuous Improvement Pay Plan," *Issues in Accounting Education* 19 (2004): 487–503.

has strengths and weaknesses.[49] Giving team members equal shares of the reward builds a sense of unity and teamwork. Indeed, equal allocation among team members seems to be the most common way of dividing team bonuses.[50] This allocation may, however, fail to motivate individuals to put forth their best effort. In contrast, dividing the reward based on performance recognizes high-achieving individuals but may undermine cooperative effort. Determining which individuals are top performers is also difficult. In some cases, team members provide peer assessments. In other cases, an outside observer, such as the supervisor, allocates the bonus. Regardless of who makes the allocation, an accurate appraisal of individual performance is essential when team rewards are divided equally. At any rate, as explained in the "Building Strength Through HR" feature, moving to team incentives often results in performance improvement.

Organizations can also reward employees for the contributions they make to teams. Rather than basing the reward on team performance, this method provides individual incentives for team contribution. In essence, then, this is an individual incentive specifically for people who offer valuable inputs to teams. Team members are rated on scales that measure their contributions to the team, and higher rewards are given to the highest-rated members. The U.S. Army Corps of Engineers Huntsville Center surveyed its employees and found strong support for this approach, which encourages both teamwork and individual effort.[51]

GAINSHARING

Who should reap the benefits when an organization reduces costs and increases production? One answer might be managers and owners. This seems reasonable if managers and owners are responsible for the improvements. But what happens if regular employees take the primary responsibility for improvement? Shouldn't these employees receive some of the reward? The question of sharing financial gains among owners, managers, and regular employees is the central issue of gainsharing. **Gainsharing** occurs when groups of workers receive a portion of the financial return from reducing costs and improving productivity. In essence, gainsharing aligns the interests of workers with the interests of company owners.[52]

As many as 26 percent of U.S. companies use some form of gainsharing.[53] The practice is particularly common in manufacturing organizations, where costs and productivity gains can be objectively measured.[54] In its most basic form, gainsharing establishes a benchmark for productivity. For instance, a tire manufacturer may examine current records and determine that producing a particular tire costs $50. Once this cost has been established, the organization then agrees to share any future cost savings beyond $50 per tire with employees who are part of the manufacturing team. Limiting the gainsharing plan to only those employees who have a direct influence on the particular product is important for maintaining line of sight. After the gainsharing plan has been developed, employees become involved in a participative effort to make production more efficient. In the case of tire production, employees might work together by focusing on such things as reducing the number of defective tires, redesigning work processes, or simply working faster. If the process becomes more efficient, the amount of money saved is split between the organization and employees. A 50–50 split is common.

An example of a gainsharing plan is the compensation practice of a Verizon unit that produces telephone directories. Standards for budgets and production costs are established, and savings are split between the company and employees. Forty-five percent is reinvested in the general funds of the company. Ten percent is placed in an improvement fund specifically targeted for training, equipment, and other improvements that directly advance the telephone directory production process. Thirty-five percent is given back to employees in a quarterly payout. This payout is adjusted for quality of output; it is increased if quality is high and decreased if quality is low and corrections are required. The remaining 10 percent of the gain is saved in a reserve fund that is shared with employees a year later when costs resulting from customers' claims of printing errors in the directories have been determined.[55]

Healthcare is a particular field that has shown increased interest in gainsharing in recent years. The costs of healthcare have been rising at a growing rate, and hospitals have begun to contract to share cost savings with physicians. Initially, the Office of Inspector General of the Department of Health and Human Services argued that such arrangements violated Medicare policies that guard against limiting services to patients. It was thought that offering physicians an incentive to reduce costs would result in lower quality of care. However, more recent decisions from the Office of Inspector General have allowed gainsharing.[56] One example of successful gainsharing in a health setting is PinnacleHealth, a five-hospital system based in Harrisburg, Pennsylvania. The gainsharing program at PinnacleHealth encouraged

Gainsharing
A group-level incentive program that rewards groups of employees for working together to reduce costs and improve productivity.

Table 12.1	*Rules for Gainsharing Success*
Rule	**Explanation**
1. Make sure the payout formula is understood by employees.	Motivation is increased when the rules by which the bonus is calculated are understood.
2. Ensure a high level of employee involvement.	Involvement increases employee commitment and trust.
3. Provide monetary rewards as close to the time of performance as possible.	Motivation is increased when rewards are clearly associated with actions and outcomes.
4. Involve gainsharing specialists who provide valuable recommendations.	Each organizational setting is somewhat different, and expert advice helps tailor the plan to the specific organization.

Source: Information from Matthew H. Roy and Sanjiv S. Dugal, "Using Employee Gainsharing Plans to Improve Organizational Effectiveness," *Benchmarking* 12 (2005): 250–259.

cardiac surgeons to reduce costs through standardizing supplies. The total savings amounted to $1 million, half of which was shared with the surgeons.[57]

Like other forms of incentive compensation, gainsharing is not equally effective for all organizations. Table 12.1 provides a list of issues that increase the likelihood of success for gainsharing programs. In general, gainsharing requires a great deal of cooperation and trust between managers and employees. Chances of success increase when employees are highly involved in developing and carrying out the plan. This makes gainsharing most beneficial in organizations where employees expect to have long careers. Given that gainsharing most frequently occurs in manufacturing settings emphasizing cost reduction, organizations pursuing Loyal Soldier HR strategies seem to be best suited for this type of group incentive.

PROFIT SHARING

Profit sharing
An organization-wide incentive program under which a portion of organizational profits are shared with employees.

Profit sharing occurs when employees receive incentive payments based on overall organizational profits. As many as 70 percent of Fortune 1000 companies participate in some form of profit sharing.[58] In most profit-sharing plans, the publicly reported earnings of an organization are shared with employees. Some organizations share the reward when the profit is reported, whereas others defer payment so that employees receive a share of the profit only if they remain employed for a number of years.

Earlier, we discussed the piece-rate incentives offered by Lincoln Electric. The company also places a large portion—frequently more than half—of company profits in a bonus pool that is shared with employees.[59] Every employee receives a portion of the bonus, but the size of each employee's portion depends in part on individual performance evaluations collected twice each year. In many instances, bonuses at Lincoln Electric can be as much as 50 percent of the piece-rate total.[60]

Profit sharing has the potential to align the interests of employees with the interests of owners. However, a major problem with profit sharing is line of sight. In many organizations, employees simply don't feel that their personal efforts will have an impact on organizational profits. This lack of a perceived link between personal effort and compensation means that profit sharing may not be a strong motivator for average employees. Another potential weakness of profit sharing is that employees come to expect bonuses and are dissatisfied in years when no bonus is available. Employees often express dissatisfaction in years when productivity is down and the bonus is not available. Many do not believe it is fair for their bonuses to be reduced by poor market conditions.[61]

Even though it has limitations, profit sharing can be an important part of an overall compensation package. Sharing profits with employees provides a strong motivator when employees perceive that their individual efforts truly influence overall profits. What about the issue of fit with the organization's human resource strategy? Here, the main concern is the timing of the profit-sharing payout. For organizations pursuing a Free Agent HR strategy, the payout should be made frequently. For organizations pursuing Committed Expert and Loyal Soldier HR strategies, it may make sense to delay the payout as part of a retirement package that builds a long-term bond with employees.

STOCK PLANS

One way to align the interests of employees and owners is by making employees owners. In corporations, this can be done through stock ownership. **Stock plans** transfer corporate stock to individual employees. In some cases, shares of stock are given directly to employees. However, most organizations instead provide **stock options**, which represent the right to buy company stock at a given price on a future date. Most stock options are granted at current stock prices. This means that the stock option has no value unless the stock price increases; after all, anyone can buy the stock at the current price. If the stock price does increase, an employee can buy the stock at the option price and reap a substantial reward. However, if the value of the stock falls below the option price, the employee can simply choose not to purchase the stock. This set of circumstances provides a long-term incentive that links an individual's financial interests with the financial interests of others who own stock.

A number of years ago, stock options were primarily reserved for top executives. However, a majority of Fortune 1000 companies, including PepsiCo and Procter & Gamble, now provide stock plans for regular employees.[62] Top-performing small companies also provide employees with stock plans. For instance, Kyphon—a medical device manufacturer located in Sunnyvale, California—provides its 535 employees with stock options and a 15 percent discount on additional stock purchases. This incentive has helped the company to become known as one of the 25 best medium-sized companies to work for in the United States and has also been credited with helping to produce a 63 percent annual increase in sales.[63]

In addition to stock options, many organizations offer **employee stock ownership plans (ESOPs)**, in which the organization contributes stock shares to a tax-exempt trust that holds and manages the stock for employees. One advantage of ESOPs is favorable tax status, since organizations are allowed to exclude the portion of stock given to employees from taxation.

Although stock plans are increasingly popular and some evidence links their use to improved organizational performance, the extent to which they are effective in actually motivating individual employees is frequenlty questioned. As with profit sharing, an employee's line of sight is often far removed from the organization's stock price. Even though CEOs and other top executives may have a clear line of sight in this area, most employees are not likely

Stock plan
An incentive plan that gives employees company stock, providing the employees with an ownership interest in the organization.

Stock options
Rights to purchase stock at a specified price in the future.

Employee stock ownership plan (ESOP)
A plan under which an organization sets up a trust fund to hold and manage company stock given to employees.

to perceive that their efforts actually influence stock prices. Stock plans are thus not expected to increase motivation for most employees.

Stock plans have other potential problems. In some instances, CEOs have been found to manipulate earnings in order to maximize their personal stock return.[64] Although widely accepted in the United States, stock plans have also met with resistance in other countries such as Germany.[65] From employees' point of view, a potential weakness of stock plans is that employees may have most of their financial investments tied up in the stock of a single company—the one that employs them. Much of their financial security depends on the performance of this company. If the company's stock performs poorly, their financial investments, such as retirement savings, can quickly disappear.

In most cases, stock options make the most sense in organizations with human resource strategies that encourage long-term employment. Stock options that require a waiting period before purchase align the long-term financial interests of employees with the financial interests of the organization. Organizations with Loyal Soldier and Committed Expert HR strategies thus tend to incorporate stock plans into their compensation plans. Organizations with Free Agent HR strategies can also use stock plans to attract high performers, but in this case the period of time between receiving the stock award and owning the stock is usually minimized.

CONCEPT CHECK

1. *How does gainsharing determine the extent of a team's bonus?*
2. *What are some common problems associated with line of sight and organization-level incentives such as profit sharing and ESOPs?*

How Do Strategic Decisions Influence a Compensation Package?

Creating a compensation package requires a number of important decisions. Figure 12.4 provides an overview of these decisions. As with other aspects of human resource management, the first task is to determine the organization's overall competitive strategy. The competitive strategy then drives the broad human resource strategy. Once the human resource strategy is determined, a number of specific compensation decisions are made to align elements of the reward system with strategy. These decisions include setting a pay level and establishing a pay structure. One critical decision is how much at-risk compensation to include in the package. Once the percentage of at-risk pay is determined, specific amounts of compensation must be allotted to base pay, benefits, individual incentives, and group incentives.

The optimal percentage of at-risk compensation depends on overall strategy. Organizations with a competitive strategy of differentiation seek innovation and recognition of top performers. Placing a high percentage of compensation at risk is thus common in organizations pursuing Free Agent or Committed Expert HR strategies. In contrast, organizations with a cost-reduction strategy prefer to pay employees lower overall wages, which is at odds with the need to pay employees more when they assume the risk of receiving less compensation if performance is poor. Organizations with Bargain Laborer and Loyal Soldier HR strategies are therefore likely to have less at-risk compensation.

As explained in Chapter 11, human resource strategy also affects pay-level decisions. Meet-the-market pay-level strategies are most frequently adopted by organizations pursuing Bargain Laborer and Loyal Soldier HR strategies. Organizations with differentiation strategies rely on hiring and retaining highly talented employees. Therefore, Free Agent and Committed Expert HR strategies are more often closely aligned with lead-the-market pay strategies.

Organizations with Bargain Laborer HR strategies tend to compensate their employees mostly in the form of base pay, usually minimum-wage compensation. Yet some organizations with this strategy do use piece-rate incentives that directly link production and labor costs.

Organizations with Loyal Soldier HR strategies also offer base pay as a high percentage of overall compensation, along with incentives that include piece-rate incentives, gainsharing, profit sharing, and stock options. These organizations also include a substantial number of employee benefits in their compensation packages.

The Committed Expert HR strategy fits with higher levels of at-risk compensation. Individual incentives associated with the Committed Expert strategy include commissions and merit pay. Group incentives include profit sharing and stock plans that have fairly long time horizons. In addition, benefits are used to build long-term commitments.

At-risk pay is often highest in organizations with Free Agent HR strategies. These organizations frequently use commission-based pay systems. Many organizations

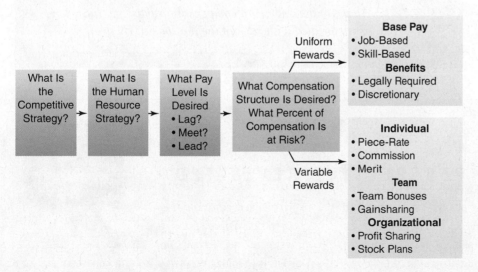

Figure 12.4 Strategic Compensation Process.

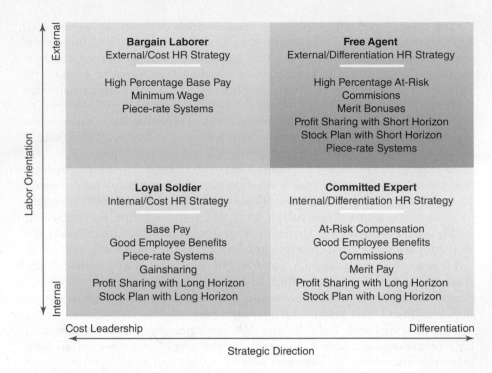

Figure 12.5 Typical Compensation Elements.

with Free Agent HR strategies offer merit bonuses to reward outstanding accomplishments. Profit sharing and stock plans that emphasize near-immediate payouts are also common in these organizations. Figure 12.5 summarizes how different incentive elements align with various human resource strategies.

CONCEPT CHECK

1. *What are some common compensation package characteristics associated with each of the four basic HR strategies?*

A MANAGER'S PERSPECTIVE REVISITED

THE MANAGER'S PERSPECTIVE THAT OPENED THE CHAPTER HAD TOWANDA CONCERNED ABOUT COMPENSATION. SHE WONDERED WHETHER INDIVIDUAL INCENTIVES SHOULD BE REPLACED WITH GROUP INCENTIVES. SHE ALSO THOUGHT ABOUT THE ADVANTAGES AND DISADVANTAGES OF CREATING A SERVICE CENTER TO HELP EMPLOYEES WITH PERSONAL TASKS. FOLLOWING ARE ANSWERS TO THE "WHAT DO YOU THINK?" QUIZ. WERE YOU ABLE TO CORRECTLY IDENTIFY THE TRUE STATEMENTS? CAN YOU DO BETTER NOW?

1. Organizations increase the value of overall compensation by providing benefits such as insurance and retirement plans. TRUE. *Tax incentives allow employers to provide greater total rewards when they include health and retirement benefits.*

2. If all members of a team are paid the same amount, some individual team members will not work as hard. TRUE. *Employees receiving group incentives may not maximize individual efforts. This is a disadvantage of group incentives.*

3. Receiving an annual raise is a key motivator for most employees. FALSE. *Annual raises in most organizations are not motivating because the value of the raise is not large enough to influence behavior.*

4. Giving company stock to employees is a poor motivational tool. TRUE. *For most employees, line of sight is so distant that stock plans do not truly motivate behavior.*

5. Most young people who are just graduating from college are willing to work long hours in boring jobs as long as they receive high wages. FALSE. *Young employees are motivated by a number of alternative rewards, such as interesting work and flexibility.*

Towanda's concern about the value of benefits is well founded. Although organizations can use benefits to provide more value to employees, most organizations do a poor job communicating the cost of benefit plans. Shifting some compensation to group incentives might help Towanda increase cooperation and teamwork. However, eliminating individual incentives will likely decrease individual effort and could have a strong negative impact on overall performance. The best approach for Towanda is to combine current individual incentives with group incentives.

SUMMARY

LEARNING OBJECTIVE 1

How do compensation packages align with strategy?

Compensation packages have four basic elements: base pay, employee benefits, individual incentives, and group incentives. Base pay and benefits foster a sense of security by providing consistent rewards. Individual and group incentives are forms of at-risk compensation that help motivate higher performance.

LEARNING OBJECTIVE 2

What are common approaches to base pay and employee benefit plans?

Base pay can be set according to either job-based analysis or skill-based analysis. Job-based analysis focuses on compensating employees for the tasks they do as part of a particular position. Skill-based analysis focuses on compensating employees for the skills they possess.

LEARNING OBJECTIVE 3

What are common employee benefit plans?

Employee benefits can be either legally required or discretionary. Legally required benefits include social security, unemployment insurance, workers' compensation, and with recent legislation healthcare plans. Because most organizations are required to provide these benefits, organizations generally offer them but gain little competitive advantage for doing so. Discretionary benefits include supplemental insurance, retirement savings, pay without work, and lifestyle benefits. Providing these benefits can be particularly helpful for creating long-term ties with employees.

LEARNING OBJECTIVE **4**

What are common individual incentives?

Individual incentives reward employees for individual contributions. Piece-rate incentives are based on the quantity and quality of output produced by individual employees. Commissions are common for sales representatives and place a high proportion of compensation at risk, creating a strong incentive. Merit pay increases provide raises based on performance, but problems with contingency and the amount of the raise often make merit increases ineffective motivators. In many cases, merit bonuses, which are one-time payments for particular contributions, are more effective than merit pay increases.

LEARNING OBJECTIVE **5**

What are common group and organizational incentives?

Group incentives encourage cooperation and teamwork. Team bonuses and incentives can be offered as rewards when groups of employees achieve specific objectives or when managers observe teams performing especially well. Gainsharing is an increasingly popular incentive that rewards small groups of employees for reducing costs and improving productivity. These programs establish a baseline for performance, and the cost savings of improving upon the baseline are shared between employees and owners.

Profit sharing provides employees with a portion of the organization's financial profits. Some plans share profits almost immediately, whereas others hold the profit until employees have been with the organization for a specified period of time. Stock plans provide an ownership stake for employees. Stock options give employees the opportunity to make future stock purchases at a given level and are a way of rewarding employees when stock prices rise. ESOPs provide tax advantages that encourage employees to collectively purchase company stock. In many cases, profit sharing and stock plans fail to motivate employees because line of sight is too distant for employees to believe their actions really influence the outcomes.

LEARNING OBJECTIVE **6**

How do strategic decisions influence a compensation package?

Creating a compensation package involves making and implementing a number of important decisions. Decision makers must first set the pay level and must then decide how much pay to place at risk. Organizations with differentiation strategies generally place a higher percentage of pay at risk than do organizations with cost reduction strategies. Finally, the organization must decide how much compensation to allocate to base pay, benefits, individual incentives, and group incentives. Specific forms of incentives are most effective when they are aligned with the organization's broad HR strategy.

KEY TERMS

At-risk pay   460
Base pay   463
Base wage   476
Commission   477
Compensation package   458
Defined benefit plan   472
Defined contribution plan   472
Disability insurance   472
Discretionary team bonus   481
Employee benefits   463
Employee stock ownership plan (ESOP)   485
Flexible benefit program, or cafeteria benefits   474

Gainsharing   483
Goal-based team reward   481
Group incentive   463
Healthcare plan   469
Health maintenance organization (HMO)   470
Health savings account (HSA)   470
Individual incentive   463
Life insurance   472
Line of sight   461
Merit bonus   480
Merit pay increase   479
Pay without work   474

DISCUSSION QUESTIONS

1. What are some specific jobs in which you would be comfortable having a high percentage of pay at risk? What are some jobs in which you would prefer having guaranteed pay? What is the difference between the jobs on these two lists?

2. What type of person do you think might be attracted to work in an organization that has relatively low wages but extensive benefits?

3. Do you think social security has benefited or harmed workers? Do you think social security will be available when you retire?

4. Is it a good idea for the government to give tax incentives to organizations for providing employee benefits? Why or why not?

5. What makes piece-rate incentive systems such effective motivators? How does a piece-rate system meet the requirements of expectancy theory?

6. What are some reasons why an organization might use incentives other than commissions to compensate a sales force?

7. What principles of motivation make gainsharing such an effective motivational tool?

8. Why do organizations continue to provide employees with stock plans even though evidence suggests they have only limited effectiveness for motivating most workers?

9. Many news articles discuss high compensation for CEOs. What justification do organizations have for paying CEOs millions of dollars each year? Do you think CEOs are paid too much? Why?

10. What are the specific elements of a compensation package that you would recommend for an organization with a Loyal Soldier HR strategy? What are your recommendations for an organization with a Free Agent HR strategy?

EXAMPLE CASE   *Best Buy*

Linda Herman joined Best Buy as senior manager, executive compensation, knowing that the pace was going to be faster than she was accustomed to at her old job in financial services.

"In retail, you need to be able to turn on a dime," she says.

That's why she shouldn't have been surprised when she came back to work after a long weekend in July to a request, by CEO Brad Anderson, to be more creative with the 2006 long-term incentive program. Specifically, Anderson asked Herman and her staff why the company couldn't offer employees a plan that provided an array of options.

Up until 2003, Best Buy relied primarily on stock options to retain and reward 2,600 managers and executives. But the Minneapolis-based electronics retailer, like many employers, realized that stock options aren't always the best retention tool, particularly during times of market volatility, Herman says. And the company knew that accounting rule changes were looming. The rules have since come to pass, and they require companies to expense options.

With all that in mind, the firm wanted to try alternatives. So in 2003, the retailer replaced its stock option plan with a mix of performance shares, which employees would get if they reach specific performance criteria, and restricted stock, which are grants of shares that vest at the end of a given period if an employee remains on staff.

The final plan, introduced on September 30, 2005, offers participants four choices.

Choice 1 is 100 percent stock options with a four-year vesting schedule and a 10-year life. Choice 2 is 50 percent stock options and 50 percent performance shares, which are based on the company's total shareholder return compared with the S&P 500 over a three-year period.

"The first two choices are catering to people who are willing to roll the dice," Herman says, adding that the payouts are vulnerable to market conditions.

The third and fourth choices are quite different. They are based on "economic value added," a metric devised by Best Buy that uses an internal formula that changes from year to year. They involve the meeting of one-year performance targets, but employees can't access the rewards for three years.

Choice 3 offers 50 percent stock options and 50 percent restricted stock, which is awarded at the end of three years for performance measured against the company's economic-value-added goal at the end of 2007. Choice 4 offers 50 percent restricted stock and 50 percent performance units, both earned at the end of three years, based on company performance against the economic-value-added goal at the end of 2007.

A majority of eligible employees opted for Choice 1 or 2, while only 11 percent took Choice 3 and 2 percent chose Choice 4. Herman attributes this imbalance to the difficulty of explaining economic value added to its employees.

QUESTIONS

1. Why do you think so many of Best Buy executives opted for Choice 1 or 2? What would you do to encourage more employees to adopt Choices 3 and 4?
2. Does this Best Buy compensation program satisfy line of sight requirements? Which of the four choices do you think has the most direct line of sight?
3. What additional compensation elements would you add to the Best Buy compensation package?

Source: Jessica Marquez, "Best Buy Offers Choice in Its Long-Term Incentive Program to Keep the Best and Brightest," *Workforce Management,* April 24, 2006, pp. 42–43.

DISCUSSION CASE   *Collegiate Promotions*

Collegiate Promotions distributes products that are marketed to students and alumni of major universities. High-selling products include coffee mugs and T-shirts that bear collegiate logos. In order to distribute its products, Collegiate Promotions has adopted an independent sales representative model. The sales representatives work for themselves and are not actual employees of Collegiate. They have independent contractor status.

Becoming an independent sales representative is easy. An interested person pays a $300 fee to obtain catalogs and other literature needed to advertise and sell the line of products. The sales representative then begins to write orders for products. A sales representative can sell to anyone through any channel. This means that there are no protected territories, so several sales representatives are often working in the same geographic location. Many representatives also sell through Internet websites.

Collegiate Promotions does not set an absolute price for its products. Instead, it uses a wholesale plus pricing strategy that allows sales representatives to sell within a relatively broad range. The range is normally 30 to 50 percent higher than wholesale. For instance, if the wholesale price of a coffee mug is $10, then the representative can choose to sell the mug at a price anywhere between $13 and $15. The sales representative receives a commission of half the amount charged over the wholesale price. If the mug sells for $13, the representative receives $1.50. If the mug sells for $15, the representative receives $2.50. Because they are independent contractors, the sales representatives receive no other compensation.

QUESTIONS

1. Do you think the compensation system at Collegiate Promotions is effective?
2. Why would a sales representative try to sell at the top of the price range? Why at the bottom of the price range? Do you predict that most sales are made at the top or bottom of the range of possible prices?
3. How does the lack of geographically protected sales areas affect salespersons' behavior?
4. How committed do you think the independent contractors are to Collegiate Promotions? What are some positive features of the independent contractor status for the organization? What might be some positive features for the independent representatives? Would you expect sales representatives to have long-term associations with the company?

EXPERIENTIAL EXERCISE   *Learning Through Interviewing*

Interview two people in different career stages. One person should be recently graduated from college and just beginning a career. The other person should be near retirement age. Try to find out their perceptions about different elements of compensation packages. Use questions such as the following to guide your conversations.

1. What types of compensation do you most value? Do you prefer high base pay and relatively low incentive pay, or do you prefer low base pay with high incentive pay?

2. How important are employee benefits to you? What type of benefits do you value most?
3. Do the compensation practices at your company increase your commitment to the organization? In what ways?
4. Do you prefer incentives to be based on individual performance or group performance?
5. Do you receive any type of company stock? If so, do you think the stock motivates you to work harder?
6. What would you change to make the compensation plan more effective for motivating you?

Using the information obtained from the interviews, do the following:

1. Identify areas in which the perceptions of the person beginning a career are different from the perceptions of the person near retirement.
2. Analyze these differences. Are there consistent differences that might result from the fact that the individuals are in different career stages?

Are there differences that seem more individual and that might result from factors such as personality?

3. Develop a list of specific compensation changes that might be made to increase motivation for each person.
4. Evaluate whether differences in competitive strategies might explain some of the differences suggested by the people you interviewed.

**INTERACTIVE
EXPERIENTIAL EXERCISE**

Is It All about Base Salary? Explaining Compensation Issues at SuperFoods
http://www.wiley.com/college/sc/stewart

Access the companion website to test your knowledge by completing a SuperFoods interactive role-play.

In this exercise, one of the managers at SuperFoods informs you that, at least in her department, the main motivator for the employees is their base salary. The rest of the compensation package, she says, is "just details." She insists that giving the employees in her department big pay increases will make all of them very happy, regardless of the rest of the compensation package. Your solid HR education and your years of diverse experience as a consultant, however, tell you that statement is likely not true, even though the company's HR strategy has always been that of Bargain Laborer. How should you respond to the manager's comments? •

ENDNOTES

1. http://www.ikea.com/ms/sv_SE/pdf/yearly_summary/ys_welcome_inside_2012.pdf
2. http://franchisor.ikea.com/concept.html
3. http://franchisor.ikea.com/
4. Bernadette Casey, "IKEA's Story: Commitment, Charity, Conservation," *DSN Retailing Today* 44, no. 22 (2005): 6.
5. Andy Meisler, "Success Scandinavian Style," *Workforce Management* 83, no. 8 (2004).
6. Christopher Brown-Humes and Peggy Hollinger, "Ikea to Give Staff World's Takings for Day," *Financial Times,* October 8, 1999, p. 2.
7. Meisler, "Success Scandinavian Style."
8. James Lewis, "Furnishing an Ethical RRSP," *Benefits Canada* 2, no. 8 (2004).
9. Meisler, "Success Scandinavian Style."
10. Meisler, "Success Scandinavian Style."
11. Bill Dibenedetto, "Furniture: Built to Last?" *Journal of Commerce,* May 26, 2008.
12. Barry Gerhart and Sara L. Ryncs, *Compensation: Theory, Evidence, and Strategic Implications* (Thousand Oaks, CA: Sage, 2003).
13. A. M. O'Leary-Kelly, J. J. Martocchio, and D. D. Frink. "A Review of the Influence of Group Goals on Group Performances," *Academy of Management Journal* 37 (1994): 1285–1301.
14. Sanford E. DeVoe and Jeffrey Pfeffer, "When Time Is Money: The Effect of Hourly Payment on the Evaluation of Time," *Organizational Behavior and Human Decision Processes* 104 (2007): 1–13.
15. Sanford E. DeVoe and Jeffrey Pfeffer, "Hourly Payment and Volunteering: The Effect of Organizational Practices on Decisions about Time Use," *Academy of Management Journal* 50 (2007): 783–798.
16. D. F. Crown and J. G. Rosse. "Yours, Mine, and Ours: Facilitating Group Productivity through the Integration of Individual and Group Goals," *Organizational Behavior and Human Decision Processes* 64 (1995): 138–150.
17. R. E. Kidwell and N. Bennett, "Employee Propensity to Withhold Effort: A Conceptual Model to Intersect Three Avenues of Research," *Academy of Management Review* 18 (1993): 429–456.
18. *Bureau of Labor Statistics News,* March 2006.
19. Max Messmer, "Benefits: Gain a Competitive Edge with Offerings Employees Want," *Strategic Finance* 88, no. 5 (2007), 8–10.
20. Marie Wilson, Gregory B. Northcraft, and Margaret A. Neale, "The Perceived Value of Fringe Benefits," *Personnel Psychology* 38 (1985): 309–320.
21. A Brief History of Social Security, www.ssa.gov/history/pdf/2005pamphlet.pdf
22. www.ssa.gov/history/pdf/48advise9.pdf
23. www.workforcesecurity.doleta.gov/unemploy/uifactsheet.asp
24. http://bls.gov/ncs/ebs/#bulletin_coverage

25. Fay Hansen, "Currents in Compensation and Benefits," *Compensation and Benefits Review* 38, no. 4 (2006): 6–24.

26. Julie Appleby, "Health Insurance Costs Rise 7.7%, Twice the Rate of Inflation," *USA Today*, September 27, 2006.

27. Gigi M. Alexander, Richard J. Cebula, and Yassaman Saadatmand, "Determinants of the Percent of the Population Enrolled in HMOs," *Journal of American Academy of Business* 9, no. 2 (2006): 32–37.

28. D. Shawn Mauldin and Patricia H. Mounce, "Health Savings Accounts: The New Benefits Plan?" *The CPA Journal* 76, no. 8, (2006): 56–57.

29. John L. Utz, "Health Savings Accounts," *Journal of Pension Planning and Compliance*, 32 no. 3 (2006): 38–98.

30. Vanessa Fuhrmans, "Citing Cost Concerns, More Workers Leave Firms' Health Plans," *Wall Street Journal*, August 25, 2006, p. A9.

31. Hanson, "Currents in Compensation and Benefits."

32. James Schulte Scott, "Let's Talk about Health Savings Accounts," *Healthcare Financial Management* 60, no. 9 (2006): 46–48.

33. Maria M. Sarli, "Nondiscrimination Rules for Qualified Plans: The General Test," *Compensation and Benefits Review* 23, no. 5 (1991): 56–67.

34. http://bls.gov/ncs/ebs/benefits/2012/benefits_retirement.htm

35. http://bls.gov/ncs/ebs/benefits/2012/benefits_retirement.htm

36. http://bls.gov/ncs/ebs/benefits/2012/benefits_retirement.htm

37. Anonymous, "Colorado Hospital Woos Clinicians, Staff with Novel Service that Picks Up Dry Cleaning, Plans Parties," *Healthcare Strategic Management* (February 2006): 11.

38. Anonymous, "Flexible Benefits: A Foundation to Perks Plan," *Employee Benefits Magazine*, September 14, 2006, p. S23.

39. Allison E Barber, Randall B. Dunham, and Roger A. Formisano, "The Impact of Flexible Benefits on Employee Satisfaction: A Field Study," *Personnel Psychology* 45 (1992): 55–75.

40. Gerald D. Klein, "Creating Cultures that Lead to Success: Lincoln Electric, Southwest Airlines, and SAS Institute," *Organizational Dynamics* 41 (2012): 32-43; Kenneth W. Chilton, "Lincoln Electric's Incentive System: Can It Be Transferred Overseas?" *Compensation and Benefits Review* 25 (November–December 1993): 21–30.

41. Thomas B. Wilson, "Is It Time to Eliminate the Piece Rate Incentive System?" *Compensation and Benefits Review* 24 (March/April, 1992): 43–49.

42. Greg L. Stewart, "Reward Structure as a Moderator of the Relationship Between Extraversion and Sales Performance," *Journal of Applied Psychology* 81 (1996): 619–627.

43. Gerhart and Rynes, *Compensation.*

44. John Schaubroeck, Jason D. Shaw, Michelle K. Duffy, and Atul Mitra, "An Under-Met and Over-Met Expectations Model of Employee Reactions to Merit Raises," *Journal of Applied Psychology* 93 (2008): 424–434.

45. Edward E. Lawler III, *Rewarding Excellence: Pay Strategies for the New Economy* (San Francisco: Jossey-Bass, 2000).

46. Erin White, "Employers Increasingly Favor Bonuses to Raises," *Wall Street Journal*, August 28, 2006, p. B3.

47. Todd R. Zenger and C. R. Marshall, "Determinants of Incentive Intensity in Group-Based Rewards," *Academy of Management Journal* 43 (2000): 149–163.

48. Jody R. Hoffman and Steven G. Rogelberg, "A Guide to Team Incentive Systems," *Team Performance Management* 4, no. 1 (1998): 23.

49. Kathryn M. Bartol and Laura L. Hagmann, "Team-Based Pay Plans: A Key to Effective Teamwork," *Compensation and Benefits Review* 24 (November–December 1992): 24–29.

50. Lucy Newton McClurg, "Team Rewards: How Far Have We Come?" *Human Resource Management* 40 (Spring 2001): 73.

51. James M. Cox and Donald D. Tippett, "An Analysis of Team Rewards at the U.S. Army Corps of Engineers Huntsville Center," *Engineering Management Journal* 15, no. 4 (2003): 11–18.

52. Luis R. Gomez-Mejia, Therea M. Welbourne, and Robert M. Wiseman, "The Role of Risk Sharing and Risk Taking Under Gainsharing," *Academy of Management Review* 25 (2000): 492–507.

53. Matthew H. Roy and Sanjib S. Dugal, "Using Employee Gainsharing Plans to Improve Organizational Effectiveness," *Benchmarking* 12 (2005): 250–259.

54. Steven E. Markham, K. Dow Scott, and Beverly L. Little, "National Gainsharing Study: The Importance of Industry Differences," *Compensation and Benefits Review* 24, no. 1, (1992): 34–45.

55. Michael J. Gaudioso, "How a Successful Gainsharing Program Arose from an Old One's Ashes at Bell Atlantic (Now Verizon) Directory Graphics," *Journal of Organizational Excellence* 20 (2000): 11–18.

56. Anjana D. Patel, "Gainsharing: Past, Present, and Future," *Healthcare Financial Management* 60, no. 9 (2006): 124–130.

57. Anonymous, "Hospital System Reports Big Savings on Cardiology Supplies Following Gainsharing Implementation," *Hospital Materials Management* 32 no. 2 (2006): 8.

58. Lawler, *Rewarding Excellence.*

59. Chilton, "Lincoln Electric's Incentive System."

60. Richard M. Hodgetts, "Discussing Incentive Compensation with Donald Hastings of Lincoln Electric," *Compensation and Benefits Review* 29, no. 5 (1997): 60.

61. Arthur M. Cummins, "Business Brief: Saturn Workers Vote to Retain Innovative Labor Pact with GM," *Wall Street Journal*, March 12, 1998, p. 1.

62. Edward E. Lawler, Susan A. Mohrman, and Gerald E. Ledford, Jr., *Strategies for High Performing Organizations: The CEO Report* (San Francisco: Jossey-Bass, 1998).

63. Ann Pomeroy, Adrienne Fox, Terence F. Shea, Leon Rubis, and Patrick Mirza, "50 Best Small & Medium Places to Work," *HRMagazine* 50, no. 7 (2005): 44–65.

64. Xiaomeng Zhang, Kathryn M. Bartol, Ken G. Smith, Michael D. Pfarrer, and Dmitry M. Khanin, "CEOs On The Edge: Earnings Manipulation and Stock-Based Incentive Misalignment," *Academy of Management Journal* 51 (2008): 241–258.

65. Wm. Gerard Sanders and Anja Tuschke, "The Adoption of Institutionally Contested Organizational Practices; The Emergence of Stock Option Pay in Germany," *Academy of Management Journal* 50 (2007): 33–56.

Chapter 13

Working Effectively with Labor

A MANAGER'S PERSPECTIVE

JOSE SENSES A TIGHTENING IN HIS STOMACH AS HE PULLS INTO THE DRIVEWAY LEADING TO THE FURNITURE MANUFACTURING PLANT WHERE HE HAS BEEN EMPLOYED AS A SUPERVISOR FOR THE PAST SIX YEARS. SEEING THE LINE OF WORKERS CARRYING PICKET SIGNS REMINDS HIM THAT THE DAY AHEAD WILL NOT BE EASY. MANY OF THE PEOPLE CARRYING SIGNS ARE PERSONAL FRIENDS WHO BEGAN A LABOR STRIKE LAST WEEK. THE EMPLOYEES HE SUPERVISES ARE MEMBERS OF A LABOR UNION SEEKING INCREASED PAY AND BENEFITS. SO FAR, MANAGEMENT HAS REFUSED TO MEET THE UNION'S DEMANDS, AND THE TWO SIDES ARE STILL FAR APART IN AGREEING ON A NEW LABOR CONTRACT.

As he inches through the picket line, Jose wonders what the plant would be like without the union. He knows that the national trend has been toward fewer and fewer employees being organized into unions. Jose wonders whether the union has really helped improve life for the plant employees. Are they treated better because of the union? Do they make more money? Does the union offer

jacomstephens/iStockphoto

protection from being fired without cause? Is Jose's own situation better or worse because of unions? What would happen if the workers voted to get rid of the union?

Jose parks his car and walks to his office. As he listens to his telephone messages, he is surprised to hear a message from a newspaper reporter who wants to talk to him. The reporter is doing a story about a proposed change to the law that would make it easier to organize unions. Jose's mind quickly races back to his early days with the furniture manufacturer. Line employees had just begun to talk about forming a union. Jose and other supervisors learned about things they were prohibited from saying and doing to resist the union efforts. In the end the employees voted to organize the union. Jose knows that the proposed legal change would make it so that a union would be recognized once a majority of employee had signed

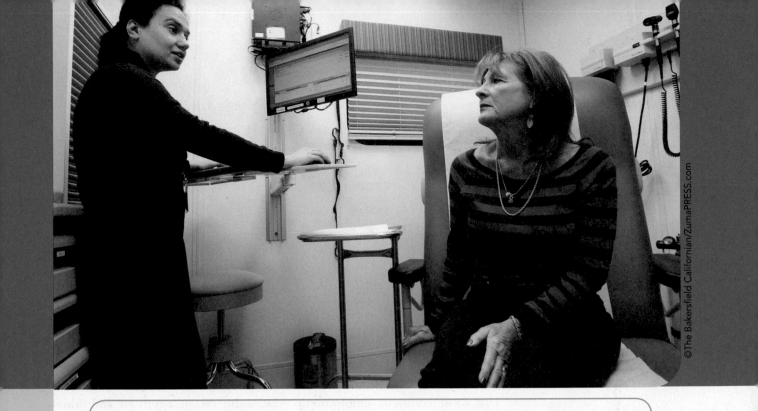

THE BIG PICTURE *Effective Organizations Manage Relationships with Organized Labor Unions to Ensure High Productivity and Fair Treatment of Workers*

cards supporting it, and that elections would no longer be needed. He is uncertain whether this would actually make it easier to form unions.

Thinking about talking to a reporter makes Jose laugh. He has enough problems of his own today. The strike means that few of the employees in his part of the plant will come to work. How will he organize the work processes to get at least something done? He hopes the strike will end quickly. He wonders what is happening in the negotiations. Why do things become so heated and emotional? Shouldn't there be a better way to arrive at a compensation agreement that is fair to both the company and the employees? The day is just beginning, yet Jose looks forward to getting through it and moving on to future days where he will once again work with his friends who are standing in front of the plant holding picket signs.

WHAT DO YOU THINK?

Suppose you are listening to a conversation between Jose and other supervisors at the furniture plant. The following statements are made in the conversation. Which of the statements do you think are true?

| T or F | Workers who are represented by unions usually make more money than workers who are not represented by unions. |

| T or F | Organizations with employees who are represented by a union invest less money in things like equipment and research. |

| T or F | Trends show that fewer and fewer employees in the United States are represented by labor unions. |

| T or F | Threatening to close the plant is an effective method for discouraging employees from voting to join a union. |

| T or F | Because unions advocate for employees during negotiations, businesses should strongly focus on company interests. |

After reading this chapter you should be able to:

LEARNING OBJECTIVE 1   Explain how unions and organized labor fit with human resource strategies.

LEARNING OBJECTIVE 2   Describe the history of organized labor in the United States, and explain how current trends are affecting labor unions.

LEARNING OBJECTIVE 3   Explain the steps that are involved in organizing a labor union, and describe managerial actions that are appropriate responses to unionization efforts.

LEARNING OBJECTIVE 4   Describe the collective bargaining process.

LEARNING OBJECTIVE 5   Explain the employee grievance process.

How Can Good Labor Relations Make an Organization Effective?

Labor union
An organization representing the collective interests of workers.

Labor relations
The dealings that result from interactions between a labor union and an employer.

The most common employment relationship is between an individual employee and a large organization. The large organization, of course, has many more resources and much more power than a single individual employee. Throughout history, this imbalance of power has at times led to abuses. Employees with no other work alternatives have sometimes been forced to accept dangerous work for low pay. Abusive managers have unfairly disciplined workers. In order to gain more power, workers have often joined together to form labor unions. A **labor union** is an organization of workers who work collectively to improve the conditions of their employment. Interactions between employing organizations and labor unions are called **labor relations**. In many—in fact, most—organizations, employees are not organized into labor unions. Nevertheless, the possibility that employees will organize into unions makes effective labor relations an essential part of almost every business operation.

Relationships between unions and employers are often adversarial. Each side focuses on getting what it feels it deserves from the other. Such relationships frequently prevent unions and employers from working together to improve overall productivity and customer service. The end result is that unions may be seen as harmful to overall productivity and organizational success.[1] A few exceptional organizations have, nevertheless, developed cooperative labor relations. Here, managers and union leaders work together to create high-performing organizations. One example of a company with an effective labor relations strategy is Kaiser Permanente.

Kaiser Permanente is the largest managed care organization in the United States. The organization operates hospitals and medical clinics in various states, including California, Hawaii, Washington, and Maryland. Kaiser has annual revenues of $481 billion and employs over 173,000 people in roles that include physician, nurse, pharmacist, and lab technician.[2]

In the mid-1990s, Kaiser was faced with many union demands. Wage cuts and layoffs had created an adversarial relationship between the organization and as many as 33 different national, international, and local labor unions. Rather than continue fighting the various unions, Kaiser formed a cooperative relationship with the American Federation of Labor and Congress of Industrial Organizations (AFL–CIO), which is a federation—or alliance—of labor unions. The cooperative relationship, known as the Labor Management Partnership, represents a vision of union members and managers working together to improve healthcare delivery. A major feature of the program is frequent meetings between top executives and union officials.[3]

The Labor Management Partnership seeks to improve competitive performance by making Kaiser a better place to work. In the early days of the partnership, union and management representatives began working together in bargaining task groups to solve problems. These groups focused on finding ways to increase profits rather than arguing about how the profits would be divided between management and employees. Creative resolutions to problems included such things as giving each union a sum of money that it could allocate among employees as it chose.[4] Inviting the union to participate more fully in such decisions built a stronger sense of ownership in and loyalty to Kaiser. As a result of working together, managers and union members began to trust one another.

Bargaining groups have now evolved into a collective bargaining agreement that covers the employees who belong to the various unions. The agreement covers issues such as wage increases, work scheduling, and worker safety.[5] In many organizations, arriving at a collective bargaining agreement involves argumentative and sometimes lengthy negotiations. Kaiser and its unions avoid this destructive situation by using interest-based negotiation. Rather than staking out claims regarding how money should be distributed, management and unions both present the interests that are important to them. Both sides then work together to find solutions that meet the needs of each side. Important skills for interest-based negotiation include active listening, joint data collection, brainstorming, and facilitative problem solving. Both sides understand that even though their interests sometimes conflict (for example, higher wages might mean less profit to invest in research), they also depend on cooperation to create value that builds a competitive advantage (the ability to deliver quality health services at a good price).[6] Strong leaders on both sides help those they represent understand the need for cooperation. Each side follows through on commitments, building a sense of trust that makes future negotiations easier.[7]

Labor and management work together to reach a new bargaining agreement every three to five years. The latest Labor Management Partnership agreement was formed in 2012 and includes not only pay and benefit issues but also methods for increasing employee engagement and improving overall performance. One example of such innovation is the formation of unit-based teams, which occur in every work unit and include supervisors, union stewards, physicians, dentists, managers, and staff members. Each team is required to work together to create an annual development plan that outlines methods for improvement, as well as metrics to assess performance.[8]

The cooperative atmosphere created by the bargaining agreement helps Kaiser focus on innovations that improve its services. For instance, Kaiser is installing computer terminals in each exam room that can be used to show patients such things as X-rays and trends in health status, which dramatically

Building Strength Through HR

KAISER PERMANENTE

©The Bakersfield Californian/ ZumaPRESS.com

Kaiser Permanente is a health-care delivery organization that operates over 37 hospitals and more than 611 medical office buildings. Human resource management at Kaiser builds competitive strength by

- Adopting a cooperative approach to labor relations that seeks to treat union members as partners rather than adversaries.
- Providing open communication channels so that union members and leaders can make suggestions for improvement.
- Using interest-based negotiation strategies that focus on identifying ways for unions and management to work together to increase profits.

improves patient satisfaction.[9] The company also has a massive database that efficiently tracks patient treatments.[10] Since the cooperative agreement was put into place, workplace injuries have fallen by over 20 percent, employee satisfaction has increased 15 percentage points, and Kaiser has achieved cost savings estimated at over $100 million.[11]

LEARNING OBJECTIVE 1

How Are Labor Relations Strategic?

Not all organizations can be expected to benefit as much from cooperative labor relations as Kaiser Permanente. For one thing, unions are more prevalent in some industries than in others. For another, the benefits of working with a union depend to some extent on an organization's competitive strategy. The effects of union representation on organizational success thus depend on human resource strategy. In general, organizations gain from partnering with unions when their human resource practices have the overall objective of creating a stable workforce where all employees are treated similarly.

A primary objective of unions is to provide job security and long-term employment. In most cases, a powerful labor union makes it difficult for an organization to dismiss workers.[12] Unions encourage organizations to provide training and better develop the specific skills of employees.[13] Such investment can be counterproductive if employees leave to work for competitors. Unions also tend to oppose workers taking on additional responsibility unless they believe that employees have secure, long-term jobs.[14] Unions are thus more compatible with organizations that seek to develop long-term relationships with workers.

Another primary objective of unions is to secure fair wages and benefits for all workers. This practice reduces pay differences between workers with different skill levels. The gap between high- and low-performing employees is thus not as high in unionized organizations as in organizations without unions.[15] Organizations with labor unions also tend to provide more-extensive benefits to a greater number of employees.[16] In short, unions have the effect of creating equality among workers. This means that labor unions fit best with human resource strategies that seek to build solidarity among workers and minimize differences between high and low performers.

Combining differences in terms of employment with differences in equality results in the grid in Figure 13.1. Organizations seeking long-term employment relationships and high levels of equality among workers are most compatible with labor unions. Unions thus seem to be most prevalent, and potentially most beneficial, in organizations pursuing a Loyal Soldier HR strategy. In contrast, unions tend to be incompatible with organizations that combine a desire for short-term relationships with an emphasis on recognizing performance differences. Organizations with a Free Agent HR strategy thus seem to have the most difficulty working cooperatively with labor unions.

As discussed in a previous chapter, an example of the difficulty with a Free Agent HR strategy occurred a few years ago at Nordstrom. The fashion retailer has a competitive strategy of differentiation, which it pursues by providing quality clothing and outstanding, personalized service. Great service comes from hiring high-performing sales representatives who act as entrepreneurs to build personal relationships with customers. The work environment at Nordstrom provides high incentives for top performers. However, some

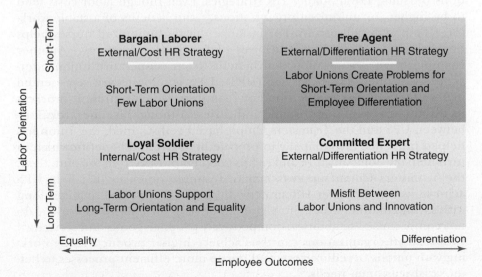

Figure 13.1 Human Resource Strategy and Labor Unions.

Nordstrom employees were covered by the United Food and Commercial Worker Union, and the union asserted that sales representatives were being pressured not to record all hours worked.[17] This meant that the sales representatives were often not receiving hourly compensation for the time that they worked to make deliveries and service the requests of loyal customers. Many representatives were willing to do this because incentives made their overall level of pay higher than that paid by competing retailers. Nevertheless, the union filed complaints of unfair labor practices and forced the company to change some of its timekeeping and compensation practices.[18] The changes made in response to the union complaint minimized some of the variation in pay between high- and low-performing employees and made it more difficult for Nordstrom to carry out its Free Agent HR strategy.

Similarly, the lack of focus on long-term employment relationships makes labor unions somewhat incompatible with Bargain Laborer HR strategies. Employees who expect to be employed for only a short period of time are less likely to form unions.[19] Unions can create problems for organizations pursuing Committed Expert HR strategies as well. Organizations with unionized employees tend to invest less of their profits back into the business, because a higher percentage of the profit goes to employees in the form of higher wages.[20] Unionized organizations generally spend less on constructing new buildings, for example.[21] They also tend to spend less on research and development,[22] which can be a particular problem for organizations seeking to innovate and differentiate products and services. Such reductions in investment may not be universal, as research found that the presence of unions in Germany does not correspond with decreased investment.[23] Nevertheless, evidence suggests that investment decreases with the type of union most frequently organized in the United States. Thus, even though companies using Committed Expert HR strategies emphasize long-term relationships, this strategy is not altogether compatible with unions.

Labor unions do frequently make a positive contribution to organizations pursuing Loyal Soldier HR strategies. Even though labor costs tend to be higher for unionized organizations,[24] the benefits of a stable workforce help maintain quality. For instance, having unionized nurses helps hospitals in California save the lives of heart attack victims.[25] Another example of an organization that benefits from cooperative union interactions is United Parcel Service (UPS). UPS employees are represented by the International Brotherhood of Teamsters, which represents workers in the transportation and freight industries. Although at times, relations between UPS and the Teamsters Union have been strained, the union has helped influence the company to provide high pay and benefits, which in turn help the company hire and retain good employees.[26] In the end, then, the Teamsters Union supports human resource practices that help UPS achieve its Loyal Soldier HR strategy. Because of increased quality, along with savings in other areas, the higher labor rates for unionized workers do not compromise the ability to competitively produce goods and services.[27] Cost-focused organizations can thus achieve higher productivity by working with unions to reduce costs and create more efficient processes to better satisfy customer needs.[28]

Building Strength Through HR

MIDSTATE MEDICAL CENTER

MidState Medical Center is a 156-bed hospital located in central Connecticut that employs 1400 workers. Approximately 30 percent of the employees are nurses who are represented by the National Union of Hospital and Health Care Employees/ AFSCME (American Federation of State, County and Municipal Employees). MidState works with union members to provide excellent healthcare and has been ranked nationally as a "Great Place to Work." Nurse turnover at MidState is less than half the statewide average. Specific actions that help MidState excel with a unionized workforce are the following:

©Hero Images/Corbis

- Top management respects union leaders and seeks to develop a sense of trust.
- Grievances are addressed quickly to resolve employee concerns.
- Cooperative negotiations have included reopening a contract to increase pay when it became apparent that wage rates were lagging behind competitors.

- Nurses are treated as contributing individuals who have access to information and participate in decision making.
- Management meets its obligations to the union but in some instances operates by bypassing the union and directly meeting the needs of employees.

Source: Information from Robert Grossman, "A Tale of Two (Unionized) Companies," *HR Magazine* 50, no. 9 (2005): 70–78; http://www.midstatemedical.org/about_facts.aspx

To sum up, as shown in Figure 13.1, labor unions encourage long-term employment, making their interests most similar to the interests of organizations emphasizing internal labor strategies. Unions also tend to emphasize equal treatment for all, which aligns with efforts to retain quality workers but not star performers. As described in the "Building Strength Through HR" feature, simply having a union can improve how the organization treats employees. Working together with labor unions is therefore most compatible with a Loyal Soldier HR strategy, as mentioned earlier, and least compatible with a Free Agent HR strategy. Nevertheless, as we will illustrate throughout this chapter, the nature of the relationship with the labor union is much more critical than the simple presence—or absence—of the union.

CONCEPT CHECK
1. *Which HR strategy is most compatible with labor unions?*
2. *What problems do labor unions pose for organizations with a Free Agent HR strategy?*

How Has Organized Labor Evolved over Time?

As a student, you may feel powerless to create changes at the institution where you study. Taking concerns or ideas to faculty and administrators doesn't usually lead to change. Complaints and suggestions are frequently seen as the views of a single student who doesn't understand the big picture. However, change efforts can sometimes be effective when students bond together and work as a collective group. Complaints about the fairness of an exam or the need for additional recreational facilities can have a much greater impact when they come from a large group than when they come from a single student. In the workplace, similar attempts to work together and improve working conditions often result in the formation of a labor union.

The rise of labor unions in the United States is a relatively recent event. Until the early 1900s, the court system generally saw employment relationships as private agreements between an employer and an individual laborer. Unfortunately, many large employers took advantage of this relationship and forced employees to work in unsafe conditions for long hours at minimal wages. Gradually, labor unions formed and gained strength, and the federal government responded with laws and regulations that significantly influenced the evolution of organized labor in the United States.

THE INFLUENCE OF GOVERNMENT REGULATIONS

Railway Labor Act (RLA)
A federal law passed in 1926 to regulate relationships between railroad companies and unions.

An early federal law related to labor unions is the **Railway Labor Act (RLA)**, passed in 1926. The RLA regulated relationships between railroads and unions and still regulates labor relations in the railroad and airline industries. The RLA was the first of a series of laws passed to recognize and regulate labor unions. The main pieces of legislation in this series are known by the names of the legislators who sponsored them and include the Wagner Act, the Taft–Hartley Act, and the Landrum–Griffin Act.

Wagner Act

Wagner Act
A federal law passed in 1935 that created the National Labor Relations Board and provided employees with the express right to organize unions; formally known as the National Labor Relations Act.

The most important legislation related to unions is the **Wagner Act**, which is actually titled the National Labor Relations Act. This federal law was passed in 1935 against a background of conflict over union activities that sometimes escalated to physical violence. Union organizers were trying to convince employees to join unions, and management was resisting these attempts vigorously. Congress took an active role in the labor debate by passing the Wagner Act, which has the central purpose of ensuring that employees have the right to participate in labor unions.[29]

The Wagner Act specifically gives employees the right to form and join unions and to assist unions in recruiting members. Employees also have the right to bargain collectively, which usually means electing representatives who bargain for the interests of the group. In addition, employees have the right to collectively refuse to work (i.e., strike), to protest unfair labor practices, and to seek higher economic rewards. When they strike, employees have the right to form picket lines. However, employees engaging in a labor strike cannot physically block access to business plants, threaten violence against nonstriking employees, or attack management representatives.

The Wagner Act prohibits management from engaging in a number of specific actions, which are labeled **unfair labor practices**. Some frequently observed unfair practices are shown in Table 13.1. The bottom line is that businesses cannot punish employees who engage in union activities. Business organizations are also prohibited from dominating or illegally assisting unions. In essence, this provision prevents management from helping to create a weak union that it can easily coerce into complying with management requests. Domination is assumed when the business organization takes an active part in organizing the union, or supports the union financially. In addition, all unions trying to organize workers must have equal access to an organization's employees. It is unfair for the organization to allow representatives of one union to meet with employees on work premises but deny the same privilege to other unions, for example.

Under the Wagner Act, employers are required to bargain with unions in good faith. This does not mean that they must accept union demands. Rather, it means that they must make efforts to work with the union to form an agreement outlining relationships between management and workers. Violations of this requirement occur when management refuses to meet with union representatives to discuss issues or refuses to provide information to the union.

A central feature of the Wagner Act was the creation of the **National Labor Relations Board (NLRB)**, which has the duty of enforcing the Wagner Act. The board consists of five members who are appointed by the president of the United States, subject to Senate approval, to serve five-year terms. The president also appoints a General Counsel. In essence, the General Counsel serves as a prosecutor, and the NLRB serves as the judge. The NLRB has two specific purposes. The first is to organize and oversee employee elections that determine whether a union will be formed in a particular workplace. The second is to investigate allegations of unfair labor practices and to provide remedies, if necessary. Currently, 28 regional offices located in major cities across the country carry out the work of the NLRB and the General Counsel.

The Wagner Act is seen primarily as pro-union legislation. It gives unions a right to organize employees and prohibits businesses from retaliating against employees who become involved in unions. It also requires businesses to bargain with unions in good faith.

Taft–Hartley Act

Labor unions formed at a rapid pace after the Wagner Act became law. However, many business organizations argued that the Wagner Act had shifted power too far toward unions. In 1947, the **Taft–Hartley Act**, formally known

Unfair labor practices
Labor practices on the part of employers or unions that are prohibited by federal law.

National Labor Relations Board (NLRB)
A board of five members appointed by the president of the United States to enforce the Wagner Act.

Taft–Hartley Act
A federal law passed in 1947 that regulates union activities and requires unions to bargain in good faith; formally known as the Labor–Management Relations Act.

Table 13.1	Unfair Labor Practices for Management
Threatening employees with loss of jobs or benefits if they join a union	
Threatening to close a plant if a union is organized	
Questioning employees about union activities or membership	
Spying on union gatherings	
Granting wage increases deliberately timed to discourage employees from forming a union	

as the Labor–Management Relations Act, was passed. Taft–Hartley shifted power back toward management interests by creating a list of unfair labor practices for unions. Some of these practices are listed in Table 13.2. The act prohibits labor unions from coercing employees to join and requires unions, like management, to bargain in good faith. Whereas the Wagner Act created guidelines for elections to organize unions, the Taft–Hartley Act describes procedures for removing a union once it is in existence.

The Taft–Hartley Act makes several union practices illegal. One such practice is the **secondary boycott**, which occurs when a labor union pressures other businesses to stop purchasing goods and services from a business with which the union has a dispute. The act also prohibits "**featherbedding**," which occurs when the union requires a business organization to pay employees wages even though the employees are not performing any services.[30]

Perhaps the most significant issue associated with the Taft–Hartley Act was the prohibition of the closed shop. To clarify this, we need to make the following distinctions:

- A **closed shop** hires only individuals who are members of a particular labor union.
- A **union shop** does not require union membership as a condition of hiring but does require employees to join the union once they are on the job.
- An **agency shop** does not require employees to join the union but requires them to pay service fees to the union.
- An **open shop** does not require employees to have any relationship with the union.

The Taft–Hartley Act specifically made closed shops illegal. In addition, it provided states with the authority to enact right-to-work laws—laws allowing open-shop arrangements. In essence, **right-to-work** laws create open shops where employees are not required to join or contribute to a union. As shown in Figure 13.2, currently, 24 states, including Indiana and Michigan as states passing legislation in 2012, have right-to-work laws.[31] Needless to say, unions are not in favor of right-to-work laws. They argue that unions provide many benefits for employees and that nonunion employees who receive these benefits without paying are getting a "free ride."

The Taft–Hartley Act also created the Federal Mediation and Conciliation Service (FMCS), which is an independent agency of the U.S. government. The agency has the mission of preventing or minimizing the impact of labor disputes. The FMCS cannot enforce laws or regulations but acts as a neutral party and independent mediator. Businesses and unions having difficulty negotiating a labor contract can ask the FMCS for mediation assistance. An important part of mediation is making sure that the parties communicate openly with each other.[32]

Secondary boycott
A boycott by unionized employees that is meant to pressure a company not to purchase goods and services from another company that is engaged in a labor dispute with a union; defined as an unfair labor practice.

Featherbedding
A practice in which a union requires a company to pay employees wages for work that is not performed; defined as an unfair labor practice.

Closed shop
An organization that hires only workers who belong to a certain union.

Union shop
An organization that requires workers to join a union as soon as they are hired.

Agency shop
An organization that requires employees to pay the equivalent of union dues even if they are not union members.

Open shop
An organization that does not require employees to affiliate with or pay dues to the union elected to represent the organization's employees.

Right-to-work laws
State laws that require open-shop labor agreements.

Table 13.2	*Unfair Labor Practices for Labor Unions*
Mass picketing in numbers that physically bar others from entering the plant	
Threatening bodily injury to other employees	
Threatening that employees will lose their jobs unless they support the union	
Entering a contract with an employer when a majority of employees have not chosen the union	
Fining or expelling members for filing unfair labor charges with the NLRB	

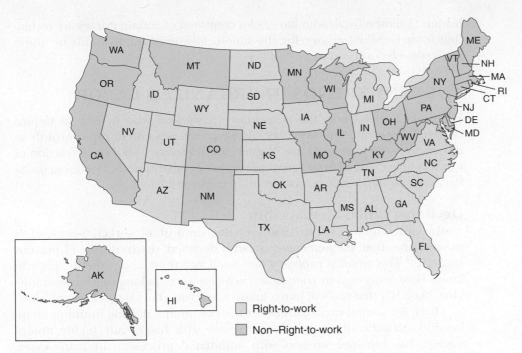

Figure 13.2 Right-to-Work States. *Note: Notice that most states that do not have right-to-work laws are located in the Northeast and on the West Coast.*
Source: Information from National Conference of State Legislatures at http://www.ncsl.org/issues-research/labor/right-to-work-laws-and-bills.aspx.

☐ Right-to-work
☐ Non–Right-to-work

Landrum–Griffin Act

As labor unions continued to grow and gain power, corrupt leadership became a problem in some unions. Union leaders used their power in unethical ways that denied union members simple rights such as the right to elect union representatives. The **Landrum–Griffin Act**, formally known as the Labor–Management Reporting and Disclosure Act, was passed in 1959. This act regulates the internal workings of unions and protects union members from abuse by corrupt leaders.[33]

A major part of the Landrum–Griffin Act is a bill of rights for union members. These rights include the following:

1. All members must have equal rights to nominate and vote for union leaders.
2. The union can only impose fees through democratic procedures.
3. All members must have the right to participate in union meetings.

Union members who feel that their individual rights are being violated by the union must first try to resolve their complaints by working with the union. However, individuals who are not satisfied with a union's responses to their claims can eventually bring lawsuits against the union.

The Landrum–Griffin Act also requires unions to report on several aspects of their inner workings. Unions must file copies of their constitutions and bylaws, for example, and must report their financial activities to the Department of Labor. The act also makes it clear that union funds can be used only for the benefit of the union and not for the benefit of individual

Landrum–Griffin Act
A federal law passed in 1959 to prevent corruption and regulate internal union affairs; formally known as the Labor–Management Reporting and Disclosure Act.

leaders. Union officials who have been convicted of certain crimes are forbidden from handling money for the union. Misuse of union funds by union leaders is a federal crime.

CURRENT TRENDS IN ORGANIZED LABOR

Figure 13.3 shows how the percentage of workers who belong to unions changed between 1950 and 2012. As we previously noted, rapid growth in unions followed passage of the Wagner Act. Yet today, only a small fraction of workers in the United States are represented by labor unions. Declining membership is an important current trend in organized labor.

Declining Union Membership

As shown in Figure 13.3, in 1950 over one third of all workers belonged to unions. After that, the percentage steadily declined, reaching only 11 percent in 2012.[34] This trend is probably obvious if you think about the people you know. How many of your friends and acquaintances belong to a labor union? How likely is it that you will join a union when you graduate and accept a job?

There are several explanations for the continuing decline in union membership. Manufacturing, which is a sector with historically highly unionization, has replaced workers with automated processes. In many cases, organizations have moved their manufacturing facilities to foreign countries where labor costs are lower. Jobs remaining in the United States are those that have not traditionally been unionized. Business organizations have also become increasingly hostile toward unions and more sophisticated at fighting attempts to unionize.[35] All of these factors make it more difficult for unions to organize workers, which in turn has led to the substantial decline of union membership.

Declines in union membership are not consistent across all jobs. The most noticeable difference in union representation is between public- and

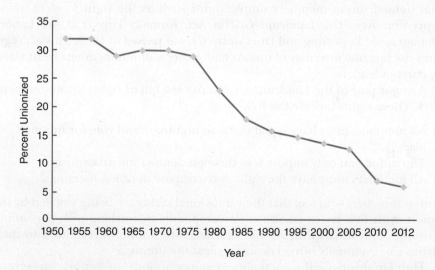

Figure 13.3 Union Membership in the United States 1950–2012.
Sources: Information from Labor Research Association, accessed online at Source: Bureau of Labor Statistics Economic News Release, at http://www.bls.gov/news.release/union2.nr0.htm.

private-sector employees. Figure 13.4 shows that the percentage of unionized employees in the private sector declined from 35 percent in 1950 to about 7 percent in 2012; this drop mirrors the overall decline shown in Figure 13.3. In contrast, the percentage of unionized employees in the public sector grew over the same period. In 2012, about 36 percent of public sector workers were union members. Public-sector jobs with high union representation include teacher, postal worker, bus driver, air traffic controller, police officer, and firefighter.

Unions in the Public Sector

The role of labor unions in the public sector is often quite different from the role of unions in the private sector. The Wagner Act, which created a legitimate role for unions in the private sector, does not apply to most public employees. Instead, public-sector union activity is regulated primarily by the laws of the individual states. Many states limit the right of public-sector employees to engage in strikes. Some states prohibit collective bargaining for public-sector employees.[36] Indeed, the state of Wisconsin recently made newspaper headlines when it passed a law prohibiting public sector workers from collective bargaining.[37]

In spite of the limitations imposed on unions in the public sector, a number of factors support the organizing of public workers. Foremost among these factors is the general desire for voice among public-sector employees. That is, these employees want a communication channel where their ideas and input can be used to improve their work lives. Improving their current work situation is particularly important for public-sector employees, who often have specialized skills that are not easily transferred to other organizations. For example, where would a firefighter work other than in a fire department? Because public-sector employees have fewer alternative jobs, they are more likely to organize unions to improve their current work situation. Furthermore, because they see themselves as public servants, they are less likely to leave their jobs when they feel dissatisfied.

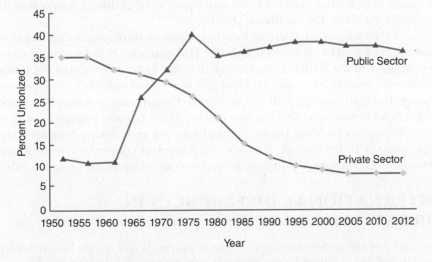

Figure 13.4 Union Membership in U.S. Public and Private Sectors, 1950–2010. *Source:* Bureau of Labor Statistics Economic News Release available at http://www.bls.gov/news.release/union2.nr0.htm.

Another factor is the high profile of many public employees. Citizens are very aware of what, say, firefighters do. Furthermore, they may see themselves as the ultimate employers of firefighters and may be uncomfortable with active efforts to deny them union organization. The result is that public-sector unions experience less resistance. Yet another factor is the exclusive domain of many public-sector endeavors. A school district doesn't face competition in the same way that a global manufacturer does. Differences in labor costs between unionized and nonunionized workers may thus not be a major issue in the public sector.[38] We should note that many public-sector organizations pursue Loyal Soldier HR strategies; given that fact, the high rate of unionization suggests that these organizations match their labor relations strategy to their competitive strategy.

Nevertheless, some trends suggest that public-sector unions are currently facing many of the obstacles that caused the decline of unions in the private sector. Increased pressure to control service costs is pressuring many governments to curtail wage growth. Public sentiment also seems to be shifting toward a less favorable opinion of unions. The example of Wisconsin clearly demonstrates this trend, as a state that has historically been favorable to unions continues to debate the merits of allowing public sector employees to engage in collective bargaining. Also, public services are increasingly becoming privatized. In sum, although the public sector is still more receptive to unions than the private sector, many trends suggest that even unions representing public employees will need to innovate and find additional ways to contribute and grow in the future.[39]

Union Responses to Current Trends

Declines in membership have led unions to rethink many of their strategies. In order for unions to continue, they must find new ways of attracting and retaining members. In order to do this, many unions are focusing on organizing part-time and professional workers. For example, medical doctors are increasingly becoming interested in joining labor unions. Unions have also made greater efforts to organize historically disadvantaged workers, such as employees who work in temporary jobs that may last only a single day.[40] An example of potential benefits from unionization of childcare workers is discussed in the "How Do We Know?" feature.

Union responses to current trends suggest that organizations pursuing Committed Expert and Bargain Laborer HR strategies may face more union organization in the future. Nevertheless, in order to be successful in the future, unions will need to innovate. Much of this innovation will likely require more cooperative relationships with organizations. Union leaders must also balance their efforts to not only meet the needs of members but also engage in external activities such as building public political support and making long-term strategic plans.[41] Today though, strategic planning and cooperative relationships between organizations and unions are still the exception rather than the rule.[42]

INTERNATIONAL DIFFERENCES IN ORGANIZED LABOR

Another key for understanding the role of unions is to explore how unions in the United States differ from unions in other countries. Would you be more likely to join a union if you lived in a country other than the United States? Are unions in other countries the same as U.S. unions? Unionization around the world will become increasingly relevant for U.S. organizations as globalization continues and more and more U.S. companies establish workplaces abroad.

How Do We Know?

CAN UNIONS MAKE LIFE BETTER FOR CHILDCARE WORKERS?

Some observers wonder what unions contribute to society today. Do unions really make things better for employees? Or do they make things worse—for example, increasing wages to the point where employers replace union workers with nonunion workers? Gordon Cleveland, Morley Gunderson, and Douglas Hyatt sought answers to these questions. They conducted a survey of 2,062 workers in licensed group childcare centers in Canada. They compared work-life characteristics and rewards for unionized and nonunionized workers.

Childcare workers who were members of a labor union received wages that were 15 percent higher on average than workers who did not belong to unions. They also received better benefits, such as paid vacations and job protection for parental leave. Providers with better qualifications and more skills received higher pay regardless of whether they were members of a union.

The Bottom Line. Unionization in the childcare industry can improve working conditions and provide greater economic rewards for employees. The demand for childcare is sufficient that many consumers appear willing to pay a higher wage rate to union members. The authors conclude that childcare workers represent a group of historically low-paid employees who should respond positively to union organizing attempts.

Source: Gordon Cleveland, Morley Gunderson, and Douglas Hyatt, "Union Effects in Low-Wage Services: Evidence from Canadian Childcare," *Industrial Relations* 41 (2002): 110–158.

Union Membership Around the World

Table 13.3 shows the percentage of the workforce organized into labor unions, as well as trends in union membership, for a number of countries. The overall percentage ranges from a high of 78 percent in Sweden to a low of 8 percent in France. As you can see, the 12 percent figure for the United States is lower than the percentages for many other countries. Looking at the third column, you can see that the overall percentage of workers organized into labor unions is generally declining throughout the world. The largest decline over the past 35 years was in New Zealand, with consistent declines occurring in Australia, Japan, Ireland, and Austria. The prevalence of unions has substantially increased in Finland, Belgium, Denmark, and Sweden.[43]

Differences Among Countries

Labor unions in the United States have the overall goal of increasing the economic well-being of workers. U.S. unions thus tend to focus on what are known as "bread-and-butter" issues, such as wages, benefits, and job security. The system of unions is modeled after the court system, with both unions and management striving to represent the rights of their constituents. Although unions in the United States often support specific political candidates, political activism is not their primary purpose. They simply favor candidates who advance their interests in securing economic benefits for laborers.

Unions in some countries are similar to unions in the United States, but unions in other countries are very different. There are two major dimensions on which unions differ.[44] One way unions differ is in their focus on economic

Table 13.3	*Unions Around the World*	
Country	**Percent Unionized**	**Percent Change Since 1970**
United States	12	−11
Canada	28	−7
Australia	23	−27
New Zealand	22	−33
Japan	20	−15
South Korea	11	−2
Germany	23	−10
France	8	−13
Italy	34	−3
United Kingdom	29	−16
Ireland	35	−18
Finland	74	+23
Sweden	78	+10
Norway	53	−4
Denmark	70	+10
Netherlands	22	−14
Belgium	55	+13
Spain	16	+3
Switzerland	18	−11
Austria	35	−27

Source: From Jelle Visser, "Union Membership Statistics in 24 Countries," *Monthly Labor Review*, January 2006.

interests. Unions in some countries are organized with the primary purpose of increasing the wealth of the employees they represent. As we've already mentioned, U.S. unions fall into this category. Unions in other countries place only limited emphasis on advancing employees' financial interests. A second way unions vary across countries is in their focus on political activities. Unions in many European nations are closely aligned with political parties. A good example is the United Kingdom, where the Labour Party represents a specific political orientation. The main emphasis of affiliated unions is promoting a social agenda that advances the broad interests of workers. Increased wages and benefits are not the primary focus of many union activities. Figure 13.5 summarizes these two dimensions.

Unions in some countries emphasize both economic and political perspectives. In Sweden, for example, labor unions not only represent a major political force but also advance the economic interests of workers. Labor union power is centralized, and strong national unions work closely with government to establish wage rates across entire industries.[45] This combination seems to work well for ensuring the place of unions. As shown in Table 13.3, Sweden has not only a relatively high percentage of workers organized into unions but also positive growth trends in unionization. Current trends, then, seem to suggest that unions have their strongest impact when they combine the economic and political approaches.

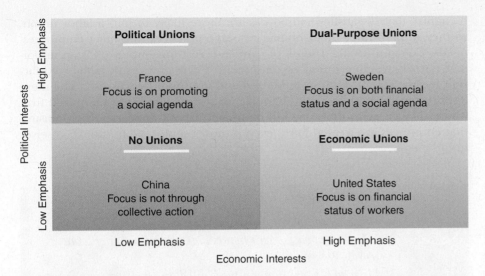

Figure 13.5 Points of Emphasis for Unions. *Source:* Information from Joseph Ofori-Dankwa, "Murray and Reshef Revisited: Toward a Typology/Theory of Paradigms of National Trade Union Movements," *Academy of Management Review* 18 (1993): 269–292.

The greater acceptance of unions in many foreign countries may affect the United States as businesses become more global. As an example, consider companies headquartered in other countries that have subsidiaries in the United States. In such cases, organizational leaders in countries with opinions more favorable to unions may pressure management in the U.S. subsidiaries to allow and even encourage union organization. These foreign executives can actually be important allies for union organizers.[46]

THE EFFECT OF LABOR UNIONS ON NONUNION WORKERS

Only a small percentage of the U.S. workforce is organized into labor unions, but most employees benefit from the existence of unions. Evidence shows that unionized workers have higher salaries than nonunionized workers performing similar jobs.[47] Union employees working for organizations that are acquired by nonunion organizations lose as much as 8 percent of their annual earnings.[48] In many cases unionized workers also report increased job security and autonomy.[49] However, unionization can also increase wages and improve working conditions for nonunionized workers.

The relatively high prevalence of unions in the public sector has helped increase wages for all employees, for example, even for employees who are not represented by a union.[50] Furthermore, industries with a higher percentage of workers who are union members tend to pay their nonunion employees higher wages than they would earn in nonunionized industries.[51] Thus, the overall effect of unions is to transfer a larger portion of profits from owners to employees, even when employees are not organized into unions. The threat of having employees join a union is sufficient to increase wages.

The threat of unionization also appears to improve working conditions. Many organizations pursue a strategy of union avoidance. These organizations recognize that dissatisfied employees are more likely to join a labor union, so they work to implement human resource practices that meet employees' needs. Communicating a sense of care and trust for employees is an important part of avoiding union establishment.[52] The end result is that satisfaction may be equally high in unionized and nonunionized firms.[53] The mere opportunity for employees to unionize, or to leave to join a unionized firm where they perceive that they will be treated better, appears to help ensure that employees are treated fairly, even if those employees are not themselves union members.

CONCEPT CHECK

1. *What major laws regulate labor unions?*
2. *What are some current trends that are influencing labor unions?*
3. *How do labor unions in the United States differ from labor unions in other parts of the world?*

LEARNING OBJECTIVE **3**

How Do Workers Become Part of a Union?

Suppose you want to organize employees where you work into a labor union. What would you need to do? Would all employees be required to join the union? What if a few didn't want to have the union? Could organizational leaders try to convince employees not to organize a union? We address these questions next.

UNION ORGANIZING CAMPAIGNS

The Wagner Act established procedures for organizing workers into labor unions, and the NLRB oversees such efforts. This legislation provided unions with legitimacy and created a way for government to oversee the fairness of union organization efforts. The general procedure for organizing a labor union begins with a campaign to determine whether employees have sufficient interest in forming a union. If they do, an election is held to determine whether a majority of workers want the union. Although lawmakers have recently debated changes to the process, the steps for organizing a union are shown in Figure 13.6.[54]

Authorization Card Campaign

Authorization card campaign
A campaign in which employees or labor union representatives seek signatures from employees requesting a vote on union representation.

The first step in organizing a union is to demonstrate that a sufficient number of employees are interested in joining. This is done through an **authorization card campaign**, in which employees sign cards stating that they wish to hold a secret-ballot election to determine whether a union will be formed. Signature sheets can be used in place of cards. Signing an authorization card or sheet does not necessarily mean that an employee supports the union. The signature just means that the employee supports holding an election. The meaning of the card campaign is, nevertheless, the key focus of many proposed changes to the union certification process. Over the past few years, legislators have introduced bills that would essentially forgo (forego = go before) elections and recognize unions once a majority of workers have signed authorization cards. This is widely seen as a method of making it easier to organize unions, yet research suggests this may not be true, as workers might be less likely to sign cards if they know that the outcome might be actual adoption of the union rather than just an election.[55]

An authorization card campaign can be initiated by current employees or by an existing union that is seeking to represent the employees at the particular workplace. For instance, the United Auto Workers might initiate a card campaign to organize employees at an automobile parts manufacturing plant, or the employees themselves might initiate the campaign. In either case, the cards must identify a specific union, and if an election is held, that election asks whether that particular union should represent the employees.

Representation Petition

Once at least 30 percent of eligible workers have signed authorization cards, a petition to hold an election can be made to the NLRB. However, in many cases, union organizers do not file the petition until they have obtained signatures from at least 50 percent of eligible workers. They do this in hopes that the strong showing of support will convince the business organization to acknowledge the union without an election.

There are some restrictions concerning when representation petitions can be filed. When employees are already represented by a recognized union, and when they are working under a collective agreement that has a total duration of three years or less, a petition for representation by a different union cannot be filed until the period 60 to 90 days preceding the expiration of the agreement. In addition, a new petition cannot be filed if a petition has failed during the preceding 12 months.

An important consideration in representation petitions is what constitutes a bargaining unit. A **bargaining unit** is defined as two or more employees who share a "community of interest" and may be reasonably grouped together

Bargaining unit
A group of employees within an organization who are represented by a particular labor union; these employees generally work in similar jobs and therefore represent a community of interest.

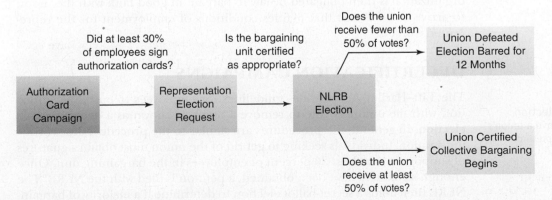

Figure 13.6 Steps Organizing a Union.

for collective bargaining purposes. The appropriateness of a bargaining unit is often determined by examining job descriptions. For instance, all production employees at a manufacturing plant might be seen as a collective bargaining unit. Because large groups of employees are often difficult to organize, labor unions often prefer small bargaining units. Management may also attempt to thwart unionization by combining employees who are sympathetic to a union with a larger group who are not. The determination of an appropriate bargaining unit can thus be a source of contention between management and the union. Disagreements are heard and settled by the NLRB. Once the bargaining unit has been determined, then a check is made to make sure that at least 30 percent of eligible employees in the unit have signed authorization cards.

Certification Election

After receiving a petition for representation, the NLRB conducts a union certification vote. Usually the election is held within 50 days of the petition filing. Managers and supervisors cannot vote in a union election. Security guards are also prohibited from voting, unless the election is for a union to specifically represent security guards as a bargaining unit.

Most elections are held at the work site, but elections can be conducted by mail when employees are spread out geographically. The NLRB conducts the election to make sure that every employee has the opportunity to cast a secret ballot. Union organizers and management are prohibited from campaigning during the election and during the 24-hour period preceding the election. NLRB officials normally count votes in the presence of designated observers from both management and the union.

Union Certification

Either management or the union can file an objection within seven days of an election. Objections concern allegations of unfair labor practices committed by the other side to unduly influence employees. A union might be accused of physically intimidating voters, for example, or management might be accused of threatening to close a plant if the union wins the election.

Evidence supporting and refuting objections to the election is heard by the NLRB, which issues a final ruling concerning the validity of the election results. The union is certified if the NLRB determines that at least 50 percent of employees in the bargaining unit voted in favor of the union. The business organization is then obligated by law to bargain in good faith with the union to arrive at a contract that defines conditions of employment for the represented workers.

DECERTIFICATION CAMPAIGNS

Decertification election
An election to remove a union's authorization to represent employees.

The Taft–Hartley Act provides guidelines for employees to end their affiliation with the union. A vote to remove a union is known as a **decertification election**. In general, the procedures are similar to the procedures for certifying a union. Individuals seeking to get rid of the union must obtain signatures of support from at least 30 percent of employees in the bargaining unit. Once enough signatures have been obtained, a petition is filed with the NLRB. The NLRB then holds a secret-ballot election to determine if a majority of bargaining unit employees agree that they should no longer be represented by the labor union.

FACTORS INFLUENCING UNION CAMPAIGNS

Of course, not all union campaigns are successful. In the 1950s, approximately 75 percent of elections supported unionization. This percentage has steadily decreased, and now only about 50 percent of elections result in union certification.[56] In a broader sense only about 16 percent of card campaigns end up with an uncontested contract.[57]

Most employers generally would prefer not to have an election in the first place. What can they do to make it less likely that employees will support initial unionizing attempts? Employees are most likely to support unionizing when they feel that the actions of management leave them powerless. Company policies that don't show respect for employees, along with ineffective management, frequently lead to union organizing campaigns.[58] Organizations can thus reduce the chance of a union election by instituting effective human resource practices that treat employees fairly.

From the union's point of view, a number of actions have been shown to increase the likelihood of success in organizing. In general, union organization efforts are more effective when the union clearly seeks to meet the needs of employees rather than pursuing national political agendas.[59] Employees support unions when they feel that the union cares about them and values their contributions.[60] Less centralized control and more supportive relationships are particularly important for women who are deciding whether to support the union.[61] In contrast to men, who focus more on money, women support unions when they have confidence that their efforts with the union will truly be effective in making the organization a better place to work.[62] Women are also more likely to join and support unions when union leadership includes women.[63]

A union that has a record of delivering on promises and leaders who are seen as being in touch with the interests of laborers are more likely to succeed in an organizing campaign.[64] Effective union organizing campaigns also tend to emphasize dignity and fairness rather than simply better wages and benefits. In addition, they often use person-to-person contacting, whereby employees who support the union personally share the message with their friends.[65] The sense of solidarity that comes from joining with people similar in race, gender, and religious identification may also increase the likelihood that employees will support organizing a union.[66]

Regardless of union organizing strategies, individual employees differ in their willingness to support and join labor unions. Workers with parents who are more supportive of unions are more likely to support unions themselves.[67] Employees who have had previous positive experiences with unions are also more likely to vote to participate in a union.[68]

CONCEPT CHECK

1. *What steps are required for employees to be organized into a union?*
2. *How can employees remove a union once it is in place?*
3. *What factors influence whether a union organizing campaign will be effective?*

What Happens During Labor Negotiations and Collective Bargaining?

Collective bargaining
The process in which labor unions and employers negotiate contracts defining the terms and conditions under which union members will work.

Once a union has been recognized to represent a group of employees, the next step is to agree on a contract that spells out terms of the relationship between the organization and the workers. The process of agreeing on a labor contract is known as collective bargaining, and it is not always easy. Professional sports represent some of the most high-profile examples of failures in **collective bargaining**. For instance, the 2004–2005 season of the National Hockey League (NHL) never occurred because of failed negotiations between team owners and the National Hockey League Players' Association (NHLPA).[69] A more recent example of failed collective bargaining occurred during the 2011 season of the National Basketball Association (NBA). The labor disagreement lasted 161 days and resulted in a reduction of regular season games from the typical 82 to 66 contests.[70] The NBA experience illustrates many of the core activities of collective bargaining, which we examine next.

BARGAINING TOPICS

Negotiations between NBA owners and the players' union focused primarily on how profits would be split between players and team owners. Owners wanted to reduce the percentage of revenue distributed to players from 57% to 47%. In order to ensure competition between teams, owners also wanted to include measures that made it difficult for some teams to pay players more than other teams. Players not only wanted to retain the higher revenue split but also opposed measures that would have the effect of decreasing the amount some teams would be willing to spend on player costs. The major sticking point of the 2011 NBA negotiations was therefore wages.

Mandatory bargaining topics
Issues, such as wages, hours, and working conditions, that must be discussed as part of collective bargaining.

Wages are a mandatory topic for labor negotiations. **Mandatory bargaining** topics represent issues that the NLRB classifies as fundamental. The NLRB requires management and unions to discuss these issues as part of the collective bargaining process. Wages include things such as minimum salary, bonus payments, and benefits. Other mandatory bargaining topics are hours and working conditions. The topic of hours focuses on work scheduling and includes holidays, vacation time, and shifts. Working conditions encompass safety rules, promotions, layoffs, and grievance procedures. A labor negotiation such as the NBA discussions must thus address the three mandatory topics: wages, hours, and working conditions.

Permissive bargaining topics
Issues, such as employee involvement and strategic direction, that are not required but are allowed to be discussed as part of collective bargaining.

Management and a labor union may choose to discuss some issues that are not related to wages, hours, and working conditions. Issues that parties are allowed but are not obligated to discuss are labeled **permissive bargaining topics**. For instance, an item of negotiation might be involvement of union members in strategic planning. The union might also wish to negotiate the right to have one of its representatives serve on the company's board of directors. The "Technology in HR" feature illustrates how the adoption of computerized processes became a permissive bargaining topic in negotiations with the International Longshore and Warehouse Union.

Technology in HR

REPLACING LABORERS WITH COMPUTERS

The industrial revolution of the late 1800s and early 1900s began a movement to automate production processes for manufactured goods, such as automobiles. The resulting processes emphasized narrow jobs with specific duties and helped create a role for labor unions. Unions protected the interests of workers by promoting job security, fair treatment, and safety. However, recent trends toward automated processes and computerized production are increasingly threatening to replace unionized workers with technology. This situation often creates tension between labor unions and organizations seeking to increase their use of technology.

An example of tension over technology is the International Longshore and Warehouse Union (ILWU). For many years, the ILWU saw the use of computers at marine terminals as a threat to employees' job security. What would happen to the jobs of marine clerks if technology enabled companies to directly input data into computer systems? The adoption of computerized systems became a critical point in labor negotiations. The ILWU finally agreed to allow more technology in exchange for higher wages, benefits, and pensions.

As expected, a number of marine clerk positions are being replaced by technology. The upside, however, is an increase in other positions. Improved efficiency from computerization has helped increase the number of containers moved

Sandra Baker/Getty Images

at each location. The greater number of containers has in turn created a need for additional manual labor. In addition, the new systems require highly sophisticated inputs from people doing computer programming and maintenance. The end result is that overall union membership has actually grown. Adopting computerized processes has led not to a decline in union members but rather to a shift in work processes. Jobs that were once completed by marine clerks have been replaced by jobs that range from manual to intellectual.

Sources: Richard Cardinali, "The Cyberknights vs. Trade Unions: Determining Workplace Futures," *Work Study* 49, no. 6 (2000): 223; Bill Mongelluzzo, "New Place at the Table," *Journal of Commerce,* June 6, 2005, p. 1.

A few topics cannot be discussed in the negotiation process. These **illegal bargaining topics** include plans to discriminate against employees because of factors such as race and gender. It is also illegal for unions and management to discuss the formation of a closed shop, which would require the company to hire only employees who are already members of the union.

Illegal bargaining topics
Issues, such as planning to engage in race or gender discrimination, that are prohibited from being discussed as part of collective bargaining.

WORK STOPPAGES

The NBA example illustrates a case in which the sides did not come to agreement during bargaining. In most cases, failure to reach agreement results in a work stoppage. The work stoppage can be initiated by either the employer or the union. In the first situation, the work stoppage is a lockout; in the second, it is a strike.

Lockout
An action in which an employer closes a workplace or otherwise prevents union members from working as a result of a labor dispute.

Lockouts

A **lockout** occurs when an employer shuts down operations during a labor dispute. Members of the union are prohibited from working and are not paid. The NBA owners used a lockout to prevent union members from playing. In the case of the NBA, this had the effect of canceling the games. A lockout can be devastating to a company that is unable to identify and hire workers who are not union members. A lockout also creates financial hardship for employees who are not being paid. During the basketball lockout, a few players accepted offers to play on teams in leagues operated in other countries

Strikes

Strike
An action in which union members refuse to perform their job duties as a result of a labor dispute.

A **strike** occurs when union members collectively refuse to perform their jobs. A well-known strike in sports happened when Major League Baseball (MLB) players refused to play during a period in 1994 and 1995. The core issues were very similar to the issues surrounding the NBA lockout. Team owners sought to impose a salary cap. Union members rejected the cap. The union and the owners could not arrive at an agreement, which created an impasse. The previous collective bargaining agreement was set to expire, and owners planned to implement the salary cap even though no new agreement had been reached. The players went on strike to prevent the owners from implementing the cap. The strike began in August and caused the cancellation of postseason play, including the World Series. Even President Bill Clinton tried to help negotiate an end to the strike. However, neither side was willing to compromise. Finally, the NLRB ruled that team owners had engaged in an unfair labor practice when they failed to negotiate in good faith. The players then went back to work and started a belated 1995 season.[71]

A strike is the union action that can be most damaging to an organization. A company without workers is unable to produce goods or services. Of course, a strike is most effective when the work cannot be done by others, such as managers or replacement workers. Striking workers may also take a number of additional actions to pressure the company to agree to their conditions. Workers who are on strike often form picket lines that publicly demonstrate their displeasure with the company. In some cases, members of other unions refuse to cross a picket line. Thus, for example, a company with striking employees may have difficulty receiving and shipping goods, because transportation workers may support the employees' strike by refusing to cross the picket line to pick up goods or make deliveries. Striking employees may also encourage consumers or other companies not to purchase the company's goods or services, which is known as a **boycott**.

Boycott
An organized action in which consumers refuse to purchase goods or services from a company; unions engaged in labor disputes may support boycotts of the companies involved in the disputes.

A strike can impose hardships on workers as well as employers. Striking workers are not paid, which of course can create financial difficulties. Most unions thus save part of their dues to create a strike fund that can be used to cover living expenses for workers who are participating in a strike.

THE BARGAINING ATMOSPHERE

Effective negotiations involve cooperative attempts to understand and resolve issues from both parties. The NBA and MLB examples both represent relatively poor bargaining atmospheres in which unions and management took adversarial positions instead of working together. The NBA agreement resulted in a reduction of the player portion of salary from 57% to 50%, but the owners failed to secure a hard salary cap that would punish teams who spent more on personnel. To many observers the overall process did not identify and implement new practices to help management and union members work together to solve ongoing revenue problems. Future failures of bargaining are likely if either party, most likely players in the NBA example, feels that their interests were not adequately addressed in an agreement.[72]

MLB labor relations offer an example of what happens when management and a union interact in a negative manner over time. Under NLRB guidelines, management and a union must negotiate to create a new collective bargaining agreement each time the previous agreement expires. Since 1972, professional baseball has had nine collective bargaining agreements expire, and in eight of those cases, a work stoppage occurred. Players have gone on strike five times, and owners have used a lockout three times. The negative relationship between owners and the players' union stems from mistrust and personality conflicts among lead negotiators from each side.[73] Over the years, negotiators and leaders have allowed their personal dislike for one another get in the way of effective labor relations.[74] As you can imagine, anger is counterproductive in negotiations and reduces the likelihood that an agreement will be reached.[75] MLB's negative labor relations atmosphere illustrates how negative interactions compound over years to the point where management and a union become competitive and unable to cooperate with each other. Fortunately these negative relationships seem to have decreased with an agreement being reached in 2011 that stretches cooperation into 2016, suggesting the possibility of a 21-year period of labor peace for the sport.[76]

Truly effective labor relations require the creation of a positive bargaining atmosphere. Table 13.4 provides a list of conditions that have been shown to influence cooperation during collective bargaining.[77] The first condition concerns the degree of trust developed during previous negotiations. Trust is built when each party perceives the other as having honest and moral intentions. In addition, the parties trust one another more when they do not feel they have been unfairly taken advantage of in past negotiations. The history of fair treatment in past negotiations is thus an important factor in the success of future negotiations.[78] A second important condition of cooperation is the expertise and style of the negotiators. Negotiators who believe that the labor–management relationship can be a win–win association are more cooperative.

Table 13.4	*Conditions Influencing Cooperation in Negotiations*	
Degree of Trust Developed During Previous Negotiations		**Clarity of Bargaining Issues**
• Are intentions honest and moral?		• Which issues are distributive in nature?
• Have there been instances of past unfairness?		• Which issues are integrative?
Expertise and Style of Negotiators		**Ability to Use Problem-Solving Techniques**
• Is there an expectation of a win–win relationship?		• Are both sides motivated to find a solution?
• Are noncompeting interests acknowledged?		• Is there social support?

Source: Information from Natasha Caverley, Bart Cunningham, and Lari Mitchell, "Reflections on Public Sector–Based Integrative Collective Bargaining," *Employee Relations* 28 (2006): 62–75.

How Do We Know?

DOES COOPERATING WITH UNIONS HELP ORGANIZATIONS SUCCEED?

Should businesses and organizations really cooperate? Can a cooperative approach promote success without compromising the position of either management or the union? Stephen Deery and Roderick Iverson sought to investigate this issue by assessing labor relations in 305 bank branches located in Australia. They first surveyed management and unions to learn about their practices in such areas as information sharing and bargaining approaches. A year later, they assessed cooperation between management and the union. They also measured employees' commitment to the organization and loyalty to the union. Performance measures, including quality of service and employee absenteeism, were then tracked for a six-month period.

Results showed that labor relations are more cooperative when management shares information with the union and has practices that are seen as fair. A union adds to the cooperative relationship by adopting an integrative approach to bargaining. More cooperative relationships increased employees' commitment and loyalty to both the union and the bank. Commitment in turn was associated with increased productivity, including better service for customers and lower absenteeism.

The Bottom Line. Relationships between management and unions are enhanced by sharing information and adopting a cooperative approach to negotiations. More cooperation is good for both the union and the organization. The authors conclude that cooperative labor–management relations do indeed contribute to improved organizational performance.

Source: Stephen J. Deery and Roderick D. Iverson, "Labor–Management Cooperation: Antecedents and Impact on Organizational Performance," *Industrial & Labor Relations Review* 58 (2005): 588–609.

Distributive issues
Issues, such as distribution of rewards and benefits, whose resolution provides value to one party at the expense of the other party.

Integrative issues
Issues, such as safety improvement, whose resolution can provide more value to both parties.

Another condition necessary for cooperation is the ability to clearly distinguish distributive and integrative issues. **Distributive issues** cover areas where rewards and benefits must be divided among parties. Dividing current profits between employees and owners is a distributive issue, for example. In labor negotiations, distributive issues involve competing interests. Here, gains for one party usually come at the expense of the other. **Integrative issues**, in contrast, can result in mutual gains, increasing the overall level of rewards and benefits for everyone. Improving employee safety, for instance, can result in greater benefits for both management and employees. Adopting new work methods to raise productivity can also increase the overall amount of rewards, benefiting both management and workers. Clearly separating distributive and integrative issues allows negotiators to match their bargaining strategies with the nature of the issue, which in turn can reduce conflict and tension.

A final condition that facilitates cooperation is adopting problem-solving techniques. One such technique is for leaders and mediators to ensure mutual motivation, which exists when both sides see the importance of arriving at a cooperative resolution. Another technique is to create a sense of equality so that neither side is allowed to dominate the other. Leaders and external consultants can also provide social support to reduce negative emotions and enhance discussions.

Benefits of cooperative relationships for both companies and unions are described in the "How Do We Know?" feature. Developing a sense of trust, choosing skilled negotiators, clarifying bargaining issues, and adopting problem-solving techniques are critical ways to increase cooperation. Such cooperation is often essential for high-quality labor relations. In many cases, the nature of the interaction is more important than the outcome of the negotiation. Managers and unions that adopt a cooperative approach to negotiation are more likely to work together and identify methods of increasing organizational productivity.

INTEREST-BASED NEGOTIATION

Interest-based negotiation represents an innovative strategy for collective bargaining. Table 13.5 lists some of the common differences between interest-based and traditional approaches to negotiation. In traditional negotiation, each side stakes out a claim and then pursues the solution that best satisfies its position. Interest-based negotiation is different in that each side explains to the other the factors that are of most interest. The two parties then work together to find the solution that best satisfies the interests of both parties. Interest-based negotiation is an important part of successful labor relations for Kaiser Permanente, described at the beginning of this chapter. There are four steps to interest-based negotiation: preparing for negotiations, opening negotiations, using integrative principles, and communicating the bargaining results.

Step 1: Prepare for Negotiations

Interest-based negotiations use data to identify key concerns. Thus, an important part of the preparation stage is for each side to collect as much data as possible. Data should include information about the interests of both sides in the negotiation. Data can be gathered through formal surveys or informal conversations. The data should be framed in a way that illustrates key interests rather than demands made on the other side.

Once data have been gathered, information is shared with the other side. Openly communicating in this way builds trust and is essential to bargaining that focuses on mutual gains. After each party has examined the data provided by the other side, the parties come together to develop a list of rules that they will follow when negotiating. These rules might include such practices as moving away from demands toward discussions of interests.

Table 13.5	*Approaches to Collective Bargaining*
Traditional Negotiation	**Interest-Based Negotiation**
Discredit and attack opponent; present and support a position	Address mutual concerns; focus on issues, not past conflicts
Pursue a specific bargaining position	Explore interests of joint concern
Use power and pressure to obtain a desired solution	Remain open-minded to possibilities; define solutions acceptable to both parties

Source: Information from Federal Mediation and Conciliation Service, *Interest-Based Negotiation: Participants' Guidebook.*

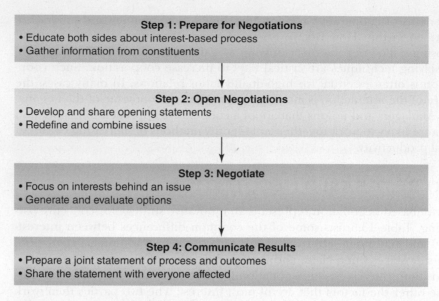

Figure 13.7 Interest-Based Negotiation Process.

Step 2: Open Negotiations

Negotiations start with each side presenting an opening statement that lists its major interests. This helps negotiators understand what issues are most important. It also clarifies the scope of problems that need to be addressed in the negotiation. An important part of this stage is clearly defining issues so that both sides are assured that they understand one another and are talking about the same concepts.

Step 3: Negotiate Using Interest-Based Principles

Once issues have been identified, the next step is to mutually arrive at a resolution for each issue. To do this, negotiators discuss the interests behind the issues. Part of the discussion includes brainstorming, in which the negotiators work together to create a list of potential solutions. They then identify a set of standards that they can use to evaluate the quality of each solution. The standards help the negotiators to determine which of the options best meets the interests of the two parties. Once the negotiators arrive at a consensus decision about what should be done, they clarify the option chosen and acknowledge its choice by writing it down.

Step 4: Communicate Bargaining Results

Once the issues have been identified and solutions have been negotiated, the final step is for management and union representatives to work together to create a joint statement that describes the negotiation process and outcome. The statement acknowledges the important interests that have been addressed from both perspectives. Publicly disseminating the solution increases the parties' commitment to follow through and implement solutions.

Figure 13.7 summarizes the four steps. One example of the benefits of interest-based principles is a negotiation between the Salt River Project, which is a major utility provider in Phoenix, Arizona, and IBEW Local 266, which is part of the

International Brotherhood of Electrical Workers. The process opened up lines of communication and fostered a sense of partnership and mutual respect.[79]

CONCEPT CHECK
1. *What topics are negotiated during collective bargaining?*
2. *How is a lockout different from a strike?*
3. *What steps are associated with interest-based negotiation?*

LEARNING OBJECTIVE **5**

What Is the Grievance Process?

A labor contract formally defines much of the relationship between employees and the organization. As might be expected, there are times when one side feels that the behavior of the other violates the agreement. One such situation may arise as a result of disciplinary procedures. Managers discipline employees for various reasons, including excessive absence or tardiness, violation of safety rules, and failure to perform basic job duties. Employees who feel that they have been unfairly disciplined— or who believe management has violated some other term of the labor contract—can file a grievance. A **grievance** is a dispute that arises between an employer and employee over the terms of the employment agreement. When a union represents workers, grievance procedures are clearly stated in the formal contract that is negotiated and accepted during collective bargaining.

Grievance
A complaint filed by an employee who perceives that he or she has been unfairly treated by an organization.

GRIEVANCE PROCEDURES

Grievance procedures generally follow a multistep process. The number of steps, and the actions associated with each step, vary across organizations. In general, however, the steps move from informal discussions to formal mediation. The grievance process normally begins when an employee feels that he or she has been treated unfairly and goes to a supervisor with this complaint. In some cases, the initial complaint is made in writing, but often the first step is simply a verbal statement that informs the supervisor of the concern. A majority of grievances are resolved at this first stage.

If the grievance is not resolved at the first step, the employee then moves to a step that involves more people. The employee often obtains help at this point from the **union steward**, who is a representative of the union that advocates for employees. Many unions also have a grievance committee and national representatives who get involved if a resolution is difficult. From management's side, additional steps in the grievance process usually involve leaders higher in the organizational hierarchy. Department or division managers listen to appeals, and human resource representatives often play a supporting role.

Union steward
A representative of the union who acts as an advocate for employees.

Arbitration
A process in which a neutral third party resolves a dispute by issuing a binding decision; in the context of labor relations, arbitration is generally the last step in the grievance process.

The final step in most grievance procedures is **arbitration**, which is a type of judicial process. Although arbitration is not carried out in the court system, the process is very similar to court proceedings. Management and union representatives act much like attorneys to present facts and arguments supporting their side of the disagreement. The arguments are heard by an arbitrator, a neutral third party who has a role similar to that of a judge. After hearing the arguments, the arbitrator makes a ruling, which is usually binding on both parties. Only about 2 percent of grievances actually reach the arbitration stage.[80]

DETERMINANTS OF GRIEVANCE FILING

A number of issues influence whether employees file grievances. One factor is the characteristics of the individual worker. As you might expect, people who file grievances have higher rates of absenteeism and more insurance claims. Workers who are younger, male, educated, and working in skilled jobs are also more likely to file grievances.[81]

Characteristics of the work environment also influence grievance filing rates. Grievance rates are higher when supervisors emphasize production rather than friendly relationships.[82] In addition, the perceived fairness of supervisors has an effect. Organizations with procedures that are seen as fairer have lower grievance rates.[83] Thus, training to help supervisors learn how to administer discipline in a fair and consistent manner can lower grievance rates.[84]

A final influence on grievance filing is union characteristics. Unions tend to initiate grievances that focus on defining the actions associated with particular jobs.[85] For instance, a grievance might be filed if an employee is asked to complete tasks that are outside the scope of his or her job.

GRIEVANCE MEDIATION

Mediation
A process in which a neutral third party attempts to help the parties reach an agreement but does not issue a binding decision to resolve the dispute; in the context of labor relations, mediation is sometimes available as part of the grievance resolution process.

Many organizations have adopted **mediation** as a step in the grievance process. When mediation is part of the process, it occurs just before arbitration. Mediation is similar in some respects to interest-based negotiation. In most organizations, mediation involves a third party—a mediator—who helps the parties work together to arrive at a mutually beneficial resolution. The process is more informal than arbitration. Each side presents facts, but there are no witnesses or cross-examination, and the mediator does not make a binding decision. If the parties do not resolve the conflict with the mediator's help, the issue goes on to arbitration.

Evidence suggests that mediation has long-term benefits. Most organizations see mediation techniques as an effective way to resolve disputes such as grievances.[86] Conflict is generally decreased with mediation, and managers, union leaders, and employees learn effective methods of resolving disagreements that make future disagreements easier to resolve.[87]

CONCEPT CHECK

?

1. *What are the common steps associated with filing a grievance?*
2. *Why do some organizations experience more grievances than others?*

A MANAGER'S PERSPECTIVE REVISITED

In the Manager's Perspective that opened the chapter, Jose was thinking about union issues. He was concerned about the strike that was taking place at the plant where he worked as a supervisor. He had also received a phone call from a reporter who was seeking an answer about union organizing issues. Following are the answers to the "What Do You Think?" quiz that followed the Manager's Perspective. Were you able to correctly identify the true statements? Could you do better now?

1. Workers who are represented by unions usually make more money than workers who are not represented by unions. TRUE. *Union workers on average make more money than nonunion workers doing the same job.*

2. Organizations with employees who are represented by a union invest less money in things like equipment and research. TRUE. *Unionized firms tend to spend less money on things that support innovation.*

3. Trends show that fewer and fewer employees in the United States are represented by labor unions. TRUE. *Union membership rates have been steadily declining* over the past 50 years or so.

4. Threatening to close the plant is an effective method for discouraging employees from voting to join a union. FALSE. *Threatening to close a plant is an example of an unfair labor practice.*

5. Because unions advocate for employees during negotiations, businesses should strongly focus on company interests. FALSE. *Interest-based negotiation is often more effective than traditional adversarial methods where each side strongly advocates its own position.*

Even though union influence is weaker than it has been in the past, Jose's concerns are experienced by many supervisors. A series of laws provide unions with a legitimate role in labor relations. The threat of union organization encourages many other businesses to treat employees more fairly. Understanding important practices associated with union organization, collective bargaining, and grievance procedures is an essential skill for many managers.

SUMMARY

How are labor unions strategic?

Unions fit best with organizations that seek a stable workforce. The emphasis on long-term employment and on equal treatment of employees makes unions most compatible with organizations pursuing a Loyal Soldier HR strategy. Organizations with a Free Agent HR strategy often encounter difficulties when their employees are unionized. Union representation is rare in organizations with a Bargain Laborer HR strategy. Lower investment of profits back into the organization can also create problems when employees of organizations pursuing a Committed Expert HR strategy are unionized.

How has organized labor evolved over time?

Labor unions became much more common in the United States beginning in the 1930s. The Wagner Act, which was passed in 1935, recognized the right of employees to organize unions. The act created the NLRB, which oversees union election campaigns and allegations of unfair labor practices. The Taft–Hartley Act shifted power back toward businesses by making it illegal for unions to engage in unfair labor practices. The Landrum–Griffin Act regulates internal governance of unions.

Union membership in the United States has been decreasing steadily since the 1950s. Overall, only about 12 percent of U.S. workers are currently organized into unions. Representation is significantly higher in the public sector, with almost 40 percent of the workforce organized into labor unions.

The role of unions in some countries is very different from the role of unions in the United States. U.S. unions focus on bread-and-butter issues, such as wages and working conditions. Unions in many European countries focus more on political activism. Union growth is currently highest in countries, such as Sweden, that focus on both economic issues and political activism.

Many workers who are not union members benefit from union activities. Wages are higher in industries that are highly unionized. Threats of union organization also encourage many businesses to treat employees fairly so that they will not vote to join a union.

LEARNING OBJECTIVE 3

How do workers become part of a union?

The NLRB oversees union elections. The first step is to obtain signatures from at least 30 percent of eligible workers. Once the signatures have been obtained, a petition for an election is filed with the NLRB. A certification election then takes place. The union is recognized as the official representative of employees if it receives the support of at least 50 percent of employees in the election. A decertification election can be used to remove a union. The process is very similar to the process for organizing a union.

LEARNING OBJECTIVE 4

What happens during labor negotiations and collective bargaining?

Collecting bargaining occurs when a union representing employees negotiates terms of the labor relationship with management. The NLRB requires unions and management to negotiate mandatory issues, which include wages, hours, and working conditions. Negotiations can also include permissive topics but not illegal topics. Work stoppages often occur when unions and management fail to reach agreement. A business can create a work stoppage by using a lockout, while a union can organize a strike.

Collective bargaining is most effective when there is an atmosphere of trust between management and the union. Interest-based negotiation helps build trust and cooperative relationships. This process uses problem-solving techniques to arrive at solutions that are acceptable to both parties. Rather than pursue their own interests, the two sides work together to make real improvements.

LEARNING OBJECTIVE 5

What is the grievance process?

Employees may file grievances when they feel they are treated unfairly. Grievance procedures generally follow a series of progressive steps. The first step is an informal discussion with a supervisor. In the next step, union stewards and managers with more authority become involved. The final step is arbitration, in which evidence is heard and an arbitrator makes a binding decision. Some organizations encourage mediation as a nonbinding step right before arbitration.

KEY TERMS

Agency shop   506
Arbitration   526
Authorization card campaign   514
Bargaining unit   515
Boycott   520

Closed shop   506
Collective bargaining   518
Decertification election   516
Distributive issues   522
Featherbedding   506

DISCUSSION QUESTIONS

1. If you were a union organizer, where would you focus your efforts? What type of people do you think are most likely to join a union today?

2. Why have U.S. labor unions and businesses adopted an adversarial approach to labor relations? Why might it be difficult for many to accept and pursue a cooperative relationship?

3. Why do unions pose problems for organizations pursuing Free Agent HR strategies?

4. What issues do you think are responsible for declining union membership? Do you believe membership will increase in the future? Why or why not?

5. Is new legislation needed to better regulate relationships between organizations and labor unions? What legal reforms do you think might be helpful?

6. Do you think union membership will decrease in the public sector? Why or why not?

7. Why do you think fewer union organizing campaigns are successful today than in the past?

8. Although you are probably not a union member, think about ways unions have influenced your life. What have unions done to improve your life? What have they done to make your life worse?

9. What do you think causes younger male workers who are highly skilled to file more grievances?

10. What issues make some labor strikes more successful than others? What factors do you think make it difficult for the National Hockey League players' union to be effective in advocating the interests of players?

EXAMPLE CASE   *Energy Co.*

Energy Co. is a pseudo name for an actual utility company with operations in the UK and overseas. In total, Energy Co. employs around 16,000 people. Energy Co. is widely recognized as an innovator in several personnel practices.

The workforce at Alpha Plant is predominantly male, and most have worked for Energy Co. for over 20 years. Union membership is around 90 percent, and the division entered a partnership with the Engineers' and Managers' Association (EMA), Amalgamated Engineering and Electrical Union, GMB, and UNISON.

Partnership was "agreed" in the Generation Business in 1995, two years prior to the election of New Labour in May 1997. Interestingly, the agreement was only signed in one division, and this remains the case today. Following privatization, industrial relations in this division were extremely poor, characterized by protracted pay negotiations and a major disagreement over the introduction of annual hours for power station personnel. It was also suggested that the generation business has always been the most progressive in relation to HR policy. Though employees in other divisions with a more stable industrial relations climate were not affected, for the ailing generation business it was hailed as "a new approach to relationships at work which recognizes that all parties—management, staff and trade unions—have many common interests."

It was based upon 13 founding principles:

1. Legitimate role of trade unions
2. Joint commitment to success, prosperity, and shared goals
3. Best in class
4. Fair treatment, mutual respect, and single status
5. Employment security
6. Flexibility
7. Opportunities for training and personal development
8. Response to change
9. Sharing in success
10. Safety, health, and welfare
11. Environment
12. Community relations
13. Information, consultation, and participation

There was a consensus that partnership was born out of a poor industrial relations climate following privatization in 1991. Indeed, several privatized utilities used the opportunity to encourage culture change toward a spirit of working together. Given ambiguity of definition, an attempt was made to understand what the partnership meant to different actors and to uncover the rationale behind the approach.

According to managers, partnership was more than just a formal agreement as it affected day-to-day working relationships:

> Partnership in its purest form within the business is a written agreement between unions and management about how we manage industrial relations, while in a broader sense it is about empowering staff and how we work on a day-to-day basis (Compliance manager).

> Where management set the goals but how we achieve these goals is very much driven by employees (Production manager).

Union representatives explained that the partnership meant trying to work together rather than against each other, as was the case with the earlier head-to-head approach:

> Partnership is a group of people working together for the betterment of the company and its employees (Amicus representative).

In terms of rationale, managers offered various explanations:

> Employees that aren't very involved get very cynical and pissed off and aren't particularly driven, I don't believe. We don't live in a military environment (Compliance manager).

For one representative it was about giving employees a say in the workplace:

> We wanted to be part of the decision-making process, rather than sit back and let management take all the decisions, and we appreciate management's right to manage but at the end of the day the more influence we can have on decisions . . . it can only be to the good (Amicus representative).

In sum, management drivers appeared to be improving industrial relations, fostering employee commitment, informing employees, and tapping into employee knowledge. From the trade union perspective, it was more about developing channels for employees' voices to be heard and engaging in more constructive relations with management.

QUESTIONS

1. How did the existence of very poor labor relations encourage the partnership?
2. What competitive strategy do you think is most appropriate for Energy Co.? How do unions fit with this strategy?
3. How does a cooperative relationship with labor unions influence worker autonomy?
4. Which of the 13 principles do you think was most difficult for management to accept? Which principles do you think are most critical for making the partnership work?

Source: Stewart Johnstone, Adrian Wilkinson, and Peter Ackers, "Partnership Paradoxes: A Case Study of an Energy Company," *Employee Relations* 26 (2004): 353–376. Used with permission from Emerald Group Publishing Limited.

DISCUSSION CASE	*Teaching Assistants at State University*

State University employs a large number of graduate students to work as teaching assistants. The teaching assistants often complain about their work. They feel that faculty and administrators demand too much. A common complaint is their low wages. The graduate students frequently point out that they do much the same work as faculty members, yet they receive only a very small percentage of the pay that faculty members receive. They also claim that faculty members frequently treat them unfairly. Teaching assistants are often asked to do large amounts of grading in very short time periods. Many also feel that faculty members are not very good at communicating expectations.

In response to the dissatisfaction of the teaching assistants, a local union representing public workers has begun efforts to organize a labor union. Union representatives have obtained campaign card signatures from 40 percent of the teaching assistants. An election is scheduled for next month. Union representatives have been busy making a case that the union can help ensure that teaching assistants are treated more fairly. They have publicized statistics showing that unionized workers make significantly more than nonunionized workers. University administrators have decided not to actively oppose union organization. They have simply stated that it is important for teaching assistants to have the opportunity to decide whether they should be represented by a labor union.

Some faculty members are sympathetic to the concerns voiced by graduate students. They publicly state their concern that wages are too low. They also express frustration when they see some of their colleagues take advantage of students by assigning them large amounts of work to complete in short time periods. Other faculty members are less sympathetic. These professors talk about how they were treated even worse when they were graduate assistants. They seem to find joy in looking back and telling war stories about "the old days." They seem to think that working hard for little pay is a right of passage that helps prepare students for future careers. Overall, the faculty at State University thus seems to be about evenly split in their support for student efforts to unionize.

A majority of the undergraduate students at State University don't seem to know anything about the unionization efforts. A few politically active students have joined public rallies supporting the unionization efforts. Others seem to have used the unionization issue to complain about the quality of teaching provided by graduate students. These students recently met with administrators to complain about having too many graduate students as instructors. Just last week the local newspaper printed an article detailing some of the problems experienced when courses are taught by graduate students.

As a community, State University thus seems to be quite divided over the unionization issue. No matter who prevails in the election, it seems likely that a large number of people will be unhappy with the result.

QUESTIONS

1. Do you think a union would help resolve the complaints of the teaching assistants?

2. What makes the position of teaching assistant different from many jobs frequently represented by unions?

3. Do you think the administration's response is appropriate?

4. If you were a graduate student at State University, would you vote for the union? Why?

EXPERIENTIAL EXERCISE | *Investigating the Labor–Management Partnership*

Visit the website that describes the labor–management partnership at Kaiser Permanente (www.lmpartnership.org/). Read the following:

1. The history of the partnership.
2. The key issues the partnership emphasizes.
3. The contracts and agreements that have been reached through collective bargaining.

Once you have visited the website, answer the following questions:

1. Are the outcomes of this agreement different from the outcomes of most other labor negotiations?
2. Why do you think Kaiser and the AFL–CIO are so willing to make this agreement public?
3. Do you think this agreement would improve the quality of your worklife if you were employed at Kaiser Permanente?

INTERACTIVE EXPERIENTIAL EXERCISE

Unions: Negotiating a New Labor Contract for Mega Manufacturing
http://www.wiley.com/college/sc/stewart

Access the companion website to test your knowledge by completing a Mega Manufacturing interactive role play.

The collective bargaining agreement at one of Mega Manufacturing's plants will expire soon, and in this exercise you've been hired to help with the contract negotiations. Recall that Mega follows a Free Agent HR strategy with an external labor orientation and a focus on differentiation. Mega's management has several concerns about the upcoming negotiations. For one thing, a major increase in healthcare costs needs to be passed along to employees, at least to some extent. In addition, the union and its members will expect bigger raises in this contract because of current conditions in the labor market. Both sides have traditionally bargained in good faith, but these contract negotiations will be especially challenging, and rumblings of strike have already surfaced. To make matters worse, the employees at another of Mega's plants are starting a union organizing campaign. What bargaining approach will you recommend that Mega follow in the contract negotiations? •

ENDNOTES

1. Richard K. Vedder and Lowell E. Gallaway, "Do Unions Help the Economy? The Economic Effects of Labor Unions Revisited," *Government Union Review and Public Policy Digest* 20, no. 4 (2003): 33–70.
2. www.kaiserpermanente.org
3. Thomas A. Kochan, "Taking the High Road," *MIT Sloan Management Review* 47, no. 4 (2006): 16–19.
4. Leib Leventhal, "Implementing Interest-Based Negotiation: Conditions for Success with Evidence from Kaiser Permanente," *Dispute Resolution Journal* 61 (2006): 50–58.
5. www.lmpartnership.org/contracts/index.html#
6. Nils O. Fonstad, Robert B. McKersie, and Susan C. Eaton, "Interest-Based Negotiations in a Transformed Labor–Management Setting," *Negotiation Journal* 20 (2004): 5–11.
7. Susan C. Eaton, Robert B. McKersie, and Nils O. Fonstad, "Taking Stock of the Kaiser Permanente Partnership Story," *Negotiation Journal* 20 (2004): 47–64.
8. http://lmpartnership.org/what-is-partnership/national-agreements/2012-national-agreement
9. Andis Robenznieks, "Calculating Satisfaction," *Modern Healthcare* 35 (2005): 32.
10. Brian Raymond, "The Kaiser IT Transformation," *Healthcare Financial Management* 59 (2005): 62–66.
11. Jeffrey Pfeffer, "In Praise of Organized Labor, Never Mind Conventional Wisdom, the Evidence Says that When Bosses Partner with Unions, It's Good for Both Workers and the Bottom Line," *Business 2.0* 6, no. 5 (2005): 80.
12. Francis Green and Steven McIntosh, "Union Power, Cost of Job Loss, and Workers' Effort," *Industrial and Labor Relations Review* 51 (1998): 363–383.
13. Alison L. Booth, Marco Francesconi, and Gylfi Zoega, "Unions, Work-Related Training, and Wages: Evidence for British Men," *Industrial and Labor Relations Review* 57 (2003): 68.
14. Wenchuan Liu, James P. Guthrie, Patrick C. Flood, and Sarah MacCurtain, "Unions and the Adoption of High Performance Work Systems: Does Employment Security Play a Role?" *Industrial and Labor Relations Review* 63 (2009): 109–127.
15. Barry T. Hirsch and Edward J. Schumacher, "Unions, Wage, and Skills," *Journal of Human Resources* 33, no. 1 (1998): 201–219; David Card, "The Effect of Unions on Wage Inequality in the U.S. Labor Market," *Industrial and Labor Relations Review* 54 (2001): 354–367.
16. Thomas C. Buchmueller, John Dinardo, and Robert G. Valletta, "Union Effects on Health Insurance Provision and Coverage in the United States," *Industrial and Labor Relations Review* 55 (2002): 610.
17. Robert Spector, "Union Says Nordstrom Owes Workers Millions," *Footwear News*, November 6, 1989.
18. Bob Baker, "Agency Orders Nordstrom to Pay Back Wages," *Los Angeles Times*, February 17, 1990; Stuart Silverstein, "Nordstrom to Change Its Timekeeping Procedures," *Los Angeles Times*, February 24, 1990.
19. Alison L. Booth and Marco Francesconi, "Union Coverage and Non-Standard Work in Britain," *Oxford Economic Papers* 55 (2003): 383.
20. Cameron W. Odgers and Julian R. Betts, "Do Unions Reduce Investment? Evidence from Canada," *Industrial and Labor Relations Review* 51 (1997): 18.
21. John W. Budd and Yijiang Wang, "Labor Policy and Investment: Evidence from Canada," *Industrial and Labor Relations Review* 57 (2004): 386.
22. Naercio Menezes-Filho, David Ulph, and John Van Reenen, "R&D and Unionism: Comparative Evidence

from British Companies and Establishments," *Industrial and Labor Relations Review* 52 (1998): 45.

23. John T. Addison, Thorsten Schank, Claus Schnabel, and Joachim Wagner, "Do Works Councils Inhibit Investment?" *Industrial and Labor Relations Review* 60 (2007): 187–203.

24. Bernt Bratsberg and James F. Ragan, Jr., "Changes in the Union Wage Premium by Industry," *Industrial and Labor Relations Review* 56 (2002): 65.

25. Michael Ash and Jean Ann Seago, "The Effect of Registered Nurses' Unions on Heart-Attack Mortality," *Industrial and Labor Relations Review* 57 (2004): 422.

26. Corey Dade, "UPS, Teamsters Begin Negotiations," *Wall Street Journal*, September 20, 2006; Corey Dade, "Pilots at UPS Ratify Labor Pact; Teamster Talks Set," *Wall Street Journal*, September 1, 2006.

27. Richard B. Freeman and Morris M. Kleiner, "Do Unions Make Enterprises Insolvent," *Industrial and Labor Relations Review* 52 (1999): 510.

28. Jody Hoffer Gittell, Andrew Von Nordenflycht, and Thomas A. Kochan, "Mutual Gains or Zero Sum? Labor Relations and Firm Performance in the Airline Industry," *Industrial and Labor Relations Review* 57 (2004): 163.

29. http://nlrb.gov/national-labor-relations-act

30. http://nlrb.gov/who-we-are/our-history/1947-taft-hartley-substantive-provisions

31. http://www.ncsl.org/issues-research/labor/right-to-work-laws-and-bills.aspx

32. www.fmcs.gov/internet/itemDetail.asp?categoryID=21&itemID=15810

33. www.dol.gov/compliance/laws/comp-lmrda.htm

34. Barry T. Hirsch and David A. Macpherson, "Union Membership and Coverage Database from the Current Population Survey: Note," *Industrial and Labor Relations Review* 56 (2003): 349; Kris Maher, "U.S. News: Unions See Members Fall by 10%," *Wall Street Journal*, January 23, 2010, p. A3.

35. Richard W. Hurd and Sharon Pinnock, "Public Sector Unions: Will They Thrive or Struggle to Survive?" *Journal of Labor Research* 25 (2004): 211–221.

36. Robert Hebdon, "Behavioural Determinants of Public Sector Illegal Strikes: Cases from Canada and U.S.," *Relations Industrielles* 53 (2004): 667–690.

37. John Helton and Tom Cohen, "Walker's Wisconsin Win Big Blow to Unions, Smaller One to Obama," CNN Politics, June 6, 2012, http://www.cnn.com/2012/06/05/politics/wisconsin-recall-vote

38. Morley Gunderson, "Two Faces of Union Voice in the Public Sector," *Journal of Labor Research* 26 (2005): 393–413.

39. Hurd and Pinnock, "Public Sector Unions," 211.

40. Anonymous, "AFL–CIO Reaches Out to Hispanics and Illegal Immigrants," *Management Report* 29, no. 12 (2006): 1.

41. Tove H. Hammer, Mahmut Bayazit, and David L. Wazeter, "Union Leadership and Member Attitudes: A Multilevel Analysis," *Journal of Applied Psychology* 94 (2009): 392–410.

42. Joel Cutcher-Gershenfeld and Thomas Kochan, "Taking Stock: Collective Bargaining at the Turn of the Century," *Industrial and Labor Relations Review* 58 (2004): 3.

43. Jelle Visser, "Union Membership Statistics in 24 Countries," *Monthly Labor Review* 129, no. 1 (2006): 38–49.

44. Joseph Ofori-Dankwa, "Murray and Reshef Revisited: Toward a Typology/Theory of Paradigms of National Trade Union Movements," *Academy of Management Review* 18 (1993): 269–292.

45. Michael Wallerstein, Miriam Golden, and Peter Lange, "Unions, Employers' Associations, and Wage-Setting Institutions in Northern and Central Europe, 1950–1992," *Industrial and Labor Relations Review* 50 (1997): 379–401.

46. Jessica Marquez, "Unions Global End Run," *Workforce Management* 85, no. 2 (2006): 1.

47. Daniel I. Rees, Pradeep Kumar, and Dorothy W. Fisher, "The Salary Effect of Faculty Unionism in Canada," *Industrial and Labor Relations Review* 48 (1995): 441.

48. Brian E. Becker, "Union Rents as a Source of Takeover Gains Among Target Shareholders," *Industrial and Labor Relations Review* 49 (1995): 3.

49. Virginia Doellgast, Ursula Holtgrewe, and Stephen Deery, "The Effects of National Institutions and Collective Bargaining Arrangements on Job Quality in Front-Line Service Workplaces," *Industrial and Labor Relations Review* 62 (2009): 489–509.

50. Dale Belman, John S. Heywood, and John Lund, "Public Sector Earnings and the Extent of Unionization," *Industrial and Labor Relations Review* 50 (1997): 610.

51. David Neumark and Michael L. Wachter, "Union Effects on Nonunion Wages: Evidence from Panel Data on Industries and Cities," *Industrial and Labor Relations Review* 49 (1995): 20.

52. Ted Pilonero, "Paying Employees Too Little Can Be Costly," *Health Care Strategic Management* 24, no. 5 (2006): 1–3.

53. John S. Heywood, W. S. Siebert, and Xiangdong Wei, "Worker Sorting and Job Satisfaction: The Case of Union and Government Jobs," *Industrial and Labor Relations Review* 55 (2002): 595; Michael E. Gordon and Angelo S. DeNisi, "A Re-Examination of the Relationship Between Union Membership and Job Satisfaction," *Industrial and Labor Relations Review* 48 (1995): 222.

54. Information about organizing a union can be found on the NLRB website at the following sites: http://www.nlrb.gov/what-we-do/conduct-elections

55. Adrienne E. Eaton, and Jill Kriesky, "NLRB Elections Versus Card Check Campaigns: Results of a Worker Survey," *Industrial and Labor Relations Review* 62 (2009): 157–172.

56. Henry S. Farber, "Union Success in Representation Elections: Why Does Unit Size Matter?" *Industrial and Labor Relations Review* 54 (2001): 329–348.

57. John-Paul Ferguson, "The Eyes of the Needles: A Sequential Model of Union Organizing Drives, 1999–2004," *Industrial and Labor Relations Review* 62 (2008): 3–21.

58. Daphne Gottlieb Taras and Jason Copping, "The Transition from Formal Nonunion Representation to Unionization: A Contemporary Case," *Industrial and Labor Relations Review* 52 (1998): 22.

59. Jack Fiorito, Paul Jarley, and John Thomas Delaney, "National Union Effectiveness in Organizing: Measures and Influences," *Industrial and Labor Relations Review* 48 (1995): 613; Linda Babcock and John Engberg, "Bargaining Unit Composition and the Returns to Education and Tenure," *Industrial and Labor Relations Review* 52 (1999): 163.

60. Lois E. Tetrick, Lynn M. Shore, Lucy Newton McClurg, and Robert J. Vandenberg, "A Model of Union Participation: The Impact of Perceived Union Support, Union Instrumentality, and Union Loyalty," *Journal of Applied Psychology* 92 (2007): 820–828.

61. Steven Mellor, John E. Mathieu, and Janet K. Swim, "Cross-Level Analysis of the Influence of Local Union Structure on Women's and Men's Union Commitment," *Journal of Applied Psychology* 79 (1994): 203–210.

62. Carrie A. Bulger and Steven Mellor, "Self-Efficacy as a Mediator of the Relationship Between Perceived Union Barriers and Women's Participation in Union Activities," *Journal of Applied Psychology* 82 (1997): 935–944.

63. Steven Mellor, "Gender Composition and Gender Representation in Local Unions: Relationships Between Women's Participation in Local Office and Women's Participation in Local Activities," *Journal of Applied Psychology* 80 (1995): 706–720.

64. Christina Cregan, "Can Organizing Work? An Inductive Analysis of Individual Attitudes Toward Union Membership," *Industrial and Labor Relations Review* 58 (2005): 282.

65. Kate Bronfenbrenner, "The Role of Union Strategies in NLRB Certification Elections," *Industrial and Labor Relations Review* 50 (1997): 195.

66. Robert Bussel, "Southern Organizing in the Post–Civil Rights Era: The Case of S. Lichtenberg," *Industrial and Labor Relations Review* 52 (1999): 528.

67. Julian Barling, Kevin E. Kelloway, and Eric H. Bremermann, "Preemployment Predictors of Union Attitudes: The Role of Family Socialization and Work Beliefs," *Journal of Applied Psychology* 76 (1991): 725–731; Kevin E. Kelloway and Laura Watts, "Preemployment Predictors of Union Attitudes: Replication and Extension," *Journal of Applied Psychology* 79 (1994): 631–634.

68. Hwee Hoon Tan and Samuel Aryee, "Antecedents and Outcomes of Union Loyalty: A Constructive Replication and an Extension," *Journal of Applied Psychology* 87 (2002): 715–722; Clive J. A. Fullager, Daniel G. Gallagher, Michael E. Gordon, and Paul F. Clark, "The Impact of Early Socialization on Union Commitment and Participation: A Longitudinal Study," *Journal of Applied Psychology* 80 (1995): 147–157.

69. Paul D. Staudohar, "The Hockey Lockout of 2004–05," *Monthly Labor Review* 128, no. 12 (2005): 23–29.

70. Howard Beck, "NBA Reaches a Tentative Deal to Save the Season," New York Times, November 26, 2011; http://www.nba.com/2011/news/09/09/labor-timeline/index.html

71. Paul D. Staudohar, "The Baseball Strike of 1994–95," *Monthly Labor Review* 120, no. 3 (1997): 21–27.

72. Seungwoo Kwon and Laurie R. Weingart, "Unilateral Concessions from the Other Party: Concession Behavior, Attributions, and Negotiation Judgments," *Journal of Applied Psychology* 89 (2004): 263–278.

73. Paul D. Staudohar, "Baseball Negotiations: A New Agreement," *Monthly Labor Review*, no. 12 (2002): 15–22.

74. Richard C. Reuben, "Baseball Strike Teaches Legal Lessons," *ABA Journal* (June 1995): 42–43.

75. Ray Friedman, Cameron Anderson, Jeanne Brett, Mara Olekalns, Nathan Goates, and Cara Cherry Lisco, "The Positive and Negative Effects of Anger on Dispute Resolution: Evidence from Electronically Mediated Disputes," *Journal of Applied Psychology* 89 (2004): 369–376.

76. http://www.foxnews.com/sports/2011/11/22/mlb-announces-new-collective-bargaining-agreement/

77. Natasha Caverly, Bart Cunningham, and Lari Mitchell, "Reflections on Public Sector–Based Integrative Collective Bargaining: Conditions Affecting Cooperation within the Negotiation Process," *Employee Relations* 28 (2006): 62–75.

78. Kathleen M. O'Connor, Josh A. Arnold, and Ethan R. Burris, "Negotiators Bargaining Histories and Their Effects on Future Negotiation Performance," *Journal of Applied Psychology* 90 (2005): 350–362.

79. George W. Bohlander and Jim Naber, "Nonadversarial Negotiations: The FMCS Interest-Based Bargaining Program," *Journal of Collective Negotiations* 28 (1999): 41–52.

80. Gilles Trudeau, "The Internal Grievance Process and Grievance Arbitration in Quebec: An Illustration of the North-American Methods of Resolving Disputes Arising from the Application of Collective Agreements," *Managerial Law* 44 (2002): 27–46.

81. Richard B. Peterson and David Lewin, "Research on Unionized Grievance Procedures: Management Issues and Recommendations," *Human Resource Management* 39 (2000): 395.

82. Brian Bemmels, "The Determinants of Grievance Initiation," *Industrial and Labor Relations Review* 47 (1994): 285–301.

83. Lawrence Nurse and Dwayne Devonish, "Grievance Management and Its Links to Workplace Justice," *Employee Relations* 29 (2007): 89.

84. Nina D. Cole and Gary P. Latham, "Effects of Training in Procedural Justice on Perceptions of Disciplinary Fairness by Unionized Employees and Disciplinary Subject Matter Experts," *Journal of Applied Psychology* 82 (1997): 699–705.

85. Bemmels, "The Determinants of Grievance Initiation."

86. Patrick E. McDermott, "Survey of 92 Key Companies: Using ADR to Settle Employment Disputes," *Dispute Resolution Journal* 50 (1995): 8–13.

87. Steven B. Goldberg, "How Interest-Based, Grievance Mediation Performs over the Long Term," *Dispute Resolution Journal* 59, no. 4 (2005): 8–15.

Chapter 14
Aligning Strategy with Practice

A MANAGER'S PERSPECTIVE

imtmphoto/iStockphoto

TAKASHI LEAVES HIS OFFICE AND WALKS ACROSS THE
COURTYARD TO THE CORPORATE BUILDING. TODAY
HE IS MEETING WITH A GROUP OF TOP EXECUTIVES
TO EXPLAIN PROPOSED CHANGES TO THE PERFOR-
MANCE APPRAISAL PROCESS. FROM PAST EXPERI-
ENCE, TAKASHI KNOWS THAT THE PROPOSAL WILL BE
MET WITH SKEPTICISM BY SOME BUT ENTHUSIASTI-
CALLY ACCEPTED BY OTHERS. DURING HIS 10-YEAR
CAREER AS A HUMAN RESOURCE SPECIALIST HE HAS
BEEN PART OF MORE THAN 30 INITIATIVES TO ALTER
PERFORMANCE MANAGEMENT PRACTICES, YET EACH
TIME HE IS AMAZED AT THE EMOTIONS GENERATED BY
CHANGE. THIS TIME HE IS PARTICULARLY NERVOUS
BECAUSE HE PERSONALLY HAS CONCERNS ABOUT THE
PROPOSAL THAT IS BEING PUT FORTH.

One of Takashi's main concerns is that hiring
practices over the past few years have been geared
toward selecting star performers. Recruits were
promised high pay and rapid advancement. For the
most part, these promises have been kept. The highest performers have been recognized and rewarded.
However, the new performance management program
puts less emphasis on identifying top performers and
seeks to treat everyone similarly. Managers will no
longer be required to
rate employees in com-
parison to each other,
and everyone in a work
group can receive the same rating. Takashi worries
that these changes to the performance management
system will send a signal that is not consistent with
other human resource practices.

Takashi recently read an article, written by an
experienced human resource professional, who
argued that human resource practices—including
work design, recruiting, selection, training, and
compensation—should fit together to create a
consistent set of procedures for attracting and
motivating workers. When he read the article, he
thought it made a lot of sense. If the company goes
ahead with the proposed performance management
changes, shouldn't it also alter the hiring process to
focus on bringing in employees who are comfortable
working in groups rather than being star performers? Shouldn't they change compensation to reward
consistent effort rather than short-term exceptional
performance? In fact, Takashi really wonders how
they will be able to make compensation decisions
once the new performance ratings make it more
difficult to identify top performers. He is just not

©Douglas Pebbles/Corbis

THE BIG PICTURE *Human Resource Management Is Most Effective When Human Resource Practices Complement Each Other and Align with Competitive Strategy*

---

sure that all the potential consequences of the new performance system have been considered.

As he nears the corporate building, Takashi greets Dave, who has been the top sales representative for the past four years. Dave tells Takashi a quick joke and then asks if the rumors about a performance management change are true. As Takashi evades the question, Dave states that he will accept a position with a competitor if things change and his excellent contributions are not recognized.

Takashi leaves Dave and lets out a sigh of frustration. He suspects that Dave will really leave the company. Experience has taught him to think carefully about how a change in one human resource practice can affect other practices. In the current case he believes that the shift away from identifying top performers will be a big problem. The next few months will be challenging. The role of an HR specialist just seems to get harder each year.

WHAT DO YOU THINK?

As Takashi makes his presentation, the executives make the following remarks. Which of the statements do you think are true?

| **T or F** | Effective human resource management can be a source of competitive advantage for an organization. |

| **T or F** | Human resource practices are most effective when they align with an organization's competitive business strategy. |

| **T or F** | The best way to choose a method of performance management is to identify and copy a practice that is successful at another organization. |

| **T or F** | Human resource policies and practices are not as important in smaller companies. |

| **T or F** | Future trends and technological advances will likely decrease the importance of human resource management. |

After reading this chapter you should be able to:

LEARNING OBJECTIVE 1   Explain the concepts of vertical and horizontal alignment.

LEARNING OBJECTIVE 2   Identify the specific human resource practices that fit within each of the basic HR strategies.

LEARNING OBJECTIVE 3   Understand how basic competitive and HR strategies can vary, what role human resources can play in strategy formulation, and why human resource management is important for small organizations.

LEARNING OBJECTIVE 4   Describe how the field of human resource management is likely to change in upcoming years.

How Can Alignment of HR Practices Make an Organization Effective?

Congratulations, you made it to the last chapter! At this point, you should be able to identify many benefits of effective human resource management. You should also be able to describe the processes associated with a number of human resource practices. Hopefully, you answered "true" to the first two "What Do You Think?" questions. You have missed some important concepts if you don't know the answer to these questions by now. Attracting and hiring the right people, and then properly training and motivating them, is critical for building a successful organization. As we have discussed in each chapter, these efforts are most beneficial when they fit with the organization's strategy.

One of the strategic issues we discussed back in Chapter 2 was the importance of bundling human resource practices. Human resource management is most effective when various practices work together to create an overall culture of excellence. Combinations, or bundles, of practices are more valuable than a single good practice in isolation.[1] A set of good human resource practices builds a strong culture. A good example of a company with a strong culture shaped by effective human resource management is Walt Disney Company. Most of us have childhood memories of Disney movies, vacations, and products. What may not be obvious is the role of human resource practices in creating such memories.

Worldwide, Disney has more than 166,000 employees and revenues exceeding $42 billion. Walt Disney World in Florida is one of the largest single-site employers in the United States.[2] Disney has a clear strategy of differentiation, with an emphasis on creativity and family entertainment. The effective execution of this strategy is seen at Disney World, where success is measured by the creation of magical experiences. Great customer service and friendly interactions between customers and employees, who are referred to as cast members, set Disney World apart from competitors. The role of employees in ensuring high-quality customer service was captured by the founder—Walt Disney himself—when he stated, "You can dream, create, design, and build the most wonderful place in the world, but it requires people to make the dream a reality."[3]

Although it pursues a differentiation strategy, success for Walt Disney World does not depend only on employees with specialized skills. Most of the jobs in the theme park are made up of relatively simple tasks, such as food service and ticket taking. The key to success in these positions is friendly employees who work together to create a fun atmosphere. Disney World uses an HR strategy for theme park workers that most resembles the Loyal Soldier model to carry out its differentiation strategy. Human resource practices are designed to build a culture of cooperation and customer service. The unique experience of working for Disney, rather than the performance of a specific job, is emphasized in every aspect of human resource management.

Work tasks at Disney World are designed around standardized procedures. Employees are told that they have three major tasks:[4]

1. To keep the park clean.
2. To create happiness.
3. To do their specific jobs.

Everyone is expected to follow company procedures, and an extensive system of standard operating procedures is in place. Standardization helps to ensure that employees know how to interact with guests in the way Disney wants. For example, employees learn that they are always "on stage," and they are encouraged to do specific things, such as maintain eye contact with guests, that will help them to create positive social encounters. Standardization also ensures that employees are treated the same no matter where they work in the park. Work design at Disney World is thus aimed at creating an atmosphere in which each employee feels responsible for making sure that guests are highly satisfied and in which teamwork is emphasized over high individual achievement.[5]

Recruiting processes help Disney World attract a sufficient number of employees who fit the company culture. Disney, which takes a flow approach to recruiting, is always looking to hire people who fit the culture. Because the demand for entry-level workers at Disney World is often greater than the number of workers available in the Orlando area, the company conducts ongoing recruiting in other locations, such as Puerto Rico and New York City.

Early in the recruiting process, potential hires are shown a video that provides a realistic picture of what it is like to work at Disney. Time off on holidays is rare, since the park is always open. Strict codes regulate employees' appearance and prohibit such things as visible tattoos. This realistic approach saves time and effort by quickly encouraging around 10 percent of applicants to decide on their own that they do not fit with the Disney culture. Those who do fit may be offered as much as $1,500 in relocation assistance.[6]

The selection process at Disney World is captured by the phrase "hire for attitude; train for skills." Managers focus on selecting employees with friendly personalities and good customer service skills. Once the company has hired the kind of employees it wants, it makes extensive efforts to retain them. The annual turnover rate is below 20 percent, which is outstanding for the industry. One practice that encourages loyalty is a high rate of internal promotions; approximately 80 percent of jobs are filled by internal candidates.[7]

Training begins as soon as employees enter the organization. New hires are taught about the Disney culture through examples and stories that emphasize the value of family-friendly entertainment and high levels of customer service. Employees learn core values such as respect, integrity, and appreciation of diversity. Everyone, including the employee who sweeps up trash in the park, is taught to smile and greet guests in a friendly manner. Classes focus on using humor to entertain guests and taking time to engage people in conversation. Managers receive ongoing training to improve their skills for creating a positive work environment that motivates and retains employees.[8]

Rewards and recognition are also an important part of the human resource package at Disney World. High-performing employees are recognized at dinner parties and celebrations. Employees receive awards when they reach milestones for years of employment. This public recognition builds loyalty and sends a clear signal that employees will be rewarded for having consistent attendance and providing quality service. Loyalty is also encouraged by providing employees with discounts and invitations to exclusive parties.[9]

Each of the human resource practices at Walt Disney World contributes to the success of the theme park. However, the true value of human resource management comes from the entire package of practices. Work tasks are designed to encourage cooperation and compliance with standard operating procedures that promote high levels of customer service. Recruiting and selection practices ensure that the people hired have personality traits that fit Disney's values. Training, as well as rewards and incentives, further emphasize the Disney culture and encourage actions that ensure good customer service. The incentive system encourages and motivates people who have the characteristics identified in the selection and recruiting process. Competitive advantage through people, then, comes not so much from any particular practice but from alignment of the various practices. The overall package is recognized as valuable enough that companies in other industries have come to Disney for human resource training and consultation. The bundle of practices that has helped make Disney a great place to work—and therefore a successful organization—is in essence sold to other companies.

Building Strength Through HR

WALT DISNEY WORLD

©Douglas Pebbles/Corbis

Walt Disney World is a theme park located in Orlando, Florida. It is owned by Walt Disney Company, an organization with over 166,000 employees and $42 billion in annual revenue. Human resource management at Walt Disney World builds competitive strength by

- Ensuring consistently high customer satisfaction by adopting standardized procedures to maintain consistently high service
- Recruiting and selecting employees who have outgoing personalities that fit with organizational culture
- Providing training and rewards that encourage loyalty and a focus on doing whatever it takes to meet the needs of guests
- Creating a consistent bundle of human resource practices that work together to create a culture of customer service

What Are Two Basic Forms of Strategic Alignment?

In earlier chapters, we often talked about aligning practices with strategies. Think for a minute about the concept of alignment. A dictionary definition of the term might involve the proper positioning of parts. For instance, an automobile works best when the tires are in alignment—in other words, when each tire is in the proper position in relation to the other tires and the rest of the automobile. This same concept applies to human resource practices. Each human resource practice is in **alignment** when it is in its proper place relative to other practices and strategic objectives. A compensation system that emphasizes and rewards loyalty and longevity, for example, is in alignment when it fits with other human resource practices and with the overall strategic objectives of the organization, as in the case of Disney.

Alignment
The state in which organizational practices are in their proper place relative to other practices.

Alignment comes in several different forms. Figure 14.1 illustrates two basic forms of alignment that are commonly discussed as part of strategic management. The first form, **vertical alignment**, refers to the positioning of an organization's human resource management strategy in relation to other organizational strategies.[10] The fundamental issue is whether an organization's human resource strategy fits with its competitive strategy. An organization might be out of vertical alignment if it seeks to differentiate

Vertical alignment
The state in which an organization's human resource strategy supports its competitive business strategy.

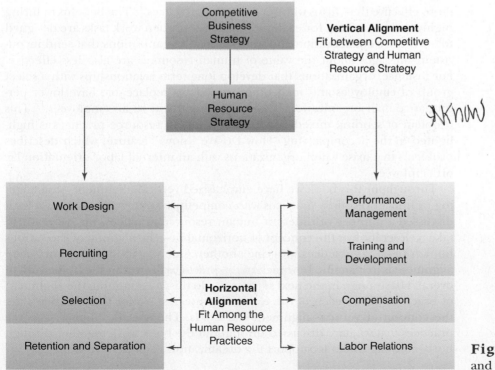

Figure 14.1 Vertical and Horizontal Alignment

its products through innovation but adopts a Bargain Laborer HR strategy, for example. A Free Agent or Committed Expert HR strategy would more closely align with the competitive strategy of differentiation through innovation. As we have seen, the contingency perspective of human resource management suggests that organizations are more effective when their approach to human resource management fits—or aligns—with their competitive approach.

Research studies support the value of vertical alignment. Successful organizations pursuing a specific organizational strategy usually have an appropriately aligned HR strategy.[11] For instance, organizations with human resource strategies that emphasize developing long-term relationships with highly skilled employees—what we have referred to as the Committed Expert HR strategy—have been shown to be more effective than their competitors because they create more new products and services. In essence, the Committed Expert HR strategy develops a climate of trust and cooperation that helps employees share knowledge and work together to innovate.[12]

The other form of fit, known as horizontal alignment, concerns the coordination of parts within the organization.[13] In the specific case of human resource management, **horizontal alignment** refers to the fit of specific practices with other practices.[14] The selection practice of seeking employees who are likely to be team players aligns with the performance appraisal practice of reducing competition among employees, for example. In contrast, practices would not be horizontally aligned if the selection practice focused on hiring team players but the performance appraisal practice emphasized competition and individual achievement.

Research studies also support the benefits of horizontal alignment. Firms with consistent bundles of human resource practices have been found to be more effective than firms without consistent practices.[15] The benefits of hiring highly skilled workers, for example, are greatest when work tasks are designed to encourage collaboration and innovation.[16] Organizations that send inconsistent messages about the value of human resources are also less effective. For instance, organizations that develop long-term relationships with a select group of employees and treat other workers as replaceable have lower performance than organizations showing commitment to all employees.[17] This problem of sending mixed signals about human resource practices is highlighted in the accompanying "How Do We Know?" feature, which describes problems that arise when organizations with an internal labor orientation lay off employees.

Throughout this book we have emphasized vertical alignment—the aligning of human resource practices with competitive strategy. Now that we have discussed a number of different human resource practices, we are ready to take a closer look at the concept of horizontal fit—the aligning of the various human resource practices with one another. One way to illustrate horizontal alignment is to examine how each of the practices fits within the framework of overall HR strategy. In the next section, we do this by examining the alignment of practices within each of the four HR strategies. Notice that, in each case, the concept of vertical alignment still holds. The specific human resource practices that we have discussed throughout the book work together through horizontal alignment to support the organization's competitive strategy.

Horizontal alignment
The state in which individual human resource practices fit together and support each other.

How Do We Know?

WHAT HAPPENS WHEN ORGANIZATIONS SEND MIXED SIGNALS ABOUT THE VALUE OF EMPLOYEES?

What happens when an organization doesn't treat employees as they expect to be treated? Will an organization that has used human resource practices to develop close relationships with employees suffer when it adopts a contrary practice? Christopher Zatzick and Roderick Iverson sought to answer this question by examining whether the effects of employee layoffs on organizational productivity depend on an organization's general approach to managing employees.

Approximately 3,000 Canadian workplaces provided reports about their human resource practices, employee layoff rates, and productivity. Employee layoffs were found to have a negative effect on productivity when organizations had human resource policies that communicated high commitment. In particular, layoffs harmed the productivity of organizations with flexible work arrangements, high

empowerment, teams, cooperative compensation, and formal training. Some of this effect was overcome, however, if the firm continued to show commitment after the layoffs.

The Bottom Line. Productivity suffers when an organization engages in a human resource practice that is not aligned with its other human resource practices. The authors conclude that layoffs can erode the competitive advantage that a firm achieves through adopting a set of human resource practices that demonstrate high commitment to employees.

Source: Information from Christopher D. Zatzick and Roderick D. Iverson, "High-Involvement Management and Workforce Reduction: Competitive Advantage or Disadvantage," *Academy of Management Journal* 49 (2006): 999–1015.

CONCEPT CHECK

1. *How do the concepts of vertical and horizontal alignment differ?*
2. *What happens when a human resource practice is not in horizontal alignment with other practices?*

LEARNING OBJECTIVE 2

How Do HR Practices Align with One Another?

Most chapters in this book have included a strategic framework describing how specific human resource practices fit with an overall HR strategy. Now that we have separately discussed all these practices, we are ready to integrate them to describe how human resource management should operate within each of the broad HR strategies. Examining practices from the perspective of each HR strategy also provides a good review of the strategic concepts we have discussed in earlier chapters.

EXTERNAL/COST: ALIGNMENT FOR BARGAIN LABORERS

The Bargain Laborer HR strategy focuses on creating efficiency with talent obtained from external labor markets. Such an approach is adopted by many fast-food restaurants and hotels. Human resource practices focus on minimizing labor costs. Most employees work in entry-level positions that require few specialized skills. Few workers feel strong commitment to the organization, and quitting to accept a better job in another organization is common. Table 14.1 lists core human resource practices associated with the Bargain Laborer HR strategy.

Work Design

Organizations that pursue a Bargain Laborer HR strategy make work as simple as possible so that employees with little skill can quickly learn their jobs. Work is structured according to concepts from the mechanistic approach to job design, and tasks are similar to machine parts—each with a specific, limited purpose. Work is broken into simple tasks that can be easily learned. Goods and services are produced by assembly lines that represent sequential processing. Autonomy is low. Employees are expected to complete specific tasks in the prescribed way, which helps ensure coordination.

Recruiting and Selection

Recruiting within the Bargain Laborer HR strategy is designed to identify a large number of candidates. An approach using a broad skill scope with external sourcing, as described in Chapter 5, is appropriate. High turnover creates a need for ongoing applications from people willing to work in relatively low-skilled positions. The lack of need for specific skills allows organizations to cast a wide net to identify potential workers. Positive aspects of the job are highlighted to encourage applicants to accept positions. Common recruiting methods include referrals, print advertising in newspapers, electronic advertising on commercial websites, and public employment agencies.

After recruiting comes selection. Organizations pursuing the Bargain Laborer HR strategy constantly hire new employees. Because the jobs they will

Table 14.1	*Practices Aligning with Bargain Laborer HR Strategy*
Practice	**Emphasis on . . .**
Work Design	• Simplified tasks
Recruiting and Selection	• Having numerous job applicants
	• Predicting dependability
Retention	• Accepting some employee turnover
Performance Management	• Ensuring minimally acceptable contribution
Training and Development	• Learning specific job duties
	• Reducing training costs
Compensation	• Minimizing labor costs
	• Limiting pay differences among employees
Labor Relations	• Labor union incompatibility with short-term employment

be performing are relatively simple, selection practices need not identify specific skills and abilities. And since no one expects employees to have a long career with the organization, there is little need to assess organizational fit. In most cases, employees are hired because they are dependable and willing to follow instructions. Common selection methods include cognitive ability testing, physical ability testing, integrity testing, drug testing, and application forms.

Retention

Frequent turnover of employees is common with the Bargain Laborer HR strategy, since low-paid workers in relatively unskilled jobs often switch employers. Good employees are encouraged to stay as long as they will, but the emphasis on cost reduction often makes it difficult to retain high performers. In addition, given the ongoing need to attract workers, low-performing employees are usually allowed to stay employed as long as they meet minimum requirements. The Bargain Laborer HR strategy and its focus on cost reduction thus accepts some employee turnover and does not strongly emphasize either retention or forced separation.

Performance Management

Performance management within the Bargain Labor HR Strategy focuses on ensuring that employees are performing above a minimally acceptable level. This means that assessments are based on absolute standards that do not compare employees with each other. Little emphasis is placed on identifying high performers.

Training and Development

Teaching employees how to perform specific job duties, with an emphasis on efficient operations, is the key focus of training for the Bargain Laborer HR strategy. Training focuses not only on learning how to do things but also on communicating the importance of following company procedures. Because of the emphasis on efficiency, training effectiveness is often assessed in terms of the costs associated with helping employees learn. Costs can be reduced by purchasing off-the-shelf training packages, reducing travel, and using current employees as part-time trainers. Long-term employee development is not common in organizations with a Bargain Laborer HR strategy, as few employees stay with the company long enough to benefit from learning skills that would be beneficial in future jobs.

Compensation

In accordance with the goal of minimizing labor costs, compensation levels tend to be relatively low in organizations using the Bargain Laborer HR strategy. These organizations set wage rates at the point necessary to attract workers but do not offer premium wages to attract and retain highly skilled employees. The level of compensation for each job depends largely on what individuals can earn in similar jobs at other organizations. Organizations that follow the Bargain Laborer strategy often use compensation that minimizes pay differences among employees and acknowledges that most employees do not have a strong commitment to the organization. The desire to reduce labor costs means that most such organizations avoid making pay contingent on performance. Employees are usually paid an hourly wage for doing what they are asked to do. In some cases, however, employees receive piece-rate compensation that ties their wages to individual productivity.

Labor Relations

A major objective of most labor unions is ensuring job security. Unions are therefore somewhat at odds with the Bargain Laborer HR strategy. Employees are less likely to organize or join unions, since they usually do not expect to have a long-term relationship with the organization.

INTERNAL/COST: ALIGNMENT FOR LOYAL SOLDIERS

The Loyal Soldier HR strategy focuses on internal talent development and efficiency. Table 14.2 lists core human resource practices associated with the Loyal Soldier HR strategy. An earlier discussion illustrated how United Parcel Service has benefited from the Loyal Soldier strategy. Government offices, such as motor vehicle departments, also frequently adopt this strategy. Organizations following such an approach seek to develop a strong culture of commitment. Human resource practices encourage long careers within the organization. Work is facilitated when employees do whatever is asked of them, with a focus on reducing costs. Even organizations that require employees to perform relatively mundane work can benefit from human resource practices that engage employees and provide them with an opportunity to participate.[18] The U.S. Navy, which is profiled in the "Building Strength Through HR" feature, provides an example of an organization that is aligned around the Loyal Soldier HR strategy.

Work Design

Organizations pursuing a Loyal Soldier HR strategy adopt standardization as a core principle of work design. As with the Bargain Labor HR strategy, work is structured according to the mechanistic approach for job design, which seeks to create an efficient machine for producing goods and services. Employees learn and carry out efficient processes and have little power to change how work is completed. Assembly lines are common, and each employee performs a limited number of tasks. The focus is on determining efficient production processes and then encouraging employees to follow prescribed methods of doing things.

Table 14.2	*Practices Aligning with Loyal Soldier HR Strategy*
Practice	**Emphasis on . . .**
Work Design	• Standardized procedures
Recruiting and Selection	• Internal promotions
	• Organizational fit
Retention	• Keeping loyal workers
Performance Management	• Parity-based assessments that encourage cooperation
Training and Development	• Teaching specific skills
	• Continual learning
Compensation	• Rewarding long-term contribution
	• Limiting pay differences among employees
Labor Relations	• Labor unions supplementing a culture of solidarity

Building Strength Through HR

U.S. NAVY

The U.S. Navy has the difficult task of recruiting and managing over 317,000 active-duty personnel, as well as 109,000 reservists. The overall HR strategy aligns closely with the Loyal Soldier perspective. Sailors are expected to perform a variety of tasks, and effort is continually directed toward encouraging reenlistment.

Each year the Navy must recruit a large number of new workers. Positions range from basic recruit to nuclear operator and doctor. Most recruits are young. Recruiting relationships are formed with school counselors and advisors. Advertising is also directed toward parents, with a message of the opportunity and benefits that come with a Navy career. Once a sailor is recruited, a relationship is developed to make him or her feel a part of the large organization. This long-term commitment is summarized by Vice Admiral Mark Ferguson, who states, "That bond with them, where they feel that we're going to invest in them and take care of them and their families, is the strongest component."

A specific staffing practice that is consistent with building a long-term employment relationship is a recent program that allows sailors to bid for jobs that pay them extra. For example, jobs at Guantanamo Bay were avoided by many sailors, but a program that allowed sailors to set their price for accepting the assignment resulted in sailors willingly taking the jobs. Paying them a premium fit with a low-cost strategy in that significant savings were realized from not having to compensate the sailors in other ways such as with extra leave time.

Training and career development are key components of human resource management within the Navy. A model called the 5 Vector Model identifies milestones for career paths from recruit all the way to admiral. The first vector is professional

©Lowell Georgia/Corbis

development and emphasizes technical skills. Qualifications and certifications, which make up the second vector, provide credentials that go beyond a sailor's specific job. For instance, many receive certification in firefighting. The third vector, personal development, emphasizes lifelong learning, wellness, and interpersonal skills. Leadership skills are emphasized as the fourth vector, and performance accomplishments are the fifth vector. Taken together, these five vectors, or areas of development, help ensure that Navy personnel advance through the ranks and develop a diverse set of skills.

Human resource practices are also tracked and coordinated with an objective measurement system. Data are collected to capture both efficiency of operation and satisfaction of managers. These data help reduce costs and standardize procedures. This helps the Navy become more effective as it works to recruit, develop, and retain a loyal workforce.

Sources: Information from Mark Schoeff, Jr., "U.S. Navy: Optimas Award Winner for General Excellence," *Workforce Management* (December 14, 2009): 14–15; Gary Kirchner, "The Navy's New War," *Training* 42, no. 7 (2005): 30–36; F. Sharkey, S. Rosenberg, K. Marti, and T.E. Winchell, Sr., "A New Model for Human Resources Performance Measurement," *Public Manager* 33, no. 3 (2004): 26–32.

Recruiting and Selection

Recruiting strategies linked to the Loyal Soldier HR strategy are designed to identify current employees who can be promoted and transferred. Using a broad skill scope with internal sourcing, the strategy focuses on getting employees to move within the organization so that they can engage in new experiences and develop broad skills. The key to success for internal recruiting is to identify people who are willing to change positions and who can benefit from new job opportunities. Applicants receive a realistic recruiting message that provides information about all aspects of the job and organization. Specific recruiting methods include job posting and electronic advertising within the company.

Recruiting for entry-level positions emphasizes locating and gaining the attention of job applicants who will become loyal employees committed to the organization. External efforts to locate entry-level employees focus on obtaining job applications from people who have personality characteristics that fit with organizational values. Common methods include employee referrals, electronic advertising, public employment agencies, and campus recruiting.

The next step is to hire people from the pool of job applicants. The emphasis is on identifying people who will fit with the organizational culture. Since employees will rotate among numerous jobs during their careers, identifying specific skills and interests is not critical. General aptitude and motivation are more important. Employees are hired more for their potential than for what they have already achieved. Common selection methods associated with the Loyal Soldier HR strategy include cognitive ability testing, personality testing, physical ability testing, drug testing, application forms, and interviewing.

Retention

Employees who fit the organization are encouraged to stay. Employee retention is thus a major part of the Loyal Soldier HR strategy. When an individual is not performing well in a particular job, he or she will likely be placed in a different position within the organization. The organization continually monitors employee satisfaction and implements programs to improve working conditions. To create a bond with employees, the organization communicates support and care about their well-being. Workers are embedded by relationships with others throughout the organization.

Performance Management

Performance management is used to motivate employees working in organizations that use the Loyal Soldier HR strategy. Employee contributions are assessed, and feedback provides guidance for improvement. Given the need for standardization, measurement focuses on how well employees follow standard operating procedures. Cooperation and teamwork are emphasized over high individual performance. Parity-based assessments compare performance against absolute standards and allow everyone to be classified as a high performer.

Training and Development

Training is critical for success with the Loyal Soldier HR strategy. As we have seen, employees are selected mostly for fit with the organization rather than with a particular job. This often makes it necessary for them to develop skills after they have been hired. Indeed, many skills will be specific to how things are done in the organization, making it so that people can learn what they need to know only after they have become employees. Training is often done on the job and focuses on specific procedures for completing tasks. This helps to minimize costs and ensure standardization of operating procedures. Ongoing training is also important, since employees will rotate through a number of jobs during their careers with the organization. Training helps these employees learn new skills each time they are transferred to positions that are very different from their past positions.

Compensation

Consistent with the Loyal Soldier HR strategy, compensation focuses on providing rewards for long-term contributions. Workers who have been with the organization for more time earn higher wages. Compensation strives to provide similar rewards to all employees. Good benefits help strengthen the bond between employees and the organization. Health insurance and retirement plans, for example, help employees meet basic needs and make it difficult for them to change employers. Most compensation takes the form of base pay, and little is placed at risk from pay period to pay period. The organization may use group incentives to encourage cooperation among workers and may offer profit-sharing and stock plans to link employee behavior with long-term organizational interests. Overall compensation under the Loyal Soldier HR strategy is designed to reward employees who are team players and who commit to long careers with the organization.

Labor Relations

We frequently see labor unions in organizations pursuing a Loyal Soldier HR strategy. The focus on ensuring long-term employment and equality among workers is compatible with this strategy. The sense of solidarity that comes from the union adds to the organizational culture of cooperation. In addition, the sense of stability that usually develops among union workers can benefit an organization that is trying to achieve efficiency through long-term relationships with employees.

INTERNAL/DIFFERENTIATION: ALIGNMENT FOR COMMITTED EXPERTS ✗ Paper Case Study

The Committed Expert HR strategy focuses on creating distinctive products and services with talent developed internally. Pharmaceutical firms such as Merck and consumer product firms such as Procter and Gamble often adopt this strategy. Human resource practices are designed to form a strong bond between the organization and its employees. Workers are encouraged to pursue long careers within the organization, and each employee is expected to become an expert in his or her chosen field. Ideally, workers will use their expertise to innovate and create unique outputs.

Work Design

Organizations pursuing a Committed Expert HR strategy emphasize high worker autonomy and reciprocal processing. In other words, such organizations give employees broad responsibilities and expect them to continually coordinate their efforts with those of others. Skilled employees have freedom to adjust their work to fit with changing demands, and they are encouraged to experiment to learn new ways to approach tasks. Groups of workers continually coordinate their efforts and adapt to changing technological innovations and shifting market conditions. Work is designed around the motivational approach to job design, which seeks to ensure that each employee knows the results of his or her activities and perceives work tasks as meaningful. The focus is on designing work in ways that provide employees with opportunities to innovate and develop ongoing relationships with others.

Recruiting and Selection

As shown in Table 14.3, recruiting strategies associated with the Committed Expert HR strategy focus first on internal candidates. The targeted skills approach, combined with internal sourcing, seeks to identify current employees with skills that have been developed through training and experience in the organization. Because of the emphasis on long careers, recruiting for entry-level positions communicates a realistic message that clearly describes the good and bad aspects of the job and organization. The key to successful recruiting of employees with required expertise is identifying people who have specific skills and who are committed to advancing through the ranks within the organization. Common recruiting sources to identify applicants already working for the company include job posting and electronic advertising in areas of the company website that are accessible only to employees. Sources for recruiting outside the organization include employee referrals and campus recruiting.

The next decision concerns whom to select from the pool of job applicants generated from internal and external sources. With the Committed Expert HR strategy, the goal is to identify individuals with potential to develop specific expertise over time. Employees don't necessarily need advanced skills before they are hired, but they should have the ability and interest necessary to develop specific skills during their careers. They also need characteristics that fit the culture of the organization. Employees should thus be selected because of fit not only with specific tasks to be performed but also with organizational

Table 14.3	*Practices Aligning with Committed Expert HR Strategy*
Practice	**Emphasis on . . .**
Work Design	• Broad work responsibilities
Recruiting and Selection	• Predicting high potential
	• Organizational and job fit
Retention	• Retaining high performers
	• Dismissing low performers
Performance Management	• Merit-based assessments that encourage good outcomes
Training and Development	• Skill training for current job
	• Development for future jobs
Compensation	• Using variable pay to reward high performers
	• Long-term benefits and employee ownership
Labor Relations	• Potential negative impact of labor unions on innovation

culture. Common selection methods used to assess potential and fit include cognitive ability testing, personality testing, assessment centers, biodata, and interviewing.

Retention

Once employees have been hired, the emphasis of the Committed Expert HR strategy is on retention of high performers and dismissal of low performers. Organizational efforts focus on creating a desirable workplace with satisfied employees. Effective discipline is used to encourage low performers to improve. The employment of those who don't improve is terminated so that the ability of the organization to produce quality goods and services is not compromised. Fortunately, if recruiting and selection methods are operating as they should, instances of discipline and dismissal are rare.

Performance Management

Performance management is a critical part of the Committed Expert HR strategy. Success depends on having employees who far exceed minimum expectations. Organizations use competition to encourage employees to stretch their efforts. Competition comes from merit-based performance appraisal, which allows high performers to stand out. Employees are compared with each other, and forced distributions ensure that only a few receive the highest rating. This approach strengthens the culture of innovation and creativity.

Training and Development

Training and development are essential for the Committed Expert HR strategy. Training teaches specific skills that employees need to perform their current jobs. Continuous improvement of employees' skills is a key to producing goods and services superior to those produced by competitors. Given that employees are expected to stay with the organization for long careers, development activities are also beneficial. Assessment and feedback programs help employees see areas where they need improvement. Developmental relationships also provide guidance and support for employees who are advancing through the organizational ranks. Training and development thus work together to help employees develop superior skills, which enable them to perform well not only in their current positions but also in future positions in the organization.

Compensation

Effective compensation is another critical element of the Committed Expert HR strategy. Because organizations using this strategy seek to hire and retain the best workers, the overall level of pay is usually higher than the level at other organizations. In addition, variable forms of compensation are used to provide extra incentives for high performance. High performers are acknowledged and paid more than average performers. A substantial amount of pay is put at risk during each pay period, and high performers are paid a risk premium. Long-term incentives such as profit sharing and stock options align the monetary interests of employees with the long-term interests of the organization. Merit pay increases provide higher pay for more years of contribution, and team-based incentives encourage cooperation among employees. Good benefits strengthen ties between the organization and employees by communicating a sense of caring and by making it somewhat costly for employees to change employers. Overall compensation within the Committed Expert HR strategy is designed to provide high incentives to top performers who pursue long careers with the organization.

Labor Relations

The long-term emphasis of the Committed Expert HR strategy is compatible with labor unions. However, unions are often incompatible with the focus on innovation—recall that in unionized companies, money that might otherwise be spent on research and development often is diverted to higher pay for employees. The practice of giving more favorable treatment to high performers is also sometimes at odds with union interests.

EXTERNAL/DIFFERENTIATION: ALIGNMENT FOR FREE AGENTS

The Free Agent HR strategy is aimed at obtaining the input of experts to create distinct products and services. Information technology firms frequently adopt this strategy. Many investment banking firms also fit with the Free Agent model. Human resource practices focus on locating external talent. Employees normally enter the organization with the skills they need to perform their work tasks. Organizations acknowledge that these employees develop careers within occupations rather than specific organizations. As a result, they are more loyal to a particular profession, such as investment banking, than to the organization. Strong bonds between the organization and employees are not encouraged. Workers are frequently replaced by new employees who have up-to-date skills. Table 14.4 summarizes HR practices that are common with the Free Agent strategy.

Work Design

Organizations pursuing a Free Agent HR strategy focus on creating a work environment in which skilled employees have the freedom and opportunity

Table 14.4	*Practices Aligning with Free Agent HR Strategy*
Practice	**Emphasis on . . .**
Work Design	• Complex tasks
Recruiting and Selection	• Assessing achievement and specific skills
	• Job fit
Retention	• Dismissing low performers
Performance Management	• Merit-based systems that create internal competition
Training and Development	• Attracting good employees by offering development opportunities
Compensation	• Providing high compensation for top performers
	• Making rewards contingent on performance
Labor Relations	• Labor unions conflicting with special treatment for high performers

to innovate and create unique outputs. Autonomy is high, and tasks are complex. Workers are expected to apply their expertise and to contribute in ways that are seldom fully understood by others in the organization. Adaptation is encouraged, and rules for accomplishing work are rare. The focus is on giving highly skilled workers freedom to accomplish the tasks they are uniquely qualified to perform.

Recruiting and Selection

Recruiting practices for the Free Agent HR strategy are designed to locate and gain the attention of skilled workers who are capable of contributing in a relatively unstructured work environment. Using a targeted skill scope and external sourcing, the approach focuses on locating specific talent outside the organization. Because only a limited number of people possess the desired skills, targeted recruiting seeks applications from a select few. Common recruiting sources include employee referrals, print advertising in specialized journals, targeted Internet sites, and private employment agencies.

Selection practices identify the individuals in the recruiting pool who are most likely to succeed. For organizations pursuing Free Agent HR strategies, these are people who clearly have the desired skills and abilities. The objective of selection is thus to assess potential employees' past achievements to determine whether they already have the skills needed for the job. Fit with the demands of a particular job is more important than fit with the organization. Common methods used for selection include work sample testing, résumés, and interviewing.

Retention

Even with careful recruiting and selection, employees will sometimes be hired who don't really have the ability and motivation to perform the necessary tasks. This is a particular problem for organizations pursuing a Free Agent HR strategy. The employee was hired to do a specific job, after all, and trouble can quickly develop if the tasks aren't being performed properly. Removing low-performing employees is thus an important part of the Free Agent strategy. Poor performance must be dealt with quickly, and employees who cannot do what is required are dismissed.

Performance Management

Performance management within the Free Agent HR strategy focuses on separating high and low performers. Organizations using this strategy create a culture of competition and excellence by comparing employees with each other and forcing distributions so that only a few receive the highest evaluation. Because of the specialized nature of the work and the unique expertise of each worker, assessments often focus on outcomes rather than behavior.

Training and Development

Training is not seen as critical for the Free Agent HR strategy, as employees are expected to have the skills they need when they enter the organization. Long-term development opportunities can, however, help the organization recruit highly skilled workers because participating in development will provide these employees with credentials that are recognized by other organizations. Formal education programs offered by universities, consultants, and trade organizations are sources of such development. Another sort of development involves certification or licensing that acknowledges specific expertise. Participation in such programs may not result in knowledge about how to perform specific tasks, and the employee may not stay with the organization long enough to actually apply much of what is learned. However, highly skilled employees are more likely to accept positions with organizations when they perceive that they will have an opportunity to continue growing their skills. Development of skills that can be transferred to other organizations is thus an important part of the Free Agent HR strategy.

Compensation

Compensation rates are relatively high in organizations pursuing the Free Agent HR strategy. To hire and retain highly skilled employees, these organizations must pay higher wages than other organizations. In addition, compensation provides higher wages to top performers. The lack of emphasis on long-term contribution means that newly hired employees are often paid the highest wages. In most cases, a large proportion of compensation is put at risk, so that people are rewarded only when they produce at a high level. Commission and bonuses are frequently part of the pay package. Overall compensation within the Free Agent HR strategy is designed to provide immediate reward for high contribution.

Labor Relations

The emphasis on short-term employment relationships, along with higher compensation for top performers, generally makes the Free Agent HR strategy incompatible with unions. In addition, most employees who work in these organizations see themselves as professional workers rather than union members. Unions are thus rare in organizations pursuing a Free Agent HR strategy.

CONCEPT CHECK

1. *What specific practices align within each of the four HR strategies?*
2. *How do recruiting and selection practices differ across the HR strategies?*

LEARNING OBJECTIVE 3

What Are Some Other HR Issues?

This is an introductory textbook, so of course we have not been able to discuss everything in the field of human resource management. There are, however, some additional issues that we should briefly review in this final chapter. One issue concerns variations on the strategies that we have discussed. Another issue relates to the role of human resource management in creating strategy. Yet another issue involves the importance of human resource management for small firms.

VARIATIONS OF BASIC STRATEGIES

Throughout this book, we have focused on four basic HR strategies: Bargain Laborer, Loyal Soldier, Committed Expert, and Free Agent. Each of these strategies is associated with a different competitive business strategy. Organizations can, however, pursue slightly different and more specific competitive strategies. Although these strategies can be seen as variations and combinations of the competitive strategies we have discussed, it is worth highlighting a few common alternative strategies to see how they fit with the basic HR strategies.

One variation of an organization's competitive approach is a **turnaround strategy**. Here, a company that is performing badly attempts to change radically and return to profitability. In many cases, employees are laid off, and new approaches to production are implemented. This strategy requires organizations to do things very differently than they have in the past, which usually makes it compatible with an external labor orientation. Low performers are dismissed, and new employees are hired for their ability to change the way work is accomplished. A Free Agent HR strategy is thus often part of a competitive strategy that emphasizes the need to turn around low organizational performance quickly.

Global expansion is another frequent variation of competitive strategy. A **global expansion strategy** focuses specifically on growing an organization's presence in foreign countries. Human resource management can play an important role in helping an organization achieve this objective. In many cases, effective implementation of the strategy requires organizations to attract and select workers who are quite different from those already employed. The human resource approach most closely aligned with the global expansion competitive strategy is the Free Agent HR strategy.

Another variation of competitive strategy is the **growth strategy**, through which a company seeks to expand into new markets. In some cases, this is done through acquisitions and mergers. Effective human resource management can be critical for reducing barriers to effective integration of organizational cultures. For example, Johnna Torsone, who is senior vice president and chief HR officer of Pitney Bowes, Inc., spends a great deal of her time integrating human resource practices. Over the past several years, Pitney Bowes has pursued a growth strategy through acquisition of other companies. Torsone and other human resource professionals have helped the company assess the talent and skills of employees in companies that might be acquired. Companies with employees and human resource practices that do not fit the Pitney Bowes model are less likely to be acquired.[19]

Turnaround strategy
A competitive business strategy that focuses on radical change to return a company to profitability.

Global expansion strategy
A competitive business strategy that focuses on increasing an organization's presence in foreign countries.

Growth strategy
A competitive business strategy that focuses on expanding products and services into new markets.

How Do We Know?

DOES WORKING IN A FOREIGN COUNTRY REQUIRE MORE SKILL?

Is working in a foreign country more difficult than working domestically? Do employees working in foreign countries need to adapt their behavior to fit the demands of the culture in order to succeed? Shung Shin, Frederick Morgeson, and Michael Campion conducted a study to answer these questions. They surveyed 1,312 midcareer professional employees working in an international agency of the U.S. government.

Employees working in 156 countries were asked to describe the skills, abilities, and personality requirements of their jobs. Expatriate employees working in foreign countries reported higher skill and ability requirements than people working in their home countries. International assignments required greater social skills, more perceptual and reasoning skills, and higher motivation to achieve and adjust. These higher requirements were primarily due to changes associated with working in a different culture.

A subset of 945 employees who answered the survey also reported the frequency of certain work behaviors. Employees working in cultures that emphasize group harmony and social relationships reported engaging in more relationship-oriented behavior. People working in cultures emphasizing power differences between managers and line workers reported more frequent administrative activity and monitoring of resources. These findings suggest that employees do indeed adapt their behaviors to fit the demands of their host country.

The Bottom Line. Working in a foreign country is more demanding than working in one's home country. The authors conclude that global organizations can benefit from using selection and training procedures to ensure that employees possess and further develop the skills necessary to succeed in international assignments.

Source: Information from Shung J. Shin, Frederick P. Morgeson, and Michael A. Campion, "What You Do Depends on Where You Are: Understanding How Domestic and Expatriate Work Requirements Depend upon the Cultural Context," *Journal of International Business Studies* 38 (2007): 64–83.

The "How Do We Know?" feature illustrates how alternative strategies that we have discussed, such as global expansion, can be affected by human resource practices. There are, of course, other variations on competitive strategies. Fortunately, the core human resource concepts can be adapted to help an organization achieve whatever strategy it is pursuing. The key is to begin by thinking about what types of worker inputs are needed to carry out the strategy successfully. Once these inputs have been identified, the organization can generally modify one of the core HR strategies to help it acquire and motivate the types of workers it needs. The four basic HR strategies thus provide a good foundation for thinking about ways to successfully manage people, but they may need to be adapted to meet the needs of a specific organization.

Rational strategic approach
An approach in which organizational leaders carefully plan a strategy before carrying it out.

HR AS AN INPUT TO COMPETITIVE STRATEGY

Throughout this book, we have taken the perspective that organizations begin with a competitive strategy and then match their HR strategy to the competitive strategy. This **rational strategic approach** assumes that organizational leaders plan what they want to accomplish and then use human resource practices to help them reach their objectives. Instead, however, many organizations appear to adopt an evolutionary approach to competitive strategy. Under an **evolutionary strategic approach**, strategy is not always planned; rather, it unfolds over time. From this perspective, an organization's human resource capabilities can be seen as part of the strategy formulation process.

The notion that human resources provide an input to competitive strategy suggests that organizations with human resource limitations may not be able to carry out certain strategies. For instance, suppose an organization produces goods that are no longer in high demand. The organization may wish to become more innovative, but it may have trouble moving to a more innovative strategy if its employees do not have up-to-date skills. In contrast, organizations with certain human resource strengths may be able to incorporate these strengths into future plans. For example, consider an organization with highly skilled employees who are capable of working in foreign countries. This pool of talent could form the basis for a decision to pursue a global expansion strategy. In sum, we need to realize that human resource capabilities can drive strategy formulation.[20]

Evolutionary strategic approach
An approach in which an organization's strategy unfolds over time in response to common issues.

THE ROLE OF HR IN SMALL BUSINESSES

Historically, the field of human resource management has focused on large organizations. But what about the role of human resource management in small organizations that employ only a few workers? Small businesses often lack elaborate HR systems and strategies. This does not, however, mean that human resource strategy and practice are less important to small businesses.

Small organizations with better strategic plans for human resource management have been shown to have a higher rate of survival.[21] In addition, small firms that place greater emphasis on recruiting, selection, performance appraisals, training, and compensation grow at a faster rate than other firms.[22] In particular, effective human resource management helps small organizations innovate, which is critical for their survival.[23]

Unfortunately, little is known about the specific human resource practices that are most effective for small businesses. In many cases, commonly accepted practices must be adapted to fit the unique demands of small organizations. In the future, the field of human resource management will benefit from additional research and investigation into the unique circumstances of small businesses.

CONCEPT CHECK

1. *What are some variations of basic competitive strategies? How do the basic HR strategies fit with these variations?*
2. *In what ways can human resource capabilities influence an organization's competitive strategy?*

What Might the Future of HR Look Like?

The field of human resource management is continually changing. In recent years, the emphasis has moved away from personnel management designed to ensure compliance with legal requirements toward a strategic model that links the management of people to competitive objectives. This trend is expected to continue. The Society for Human Resource Management (SHRM), which is the primary professional organization for HR professionals—and an organization we recommend students interested in the field join—recently asked members to identify the top issues that they think HR executives will face in the next 10 years. Results of the survey are shown in Figure 14.2. These human resource professionals identified retaining top performers and developing corporate leaders as the greatest challenges. Interestingly, the emphasis on global issues seems to be waning, perhaps because organizations have already made progress in this area.

As part of another research project, SHRM had a panel of experts identify top trends. Numerous important trends were identified. In the following

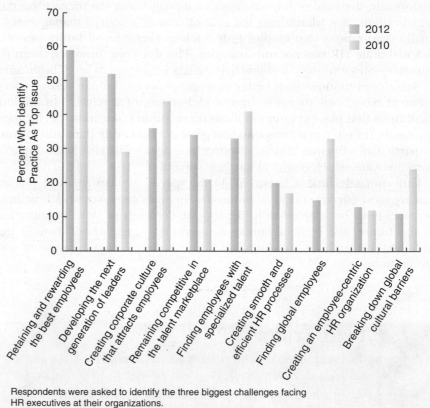

Respondents were asked to identify the three biggest challenges facing
HR executives at their organizations.
Percentages do not total 100% because respondents chose three options.

Figure 14.2 Challenges Facing HR Executives *Source:* SHRM Research Spotlight: Future HR Challenges and Talent Management Tactics, www.shrm.org/research.

sections, we discuss five key trends that we see as especially critical to the future of human resource management: volatile economic conditions, increased emphasis on sustainability, growth of social networking, balancing of work and family, and adaptation to healthcare legislation.[24]

VOLATILE ECONOMIC CONDITIONS

The recent recession made clear the uncertainty of economic conditions. For many companies, declining profits made it difficult to maintain not only stable business relationships but also employee morale. The focus often shifted away from hiring more workers to reducing the workforce. HR has thus been forced to think more strategically and become better at using data to drive decisions. As explained in the "Building Strength Through HR" feature, one company that benefitted from human resource management during the recession is Ford Motor Company.

 # Building Strength Through HR

FORD MOTOR COMPANY

Ford Motor Company has annual revenue exceeding $132 billion It was the only U.S. automaker not to receive government bailout assistance during the recent recession. Effective management of people is one reason why Ford has been able to outperform its competitors.

A few years back, Ford began a Way Forward plan. Much of the plan focused on cutting the workforce and reducing labor costs. However, Ford also began major changes in the ways that it trains and motivates employees. Increased emphasis was placed on training workers to reduce waste and improve productivity. Layers of management were cut, and employees were given more responsibility and access to top bosses. The prototypical employee became someone who works well in a team to find better ways of accomplishing tasks. Taking initiative was emphasized and rewarded.

The management of a subsidiary provides an example of Ford's commitment to employees and the company's understanding of the value of effective human resource management. Over a decade ago, Ford spun off its parts supplier Visteon. After a few years Visteon was nearly bankrupt, but Ford bought part of the company back and created a unit known as Automotive Components Holdings. Ford worked to return the subsidiary

plants to profitability. Better management of people was the key to the turnaround. Employees were given incentive pay to motivate them to work harder. Alliances were formed with local colleges to provide needed training. Communication with employees was emphasized and enhanced. These efforts resulted in 5 to 10 percent improvements in quality and cost during the first 8 months. Also important to Ford, better treatment of employees helped ensure a consistent flow of parts.

Today, Ford Motor Company employs 164,000 people and is seen by many as the top U.S. automobile manufacturer. Success is facilitated by the following human resource practices:

- Training workers to reduce cost and improve quality.
- Reducing managerial layers and empowering employees.
- Restructuring jobs and transforming labor relationships.

Sources: Jessica Marquez, "Ford Recovery Plan Includes Long-Term People Investment in Short-Term Business," *Workforce Management* 85, no. 13 (2006): 46–47; Laura Egodigwe, "In Perfect Alignment," *Black Enterprise* 39, no. 11 (2009): 49; Irwin Speizer, "The Right Way Forward?" *Workforce Management* 85, no. 6 (2006): 25–30; John Reed and Bernard Simon, "Ford Back in the Black after 'Pivotal' Year," *Financial Times*, January 29, 2010, p. 17; http://www.sec.gov/Archives/edgar/data/37996/000003799612000007/f12312011-10k.htm.

INCREASED EMPHASIS ON SUSTAINABILITY

Society is increasingly paying attention to the effect of business practices on the natural environment. Companies are examining their business practices to determine areas where improvement is needed. Regulations requiring environmental protection are growing in many countries. Many organizations are also engaging in corporate philanthropy to give back to the communities where they are located. HR plays an important role in many of these efforts. Job roles and responsibilities must be updated. Efforts to engage individuals in community activities are also often coordinated by human resource professionals.

GROWTH OF SOCIAL NETWORKING

Social networking is a common activity for most college students. Platforms such as Facebook, LinkedIn, and Twitter are a key part of life. Employees are increasingly expecting organizations to integrate human resource activities with these tools. Having a presence in network circles provides organizations with a tool to increase employee engagement. Unfortunately, social outlets are often used to post negative information about a company, and in some cases to harass co-workers. Mobile apps will become more and more common as the primary method for accessing information about benefits and compensation. Many organizations have also begun to obtain information from social network sources before extending job offers. Students and potential employees thus need to carefully manage their social media presence.

BALANCING OF WORK AND FAMILY

People are increasingly struggling to balance work and family commitments. This balance is particularly difficult for women, as illustrated by the content and reaction to Facebook COO Sheryl Sandberg's recent book *Lean In: Women, Work, and the Will to Lead*. The book suggest that women can benefit from more fully engaging in work, but many critics have argued that such talk puts too much pressure on women and ignores their important family roles.[25] Given challenges in balancing life pressures, HR must continue to develop flexible career paths. Many new workers are also looking for intrinsic work rather than employment that simply provides a paycheck.

ADAPTATION TO HEALTHCARE LEGISLATION

Over the past few years, HR has played a key role in initiatives to reduce the cost of healthcare.[26] Healthcare reform was a major issue during the past presidential election; implementation of the Affordable Care Act (Obamacare) has now become a major focus of many organizations. In most cases, HR is taking the lead to ensure that companies comply with new regulations. Wellness programs are also an increasing priority for organizations seeking to improve the overall health of employees.

Each of the five trends suggests that the role of human resource management is increasingly important for modern organizations. As you finish this book, we hope you have come to see human resource management as a dynamic and evolving field. You may not choose a career in HR, but you can apply the principles we have discussed to help you become more effective in whatever you do. Most great leaders acknowledge the importance of surrounding themselves with highly skilled people who are motivated to succeed. The strategic principles and practices that we have discussed can help you do the same by more effectively managing people at work.

CONCEPT CHECK

1. *What issues are expected to become priorities for HR executives in the next 10 years?*
2. *What trends are shaping the future of human resource management?*

A MANAGER'S PERSPECTIVE REVISITED

imtmphoto/iStockphoto

IN THE MANAGER'S PERSPECTIVE THAT OPENED THE CHAPTER, TAKASHI WAS THINKING ABOUT PROPOSED CHANGES TO THE PERFORMANCE MANAGEMENT PROCESS. HE WAS CONCERNED THAT THE CHANGES HAD NOT BEEN CAREFULLY DESIGNED TO FIT WITH OTHER AREAS OF HUMAN RESOURCE MANAGEMENT. FOLLOWING ARE THE ANSWERS TO THE "WHAT DO YOU THINK?" QUIZ THAT FOLLOWED THE CASE. WERE YOU ABLE TO CORRECTLY IDENTIFY THE TRUE STATEMENTS? COULD YOU DO BETTER NOW?

1. Effective human resource management can be a source of competitive advantage for an organization. TRUE. *That has been an important theme throughout this book. A system for obtaining and managing people is an important resource that is difficult for competitors to imitate.*

2. Human resource practices are most effective when they align with an organization's competitive business strategy. TRUE. *As we have explained throughout this book, organizations are more effective when they align human resource management with competitive strategy.*

3. The best way to choose a method of performance management is to identify and copy a practice that is successful at another organization. FALSE. *Human*

resource practices, such as performance management, are most effective when they are aligned with an organization's business strategy and other HR practices.

4. Human resource policies and practices are not as important in smaller companies. FALSE. *Effective human resource management appears to be equally important for small and large businesses.*

5. Future trends and technological advances will likely decrease the importance of human resource management. FALSE. *Upcoming labor shortages are expected to increase the value of good human resource management.*

Takashi is wise to think about how changing one human resource practice might affect other practices. The concept of horizontal alignment acknowledges that human resource practices are best when they operate in concert to obtain and motivate the right type of employee. This chapter illustrates how HR practices can combine to support each of the four basic HR strategies. It also touches on a few additional issues and identifies some areas of human resource management likely to be important in the future.

SUMMARY

What are two basic forms of alignment?

Alignment occurs when human resource practices are in their proper place relative to other practices and strategic objectives. Vertical alignment refers to the positioning of human resource management in relation to competitive strategy. Horizontal alignment refers to the fit of specific human resource practices relative to each other. Research suggests that organizations are most effective when they have both vertical and horizontal alignment.

How do human resource practices align with one another?

The Bargain Laborer HR strategy focuses on efficiency and cost reduction. Work tasks are simplified. Ongoing recruiting efforts seek a large number of job applicants. Selection is based on dependability and willingness to perform unskilled tasks. Some turnover of employees is expected. Performance measures ensure that employees perform at a minimally acceptable level. Training focuses on efficiently teaching employees how to perform specific tasks. Compensation provides relatively low wages with minimal differences among employees. Labor unions are rare.

The Loyal Soldier HR strategy focuses on building a strong culture and creating talent internally. Work is structured around standardized procedures. Employees are promoted from within the organization. Selection focuses on identifying individuals who fit with the organizational culture. Parity-based performance assessments encourage cooperation among workers. Training and development teach not only skills for the current job but also skills needed for future positions. Compensation minimizes differences among workers and rewards employees who have long careers with the organization. Labor unions can supplement the culture of solidarity and stability.

The Committed Expert HR strategy uses internally developed talent to produce distinctive goods and services. Employees are given broad task responsibilities. Recruiting focuses on obtaining job applicants who have aptitude in specific areas. Employee selection decisions are based on both organization fit and job fit. Efforts are made to retain high performers, but low performers are dismissed. Merit-based performance assessment creates a sense of competition and innovation. Training teaches skills that are beneficial for current jobs, and development extends abilities so that employees can be promoted. Compensation builds long-term ties to the organization, and high performers receive greater rewards than low performers. Labor unions are compatible with the emphasis on long-term employment relationships but sometimes incompatible with the need for innovation.

The Free Agent HR strategy obtains labor inputs from experts. Work is designed to give employees the autonomy they need to carry out tasks they are uniquely qualified to perform. Targeted recruiting focuses on job applicants who already have the skills needed to perform a specific job. Employee selection is based on past achievements. Merit-based performance appraisal systems assess outcomes and recognize outstanding performers. Training is rare, and development opportunities are provided mostly as a tool for attracting good employees. Compensation is at risk and provides extraordinary rewards for high performers. Labor unions are generally incompatible with the Free Agent HR strategy.

What are some other HR issues?

One important additional issue concerns variations on the four basic HR strategies we have discussed. Common variations on competitive strategies include the turnaround strategy, global expansion strategy, and growth strategy. In most cases, variations of the core HR strategies can be adapted to fit these specific competitive strategies.

Another issue involves the role of human resources in shaping strategy. We have focused on the rational strategic approach, in which human resource strategy is designed to fit competitive strategy. In contrast, the evolutionary strategic approach suggests that human resource capabilities can drive competitive strategy. When this approach is used, the nature of employee skills and abilities can serve as an important input into strategic decisions.

A third issue concerns the role of HR management in small organizations. Effective human resource management is critical for small businesses. More research is needed to understand

methods of applying human resource strategy to small businesses, however.

LEARNING OBJECTIVE 4

What might the future of HR look like?

Trends suggest that key issues faced by HR executives in the next ten years include retaining top performers and developing corporate leaders. Adaptation to globalization appears to be less of an issue than it was two years ago. Future trends relevant to human resource management include increased emphasis on sustainability, growth of social networking, balancing of work and family, volatile economic conditions, and adaptation to healthcare legislation.

KEY TERMS

Alignment   541
Evolutionary strategic approach   557
Global expansion strategy   555
Growth strategy   555

Horizontal alignment   542
Rational strategic approach   556
Turnaround strategy   555
Vertical alignment   541

DISCUSSION QUESTIONS

1. How is horizontal alignment different from vertical alignment?
2. Which do you think is more important: vertical alignment or horizontal alignment?
3. What might happen if an organization combines a merit-based performance appraisal system with compensation practices that limit differences in employee pay?
4. Within the Loyal Soldier HR strategy, how does the approach of parity-based performance appraisal support the work-design goal of standardization?
5. What difficulties might an organization face when it attempts to change its human resource practices?

6. What are some specific HR practices that could be used to support a global expansion strategy?
7. What specific methods of selecting and compensating employees do you think a small business should use?
8. How do you believe current societal trends will influence future human resource strategies and practices?
9. What advice do you think would be helpful for someone beginning a career as a human resource professional?
10. How would you summarize the most important concepts you have learned about human resource management?

EXAMPLE CASE | *Portman Ritz-Carlton in Shanghai, China*

In the following interview, Mark DeCocinis, general manager of the Portman Ritz-Carlton and regional vice president, Asia-Pacific, of the Ritz-Carlton Hotel Company, shares his successful formula with Arthur Yeung, Philips Chair Professor of Human Resource Management at the China Europe International Business School.

Arthur Yeung: The Portman Ritz-Carlton has been consistently selected the Best Employer in Asia. What's your secret to success in people management?

Mark DeCocinis: The secret is constancy in execution. Our priority is taking care of people. We're in the service business, and service comes only from people. It's about keeping our promise to our employees and making that an everyday priority. Our promise is to take care of them, trust them, develop them, and provide a happy place for them to work. The key is everyday execution.

Arthur Yeung: The idea is to set up people for success so they have pride in their jobs. But in China, where employees have relatively poor service attitudes and skills, what management practices do you put in place to help them succeed?

Mark DeCocinis: The key starts with selecting the right people. Our selection focuses on talent and personal values because these are things that can't be taught. Our culture is special, and we can't expect to bring someone into this culture if they don't have the same values and purpose.

We focus on a person's theme. What do they enjoy? What's their purpose in life? What motivates them? We look for people who genuinely enjoy contact with people and helping others. It's not about being introverted or extroverted; it's about caring for and respecting others. You can work at the front desk or behind the scenes, but you must enjoy contact with others, whether they are guests or other employees.

Arthur Yeung: How many people are promoted from within? What's the average tenure of employees here?

Mark DeCocinis: Many senior positions are filled from within the hotel or within the company, approximately 70 to 80 percent of the leadership positions. We took over management of the hotel in January 1998. Over 60 percent of the employees have tenure of more than five years, and over 30 percent have tenure of eight years or more.

Arthur Yeung: Besides the selection process, what else does the Ritz-Carlton do to motivate its employees to provide excellent service?

Mark DeCocinis: We spend two days of orientation with new employees before they come into contact with any guest. They must understand our culture and philosophy. The general manager, the executive team or guidance team, and HR are all involved. Each of them explains our Credo (we are here to take care of our guests); our Employee Promise (we are to take care of you); our 20 Basics; and our Motto (we are ladies and gentlemen taking care of ladies and gentlemen).

Then they receive 30 days of training with a certified trainer from the department. Following that, we have reinforcement training on the 21st day, and we get feedback on how we can improve our training program for future retraining and recertification. Then, throughout the year we provide a minimum of 130 hours of training for every employee, including specific training for their department and training on culture, language, and computer skills.

Arthur Yeung: You start with a philosophy that employee satisfaction leads to guest satisfaction, which in turn leads to good financial results. How do you know such a relationship really exists?

Mark DeCocinis: I'll give this hotel as an example. Our employee satisfaction rate is 98 percent. In the last five years, it's been 95, 97, and 98 percent. Our guest satisfaction is between 92 and 95 percent. If employee satisfaction were to decrease, I guarantee the other factors would decline. Let's say the employees are happy but the guests are not, that means we are not balanced.

QUESTIONS

1. How do selection, retention, and training practices work together at the Portman Ritz-Carlton?

2. Which of the HR strategies do you think the Portman Ritz-Carlton is pursuing?

3. Why do you think employee satisfaction leads to customer satisfaction?

Source: Arthur Yeung, "Setting People Up for Success: How the Portman Ritz-Carlton Hotel Gets the Best from Its People," *Human Resource Management* 45 (2006): 267–275. Reprinted with permission of John Wiley & Sons, Inc.

DISCUSSION CASE | *Technology Consultants*

Technology Consultants is a company started by a computer science professor. Five years ago, the professor hired three graduate students and began offering computer and technology services to local companies. The company grew rapidly and currently employs 30 consulting specialists. The typical specialist recently graduated from college with a degree in information management or computer science. Each specialist is assigned to work as part of a team that focuses on servicing the needs of specific customers. To date, Technology Consultants has not felt a need to formalize personnel practices. The professor spends most of his time hiring and training new consulting specialists. He also has a part-time administrative assistant who helps with personnel activities such as payroll.

Some customers complain about the high turnover of consulting specialists. It seems that most consultants leave within a year after being hired. From the customers' perspective, specialists leave just when they are beginning to understand how to provide quality service. The professor knows this is a problem, and she worries that such turnover may eventually lead customers to cancel their contracts for service. In the past, she and a few key employees were able to form long-term relationships with most clients, but this is becoming increasingly difficult as the company grows.

Technology Consultants recruits at two local universities. This practice seems to be effective, as most graduates from the programs have the technological skills needed to serve clients. The hiring process consists of a series of interviews. The professor and two other employees conduct informal interviews and then offer jobs to individuals they feel will be successful. They don't worry much about personality traits or past achievements; they simply focus on assessing technical skills. The performance of each consulting specialist is measured against the performance of peers, and only a few employees receive the highest ratings. Since most employees are expected to possess the technological skills they need when they are hired, Technology Consultants does not offer opportunities for training and development. Compensation has been a difficult issue for the company's founder. She wants to encourage teamwork, so she has chosen to structure pay so that most employees receive similar wages. She doesn't want to have some employees earning a lot more than others. New hires are paid approximately the same as other consulting specialists. So far, the company has found it difficult to offer employee benefits. The professor feels that the cost of the benefits is too high.

QUESTIONS

1. Which human resource practices would you recommend that Technology Consultants change?
2. How well do the company's human resources practices align with one another?
3. How would you approach human resource management if you were starting a company like Technology Consultants?

EXPERIENTIAL EXERCISE — *Learning about Company Cultures*

Identify three friends or family members who work at different companies. Ask each of them to describe the culture of the company. What words would most employees use to describe the company? How would customers describe the company? What does it feel like to work for the company? What type of employees succeed? How does management interact with the employees? What kind of relationships do employees have with each other?

Once friends and family members have described the company culture, ask them about human resource practices. How are work tasks assigned to specific employees? What sources are used to inform potential applicants about work opportunities? How are people hired? What is done to keep employees from leaving for jobs with other companies? Are many people dismissed for low performance? What kind of training and development are offered? How is pay structured? Do some employees make a lot more than others? How much of pay is put at risk? Are employees organized into labor unions?

Examine the companies' cultures and human resource practices by answering the following questions:

1. How are the company cultures different?
2. Is there any evidence that human resource practices create company culture? How do recruitment and selection seem to influence culture? How does compensation influence interactions between employees?
3. Within each organization, identify human resource practices that are aligned. Are there some practices that seem to be out of alignment?

INTERACTIVE EXPERIENTIAL EXERCISE — *A Final Journey: Communicating the Strategic Importance of HR*
http://www.wiley.com/college/sc/stewart

Access the companion website to test your knowledge by completing an interactive role play.

Through your diverse consulting experience, you have learned a great deal about how HR should align with competitive strategy (vertical alignment) and how HR practices should align with each other (horizontal alignment). In this exercise you are traveling to an HR conference and meet a corporate executive who has a very negative opinion of HR as a whole. He tells you that HR is the same in every company; that is, it adds no value to organizations, and that HR people are unable to think strategically. You recall what you've learned about the four basic HR strategies and the four companies you've recently helped—Mega Manufacturing, Graphics Design, Global Telecommunications, and SuperFoods. How will you convince the executive that he's wrong about HR? •

ADDITIONAL WEB RESOURCES

The Companion website for *Human Resource Management* contains myriad tools and links to assist you in the course.

Web Quizzes

This resource offers online quizzes, with questions varying in level of difficulty, designed to help you evaluate your individual progress through a chapter. Each chapter's quiz includes 10 questions, including true/false and multiple-choice questions. These review questions were created to provide an effective and efficient testing system. Within this system, you'll have the opportunity to "practice" the type of knowledge you'll be expected to demonstrate on exams.

WileyPLUS

If your instructor has adopted WileyPLUS, you'll have access to a variety of study tools:

- Video clips
- mp3 downloads—audio overviews of each chapter
- Business simulations
- Team evaluation tools
- Experiential exercises
- Self-assessments

ENDNOTES

1. James Combs, Yongmei Liu, Angela Hall, and David Ketchen, "How Much Do High-Performance Work Practices Matter? A Meta-Analysis of Their Effects on Organizational Performance," *Personnel Psychology* 59 (2006): 501–528.
2. http://a.media.global.go.com/investorrelations/annual_reports/WDC-10kwrap-2011.pdf; Douglas P. Shuit, "Magic for Sale," *Workforce Management* 83, no. 9 (2004): 35–40.
3. Liana Cafolla, "Investing in HR Is No Mouse Feat," *China Staff* 12, no. 8 (2006): 8–11.
4. Hoai Anh Nguyen and Brian H. Kleiner, 'Effective Human Resource Management in the Entertainment Industry," *Management Research News* 28, no. 2/3 (2005): 100–107.
5. Jeffrey Hickman and Karl J. Mayer, "Service Quality and Human Resource Practices: A Theme Park Case Study," *International Journal of Contemporary Hospitality Management* 15 (2003): 116–119.
6. Anonymous, "'Theme Parks Find They Must Take Innovative Steps to Fill Summer Jobs," *Wall Street Journal*, May 30, 2000; Dennis Blank, "Short-Staffed Disney, McD Siphon Offshore Labor Pool," *Nations Restaurant News* 33, no. 28 (1999): 1–6; Shuit, "Magic for Sale."
7. Shuit, "Magic for Sale"; Hickman and Mayer, "Service Quality and Human Resource Practices."
8. Cafolla, "Investing in HR Is No Mouse Feat."
9. Nguyen and Kleiner, "Effective Human Resource Management."
10. John E. Delery, "Issues of Fit in Strategic Human Resource Management: Implications for Research," *Human Resource Management Review* 8 (1998): 289–309.
11. Jeffrey B. Arthur, "The Link Between Business Strategy and Industrial Relations Systems in American Steel Mini-Mills," *Industrial and Labor Relations Review* 45 (1992): 488–506.
12. Christopher J. Collins and Ken G. Smith, "Knowledge Exchange and Combination: The Role of Human

Resource Practices in the Performance of High-Technology Firms," *Academy of Management Journal* 49 (2006): 544–560.

13. Ravi Kathuria, Maheshkumar P. Joshi, and Stephen J. Porth, "Organizational Alignment and Performance: Past, Present, and Future," *Management Decision* 45 (2007): 503–517.

14. Delery, "Issues of Fit in Strategic Human Resource Management."

15. John Paul MacDuffie, "Human Resource Bundles and Manufacturing Performance: Organizational Logic and Flexible Production Systems in the World Auto Industry," *Industrial and Labor Relations Review* 48 (1995): 197–221; Casey Ichinowski, Kathryn Shaw, and Giovanna Prennushi, "The Effects of Human Resource Management Practices on Productivity: A Study of Steel Finishing Lines," *American Economic Review* 87(1997): 291–313.

16. Mohan Subramaniam and Mark A. Youndt, "The Influence of Intellectual Capital on the Types of Innovation Capabilities," *Academy of Management Journal* 48 (2005): 450–463.

17. Joseph P. Broschak and Alison Davis-Blake, "Mixing Standard Work and Nonstandard Deals: The Consequences of Heterogeneity in Employment Relationships," *Academy of Management Journal* 49 (2006): 371–393.

18. Derek C. Jones, Panu Kalmi, and Antti Kauhnen, "How Does Employee Involvement Stack Up? The Effects of Human Resource Management Policies on Performance in a Retail Firm," *Industrial Relations* 49 (2010): 1.

19. Anonymous, "How Two HR Professionals Help Sustain Their Companies' Business Strategies," *HR Focus* 81, no. 12 (2004): 5–7.

20. Charles C. Snow and Scott A. Snell, "Staffing as Strategy," in Neal Schmitt, Walter C. Borman and Associates (Eds.), *Personnel Selection in Organizations* (San Francisco: Jossey Bass, 1993), pp. 448–480.

21. Theresa M. Welbourne and Alice O. Andrews, "Predicting the Performance of Initial Public Offerings: Should Human Resource Management Be in the Equation," *Academy of Management Journal* 39 (1996): 891–919.

22. Dawn S. Carlson, Nancy Upton, and Samuel Seaman, "The Impact of Human Resource Practices and Compensation Design on Performance: An Analysis of Family-Owned SMEs," *Journal of Small Business Management* 44 (2006): 531–543.

23. Michael L. Menefee, John A. Parnell, Ed Powers, and Chris Ziemnowicz, "The Role of Human Resources in the Success of New Businesses," *Southern Business Review* 32 (2006): 23–32.

24. Society for Human Resource Management, "Future Insights: The Top Trends for 2012 According to SHRM's Subject Matter Expert Panels," http://www.shrm.org/research/futureworkplacetrends/documents/11-0622%20workplace%20panel_trends_symp%20v4.pdf

25. Katherine Wintsch, "Working Moms: Lean In and Listen Up," Richmond Times Dispatch, April 7, 2013, http://www.timesdispatch.com/opinion/their-opinion/columnists-blogs/guest-columnists/working-moms-lean-in-and-listen-up/article_d59d5c84-ebcd-5122-aa49-2ef3dc67283f.html

26. Beth Mirza, "Rethinking Strategies During the Recession," *HR Magazine* 54 (2009): 12.

GLOSSARY

A

Absolute measures Performance ratings that assess an employee's contribution in comparison to a fixed standard or benchmark.

Acceptability A characteristic of selection methods that reflects applicants' beliefs about the appropriateness of the selection methods.

Achievement A selection approach emphasizing existing skills and past accomplishments.

Action planning A process in which employees plan how they will achieve their goals.

Adverse impact Discrimination that results from employer practices that are not discriminatory on their face but have a discriminatory effect.

Affinity group A group of similar employees that meets to support one another.

Affirmative action plan A plan aimed at increasing representation of employees from protected classes who have historically been victims of discrimination.

Agency shop An organization that requires employees to pay the equivalent of union dues even if they are not union members.

Agency theory An economic theory that uses differences in the interests of principals (owners) and agents (employees) to describe reactions to compensation.

Alignment The state in which organizational practices are in their proper place relative to other practices.

Alternate-forms method A process of estimating reliability that compares scores on different versions of a selection assessment.

Arbitration A process in which a neutral third party resolves a dispute by issuing a binding decision; in the context of labor relations, arbitration is generally the last step in the grievance process.

Assessment center A complex selection method that includes multiple measures obtained from multiple applicants across multiple days.

At-risk pay Compensation where the amount varies across pay periods depending on performance.

Attitudes An evaluative reaction to particular categories of people, issues, objects, or events.

Authorization card campaign A campaign in which employees or labor union representatives seek signatures from employees requesting a vote on union representation.

Autonomy The extent to which individual workers have freedom to determine how to complete work.

B

Banding approach The process of treating people as doing equally well when they have similar scores on a selection assessment.

Bargain Laborer HR strategy A human resource strategy that combines emphasis on short-term employees with a focus on reducing costs (an external/cost approach).

Bargaining unit A group of employees within an organization who are represented by a particular labor union; these employees generally work in similar jobs and therefore represent a community of interest.

Base pay Compensation that is consistent across time periods and not directly dependent on performance level.

Base wage Target compensation for a job, which is determined in comparison to the wage that similar employees are being paid by other organizations.

Batch approach Recruiting activities that bring new employees into the organization in groups.

Behavioral contract An agreement specifies what the trainee and his or her manager will do to ensure training is effective.

Behavioral interview Type of structured interview that uses questions concerning behavior in past situations.

Biographical data Assessment focusing on previous events and experiences in an applicant's life.

Bona fide occupational qualification (BFOQ) Characteristic of members of a specific group that is necessary to perform a certain job.

Boycott An organized action in which consumers refuse to purchase goods or services from a company; unions engaged in labor disputes may support boycotts of the companies involved in the disputes.

Broad skill scope A recruiting strategy that seeks to attract a large number of applicants.

Broadbanding The practice of reducing the number of pay categories so that each pay grade contains a large set of different jobs.

Burnout A psychological phenomenon involving emotional exhaustion, cynicism, and a decline in feelings of competence about work.

Business-level strategy A competitive strategy that concerns how an organization, or part of an organization, will compete with other organizations that produce similar goods or services.

Business management and strategy The human resource function concerned with strategic planning, change processes, and evaluating organizational effectiveness.

C

Capability builder competency Knowledge and skills related to understanding what the organization is capable of doing successfully.

Career The pattern of work experiences a person has over his or her lifetime.

Career development Activities that help people manage the progression of their work experiences across their lives.

Career development process A series of steps that people can use to identify and pursue their long-term career goals.

Career ladder A career characterized by step-by-step, hierarchical transitions from jobs with lower pay and responsibility to jobs with higher pay and responsibility.

Career path The series of work experiences that prepare an employee for higher-level jobs.

Causal analysis A process used to determine the underlying causes of a performance problem.

Central tendency error A rating error that occurs when raters give almost all employees scores in the middle of the scale.

Certification An optional designation of competence within a professional field.

Change champion competency Knowledge and skills necessary to initiate and carry out change.

Citizenship performance Employee behavior that helps others and creates a positive work environment.

Closed shop An organization that hires only workers who belong to a certain union.

Coaching When a person works with others to equip them with the tools, knowledge, and opportunities they need to become more effective at work.

Cognitive ability testing Assessment of a person's capability to learn and solve problems.

Collective bargaining The process in which labor unions and employers negotiate contracts defining the terms and conditions under which union members will work.

Commission An individual incentive program in which each employee is paid a percentage of the sales revenue that he or she generates.

Commitment strategy A human resource bundle that builds strong attachment to the organization and emphasizes worker empowerment.

Committed Expert HR strategy A human resource strategy that combines emphasis on long-term employees with a focus on producing unique goods and services (an internal/differentiation approach).

Communal stage Second stage in the organizational life cycle; focuses on expansion and innovation.

Comparable worth A measure that assumes that each job has an inherent value to the organization and that dissimilar jobs can be compared to determine whether the pay for these jobs reflects this value.

Compensation and benefits The human resource function concerned with managing employee pay and benefits.

Compensation package The mix of salary, benefits, and other incentives that employees receive from the organization.

Competencies Characteristics and capabilities that people need to succeed in work assignments.

Competency modeling An alternative to traditional job analysis that focuses on a broader set of characteristics that workers need to effectively perform job duties.

Competitive business strategy Strategy that focuses on different ways to provide goods and services that meet customer needs.

Compressed workweek Working more than eight hours in a shift so that 40 hours of work are completed in fewer than five days.

Concurrent validation strategy A form of criterion-related validity estimation in which selection assessments are obtained from people who are already employees.

Contamination A problem with performance appraisal that occurs when things that should not be included in the measurement are included.

Content validation strategy A process of estimating validity that uses expert raters to determine if a test assesses skills needed to perform a certain job.

Contingency A reinforcement principle requiring that desirable consequents only be given after the occurrence of a desirable behavior.

Contingency approach A human resource perspective that seeks to align different ways of managing people with different competitive strategies for producing goods and services.

Contingent workers People working without either an implicit or an explicit contract and who are not required to work a minimum number of hours.

Contrast error A rating error that occurs when raters unknowingly allow comparisons among employees to influence ratings.

Control strategy A human resource bundle that emphasizes managerial control and tries to streamline production processes.

Corporate-level strategy A competitive strategy that concerns the different businesses and diversity of products and services that an organization produces.

Correlation coefficient A statistical measure that describes the strength of the relationship between two measures.

Cost leadership strategy A business-level strategy that seeks to produce goods and services inexpensively.

Cost measures Methods of assessing recruiting effectiveness that focus on expenses incurred.

Cost per applicant The measure of recruiting effectiveness that assesses how much it costs to entice each person to submit an application for employment.

Cost per hire The measure of recruiting effectiveness that determines the expense incurred to find each person who is eventually hired.

Counterproductive performance Employee behavior that is harmful to the organization.

Credible activist competency Knowledge and skills for influencing others through acting with integrity, sharing information, and building trust.

Criterion-related validation strategy A process of estimating validity that uses a correlation coefficient to determine whether scores on tests predict job performance.

Critical-incidents technique A method of job analysis in which job agents identify instances of effective and ineffective behavior exhibited by people in a specific position.

Culture shock Stress caused by uncertainty and confusion that may arise when people must deal with an unfamiliar culture.

D

Decertification election An election to remove a union's authorization to represent employees.

Declarative knowledge An employee's understanding of the tasks that need to be done to perform job duties.

Defamation of character Information that causes injury to another's reputation or character; can arise as a legal issue when an organization provides negative information about a current or former employee.

Deficiency A problem with performance appraisal that occurs when things that should be included in the measurement are not included.

Defined benefit plan A retirement plan under which an organization provides retired individuals with a fixed amount of money each month; the amount is usually based on number of years employed and pay level at retirement.

Defined contribution plan A retirement plan under which the employer and/or the employee contribute to a fund for which only the contributions are defined and benefits vary according to the amount accumulated in the fund at retirement.

Differentiation The process of dividing work tasks so that employees perform specific pieces of the work process, which allows them to specialize.

Differentiation strategy A business-level strategy that seeks to produce goods and services that are in some manner superior to what is produced by competitors.

Disability insurance A form of insurance that provides benefits to individuals who develop mental or physical conditions that prevent them from working.

Discipline Organizational efforts to correct improper behavior of employees.

Discretionary team bonus A group-level incentive provided to members of a team when a supervisor observes high collective performance.

Discrimination In the context of employment, unfair treatment that occurs when people from particular groups are not given the same employment opportunities as people in other groups.

Disparate treatment The practice of treating job applicants and employees differently based on race, gender, or some other group characteristic.

Distributive issues Issues, such as distribution of rewards and benefits, whose resolution provides value to one party at the expense of the other party.

Distributive justice Perceptions of fairness based on the outcomes (such as pay) received from an organization.

Downsizing Widespread layoffs with the objective of permanently reducing the number of employees.

Downward move A career move resulting in a decrease in responsibility, pay, and status; also known as a demotion.

Due process A set of procedures carried out in accordance with established rules and principles and aimed at ensuring fairness.

Dysfunctional turnover Undesirable employee turnover that occurs when good employees quit.

E

Education and training trends Trends concerning the knowledge and skills workers will need in the future.

Elaboration stage Final stage in the organizational life cycle; focuses on reinvention and adaptation to change.

e-Learning Training delivered through computers and network technology.

Electronic advertising Using electronic forms of communication such as the Internet and email to recruit new employees.

Embeddedness The extent to which an employee is tied to an organization and to the surrounding community.

Emergency action plan standard The OSHA requirement that organizations develop a plan for dealing with emergencies such as fires or natural disasters.

Employee advocate role A human resource role concerned with looking out for the interests of employees and ensuring that they are treated fairly.

Employee and labor relations The human resource function concerned with building and maintaining good relationships with employees and labor unions.

Employee benefits Rewards other than salary and wages; typically include things such as retirement savings and insurance.

Employee compensation The human resource practice of rewarding employees for their contributions.

Employee development Activities that influence personal and professional growth.

Employee recruiting The process of getting people to apply for work with a specific organization.

Employee retention The act of keeping employees; retaining good workers is particularly important.

Employee selection The process of testing and gathering information to decide whom to hire.

Employee separation The act of terminating the employment of workers.

Employee stock ownership plan (ESOP) A plan under which an organization sets up a trust fund to hold and manage company stock given to employees.

Employee turnover The process in which employees leave the organization and are replaced by other employees.

Employment opportunity trends Trends concerning the types of jobs that will be available in the future.

Entrepreneurial stage First stage in the organizational life cycle; focuses on survival.

Equal employment opportunity Absence of discrimination in the workplace; the condition in which people have an equal chance for desirable employment regardless of belonging to a certain race, gender, or other group.

Equal Employment Opportunity Commission (EEOC) A federal agency with responsibility to oversee, investigate, and litigate claims of employment discrimination.

Equity theory A justice perspective suggesting that people determine the fairness of their pay by comparing what they give to and receive from the organization with what others give and receive.

Ergonomics An approach to designing work tasks that focuses on correct posture and movement.

Evolutionary strategic approach An approach in which an organization's strategy unfolds over time in response to common issues.

Exempt employees Workers, such as executives, administrators, professionals, and sales representatives, who are not covered by the FLSA.

Exit interview Face-to-face discussion conducted by an organization to learn why an employee is quitting.

Expatriate An employee who goes to another country for a time to work.

Expectancy An individual's belief that he or she can do what is necessary to achieve high performance.

Expectancy theory A psychological theory suggesting that people are motivated by a combination of three beliefs: valence, instrumentality, and expectancy.

External environment Forces outside the organization's boundaries that influence the organization and its outcomes.

External equity Employee perceptions of fairness based on how much they are paid relative to people working in other organizations.

External labor orientation A human resource perspective that limits attachment to a specific organization and emphasizes hiring workers who already possess the skills they need to complete specific tasks.

External sourcing A recruiting strategy that fills job openings by hiring people who are not already employed by the organization.

F

Fair Labor Standards Act (FLSA) Federal legislation that governs compensation practices and helps ensure fair treatment of employees.

Fairness A characteristic of selection methods that reflects individuals' perceptions concerning potential bias and discrimination in the selection methods.

Family-to-work conflict Problems that occur when meeting family obligations negatively influences work behavior and outcomes.

Featherbedding A practice in which a union requires a company to pay employees wages for work that is not performed; defined as an unfair labor practice.

Feedback Information given to employees to communicate how well they are performing.

Feedback specificity The level of detail in communication, which can range from broad information about overall performance to specific information about certain actions.

Flexible benefit program, or cafeteria benefits A benefit program that allows employees to choose the benefits that they want from a list of available benefits.

Flextime A scheduling policy that allows employees to determine the exact hours they will work within a specific band of time.

Flow approach Recruiting activities that are ongoing and designed to constantly find new employees.

Forced distribution Performance ratings that spread out ratings by requiring raters to place a certain percentage of employees in each category.

Forced ranking A rating format that asks raters to directly compare the contribution of an employee with the contribution of other employees.

Formalization stage Third stage in the organizational life cycle; focuses on establishing clear practices and procedures for carrying out work.

Four-fifths rule Evidence of adverse impact that occurs when the hiring rate of one group is less than 80 percent of the hiring rate of another group.

Frame-of-reference training Training that focuses on building consistency in the way different raters observe and evaluate employee behaviors and outcomes.

Free Agent HR strategy A human resource strategy that combines emphasis on short-term employees with a focus on producing unique goods and services (an external/differentiation approach).

Free distribution Performance ratings that allow raters to place as many employees as they wish into each rating category.

Functional expert role A human resource role concerned with providing technical expertise related to functions such as hiring, training, and compensating employees.

G

Gainsharing A group-level incentive program that rewards groups of employees for working together to reduce costs and improve productivity.

General performance factor A broad factor of performance that represents an employee's overall contribution to the organization.

Global expansion strategy A competitive business strategy that focuses on increasing an organization's presence in foreign countries.

Globalization trends Trends concerning the process in which companies move from doing business within one country to doing business in many countries.

Goal setting A process in which employees set milestones or desired achievements for the future.

Goal-based team reward A group-level incentive provided to members of a team when the team meets or exceeds a specific goal.

Goal-setting theory A psychological theory suggesting that an individual's conscious choices explain motivation.

Graphic ratings A rating format that asks raters to provide a numerical score for an employee on each of several dimensions of performance.

Grievance A complaint filed by an employee who perceives that he or she has been unfairly treated by an organization.

Group incentive A reward that depends on the collective performance of a group of employees.

Growth strategy A competitive business strategy that focuses on expanding products and services into new markets.

H

Halo error A rating error that occurs when raters allow a general impression to influence ratings on specific dimensions of performance.

Harassment In the workplace, improper actions or words of coworkers that cause an employee to feel persistently annoyed or alarmed.

Hazard communication standard The OSHA requirement that organizations identify and label chemicals that might harm workers.

Healthcare plan An insurance plan that provides workers with medical services.

Health maintenance organization (HMO) A healthcare plan under which the provider receives a fixed amount for providing necessary services to individuals who are enrolled in the plan.

Health savings account (HSA) A personal savings account that an employee can use to pay healthcare costs.

Holland typology A classification, developed by Dr. John Holland, of people's interests, values, and skills and of job environments; the typology asserts that people will be more satisfied and more successful in jobs that closely matches their characteristics.

Horizontal alignment The state in which individual human resource practices fit together and support each other.

Hostile environment In the context of sexual harassment, a form of harassment that occurs when employees create an offensive environment in the workplace that interferes with an individual's ability to perform work duties.

HR innovator and integrator competency Knowledge and skills that ensure HR practices such as work design, staffing, and compensation are aligned in ways that facilitate organizational success.

Human capital developer role A human resource role concerned with facilitating learning and skill development.

Human resource bundles Groups of human resource practices that work together to create a consistent work environment.

Human resource development The human resource function concerned with helping employees learn knowledge and skills.

Human resource management The field of study and practice that focuses on people in organizations.

Human resource planning The process of forecasting the number and type of employees that will be needed in the future.

Human resource strategy Strategy that focuses on different ways of managing employees of an organization.

I

Idealistic messaging The recruiting practice of communicating only positive information to potential employees.

Illegal bargaining topics Issues, such as planning to engage in race or gender discrimination, that are prohibited from being discussed as part of collective bargaining.

Immutable characteristics Personal characteristics that cannot reasonably be changed, such as race and sex.

Independent contractors Individuals who actually work for themselves but have an ongoing relationship with an organization.

Individual incentive A reward that depends on the performance of the individual employee.

Informal learning methods Natural learning that is neither planned nor organized.

Instrumentality The belief in the likelihood that the reward will actually be given contingent on high performance.

Integration The process of coordinating efforts so that employees work together.

Integrative issues Issues, such as safety improvement, whose resolution can provide more value to both parties.

Integrity testing Assessment of the likelihood that an individual will be dishonest.

Interdependence The extent to which a worker's actions affect and are affected by the actions of others.

Internal equity Employee perceptions of fairness based on how much they are paid relative to others working in the same organization.

Internal labor orientation A human resource perspective that emphasizes hiring workers early in their careers and retaining those workers for long periods of time.

Internal sourcing A recruiting strategy that fills job openings by transferring people who are already working in the organization.

Interpersonal citizenship behavior Positive employee actions aimed at helping specific coworkers succeed.

Inter-rater method A process of estimating reliability that compares assessment scores provided by different raters.

Involuntary turnover Employee separation that occurs because the employer chooses to terminate the employment relationship.

J

Job A collection of tasks that define the work duties of an employee.

Job analysis The process of systematically collecting information about the tasks that workers perform.

Job analysis interview Face-to-face meeting with the purpose of learning about a worker's duties and responsibilities.

Job analysis observation The process of watching workers perform tasks to learn about duties and responsibilities.

Job analysis questionnaire A series of written questions that seek information about a worker's duties and responsibilities.

Job-based fit Matching an employee's knowledge and skills to the tasks associated with a specific job.

Job-based pay A determination of how much to pay an employee that is based on assessments about the duties performed.

Job characteristics model A form of motivational job design that focuses on creating work that employees enjoy doing.

Job description Task statements that define the work tasks to be done by someone in a particular position.

Job design The process of deciding what tasks will be grouped together to define the duties of someone in a particular work position.

Job enrichment The addition of challenges or new responsibilities to jobs.

Job performance The contribution that individuals make to the organization that employs them.

Job posting Using company communication channels to communicate job vacancies.

Job redesign The process of reassessing task groupings to create new sets of duties that workers in particular positions are required to do.

Job rotation A time-limited lateral work assignment for the purpose of helping employees develop new knowledge and skill.

Job satisfaction Employees' feelings and beliefs about the quality of their jobs.

Job specifications Listing of the knowledge, skills, and abilities needed to perform the tasks described in a job description.

Job transfer A permanent lateral work assignment for the purpose of helping employees develop new knowledge and skills.

Justice theory A psychological theory suggesting that motivation is driven by beliefs about fairness.

K

Knowledge Memory of facts and principles.

L

Labor force trends Trends concerning the number and types of people who are working or looking for work.

Labor relations The dealings that result from interactions between a labor union and an employer.

Labor union An organization representing the collective interests of workers.

Lag-the-market strategy A compensation decision to pay employees an amount below what they might earn working for another organization.

Landrum–Griffin Act A federal law passed in 1959 to prevent corruption and regulate internal union affairs; formally known as the Labor–Management Reporting and Disclosure Act.

Layoff survivors Individuals who continue to work for an organization when their coworkers are laid off.

Layoff victims Individuals whose employment is terminated in a layoff.

Layoffs Large-scale terminations of employment that are unrelated to job performance.

Lead-the-market strategy A compensation decision to pay employees an amount above what they might earn working for another organization.

Learning A change in knowledge, skill, or attitude that results from experience.

Learning objective The individual learning outcome sought by training.

License A required designation of competence within a professional field.

Life insurance A form of insurance that pays benefits to family members or other beneficiaries when an insured person dies.

Line of sight The extent to which employees can see that their actions influence the outcomes used to determine whether they receive a particular reward.

Lockout An action in which an employer closes a workplace or otherwise prevents union members from working as a result of a labor dispute.

Long-term generalists Workers hired to perform a variety of different jobs over a relatively long period of time.

Long-term specialists Workers hired to develop specific expertise and establish a lengthy career within an organization.

Loyal Solider HR strategy A human resource strategy that combines emphasis on long-term employees with a focus on reducing costs (an internal/cost approach).

M

Mandatory bargaining topics Issues, such as wages, hours, and working conditions, that must be discussed as part of collective bargaining.

Market-based pay A compensation approach that determines how much to pay employees by assessing how much they could make working for other organizations.

Material safety data sheet (MSDS) An OSHA-required document that describes the nature of a hazardous chemical and methods of preventing and treating injuries related to the chemical.

Mediation A process in which a neutral third party attempts to help the parties reach an agreement but does not issue a binding decision to resolve the dispute; in the context of labor relations, mediation is sometimes available as part of the grievance resolution process.

Medical and first aid standard The OSHA requirement that an organization make medical and first aid resources available to workers who may become injured.

Meet-the-market strategy A compensation decision to pay employees an amount similar to what they can make working for other organizations.

Mental disabilities Impairments of the mind that substantially limit an individual's ability to engage in normal life activities.

Mentoring When an experienced person helps a less experienced person learn and grow.

Merit bonus A one-time payment made to an individual for high performance.

Merit pay increase An individual incentive program in which an employee's salary increase is based on performance.

Merit-based system A performance management system that specifically seeks to identify and recognize the contributions of high performers.

Minimum cutoffs approach The process of eliminating applicants who do not achieve an acceptable score on each selection assessment.

Minimum wage A compensation rule requiring organizations to pay employees at least a certain amount for each hour they work.

Motivation The sum of forces that cause an individual to engage in certain behaviors rather than alternative actions.

Multiple hurdles approach The process of obtaining scores on a selection method and only allowing those who achieve a minimum score to take the next assessment.

Multisource assessments and feedback A process in which an employee's managers, peers, and sometimes subordinates and customers answer questions about the employee. Responses are combined and provided as developmental feedback to the employee.

Multisource performance ratings Performance ratings obtained from a variety of raters such as customers, coworkers, supervisors, and self.

N

Narrative ratings A rating format that asks raters to provide a written description of an employee's performance.

National Labor Relations Board (NLRB) A board of five members appointed by the President of the United States to enforce the Wagner Act.

Needs assessment A process for determining what training to offer and who should be trained.

Negative feedback Information that communicates things an employee needs to change in order to improve.

Negligent hiring A legal issue that can arise when an organization does not thoroughly evaluate the background of an applicant who is hired and then harms someone.

New employee orientation A process in which organizations help new employees adjust so they can perform their work effectively.

Nonexempt employees All employees who are not explicitly exempt from the FLSA, sometimes referred to as hourly workers.

O

Objective performance measures Performance measures that are numerical and based on counts of behaviors or outcomes.

Occupational Information Network An online source of information about jobs and careers.

Open shop An organization that does not require employees to affiliate with or pay dues to the union elected to represent the organization's employees.

Opportunities Positive elements of an organization's external environment.

Opportunity to perform Allowing employees a chance to use the skills they learned in training back on the job.

Organizational analysis A process used to identify characteristics of the organizational environment that will influence the effectiveness of training.

Organization-based fit Matching an employee's characteristics to the general culture of the organization.

Organizational citizenship behavior Positive employee actions aimed at helping the organization as a whole to succeed.

Organizational life cycle Stages through which an organization moves after its founding.

Organizational objective The organization result sought by training.

Outplacement services Professional assistance provided by an employer to help employees who have been dismissed to cope with job loss and find new positions.

Overtime A compensation rule requiring organizations to pay a higher hourly rate for each hour that a nonexempt employee works beyond 40 hours in a one-week period.

P

Parity-based system A performance management system that seeks to recognize contributions from all employees without elevating some above others.

Pay-for-performance Compensation practices that use differences in employee performance to determine differences in pay.

Pay level The compensation decision concerning how much to pay employees relative to what they could earn doing the same job elsewhere.

Pay survey Gathering information to learn how much employees are being paid by other organizations.

Pay without work Compensation paid for time off, such as holidays.

Perceived organizational support Employees' beliefs about how much their employer values their contributions and cares about their personal well-being.

Performance appraisal The process of measuring what employees contribute to the organization.

Performance management The process of measuring and providing feedback about employee contributions to the organization.

Permissive bargaining topics Issues, such as employee involvement and strategic direction, that are not required but are allowed to be discussed as part of collective bargaining.

Person analysis A process used to identify who needs training and what characteristics of those individuals will influence the effectiveness of training.

Personal aggression Harmful employee actions that seek to personally harm coworkers.

Personality testing Assessment of traits that show consistency in behavior.

Physical disabilities Body impairments that substantially limit an individual's ability to engage in normal life activities.

Piece-rate incentive An individual incentive program in which each employee is paid a certain amount for each piece of output.

Point system A process of assigning numerical values to each job in order to compare the value of contributions within and across organizations.

Political deviance Harmful employee actions designed to harm the performance and careers of other employees.

Population trends Demographic trends related to the characteristics of people in a certain population.

Position Analysis Questionnaire (PAQ) A method of job analysis that uses a structured questionnaire to learn about work activities.

Positive feedback Information that communicates things that an employee is doing well.

Potential A selection approach emphasizing broad characteristics that foreshadow capability to develop future knowledge and skill.

Predictive validation strategy A form of criterion-related validity estimation in which selection assessments are obtained from applicants before they are hired.

Predictor weighting Multiplying scores on selection assessments by different values to give more important means greater weight.

Primacy error A rating error that occurs when raters place too much emphasis on performance observed at the beginning of the measurement period.

Private employment agency A business that exists for the purpose of helping organizations find workers.

Proactive needs assessment A systematic process for determining and prioritizing the training programs to be developed and delivered by an organization.

Problem definition The gap between desired and actual performance.

Procedural justice Perceptions of fairness based on the processes used to allocate outcomes such as pay.

Procedural knowledge and skill Information and expertise that an employee needs to have in order to carry out specific actions.

Production deviance Harmful employee actions aimed at reducing the speed and accuracy of production processes.

Profit sharing An organization-wide incentive program under which a portion of organizational profits are shared with employees.

Progressive discipline Discipline involving successively more severe consequences for employees who continue to engage in undesirable behavior.

Property deviance Harmful employee actions aimed at destroying assets of the organization.

Protean career A career characterized by personal responsibility, continuous and self-directed development, and an emphasis on psychological success.

Protected classes Groups of people, such as racial minorities and women, who are protected against discrimination by law.

Public employment agency Government-sponsored agency that helps people find jobs.

Punitive damages Payments ordered by courts that exceed actual damages and are designed to punish a defendant—for example, to punish a company for discrimination.

Pygmalion effect A process whereby performance increases when leaders have high expectations about the skills and capabilities of followers.

Q

Qualified benefit plan A benefit plan that meets federal guidelines so that the organization can provide nontaxable benefits to employees.

Quality measures Methods of assessing recruiting effectiveness that focus on the extent to which sources provide applicants who are actually qualified for jobs.

Quantity measures Methods of assessing recruiting effectiveness that focus on the number of applicants and hires found by each source.

Quid pro quo In the context of sexual harassment, a form of harassment that makes continued employment and advancement contingent upon sexual favors.

R

Race-norming The practice of evaluating an applicant's score by comparing the score only with scores achieved by people of the same race.

Railway Labor Act (RLA) A federal law passed in 1926 to regulate relationships between railroad companies and unions.

Rapid model of instructional design A process used to create training programs in which assessment, design and delivery, and evaluation overlap in time.

Rater bias Bias that occurs when a rater unfairly provides lower ratings to certain groups of people, such as women and minorities.

Rational strategic approach An approach in which organizational leaders carefully plan a strategy before carrying it out.

Reactive needs assessment A problem-solving process used to determine whether training is necessary to fix a specific performance problem and, if training is necessary, what training should be delivered.

Realistic job previews Information given to potential employees that provides a complete picture of the job and organization.

Realistic messaging The recruiting practice of communicating both good and bad features of jobs to potential employees.

Reality check A process in which employees determine the accuracy of their self-assessments and how those assessments fit with opportunities in the environment.

Reasonable accommodation Under the ADA, an alteration of the work environment that enables a qualified individual with a disability to perform essential tasks.

Recency error A rating error that occurs when raters place too much emphasis on performance observed right before the measure is taken.

Reciprocal processing Work organized around teams such that workers constantly adjust to the task inputs of others.

Reinforcement theory A psychological theory suggesting that people are motivated by antecedents (environmental cues) and consequents (rewards and punishments).

Relapse prevention training A transfer enhancement activity that helps prepare trainees to overcome obstacles to using trained behaviors on the job.

Relational commitment A sense of loyalty to an organization that is based not only on financial incentives but also on social ties.

Relative measures Performance ratings that assess an employee's contributions through comparison with the contributions of other employees.

Reliability The degree to which a selection method yields consistent results.

Repatriation The process of adjusting to a home culture after returning from living and working in another culture.

Return on investment (ROI) An efficiency measure created by dividing the monetary value of training benefits by the costs of delivering training and multiplying the result by 100.

Right-to-work laws State laws that require open shop labor agreements.

Risk management The human resource function concerned with employees' physical and mental well-being.

S

Salary compression A situation created when new employees receive higher pay than employees who have been with the organization for a long time even though they perform the same job.

Scientific management A set of management principles that focus on efficiency and standardization of processes.

Secondary boycott A boycott by unionized employees that is meant to pressure a company not to purchase goods and services from another company that is engaged in a labor dispute with a union; defined as an unfair labor practice.

Self-assessment A process in which employees determine their interests, values, personalities, and skills.

Sequential processing Work organized around an assembly line such that the completed tasks of one employee feed directly into the tasks of another employee.

Severance compensation Money provided to an employee as part of a dismissal package.

Sexual harassment In the workplace, improper words or actions that are sexual in nature or that are directed toward workers of a specific sex or sexual orientation.

Short-term generalists Workers hired to produce general labor inputs for a relatively short period of time.

Short-term specialists Workers hired to provide specific labor inputs for a relatively short period of time.

Sick leave Compensation paid to employees who are unable to work because they are ill.

Situational influences Factors that affect performance but that are outside the control of the employee being rated.

Situational interview Type of structured interview that uses questions based on hypothetical situations.

Situational judgment test Assessment that asks job applicants what they would do, or should do, in a hypothetical situation.

Situational specificity The condition in which evidence of validity in one setting does not support validity in other settings.

Skills Proficiency at performing a particular act.

Skill-based pay A determination of how much to pay an employee that is based on skills, even if those skills are not currently used to perform duties.

Social security system A federal program that requires workers to pay into a retirement fund, from which they will draw when they have reached a certain age.

Socialization The process in which a new employee learns about an organization and develops social relationships with other organizational members.

Split-halves method A process of estimating reliability that compares scores on two parts of a selection assessment.

Stakeholders Individuals or groups who are affected by or who affect an organization.

Standard rate The rate of pay that an employee receives for producing an average number of output units.

Stock options Rights to purchase stock at a specified price in the future.

Stock plan An incentive plan that gives employees company stock, providing the employees with an ownership interest in the organization.

Strategic partner role A human resource role concerned with providing inputs that help an organization put its competitive strategy into action.

Strategic positioner competency Knowledge and skills associated with accurately placing an organization in its business context through understanding finance, strategy, stakeholders, and competitive context.

Strategy Coordinated choices and actions that provide direction for people and organizations.

Strengths Positive elements that define areas in which an organization has high internal capability.

Strike An action in which union members refuse to perform their job duties as a result of a labor dispute.

Structured interview Employment interview that incorporates multiple raters, common questions, and standardized evaluation procedures.

Subjective performance measures Performance measures that represent judgments made by raters.

T

Taft–Hartley Act A federal law passed in 1947 that regulates union activities and requires unions to bargain in good faith; formally known as the Labor–Management Relations Act.

Talent wars Negative competition in which companies attempt to hire one another's employees.

Targeted skill scope A recruiting strategy that seeks to attract a small number of applicants who have specific characteristics.

Task analysis A process used to describe the work activities of employees, including the knowledge and skill required to complete those activities.

Task analysis inventory A method of job analysis in which job agents rate the frequency and importance of tasks associated with a specific set of work duties.

Task performance Employee behavior that directly contributes to producing goods or services.

Technology proponent competency Knowledge and skills used to help organizations effectively adopt technology to manage information and connect individuals.

Telework Completion of work through voice and data lines such as telephone and high-speed Internet connections.

Temporary workers Individuals who are employed by an outside staffing agency and assigned to work in an organization for a short period of time.

Test–retest method A process of estimating reliability that compares scores on a single selection assessment obtained at different times.

Threats Negative elements of an organization's external environment.

Time measures Methods of assessing recruiting effectiveness that focus on the length of time it takes to fill positions.

Title VII The portion of the Civil Rights Act of 1964 that focuses specifically on employment discrimination.

Traditional model of instructional design A process used to create training programs in which needs assessment is followed by design and delivery and then by evaluation.

Training A planned effort to help employees learn job-related knowledge, skills, and attitudes.

Training climate Environmental factors that support training, including policies, rewards, and the attitudes and actions of management and coworkers.

Training effectiveness The extent to which trainees and their organizations benefit as intended from training.

Training efficiency The extent to which the benefits of training exceed the costs of developing and delivering training.

Training media How training content and the associated methods are delivered to the learner.

Training methods How training content is organized and structured for the learner.

Training vendors Organizations that sell existing training programs or services to develop and deliver training programs.

Transactional commitment A sense of obligation to an organization that is created primarily by financial incentives.

Transfer of training Application on the job of knowledge, skills, or attitudes learned in training.

Turnaround strategy A competitive business strategy that focuses on radical change to return a company to profitability.

U

Undue hardship Under the ADA, a severe economic or other hardship placed on an employer by the requirement to make accommodations for workers with disabilities; an employer is not required to make accommodations that impose undue hardship.

Unemployment insurance A network of state-mandated insurance plans that provide monetary assistance to workers who lose their jobs through no fault of their own.

Unfair labor practices Labor practices on the part of employers or unions that are prohibited by federal law.

Uniform rewards A reward system that minimizes differences among workers and offers similar compensation to all employees.

Union shop An organization that requires workers to join a union as soon as they are hired.

Union steward A representative of the union who acts as an advocate for employees.

Universalistic approach A human resource perspective that seeks to identify methods of managing people that are effective for all organizations.

Upward move A career move resulting in an increase in responsibility, pay, and status; also known as a promotion.

Utility A characteristic of selection methods that reflects their cost effectiveness.

Utilization study An assessment to determine how closely an organization's pool of employees reflects the racial and gender profile of the surrounding community.

V

Valence The value that an individual places on a reward being offered.

Validity The quality of being justifiable. To be valid, a method of selecting employees must accurately predict who will perform the job well.

Validity generalization The condition in which evidence of validity in one setting can be seen as evidence of validity in other settings.

Variable rewards A reward system that pays some employees substantially more than others in order to emphasize difference between high and low performers.

Vertical alignment The state in which an organization's human resource strategy supports its competitive business strategy.

Vested Eligible to receive the benefits of a retirement plan; individual employees must often work a certain period of time before such eligibility is granted.

Voluntary turnover Employee separation that occurs because the employee chooses to leave.

W

Wagner Act A federal law passed in 1935 that created the National Labor Relations Board and provided employees with the express right to organize unions; formally known as the National Labor Relations Act.

Walking/working surfaces standard The OSHA requirement that an organization maintain a clean and orderly work environment.

Weaknesses Negative factors that define areas in which an organization has low internal capability.

Withdrawal The process that occurs when employees begin to distance themselves from the organization by working less hard and planning to quit.

Work design The process of assigning and coordinating work tasks among employees.

Work sample testing Assessment of performance on tasks that represent specific job actions.

Workers' compensation State programs that provide workers and families with compensation for work-related accidents and injuries.

Workforce planning and employment The human resource function concerned with designing jobs and placing people in those jobs.

Work-role centrality The degree to which a person's life revolves around his or her job.

Work-to-family conflict Problems that occur when meeting work obligations negatively influences behavior and outcomes at home.

Name and Company Index

Subject Index

APPENDICES: Available online at http://www.wiley.com/college/sc/stewart

Appendix A: Occupational Outlook for HR Managers and Specialists

Every few years the U.S. Department of Labor updates what it calls the *Occupational Outlook Handbook*. The *Handbook* offers the following information for over 250 different occupations covering 9 out of 10 jobs in the U.S. economy: What employees with this title do, work environment, how to obtain a job with this job title, pay, job outlook, and similar occupations. This appendix, drawn from the 2012–2013 edition of the *Handbook*, includes entries of both "Human Resource Specialists" and "Human Resources Managers."

Appendix B: HR Certification Institute Body of Knowledge

The HR Certification Institute (HRCI) is an independent, internationally recognized certifying body for the HR profession. HRCI certifications require professionals to demonstrate their expertise in the core principles of HR practice by taking examinations. The material in this appendix covers the body of knowledge for the Professional in Human Resources (PHR) and Senior Professional in Human Resources (SPHR) exams.

Appendix C: HR People & Strategy Pillars of Knowledge

HR People & Strategy (HRPS), formerly the Human Resource Planning Society, is an organization for influential HR executives and innovative HRM professionals. HRPS has designated what they believe to the most critical and strategic areas of knowledge for HR professionals. This appendix summarizes these five areas of knowledge.

Appendix D: Organizations of Interest to HR Students and Professionals

This appendix lists names and websites of both U.S.-based and international professional associations related to HR. In addition, the appendix contains the names and websites of major US employment unions and U.S. government agencies.

Appendix E: Journals Useful to HR Students and Professionals

This appendix lists both research and practice-oriented periodicals, often referred to as journals. Journals are organized under two headings: HR and Behavioral Science, and General Management.